THE PURSUIT OF SODOMY:

MALE
HOMOSEXUALITY
IN
RENAISSANCE
AND
ENLIGHTENMENT

EUROPE

KENT GERARD
GERT HEKMA

EDITORS

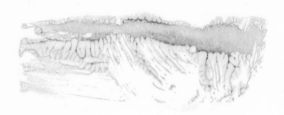

The Pursuit of Sodomy: Male Homosexuality in Renaissance and Enlightenment Europe

The Pursuit of Sodomy: Male Homosexuality in Renaissance and Enlightenment Europe

Kent Gerard
Gert Hekma
Editors

The Pursuit of Sodomy was simultaneously issued by The Haworth Press, Inc., under the same title, as a special issue of the *Journal of Homosexuality*, Volume 16, Numbers 1/2 1988, by Kent Gerard and Gert Hekma, Guest Editors, John De Cecco, Editor.

Harrington Park Press
New York • London

ISBN 0-918393-49-3

Published by

The Haworth Press, Inc., 10 Alice Street, Binghamton, NY 13904–1580
EUROSPAN/Haworth, 3 Henrietta Street, London WC2E 8LU England

Harrington Park Press, Inc., is a subsidiary of The Haworth Press, Inc., 12 West 32 Street, New York, New York 10001.

The Pursuit of Sodomy: Male Homosexuality in Renaissance and Enlightenment Europe was originally published as *Journal of Homosexuality*, Volume 16, Numbers 1/2 1988.

Cover design by Marshall Andrews.

Library of Congress Cataloging-in-Publication Data

The Pursuit of sodomy : male homosexuality in Renaissance and enlightenment Europe / Kent Gerard, Gert Hekma, editors.
    p.   cm.
    "Originally published as Journal of homosexuality, volume 16, numbers 1/2 1988."
    Includes bibliographies and index.
    ISBN 918393-49-3
    1. Homosexuality, Male – Europe – History. 2. Sodomy – Europe – History – Sources. 3. Social history, Modern – 1500- I. Gerard, Kent. II. Hekma, Gert. III. Journal of homosexuality.
HQ76.2.E9P87 1989
306.7'66'094 – dc19   88-38811
                                                                                   CIP

CONTENTS

ABOUT THE EDITORS

Kent Gerard, has taught in the history and economics departments at the University of California, Berkeley. During his graduate training in the social and economic history of Early Modern Europe, he spent some time working under Foucault's direction on topics in the history of sexuality in the seventeenth and eighteenth centuries. He has lectured widely in the United States and the Netherlands on the history of sexuality, and has published a number of scholarly articles, several essays on gay academia for the gay press, and translations of contemporary Dutch gay poetry.

Gert Hekma, Lecturer in Gay Studies and Sociology, holds the (male) co-directorship of the Gay Studies Program at the University of Amsterdam's Sociologisch Instituut. He has been a pivotal figure in both gay scholarship and gay activism in the Netherlands since they burst onto the Dutch scene in the late 1970s. He served as one of the four main organizers of the first international gay-studies conferences ever held. His publications include over thirty articles on various aspects of gay history, politics and culture.

The Pursuit of Sodomy: Male Homosexuality in Renaissance and Enlightenment Europe

Introduction

Male homosexuality has a history, but this history consists principally of sodomites and buggers, pederasts and catamites, *berdaches* and *"contrary lovers"* rather than homosexuals or gays in the modern sense. As demonstrated in this volume the differentiation of the cultural and historical forms of homosexual behavior and its social expression has enriched and broadened the history of sexuality. Assembled here for the first time are articles on most of the countries of Western Europe during the early modern era (1400-1800). Previous publications have covered only one country or one city during part of this period, or have had a more general focus, such as "illicit" or "unauthorized" sexual behavior. This collection is more comprehensive than any appearing before.

The title of this volume may be appreciated in a threefold sense: the pursuit of sodomy by early modern sodomites; the pursuit of sodomites by those authorities opposed to them; and the pursuit by contemporary scholars of the documentary evidence for these activities. Most historical research on male homosexuality in early modern Europe has focused on the persecution of sodomites. This is understandable, in that the largest body of extant evidence consists of court records and other forensic documents concerning sodomy trials and related investigations. Most of the articles in this volume draw data from legal archives. Such data provide representations of the pursuit of sodomy, and the persecution of sodomites, as seen through the eyes of officials. But frequently, something of the accused persons' views of their lives and activities is preserved in the records of legal proceedings. The juridical focus was on acts of sodomy, so there are more data on sexual practices in the accusations and confessions than there are about any other aspect of accused sodomites' lives. How sodomites viewed sodomy, sexual behavior in general, and the implications of sexual behavior for self-meaning is not as easily recoverable from the surviving forensic records. In confronting the limitations of their sources, the contributors to this volume demonstrate the possibilities for surmounting these silences, and indicate the hazards involved. They have intensively mined their materials to produce valuable new insights and interpretations.

The notion of sodomy—"that utterly confused category," in Foucault's felicitous phrasing—has provided the most important discursive thread for research on the history of early modern homosexuality. Two other promising topics for this history that often intertwine are also addressed in this volume: the classical heritage of "Socratic love," and the tradition of friendship. In an era when educated society communicated in Latin, the Greek and Roman texts on male eros must have been an inspiration for male lovers. Each of the predecessors of modern homosexual emancipation, such as Ulrichs, Pater and Symonds, was influenced by this classical heritage. Its significance for elite circles in particular can be traced from the Renaissance onward. Regarding the tradition of friendship: in a society where social relations were often limited to one gender, and thus were homosocial, friendships often had their erotic or sexual aspects. Most of early modern Europe had not yet experienced the "tabooization" of physical affection between males with which we are familiar today. Further light is shed in this volume upon male intimacies in homosocial institutions and settings, such as armies and monasteries, in the workshop and on shipboard.

The editors hope this collection on the pursuit of sodomy will prove an important breakthrough. We hope the way is now paved for more thorough investigations of the similarities and differences of the practices and meanings of male love in diverse eras and regions. Major cultural changes in early modern Europe, such as the rise of sodomite subcultures in Northwestern Europe around 1700, can now be discerned. Existing research gaps can now be more properly ascertained and evaluated: England and the Netherlands are more extensively represented here than Central and Southern Europe, for example; and the absence of work on Eastern and Southeastern Europe points to major tasks for future scholars. We hope that investigators of the history of male love will be stimulated to further ventures and to new analyses.

It has been several years since the initial insemination of this project. We want heartily to thank all the contributors, who have shown great patience in waiting for the appearance of this publication. We believe the final result will please them and our readers. We have appreciated the indispensable help of the staff of the *Journal of Homosexuality*, especially its editor-in-chief, John P. De Cecco, as well as Corlynn J. Cognata, John P. Elia, and Ann Schifter. The Haworth/Harrington Park Press production staff, including Linda Cohen, Ellen C. L. Cotter, Carol Jenkins, Karen Hammond, Ida Walker, and Ann Schwartz Willsie, have shown patience and fortitude along with their professionalism. Those scholars who served as referees or translators, or otherwise helped to facilitate this project, also deserve our commendation: among them, Guido Ruggiero, B. R. Burg, Judith Brown, Richard Trexler, E. William Monter, and especially Louis Crompton. Those authors appearing in this volume who also deserve praise for service in these capacities include Randolph Trumbach, Theo van der Meer, James Steakley, George Rousseau, Wayne Dynes, and, in particular, Stephen Murray. Lastly, for their unstinting emotional support, we wish to thank Katherine Day and Mattias Duyves.

Kent Gerard
University of California, Berkeley

Gert Hekma
University of Amsterdam

I. ITALY AND IBERIA

Sodomites in
Fifteenth-Century Tuscany:
The Views of Bernardino
of Siena

Michael J. Rocke, PhD (cand.)

Whenever you hear sodomy mentioned, each and every one of you spit on the ground and clean your mouth out well. If they don't want to change their ways by any other means, maybe they will change when they're made fools of. Spit hard! Maybe the water of your spit will extinguish their fire. Like this, everyone spit hard!

And with a noise that "seemed like thunder," as the scribe recorded, the great mass of Florentine faithful spat disgustedly on the stone pavement of Santa Croce to deride their city's sodomites. Two days later, on 9 April 1424, Bernardino of Siena urged his followers once again to join him in a more ominous public mockery. "To the fire!" he cried. "They are all sodomites!" His congregation, inspired by Bernardino's three consecutive sermons on the vice of sodomy and this last one on lust, needed no further prompting. Rushing out of the church to the vast *piazza*, at whose center had been prepared a huge pile of clothing, wigs, cosmetics, and other "vanities," they watched approvingly as the preacher set the heap aflame. Thus ended Bernardino's first extant Lenten sermons to the Florentines on sodomy, with a fiery warning of the

Michael J. Rocke is a PhD candidate at the State University of New York at Binghamton.

The author would like to thank Richard Trexler and Sharon Strocchia for their critical reading of an early version of this article.

7

destruction awaiting them on account of their vices. Four times in the next three years he would again attack his comtemporaries' sexual practices, delivering two more sermons on sodomy in Florence the following year, another in 1425 in nearby Siena, and yet another, his longest, to the Sienese in 1427.[1]

The sermons of Bernardino of Siena are probably the most extensive and vivid commentary on sodomy in late medieval Italy that we possess by a single contemporary. One of Italy's most popular and authoritative preachers, canonized in 1450, Bernardino was an astute observer and critic who was highly sensitive to the social and political problems of his culture.[2] And few activities aroused more concern and provoked more repression in fifteenth-century Tuscany than did male homosexuality.[3] Within his own lifetime, Bernardino had seen far-reaching changes in the legal and judiciary status of sodomy that reflected a heightened and pervasive fear of "the detestable vice." Once rarely prosecuted even though long illegal, consensual sexual relationships between males in Florence, for example, were being tried and condemned with increasing frequency.[4] Local authorities across Tuscany, many of whom were of Bernardino's own generation, were promoting various efforts to suppress homosexual activity, including official sponsorship of female prostitution, new and harsher laws, and more effective police surveillance.[5] Just a few years after Bernardino's apocalyptic message, Florence (in 1432) and Lucca (in 1448) created civic magistracies whose sole task at their inception was to prosecute the crime of sodomy.[6] The scope of these new institutions was enormous. In Florence, during their seventy-year tenure until 1502, the Officers of the Night, as this court was known, adjudicated cases involving at least ten thousand men and boys, and convicted an estimated two thousand, for homosexual relations.

But it is not only their strategic chronological link to this intensifying campaign that makes Bernardino's sermons so compelling. Perhaps partially intended to whip up popular pressure on foot-dragging authorities, his sermons also seem to have had a related instructional goal; that is, to bring into sharper focus the image of the "sodomite" and to isolate those social and cultural conditions that produced his "unnatural" sexual behavior. This article reconstructs this "persona" of the sodomite envisaged by Bernardino in his Florentine and Sienese sermons. Following the preacher's distinctions, I trace the development of this persona through the characteristic stages of his life, from childhood and adolescence to youth, and finally maturity when, according to Bernardino, the sodomite usually betrayed himself as such by choosing not to marry. Where reference to judiciary or demographic sources can illustrate or clarify his remarks, I have done so by drawing upon samples from the trial proceedings of the Florentine Officers of the Night and other Florentine records. The preacher's view of the sodomite was negative, to be sure, often marked by apparent commonplaces and polemical exaggeration. Yet in order to arouse and persuade, Bernardino did not invent novel images. Rather he built on ones already present, convincing because they were familiar. Bernardino's sodomite was not some moral abstract, but a figure his fellow Tuscans would have easily recognized.

* * *

Bernardino was convinced that sodomites were made, not born, and that more than anything else Tuscan home life was to blame. For this reason, the preacher fervently denounced his contemporaries' child-rearing practices which, he was sure, steered young boys into homosexual activity. Whether it was for their negligence and lack of love, or for their vanity and greed, Bernardino condemned parents as the "pimps" of their own sons.[7]

Young boys learned about homosexual activity as early as age five or seven, the preacher warned, and were thus predisposed to it by the time they reached the ages of discretion and puberty. He claimed that some boys learned about it directly from their fathers who were sodomites themselves.[8] Others picked up knowledge of sodomy from the endless jokes about it in the streets or among their school companions, or, more likely, at home where their parents blithely invited their sodomite friends to the house and never discouraged their constant "chatter about sodomy and lewdness."[9] At the workshop or in the school, at home or in the *piazza*, talk about sodomy was ubiquitous, Bernardino seemed to suggest, and its very mention was corrupting. "They aren't dry behind the ears," he complained, "and already they're polluted and sodomites! Look at them, fathers and mothers, it's astonishing that they're of such a tender age and already they're defiled by sodomy!''[10]

As the boys grew older and moved from talk about sodomy to action, some parents tried to defend their sons by claiming that their sexual misdeeds were only innocent boyish foibles. But this "boys will be boys" attitude did not satisfy the preacher, and he reminded his listeners that when a boy began to recognize natural reason, as early as eight or ten, the Church considered his sexual lust a mortal sin.[11] Florentine boys matured especially early, he instructed, because the city's moral condition was so debased that it precociously introduced them to the knowledge of sin. "First [the boy] may be in such a condition and of such an understanding that very rapidly and early he can sin mortally. Secondly, sometimes it depends on the circumstances of one's native land, and if any country is stained, it's this one of Florence.''[12] While the youngster would ultimately be held responsible for his own actions, Bernardino made it very clear that his parents were to blame for placing him in mortal danger.

> I heard it from a very worthy man, who said he believed that more [boys] are ruined from the age of eight to fifteen than at any other age. And only one thing is to blame: that parents and those who are responsible for governing and correcting these youngsters think little of their sins, and for this reason they never make them confess, letting them off because of their ignorance. "But they're only boys!" It's not enough.[13]

Bernardino only sketched these childhood developments, however, for his real concern was with the adolescent boy. Already inclined to homosexual activity due to the loose talk of his childhood, forgiven by his parents when he began to experiment, once a boy reached adolescence his sexual energy knew no bounds. From age fourteen to twenty-five, Bernardino specified, young males lost all sense of reason on account of their wicked lustfulness.[14] The Florentines needed no reminder. Local tradition had long associated this age group with disorder, violence, and reckless sexuality.[15] Despairing that parents had the will or the authority to rein in these "unbridled horses," indeed condemning parental complicity,

Bernardino focused his attention on the wayward youngsters. He reasoned that Florentine adolescents needed firmer and more effective guidance because their parents had abandoned their own moral responsibilities.[16]

Evidence from the judiciary sources illuminates this age group's sexual behavior and helps to explain our preacher's concerns. Because Bernardino delivered his sermons on sodomy before the Florentine campaign against male homosexuality found its fullest expression in the courts, judiciary records from the 1420s and 1430s unfortunately do not provide a satisfactory contemporary data base for assessing the preacher's claims. Our best evidence comes from some fifty years later, when the extensive data from the trial proceedings of the Officers of the Night overlaps with Florentine demographic sources. While this criminal data cannot be considered an objective "census" of homosexual activity, it can furnish general, more or less accurate, indications of the nature of Florentine homosexuality which can illustrate Bernardino's remarks.

From 1478 to 1483, the years of our sample, adolescents aged twelve to twenty-five years made up at least half of the nearly one thousand Florentine males denounced before the Officers of the Night for homosexual activity. By comparing this group to its age cohort in the general population, it can be roughly estimated that as many as one of every twelve Florentine boys in this age group came to the attention of the sodomy court during this five-year period.[17] This substantial figure does not, of course, indicate the actual extent of homosexual activity in Florence. But the high proportion of youngsters whose homosexual relations came to light suggests that such activity was probably widespread among young Florentine males.

The judiciary sources also provide some crucial refinements to Bernardino's general statements, especially on the link between age and sex roles. Florentine sodomy legislation categorized sodomy into "active" and "passive" roles, and court practice generally followed this distinction. The vast majority of cases prosecuted by the Officers of the Night involved an adult man who assumed the "active" role with a "passive" adolescent partner. Only 10 percent of the relationships involved two adolescents both under the legal age of eighteen, and there were no cases of an "active" adolescent with a "passive" adult. Of those described as passive, then, whose ages we can document precisely, nearly 95 percent were between twelve and nineteen years old. Two ten-year-old boys were the youngest of the group of passives, while the eldest were one adolescent aged twenty and another aged twenty-three. Their mean age was fifteen.[18] It was these mainly teenaged boys who Bernardino intended when, leaving us with a vivid image of this behavioral pattern, he lamented, "The *fanciulli* are the idols of old men, who consider them gods."[19]

Bernardino was convinced that, in Tuscany, parents themselves not only provided the raw materials but also fashioned the essential forms of the sodomite's idols. They did so in part, he accused, by dressing up their sons in immodest and provocative clothing, thinking they were making their boys attractive when in truth they were only turning them into seductive targets for sodomites. Didn't parents know it was a serious sin, the preacher asked them, "to make [their sons] a doublet that reaches only to the navel [and] stockings with a little piece in front and one in back, so that they show a lot of flesh for the sodomites"?[20] For those parents who never taught their sons about God or their souls, but only how to deceive their companions and to make and spend money, it was satisfaction enough, he claimed, "just to send them out wearing see-through shirts, with little doublets that don't cover half their bodies, with flamboyant clothes and stockings slit up the legs, with braids in their hair."[21]

To his fellow Sienese, he cautioned parents on the likely consequences of sending such enticingly groomed boys outdoors. Alluring boys, the horrified preacher threatened, risked being taken by force and raped in the streets. "Send your girls out instead," Bernardino urged mothers, "who aren't in any danger at all if you let them out among such people." Bernardino was so disturbed at the prospect of boys being raped that he admitted that violation of young girls, in the event, was less mortally dangerous and sinful. "If there is no other way," he concluded, "I consent to this as being less evil."[22]

Like other fifteenth-century Florentine moralists, Bernardino often singled out mothers as being most susceptible to the temptation to groom their sons appealingly. "Oh women," he scolded, "you also make your sons into sodomites! When you send them outdoors, you spruce them up too much! . . . Oh don't you care that you make yourselves into their pimps?"[23] Women indulged their own vanity, the scandalized preacher claimed, by trying to turn their boys into mirror-images of themselves, emasculating their young sons. "Oh silly, foolish women, it appears that you make your son look like yourself, so that to you he's quite becoming: 'Oh, isn't he the handsome lad!' and even, 'Isn't he the pretty girl! *Oimmè, oimmè, oimmè!*' "[24]

While Bernardino reserved many of his criticisms for these maternal excesses, he recognized that fathers, no less than mothers, perhaps welcomed the possibility that their well-dressed, attractive sons might turn heads in the streets. "All of you, both women and men, sin too much," he reproved, "in sending your sons out so spruced up that you make them sodomites."[25] Men were equally responsible for "these young boys of yours turned into girls. . . ." "Punish them," he urged fathers, "keep them at home at night and take them with you, . . . right beside you, and don't send them out enticing like maidens."[26] Indeed, Bernardino suggested that fathers, being men in a society where women counted but little, took a special, vain pride, "in seeing [their sons] possessed and loved and looked after and served" by other men, the "citizens of the devil" in the preacher's eyes.[27]

Why might parents experience pleasure, rather than outrage, when their adolescent sons won the attention of adult men? For Bernardino the answer was clear. Both fathers and mothers potentially stood to gain much when their sons attracted an influential suitor. "There are some parents who permit their sons to do every possible disgraceful, evil, and sinful thing, and the reason they allow it is to obtain civic offices or money." As the preacher specified, "mothers permit it so they can get the money, and fathers allow it to gain influence with the right people."[28] Other parents, he claimed, perhaps less ambitious or at least less willing deliberately to prostitute their sons, nonetheless accepted money or gifts from their sons' lovers in exchange for not protesting and to avoid public scandal. "[Parents] keep quiet about [their son's activities] because they are afraid of scandal, etc. Oh you understand me very well! *Oimme*, fathers and mothers, for this reason alone you permit this sin to be committed for a handful of things or money!"[29]

Such polemical contentions are hard to prove. Nonetheless, evidence from the judiciary sources indicates that many other Florentines perceived homosexual relations and their rites in ways that resembled Bernardino's arguments. For example, probably the most common phrase used by anonymous writers to describe and denounce homosexual relations before the sodomy court was not "Giovanni sodomizes Jacopo" but "Giovanni keeps [*si tiene*] Jacopo." The wording can imply both an ongoing sexual partnership and some sort of maintenance of the younger partner by the elder. Denunciations often described such support (usually gifts of clothing) and evidence of it could be offered as proof of suspicious relations between a man and a boy, as in this writer's claim: "I am certain if you pick up the boy . . . he will tell you the truth, and especially about him, that is Piero [Gerini], because Piero with his own mouth has said and says that [the boy, Piero Panichi] is costing him as much as fifty florins this year. . . ."[30]

A second writer shows how parents might have been involved in and profited from their sons' relationships:

> [Andrea] is kept by several persons with the consent of Fioravante his father and . . . of Mona Francesca his mother. . . . Andrea and his parents have gone to stay in Castel San Giovanni di Val d'Arno for fear [of the authorities], and his lovers provide for all their needs. . . . The mother is a scoundrel and the father a villain because they have squandered 200 florins [given to them] by these lovers.[31]

These sources have not yielded any direct evidence that lovers extended political favors as well as other gifts. But given the Florentine context, in which civic offices were highly prized, patronage networks were widespread, and homosexual activity appears to have been frequent among representatives of the politically privileged class, Bernardino's repeated insinuations cannot be taken lightly.[32]

Such traditional courting rituals as the pursuit of the beloved through favors or gifts tend to reinforce the cultural assumptions associated with the strict observance of "active" and "passive" sex-role distinctions. Yet Bernardino sometimes confounded these notions by emphasizing the "active" role of the boys themselves in soliciting and maintaining relationships with men. Some boys knew very well they were desirable, the preacher noted, and not only capitalized on their attractions but also incited others to do the same. "I've heard of those boys who dress themselves up and go around boasting about their sodomizers, and they make a practice of it for pay, and go about encouraging others in the ugly sin."[33] Adolescent boys seemed to exert a strange allure and power over grown men that even Bernardino found difficult to explain. In the end, the astonished preacher admitted to a sort of mutual manipulation in which both partners gained. The suitor may have showered a boy and his family with gifts in return for the adolescent's sexual favors. But the boy's charms and beauty captivated his lover, making him "always irritated and upset, and he's so afraid he will fall out of the good graces of the wicked *fanciullo*."[34] Such a man "servilely obeys the *fanciullo*, and does everything he can at his asking."[35] This topsy-turvy aspect of male homosexuality, in which both traditional gender boundaries and power relations become confused, with parents abandoning their sons to the "unnatural" affections of strangers, must have provided Bernardino's congregations with a profoundly unsettling and provocative image of their society.

Who then were those men who idolized young boys, who worshipped "the beauty of youths, [holding it constantly] before their eyes, both mental and physical," as if adoring the image of the apocalyptic beast?[36] To earthy Tuscans, another of Bernardino's characterizations may have seemed more appropriate: those men who were "like a dog tailing a bitch [in heat], so that a boy can't even pass nearby without having the sodomite on his tail."[37] Bernardino had implied that all Florentine adolescents, regardless of their class or other social attributes, were involved in homosexual activity. He was equally imprecise about social status when describing the boys' lovers, but he was a good deal more discriminating about other characteristics.[38] First, let us look at his views on age.

Observing the sexual behaviors of his fellow Tuscans, Bernardino noted that male youths — the "giovani" in local usage, roughly young men in their twenties and thirties — not surprisingly were more sexually active than their elders. Moreover, among those he described as "mature" and "old" men, from the early forties to age seventy, he detected different sexual behavior patterns to which he attributed various meanings.[39] Some in these latter two groups, Bernardino thought, had never stained themselves with the vice of sodomy, always regarding it with "hatred and horror and revulsion." Others of the mature and old men had either been "defiled in their youth" but had later given up the practice entirely, or had only occasionally fallen into the sin, immediately afterwards repenting and reforming.

Finally, Bernardino identified some of each of the two groups as confirmed sodomites. Among the old men, he pointed out, there were those "who had [already] grown aged and hardened in the sin against nature. Crazy old men," he cried at them, "crazier in your old age than in your youth!" A number of the mature men, too, "defiled at this age, grow hard and don't want to repent or correct themselves. Instead they justify the sin," the preacher suggestively added, "saying that all the leading men [uomini da bene] make a practice of it."[40] When he finally arrived at the sexual behavior of the "unrestrained and crazy young men," Bernardino apparently abandoned all attempts at classification. Such nuances were useless because "all your evil youths," he declared, "will be burned and consumed by the wrath of God" for their sodomy.[41]

Bernardino obviously used his schema to represent patterns or impressions, not proportions. An examination of the ages of adult males denounced to the Officers of the Night, again between 1478 and 1483, tends to bear out what he saw and described. For example, the mean age of those "active" partners whose ages I have precisely documented was slightly under thirty-four. The average male, then, accused of having sexual relations with an adolescent in these years fell exactly into the middle of the *giovani*, among whom Bernardino found the most homosexual activity. The overall proportion of youths appearing in these records is also striking. Of all the legal adults — that is, those over the court's majority of eighteen years — implicated in homosexual relations, nearly three-fourths were between the ages of nineteen and forty. One in six was between forty-one and fifty, while only one in ten men implicated was between the ages of fifty-one and seventy.[42] These figures, of course, cannot confirm Bernardino's interesting taxology of sexual behavior, but they do support his impressions that a great many youths were involved in homosexual activity and that some men continued well into their maturity and old age to have relations with boys.

Considering his general line of thinking, Bernardino probably assumed that most of these youths had gained their first homosexual experiences as "passive" *fanciulli*. Nowhere, however, did he elucidate the transition from adolescence to youth that, as we know from both the preacher's remarks and the judiciary evidence, would have entailed a change of roles, from "passive" to "active," from beloved to lover. Nor can my research yet clarify the question. Only an ongoing systematic study of case histories and individual biographies over an extended time period will be able to determine whether those boys who confessed to relationships as adolescents continued to appear in the judicial records as they grew older.[43]

Whatever light further research may shed on this problem, Bernardino stressed that once a boy or youth began to engage in homosexual activity, he would find it too entangling or too attractive to stop, and there was precious little parents or others could do to induce him to change. "When he begins to get involved in sodomy," the preacher sadly warned, "our hands are tied."[44] In fact, he doubted that any young man would willingly give up his affairs and friends: "Whenever youths are seized by this baleful ruin, only with force are they ever cured. . . ."[45] Despite the difficulties, he urged youths to reform while they still had time, because if they reached the age of thirty-two still heavily involved, he warned, "you can just about give up hope."[46] "This cursed vice is rarely abandoned, especially when you have grown old in it, that is, until you are thirty-two years old."[47] Once a youth "passes thirty-three years of age," Bernardino despaired "it is practically impossible for him to turn around. He still can, but it's terribly difficult to get out of it. . . . I tell you, it's just about impossible."[48]

Bernardino's curious insistence that thirty-two or thirty-three was a crucial turning point in a young man's sexual life can only be understood in light of two further considerations. Florentine demographic studies have shown that precisely during the years Bernardino was preaching in Florence, men married at an average age of around thirty or thirty-one.[49] This might not necessarily have had much bearing on Bernardino's argument were it not for a second point: the preacher insisted equally strongly that men who failed to marry were or became sodomites.

> Woe to him who doesn't take a wife when he has the time and a legitimate reason! For remaining single they become sodomites. And take this as a general rule. When you see a man the right age and in good health, who doesn't take a wife, take it as a bad sign about him, if he hasn't already been practicing chastity for spiritual reasons.[50]

Nor was Bernardino alone in suspecting a relationship between this particular age, bachelorhood, and homosexuality. Even before Bernardino made the association, the Florentine government in 1421 had tried to prohibit unmarried men between the ages of thirty and fifty from holding civic offices, probably a veiled effort to bar suspected sodomites from public life as well as to prompt citizens into marrying.[51] Denial of political privileges was no mean threat in republican Florence, where office-holding was an individual's and a family's badge of social and political prestige. The attempt in 1421 failed, but when Bernardino arrived three years later the question was still not dead. "All those who don't live spiritually in chastity, and don't have a wife," he demanded, "drive them out of the city, deprive them of the offices. . . ."[52] In this region that had been wracked by plague and was acutely conscious of its stagnant population, it appears that any man failing to marry when most of his cohorts did so fell under suspicion of sodomy.[53]

   While many Florentines apparently realized the claim that all unmarried men were sodomites could not be sustained, our evidence in fact suggests that most men implicated in homosexual relationships were not married. A study of the marital status of the men incriminated for sodomy from 1478 to 1483 reveals that fully three-fourths of all such men aged nineteen to seventy were unmarried. The proportion of single men is even higher (81 percent) among men who voluntarily turned themselves in to the sodomy officials to take advantage of an immunity clause in the office's statutes.[54] Table 1 reports the marital status of these respective groups according to age. I also present the proportions of males married in the popu-

Table 1. Marital status of men denounced for sodomy, 1478-1483.

age	full sample[a]			self-accusers,[a]			1427[b]
	married	total	%	married	total	%	%
18-30	3	58	5,2	0	12	0,0	21,3
31-40	14	32	43,7	5	12	41,7	63,4
41-50	10	20[c]	50,0	3	7	42,9	82,2
>51	3	11	27,3	1	4	25,0	84,2
unknown[d]	0	3	0,0	—	—	—	
total	30	124	24,2	9	35	25,7	56,7

a. Source: ASF, Ufficiali di Notte 19-23 (1478-1483); ASF, Catasto (1480).

b. Source: D. Herlihy and C. Klapisch-Zuber, Les Toscans, Appendix V, Table 2.

c. Includes two men who possibly were widowers.

d. Includes active partners only.

lation at large in 1427, the only year for which such figures are currently available. Using the 1427 figures cautiously as a rough comparative guide, we see that in every age group in both samples, but especially among the self-accusers, a substantially lower proportion of men was married than one would expect to find in the general male population. Now this striking pattern may, of course, partly reflect the "targeting" of bachelors, who were likely to arouse suspicion as candidates for homosexual relations simply because they remained unattached heterosexually. It should also be emphasized that even repeated denunciations for sodomy, regardless of marital status, do not constitute proof of exclusive homosexual behavior because these records cannot divulge heterosexual activity outside the interests of the court. Yet such cautionary points merely qualify without discrediting Bernardino's interpretation. Just as it took great effort for youths to be "cured" of sodomy, as he suggestively put it, so perhaps "only by force and late in life, if ever, do they permit themselves to be united in marriage."[55]

The preacher had a ready explanation of this characteristic behavior. "The sodomite hates women," he claimed, indeed "can't bear the sight of women."[56] And women, in turn, justifiably disliked sodomites, Bernardino responded even as he encouraged this gender hostility.

> It's the nature of women to hate sodomites, just as sodomites hate women. There is enmity between them: the one hates the other. . . . And I tell you that if you women bear enmity towards [sodomites] you have good reason, in fact it seems more than reasonable. It's like sawing something in two: you dislike me, and I dislike you.[57]

He reasoned that women's "natural" hatred for sodomites derived from the ancient enmity God ordained between Eve and her daughters and the deceptive serpent, who was embodied in sodomites. Yet when he explained why sodomites hated women, Bernardino employed cultural, not biblical, arguments that center the problem in contempt of women. "There are those men so completely wrapped up in [sodomy] that they don't esteem a single woman, so base do they consider them."[58] As he argued on another occasion that God had created men and women to be equal, he also acknowledged that some in his congregation might disagree: "Isn't there any sodomite here," he wondered, "who dislikes women, and says that they're not worth as much as men? We're talking here about those cursed sodomites who are so blind in this their cunningness that, no matter how beautiful a woman is, to him she stinks and isn't pleasing, nor will he ever want to yield to her beauty."[59] The disdain of women Bernardino described was plainly characteristic of this intensely male culture where male and female spheres seldom mixed and women and feminine values were highly scorned.[60] Only the rare fifteenth-century Florentine male would have admitted to Bernardino that women were "worth as much as men." Yet the preacher went a step further and singled out sodomites because they considered women sexually unappealing. Such men's alleged contempt of women may have caricatured more widespread male attitudes, but Bernardino evidently saw sodomites' rejection of women as stemming from their basic erotic orientation.

For those few sodomites who did marry, and for their wives, Bernardino warned, this antagonistic impulse and sexual disinterest would be the source of endless marital strife and unhappiness. "As a general rule," he proposed to his congregation, "the greater a sodomite he is, the more he hates his wife, as pretty as she may be in her own fashion."[61] For this reason, the preacher urged fathers not to give their daughters in marriage to a sodomite, for the frustrated women would never have an hour of contentment.[62] On one occasion, he even advised that a woman would be better off dead than married to a sodomite: "One would rather want to cut her throat than to marry her off to such wicked sodomites of every evil race. Perhaps by murdering her you would save her soul, whereas in marrying such men, giving her to insane sodomites, [she] loses both soul and body."[63] Basically, Bernardino stressed, a married sodomite was still a sodomite, and his erotic nature was such that his wife should not delude herself. There was little she could do to please, much less reform, such a husband. "Oh woman, get it into your head that you will never be able to satisfy [your husband] if he is caught up in this vice. Whatever you do, he will always complain about it, always."[64] He scoffed at wives' futile attempts to seduce their husbands by using cosmetics, teeth-whiteners, provocative dress, and other "vanities": "A note to those women who consider themselves among the elite," he advised. "What do you think you're doing wearing all those things and the styles that the prostitutes wear?" Putting the answer into their mouths, he continued, "[I do it] to please my husband, so that I'm more attractive to him, and he doesn't fall into sodomy."[65] Didn't they realize, he demanded, that their beauty-aids and courtesans' dress would make them more ridiculous and disgusting to their sodomite husbands? Such vanity would have the same effect on her spouse as if she made herself physically repulsive by eating too much, or if she told him she were menstruating.[66] Never too keen anyway on satisfying his conjugal responsibilities, the preacher intimated, her husband would be all too happy for this excuse to avoid having sexual relations with her, and he would flee with relief to his pretty *fanciullo*.

* * *

If questioned, Bernardino probably would have insisted, on the authority of sacred books and patristic heroes of the Christian church, that homosexual behavior was a sin simply because it offended God, regardless of its particular characteristics. As he explained this to his congregations, however, the preacher resorted as much to contemporary social categories as to timeless moral ones to get his points across. His emphasis on life stages, age groups, and social relations shifts the terms of the fifteenth-century discourse about male homosexuality away from morality and criminality, strictly speaking, and toward sexuality and general cultural problems. Only through close attention to the roles of such nonsexual aspects of social organization in shaping homosexual experience and reactions to it can we begin to unravel the complex meanings associated with homosexual behavior and its regulation in this period. In conclusion, we can illustrate these connections by considering two distinct but related sets of issues that underlie Bernardino's views on sodomy and that largely conditioned the problem of male homosexuality in Tuscany.

The most pressing of these concerns was the current demographic crisis. Constantly reminding his audiences of their dramatic population losses, Bernardino placed the blame squarely on sodomites. "Aren't you aware," he demanded, "that this is the reason why you have lost half of your population in the last twenty-five years? Tuscany has fewer people than any country in the world, only because of this vice. . . .'"[67] It is this heightened sensitivity to reproductive problems that probably accounts for Bernardino's piercing attention to such socio-sexual factors as critical ages for males, sodomites' erotic preferences, and marital status. Because of their perceived link to reproductive potentials, these same characteristics undoubtedly influenced the nature of governments' political responses to sodomy. In Florence, for example, the creation of a special sodomy court in 1432 was clearly only one of a broad range of measures that, taken as a whole, were intended to strengthen the institution of marriage and to encourage procreation.[68] If later sentencing patterns are any indication, such social considerations continued to play a large role in shaping the court's police activities. As late as 1480 the officials were convicting proportionally four times as many single men as married men, a less than subtle message to men who may have been wavering before the marriage bed.

Like Bernardino, other Tuscans also discriminated about the problem of generations or life stages in homosexual behavior. One obvious indication of this was their alertness to the relationship between age and sex roles. As we have seen, sex roles in homosexual interactions were fairly rigidly associated with particular stages in males' lives. Such role expectations seem to have been conventional, although they were also reinforced by law. Judiciary practice generally helped maintain these roles by meting out unusually severe penalties to those few adults who were incriminated as passive partners.[69] Even in periods when such condemnations were rare, however, most boys apparently abandoned the passive role as they moved out of their teens.

As with adolescents, the homosexual activity of youths — especially unmarried youths — was thought to be linked to their age and social condition. Bernardino had characterized youthful homosexuality almost as a "phase," no less wrong for that, but one that would usually pass with the assumption of marital and political responsibilities. In their policing of homosexual activity, Florentines would continue to treat youth as a special case. For example, the Officers of the Night in 1478 to 1483 convicted thirty-five percent of the men in our sample aged nineteen to thirty, but only twenty-two percent of those aged thirty-one to forty. The proportion of condemned youths rose even higher in the following decade, when under the influence of Savonarola the government waged a repressive campaign against homosexual activity. Probably in part for this reason, youths figured prominently in the opposition to Savonarola; it was youths again who, some fifteen years later, marched on the government palace to protest yet another crackdown.[70] Finally, the Florentine government acknowledged through legislation the special sexual status of youth by introducing graduated penalties for adult sodomy offenders based on their ages. A law of 1514 created reduced fines for young men between eighteen and twenty-five, while men above that age were to be fined at twice the lower sum. In 1527 another law extended this principle by adding a much higher fine level for men over thirty. The new sodomy measures both carved out a distinct legal status for youth, something long established in cultural and judicial convention, and also guaranteed, if only temporarily, youths' relatively preferential treatment under the law.[71]

These brief examples show some of the ways late medieval and early modern Tuscans organized their society's experience of male homosexual behavior. They emphasize, as do the sermons of Bernardino, the complex and variable significance of sodomy in this culture. Bernardino gave us some useful guides in this matter, but of course he did not intend to speak for all Tuscans. Chiefly lacking are the voices of the powerless, those men and boys whom he and his society castigated as sodomites. While we can begin to chart their social characteristics, and while we can calculate the violence done to them by the authorities, we can only dimly discern how these men and boys themselves interpreted their homosexual activities.

Before the repression had begun in earnest, however, Bernardino had hinted that such men's own image of themselves—radically different from the preacher's—was as dangerous as their behavior. "You see such excited delight among the passionate sodomites who, delight upon delight, abandon God. They have lost all shame, and nothing worries them."[72] And this, for Bernardino and many others, was intolerable.

NOTES

1. I have used the following editions of Bernardino's sermons: Bernardino da Siena, *Le prediche volgari*, ed. C. Cannarozzi, Florentine sermons, 1424, 2 vols. (Pistoia: Tip. Cav. Alberto Pacinotti & Co., 1934); Florentine sermons, 1425, 3 vols. (Florence: Libreria Editrice Florentina, 1940); Sienese sermons, 1425, 2 vols. (Florence: Tip. E. Rinaldi, 1958); and *Le prediche volgari*, ed., P. Bargellini, Sienese sermons, 1427 (Milan: Rizzoli, 1936). See also *S. Bernardini senensis Opera Omnia*, 8 vols. (Florence: Typographia Collegii S. Bonaventurae, 1956), T. 3: 267-284: "De horrendo peccato contra naturam." These sermons will be referred to by the city in which they were preached and their date. All translations are mine. Passages cited: (Florence, 1424) 2: 48, 87. For an extended study of homosexuality in Florence, see my forthcoming "Sodomy in Florence (1300-1550): The Politics and Sociability of Male Homosexuality," PhD dissertation, State University of New York, 1988.

2. On the life and influence of Bernardino, I. Origo, *The World of San Bernardino* (New York: Harcourt, Brace and World, 1962); A. G. Ferrers Howell, *San Bernardino of Siena* (London: Methuen and Co., 1913).

3. While the term "sodomy" in Tuscany, as elsewhere in this period, generally intended all nonprocreative sexual acts regardless of the sex of the partners involved, it was male homosexual relations that preoccupied Tuscans and spurred the antisodomy campaign into life. This is plainly the sense in which Bernardino used the term in the discussion of his views that follows. The matter of terminology in the premodern period has engendered a good deal of debate. For now, I have tried to strike a not-always-satisfying compromise by avoiding the use of "homosexual" as a substantive in favor of the contemporary "sodomite."

4. I am grateful to Gene Brucker for kindly furnishing me with valuable references and advice on this point. Published samplings of fourteenth-century Florentine criminal records have turned up only scattered prosecutions for sodomy; see S. Cohn, *The Laboring Classes in Renaissance Florence* (New York: Academic Press, 1980), apps. H.1 and H.2; U. Dorini, *Il diritto penale e la delinquenza in Firenze nel secolo XIV* (Lucca: Domenico Corsi, 1923), 72.

5. On the public administration of brothels in Florence, R. Trexler, "La prostitution florentine au XVe siècle: patronages et clientèles," *Annales E. S. C.* 36 (1981): 983-1015; for Siena, T. Compton, "Sodomy and Civic Doom," *Vector* 11, n. 11 (November, 1975), 57; for similar developments in Lucca, *Inventario del R. Archivio di Stato in Lucca*, 5 vols. (Lucca: Tipografia Giusti, 1872-1946), 213-214; and outside Tuscany, E. Pavan, "Police des moeurs, société et politique à Venise à la fin du Moyen Age," *Revue historique* 264 (1980); 241-288. In 1403 the government of Florence undertook with only partial success a major revision of its legal and institutional arrangements for prosecuting sodomy; (A)rchivio de (S)tato di (F)irenze, Provvisioni, Registri 92, fols. 9r-10r (24 April 1403); ibid., fols. 323r-324r (13 March 1403) Florentine calendar, 1404 modern style. Such dates will hereafter be rendered 1403/04). For continuing Florentine

efforts in the 1410s to devise a new strategy against sodomy, see the passages published in G. Brucker, *The Society of Renaissance Florence. A Documentary Study* (New York: Harper and Row, 1971), 201-3. Siena and neighboring Perugia instituted harsh new laws against sodomy in 1425 under the direct influence of Bernardino; Origo, *World*, 152. Venice was also a leader in the Italian crusade against sodomy; that city's extensive repression has recently been documented in G. Ruggiero's important *The Boundaries of Eros. Sex Crimes and Sexuality in Renaissance Venice* (New York: Oxford University Press, 1985); and E. Pavan, "Police." I wish to thank Professor Ruggiero for allowing me to read his manuscript chapter on homosexuality in Venice before his book's publication.

6. The law instituting the *Ufficiali di Notte* in Florence is in *ASF, Provisioni Registri* 23, fols. 31v-36v (13 April 1432), a small portion of which is published in G. Brucker, *Society*, 203-4. In August 1433, the task of safeguarding the inviolability and honor of female convents was added to the office's original competence, but throughout the fifteenth century such cases constituted only a tiny fraction of its entire proceedings. For the *Offizio sopra l'Onestà* in Lucca, *Archivio di Stato di Lucca, Consiglio Generale* 16, fol. 796v (8 March 1448).

7. Bernardino repeatedly used this term to describe parents. See *Prediche* (Florence, 1424), 2: 41.

8. *Prediche* (Siena, 1427), 898.

9. On jokes among schoolboys, ibid. (Florence, 1425), 3: 42; sodomite friends invited to the house, ibid. (Florence, 1424), 2: 40, 41; on "chatter," ibid. (Florence, 1424), 2: 49. At the end of the century, Savonarola would still be complaining about the Florentine habit of "talking and chattering about the vice"; cited in Trexler, "Prostitution," 1006.

10. *Prediche* (Florence, 1425), 2: 274.

11. Ibid. (Florence, 1425), 3:41. Elsewhere, Bernardino specified age twelve as the age of discretion; cf. D. Herlihy and C. Klapisch-Zuber, *Les Toscans et leurs familles* (Paris: Fondation Nationale des Sciences Politiques, 1978), 571.

12. *Prediche*, (Florence, 1425), 3: 39.

13. Ibid., 42.

14. Ibid., 44.

15. On Florentine attitudes toward male adolescents and youths, equated with women and the lower classes because of their uncontrollable passions, see R. Trexler, *Public Life in Renaissance Florence* (New York: Academic Press, 1980), 16. Trexler studies the disruptive festive activities of boys' groups in "De la ville à la Cour. La déraison à Florence durant la République et la Grand Duché," in *Le Charivari*, eds. J. Le Goff and J. C. Schmitt (Paris: Mouton, 1981), 165-176.

16. In this regard, Bernardino's preoccupation with adolescence clearly reflected, and perhaps encouraged, the formation of confraternities specifically for adolescents for their instruction in moral values and decorous behavior. As Richard Trexler has shown, these companies, which were just beginning to appear in the 1410s and 1420s, grew steadily throughout the fifteenth century, laying the groundwork for Savonarola's city-wide brigades of *fanciulli* at the end of the century. Savonarola's mobilization of these thousands of youngsters was part of a

vast "moral purity" campaign that included a frontal assault on male homosexuality; R. Trexler, "Ritual in Florence: Adolescence and Salvation in the Renaissance," In *The Pursuit of Holiness in Late Medieval and Renaissance Religion*, eds. C. Trinkaus and H. A. Oberman (Leiden: Brill, 1974): 200-64.

17. These estimates are derived from a detailed analysis of the *Ufficiali di Notte* records from 1478 to 1483. In these five years, a total of 1,117 individuals came to the attention of the magistrates, 18 of whom were accused of entering convents without a license, 9 implicated for heterosexual sodomy, and 1,090 (97.6%) incriminated for homosexual relations. Of the latter, 970 were residents of Florence or its immediate environs, and the remaining 120 came mainly from other towns in the Florentine territory, especially Prato, Pistoia, and Pisa. The information on ages and other social characteristics I use here results from a sample of 183 Florentine men and boys accused of sodomy who I was able to identify in the Florentine *Catasto* of 1480, a tax that also furnishes detailed data on household composition and wealth. Anthony Molho's kind assistance greatly facilitated my work in the 1480 *Catasto*. I have drawn the basic age data for the general population from D. Herlihy and C. Klapisch-Zuber's fundamental study of Tuscan demographic structure, *Les Toscans*, based on their computerized analysis of the 1427 *Catasto*. For my purposes, Appendix 5, Table 2 has been invaluable. For an updated and expanded study of the homosexual sodomy cases prosecuted by the Officers of the Night from 1478 to 1502, see M. Rocke, "Il controllo dell'omosessualità a Firenze nel XV secolo: gli *Ufficiali di Notte*," *Quaderni Storici* 66, n. 3 (1987), 701-723.

18. These figures are based on the fifty-eight passive partners among the Catasto group of 183 (see above, note 17). Almost exactly the same age characteristics for passives are described for Venice by E. Pavan, "Police," 284. Despite the reservations expressed by J. Boswell, in the late middle ages in Italy, at least, passivity was in general closely associated with adolescence, and was not simply a "cultural convention"; *Christianity, Social Tolerance and Homosexuality* (Chicago: University of Chicago Press, 1980), 28-30. The following table expresses sex role differences by age (up to thirty) for those boys and youths whose ages I could identify precisely in the *Catasto*.

AGE	PASSIVE	ACTIVE	AGE	PASSIVE	ACTIVE
10	2	0	21	0	2
11	0	0	22	0	8
12	5	0	23	1	2
13	7	2	24	0	4
14	9	0	25	0	1
15	13	0	26	0	4
16	9	2	27	0	6
17	3	2	28	0	2
18	5	5	29	0	4
19	3	1	30	0	2
20	1	9			

19. *Prediche* (Siena, 1425), 2: 106.

20. *Prediche* (Florence, 1425), 3: 42.

21. Ibid., (Florence, 1424), 2: 39; cf. ibid. (Florence, 1424), 2: 46.

22. Ibid., (Siena, 1427), 908. Pavan attributes an important role to violence in determining the character of sodomy in Venice; "Police," 284-86. For Florence, however, I have found only scattered evidence of violence or homosexual rape.

23. *Prediche* (Siena, 1427), 904.

24. Ibid.

25. Ibid. (Florence, 1425), 2: 184.

26. Ibid. (Florence, 1424), 2: 35.

27. Ibid., 2: 47. Considering Bernardino's opinions that men no less than women in Florentine society were responsible for "effeminizing" their sons and instilling in them refined tastes and manners, D. Herlihy's exclusive emphasis on women's assumed predominant role in the transmission of such cultural values is not justifiable. See his important "Vieillir à Florence au Quattrocento," *Annales, E.S.C.* 24 (1969): 1338-52, esp. 1345.

28. *Prediche* (Siena, 1425), 2: 100.

29. Ibid. (Siena, 1427), 898.

30. *ASF, Ufficiali di Notte* 30, fol. 43v (11 December 1495).

31. Ibid., fol. 54r (19 January 1495/96).

32. In 1478-83, approximately 20 percent of the "actives" and 30 percent of the "passives" bore surnames, a rough indicator in Florence of elevated social position. A list of these individuals would include many of the more ancient and important family names in Florence. On political factions and patronage in Florence see, for example, D. V. and F. W. Kent, *Neighbours and Neighbourhood in Renaissance Florence: The District of the Red Lion in the Fifteenth Century* (Locust Valley, NY: J. J. Augustin, 1982); D. Kent, *The Rise of the Medici: Faction in Florence 1426-1434* (Oxford: Oxford University Press, 1978).

33. *Prediche* (Florence, 1425), 3: 42. The kind of informal prostitution Bernardino describes here was apparently frequent; evidence for it abounds in the judiciary sources from the end of the century.

34. Ibid. (Siena, 1427), 897.

35. *Prediche* (Siena, 1427), 898.

36. Ibid. (Florence, 1424), 2: 59.

37. *Prediche* (Siena, 1427), 897. This description, with the addition "in heat," occurs frequently in the anonymous denunciations to the *Ufficiali di Notte* sixty and seventy years after Bernardino's sermons. It appears to have been a standard expression in the vocabulary of Florentine sexual imagery.

38. Bernardino's curious inattention to social status is probably due more than anything else to the difficulty in distinguishing these men from the rest of the population solely on the basis of their occupation or wealth. The men incriminated for sodomy in 1478 to 1483 represent more or less a social cross-section of Florentine society.

39. *Prediche* (Florence, 1424), 2: 49-51. Bernardino did not specify these ages, but he was surely following typical Florentine usage. On age group designa-

tions, see D. Herlihy, "Vieillir," 1339; R. Trexler, "Adolescence," 201, n. 2; the same author's *Public Life, passim.*

40. In this rare allusion to social status, Bernardino intriguingly implies that among certain men vying for social and political prestige, homosexual affairs may have been seen as a mark of distinction.

41. *Prediche* (Florence, 1424), 2: 51.

42. The mean age of "active" partners is derived from the ages of 120 males so defined among my demographic sample of 183 individuals, including 11 active minors eighteen or under. The proportions for all adults, active and passive, are as follows: 19-30, 50 (43.9%); 31-40, 34 (29.8%); 41-50, 18 (15.8%); 51-60, 6 (5.3%); 61-70, 6 (5.3%). Lacking precise population figures for 1480, it can only be estimated, on the basis of 1427 figures, that the nineteen- to forty-year olds are proportionately more numerous, and the fifty-one- to seventy-year olds less numerous, than their respective age cohorts in the population at large.

43. Individual examples of such a transition, however, are not infrequent. Berto di Salvi Salvolini, for instance, was nineteen when in 1479 he first appeared before the Officers of the Night, confessing that he had been sodomized by eleven different men within the preceding year. In the next couple of years he turned up several more times, both as the passive and, occasionally, as the active partner in various relationships. Finally, after a decade in which he is lost to view, Salvolini, now in his early thirties, appeared with seven different partners between 1491 and 1494, always as the active partner with adolescent boys. His cases appear in *ASF, Ufficiali di Notte,* vol. 19 books 2 and 3, and vols. 20, 22, 27, 28, and 29.

44. *Prediche* (Florence, 1424), 2: 45.

45. *Opera omnia,* 2: 83.

46. *Prediche* (Siena, 1427), 919.

47. Ibid. (Florence, 1424), 2: 35.

48. Ibid. (Siena, 1425), 2: 109.

49. Women, on the other hand, married at an average age of less than eighteen in 1427; D. Herlihy and C. Klapisch-Zuber, *Les Toscans,* 204-9, and chap. 14, "Le mariage"; D. Herlihy, "Vieillir," 1347-49, comments on the possible relationship between late age at marriage for males and homosexuality. Cf. J. Kirshner and A. Molho, "The Dowry Fund and the Marriage Market in Early Quattrocento Florence," *Journal of Modern History* 50 (1978); 403-38, esp. 431-34; and the same authors' "Il Monte delle Doti a Firenze dalla sua fondazione nel 1425 alla metà del sedicesimo secolo. Abbozzo di una ricerca," *Ricerche storiche* 10 (1980): 21-47, esp. 41-42, where their calculations put the average age at marriage for males slightly higher.

50. *Prediche* (Florence, 1424), 1: 416.

51. *Biblioteca Nazionale di Firenze, Conventi Religiosi Soppressi,* C.4.895, Priorista di Paolo Pietrobuoni, fol. 105r. The government of Lucca passed a similar law in 1454, and Città di Castello followed suit in 1465; R. Trexler, "Prostitution," 1007, n. 7, citing G. Rezasco, "Segno delle meretrici," *Giornale ligustico* 17 (1890), 188 ff.

52. *Prediche* (Florence, 1424), 2: 47.

53. The population of Tuscany fell drastically in the fourteenth and early fifteenth centuries, due chiefly to the great plague of 1348 and its recurrent manifestations. The population of Florence, for example, declined from an estimated one hundred twenty thousand in the 1340s to less than forty thousand in 1427, from which point it expanded only slightly through the fifteenth century; D. Herlihy and C. Klapisch-Zuber, *Les Toscans*, 176, 183 (Table 16).

54. For the immunity clause, *ASF, Provvisioni, Registri* 123, fol. 35r (17 April 1432). Self-denunciations worked well for both parties, because the self-accuser was absolved completely from those sexual relations to which he confessed, while the officials had a sure suspect in his partner(s). The obvious but perhaps not sole motive in such cases was to avoid having to pay the stiff fines imposed on convicted offenders. The relationships divulged through such self-accusations, presumably true, are clearly invaluable for understanding the nature of homosexual behavior in Florence without having to depend entirely on the problematic conviction patterns.

55. *Opera omnia*, 2: 83. For some men homoerotic relationships may have been seen as an alternative to heterosexual marriage. An anonymous individual wrote to the Officers of the Night that "Niccolò, son of Brunetto, shoemaker . . . retains Bastiano his apprentice, [who is] about sixteen years old. He keeps him at home like a wife. And in fact he isn't married, so that his wife is Bastiano"; *ASF, Ufficiali di Notte* 30, fol. 43r (9 December 1495).

56. *Prediche* (Florence, 1425), 2: 276; (Siena, 1427), 917.

57. Ibid. (Siena, 1427), 910-11.

58. *Prediche* (Siena, 1425), 2: 105.

59. Ibid. (Siena, 1427), 410.

60. For negative attitudes toward women in this society, see cited remarks of various Florentine moralists and others in D. Herlihy, "Vieillir," 1342-45. The many articles of C. Klapisch-Zuber provide the most sensitive analyses of women's position in this society; some of them are now collected in *Women, Family, and Ritual in Renaissance Italy* (Chicago: University of Chicago Press, 1985).

61. *Prediche* (Florence, 1425), 2: 276.

62. Ibid.

63. Ibid. (Florence, 1424), 1: 387. Bernardino claimed that sodomy between husband and wife was the worst of all forms of sodomy; ibid. (Florence, 1425), 2:184; (Siena, 1427), 435.

64. Ibid. (Siena, 1427), 897.

65. Ibid. (Florence, 1424), 2: 141.

66. On the use of cosmetics and their effect on husbands, ibid. (Siena, 1427), 853; wives making themselves physically unappealing, ibid., 428-29; danger of telling husband she is menstruating, ibid., 436.

67. *Prediche* (Florence, 1424), 2: 20; cf., ibid. (Siena, 1425), 2: 106, 107; and ibid. (Siena, 1427), 906-8.

68. I treated this subject more fully in a paper presented at the International Congress on Medieval Studies, Western Michigan University, Kalamazoo, 9-12 May 1985, entitled, " 'A Court for Sodomites': Sexual Politics and the Regula-

tion of Male Homosexual Activity in Fifteenth-Century Florence." See also R. Trexler, "Prostitution," 984.

69. One among several possible examples is the case of nineteen-year-old Giovanni di Giorgio Albanese, fined twenty-five florins when passives under eighteen were absolved and actives over eighteen normally received fines of only ten florins; *ASF, Ufficiali di Notte* 25, fol. 48r (21 September 1490).

70. The youth group known as the *Compagnacci*, formed in 1497, terrorized Savonarola's followers. Many of the group's leaders whose identities are known, had earlier been or were in these years prosecuted by the Officers of the Night. In 1512 a group of youths demanded that the government release men recently jailed for sodomy; G. Cambi, *Istorie di Giovanni Cambi, cittadino fiorentino*, in *Delizie degli eruditi toscani*, ed. I. di San Luigi, 24 vols. (Florence: per Gaetano Cambiagi stampator granducale, 1770-86), 21: 308:09.

71. *ASF, Miscellanea Repubblicana* busta 66, fol. 361rv (24 January 1513/14); *ASF, Provvisioni, Registri* 206, fols. 17r-18v (16 June 1527); L. Cantini, *Legislazione Toscana* 32 vols. (Florence: nella Stamperia Albizziniana da S. Maria in Campo, 1800: 211-13 (8 July 1542).

72. *Prediche* (Florence, 1424), 2: 48.

"Socratic Love" as a Disguise for Same-Sex Love in the Italian Renaissance

Giovanni Dall'Orto

The recent stimulating discussion about the "historical construction of the homosexual" (fostered by authors such as Plummer, Weeks, Foucault, and others) deals with the problem of when who we now call "homosexual people" began to identify themselves as a "different" category, and when society began to see them as a distinct minority. In other words, when did the "homosexual" take the place of the "sodomite." Recently, the original hypothesis that the category of homosexuality was created about 1850 through the diagnostic and classificatory work of physicians, psychiatrists, and neurologists has yielded to other theories, and the beginning of a homosexual subculture, with features comparable to the modern ones, has been fixed—for now—at the beginning of the eighteenth century.

Some participants in the debate assume that before the eighteenth century no homosexual self-consciousness, self-labeling, and subculture could occur: they claim that our ancestors could only perceive individual sodomitical acts, inasmuch as the idea of a "sexual drive" as part of one's core identity was simply nonexistent. Therefore, homosexual people in the past were defined as "single-act sinners." In support of their point of view, they cite the absence in the historical documents of hints about any homosexual subcultures, and especially the absence of any concept similar to that of "homosexuality" as we know today.

Giovanni Dall'Orto can be reached at Edilnord, Fontana 203, Via Volturno 80, I 20067 Brugherio (MI), Italy.

My point of view is somewhat different. This article will seek to prove that the purported "silence" of the old historical documents is in reality very noisy. The research of the scholars whose ideas I have alluded to focused on modern and contemporary history and asked the right questions for the period they were studying, but they missed some important points from earlier centuries. I think that what has deceived many until now was their attempt to discover in the old mentality a concept similar to that of "homosexuality." However, such a concept does not seem to have existed before the eighteenth or nineteenth century.

The "birth" of the homosexual in the eighteenth century seems simply to have been the outcome of a process which took many centuries, and it is possible to recognize the emergent features of the homosexual much earlier. The eighteenth century merely *sanctioned* the existence of a reality which was well known before although not officially recognized.

Long before 1700 we find documents revealing beneath the "single-act sins" of sodomy a meaning that theoretically (according to official mentality) should not exist.[1] Until now we have been looking for germs of "homosexual self-consciousness" in the past in terms of defenses or exaltations of "homosexuality" in the etymological meaning. We have in fact been searching, with little success, for discussions of *sexualitas* — that is to say, in the old terminology, of "sodomy." But this is exactly what the older society condemned and punished.[2]

In any event, the word "homosexuality," as we generally use it, also includes the concept of "homoeroticism." Therefore, it would seem wise to approach the question from the other side, by looking for testimonies of *homoeroticism* in the historical literature. After all, while sodomy was always condemned, homoeroticism was not always condemned. Moreover, not all nonconformists choose to fight, openly opposing the society they live in. On the contrary, most of them try to find agreement and strive to demonstrate that the new ideas they propose are mere orthodox extensions of those ideas that they reject.

This article will analyze a phenomenon that until now has been virtually ignored by gay scholars: *amor socraticus* as theorized in Italy during the fifteenth and sixteenth centuries.[3] By referencing new or little-known documents, I will strive to demonstrate that this concept can amount to a coherent strategy to justify what we now call a "homosexual drive," allowing a person to express it openly (or at least as openly as possible). Moreover, we shall see how a very different strategy from those we know today can be as successful as modern ones—if not more so.

I need not describe the philosophical evolution of the concept of amor socraticus, a task already accomplished by many other scholars.[4] I merely want to analyze the connection (if any) between what we now call "homosexual love" and what our ancestors called amor socraticus.[5]

THE ITALIAN RENAISSANCE
AND THE SODOMITE

One of the most interesting questions awaiting analysis in this field of research is the following: our age seems not to have been the only one in which same-sex behavior has been ascribed to an inborn condition. Yet at least two historical periods, ancient Greece and the Italian Renaissance, seem to share this point of view in some way.

Unlike the official Church position, in which same-sex contacts were considered as *acts*, sins fueled by devilish impulses, it seems that many people hold the opinion that sodomy was a sort of sickness, a mania. At the same time, it also seems that many sodomites made every possible effort to avoid self-labeling as such (intercrural, rather than anal copulation, is common in fourteenth- and fifteenth-century trials, even in cases of rape) and successfully managed to defend their behavior and feelings. Many "sodomites," for instance, alleged that inasmuch as kings, popes, and even ancient gods practiced sodomy, how could it really be evil?[6] Others kept their feelings of guilt under control assuming that before dying they would confess and repent, and thus be saved.[7] Those who were closer to "libertine" thought and stated that religious morality was a fraud, invented to keep people under control.

Obviously, there must have been people (especially in towns) aware of what sodomy was and who, being "good Christians," abstained from it throughout their lives. These people did not need to wonder whether or not they were sodomites: the very fact of being subject to temptation was a normal feature of human nature. They might have fallen in love with other men, but in an age when "homosociality" allowed among people of the same sex an intimacy now shunned, their feelings were probably perceived, as mere "friendship." Medieval literature is full of examples of such a "faithful" friendship, which was also affection, devotion – in sum, "love."[8] That sexuality and affectivity can be experienced in separate spheres is commonly accepted. Experiencing strong, involving love for someone of the same sex, without anything openly unchaste, is essentially what "Socratic love" meant to fifteenth-century society.

"SOCRATIC LOVE"

Amor socraticus is one of the names given to a "new form" of love, the rediscovery of platonic love made by Marsilio Ficino (1433-1499) in the very period when scholars rediscovering ancient Greek authors were achieving important results. Ficino himself translated the works of Plato from Greek into Latin, thus allowing a much wider public to read them. He not only popularized Plato, but also worked hard to fit his thought into the Christian mould, to demonstrate that nothing in Plato was against the "true faith." So passionate was his Neoplatonism that he was dubbed *"Plato redivivus."*

Together with the rest of Plato's philosophy, Ficino also rediscovered the ancient's theory of love, which he adopted as his own. Following Plato, Ficino declared that through the beauty of the human body we can admire a reflection of God's own beauty, which is its model, its "idea." In Ficino's thought, the human body is seen as a link connecting the tangible world and God: it stands halfway between the two. Moreover, only love can grasp the reality of God, which is the source and idea of any human love, whereas the human mind is limited, and can know only a part of the truth.

Of course, true love must not be tainted by lechery, nevertheless, this does not mean that "vulgar love" is to be banned from human life, but rather that it must be kept under control to avoid its transformation into *amor ferinus*, "beastly love," or its encroachment upon heavenly love. Ficino does not expect all human beings to become chaste, but simply hoped for heavenly love to prevail over vulgar love.

The Ficinian popularization of Plato's conception of love did not try to change or minimize its homoerotic overtones. Here is how Ficino dealt with the question in his *Commentarium in Platonis Convivium* (written 1469), book 6, chapter 14:

According to Plato, the soul is as pregnant as the body, and they are both aroused to procreation by the stimuli of love. But some men, either on account of their nature or their training, are better equipped for offspring of the soul than for those of the body. Others, and certainly the majority of them, are the opposite. The former pursue heavenly love, the latter earthly. The former, therefore, naturally love men more than women and those nearly adults rather than children, because the first two are much stronger in mental keenness, and this because of its higher beauty is most essential to knowledge, which they naturally wish to generate. But the others are just the opposite, because of their passion for the physical union of love, and the sensuous effect of bodily generation. But, since that genital force of the soul has no power of cognition, it makes no discrimination between the sexes; but is, naturally, aroused for generation whenever we see any beautiful object, and it consequently happens that those who associate with males have intercourse with them in order to satisfy the urge of their genital parts.

This is especially frequent in people for whom Venus was in the masculine sign and in conjunction, or in termination or opposition, with Saturn. [It is not pleasant to do,] but we ought to have noticed that erections of the genital parts do not naturally bring about this ejaculation in vain, but for the purpose of fertilization and procreation, and the carrying of that part from the male to the female. We think that by some error of this sort that wicked crime arose which Plato in *The Laws* most severely condemns as a form of homicide. Certainly he is no less to be censored as a homicide who snatches from life a man about to be born than one who carries him out of mid-life when he has been born; very bold indeed is he who interrupts present life, but more cruel still is he who begrudges the light to the infant about to be born and denies life to his still unborn children.[9]

Interestingly enough, in this explanation is the implicit idea that *some* people are more inclined toward same-sex love — although "the genital force of the soul makes no discrimination between the sexes" — not because of the devil's temptation, but for an inborn reason. Ficino explained in fact the proclivity to make love with males as fostered by a "natural" phenomenon: birth during the conjunction of the planets Venus and Saturn. This explanation could have been another pretext to justify one's drive toward male love.[10]

After condemning sexual intercourse between males, in the same work Ficino recommended *love* between men as a real, useful, and good feeling. In book 7, chapter 16, he wrote:

Do you ask for what the Socratic Love is useful? First, indeed, it avails most to a man for recovering those wings by which to fly back to his fatherland. Second, it avails greatly to his state for living honestly, and happily. Truly, "men, not stones, make up a state." But men, from their youth, like trees, have to be protected from weaker men and trained for the best fruit. Parents and teachers have the care of children, but youths no sooner escape the supervision of parents and teachers than they are debased by wicked association with the mob. Certainly they would follow that higher level of living received from their master, if they were not deflected from it by the intimacy and the companionship of wicked men, especially those who flatter them. . . .

So the true love, like a shepherd, keeps his flock of lambs safe from false lovers as from the ravage of wolves and disease. Since, in fact, equals are easily congregated with equals, he makes himself equal with the young man in purity of life, in simplicity of language, games, jokes, and witticisms. He makes himself a boy instead of an old man in the first place, so that he may at some time make boys into mature men by his personal and pleasing intimacy.[11]

In these passages we see how Ficino carefully separated sodomy and homoeroticism into two distinct spheres. If we consider homosexuality as only a social construction, we may find this separation of same-sex love and same-sex behavior very natural. We may assume that it also seemed natural to everyone, before the "invention" of the homosexual, a concept which combines two aspects of human life which, in themselves, have nothing necessarily in common.

Yet this is not what actually happened. The history of the concept of Socratic love became a struggle against the identification of same-sex love with same-sex behavior. The efforts of philosophers notwithstanding, the two concepts became intertwined, thus condemning Socratic love to death after less than one century. Of course, the fact that sixteenth century people could not restrain themselves from identifying same-sex love with same-sex behavior does not prove that these things are intrinsically linked, but it does demonstrate that some people in the sixteenth century already had a point of view about same-sex behavior close to our view of homosexuality.

SOCRATIC LOVE AS A DISGUISE FOR HOMOSEXUAL LOVE

Ficino presented amor socraticus as a delicate, refined form of relationship among highly cultivated individuals. When recognizing the mystical aspects of Ficino, one must avoid dismissing his deep, sincere love toward God as a mere tribute paid to social convention. Amor socraticus was a very philosophical, highly stylized, and rather mystical way of interacting between two men. To work properly, it required of both partners the will *to go beyond*; that is, to use the other's beauty and knowledge to reach what was beyond both, to true beauty, to true knowledge, to God. This high ideal could work only in a semi monastic, closed philosophical setting such as the Neoplatonic circle. When popularized among less cultured and more earthly people (which happened when Ficino himself translated his *Commentarium* into Italian) the loss of these delicate features was probably unavoidable.

With the wisdom of hindsight, we realize that most people who allegedly adopted Ficino's conception of love were merely reviving *Stilnovismo* (whose supreme expression is in Dante's work): through the beauty of a woman, and love toward her, the soul of a man can reach God. This said, it is easier to understand why from the beginning amor socraticus had tended in the mind of outsiders to be identified with sodomy.

George of Trebizond (1396-1486) and Cardinal Bessarion (1403-1472)

We must admit that amor socraticus was born under ill omens. In fact, a heated dispute before its birth involved the Italian intelligentsia. George of Trebizond, a Byzantine Aristotelian, launched an attack against Plato in his book *In comparationes Aristotelis et Platonis* (1455). In it he condemned Plato's opinions, which he judged subversive of Christian honesty, charity, and orthodoxy.

About platonic love he wrote (book 3, chap. 17):

> O ignavas principum christianorum mentes! O animos potentum non omnium, sed Platonicorum in clunibus puerorum turpiter inclusos! . . . Multa possunt viri decori, cum velint; volentque forsan, si Platonem contemnent et nates relinquent.[12]

And he went even further. In book 3, chapter 16, he called sodomy *Platonica venus*: "Sed doleo, quoniam, quemadmodum sancta orientalium monachorum vita in Platonicam ex ipsa Platonis lectione venerem lapsa [est]."[13]

Cardinal Bessarion answered at length in his *In calumniatorem Platonis libri IV* (Greek text 1457-58, Latin translation printed in Rome in 1469), writing that Plato reproved sodomy very harshly and that George was simply exploiting the fact that the word amor, "love," is used to describe different phenomena. Even the Bible speaks of love, but this does not authorize us to think of anything sensual or lecherous. A chaste, heavenly, almost "Christian" love; this is what Plato recommends.[14]

Other Italian writers subsequently attacked George, and eventually public opinion came to favor Bessarion's position. Such was the situation in Italy when Ficino wrote his *Commentarium*.

Marsilio Ficino and Giovanni Cavalcanti (1444?-1509)

Given this situation, Ficino must have been aware of the possible "misinterpretations" of his Neoplatonic conception of love. He therefore *willingly* chose to think that nothing in Plato's writings suggested what George said. This is why Ficino refused to do what was later done by Castiglione and Bembo—to "heterosexualize" platonic love. There were philosophical and personal elements to his decision. As the dispute between George of Trebizond and Cardinal Bessarion demonstrated, the Italian intelligentsia in that period felt more at ease with the interpretation of the latter. Neoplatonism meant a new approach to the world. People were "hungry" for it, and it became a fashion, a craze, just as existentialism did in Europe after World War II. So it was very easy to dismiss the Aristotelian George, and Ficino was not the only one who chose to ignore George's objections. The cultural climate of the period suffices to explain his choice.

Nevertheless, there was another aspect to his choice—a personal one. To say it plainly, Ficino was probably a homosexual man. This does not mean that he was attracted to Neoplatonism for this reason.[15] In my opinion, his homosexuality had no effect on his philosophical ideas, but rather on his willingness to *live*, to *embody* the type of love he theorized. Such a decision did not simply reflect the "cultural climate of the period"; it required a personal motive.

Ficino enthusiastically sought a love relationship with Giovanni Cavalcanti, a young man to whom he dedicated the *Commentarium*, and who is called his "only true friend" (*amicus unicus*) in his letters. When writing to Cavalcanti, Ficino sometimes rebuked him a bit peevishly, asking him to write longer or more frequent letters or to write first. From his correspondence with Cavalcanti, it appears Ficino was really "in love" with Giovanni, who, however, was much less inflamed and behaved "only" as a friend, not as a lover. Ficino reproached him: *Amatorias posco literas, non mercatorias!"* But while accepting the same Neoplatonic approach to life as Ficino, Cavalcanti did not share the burning flame that kindled the heart of his infatuated friend.

It is also remarkable that, although according to Ficino (who gave him a prominent role in the *Commentarium*), Giovanni was a real genius, nothing of his has survived. An outstanding scholar of Ficino generously declared that: "Si l'on juge par tous les traités ou dialogues, où il est question de lui, on peut assurément le considerer comme un des représentants les plus qualifiés de la pensée platonicienne, et un des humanistes les plus distingués."[16] But among his contemporaries (Ficino excepted), Cavalcanti passed quite unnoticed. Maybe the most likely explanation is the simplest one: Ficino overvalued him. He was attracted by his beauty (*"Cum amorem dicimus, pulchritudinis desiderium intelligite,"*)[17] and thus forged a fictitious mental acuity to harmonize the reality of his all-too-earthly desire with the philosophic meaning of his theory.

Love and desire are quite evident in Ficino's letters. Even if Marsilio wanted them to be examples of classic Latin style and of noble, serene feelings, a good deal of anguish, frustrated love, and desire transpire from them. For instance, on 5 January 1474 Ficino wrote:

> Marsilius Ficinus Ioanni Cavalcanti amico unico.
> Non potest manus calamum ducere, nisi ipsa moveatur ab animo. Non poterat his temporibus scribere Marsilius ad Heroem [i.e., Cavalcanti], nisi ante invitatus ab Heroë. Sed unum mihi molestum est prae caeteris, quod ideo scribis ad me, quia promiseris, ergo pactioni istud tribuo, non amori. Amatorias posco literas, non mercatorias, an es etiam pacto meus, scilicet quia ego sum tuus, amore volo sis meus. Vale.[18]

And on an unknown date, he added:

> Magni plerique cives, o Marsili, aiunt, cur tandiu solus in urbe? Quia solum incedere nunc me vult, qui numquam sinit esse me solum. Nondum rediit ergo? Nondum. Non habeo praesens aliud, quod ad te scribam. Scripsi ad te urbana negotia. Scribe ad me tu rustica. Hei mihi erravi, ne scribas volo, sed dicas. Si colloquemur, loquemur mi Heros eadem, dum scribimus, scribimus de diversis. Ego de memoria, de oblivione Ioannes. Sed nolim dixisse istud. Non oblitus est mei meus, quia neque sui. Imo venit iam obsecutus mihi, ecce venit, occurrite mei huic fortunati pedes, excipite foelices ulnae.[19]

And again:

> Amice, quid tamdiu certatim silemus? Quid tandem victori lu-
> cri accedet, victo quid damni? Ego vero in hac silendi pertina-
> cia vinci abs te satius censui, ut in loquendi certamine vin-
> cerem. Ita post hac primae tibi in tacendo partes, mihi primae
> in loquendo dabuntur. Semper ne calcaribus indigebis in sta-
> dio? Nunquam tua sponte curres? Cur mecum tam dure?
> Acrius forsitan iocari tecum videor mi Ioannes. Tu autem agis
> acerrime, acerrime, quoque responde si placet, modo re-
> sponde, sin minus placet, dulciter sile. Meae certe huic ver-
> borum acrimoniae cordis affectum melle dulciorem subesse
> putato. Vale, & tamdiu abesto, quam tua res postulat. Satis
> enim mihi fit cum res agitur tua. Nonis octobris Charegij.[20]

Giovanni Pico della Mirandola (1463-1494) and Girolamo Benivieni (1453-1542)

Ficino was not the only person willing to *live* the amor socraticus. For instance, two other philosophers of his circle, Giovanni
Pico della Mirandola and Girolamo Benivieni, resolved to be buried
together, in a decision that for centuries symbolized love and intimacy between two persons. The words engraved in 1530 by Girolamo Benivieni read:

> Here lies Giovanni Mirandola, the rest know both the Tagus
> and the Ganges and maybe even the Antipodes. He died in
> 1494, and lived for 32 years. Girolamo Benivieni, to prevent
> separate places from disjoining after death the bones of those
> whose souls were joined by Love while living, provided for
> this grave.

Someone later added some Italian verses:

> I pray God Girolamo that in peace
> also in Heaven you may be joined with your Pico
> as you were on earth, and as now your dead
> corpse together with his sacred bones here lies.[21]

Enthusiastic as these philosophers were over the ideal of *amor socraticus*, they were not oblivious to its ambiguity, but like Ficino they preferred to dismiss it as nonexistent or trivial. So Pico della Mirandola stated in his *Commento* to Girolamo Benivieni's *Dell'amore celeste e divino* (written shortly after 1486):

> Socrates loved out of this chaste Love not only Alcibiades, but almost all of the wisest and handsomest men in Athens; and in the same way Zeno was loved by Parmenides, Musaeus by Orpheus, Nicohachus by Theophrastus, Clinias by Xenophon, all of whom did not wish to perform with their beloved ones any filthy actions (as believed by many people, who judge the heavenly thoughts of those philosophers with the measure of their shameful desires), but only to get incitement from the body's outward beauty to look at that of the Soul, from which proceeded and came the bodily one.[22]

Pomponio Leto (1428-1497) and Niccolò Lelio Cosmico (1420-1500)

"They did not wish to perform with their beloved ones any filthy actions," states Pico. Again, we find a specific refusal to identify Socratic love with sodomy. This leads us to suspect that those "many people" represented a significant portion of the educated in Italy, and that Ficino chose to reject the commonsense belief (followed, as we saw, by most Italian intellectuals) when he separated same-sex love from same-sex behavior. Did this "natural" separation seem unclear to Italians during that period and later? Can we say that Ficino's theory was tainted with an intrinsic ambiguity and that the way it was formulated could serve to protect one's proclivity for same-sex behavior?

We can easily perceive the ambivalence of Socratic love in certain documents by two of Ficino's contemporaries. The first, Pomponio Leto, was jailed in 1468, one year before Marsilio wrote his *Commentarium*, on the charge (among others) of alleged sodomy for being too attached to two boys whose beauty he had praised in Latin writings. In the same year, Pomponio wrote a *defensio* to refute the charges. Pomponio admitted having praised the boys' beauty, but he said this was only because their father had done him many favors, appointing him as tutor to the boys and treating Pomponio more as a relative than as a teacher. The boys were like sons to Pomponio.

At this point, Pomponio added: "Rursu de forma exemplum habeo Socratis, qui fuit parens morum et severitatis. Is enim formosis adolescentibus speculum admovebat inquiens: ubi natura tale tibi donum dedit, age ne in moribus ac litteris turpis videare." And after a few more examples, he drew this conclusion: "Nolo bibliothecas excutere, scio enim vos exemplorum omnium refertissimos esse, et satis esse pro tutela mea unius Socratis testimonium."[23]

It is not likely that Pomponio would have quoted Socrates had he not been sure that in the mind of the judges (to which the *defensio* was addressed) no connection could exist between Socratic *mores* and sodomitic ones. He was sure that among cultured people, Socrates and his way of loving conveyed nothing suspect; thus Pomponio could present him as a model.

Yet, only fifteen years later, Niccolò Lelio Cosmico revealed an opposite point of view. In about 1483 he wrote a Latin poem for a Negro boy (almost surely a slave owned by Lorenzo the Magnificent). In the poem, after praising the beauty of the boy's black skin with many hyperboles, Cosmico asked him not to be cruel and to yield. While doing so, the author quoted as an accomplice to his desires the author of the *Symposium*, Plato himself:

> Nec probitas ab amore trahit, sed dura severos rusticitas trucibus nec toleranda feris. Illa et inexpliciti mens observata Platonis, quamvis neglecto corpore casta foret, nec tamen erubuit querulo suspiria motu haec. . . . [lacuna] ludere carminibus: "suggere dilectum puerum dum nitor hiulco suaviolo, ut flores dedala suggit apis." . . . Aspice quam blande ingenuo lascivit amore unquam laudatus non satis ille senex.[24]

There is no doubt as to the meaning Cosmico attached to those "kisses." Here is how another poem of his begins: "Iane, meum certe vix excusabile crimen tot tecum noctes, tot iacuisse dies."[25] ("Janus, my crime is barely forgivable having laid with you for so many nights, so many days.")

Baldassarre Castiglione (1478-1529)
and Carlo Sigonio (1520-1584)

Things were not destined to improve. As time passed, the identification of the love of Socrates and Plato with sodomy became more
and more frequent. A generation after Marsilio Ficino, Baldassarre
Castiglione had two characters of his famous *Il Cortegiano* (written
around 1518, published 1528) discuss continence as follows:

> I myself saw it—Master Cesare answered—therefore I am
> much more sure than you or anybody else could be sure that
> Alcibiade rose from Socrates' bed as pure as sons get up from
> their fathers' beds. A very strange place and time were in fact
> the bed and the night to admire that pure beauty, that Socrates
> is said to have loved without any indecent desire, especially
> loving more the beauty of the soul than the bodily one, but in
> boys and not in old men, although the latter are wiser.[26]

A few years later, the irony of Master Cesare became a certitude
in a letter by Carlo Sigonio, then a young student, to Ludovico
Montio, on 17 November 1538. After accusing the *pedanti* (school
teachers) of being vicious and, above all, of being sodomites, he
added:

> I am sure that before I could carry on with my speech, you
> would interrupt me with examples, to show to me that there
> are, and there have been, pedants who were very learned and
> very noble men, and if I condemn all of them as I am doing, I
> shall offend them. And here you will offer Socrates as an ex-
> ample, saying: "He taught young people too: do you really
> think that he was tainted by so many, and such vices?" To
> which question I shall answer as directly as possible, indicat-
> ing how I feel about it.
>   Socrates was very wise, but even he sinned as a mortal man.
> This is why therefore, I harm no one's honor in not naming
> him in particular, and if by chance somebody wanted to rise to
> defend him, I shall say that not only is he vicious himself, but
> also willing to cover up other people's vices, and to defend
> them by means of a shameless impudence.[27]

Giovanni Della Casa (1503-1556)
and Flaminio Nobili (1530-1590)

In this situation, the shy defense of Socrates made by Giovanni della Casa in his *Galateo* (1558) was not very convincing. Moreover, throughout the *Galateo*, "Platonic Love" was completely "heterosexualized"; the conception of amor socraticus disappeared.

Della Casa stated that most people did not reproach addiction to drinking for fear that "by chance there could happen what happened to Socrates himself for his excessive blaming of everybody, since out of envy he was charged with heresy and other filthy sins, so that he was condemned, although for false reasons, because he was orthodox, according with their false idolatry."[28]

A similar attitude was revealed by Flaminio Nobili in his *Trattato dell'amore humano* (written 1556, published 1567). In it we rediscover, apparently unchanged, the Ficinian-Platonic theory of love:

To incite the love desire of the intellect, Plato and other learned men deemed more convenient the beauty of a young man than that of a young woman; and indeed those who love men are judged by him fecund and pregnant more in their souls rather than in their bodies.[29]

Nobili displayed candid astonishment when confronted with the possibility that things need not follow the normal course: who else, except women, would ever elicit a sexual urge?

Certainly, looking at the nature of things, it seems likely to me that the beauty of males is not suitable to engender carnal concupiscence, as is women's beauty, which was created to excite in us the desire to procreate corporally. But in this matter it is appropriate to trust Plato, and his followers, who loving males, having not allowed themselves to be seized by that indecent appetite, repugnant to Nature in everything, developed a burning desire to avail themselves to them, and make them brave, and wise. And when they obtained it, they thought they had achieved the true aim of their love.[30]

Once more we find same-sex love and sodomy treated together; once more the connection between the two was suggested, even if only to be denied afterwards. The very need to pinpoint this difference is proof that it was not very clear. Why insist on demonstrating what should have been self-evident since the "nature of things" teaches that "the beauty of males is not suitable to engender carnal concupiscence"? Yet Nobili departed even further from Plato and Ficino when he added "women, who have something manly in them" to the list of possible candidates for Socratic love. This was a consequence of growing "heterosexualization" of Socratic love in that period, proposing that women were a proper object for "platonic" passions:

> Therefore the main aim of love is not enjoying human beauty, since Nature cannot have such a base purpose as pleasing the sight by means of a handful of colored dust, or contemplating a still unripe soul, that cannot be capable of much perfection. But by means of male beauty, and perhaps also that of women who have something manly in them, [Nature] fosters us in begetting spiritual sons, and by means of the other, more lecherous beauty, begetting bodily sons.[31]

While apparently agreeing with Ficino, Nobili revealed his skepticism about "Socratic love" as a form of "erotopedagogy": "a still unripe soul cannot be capable of much perfection."

It is now clear why, given these changes, those who insisted in keeping alive the original Ficinian vision of platonic love — as a real passion among people of the same sex — were by this time misunderstood. It is also clear why most (if not all) of them would be defined today as "homosexual" people.

Giordano Bruno (1548-1600)

A little more than a century after the *Commentarium*, the parabola of Socratic love came perfectly to an end when Giordano Bruno, described Socrates as a person having a homosexual *drive (inclinatione)*.

In *De la causa, principio e uno* (1584), Bruno wrote about a *pedante* (a character who, like hairdressers or dancers today, was considered the typical representative of "that" vice): "This sacrilegious pedant comes fourth, one of the philosophers' strict faultfinders, hence he calls himself Momo;[32] a man very attached to his flock of pupils, whence he calls 'Socratic' his love; an everlasting enemy of the female sex."[33] Socratic love was therefore presented as typical of pedants, which at the time was the same as saying sodomy.

But there is more. In his *Spaccio della bestia triunfante* (1584), Bruno argued that continence is not a virtue for those people who, being too "cold" or too old, experience little or no sexual urge, whereas it is a virtue for those who experience it acutely. Therefore:

> If you think of it more profoundly, it is false that Socrates revealed any blemish of his, but rather became much more worth praising for his continence, when he approved the physiognomist's judgement concerning his *natural leaning towards the filthy love of boys (la sua natural inclinatione al sporco amor di gargioni)*.[34]

Although not even Bruno dared doubt Socrates' chastity, he made Socrates something different from a *verus amator*, something we now would call a homosexual. What connection is there between "single-act" sinner and a man experiencing a "natural leaning" toward the "filthy love of boys"? If sodomy is nothing but an act (a *single* act), which is the meaning of the expression "natural leaning" toward it when speaking of a person who, being chaste, never indulged in it?

Moreover, Bruno wrote that lecherous leanings are different from person to person, and immediately after stated that Socrates was a very virtuous man because, although very "inclined" toward love for boys, he resisted it. The corollary, clearly stated by Bruno himself, is that there is no virtue in resisting weak or nonexistent leanings. In sum, the leaning toward people of the same sex, according to Bruno, is different from person to person; it is not a datum which is the same for every man in the same way.

Bruno expressed this opinion while retelling an anecdote by Cicero (*Tusculan disputations*, IV, 37): the physiognomist Zopyrus declares that he sees in Socrates many a vice. Socrates' friends scorn him, but the philosopher himself agrees, admitting having been born with those bad leanings, but to have got rid of them by means of the control of Reason (*cum illa sibi insita, sed ratione a se deiecta diceret*). There are two possibilities: Bruno based his point of view either on the Latin anecdote (revealing that in the Hellenistic world same-sex behavior was seen as a result of a "leaning") or on the cultural *humus* of his own time. In either case, the concept of the "homosexual" being such "by natural leaning" thus appeared long before the alleged "medical construction of homosexuality."

THE HOMOSEXUAL ANSWER: PART 1, MICHELANGELO BUONARROTI (1475-1564)

In the mid-sixteenth century, when ironies, suspicions, and doubts about the real nature of Socratic love were multiplying, many homosexual writers embraced it because they saw it as a valid and prestigious means by which to express their feelings. Space limitations do not allow me to mention all of these writers. Therefore, I will focus upon two well-known authors, Michelangelo Buonarroti and Benedetto Varchi, in order to examine what they wrote and what their contemporaries thought about their defense of Socratic love.

While a boy at the court of Lorenzo the Magnificent, Michelangelo met and was influenced by Ficino himself. It is not surprising then that for the rest of his life he expressed in Neoplatonic terms his feelings toward the boys he loved, especially Tommaso de' Cavalieri. For instance, this is how Michelangelo addressed Cavalieri in 1532:

> If love be chaste, if virtue conquer ill,
> if fortune bind both lovers in one bond,
> if either at the other's grief despond,
> if both be governed by one life, one will;
>
> if in two bodies one soul triumph still,
> raising the twain from earth to heaven beyond,
> if Love with one blow and one golden wand
> have power both smitten breasts to pierce and thrill;

If each the other love, himself forgoing,
with such delight, such savour, and so well,
that both to one sole end their will combine;

If thousands of these thoughts, all thought outgoing,
fail the least part of their firm love to tell:
say, can mere angry spite this knot untwine?[35]

In the same year, Michelangelo left testimony, addressed to Cavalieri regarding the difficulty he experienced in convincing other people to accept his vision of love among men:

If the undying thirst that purifies
our mortal thoughts, could draw mine to the day,
perchance the lord who now holds cruel sway
in Love's high house, would prove more kindlywise.

But since the laws of heaven immortalise
our souls, and doom our flesh to swift decay,
tongue cannot tell how fair, how pure as day,
is the soul's thirst that far beyond it lies.

How then, ah woe is me! shall that chaste fire,
which burns the heart within me, be made known,
if sense finds only sense in what it sees?

All my fair hours are turned to miseries
with my loved lord, who minds but lies alone;
for, truth to tell, who trusts not is a liar.[36]

But Michelangelo, when speaking of "love between two souls," lied about the nature of his love and was aware of doing so. In a sonnet written in 1553 he wrote:

But soon I knew how wrong man's mind can be:
who, wingless, like an angel hopes to run,
he casts a seed on stones, his words are none
but wind, his thoughts of God, mortality.[37]

It is easy to remember that the metaphor of "sowing seed on stones" was used by Plato in his *Laws* to condemn sexual intercourse among men, whereas the idea that "chaste love" "gives wings" to the souls came from Plato's *Phaedrus*.

Keeping in mind those antithetic metaphors, we realize that Michelangelo expressed, in a coded way, the conception that if love between two men cannot achieve the high moral standard required by Plato, it falls into "sowing seed on stones." Michelangelo himself experienced what this sort of "sowing" was like. This is revealed, for instance, by one of the epitaphs he wrote for the young Cecchino Bracci (who died in 1535 at age sixteen) not intended for publication. The epitaph read:

The flesh, now earth, and my few bones, now ridden,
of my sweet eyes and of my pleasing sight,
remind the one to whom I gave delight
of the dark jail in which my soul was hidden.[38]

But the manuscript also bears a different conclusion, where the last two verses read:

Remind the one to whom I was grace in bed,
whom I embraced, and in whom my soul still lives.[39]

Even if we lacked these epitaphs, a letter written by Michelangelo in 1514 would reveal the rumors about his sexuality. In this letter, the then thirty-nine-year-old author complained about a father who at any cost wanted to convince Michelangelo to accept his son as an apprentice. When Michelangelo kindly but firmly refused to do so, the man replied "that if I had seen the boy, not only would I have liked to have him in my house, but in my bed as well." To which Michelangelo hastened to add to his correspondent: "I can tell you that I don't know what to do with this solace, and I don't want to take it away from him.[40]

But the oddity of Michelangelo's view of "Platonic love" became so great that by 1550 even his "official" biographer, Ascanio Condivi (1525-1574) unwillingly demonstrated by his words that he himself could not understand its meaning any more. When writing his *Vita* (published 1553), Condivi was probably guided by Michelangelo himself to such an extent that some consider Condivi's biography a sort of "as-told-to" book. Condivi attempted to remove any suspicions of sodomy from Michelangelo, but did it so awkwardly that he actually confirmed that Michelangelo had been suspected of sodomy:

> He also loved corporeal beauty, being a person who knew it very well, and loved it in a way that was the pretext, among some carnal men who cannot conceive any love of Beauty unless it is lecherous and shameful, to think and to speak badly of him, as if Alcibiades, a very handsome young man, had not been very chastely loved by Socrates, about which the young man used to say that when they slept together, he got up from bed as if he had slept with his own father.
>
> I myself heard Michelangelo reasoning and discussing about love, and I heard afterwards from those who attended that he spoke about love in the same way that can be read in Plato, and not elsewhere.[41]

It was a gamble to cite Socrates and Alcibiades in a period when such an example provoked ironic comments. Yet an even worse mistake was for Condivi to reveal himself as an enthusiastic disciple, rather than a shrewd controversialist:

> As for me, I don't know what Plato says about the matter, but I know very well myself that having associated with him so long and so closely, I never heard from his mouth anything but very honest words, having the power to extinguish in young people every disordered and unbridled desire that could be in them.[42]

Condivi's words do not prevent us from thinking that Michelangelo could have secretly indulged in what he publicly condemned because a few lines after stating that Michelangelo's love could not be base because it was the same as taught by Plato, Condivi admitted to not knowing what Plato actually wrote. Condivi probably wrote what Michelangelo suggested to him without understanding it himself. Socrates, Plato, and Socratic love were for Condivi part of another world, a world belonging to his master, not to himself.

THE HOMOSEXUAL ANSWER:
PART 2, BENEDETTO VARCHI (1503-1565)

No better was the reputation that another writer, Benedetto Varchi, got from his platonic sonnets. The bad reknown was in this case well-deserved for deluging his contemporaries with a tidal wave of "Platonic" sonnets. When one reads the hundreds and hundreds of sonnets Varchi wrote, a word immediately comes to the mind to explain the crisis of Socratic love: *inflation*. Every time Varchi takes pen in hand, wings suddenly sprout on his soul, Beauty raises him to Heaven, sacred flames burn, chaste kisses smack . . . Burning, languishing, loving, he undergoes yokes, chains, and shackles of love, rejoicing in beams of "earthy suns." Varchi thus sanctioned the trivialization of the imagery of Socratic love. He could not write a sonnet to anyone without speaking of Love, Heaven, Divine Soul, and so on. Although he often harshly condemned those who practiced "filthy loves," he nevertheless had to endure suspicion, skepticism, gossip, and eventually ostracism and the condemnation of his love sonnets.

Varchi reached the height of his imprudence when, about 1552, he fell for his 16-year-old pupil, Giulio della Stufa. Benedetto addressed many passionate sonnets to Giulio. For example:

> What a wonder is there, my lord, if you
> descended from Heaven, look like an angel, and so many
> gifts you have, and so rare, within and outwardly your body
> that you make Heaven rich, and us blissful?
> As for me, since I heard your voice and the two
> lights of your face I stared, such and so many
> sparks I felt in my heart, and so holy,
> that every mortal thing seems annoying to me.[43]

Like Michelangelo, Benedetto protested that Giulio's beauty was trifling in comparison with his moral qualities, although people could not understand it:

> Your beauty and sweetness, which appear outwardly,
> in you, although great, are nothing in comparison with
> the good, that I perceive with my mind within you:

but I must stop speaking, my lord, since I realize
how much for praising you I shall be blamed.[44]

But Varchi cared very little about blame. His Latin poems (except
the few of them for Giulio) were extremely imprudent, such as *Ad
Iolam*:

Quid petet a puero caste dilectus amato
castus amans, si non oscula casta petet?
Quidve dabit casto caste dilectus amanti
ille puer, si non oscula casta dabit?
Basia divino pulcherrime Phaedre Platoni
casta dabas, casto quot dabat ille tibi . . .

Accipe, daque tuo castissima basia amanti.
Dedecet in sancto vilis amore pudor.[45]

Even if he repeated in every line that word "chaste," this poem is
anything but chaste. One has the feeling that Varchi's intentions
were far less chaste than Ficino's. So he spoke again in another
poem *Ad Iolam*:

Te solum video, solum te cogito, solum
te loquor, in te uno spesque salusque mihi est:
nec tamen obscoenum quicquam speroque voloque,
sed magis in puro castus adurit Amor.[46]

These high and noble ideals notwithstanding, in 1545 Varchi was
unfortunately involved in a grave scandal—a rape, possibly of a
very young girl (we do not know the sex of his victim)—and
avoided imprisonment thanks only to the intervention of some of his
influential friends. In light of that incident, the credibility of
Varchi's declarations of chastity is suspect.

The least we could expect from Giulio della Stufa's relatives in
this case was suspicion. Here is what Varchi was compelled to write
to justify himself to Piero Stufa (probably Giulio's uncle):

Candidissime Stupha mi vacare
culpa, ac nil sibi turpe, nil iniquum
conscire, est adeo potens, ut omnes

floccipendere debeat malorum
tecnas, ac probra ficta nil vereri.⁴⁷

During his father's and uncle's absence, Giulio wrote a letter to
Varchi on 8 March 1553 explaining the reasons for his own behavior, which he could not have explained in the presence of other
people. First, Giulio refused to give letters to Varchi secretly, as his
teacher had asked him to do: Giulio insisted that he would give
them only to Varchi's servant Matteo, "although I prefer that you
send him the least you can, and also send fewer letters, since Messer Agnolo and also Ser Piero seem to have been very suspicious
about nothing. And to avoid giving both of them any reasons to
suspect that Your Lordship writes to me, do not send Matteo so
frequently."⁴⁸ Then Giulio asked Varchi to talk to Angelo, his father, to know "for which reason does he behave that way, since I
have not any other desire than staying with Your Lordship to learn
something."⁴⁹
Eventually, he added:

> I would also like you (as I repeated many times) if you send
> me any sonnets, such as the one answering mine that you sent
> me today, not to use words such as "like a flame in my heart
> burning and shining," because the two [i.e., Piero and Agnolo] take then these words as they please, although they do so
> because they can not understand their real meaning, and they
> can not consider further. Also the correction that Your Lordship made to my sonnet where it said "the holy love," that
> you corrected into "the holy ardor," caused Messer Agnolo,
> when he heard it, to burst out: "This is nonsense! What a love
> is this?! What an ardor?" Therefore I should rather like to
> keep the word "love," being more proper.⁵⁰

In essence, Giulio very tactfully gave his teacher a scolding for
his imprudence, adding:

> About my going tomorrow to your house, I think that it is not
> appropriate, because I think Messer Agnolo would not like it:
> never mind! And as for your coming here, take it as you will,
> but in my opinion it is for this reason that Messer Agnolo had

had Ser Piero tell you those words, that is, because in Florence somebody tells it in one way, somebody else in another, and sonnets have even been written about it; therefore it would be better if you did not come so often.[51]

Some of the sonnets which worried poor Giulio and his family have been preserved, for instance those written by Francesco Grazzini (1503-1584), who not only mocked Varchi, but also ridiculed his pretention to love "the Platonic way." The most revealing is the following;

O father Varchi, new Socrates
— or should we rather say "Pythagoras the second"? —
to you should come scores and scores
of pupils from all the world,
since your high and profound knowledge
you thrust into their brains so fast;
but you don't like the thing
if the pupil is not young and handsome.
Alcibiades and Phaedrus were perfect
pupils, as Athens saw and knew,
since they were handsome and young:
and since beauty comes from God,
straight judgement and intelligence
only handsome youths have, and they learn soon and well.[52]

Obviously, in his mockery of Varchi and the "orthodox" Neoplatonism, Grazzini intended to accuse Varchi of sodomy:

His arms open and his trousers down: this is how
your Bembo is waiting for you in the Elysian Fields. . . .

But where Varchi, alas, where will you leave
your handsome and lovely Narcissuses?
Except for speaking and gazing at each other
those lucky people can do nothing else.
There you cannot do as Thomas did,
since touching and eating is not possible,
as well as the other feeling, which I shall not name.[53]

Grazzini's mockery was prompted not only by Varchi's personality, but also by the overall negative attitude that Italian society held by 1550 toward the ideal of amor socraticus.

Consider, for example, what Girolamo Muzio (1496-1576) wrote to Ludovico Capponi:

> Concerning the sonnets by Varchi I already wrote you in my last letter; and since I saw them I have become even more convinced that, although he calls "holy" and "chaste" the fact of loving corporeal beauty that he celebrates in that boy, they are more wanton and filthy than chaste and honest; moreover, his dealing always with eyes, forefront, cheeks, lips and neck in my opinion has nothing holy, nor has his "big kiss" anything chaste no matter what the Platonists say. Then his lying alone in the grass, wishing to die not to be deprived of beauty from the passing time, is definitely ugly. To tell it in a few words, I should be ashamed if those sonnets were read under my name.[54]

Even Tullia d'Aragona (1508-1556), who made Varchi her teacher and interlocutor in her dialogue *Dell'infinità d'amore* (1547) showed that she knew very well the rumors about the nature of Plato and Socrates' love: "I heard that Socrates and Plato not only openly loved young men, but even took a pride in it, and made dialogues about it, as we can see about Alcibiades, and Phaedrus, where they talk very amorously about love." To which Varchi replied: "I do not deny that Socrates and Plato openly loved young men, and that they took a pride in it, but I add that they did not love them for the reason that the vulgar herd thinks, and that also you seem to think."[55]

Afterwards, Varchi explained the "orthodox" theory of amor socraticus, adding that in this way not only can women be loved, but they must be. Once more we see that whenever the "herd" thought of amor socraticus, they immediately mistook it for sodomy. (How rash were Condivi and Michelangelo to emphasize, in the same years, the connection between Socrates and Buonarroti.)

Last, but not least, Scipione Ammirato (1531-1601) wrote about Varchi in his *Vite* (1583), dealing with Socratic love as if it were an indecent cover-up for filthy actions:

He was known, loved and honored by all the main men of letters who lived then in Italy. But since he was always inclined [*inclinato*] to boy-love [*amori fanciulleschi*] and, as he called them, *Platonic* [loves], often disguising the names of those he loved, he greatly lessened the reputation that would have been rightfully appropriate for his age, for his condition (since he died a Priest) and for Letters.[56]

It is not surprising that Michelangelo "the younger," when he edited his great-uncle's poems, prudently decided to bowdlerize them, converting into women all the boys to whom they were addressed. Although Michelangelo struggled until the end of his life to keep the flame of the Ficinian concept of "heavenly love" burning, after he died his contemporaries could see the concept as nothing but a flimsy shield for filthy sodomy.

Varchi's battle for the same reason, sometimes fought with much courage, was hopeless, and he lost it.

CONCLUSIONS

Amor Socraticus had a strange destiny. As soon as it learned to walk by itself, and escaped from Ficino's "Academy," it marched faster and faster toward unification with sodomitical behavior. But, before merging with the concept of "sodomy," it gave birth to a heterosexual form of "Platonic love," that was par excellence the dominant style of courtly love in the Cinquecento. What was the reason for such an evolution that in less than one century consumed the concept of amor socraticus so completely that in 1764 Voltaire, in his *Dictionnaire philosophique*, entitled the chapter dealing with sex among men *"Amour nommé socratique"*?

Why did Johann Gesner feel compelled in 1743 to compose a pamphlet, *Socrates, sanctus paiderastès*, in which he strove, with all the erudition he could muster, to demonstrate that Socrates' love for boys had always been chaste? To this extent, the original meaning of Socratic love had been forgotten!

Today, the general tendency is to say that earlier societies were incapable of considering what we call "homosexual" acts as anything more than isolated actions, without any common or intrinsic meaning except that of a "simple" sin. This may be truth, but it is not the whole truth. In fact, we cannot and must not ignore the instrumental use that Renaissance Italy made of amor socraticus to give meaning not only to friendship and affection among men, but to a whole field of same-sex feelings and behaviors that omitted only sexual intercourse. But if Socratic love could not, by definition, include sexual intercourse among men, why were these two so thoroughly confused by 1550? Could it be the result of an intrinsic ambiguity in Plato's thought? (One thinks of the jokes made by some characters in Plutarch's *Erotikos* [751 F and 1073 A-C]; of Cicero [*Tusculan disputations*, IV, 33, 70]; of Juvenal, who calls a sodomite *inter socraticos notissima fossa cinaedos* [II, 10]; as well as of the indignant defense of Socrates made by Maximus of Tyre in his *Dialogues*.) Or is it something more?

The evolution traced in this article was intended to show that, in our ancestors' minds, same-sex behavior and homoeroticism were considered more closely related than we are willing to accept today. Our ancestors were not blind toward the erotic meaning that "adhesiveness" among people of the same sex can have. It is also false that homosexual people in the past endured their "sodomite" condition without trying to understand its meaning nor seeking some justification for it. What happened to Socratic love shows very well that as soon as Renaissance Italian society gave homosexual people implicit permission to speak for themselves at little risk, they immediately did so. (Anyway, Castiglione, rather than Ficino, won the war of the words.)

Today, the expression "Platonic love" is used in many languages mainly to mean a nonsexual love between a man and a woman. Rarely do we hear or read about "Platonic love" between people of the same sex. We hear or read about "friendship," and "comradeship," but not about "Platonic love," because referring to it as such would mean giving same-sex love the rank and dignity of heterosexual love. To divide the two concepts it was necessary to strip away from "love-as-Plato-saw-it" one important feature: its character of same-sex love.

Also implicit in this "Platonic" evolution is the idea that heterosexual love can be chaste, but that homosexual love cannot. Was it considered too dangerous in past historical times to give space to a chaste same-sex love? Was it perceived as a first step toward legitimation of "sodomy"? Actually, if we accept the legitimacy of *two* types of love, we are obliged to postulate *two* types of sexuality connected with them—a risk that our ancestors wanted to avoid. From time to time the *topos* of the "struggle between two loves" has appeared in literature, from Achilles Tatius' *Ktesiphon and Leucippes*, to Plutarch's *Erotikos*, to the *Erotes* by pseudo-Lucian and its medieval descendants like the *Thousand and One Nights*, the *Altercatio Ganymedis et Helene*, the poem *Post aquile raptus*, and so on. It is not by chance the idea of "two loves" re-emerges in the writings of an author we have seen who considers same-sex behavior to be caused by a *drive*: Giordano Bruno. In the *Spaccio della bestia triunfante*, we find a scene where Cupid has been jokingly dressed to avoid the scandal of his naked buttocks, and he has been "strictly obliged not to dare throw arrows except the 'natural' way."[57] Cupid, therefore, is the source of two types of love, the "natural" and the "unnatural."

In Bruno's writings, we already encounter the trend of "libertinism," which can be considered the cultivated/conservative answer to the Catholic Reformation. "Libertines" believed in only one love, a two-faced love that could express itself in two different types of sexuality. Both, being expressions of the same drive, were legitimate, even if the heterosexual one was considered more polite and in better taste.

In sum, our ancestors failed to "recognize" homosexuality as "the other love," not because they could not see the homosexual drive, but because they refused to do so, because *recognizing means legitimizing*—even when recognition was made only in order to condemn. From this point of view, Michel Foucault was right when he wrote that the condemnation stemming from nineteenth-century "medical discourse" legitimized homosexuality's existence. But it would be incorrect to say that it was from this condemnation/legitimization that the modern concept of homosexual was born. Hössli preceded Westphal, Ulrichs wrote before Krafft-Ebing, and Casper's anonymous correspondent came before Casper. The homosexual realized he was "different" long *before* "medical discourse" revealed it.

What was lacking in the past was not the perception of homosexuality as "the other love," but rather the will of legitimation. The

Italian Cinquecento not only saw the connection between homosexuality and homoeroticism, but could see it so clearly that it could not distinguish homoeroticism (as theorized by Socratic love) from sodomy. Because *amor socraticus* was felt to be so close to sodomy, but so central to Platonism, "Platonic love" had to be, and was, heterosexualized.

NOTES

1. For instance, in a ninth-century book about "monsters," the *Liber monstrorum de diversis generibus*, the author began with the description of a "man of both sexes" whom he claimed having met. This person looked like a man, and his body was manly, but he liked female work and tried to make love with other men. This individual was not, therefore, recognized as a "sodomite" by the monk who wrote the book, who tried to explain his condition with a "third sex" theory we find again in the nineteenth century (Ulrichs).

2. For instance, the statute of Florence promulgated in 1325, explicitly states that: *quicumque de tam turpi scelere faceret vel cantaret aliquam cançonem* [song] *vel aliquod simile, condempnetur in libris decem, et quotiens*. R. Caggese, ed., *Statuti della Repubblica fiorentina*, (Firenze: Ariani, 1921), 2:219.

3. I must stress that Ficino himself did not often use the words *amor socraticus*, but preferred speaking about *verus amor*. However, to avoid confusion, I have chosen to use only the first expression. For the purpose of this article, therefore, *amor socraticus* is defined as *"Platonic love* between two men."

4. The reader seeking a description of the evolution of *amor socraticus* in Italian Quattrocento and Cinquecento, can consult Edouard Meylan, "L'evolution de la notion d'amour platonique," *Humanisme et Renaissance* 5 (1938): 418-42. Another essential reference is: John Charles Nelson, *Renaissance Theory of Love* (New York: Columbia University Press, 1958), where the reader will find further information about all the authors dealt with in the present article. Regarding Ficino, please see Raymond Marcel, *Marsile Ficin*, (Paris: Les Belles Lettres, 1958).

5. Further information concerning the philosophical aspects of Ficino's ideal of love, can be found in Raymond Marcel, *Marsile Ficin*. (Paris: Les Belles Lettres, 1958).

6. *Pedicant reges, at non furantur. Amarunt Dii pueros: quidni si Cavichio lus amet?*, says the character of a fifteenth-century comedy, the *Conquestio uxoris Cavichioli papiensis* (found in: Vito Pandolfi and Erminia Artese, eds., *Teatro goliardico dell'umanesimo* [Milan: Lerici, 1965], 44). This argument is found again and again through the centuries, and is a source of constant self-justification for many homosexual people. On self-justification strategies, as well as on homosexual lifestyles, see my: "La fenice di Sodoma. Essere omosessu a le nell' Italia del Rinascimento," *Sodoma* 6 (1988).

7. Bernardino da Siena (1380-1444) preaching in 1427 denounced sodomites who calculated "Oh, when I am close to death, I shall confess it and repent," refusing to give up their "vice" before that day. (See Bernardino da Siena, *Le prediche volgari* [Milan: Rizzoli, n.d.], 914.)

8. Perhaps the most interesting and beautiful of these texts is the story of Ami and Amile (English translation: *Ami and Amile* [New Haven, CT: French Literature Publications Company, 1981]) and *De spirituali amicitia* by Aelred of Rievaulx (English translation in *The Works of Aelred of Rievaulx* ed. by D. Knowles [Spenser, MA: Cisterc. Publications, 1971]), vol. 1: *Treatises*.

9. Translation by Sears Reynolds Jayne, ed., *Marsilio Ficino's Commentary on Plato's Symposium* (Columbia, MO: University of Missouri Studies) 19 n.1, 207-8. Preferable to the Latin text published in this edition is the critical edition by Raymond Marcel (*Commentaire sur le banquet de Platon*) who discovered the original manuscript, dated 1469.

10. It must be remarked that the Greek authority Ptolemy in the *Tetrabiblos*, 3:13, said that those born when Venus was joined with Mercury are "in affairs of love, restrained in their relationships with women, but more passionate for boys." Ptolemy, *Tetrabiblos* (London: Heinemann, 1956), 359. In addition, Ascanio Condivi, in his *Vita de Michelangelo Buonarroti* (Milan: Cogliati, 1928) tells us that Michelangelo was born "having Mercury joined with Venus" (p. 32). This could be a self-explanation by Michelangelo himself concerning his love toward boys. (I owe these remarks to the kindness of Prof. Wayne Dynes.)

11. Sears Reynold Jayne (ed.), *Commentary on Plato's Symposium*, 233-35.

12. Quoted by Nicolò Perotti in his *Refutatio deliramentorum Georgi Trapezuntii* (1471). Published in Ludwig Mohler (ed.), *Kardinal Bessarion als Theologe, Humanist und Staatsmann*, vol. 3, Neudruck der Ausgabe Padeborn (1943; reprint, Ferdinand Schoningh Padeborn: Scientia Verlag Aalen, 1967), 370. There exists also a reprint of George's text (Frankfurt a.M.: Minerva GmbH, 1965) based on the edition by J. Pentius da Leuco, Venice 1523, but I could not consult a copy of either.

13. Ivi.

14. The text is republished in Ludwig Mohler, ed., *Kardinal Bessarion*, vol. 2, 1967 (Greek text and Latin translation).

15. An interesting discussion on whether a philosopher's homosexuality can affect his thought was made, taking Wittgenstein as an example, by W. W. Bartley in: "Wittgenstein and Homosexuality," *Salmagundi* 58-59 (Fall 1982-Winter 1983): 166-96. He concluded that no such link can be found.

16. Raymond Marcel, *Commentaire*, 34.

17. *Commentarium*, Oratio 1, cap. 4.

18. Marsilio Ficino, "Epistolarium," in: *Opera Omnia*, Basileae (1626; reprint, Turin: Bottega d'Erasmo, 1959-62), 2:626.

19. Ivi.

20. Ibid., 625.

21. Quoted in Isidoro Del Lungo, *Florentia*, (Florence: Barbera, 1897), 277-78. Except where otherwise stated, all of the following translations are mine.

22. Giovanni Pico della Mirandola, *Commento*, to G. Benivieni's *Canzone: Dell'amore celeste e divino* (Lucca: Marescandoli, 1731), chap. 3, 83-84.

23. Text in Isidoro Carini, *La "difesa" di Pomponio Leto*. Abstract from: *Nozze Cian/Sappa-Flandinet* (Bergamo: 1894). My quotation from pp. 36-37.

24. Text in Vittorio Rossi, "Niccolò Lelio Cosmico, poeta padovano del sec. XV," *Giornale storico della letteratura italiana* 13 (1889), 155. The last two lines hint at two apocryphal epigrams given to Plato in the *Greek Anthology*.

25. Ibid., 157.

26. *Il Cortigiano*, in Baldassarre Castiglione, Giovanni Della Casa, Benenuto Cellini, *Opere* (Milan and Naples: Ricciardi, 1960), 253.

27. Published as "Una lettera di Carlo Sigonio contro i pedanti," *Giornale storico della letteratura italiana* 15 (1890): 459-61.

28. Giovanni Della Casa, *Galateo*, in Baldassarre Castiglione et al., *Opere*, 437.

29. Flaminio Nobili, *Trattato dell'amore humano*, (Lucca: Busdraghi, 1567), 17a. Also reprinted by Loescher, Rome, 1896.

30. Ibid., 17b.

31. Ivi.

32. The fault-finder of gods.

33. Giordano Bruno and Tommaso Campanella, *Opere*, (Milan and Naples: Ricciardi, 1956), 321.

34. Ibid., 538. Italics mine.

35. Michelangelo Buonarroti, *The Sonnets of Michelangelo*, trans. J. A. Symonds (London: Vision Press, 1950), 81.

36. Ibid., 91.

37. Michelangelo Buonarroti, *The Complete Poems of Michelangelo*, trans. J. Tusiani (New York: Humanities Press, 1969) 79. Symonds, as a good Victorian, preferred here to translate the Italian *seme* (seed) as "dew."

38. Ibid., 63 (missing in Symonds' translation).

39. *"Fan fede a quel ch'i' fui grazia nel letto/che abbracciava e'n che l'anima vive."*

40. Noè Girardi (ed.), *Lettere di Michelangelo Buonarroti*, (Arezzo: Ente prov. per il turismo, 1976), 94.

41. Ascanio Condivi, *Vita di Michelangelo Buonarroti*, 192-93.

42. Ivi.

43. Benedetto Varchi, *Opere*, (Trieste: Lloyd Austriaco, 1859) vol. 2, sonnet 385, 889.

44. Ibid., sonnet n. 389, 890.

45. Text in *Carmina quinque hetruscorum poetarum*, (Florence: Giunti, 1562) 141-42.

46. Ibid., 141.

47. Ibid., 157.

48. Text in Guido Manacorda, "Benedetto Varchi: L'uomo, il poeta, il critico," *Annali della R. Scuola Normale di Pisa* 17 (1903): pt. 2, 13-14.

49. Ivi.

50. Ivi.
51. Ivi.
52. Antonio Grazzini, *Rime burlesche*, (Florence: Sansoni, 1882), 29-30.
53. Ibid., 31.
54. Quoted by Guido Manacorda, "Benedetto Varchi," 78.
55. Tullia d'Aragona, "Dell'infinità d'amore," in *Trattati d'amore del Cinquecento*, ed. Mario Pozzi (Bari: Laterza, 1980), 228.
56. Scipione Ammirato, *Opuscoli*, (Florence: Maffi, 1637), 2:254.
57. Giordano Bruno, *Opere*, 479.

The "Nefarious Sin" in Early Modern Seville

Mary Elizabeth Perry, PhD

Seventy-one men were burned to death in Seville, Spain between 1567 and 1616 for the crime of *pecado nefando*, the nefarious sin of anal intercourse or intercourse with an animal.[1] Even in this city, where deviance flourished and crime became commonplace, their offense was considered so serious that it required the most severe punishment. While whippings, exile, or hanging punished most other offenders, authorities reserved the ultimate penalty, burning alive, for people convicted of pecado nefando and those whom the Inquisition found guilty as recalcitrant heretics and apostates.

The association between religious deviance and sexual "crimes against nature" should be noted, particularly in Seville. Famous as the port where transients gathered on their way to the New World or other parts of Europe, Seville was also a center of Catholic piety. The first permanent tribunal of the Holy Office had been established here after Ferdinand and Isabella won papal approval for their Inquisition. Religious orders built convents and monasteries that housed the city's expanding clerical population.[2] Women who wanted to dedicate their lives to God and chastity lived together in the "beaterios" of Seville, and thousands of men joined lay confraternities that were dedicated to good works and religious devotion.[3] Popular religious enthusiasm supported a local sect of illuminists

Dr. Mary Elizabeth Perry is affiliated with the UCLA Center for Medieval and Renaissance Studies, 212 Royce Hall, Los Angeles, CA 90024.

Funding for this study was provided through a Hays-Fulbright Fellowship and a generous grant from the Del Amo Foundation. The author wishes to acknowledge the assistance of the members of the Informal Interdisciplinary Works in Progress Seminar at UCLA who read and criticized an earlier draft of this article.

67

that the Inquisition estimated to number some seven hundred in the early seventeenth century. It also supported a very strong movement to win papal approval for teaching the Immaculate Conception of the Virgin Mary.⁴ The inhabitants of this Catholic city knew very well the dangers of heresy and sin: heresy defied God's truth revealed to His Church, and pecado nefando defied God's order revealed in nature.⁵

Sodomy executions in Seville became a morality play about God's natural order and human imperfection. Staged as a spectacle for public witness, they presented the climax of a struggle between protagonists who played well-known roles. Authorities acted as definers, examiners, judges, and punishers of prohibited sexual activity. To the accused fell the roles of perverts, victims, seducers, and defilers.

Historical evidence of pecado nefando in Seville demonstrates very clearly how sexuality has functioned as a theater of power.⁶ The social conditions of the city provide the setting of this theater, and they also help to explain why prosecutions for sodomy occurred unevenly. Cases of pecado nefando dramatize the conflict between officials who defined sexual deviance and those they accused. Before one considers specific cases reported by people living in this city, however, it is helpful to examine the larger context of sexuality and sexual deviance in sixteenth-century Spain.

* * *

Laws provide many insights into the definition of acceptable and unacceptable sexual behavior in early modern Spain. *Las Siete Partidas*, the code of law compiled under Alfonso X in the thirteenth century, defined marriage as a state necessary "to avoid quarrels, homicides, insolence, violence, and many other wrongful acts that would take place on account of women if marriage did not exist."⁷ In this view, marriage could safely contain sexual expression that otherwise would erupt in violent, antisocial behavior.

Extramarital sexual activity threatened disorder, but sexuality within marriage was valued because it could produce new citizens. Although chastity received the greatest respect in this Catholic kingdom, marriage provided an honorable estate for those who would be sexually active, and it also insured the kingdom against depopulation. In the sixteenth century, a group of economic essayists, the *Tratadistas*, wrote of their great concern that young men were not marrying. They argued that the falling rate of marriages harmed economic stability and left young women single and perishing from hunger.[8] While the Council of Trent used theological arguments to support a vigorous defense of Christian marriage, people in every community could recognize a practical reason, besides.

Bigamy, or having more than one living spouse, challenged both the utilitarian and Christian view of marriage. In the early modern period, the Inquisition prosecuted cases of bigamy as expressions of heresy that contradicted Church teachings. Both men and women were denounced as bigamists to the Holy Office, but nearly three-quarters were men. Usually, they were sentenced to wear the special insignia of the bigamist as they marched in a public procession to an *auto de fe*, the religious ceremony in which the Inquisition penanced those it found guilty. This ritual served both to demonstrate the powerlessness of the accused to defy Church teachings and to remind others in the community of the importance of monogamy.[9] On an average, bigamy cases accounted for 10 percent of those people penanced by the Inquisition between 1559 and 1648 in Seville. In some years, however, the Holy Office convicted no one of bigamy. The greatest number of these cases occurred in 1604, when the nineteen people convicted of bigamy accounted for 42 percent of all people penanced in that year by the tribunal in Seville.

Between 1559 and 1648, the Inquisition prosecuted 180 people for "simple fornication," or heterosexual sexual relations outside marriage. As an offense punished by the Inquisition, fornication offended not through actual sexual relations outside marriage, but through statements which denied that this was a mortal sin. Many men accused of fornication defended themselves by distinguishing between sexual relations with a married woman, and sexual relations in exchange for money that was given to the woman.[10] In some cases this defense was not acceptable, even when the accused man insisted that he had only had sexual relations with a female prostitute whom he had paid.[11] Seventy-four percent of those penanced for fornication by the Inquisition were men, and those few women so penanced were usually single or "women of the world."[12] A married woman accused of having sexual relations with a man who was not her husband was more generally prosecuted by secular officials as an adulteress.[13] Approximately 11 percent of those people penanced by the Inquisition in Seville between 1559 and 1648 were convicted of fornication.

As private auricular confession became more common after the middle of the sixteenth century, the Inquisition began to prosecute clerics who were denounced as "solicitantes." Both monks and priests were accused of making sexual advances in the confessional. Men, women, and children testified that the cleric had said "scandalous" words to them or that he had engaged in "dishonest touchings."[14] Customarily, the Holy Office penanced these clerics with reclusion in a monastery and loss of the privilege of hearing confessions. In some cases, the accused clerics were forbidden to hear confessions from both men and women.[15] The tribunal in Seville never penanced more than seven men for solicitation in any one year, presumably because it left the disciplining of most accused clerics to their religious orders. Only 3 percent of all those sentenced by the Inquisition in Seville were accused of soliciting.

Despite Inquisition action against illicit sex, not all sexual activity was confined to marriage. *Las Siete Partidas* established the legal status of concubines and the children of prostitutes. In addition, countless towns and cities throughout Spain provided legal brothels.[16] As long as they did not boast that their action was not a mortal sin, males could visit prostitutes in legal brothels because prostitution, in the words of a sixteenth-century cleric, offended God less than adultery, fornication, rape, incest, or sodomy, which would otherwise occur.[17] Many accepted the traditional Augustinian argument that a brothel was as necessary to a town as a cesspool was to a house. Males were expected to have sexual relations only with female prostitutes in these brothels, which came under increasing regulation in the later sixteenth and seventeenth centuries.[18]

Homosexual relations troubled clerics and officials much more. *Las Siete Partidas* provided the death penalty for sins "against nature," except for those people forced against their will or for children younger than fourteen.[19] The possibility of lesbianism evidently did not concern these men, for few commented on sexual activity between women.[20] In contrast, male homosexuality appeared so dangerous that males accused of homosexuality were isolated from others in the Royal Prison of Seville, their deviance regarded as a contagion that could easily infect others.[21] Preachers and moralizers warned of the wickedness of sodomy, the temptations of allowing men to share a bed, and the danger implicit in those men who let their hair grow long and dressed in extravagant fashion.[22]

Many cases of male sodomy appear in the Inquisition records from the tribunals of Aragon. Unlike the Holy Office in Castile, the Aragonese Inquisition held jurisdiction over cases of pecado nefando. Secular justice shared this jurisdiction, but accused sodomites probably preferred to be tried by the Inquisition rather than by the secular courts because punishments prescribed by the Holy Office usually included exile, a whipping, or suspension from a religious order, whereas secular law required death by fire.[23] Noting that the number of sodomy cases increased between 1560 and 1590, historian Bartolomé Bennassar pointed to a similar increase in bigamy cases and suggested that both reflected the strong campaign against sexual crimes launched by the Council of Trent in defense of Christian marriage.[24] Ricardo García Cárcel, who has also used Inquisition records from Aragon to examine sodomy, has described the Inquisition in this region as a custodian of the established morality.[25] Sodomy concerned inquisitors who sought to mark the boundaries of "counter-natural" sexual behavior. For these men, and for all faithful Christians in this period, religion, "with its rigorous obsession of chastity, had a vocation profoundly repressive in all the complex world of the sexual."[26]

The studies of García Cárcel, Bennassar, and Jaime Contreras indicate the large number of sodomy cases between 1540 and 1700 in the Crown of Aragon. In Valencia, the Holy Office prosecuted 379 people for sodomy and bestiality; the Barcelona tribunal prosecuted 453 people for these offenses; and the tribunal in Saragossa prosecuted 791 people.[27] These figures strongly contrast with the numbers of known cases of pecado nefando in Seville, for in this city the secular justice, which had sole jurisdiction, punished only seventy-one known cases of sodomy. Table 1 compares sodomy cases in Seville with those of other sexual deviance prosecuted by the Inquisition.

A comparison using the data in Table 1 suggests a complex relationship between convictions for sodomy and those for other forms

Mary Elizabeth Perry

Table 1: Convictions for Sodomy and Bestiality*

SODOMY

Decade	Prosecutions	# of Defendants	Convictions	True Bills
1740-9	2	2	0	1
1750-9	3	3	0	1
1760-9	7	5	0	3
1770-9	4	3	0	0
1780-9	3	3	3	0
1790-9	8	4	1	2
1800-9	6	6	0	1
1810-9	12	9	5	1
1820-9	8	6	1+1	5
1830-9	2	1	0	2
1840-9	0	0	0	0

55 offenses

BESTIALITY

Decade	Prosecutions	# of Defendants	Convictions	True Bills
1740-9	2		0	0
1750-9	1		0	0
1760-9	0		0	0
1770-9	2		0	0
1780-9	1		0	0
1790-9	1		0	0
1800-9	1		0	0
1810-9	8		4	0
1820-9	6	4	4	0
1830-9	2		0	1
1840-9	3		0	3

27 offenses

*This includes felonies and misdemeanors; some of the sodomy convictions were for common assault or aggravated assault. True bills are included as possible convictions. Assize causes are included until 1828.

of sexual deviance. The smaller number of sodomy convictions may be the result of less complete records, a problem of evidence which is discussed below. Another explanation for the smaller number of sodomy convictions is that city officials, who prosecuted sodomy, lacked the bureaucratic resources that the Inquisition had to prosecute larger numbers of accused deviants. Secular authorities also may have hesitated to convict more people of sodomy because its penalty of death by fire was so much more severe than penalties prescribed for other offenses. Significantly, the Inquisition penanced no one for bigamy, fornication, or solicitation during seventeen of the twenty-two years in which secular authorities burned convicted sodomites. Sodomy cases in Seville, therefore, did not simply parallel those of other sexual deviance, nor can they be so easily combined with bigamy cases as a Tridentine expression of concern about marriage, as Bennassar found in Aragon.[29] Possibly, secular and Inquisition officials carried out their prosecutions in apposition in order to heighten their impact on the public. Although sodomy convictions clearly occurred within a larger context of punitive rituals for many forms of sexual deviance, their significance as a theater of power may best be explored by focusing on them more exclusively.

* * *

Evidence of homosexual activity in early modern Seville comes only from accounts of criminal prosecutions and descriptions of the city's prisons. To my knowledge, neither literature nor art of the city presents a more tolerant view of homosexuality than the disapproval apparent in laws, judicial proceedings, and ecclesiastical records. Primary sources for information include: (1) the report of Pedro de León, a Jesuit who worked with people in the Royal Prison of Seville between 1578 and 1616; (2) accounts of sexual deviance confessed to the tribunal of the Inquisition in Seville; (3) an anonymous chronicle of events entitled "Efemérides" in a collection of the Conde de Águila; (4) a description of the Royal Prison written by Cristóbal de Cháves, an official who may have emphasized its most bizarre qualities; and (5) a history of the city written in the early seventeenth century by Francisco de Ariño.

The limitations of these sources should be acknowledged. In the first place, they do not provide a complete record of the actual practice of sodomy. All of the sources describe only those cases of sodomy or bestiality that were reported to secular or ecclesiastical authorities. Because the Inquisition in Castile lacked jurisdiction over these cases, the reports of the Holy Office between 1559 and 1648 contain only three cases of sodomy, and two of these mentioned sodomy only in the confessions of people prosecuted for other transgressions.[30] Unfortunately, records for the secular justice system in the sixteenth and seventeenth centuries have disappeared, victims perhaps of attacks such as that on the judicial buildings in 1652.[31] In their absence, Pedro de León's reports provide valuable descriptions of sodomy and bestiality. However, his ministry was limited to the years between 1578 and 1616, interrupted by several short absences from the city. The Jesuit recognized that many others practiced pecado nefando in addition to the fifty-four men he listed as having burned for this crime. Moreover, Pedro do León realized that some among the fifty-four condemned men were innocent victims of false testimony given under torture or in fear of it.[32]

Each of the sources of information was affected by the motives of the authors. Inquisition records reflect a desire to protect the reputation of the Church, as well as to purify the faith. For this reason, accounts of clerics accused of improper behavior in the confessional refer only obliquely to homosexual activity. The *Compendio* of Pedro de León reveals his abhorrence of homosexuality and his desire to show that each of the condemned men had confessed and received Christian counseling before execution. Ariño's concern to glorify Seville led him to ignore details of people executed for sodomy, while Cháves' interest in scandalizing readers led him to emphasize the bizarre aspects of homosexuality in the prison. The anonymous authors of the "Efemérides" dutifully recorded the most noteworthy events for each year in Seville, but the scope of their project may have caused them to write very little about executions for pecado nefando.

Pedro de León's account of his ministry to the people in the Royal Prison of Seville provides the most complete information about pecado nefando. In the first appendix to Part 2 of his *Compendio*, the Jesuit listed 309 people he had counseled before execution. Nearly one-fifth of these cases involved a sexual crime, including four cases of rape, two cases of adultery, two cases of intercourse with an animal, and fifty-two cases of male sodomy. The case of Miguel, burned for pecado nefando in 1586, should probably more accurately be described as child molestation or rape because he was accused of forcing sodomy on a four-year-old boy.[33]

Evidence for sodomy prosecutions indicates that they occurred in waves, as represented in Figure 1:

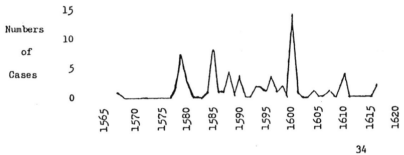

Figure 1:   Sodomy Convictions in Seville, 1567 to 1616[34]

The lack of any sodomy prosecutions in certain years may simply reflect a lack of historical records, or it may reveal a fear that led to greater caution among men in the period immediately following a public burning of those convicted of sodomy.

The undulating pattern of prosecutions resulted at least partially from methods of questioning the accused under torture about "accomplices." Sodomy, after all, was not an activity that one practiced alone—although a merchant in the royal prison was whipped for sodomizing himself.[35] It should be noted that eleven of the reported cases involved prosecutions of men in groups of two or more. The use of torture as an accepted method of interrogation may have caused an accused individual to implicate others. Pedro de León noted that people under torture often confessed to whatever the questioners wanted to hear. He referred to the "encartados," or those listed by accused sodomites, and said that some were subsequently convicted, even though he believed they were innocent.[36]

Prosecution of sodomy appears similar in certain respects to witch accusations in early modern Europe. In both cases, a full confession required the accused to list the names of accomplices.

Both offenses involved the anus, "unnatural" sexual behavior, and criminal use of children. In Spain, where so few witches were executed, sodomy cases may have functioned as a substitute strategy for punishing deviant males.[37] They also provided a forum for examining anal sex and may have served as expressions of homophobia, which officials in other regions expressed through hanging male witches.

Increases in reported sodomy cases could indicate an actual increase in the practice of sodomy, or an increase in official concern with it. It is misleading to conclude that all homosexual activity was simply symptomatic of social pathology, but waves of sodomy prosecutions appeared to occur in close association with social dislocations in Seville. The convoy system of shipping between Seville and the New World periodically placed a severe burden on the city. In 1579, for example, city officials complained to Philip II that provisioning a fleet took so much of the area's food supply that food prices had increased dramatically, "an obvious injury, especially to the poor, also to the landowners."[38] In the same year, the powder mill exploded in Triana, the parish across the river from the city center. The midday explosion destroyed more than forty houses and killed more than fifty people, causing many to believe, according to a chronicler, that it was the end of the world.[39] Prosecuting sodomites may have relieved the anxiety of this period, and the burning of seven in 1579 may have represented a social response to the disasters. They may also have reflected an actual increase in homosexual activity as some anxious men and boys turned to one another, discouraged from extramarital relations with women by the increase of fornication prosecutions during the preceding sixteen years.[40]

Several problems may have accounted for increased sodomy prosecutions in the 1580s. After an uprising of Moriscos in the mountains near Granada in 1568, Philip II ordered the resettlement of more than four thousand of these people in Seville. Resentment of the outsiders, added to a traditional association of Muslims with homosexuality, may have led to more accusations not only against Moriscos, but also against any man suspected of approving of their practices. Popular feeling against Moriscos led a crowd in 1585 to stone the body of a Morisco hanged for robbery, then seize his body and burn it, in accordance with the punishment reserved for apostates, heretics, and sodomites.[41]

There is also reason to believe that marriage rates declined after 1580.[42] Foreign wars and voyages to the New World disrupted the lives of many young people of marriageable age. Clusters of prosecutions for sodomy may have resulted as officials became more concerned that young men were not marrying, ignoring God's "natural order" and their responsibility to it. In a society in which religion exalted chastity, it may have seemed all the more important that any sexual activity be procreative. Waves of prosecutions for sodomy may also have reflected an actual increase in homosexual contacts as single males found in one another the intimacy and sexual contact unavailable to them through marriage.

Finally, the great epidemic of 1599 and 1600 caused severe dislocations that may explain the very large number of prosecutions for sodomy in 1600.[43] As families disintegrated under the onslaught of disease, many may have concluded that an apocalypse was upon them that could only be met with renewed determination to defend God's order against perversions such as sodomy. In addition, homeless boys and disoriented men may have found some solace together in a world that seemed to have turned upside down.

* * *

Pedro de León's report provides valuable information about sodomy, even though it reveals much more about official perceptions than of actual sexual practices. The Jesuit did not question the power of secular authorities to investigate and punish intimate sexual behavior. He saw his own role as that of encouraging the accused to confess so that God could forgive him, even if human authorities did not. Yet he also believed that he should play a mitigating role that could cushion the impact these authorities had. He argued that some men who confessed to sodomy were too young to be burned alive, and he warned that people who felt the awesome power of torture could as easily make false accusations as finally tell the truth.

The chaplain's *Compendio* suggests a concern with the power of youth. It does not give ages for all the men accused of pecado nefando, but it does report that their ages ranged from seventeen to fifty-six. Of the seven men for whom ages were given, two were seventeen, three were eighteen, one was twenty-two and one was fifty-six. In addition, he described six men burned for pecado nefando as "youths." Boys younger than seventeen were considered accomplices rather than culprits, and those who were caught were punished according to their ages and the accusations against them. Sixteen-year-olds, for example, were sent to the galley, while younger boys who seemed to have been merely passive partners were whipped or sentenced to watch the burning of their adult partners. Some young boys, however, who had taken a more willing or active role in male sodomy were held so their bodies "passed through the fire" which burned their adult partners. Pedro de León believed, as others must have, that this ritual helped to purify them from their infection with the crime.[44] It may also have expressed hostility toward youth and their ability to tease and entice adults.

Twenty of the cases of pecado nefando reported by Pedro de León involved sodomy between young boys and older men, although Felipe Proner, an eighteen-year-old Frenchman burned in 1588, was probably not much older than his youthful accomplice.[45] Pederasty may have accounted for a significant amount of male homosexual activity in this period, but the evidence is inconclusive. Cases involving children may have been more visible because they were much more likely to be prosecuted. Historical sources do not explain why they were more likely to be prosecuted, but they imply that contemporaries felt a great concern about the sexual use of children, perhaps because some idealized children as the innocent nonsexual beings portrayed in the paintings of Bartolomé Murillo in the seventeenth century.[46] This view of childhood innocence, still noted by anthropologists in twentieth-century Spain, must have perceived children as particularly vulnerable to exploitation by adults who offered them money, gifts, or a place to sleep.[47]

It is possible that boys exploited their gift-giving elders, although they were much more often described as victims of older men. Perhaps officials hesitated to regard children as instigators because this could have acknowledged that the usual adult-child power relationship could be inverted. In actuality, some children may have been responsible for initiating a homosexual contact. It is also possible that relationships between men and young boys reflected the human needs in a city of many orphans and transients, clerics, and women sworn to celibacy. Neither families nor charity could provide for all the needs of the people of Seville.

With one exception, all of the reports of pecado nefando in this city involved males only. In 1612 a forty-year-old cleric, Joan de Buendía, confessed to inquisitors that he had committed pecado nefando three times with a woman who was his "friend."[48] Penanced as a "solicitante" guilty of sexual misbehavior in the confessional, he escaped with a reprimand, exile, one-year reclusion in a monastery, and loss of the privilege to hear confession. Because no other case involved females, it seems likely that heterosexual sodomy was not considered as serious a crime against nature as was homosexual intercourse. This implies that the real crime of sodomy was not in ejaculating nonprocreatively, nor in the use of the anus, but in defiling or invading the male recipient's body.

A commonly accepted sixteenth-century commentary on the law against "unnatural crime" acknowledged that it prohibited sexual activity between women as well as between men. However, one interpretation of this law called for a lighter punishment when sexual activity between women did not involve an instrument for penetration.[49] Concern with an instrument for penetration implies a perception of the body that insisted on its integrity as a whole and the danger of venturing into forbidden passages. Attaching an appendage to the body for sexual purposes may have been seen to be as unnatural as the tree branches tied to the head of a man to signify the horns of a cuckhold. It seems significant that the only two reports on female homosexual activity included the use of false genitalia. However, the women that Cháves describes in the Royal Prison were not burned, but whipped and exiled. In the second case, a woman who used a false penis with other women was hanged in 1624 for "robberies, murders, and audacity."[50]

Pedro de León's records implicated many clerics in homosexual practices. Writing that sodomy was a serious problem among regular and secular clerics of "good family," he recorded a conversation in which another Jesuit told him that his brothers had no problem in avoiding sin with women because they had young students and novices as sexual partners.[51] He wrote that the Inquisition penanced one cleric in a private *auto de fe* because he had solicited young boys in the confessional. Adding that many clerics were imprisoned for pecado nefando, he stated that some of them were released to the superiors of their orders for disciplining, while others

were burned for their crimes. Although Pedro de León gave neither
names nor numbers of cases, his statements support literary implications of homosexual activity among clerics, such as the mercedar-
ian monk in the fourth tratado of *La vida de Lazarillo de Tormes*.[52]
Periodically, ecclesiastical officials moved to contain this deviant
subculture within clerical discipline, perhaps when homosexual activity became too visible or when their own homophobic responses
became too strong. They probably released to secular justice for
burning those culprits who had become too flagrant in their sexual
behavior, particularly in their use of children. Prosecution for sodomy, then, became one of the few acceptable ways that secular
authorities could reduce the influence of the clergy.

Of the five cases reported by Pedro de León that involved clerics,
one especially reveals the concerns of ecclesiastical and secular authorities.[53] Pascual Jaime, chaplain to the Duke of Alcalá, was
noted for his elegant and trim appearance. However, he also
dressed "curiously," and he often walked about accompanied by
young boys who were painted and dressed up. One day a law officer
went to Jaime's house and caught him in a compromising position
with a young boy. Whether the officer had received a tip from another boy or acted to embarrass the powerful Duke of Alcalá, he
moved swiftly. Arresting both the cleric and his young friend, he
took the youth to the Royal Prison and released the cleric to the
archbishop.

Pascual Jaime confessed under torture that he had committed
sodomy with males for forty-eight of his fifty-six years. He said that
he had had many accomplices, but most of them were no longer in
Seville. He had found many of them as young strangers, poor and
wandering the streets of the city. He took them home and dressed
them in fine clothing. After he had "used" them, he looked for
others. Perhaps because the archbishop realized that this was a case
that could not simply be turned over to a religious order for discipline, the church official ordered Pascual Jaime defrocked and released to the secular arm of the law for execution by burning. With
"enormous numbers" of people attending, the cleric stepped onto a
platform erected in the gateway of the archbishop's palace, where
he was publicly degraded. A few days later he died in a bonfire.

Francisco Legasteca, the youth arrested with him, was very

young and "cried as a boy," according to Pedro de León. Legasteca said that the cleric had tricked him by giving him clothing and presents. His protests did not save him, however. He, too, was burned, although not at the same time as Pascual Jaime. Officials may have decided not to be lenient with this young accomplice because they wanted to make an impression on the many others who had been involved with the cleric.

Nine of the cases reported by Pedro de León involved mulattos, Negroes, Turks, or "Berberiscos." One of these men was burned in 1580, but only after he had been converted, catechized, and baptized.[54] Mayuca, a Negro burned in 1585, was reported as "famous for his dealings with men."[55] Pedro de León referred to him as a procurer, rather than a man who actually engaged in pecado nefando. Francisco Bautista, a mulatto who was burned in 1596, was only twenty-two years old when he was accused of engaging in pecado nefando with boys from the Casa de Misericordia, a charitable institution.[56] A fourteen-year-old boy from this house was also condemned to burn for being a partner with the mulatto. His sentence was changed to two-hundred lashes, however, when Pedro de León urged officials to consider his very young age. The two mulattos burned in 1610, Juan Pérez de Mansilla and Antón de Morales, presumably committed pecado nefando together.[57] Two Negroes were burned in 1616, but their relationship was not described. Hamete, a Negro Turk, was accused of forcing sodomy on a boy of nine or ten. He also told of being paid eight ducats each time he took the active role in male sodomy, and he said that Moors and Turks were sought by other men because they were believed to be "very potent" and had large genitals.[58]

Pedro de León's records indicate the social status of several other men condemned for pecado nefando. Two of the culprits had been teachers, providing justification, perhaps, for the city government's concern with examining the aptitude and morality of teachers.[59] Three of the condemned men had been soldiers, and Pedro de León noted that military companies could bring to the city "many evils and many dangerous things," such as men sleeping together in one bed.[60] One culprit had been a slave, whom Pedro de León described as "Berberisco," and one was a sheriff who had a gambling house in which he kept young boys for sexual use.[61] Some of the boys were kept merely for "touching," but others were sodomized. A "youth" was burned with the sheriff, but Pedro de León did not indicate whether he had been one of the kept boys or one of the men who used them.[62]

Only one noble appears in the Jesuit's description of men condemned for pecado nefando.[63] In the 1590s don Alonso Girón held the very important position of alguacil mayor of Seville, even as he held significant offices for the dukes of Osuna and Alcalá. When the Duke of Alcalá died, Girón became embroiled in a lawsuit over property in the ducal estate and the death of his wife. The case quickly became much more serious, as he was accused of committing sodomy with one of his servants. Despite his noble status, it was decided that he should be burned as any other person guilty of pecado nefando. Seated on a mule covered with the black trappings of mourning, he was driven to the bonfire with the page with whom he had engaged in sodomy. Ariño's account emphasized the "consternation" of city residents and declared that no nobles left their homes during that day.[64] He implied that people felt very upset because a noble of such status had committed such a terrible crime, yet their concern might also have been that the city government would prosecute a noble and execute him as it did any base criminal.

Only three of the men condemned for pecado nefando were foreigners. Two Frenchmen were burned in 1588, although it is not clear that they had been partners because the young accomplice of one, Felipe Proner, was sentenced to the galleys.[65] Nine years earlier, a man from Naples was burned.[66] Pedro de León reflected a belief that Italians were especially likely to practice sodomy. He described two other condemned men as belonging "to a religion of a habit of Italy," which evidently was a euphemism for sodomy or homosexuality.[67] He also related the story of a young student who bound a basket tightly around his buttocks as a "defense" when he went to an Italian barber to have his hair cut.[68]

Francisco de Iniesta, who was penanced by the Inquisition in 1603, told three men that he had first committed sodomy with an Italian while he was a soldier.[69] Denounced to the Inquisition because he had said this was not a sin, he tried to defend himself by saying that it was not a sin because he had paid for it. Moreover, he said that another man had told him that one remedy for hemorrhoids was to be sodomized by a male. Under questioning, however, Iniesta confessed that the devil had made him say these things. The Italian connection was not so serious in this case, for his inquisitors merely reprimanded him and sentenced him to hear mass as a penitent.

Iniesta's is not the only case in which male prostitution appeared. Mayuca, the Negro sentenced in 1585, apparently acted as a procurer in finding male clients for his "handsome, painted young gallants."[70] Moreover, the sheriff who kept boys in his gambling house may have regarded them as a commercial enterprise, as well as a diversion for his own pleasure.[71] Hamete, the Negro Turk sentenced in 1616, had boasted that he was paid eight ducats each time he agreed to engage in sodomy, and an actor who was condemned for pecado nefando told the judge that he was given 100 *reales* each time he took the active role in sodomy.[72] None of these cases referred directly to male prostitution, but this is not surprising in a city where prostitution was believed to be a female service for male clients.[73]

Information from several of the cases implies the existence of a male homosexual subculture. Pedro de León described a "quadrilla," or little squad, of sodomites led by Diego Maldonado, who was punished in 1585.[74] Eight men burned in that year were reported to meet in an area just outside the city walls called the Huerta del Rey, where fig trees helped conceal their illicit activity.[75] It is also likely that men met male sexual partners in gambling houses, such as that owned by the sheriff punished in 1590.[76] The fact that fifteen men were burned together for pecado nefando in 1600 suggests the existence of a group of sodomites, although the records report nothing more about them.[77]

Descriptions of the physical appearance of those condemned for sodomy may also indicate that they were perceived as a male homosexual subculture. Francisco Galindo, for example, "walked with such charm and appeared more woman than man" in his dress and demeanor.[78] The boys kept in the sheriff's gambling house were described as "painted" and "handsome."[79] Pedro de León described Mayuca as wearing a wig, large lace ruff, and facial cosmetics, although this may have been how he was sentenced to appear at the bonfire, rather than how he usually adorned himself.[80] It seems likely that the criminal justice officials deliberately caricatured his appearance in order to humiliate him and better impress the public with his crimes. Pedro de León noted that many "honorable gentlemen" who attended his burning said that wigs, hairpieces, and lace collars should also go into the fire.[81] Not all men who wore these things were considered homosexuals. Nonetheless, moralists such as Francisco de León preached with vigor against "men converted into women" and "effeminate soldiers, full of airs, long locks, and plumes."[82] His description contrasts with the sodomite whom Quevedo described in *La vida del Buscon* as a "mean-looking fellow" with one eye, "a moustache and broad shoulders covered with whip scars."[83]

* * *

Secular and ecclesiastical officials perceived sodomy in early modern Seville as a fearsome contagion that especially infected clerics and young boys.[84] It posed a dangerous threat to the welfare of the community, as well as a blasphemous attack against God's natural order. More than simply wanting to punish sodomy as a crime, officials wanted to cure it at its roots. Yet they had to prosecute men for sodomy again and again. Their bonfires to purify the city from the contagion of sodomy seemed as ineffective as those that they set to purify infected air during an epidemic.[85]

Sodomy prosecutions in Seville between 1567 and 1616 reveal an awesome power held by officials, but the small number of convictions also suggests a remarkable restraint. Perhaps they punished fewer men for sodomy than officials in neighboring Aragon because they could ignore this deviance when it was not too flagrant and when social disasters did not require apocalyptic response. Perhaps in the early modern period, a developing criminal justice system did not have to confront all deviance because people believed that periodically God directly intervened to restore order in His universe; with Pedro de León they could conclude that sodomy, as "contemptible" and "abhorrent" as it was, would finally be "punished by divine justice."[86] In addition, perhaps officials knew that sex held enormous potential as a theater for power in which they struggled to establish dominance over the behavior and bodies of those they ruled. The power they could gain in this struggle was so great that it would be tolerated only if it appeared to be limited.

NOTES

1. *Pecado nefando* is a term that has been used for centuries in Spanish law to describe both sodomy and sexual intercourse with an animal. It is sometimes merely referred to as "the sin," although *Las Siete Partidas*, the thirteenth-century code of law compiled under Alfonso X, uses the term "sin of lust against nature" and "sin against nature." See vol. 4, 329-31 of the 1884 edition published in Barcelona. Evidence of sodomy cases in Seville is in the Archivo Municiple de Sevilla (hereafter AMS), Sección Especial, Papeles del Conde de Águila; Francisco Ariño, *Sucesos de Sevilla de 1592 a 1604* (Sevilla, 1873); and Pedro de León, *Compendio de algunas experiencias en los ministerios de que vsa la Comp a de IESVS con q practicamente se muestra con algunos acaecimientos y documentos el buen acierto en ellos* (Granada, 1619).

2. Antonio Domínguez Ortiz and Francisco Aguilar Piñal, "El Barroco y la ilustración," *Historia de Sevilla*, vol. 4 (Sevilla: Universidad de Sevilla, 1976), 103-13.

3. For beatas, see Mary Elizabeth Perry, "Beatas and the Inquisition in Early Modern Seville," in *Inquisition and Society in Early Modern Europe*, ed. Stephen Haliczer (London: Croom helm, 1986), 147-68. For lay confraternities see José Bermejo y Carballo, *Glorias religiosas de Sevilla: Noticia histórico de todas las cofradías de penitencia, sangre y luz, fundadas en esta ciudad* (Sevilla, 1882).

4. Dominguez Ortiz and Aguilar Piñal, "El Barroco," 107-9, discussed the effort to win papal approval of the Immaculate Conception; Perry, "Beatas," discussed the illuminist sect.

5. See the discussion by Bartolomé Bennassar, "Le modele sexuel; L'Inquisition d'Aragon et la repression des peches abominables," in *L'Inquisition espagnole, XVe-XIXe siècle*, ed. Bartolomé Bennasar et al. (Paris: Hachette, 1979), 339-40. John T. Noonan, *Contraception: A History of its Treatment by the Catholic Theologians and Canonists* (Cambridge, MA: Harvard University Press, 1966), 240, discussed St. Thomas Aquinas' description of sin and nature.

6. Michel Foucault, *The History of Sexuality*, vol. 1, trans. Robert Hurley (New York: Pantheon, 1978). See esp. 86-103.

7. *Las Siete Partidas*, trans. and notes Samuel Parsons Scott (Chicago: Commerce Clearing House, 1931), 886.

8. *Memoriales y discursos de Francisco Martínez de Mata*, ed. Gonzalo Ánes Álvarez (Madrid: Moneda y Crédito, 1971), 129.

9. For a broader discussion of bigamy, see Jaime Contreras, *El Santo Oficio de la Inquisicion de Galicia (poder, sociedad y cultura)* (Madrid: Akal, 1982), 643-53; and Jean-Pierre Dedieu, "Le modele sexuel: La defense du mariage chretien, in Bennassar, *L'Inquisition*, 313-38. Reports of the tribunal of the Inquisition in Seville are in the Archivo Histórico Nacional (hereafter AHN), *Inquisición*, legajos 2072, 2074, and 2075. Please note that these records do not refer to each year between 1559 and 1648. In addition, two different sets of records exist for the years 1562, 1599, 1605, and 1609.

10. For example, see the case of María Despirosa in AHN, *Inquisición*, legajo

2075, no. 19, for her statement that she did not believe it was a mortal sin for her to have carnal relations with a man because she was not married.

11. For example, see AHN, *Inquisición*, legajo 2074, no. 9. Prostitution was legal in this city if it was carried out in the city brothel; see Mary Elizabeth Perry, "Deviant Insiders: Legalized Prostitutes and a Consciousness of Women in Early Modern Seville," *Comparative Studies in Society and History* 27 (January 1985): 138-58.

12. AHN, *Inquisición*, legajo 1075, no. 5, Luisa Vásquez.

13. Examples are in "Serie histórical," Memorias eclesiasticas, Biblioteca Capitular, 84-7-19, fols. 46r-47; and AMS, Papeles del Conde de Aguila, Seccion Especial, Tomo 64 en fol., Numero 3.

14. Henry Charles Lea, *A History of the Inquisition of Spain*, vol. 4 (New York: Macmillan, 1922), 96-135.

15. AHN, *Inquisición*, legajo 2075, no. 7, contains many examples.

16. *Las Siete Partidas*, Partida 4, Title 15, Law 1. See also Perry, "Deviant Insiders."

17. Francisco Farfan, quoted in Perry, "Deviant Insiders," 143.

18. Perry, "Deviant Insiders," 142-49.

19. *Las Siete Partidas*, Partida 7, Title 21, Laws 1 and 2.

20. One source that reported homosexual activity between women was a manuscript by Cristóbal de Cháves entitled "Relación de las cosas de la cárcel de Sevilla y su trato," Tomo B-C in AMS, Papeles del Conde de Águila, Sección Especial. The second source was an addenda to the report for 1624, in AMS, Sección Especial, Tomo 20. Gregorio López, who wrote the gloss for the edition of *Las Siete Partidas* that was widely accepted in the sixteenth century, declared that sodomy was a crime possible between women, as well as between men or between men and women (see the 1884 ed., vol. 4, 330-31).

21. Cháves referred to segregation within the prison in both Part 1 and Part 2 of his "Relación." Pedro de León referred to homosexuality as a contagion in Case 129 of Appendix 1 to Part 2 of his *Compendio*. All subsequent references to his report will be from this appendix unless otherwise stated. See also the discussion in Pedro Herrera Puga, *Sociedad y delincuencia en el Siglo de Oro* (Madrid: Biblioteca de Antores Cristianos, 1974), 262.

22. Pedro de León, esp. Cases 7, 8 and 122; Juan de Mora, *Discursos morales* (Madrid, 1598); Fray Francisco de León, quoted in Carmelo Viñas Mey, *El problema de la tierra en la España de los siglos XVI y XVII* (Madrid: C.S.I.C., 1941), 47; Juan de la Cerda, *Vida política de todos los estados de mugeres* (Alcalá de Hénares, 1599), Tomo 5, Capítulos 17-24, discussed the danger of women becoming involved in carnal lust, following Capitulo 16, which described women who disguised themselves as men.

23. Bennassar, "Le modele sexuel," 344. Lea, vol. 4, 362, cited Juan Antonio Llorente, *Anales de la Inquisición de España*, vol. 1 (Madrid, 1813), 327, as declaring that twelve "sodomites" were burned alive by the Inquisition in Seville in 1506, but I have found no supporting evidence for Llorente's assertion. It may

be that those twelve people had been convicted of heresy or apostasy and were further discredited by accusations of a serious sexual crime.

24. Bennassar, "Le modele sexuel," 347.

25. Ricardo García Cárcel, *Herejía y sociedad en el siglo XVI; La inquisición en Valencia 1530-1609* (Barcelona: Ediciones 82, 1980), 261.

26. Ibid.

27. Ibid., 288. It should be noted that not all those prosecuted were executed. E. W. Monter has found that between 1560 and 1640 the Inquisition prosecuted 477 people in Saragossa for pecado nefando, but executed only 95; 248 in Valencia, where they executed only 50; and 189 in Barcelona, where only 5 were executed. This is from his paper presented at the University of Wisconsin, Madison, March 1985.

28. Pedro de León listed fifty-four men burned for sodomy in his Appendix 1 to Part 2; the "Efemérides" stated that fifteen men were burned in April 1600 for pecado nefando (a period of time when Pedro de León was absent from Seville). The "Efemérides" also recorded that Alonso Henriques de Guzmán was condemned in 1567 for pecado nefando, and it recorded the burning of a deaf and blind old man for pecado nefando in July 1604. Arino described the arrest and subsequent burning of a man for sodomy in 1596. Note that the cases of Francisco Iniesta (1603) and Joan de Buendía (1612) disclosed accusations of sodomy, but they were penanced by the Inquisition as solicitantes, recorded in AHN, *Inquisición*, legajo 2075, nos. 13 and 22. Figures for bigamy, fornication, and soliciting are from AHN, *Inquisición*, legajos 2072, 2074, and 2075.

29. Bennassar, "Le Modele sexuel," 347.

30. In addition to the two individuals in AHN, *Inquisición*, legajo 2075, nos. 13 and 22, see no. 23 and the case of Alonso Miguel, who denounced himself to the Inquisition in 1617 for committing pecado nefando twenty or twenty-three times with donkeys, dogs, a goat, and a mule.

31. Perry, *Crime and Society in Early Modern Seville* (Hanover and London: University Press of New England, 1980), 252-53.

32. Pedro de León, Cases 13 and 255 were condemned for sexual intercourse with animals. See his Cases 278 and 281 for discussion of the problem of innocent people. He also discussed torture and its effects on innocent people in Chapter 28 of Part 2 of his *Compendio*.

33. Pedro de León, Case 142.

34. Sources include "Efemérides," Pedro de León, and Ariño. Note that these are incomplete records.

35. Cháves, pt. 1.

36. Pedro de León, Cases 168 and 169. See also the discussion of confessions in Gustav Henningsen, *The Witches' Advocate: Basque Witchcraft and the Spanish Inquisition (1609-1614)* (Reno, Nevada: University of Nevada Press, 1980), 20-22.

37. See Henningsen's study especially. Note, however, that the majority of those identified as witches in other parts of Europe were females rather than males. Prosecutions for pecado nefando could not provide an alternative in Spain

for punishing deviant females, but increased prosecutions of beatas by the Inquisition may have.

38. Quoted in Joaquín Guichot y Parody, *Historia del Exmo. Ayuntamiento de la muy noble, muy leal, muy heróica e invicta ciudad de Sevilla*, vol. 2 (Sevilla, 1896), 89-90. See also Perry, *Crime*, 34-43.

39. "Efemérides," Noticias y casos, número 1.

40. See Table 1 in text.

41. Pedro de León, Case 116. For a broader discussion of Moriscos, see Celestino López Martínez, *Mudéjares y moriscos sevillanos* (Sevilla: Tipografía Rodríguez, Giménez, 1935). Also see John Boswell's discussion of Islamic culture and gay culture in his *Christianity, Social Tolerance, and Homosexuality: Gay People in Western Europe from the Beginning of the Christian Era to the Fourteenth Century* (Chicago: University of Chicago Press, 1980), especially 194-97.

42. Martínez de Mata, 129; Perry, *Crime*, 192-93 and 215.

43. For reports of dislocations resulting from this epidemic, see AMS, Siglo 16, Sección 3, Escribanías de Cabildo, Tomo 7, No. 17; Tomo 13, No. 73.

44. Ibid. Cases 7 and 8 describe the two seventeen-year-olds; Case 153 describes young accomplices whipped and sentenced to galley service for four years; accomplices in Cases 218 and 222 were passed through the fire; the accomplice in Case 223 was condemned to stay in prison; accomplice in Case 263 received 200 lashes.

45. Ibid., Case 173.

46. Perry, *Crime*, 190.

47. William A. Christian, Jr., *Person and God in a Spanish Valley* (New York: Academic Press, 1972), 156-57.

48. AHN, *Inquisición*, legajo 2075, no. 22.

49. Antonio Gómez, who wrote *Variae resolutiones, juriscivilis, communis et regii* in the sixteenth century, quoted in Louis Crompton, "The Myth of Lesbian Impunity: Capital Laws from 1270 to 1791," *Historical Perspectives on Homosexuality*. Research on Homosexuality Monograph Series, vol. 2, ed. Salvatore J. Licata and Robert P. Petersen. (New York: The Haworth Press, 1981) See p. 19.

50. AMS, Sección Especial, Tomo 20; Cháves, pt. 1.

51. Pedro de León, pt. 2, chaps. 7 and 26.

52. I am indebted to Prof. Anne J. Cruz, University of California, Irvine, who discussed this passage with me. See Harry Sieber, *Language and Society in La Vida de Lazarillo de Tormes* (Baltimore: The Johns Hopkins University Press, 1978), who developed the sexual meaning of this tratado, 45-58. Julio Caro Baroja, *Las formas complejas de la vida religiosa (Religión, sociedad y carácter en la España de los siglos XVI y XVII)* (Madrid: Akal, 1978), found a common association in sixteenth- and seventeenth-century Spanish literature between monks, woman-like spiritual excesses, and homosexuality, 470.

53. Pedro de León, app. 1 to pt. 2, Cases 168 and 169.

54. Ibid., Case 38.

55. Ibid., Case 122.

56. Ibid., Case 218.

57. Ibid., Cases 280 and 281.
58. Ibid., Cases 308 and 309.
59. Ibid., Cases 10 and 167. A 1581 petition regarding teachers appeared in AMS, Siglo 16, Sección 3, Escribanías de Cabildo, Tomo 11, no. 57.
60. Pedro de León, Cases 7, 8, and 194.
61. Ibid., Cases 309 and 180.
62. Ibid., Cases 180 and 181.
63. Ibid., Case 200. See also "Efemérides," Noticias y casos, número 1 for 1597; and *Papeles varios*, 85-4-11, Biblioteca Capitular of Seville.
64. Ariño, 42.
65. Pedro de León, Cases 166 and 173.
66. Ibid., Case 12.
67. Ibid., Cases 120, 121, and 128. Caro Baroja referred to the association of Italians with homosexuality during this period, 470.
68. Ibid., Case 309.
69. AHN, *Inquisición*, legajo 2075, no. 13.
70. Pedro de León, Case 122.
71. Ibid., Cases 180 and 181.
72. Ibid., Case 308; and Pedro de León, pt. 2, chap. 26.
73. The legal concept of male prostitution was undoubtedly poorly developed here as in nineteenth-century England, discussed by Jeffrey Weeks in "Inverts, Perverts, and Mary-Annes: Male Prostitution and the Regulation of Homosexuality in England in the Nineteenth and Early Twentieth Centuries," in Licata and Peterson, 115-17.
74. Pedro de León, Cases 127 and 128.
75. Ibid., Cases 107, 120, 121, 122, 124, 127, 128, and 129.
76. "Efemérides," Noticias y casos, número 1.
77. Ibid., Case 180. See also the discussion in Herrera Puga, 257-58.
78. Pedro de León, Case 129, also described in Cases 120 and 121.
79. Ibid., Cases 180 and 181.
80. Ibid., Case 122.
81. Ibid.
82. From a sermon in 1635, quoted in Viñas Mey, 47.
83. Francisco de Quevedo Villegas, *Historia de la vida del Buscon* (Zaragoza, 1626), reprinted in *Novela picaresca: Textos escogidos* (Madrid: Taurus, 1962), 531; and translated by Michael Alpert as *The Swindler in Two Spanish Picaresque Novels* (Middlesex: Penguin, 1981), 172.
84. See especially Pedro de León's discussion in Case 129.
85. Perry, *Crime*, 227-29, and 237-46.
86. Pedro de León, Case 129.

Love's Labors Lost:
Five Letters
from a Seventeenth-Century
Portuguese Sodomite

Luiz Mott, PhD
Aroldo Assunção

Buried among the vast archives of the Portuguese Inquisition are the earliest known collection of homosexual love letters in any European vernacular. These are not, however, the oldest in Western civilization. John Boswell has persuasively identified some of Alcuin's Epistolae, eight centuries older than these, as authentically homoerotic.[1] But most surviving love letters from one man to another date only from the late nineteenth century and afterwards. Martin Duberman stressed the relatively early date of Jeffrey Withers' two love letters to Jim Hammond, written in South Carolina in 1826.[2] The particular series discussed in this article was composed in a small town in southern Portugal in 1664.

Although at first glance it may seem odd to discover these documents in Lisbon, there are good reasons why seventeenth-century Portugal can claim this particular "first" in gay history. To begin with, medieval Portugal developed a tradition of lyric poetry set to music (cancioneiro medieval) with its famous "Songs for a Friend" (Cancoes de Amigo) where coitus per anum is mentioned several times in the most natural way.[3] In the second place, Portugal seems to have been relatively tolerant of homoerotic activities in the mid-

---

Luiz Mott and Aroldo Assunção are associated with the University of Bahia. The authors wish to thank the Conselho Nacional de Pesquisas for a grant covering eight months of study at the Tombo in Lisbon. The authors also wish to thank Osiris Guimaraes and Professor William Monter for the English translation.

seventeenth century. It was relatively common knowledge that effeminate homosexuals (*fanchonos*) made assignations in a rooming house near the palace of the Inquisition. In Rocio place, near the center of Lisbon, a homosexual dance (*danca dos fanchonos*) took place, with boys dressed as women. Some Portuguese expressed their homosexual preferences in their nicknames, such as "Rafael Fanchono" or "Manoel Maricas," a fruit-seller in Coimbra. Inquisitorial trial records show that homosexual activities sometimes occurred even within its own prisons, with its own officials participating in them. Last but far from least, the King of Portugal at the time these letters were written, D. Affonso VI (1656-1683), was himself a notorious homosexual.[4]

These five letters were written by Francisco Correa Netto, the sacristan of the cathedral of Silves, during the Lenten season of 1664. They were sent to Manuel Viegas, a guitarist and maker of musical instruments, who turned them over to the Vicar of Silves, Manuel Luiz Coelho, on 29 March 1664. He in turn sent them on to the Inquisition of Evora (responsible for the Algarve, the district in which Silves is located) in order to denounce Correa for "sodomy."

Today a small city of fewer than ten thousand, Silves then was a Moorish mining center whose Gothic cathedral—where both Correa and his denouncer held positions—had been converted from a mosque in the thirteenth century.[5] We know very little about the sacristan, the author of these letters, except that the Vicar had also charged him with being one-quarter Jewish (*cristão novo*) because he had been unable to produce valid witnesses to speak about his grandparents' ancestry when demonstrating the "purity of blood" necessary for Minor Orders. Correa was also accused of sacrilege by the Vicar because the sacristan had given a consecrated Host to another man in a sack (*bolsa de mandinga*), presumably to be carried as an amulet to preserve him from harm. We know even less about the sacristan's lover, apart from the information contained in these letters—which amply demonstrate his bisexuality—and the fact that he handed them over to his lover's mortal enemy—which amply demonstrates his character.

The five letters from Correa to Viegas, preserved *Caderno do*

Nefando #2 from the Inquisition of Evora in Lisbon's Arquiva da Torre do Tombo, which we present here in annotated translation, tell a vivid story of love and loss.

LETTER NUMBER ONE

Senhor Manoel Viegas:

If men sleep with me, it is not to find a pussy. They place the cock between my legs, and there they have their way. I do not achieve it. If Your Grace (*Vossa Merce*) would wish the same, dispose of me, I am at your service, to whom I swear unto death, to offer what is needed, and the losses are mine.

Francisco Correa Netto

Commentary

This is a remarkably courageous and explicit letter. Correa's offer is made simply, without ceremony; the pompous-sounding "Your Grace" was common seventeenth-century Portuguese usage among social equals, and even sexual intimates.

The sexual act "between the legs" (*entre as pernas*) was a common practice among homosexuals who feared punishment at the hands of the Inquisition. It enabled them to avoid the canon law definition of anal intercourse with emission of semen as constituting the "true" crime of sodomy (*sodimia completa*). Canon law considered both masturbation (*punheta*) and friction to completion between legs (*coxeta*) as mere sins of the senses, rather than crimes.

Correa's remark that "I do not achieve it" (*Eu, nao me vem nada*) may reflect his intention to satisfy his partner without experiencing an erection and ejaculation himself. This allegation was made against pseudo-hermaphroditic sodomites like the famous priest called "Paula de Lisboa," whose sexual partners all declared that they never saw the Padre's member, even though the Inquisition's surgeon testified that "Paula" lacked female characteristics.[6]

The letter seems to have had its desired effect: Viegas began a relationship with the sacristan. The Vicar of Silves commented in his denunciation that "This letter was written in front of the most holy Sacrament" (another attempt to indict Correa for sacrilege in addition to sodomy and possibly Judaism).

LETTER NUMBER TWO

Tender gift to me and longing of my senses, the tranquility of my thoughts about you is the proof of how much I desire and love you!

Now I shall not have peace nor hope of having you, because I see that not even with the best argument will my pledge serve you, heart wounded to death, heart never to be released from my affection for you.

My love and bounty: my feelings cannot rest an hour, either by day or night, without bringing to mind your companionship and your sweet words that are continually reflected in my memory.

Mirror of my sight and joy, if I have any right to you, bring peace to my heart and confirm the news I received this evening, that you were betrothed to a niece of Francisco Luiz last Monday. I would have said that by Easter you would be betrothed to me. You implied that often, and you gave your word on it. But do as you please: in spite of this I shall not stop doing what I can to be at your service. And remembering your arms and the kiss you gave me, that is what torments me most! And you know this subject well, in that heart of your loins, it was that which desired me, with its craving to fly up. There was no Lent for that heart in your loins, when I touched it with my fingers, and instantly it sprang up! And you, so evil, who did not want to do what comes so naturally!

Goodbye, my darling, my happiness, my true love!

My idea is that, even though you may be married, you do not have to break your promise to be the betrothed of your devoted Francisquinha. It seems to me you told Manoel da Costa that if I complied with your whims, even then you would not come to me, because you do not care, and it was all sham.

Here is paper to answer: Now you have no excuse not to write for lack of paper.

Commentary

This is the most ardent of the letters. Francisco Correa Netto is hopelessly enamored of his guitarist, aroused by his kisses and embraces. Manoel Viegas is also interested, even though he refused the sacristan's offer of *coxeta*. Correa now avoids using the word *caralho* (cock)—still a common term in Portugal as well as Brazil—and instead employs the rather poetic euphemism *coracao da barguilha*, literally "heart trouser fly" (which we have translated as "heart of his loins"), which Correa describes as always erect (*alevantado*) even during the Lenten season.

As the sacristan would subsequently remark, "he who is most loved, least deserves it," and this second letter begins to worry and suggest suffering: Correa has received news that Viegas intends to marry. The sacristan ("Francisquinha") accepts the possibility of sharing his lover with a woman, adopting the traditional resignation of women in the Algarve who had long been accustomed to Islamic polygamy and its successor, Christian concubinage. At the end of the letter, Correa suspects that the favorable signals from his lover are either social convenience or else hypocrisy, and he shifts strategy, remaining expectant that his lover will take the initiative and seek him out. Once again the Vicar-denouncer added his own gloss: "Observe the fatuity of this whore of a sodomite (*puto do somitigo*). Ha! How pious he seems!"

Correa's use of a female nickname, "Francisquihna"—"Francisco" in the "cute," diminutive feminine form—was a common strategy among seventeenth-century Lusitanian homosexuals. One cleric tried for sodomy, Padre Joao Mendonca de Maia, used a flock of female nicknames for his friends and lovers, such as "Miss Turk" (*A Turca*), or "Miss Galicia" (*A Galega*), while he himself was known as "Miss Chief Synagogue" (*A Arquisinagoga*).[7] Two other Portuguese priests tried for the *abominavel pecado* appeared

under the names "Isabel do Porto" and the previously named
"Paula de Lisboa." It seems superfluous for the Vicar-denouncer
to have added that the sacristan must be the passive partner (*paciente*) in this relationship.

LETTER NUMBER THREE

Manual Viegas:

Our Lord allow you to live as many happy years as you
desire!
I was not so black-hearted that you should say publicly that I
should not go to your house. If you wished to say that, you
should write or tell me privately. However, not even for this
affront will I become your enemy; and if you need something,
advise me in writing.
I sent your clothes to be washed. Go to the house of Matias
Araujo to order some shoes. And I will give you everything I
have promised. And for the fiancee, thirty *alqueires* of wheat.
As for my letters, tear them up, as I will destroy yours. Make
me a guitar (*viola*) by your own hand, for which I will pay
you. Heaven guard you all the years you desire, friend.

Francisco Correa Netto

Commentary

Although the sacristan has now been publicly humiliated, he does
not desist, but rather offers his lover several gifts in hope of winning him back. Thirty *alqueires* of wheat (equivalent to five sacks
weighing three hundred kilos) would feed a family of four for a
year — a very significant gift in dry Algarve, which often needed to
import wheat from other parts of Portugal. Correa's courtship of
Viegas is marked throughout by a continuous lavishing of presents,
a sort of bribery for affection. In this context, it appears almost as
an attempt to outbid the dowry which his fiancee would bring to
Viegas.
Finally, the sacristan begins to worry about his letters, and urges

his lover to destroy them. We know that he really did destroy Viegas' letters to him.

LETTER NUMBER FOUR

False Traitor!

False deluded love: with what words can I express this sentiment? After Your Grace (*Vossa Merce*) left, news came to me that Your Grace intended to possess Maria Nunes, who does not conceal this from anyone, not even from me, saying that Your Grace gave her some beads and pin money, saying that you desired her much. And en route to the shoemaker's to repair some shoes, we talked about biscuits, and she said that Your Grace gave her some, and she said there were none so perfect. So it seems that Your Grace has a great love for her, because she says that you come from your lovers, bringing her their gifts.

My destiny is wretched. I was confident until this, thinking that I possessed Your Grace. Better that I were put to death a thousand times than to live with something that I remember that I did to some person some time ago. But after all, if she goes around telling everyone that she saw what you gave me on my finger, my heart will burst within my chest, and I had to excuse this by saying that I had purchased the ring from Your Grace. *Vossa Merce* has left my heart besieged, with my sentiments manifest in my tears; and when I see the person I desire, I am sad and jealous, and so Your Grace grows happier. As the proverb says, "One remembers where the honey was" (*"O mel faz por onde o lembrem"*), and this is how I must be with Your Grace, inasmuch as Your Grace pays so little attention. Your Grace has so many, and one will be the worse for it, and I am that one, because I had such love for Your Grace, that just seeing you made me so happy that I could not eat. It is certain that "whoever loves more strongly deserves least" (*quem mais ama, menos merece*). I will leave my heart afar, and I will look at the ground whenever I pass Your Grace.

Heaven protect Your Grace for the sake of your two lovers!

Commentary

Jealousy now dominates the wounded sacristan; the exquisite biscuits that he had given the guitarist were shared with his rival! Although he feigns indifference for a moment, hoping that his lover will miss the "honey" he has received in the past, Correa ultimately realizes that he has been defeated by a woman and ironically invokes Heaven's protection on Viegas for both their sakes. Maria Nunes' comments were surely made with the intention of wounding Correa and making him jealous. The whole affair had become entirely too public, thanks primarily to the bisexual guitarist who had apparently described the sacristan's amorous siege to her.

LETTER NUMBER FIVE

False and Flatterer:

If I could mock, scoffing at someone in love! But in the end, *quem mais ama menos merece.* For me there were only tears, tears caused by you and by so many skirts. Now she has what I desired. So often I have sent you word not to pay attention to me, but why do you dine with your women friends rather than with me, and then why do you send me notes that are lies? Those women were jealous of me because I wore someone else's ring. They said that I should return it to its owner. And here it is. I don't want anything of yours in my possession. Do the same with what you have of mine, and that will give me much pleasure. Do not ever speak to me or look at me again. I return the ring to encourage the hilarity of your lady friends.

Commentary

This is the proverbial straw that broke the camel's back: enough ridicule, enough humiliation, enough tears, enough false hopes. Enough of the honorific *Vossa Merce,* "My Gift" (*Prenda Minha*) — as though Senhor Manuel Viegas had been his gift from Heaven — enough "Mirror of my Sight and Joy": the sacristan now begins with *falso e lisonjeiro.* As a final gesture, he returns Viegas' ring and burns his letters. He of course requested Viegas to do the same. But as we know, the guitarist turned these five letters over to the Vicar of Silves (there were originally six; one has been lost), who promptly used them in an attempt to get Correa convicted of sodomy by the Portuguese Inquisition.

However, one of the happier aspects of this story is that the sacristan of Silves was apparently never put on trial for *nefandum*. The official rules of the Holy Office (*Regimento do Santo Oficio*) required two denunciations before any suspect could be imprisoned for sodomy, and it required two completely consummated homosexual acts (*penetratio cum seminis effusione*) before handing a defendant over to the secular courts to be burned. An isolated accusation — even one as unusually well-documented as this one, backed up by the Vicar's claim that the mayor of Silves, another priest, and various other residents were prepared to swear on the Holy Gospel that the sacristan was openly infamous as a sodomite — was not enough to have Correa arrested and put on trial. The Vicar, Luiz Coelho (who may have been related to Viegas' fiancee), included along with these love letters an official letter to the Commissioner of the Inquisition in Evora, claiming that "We have long had a clandestine sodomite in this city who by God's will is now discovered," and zealously warning the Holy Office that "it is important to put an end to these things before something else happens." But he did not get his revenge. Perhaps the lovesick sacristan's humiliation was punishment enough.

The overall record of the Portuguese Inquisition in dealing with cases of *nefandum peccatum* is marked more by compassion than justice (*Misericordia* and *Justitia* being major watchwords of this institution). In the first place, homosexuality comprised only a small part of the Holy Tribunal's business: Jews and other heretics represented at least 80 percent of its cases, while such other crimes as bigamy and witchcraft filled up much of the rest. Nonetheless, the Portuguese Inquisition managed to compile two large "Catalogues of Sodomites" (*Repertorios do Nefando*), listing alphabetically everyone denounced for or confessing this crime from 1587 to 1794 and containing a total of 4,419 names. Among these, we have thus far discovered only 408 who were actually put on trial for the "abominable sin of sodomy," a scant 10 percent of those accused.

In other words, there were nine chances in ten that an accusation like that made against our sacristan would not lead to his imprisonment and trial. Moreover, of those 408 actually tried, only about thirty were ever convicted of the two "complete acts" and handed over to secular justice to be burned—only about a 7 percent conviction rate. Thus, only about 0.6 percent of those originally accused eventually received capital punishment. If one considers the thousands of homosexuals murdered in Nazi concentration camps, or the more than one thousand "Judaizers" executed by the Portuguese Inquisition, it is clear that these early modern homosexuals paid a much smaller price for being homosexual.

Correa's love letters are not the only surviving documents of this type among these abundant Portuguese records. We have also located six unpublished letters written by a choir priest of the Hieronymite Monastery in Lisbon to another cleric, which describe an intense homoerotic relationship that lasted until 1690. They are longer than our sacristan's correspondence, more erudite, and more romantic, but they express the same high passion of prohibited feelings that are apparent in Correa's letters—feelings heightened perhaps by the risk of eventual discovery, but nevertheless set down on paper. Both collections share the image of the "heart bursting within one's breast" (*coracao estalando dentro do peito*), which impelled their authors to write of their "vile feelings," and both expressed their fears of discovery. All these letters reveal an intensely intimate mixture of love, sexual attraction, and tenderness with fear of discovery. Fortunately for us, in the end their passions overcame their prudence: *o amor foi mais forte que o medo da morte* (love was stronger than fear of death).

NOTES

1. John Boswell, *Christianity, Social Tolerance and Homosexuality* (Chicago: University of Chicago Press, 1980), 190.

2. Martin B. Duberman, "Writing Bedfellows, 1826: Two young men from antebellum South Carolina's ruling elite share 'extravagant delight,'" *Journal of Homosexuality*, 6 (1980-81): 85-101.

3. See *Cancioneiro Portugues da Vaticana* (Lisbon: Imprensa Nacional, 1878), and *Canconeiro da Biblioteca Nacional* (Lisbon: n.p., n.d.), Vol. 6, nos. 1252, 1267, 1505, 1530.

4. Asdrubal D'Aguiar, "A Evolucao da Pederastia e do Lesbianismo na Europa," *Separta do Arquivo da Universidade de Lisboa* 11 (1926): 504.

5. J. Pinheiro Correia and Francisco Figueiras, *Silves, Cronologia e Historia* (Silves: Edicao Silgarve, 1981).

6. Arquivo Nacional da Tore do Tombo, Inquisicao de Lisboa, Processo no. 7622.

7. Ibid., no. 5007.

II. FRANCE, GERMANY, AND SCANDINAVIA

Homosexuality and the Court Elites of Early Modern France: Some Problems, Some Suggestions, and an Example

Robert Oresko, PhD

Most of the significant contributions to the history of what twentieth-century observers would view as homosexual behavior in early modern Europe have concerned themselves with men who were not part of the political nation of the *ancien régime*. Randolph Trumbach's London sodomites,[1] Arthur Gilbert's sailors,[2] the tradesmen and craftsmen whom William Monter has detected in the Suisse Romande,[3] and the victims of the Parisian *mouches* analyzed by Michel Rey[4] occupied, at most, middling positions within the social hierarchies of their day. Some, as Trumbach's evidence would suggest, constituted a homosexual subculture, an urban phenomenon;

Dr. Robert Oresko is chairman of the Italian history seminar at the Institute of Historical Research, University of London.

This is a very different version of a paper delivered at the Institute of Historical Research, the University of London, in March 1984, and I am very grateful to Michael Hunter for having invited me to address the seminar there devoted to radicalism and deviancy in early modern Europe, of which he was co-chairman. A large number of friends and colleagues gave advice, encouragement, and cautionary warnings, of whom: Lucien Bély, Barry Bergdoll, Vincent Bouvet, Rohan Butler, Père Jean-Marie Charles-Roux, Michael de Cossart, Claude Courouve, the late Jeffery Daniels, Ragnhild Hatton, Suzanne d'Huart, Margaret Jacobs, Alastair Laing, David McFadden, Roger Mettam, Bruno Neveu, William Ritchey Newton, John Rogister, Alfred Soman, Randolph Trumbach, Richard Vann, Michel Vorsanger, David Watkin and Andrew Wilson. Alexander Clark and David Parrott merit a special expression of gratitude. My debt to Roger Clark is so great that any attempt to measure its extent would be futile. This article is dedicated to Robert Halsband.

105

others clearly did not. Historians have been able to study these men because they were caught behaving illegally, or were perceived to be about to do so, and because many of them subsequently were prosecuted. They have left their traces in police reports and trial records. These men from different countries, different centuries, and different milieux are united by the common factor of belonging to sections of society subject to the full workings of the legal system; few had access to the range of immunities which grew with ascent in the hierarchical establishments. E. J. F. Barbier observed in his journal in July 1750, following the trial and execution of Bruno Lenoir and Jean Diot for sodomy, that "as these two workmen (*ouvriers*) had no relations with people of distinction, be it at court, be it in the town, and as apparently they implicated no one, this example can be made without subsequent consequences."[5]

The reasons for concentrating upon legal evidence are easy enough to understand. Accounts of trials and the confessions of the accused provide the kind of proof that two men actually had sex with one another which is viewed as more reliable than the allegations, the speculation, and the veiled references in letters, *mémoires*, propaganda pamphlets, and gazettes. Proof of sexual contact can be easier for heterosexual relations. Put at its most extreme, we know that Louis XIV had a physical relationship with Mme. de Montespan, not because we read the observations of his courtiers, but because the king admitted as much by recognizing and legitimizing the children of his union. The absence of such "human" evidence for historians to decide whether two men had a physical relationship has increased the importance of legal evidence for the study of the history of homosexuality. But the very nature of this evidence has, in turn, anchored the subject in those areas of society affected by the enforcement of the law.

One departure from this near "monopoly" exercised by the *petites gens* over the history of homosexuality during the ancien regime, Caroline Bingham's study of the Castlehaven case,[6] is an exception which helps to prove the rule. In 1631, Mervyn Touchet, second earl of Castlehaven, was tried and found guilty of "committing sodomy with his servants." Castlehaven's downfall was engineered by his second wife, Anne Stanley, daughter of Ferdinando Stanley, fifth earl of Derby, widow of Grey Brydges, Lord Chandos, and a woman of formidable energy and powerful connections. We know the identity of Castlehaven's sexual partners, what they said to each other, even what they did in bed—the kind of information which is scarce for members of the *élites*, but which is available, thanks to police reports, for men of inferior position—because one member of the élite was determined to destroy another member of the élite and had recourse to the legal system in order to do so.

Short of an extraordinary situation, such as the Castlehaven case, it has been difficult to *prove* homosexual relations between men who were immune from the vigilance of the police. The absence of this final certainty that two men had a physical relationship, however great the corpus of speculation and circumstantial evidence surrounding a given friendship, however great the probability, colors the study of homosexuality above the levels of those men prey to legal prosecution. Lacking the evidence of police reports, trials, and confessions, how do we know that any specific pair of men had sex with each other in the sixteenth, seventeenth, and eighteenth centuries?

The survival of private correspondence can be misleading, a mixed blessing when seventeenth-century sentiment is forced into a twentieth-century context, as Georges Dethan has warned in his analysis of the obviously intense friendship between the young Mazarin and Carlo Colonna, duca di Marsi.

> The sentiments of the baroque age disconcert us by their excess. More than once, without doubt, the reader will have occasion to be startled by the warmth of certain expressions of friendship, by the fervor of certain attachments. . . . Above all it is necessary to persuade ourselves that at the beginning of the seventeenth century . . . the *grandes dames* or cardinals, bourgeois or men of letters did not seek to dissimulate their sentiments but rather to "exaggerate" them, as they said themselves, without endowing this verb with a pejorative nuance.[7]

Dethan's caution may well be viewed as excessive, and his naive rejection of a homosexual relationship between Mazarin and Colonna, as precluded by the future cardinal's rumored gallantries with

women in Spain at about the same time, may betray a determination
not to see in the subject of his biography a man of complicated
emotions, a man whom the author would prefer not to have been, in
his view, sexually "flawed." Yet Dethan's main point remains
valid: The letters exchanged by Mazarin and Carlo Colonna are
intensely, exaggeratedly affectionate, but there is no reference in
them to sex and without such a reference we have no proof. Even
the frank letter of 1 June 1727, written by John, Lord Hervey to
Stephen Fox, which may well refer to love bites, draws a judicious
comment from Robert Halsband. "Unlike proof of his heterosexual
activity (his children), the evidence for his homosexuality is necessarily vague and oblique."[8] It seems most probable that the relationship between Lord Hervey and Fox was a good deal more than
"sentimental sodomy," but the concrete evidence is very sparse.

I am resigned to the conclusion that we shall probably never have
the wealth of detailed information about the homosexual activities
of members of the élite, or even of the merely privileged and pros-
perous of the *ancien régime*, that we have for the *petites gens* who
were unfortunate enough to be arrested. The research of Michel Rey
in the Archives de la Bastille at the Bibliotheque de l'Arsenal have
produced some fragments of information about men of superior station, but the case of the comte de Medaillon, *lieutenant de la gen-
darmerie* and a relation of the *première dame d'honneur* of the
duchesse d'Orleans, warns against expecting too much from the
archival sources of the police. Observed importuning and arrested
in the Tuileries gardens on 8 July 1725, Medaillon was released
after what would seem to have been a spontaneously assembled
group of people of rank, informed of his detainment, threatened to
alert the duchess. They complained "of such an affront, that it was
horrid (*affreux*) that one should thus arrest *gens de condition.*"[9]

The Paris police of the eighteenth century were obviously aware
that the apprehended *petites gens* were not the only homosexuals in
the city, but they simply had dramatically less freedom of action if
the observed offenders were *gens de condition*. Claude Courouve
has unearthed a *"grande mémoire,"* also from the Bibliothèque de
l'Arsenal, containing the names of 113 "sodomites," among them
the duc de Lorges, the duc de Villars Brancas, and the marquis de
Villars, son of Louis XIV's marshal.[10] But apart from making lists

of homosexuals among the élite, there was little that the police could do, unless the authorities had the cooperation of the suspect's family.

One of the rare instances of a detailed account of homosexual activity in court circles is enshrined in the journal of Mathieu Marais, who had privileged access to information because of his position as man-at-law to Prince Charles de Lorraine, Grand Ecuyer de France. Marais noted, on 31 July 1722, that the young duc de Boufflers and the marquis d'Alincourt had been detected in a *bosquet*, both attempting to sodomize (*violer*) the marquis de Rambure: Boufflers could not manage it, whereupon d'Alincourt, Bouffler's own brother-in-law, took over with the willing Rambure, who "made no attempt to defend himself."[11] Much of this could have been court tittle-tattle, but a few days later Marais reported a conversation, the source of which was, most likely, Prince Charles. The aged maréchal de Villeroy, d'Alincourt's grandfather, had obtained a *lettre de cachet* to exile his grandson from court; Boufflers was disgraced as well. Marais observed,

The marshal is censured by everyone: He has dishonored his family at his pleasure. . . . When he spoke to Prince Charles, his nephew, of his plan, the prince said to him: "Monsieur, one does not have one's children disciplined by the king, there are other ways of doing it, and for my part, I would have done nothing."[12]

Given the privileges and the *de facto* immunities enjoyed by someone in the position of the comte de Medaillon, and the counsel of discretion urged by Prince Charles de Lorraine, it is scarcely surprising that the sort of firm evidence which has been extracted from police reports and which has assisted a retrieval of "the life, the actions, the words" of Paris homosexuals[13] is missing for the *gens de condition*.

This is a profoundly ironic situation for, as Trumbach has pointed out, "the [British eighteenth-century] public . . . believed . . . that sodomy was a fashionable vice — the final corruption of the aristocracy."[14] Rey has detected this attitude in some of the reports of the Paris police, who should have known better, and argues that some officials seemed convinced that the "vice" should be confined to the court and should be prevented from infecting those who were viewed as constituting "the people."[15]

The mythic view of early modern homosexuality as the exclusive preserve of aristocracies has been fed by generations of fluent practitioners of *petite histoire*. Their biographies and *chroniques scandaleuses* rely heavily upon anecdotes culled from the series of memoires, journals, and letters dating from the *ancien régime* which appeared, from about 1800 onward, in editions which stand as monuments to the energy of scholars and the enterprise of publishers in nineteenth-century France. Although some historians, especially those belonging to the first generation to feel the impact of what is popularly viewed as quantitative history, have disparaged the usefulness of such sources, dismissing them as fodder exclusively for the consumption of the historical novelist, others have adopted a more flexible approach. François Bluche of the Université de Paris X-Nanterre has encouraged his students to return to the published memoires and to reappropriate them for scholars not by attempting to write biographies or *histoire evenementielle* of the political, military, and diplomatic developments of successive reigns, but rather by extracting from them vital information about the structure and the practical workings of life at court. By rereading the memoires with this in mind, complicated systems of clientage and patronage, the manipulation of favor, the significance of marriage and the plotting of family strategies, the overlapping of social and political groupings — in short, the functioning of a sophisticated machine, harboring a complex social life — can move more clearly into focus.

Michel Vorsanger's 1983 *maîtrise* drew upon the memoires of the marquis de Sourches to reveal the use of royal disgrace or disfavor as a means of social control and to evaluate the varying extents of liberty of action among the courtiers surrounding Louis XIV.[16] This technique has interesting implications for historians of homosexuality. By sifting the memoires not for the colorful *historiette*, but rather for the identities of men reputed to have had emotional or sexual relations with other men, we can, with great caution, piece together a list of members of the French court who were probably homosexual and attempt to uncover systems or networks within the court based, at least in part, upon this sexual affinity.

At this point, a specific example might be helpful. As my own work centers upon the dynastic and familial structures of the Houses of Savoy, Lorraine, and Orléans, I shall now look at the life of Louis XIV's only brother, Philippe de France, duc d'Orléans (1640-1701) and his relationship with his acknowledged favorite, Philippe de Lorraine, the "chevalier de Lorraine" (1643-1702).[17] Most twentieth-century historians accept that Philippe de France, styled "Monsieur" in court parlance, was homosexual. For John Wolf, he was "Poor Philippe, a homosexual whose rouge, jewels, ribbons and lace brought smiles to many faces."[18] Ragnhild Hatton cites "the homosexuality and feminine aspect of Philippe's personality,"[19] while cautioning against stressing these elements and pointing to Monsieur's two marriages and three surviving children.

What is the evidence for assuming that Monsieur was homosexual? Madame, Monsieur's second wife, burnt, without reading them, "all the letters the boys (*die Buben*) wrote him,"[20] immediately after her husband's death. Of all the ducs d'Orléans of the Bourbon line whose papers have been preserved in the Archives de la Maison de France,[21] Monsieur is the least well-represented. The one *carton* of his personal papers, shared with those of his uncle Gaston, would seem to include only documents relating to family arrangements.[22] The answer, again, lies with the published memoires and letters. Mme. de La Fayette, who left an account of the life of her friend, Monsieur's first wife, Henrietta Anne Stuart of England (1644-1670), commented with characteristically exquisite tact that "the miracle of inflaming the heart of this prince was reserved to no woman of this world."[23] Such reticence was avoided by other contemporary commentators, who dwelt on Monsieur's effeminacy, his delight in dressing in women's clothes, the dominance of male favorites; there are also unspecified references to debaucheries, too vague to be considered evidence.

The major source which has determined much of our view of Monsieur's life and personality is the published correspondence of his second wife, Elisabeth-Charlotte of the Palatinate (1652-1722).

As the extraordinary letters of the second Madame are such a rich source of homosexual gossip, albeit frequently of the nature of who-had-tried-to-seduce-whom, with a range of information on homosexual *coteries* at court, they are a beguiling collection for any historian of homosexuality during the *ancien régime*, such a historian too often deprived of the immediacy of observation and the frankness of discourse which Madame's correspondence offers. It is best to pause and to evaluate the undeniable importance of these letters more coolly.

All published editions of Madame's letters are very fragmentary. By the time of Monsieur's death in 1701, Madame wrote at least once each week to her daughter at Lunéville, Elisabeth-Charlotte, Duchess of Lorraine, to her stepdaughter at Turin, Anne, Duchess of Savoy, and to her cousin, the Duchess of Modena, Charlotte Felicitas of Brunswick. She wrote nearly as frequently to Madrid to successive Queens of Spain. None of these letters has been unearthed. This is a pity as many of them must have been written in French, notably those to the Duchess of Savoy, which would represent a run of correspondence of nearly forty years, and those to the Duchess of Lorraine, whose relationship with her mother was especially close. The vast bulk of the letters which have come to light and which form the basis of all published editions were written in German. Despite this, nearly all English-speaking historians and, it would seem every French historian, use one of the French translations of these letters. This is Madame very much at second hand and a Madame who speaks with the voice of a nineteenth-century woman of letters.

Apart from the letters to Leibnitz, the correspondence which has attracted most attention was dispatched to two recipients, Madame's aunt, the Electress Sophia of Hanover, and Madame's morganatic half-sister, Luise, Raugräfin von Degenfeld. The letters sent to Sophia have the intimacy not only of a correspondence exchanged between people of the same rank, but also of one between people who were deeply fond of each other, a bond formed when the adolescent Elisabeth-Charlotte, in the wake of her parents' separation, found refuge at her aunt's court. The difficulty with these letters is that they were all written during Louis XIV's lifetime: The Electress died in 1714, the king the following year. Madame was aware that all her correspondence was opened and read, and although she was still indiscreet, she did have to exercise some caution, especially at critical points when she needed either her brother-in-law's favor or the grudging support of Mme. de Maintenon.

Louis's death in 1715 and the assumption of the regency for Louis XV by Madame's son brought the end of epistolary surveillance, and the untrammeled flow of letters to her half-sister, which ended only with Madame's death, is of vital importance for historians of the Orléans regency. The rather freer Degenfeld correspondence of this last period also contains much about Monsieur, but written, of course, at the very least fourteen years after the events described took place. One other virtue of the Degenfeld letters is that the Raugräfin was not a woman of the court, and Madame took pains to explain the relationships and workings of Versailles with great precision, knowledge of which Madame took for granted when writing to her aunt. The Raugräfin's ignorance is a blessing for twentieth-century historians.[24]

Bearing these caveats in mind, we can piece together a view of the structure within which the king's brother led his life by the judicious use of: (a) Madame's letters; (b) the memoires of Daniel de Cosnac, future archbishop of Aix-en-Provence but, as Monsieur's *premier aumonier*, a member of the Orléans household before Philippe's second marriage in 1672; (c) the memoires of Saint-Simon, whose close ties to the Regent and the Orléans machine give his observations special value despite their compilation decades after the events described; (d) the memoires of abbé de Choisy, a boyhood friend of Monsieur and one attuned to the attraction of transvestism; and, (e) the journals and memoires of two of the most meticulous commentators on the daily routine of court life, the marquis de Sources and the marquis de Dangeau.

All of these writers agree on one central element: the overwhelming importance of the chevalier de Lorraine, whose style derived from an early but never finalized membership in the Order of Malta. Writing in 1681, Sources commented that Monsieur "was too governed by the chevalier de Lorraine, who for a long time has had an absolute empire over his soul."[25] Saint-Simon stated simply that "the chevalier de Lorraine governed Monsieur for all time: the taste of Monsieur was not for women and he never hid this; this same taste gave him the chevalier for master and such he remained all of his life."²⁶ Saint-Simon's detached tone may have owed something to the friendly relations between the chevalier and Monsieur's son, the future Regent, even after Monsieur's death.

Philippe de Lorraine was the second son of Henri de Lorraine, comte d'Armagnac and Grand Ecuyer de France. As a member of the House of Lorraine, competent to succeed to the sovereign duchy of Lorraine, Philippe, as with all his family, took the precedence at the French court of a *prince étranger*. The straitened financial circumstances of the Armagnac line were observed by contemporary commentators,²⁷ and for a younger son of a family of princely standing but of limited means, a career in the church, either as the occupant of commendatory abbeys or a member of the Order of Malta, provided the almost inevitable resolution to the problem of finding an establishment. According to Cosnac, the chevalier's annual income before attaching himself to Monsieur was a mere 1,000 écus.²⁸

But if the chevalier was financially impoverished, he had as compensation a wealth of physical beauty. Writing to her daughter in 1672, Mme. de Sévigné referred to "The chevalier with that beautiful, open physiognomy which I love and which you do not,"²⁹ and even the second Madame recollected for the Raugräfin, fourteen years after Philippe de Lorraine's death, that "he was a handsome man, well made; if the interior had been as good as the exterior, I would, never in my life, have had anything to say against him."³⁰ It was, however, Saint-Simon who made the necessary connection between beauty and favor. Writing of the chevalier and the young Châtillon, the duke observed that "they had made a great fortune by their figures of which Monsieur had been more intoxicated than of any others."³¹

Monsieur's favor brought the chevalier a stream of gifts, including four benefices which provided an annual income, this despite Louis XIV's reluctance to endow members of Monsieur's circle with abbeys, which brought a degree of financial independence, instead preferring to bestow pensions, which were revocable. Madame, writing in 1716, put the chevalier's yearly revenue at the time of his death in 1702 at 100,000 écus.³² Both Cosnac and Madame were hostile to the chevalier, and I have yet to discover any tabulations of income for the Lorraine prince's residence in France. But a comparison of the 1,000 écus cited by Cosnac and the figure given by Madame gives at least a rough indication of the spectacular improvement in the chevalier's finances, owed either to Monsieur's direct generosity or to Monsieur's intervention with the king on the chevalier's behalf.

One early major problem was posed by the official role which Philippe de Lorraine assumed in Philippe de France's life. It was impossible for the chevalier, as a prince, to hold a position, a *charge*, in Monsieur's household. Not until 1684 did Monsieur acquire the privilege of being served by dukes and duchesses, a right no previous *fils de France* had been accorded. In the late 1660s, however, the chevalier pressed for a public declaration of his role as Monsieur's favorite.

> He wants absolutely to attach himself to me; but he makes one condition . . . that, in giving himself to me, it means to renounce entirely all the graces he could obtain from the king, and that nothing could compensate for this loss apart from declaring him publicly as my favorite; that this is the means to bring him the consideration (*le faire considérer*) of the king.[33]

Monsieur was obviously inclined to grant this request and justified his willingness by citing an episode from the life of his uncle, Gaston de France, duc d'Orléans. Cosnac recorded Monsieur depicting the chevalier as wanting to have "for his person [Monsieur's] the same attachment that the late M. de Montmorency had for the late Monseigneur the duc d'Orléans, his uncle, and that it would be for him more glorious, this chevalier being a prince, whereas M. de Montmorency was only a gentleman."[34] This statement is striking both for its reliance upon precedent as the justification for an openly acknowledged male favorite and for the introduction of notions of dynastic suitability in making the choice.

The chevalier's request was granted, and his position became official enough to receive the recognition of the massive compendiums dealing with the French royal house and court which appeared in the eighteenth century. Among the chevalier de Lorraine's benefices,

Orders, and military exploits, Père Anselme noted for posterity that he "merita l'affection de Philippe de France, duc d'Orléans," and this formula was repeated word-for-word in the *Dictionnaire de la noblesse*.[35]

Although the chevalier occupied the central position in Monsieur's life from the late 1660s until the duc d'Orléans's death in 1701, succeeding decades produced a sequence of men who enjoyed such notable favor from Monsieur that it is possible to discern at least the shape of their careers from the published *mémoires* and letters. The lives of these other favorites have many elements in common. As none was a duke or prince, they made their way through the apparatus of the Orléans household.

Antoine Coeffier-Ruzé, marquis d'Effiat (1638-1719) entered the establishment of Monsieur in the 1660s as *capitaine des chasses* at Montargis, one of the component parts of the Orléans *apanage*, but rose quickly to become *premier veneur* and *premier écuyer* of Monsieur's entire household. Although d'Effiat seems to have had the good opinion of Louis XIV and played an active role in the government of the regency under Monsieur's son, the debauches of his private life were considered of such public knowledge that the king intervened in 1689 to block his appointment as the *gouverneur* to the future Regent, then duc de Chartres. Writing in 1689 to Sophia of Hanover, Madame reported an exchange with Monsieur which leaves no doubt what these debauches were: "It seems to me that it would not be an honor for my son if people believed he was the mistress of d'Effiat, and it is certain that there is no greater sodomite than he in all of France." Even Monsieur, who had enthusiastically supported this appointment, had to concede that d'Effiat "had been a *débauché* and that he had loved young men."[36]

In 1696 and 1697, François-Gabriel-Thibault de La Carte also moved rapidly through the Orléans household, from the position of *maître d'hôtel* of Monsieur to that of captain of his guards and then to the charge of governor of Monsieur's principality of Joinville. As was the chevalier de Lorraine, some of the other favorites were younger sons and many were drawn from the ranks of the impoverished provincial nobility, La Carte from Gascony, Beuvron from Normandy. Acquisition of office within the Orléans household helped to remedy their relative poverty, and income from charges could be complemented by social and hierarchical advancement thanks to the arrangement, under the aegis of Monsieur, of an advantageous marriage. Despite the virulent opposition of most of the bride's family, Monsieur engineered the wedding of La Carte to the daughter of the duc de La Ferté with the provision that La Carte assume the La Ferté name and arms by means of an Orléans guarantee of 200,000 livres against the duc de La Ferté's debts.

Again, as with the chevalier de Lorraine, all favorites seem to have been beautiful. Of Alexis-Henri, chevalier de Châtillon, Saint-Simon wrote that he "was the best-made man in France and his figure made his fortune with Monsieur,"[37] a factor in the evolution of his career noted with more choler by Primi-Visconti, when observing of Châtillon that "for his beauty he was raised from the muck of the streets to captain of the guards."[38]

There are also stray references to men whose careers seem to have been more transitory. A page named Bolgar was rumored to have been given a sword worth 2,000 pistoles,[39] and Madame informed her aunt in 1692 that Monsieur had spent 200,000 gulden on positions in the guards regiments "as recompense for young men (*um junger Bürscher zu recompensiren*),"[40] an expenditure for which an archival source has so far proved elusive. Moving further down the social scale, Madame reported in 1698 that "Monsieur is more than ever taken with boys (*Buben*), he takes lackeys out of the antechamber.[41] Everything he has he squanders in this way . . . and allows himself to be ruled by these lewd boys (*Bursch*)."[42]

Clusters of anecdotes have gathered around all of these young men who made considerable fortunes in the service of Monsieur, anecdotes which suggest, at least obliquely, that one of the vital mechanisms of this system of favor was sex. The tone of coy but knowing reticence which informs so many of these stories is clear in a passage written by Primi-Visconti which describes Châtillon's elder brother, who

never had the wherewithal to have a suit of clothes appropriate to his rank. Being an officer (*exempt*) of the *gardes du corps* of the king, he complained once to the king that, being the elder, he had not made his fortune in His Majesty's service, whereas his younger brother had been so greatly advanced by the younger brother of His Majesty. The king answered him: "One finds one's fortune with my brother by certain means which, when practiced, lose favor with me."[43]

What were these means? The strong implication is that the favorites of Monsieur progressed in their careers by having sex with him. None of the writers of the *mémoires* and letters say so in as many words, although it is worth bearing in mind that Claude Courouve's citation from Barbier for the execution of Lenoir and Diot came from an inspection of the Barbier manuscript, not from the published version.[44] Many editions of Barbier omit references to sodomy, and there is at least a possibility that other passages dealing with homosexuality in other collections of *mémoires* were gently expunged from the manuscript originals by nineteenth-century editors. (Such originals should now be re-explored by historians of homosexuality.)

To twentieth-century eyes, the existence in the Orléans household of a homosexual network which advanced careers and brought riches may seem obvious, but the hard evidence for the sexual mechanism is all but nonexistent. Primi-Visconti's commentaries are more direct than some: "The chevalier de Lorraine was reputed to be a protector of the beautiful youth (*la belle jeunesse*): moreover, he himself, although thirty years old, was not *hors des rangs*, which made of him a special favorite."[45] We have much testimony to the depth of Monsieur's emotional attachment to the chevalier, but can we automatically assume that their relationship was physical? It is doubtful that historians will ever have adequate information to be certain, however great the probability may be, that the two Philippes ever had sex with each other.

This need not, however, be the end of our inquiries. The layers of evidence for the importance of homosexual affinities and physical beauty lie too heavily upon the history of the evolution of the Orléans household to be ignored. We must explore more closely the structure of Monsieur's establishment. Philippe de France has frequently been dismissed as a vain and frivolous man who had been denied, by his brother, any access to power. If power is measured in terms of the extent of influence upon the direction of state policy, a definition propounded unquestioningly by nineteenth- and early-twentieth-century political, diplomatic, and military historians, then this evaluation of Monsieur has substance. But one of the more fruitful historiographical developments of the past few decades has been the exploration of how different types of power were manipulated within a court society, specifically the power of patronage working through clientage systems.[46]

Some historians have suggested, or at least pointed to, the possibility of links between homosexual groupings and the distribution of favor. Piers Mackesy's biography of Lord George Sackville points to the promotion of the careers of young men for whom Lord George felt homosexual affection during his tenure as Secretary of State for the American Colonies (1775-1782).[47] Georges Dethan has analyzed the household in Rome of Cardinal Antonio Barberini (1607-1671), the younger of the two cardinal-nephews of Pope Urban VIII, and the central role played in this establishment by the castrato Marco Antonio Pasqualini, called Malagigi. Pasqualini was granted control over the expenditure of large sums of money and, at least as important, over access to the cardinal himself.[48]

Moving to a period apart from the *ancien régime*, Isabel Hull has investigated the bonds between a homosexual *coterie*, that of Prinz Philipp zu Eulenburg, and the deployment of political influence in the second Reich of Emperor Wilhelm II. But here again, we are dealing with questions of appointments rather than "the actual content of policy"[49] and its implementation. One of the gravest charges Maximilian Harden launched at Eulenburg was that "no important post was filled without his help."[50] This is the language of patronage, not necessarily of high state policy goals. Monsieur may have been deprived of military command and the government of provinces, but his powers in bestowing offices and benefices, in securing pensions, in arranging marriages and establishing recognition of dubious titles, in supporting advancement within the hierarchy of the court, in dispensing gifts either from his own purse or through intercession with his brother, were immense.

As suggested by the establishment of Cardinal Antonio Barberini and Pasqualini, the question of access to the fount of favor had vital importance. For nearly every day of his adult life (with the obvious exception of campaigns), Monsieur saw the king alone in Louis's study between the meeting of the Council and the *Petit Couvert*.

Apart from Louis's wives and mistresses, no one had such regular and private access to the sovereign.[51] Access to the king has been seen as a major factor in the structuring of daily routine at Versailles,[52] and frequent contact with Louis brought with it occasions to present petitions and to ask for favor, either for oneself or on behalf of someone else—a relation or a member of the courtier's household or clientage system.

Some of the favor which Monsieur's intimates enjoyed came directly from Louis. In 1685 the king gave the chevalier de Lorraine 100,000 écus and in 1688 included him, his two brothers, his nephew, d'Effiat, and Châtillon in the promotion to the Order of the Saint-Esprit, adding the further grace of confirming the precedence of the four Lorraine princes before the *ducs et pairs* within the Order.[53] Monsieur's role in interceding with his brother was important. In 1683, Madame informed her aunt of "all the good treatment the king daily gives to the chevalier, to which end my husband applies all his favor,"[54] and this only one year after Louis ordered the chevalier to enter his presence less frequently as a result of his implication in the homosexual "confrérie" of 1682.[55]

But much of the patronage bestowed upon the Orléans favorites was in the direct gift of Monsieur. The pioneering work of Beatrice Hyslop on the *apanage* of Monsieur's descendant, Louis-Philippe be Bourbon, duc d'Orléans (1747-1793), known as "Philippe-Egalite," provides at least a starting point for an appreciation of the vast resources at Monsieur's disposal.[56] Monsieur's *apanage*, created in March 1661, comprised the duchies of Orléans, Valois, and Chartres, and the *seigneurie* of Montargis. It was supplemented in April 1672 with the duchy of Nemours, the counties of Dourdan and Romorantin, and the marquisates of Coucy and Folembray, and it continued to grow by gift and purchase throughout Monsieur's lifetime. In some parts of the apanage Monsieur was granted the critical right of presentation of ecclesiastical benefices.[57] Significant additions to the fortune were made by the dowry brought by Mlle de Blois in 1692 on her marriage to the duc de Chartres and by the testament of the duchesse de Montpensier, who, on her death in 1693, named Monsieur as her universal heir.

Although their spectacular fortune is frequently viewed as an eighteenth-century phenomenon, the Orléans dynasty ranked among the wealthiest families of Europe during Monsieur's lifetime. This position was reflected in the elaboration of their establishments, notably at Saint-Cloud and at the Paris residence, the Palais-Royal. The households of Monsieur and Madame and, after 1692, of the duc and duchesse de Chartres, their son and daughter-in-law, were the most extensive and elaborate of the princely establishments in France, constituting veritable courts with a range of offices, nearly all of which were venal. We have seen how most of Monsieur's favorites advanced through this system of non-royal office holding.

Hyslop's study and those devoted, on a less ambitious scale, to the fortunes of two other branches of the House of Bourbon, the Condé and Conti,[58] are of primary importance because they permit an estimation of the extent of individual princely resources. As some of these princes were very wealthy indeed and had sophisticated systems for dispensing favor independently of the king, it is necessary to modify the view of Louis XIV's Versailles as a homogeneous social unit in which advancement came from only one source, the crown. There were other options. But as crucial as Hyslop's work is for the historian of patronage, such a study provides only half the story. Once we know how a princely fortune was accumulated and administered, we then must ask how it was spent. Expenditure was, after all, the essence of patronage. Here we meet a large problem, as the surviving accounts for the Orléans treasury during Monsieur's lifetime are, at best, fragmentary. We do not have a consecutive run of ledgers which would enable us to tabulate the sums of money disbursed to members of Monsieur's circle. Much of what we know about specific grants and the changes within the personnel of the Orléans establishment comes, again, from *mémoires*.

Art historians and architectural historians dealing with early modern France have addressed themselves with great profit and ingenuity to the notarial records preserved in the Minutier Central of the Archives Nationales. As early as 1900, Victor Champier, frustrated by the absence of registers of Monsieur's treasury, turned to the notarial archives in order to piece together elements of the history of the interior decoration of the Palais-Royal during Monsieur's tenure.[59]

The world of the *ancien régime* notary has much to offer the historian of homosexuality as well. From the *inventaire après décès* of Monsieur himself[60] we can construct a picture not only of the extent of the Orléans collections in 1701, but also of the living arrangements in Monsieur's establishment. The inventory specifies the contents and suggests the location of the apartments assigned at Saint-Cloud to both the chevalier de Lorraine and the marquis d'Effiat, and the importance of these apartments is underlined by the relative reticence of the inventory on the identity of the occupants of the other apartments at Monsieur's château.[61] This suggests that these two suites of rooms were permanent establishments incorporated within the Orléans household.

Monsieur's inventory was entrusted to the notary Bellanger le jeune, and it was this same Bellanger who helped draw up the inventory of the chevalier de Lorraine following his death, one year after that of Monsieur.[62] I am currently sifting through Bellanger's documents to see which other members of the Orléans machine used his services. Monsieur's inventory notes that his testamentary executor was Achille de Harlay, comte de Beaumont and Premier Président of the Parlement de Paris, a man whom Maurice Lever has recently singled out as a rare example among the noblesse de robe of a target of homosexual satire.[63] It is at least possible that the ties between Monsieur and Harlay were due, perhaps only partially, to shared sexual affinities.

Once the name of the notary dealing with the affairs of a courtier rumored to have been homosexual is known, it becomes possible to search in the Minutier Central for at least copies of those papers which were the very stuff of clientage systems—receipts of pensions, records of loans raised for the purchase of office, contracts for the reversion of office, matrimonial and testamentary documentation. But in the ultimate analysis, the basis for identifying such courtiers (in this case, Monsieur's intimates) is gossip, however well-informed and "contemporary" the source may have been. Investigation based on individual cases will inevitably yield a fragmentary image of the workings of the patronage machine as a whole: some people's papers will have survived, others not. It is particularly frustrating that the chevalier de Lorraine seemed reluctant to set pen to paper. Nevertheless, a judicious marriage of published *mémoires* and letters, on the one hand, and notarial sources, on the other, can produce not only a clearer view of the structure of the clientèle in an establishment of which the head was a homosexual with an acknowledged male favorite, but also a firmer basis from which to launch informed speculation about what I have consistently called the "sexual mechanism" embedded in this system.

Moreover, such a model could well be applied to other princely households in early modern France. Louis de Bourbon, prince de Condé, François-Louis de Bourbon, prince de Conti and Louis-Joseph de Bourbon, duc de Vendôme were all perceived by some of their contemporaries as having male favorites or as being sexually attracted to men. (Conti was implicated in two of the major homosexual scandals of Louis XIV's reign.) These three princes all had important establishments, all maintained residences in Paris and a major household detached from the court (Condé at Chantilly, Conti at l'Isle Adam, and Vendôme at Anet—the equivalents of Monsieur's Saint-Cloud), and, bearing in mind Madame's report of Monsieur's expenditures for military *charges*, all had close links with the army, especially the gifted Vendôme, whose supposed private use of individual patronage during the War of the Spanish Succession has a secure place in the history of early eighteenth-century propaganda and pamphlet literature.

The questions of clientage and advancement are by no means the only ways of approaching homosexuality among the *élite* at the French court. I shall address myself elsewhere to the homosexual scandals of the 1680s in an attempt to elucidate their political and social aspects and to evaluate the role of homosexuality in binding courtiers together into perceptible groupings of shared dynastic background or of social and financial interests and political goals held in common. The role played by sex—and, also of great importance, friendship—in the creation of circles at Louis XIV's court could provide another means of studying homosexuality among the *élite*. These groupings concerned themselves with all means of preferment, from the acquisition of important provincial governments to the occupancy of specific apartments at Versailles. They supported specific artists, architects, writers, and musicians in preference to others who were backed by opposing circles. They arranged themselves around the religious controversies which lacerated the fabric of spiritual unanimity and which affected the allocation of ecclesiastical benefices. They attached themselves to individual ministers of the king (Monsieur's close friendship with Louvois and tense relations with Colbert call for more attention). They were much occupied with the distribution of military commands, with the rise and fall of royal mistresses, and, as the king grew older, with the entourages which surrounded those who were perceived as Louis's immediate successors, the Dauphin and the duc de Bourgogne. Some had close family links to dynasties on the other side of the Rhein and the other side of the Alps. (Homosexual attachments seem to have been among the significant elements drawing together certain groups of princes and dukes in those regions as well.)

We shall probably never be able to recreate the daily habits of a court homosexual or the practical arrangements leading to sex between men in the way that Michel Rey has so convincingly reconstructed the cruising itineraries of, and compiled conversational exchanges among, the Parisian sodomites of the eighteenth century. But the study of homosexuality among the *élite* may provide a few more tools for those historians who have begun to dismantle the myth of a homogenized, subservient, and controlled court life, a central notion in the propaganda of absolutism.

NOTES

1. Randolph Trumbach, "London's Sodomites: Homosexual Behavior and Western Culture in the Eighteenth Century," *Journal of Social History* (1977).
2. A. N. Gilbert, "Buggery and the British Navy, 1700-1861," *Journal of Social History* (1976).
3. William Monter, "La Sodomie à l'Epoque Moderne en Suisse Romande," *Annales E.S.C.* (1974).
4. Michel Rey, *Les Sodomites Parisiens au XVIIIe siècle*, unpublished maîtrise d'historien, Université de Paris VIII-Vincennes (1979-80). I am grateful to Alfred Soman for drawing this work to my attention.
5. This important entry from Barbier's journal comes not from a published edition of this crucial source for eighteenth-century French history, but rather from the pioneering researches of Claude Courouve, who consulted the original manuscript (Bibliothèque Nationale, ms. fr. 10289, fo. 152) and published Barbier's account in *L'affaire Lenoir-Diot* (Paris: 1980).
6. Caroline Bingham, "Seventeenth-Century Attitudes to Deviant Sex," *Journal of Interdisciplinary History* (1971).
7. Georges Dethan, *Mazarin et ses Amis* (Paris: 1968), 59-60.
8. Robert Halsband, *Lord Hervey* (Oxford: 1973), 90.

9. Michel Rey, *Les Sodomites*, xxvi. The report comes from the Bibliothèque de l'Arsenal, ms. 10256.

10. Claude Courouve, *Les Gens de la manchette* (Paris: n.p., 1981), 12-13.

11. Mathieu Marais, *Journal et mémoires*, vol. 2, ed. M. Lescure (Paris: 1863-68), 319-320.

12. Ibid., vol. 2, 321-22.

13. Michel Rey, *Les Sodomites*, 3.

14. Randolph Trumbach, *London's Sodomites*, 19.

15. Michel Rey, *Les Sodomites*, 21-23.

16. Michel Vorsanger, *Quand Louis XIV disgraçiait*, unpublished maîtrise d' historien, Université de Paris X-Nanterre (1983-84).

17. There is no satisfactory biography of Monsieur. Philippe Erlanger's *Monsieur, frère du roi* (Paris: 1970) is at best an entertaining summary of court gossip, with some interesting speculation about the political motivation behind the structure of Monsieur's education. Guy de La Batut's *La cour de Monsieur* (Paris: 1927) is a slightly more ambitious undertaking and was certainly written with a greater attention to archival sources. Unfortunately, there is such a clutter of minor factual error that considerable wariness is recommended. Nancy Barker of the University of Texas, Austin, is, however, preparing a biography of Monsieur.

18. John Wolf, *Louis XIV* (New York: 1968), 605.

19. Ragnhild Hatton, *Louis XIV and his World* (London: 1972), 12. The most recent account in French, François Bluche, *Louis XIV* (Paris: 1986) also refers to Monsieur's 'ambiguïté', to his attachment to the chevalier de Lorraine and to Madame's awkward position as 'l'épouse d'un sodomite' (529-30). At the same time, Bluche draws attention to the role Monsieur played, almost as Louis's representative, in Paris, and to the importance of Louis's reaction to Philippe's military successes.

20. *Aus den Briefen der Herzogin Elisabeth Charlotte von Orléans an die Kurfürstin Sophia von Hannover*, ed. Eduard Bodemann (Hanover: 1891), vol. 2, 4: letter of 30 June 1701. See note 24 below.

21. Suzanne d'Huart, *Archives de la Maison de France* (Paris, 1976).

22. Archives Nationales, 300.AP.I.115.

23. Marie-Madeleine Pioche de La Vergne, comtesse de La Fayette, *Histoire de Madame Henriette d'Angleterre*, ed. Gilbert Sigaux (Paris: 1982), 36.

24. The problem of the editions of Madame's letters is a thorny one. The basic German editions are: *Aus den Briefen der Herzogin Elisabeth Charlotte von Orléans an die Kurfürstin Sophia von Hannover*, ed. Eduard Bodemann (Hanover: 1891), and *Briefen der Prinzessin Elisabeth Charlotte von Orléans an die Raugräfin Louise, 1677-1722*, ed. Wolfgang Menzel (*Bibliothek des Literarischen Vereins in Stuttgart* (Stuttgart: 1843). Bodemann's *Briefe der Herzogin Elisabeth Charlotte an ihre frühere Hofmeisterin A.K. Harling . . .* (Hanover: 1895) is also important, but, as these letters were not written to relations, they fall into a different category. The most recent German edition, *Die Briefe der Liselotte von der Pfalz*, ed. Margarethe Westphal (Ebenhausen-bei-München: 1958, 1984) claims to be based on a 1911 edition of the letters selected by Wilhelm Langewiesche. As

various letters have been abridged, as Madame's idiosyncratic spelling has been modernized, and as the editor has not bothered to indicate the sources for the letters, it is difficult to know of what possible use this selection can be for scholars. The classic French edition is that by G. Brunet (Paris: 1857), relying largely on the Degenfeld letters and complicating matters by including translations of some letters to the Raugräfin which escaped Menzel's notice, but for which no references are given (see notes 30 and 32 below). The most recent French edition is by Olivier Amiel (Paris: 1981). Maria Kroll has produced (1970) *Letters from Liselotte*. Comparison of twentieth-century editions of Madame's letters with the published German versions of Bodemann and Menzel leaves me with the disquieting notion that some translators are producing new translations based exclusively upon the older translations. I have not yet seen Elborg Forster's *A Woman's Life in the Court of the Sun King: Letters of Liselotte von der Pfalz* (Baltimore: 1984). Jürgen Voss has recently discovered a previously unknown collection of Madame's letters to Mme de Ludres, and much of the muddle surrounding the correspondence of Monsieur's second wife should be clarified by Dirk van der Cruysse's forthcoming edition of the letters.

25. Louis-Francois de Bouchet, marquis de Sourches, *Memoires*, ed. Gabriel-Jules de Cosnac and Edouard Pontal (Paris: 1882-93), vol. 1, 11.

26. Louis de Rouvroy, duc de Saint-Simon, *Mémoires*, ed. Arthur de Boislisle (Paris: 1879-1930), vol. 1, 60-61.

27. The finances of several of the cadet princes of the House of Lorraine were in disorder in the second half of the seventeenth century. Savoyard observers at Chambéry noted that the toilette of the Lorraine princesse de Lillebonne, delegated to accompany Monsieur's daughter, Anne, to her wedding with Vittorio Amedeo II, was so inadequate that she and her daughter had to absent themselves from mass at the Sainte-Chapelle. See G. Claretta, "L'arrivée d'Anne d'Orléans . . . à la cour de Savoie en 1684," *Mémoires et Documents publies par la Société Savoisienne* (1895).

28. Daniel de Cosnac, *Mémoires*, ed. Gabriel-Jules de Cosnac (Paris: 1852), vol. 2, 61.

29. Marie de Rabutin-Chantal, marquise de Sévigné, *Lettres*, ed. Roger Duchêne (Paris: 1972-78), vol. 1, 469.

30. *Correspondance complète de Madame, duchesse d'Orléans*, ed. G. Brunet (Paris: 1857), vol. 1, letter of 13 July 1717. This is one of the Degenfeld letters not included in Menzel's collection. See note 24.

31. Saint-Simon, *Mémoires*, vol. 8, 342.

32. *Correspondance complètè de Madame*, vol. 1, 225: letter of 31 March 1716.

33. Cosnac, *Mémoires*, vol. 2, 64. This citation can be misleading as Cosnac has Monsieur slipping from the first person to the third person when referring to himself. I have, for my translation, maintained the first person throughout.

34. Ibid., vol. 2, 61-63. See also Ibid., vol. 1, 360 for another reference to the Montmorency precedent.

35. Père Anselme, *Histoire Généalogique . . . de la Maison Royale de*

France, 3d ed. (Paris, 1733), vol. 3, 500; Francois-Alexandre Aubert de La Che-
naye-Desbois, *Dictionnaire de la noblesse* (Paris, 1770-86), of which the most
accessible edition is the reset and slightly rearranged version of 1863-76, vol. 12,
col. 432.

36. *Aus den Briefen der Herzogin Elisabeth Charlotte*, vol. 1, 111: letter of 26
August 1689.

37. Saint-Simon, *Mémoires*, vol. 14, 119-20.

38. Giovanni Battista di Primi-Visconti, conte di San Maiole, *Mémoires*,
trans. and ed. Jean Lemoine (Paris: 1908), 130. I have not been able to consult an
Italian version of these *mémoires*. Jean-François Solnon has announced a new
edition of Primi-Visconti's *Mémoires* for the near future.

39. Ibid., 130.

40. *Aus den Briefen der Herzogin Elisabeth Charlotte*, vol. 1, 184: letter of 28
June 1693. Although Madame probably meant "youths," the word "Bürscher"
can, of course, refer to "orderlies" as well.

41. The part played by lackeys in the arrangements of households and their
possible role as procurers and *entremetteurs*, the link between the household and
the outside world, need more investigation. The list of sodomites included in the
"grande mémoire" of which selections were reproduced by Claude Courouve in
Les gens de la manchette (see note 10) links employers and their lackeys. Ludovico Hernandez's *Les proces de sodomie aux XVIe, XVIIe et XVIIIe siècles*
(Paris: 1920) gives instances of lackeys procuring for their masters, although it
should be noted that the authenticity of some of Hernandez's source material has
been doubted. The letters of the baron von Pollnitz, published in 1737 in Amsterdam, note the proliferation of lackeys in Parisian households: several lackeys are
"the customary peers and companions of their masters . . . [others] enjoy the
favor of their young masters in a manner so little in conformity with ordinary
usage that one does not know what to think of it. . . . But such is the spirit of
débauche that it has possessed itself of the larger part of the youth of the court"
(vol. 3, 92-93). This passage from Pöllnitz's letters came to my attention first in
Guillaume Depping's "Madame, mére du Régent, et sa tante l'Electrice Sophie
de Hanovre," *Revue historique* (1894). For a general consideration of the question see Jean-Pierre Gutton, *Domestiques et serviteurs dans la France de l'ancien
régime* (Paris: 1981).

42. *Aus den Briefen der Herzogin Elisabeth Charlotte*, vol. 1, 327: letter of 16
March 1698.

43. Primi-Visconti, *Mémoires*, 130-31.

44. Claude Courouve, *L'affaire Lenoir-Diot* (n.p.), 5.

45. Primi-Visconti, *Mémoires*, 130-31.

46. Norbert Elias, *Die höfische Gesellschaft* (Darmstadt and Neuwied: 1969),
and Jürgen, freiherr von Kruedener, *Die Rolle des Hofes in Absolutismus* (Stuttgart: 1973) are two examples.

47. Piers Mackesy, *The Coward of Minden: The Affair of Lord George Sackville* (London: 1979), 257.

48. Georges Dethan, *Mazarin*, 93-96. Pasqualini was the subject of Andrea

Sacchi's extraordinary portrait, now in the Metropolitan Museum of Art, New York, for which see Ann Sutherland Harris, *Andrea Sacchi* (Oxford: 1977), 82-84, no. 51.

49. Isabel Hull, "Kaiser Wilhelm II and the 'Liebenberg Circle'," *Kaiser Wilhelm II*, eds. John Röhl and Nicolaus Sombart (Cambridge: 1982). See also Isabel Hull, *The Entourage of Kaiser Wilhelm II* (Cambridge: 1982).

50. Ibid., 208.

51. Saint-Simon, *Mémoires*, vol. 2, 258.

52. Hugh Murray Baillie, "Etiquette and the Planning of State Apartments in Baroque Palaces," *Archaeologia* (1967).

53. Pére Anselme, *Histoire Généalogique*, vol. 9, 216-17. Louis de Lorraine, comte d'Armagnac, Henri de Lorraine, comte de Brionne (his son), Philippe de Lorraine and Charles de Lorraine, comte de Marsan were ranked second, third, fourth, and fifth in the promotion, immediately after the duc de Vendôme, a *prince légitimé*. Apart from clarifying, in favor of the Lorraine princes, the always difficult problem of the status of the *princes étrangers* in opposition to the claims of the *ducs et pairs gentilshommes* at the French court, Louis's decision was an act of unprecedented favor: I know of no other instance of four members of the same family, apart from members of the House of France, indeed of the same branch of the same family, being included in the same promotion throughout the history of the Order. The promotion consisted of four cardinals and seventy knights; d'Effiat was ranked fifty-third and Châtillon sixty-fourth.

54. *Aus den Briefen der Herzogin Elisabeth Charlotte*, vol. 1, 59, letter of 29 August 1683.

55. Sourches, *Mémoires*, vol. 1, 118-19.

56. Beatrice Hyslop, *L'apanage de Philippe-Egalité* (Paris: 1965). Nancy Barker, 'Philippe d'Orléans, frére unique du Roi: Founder of the Family Fortune', *French Historical Studies* (1983) analyses the extent to which Monsieur's *apanage* served as a base for Orléans wealth in the eighteenth century and the process of its compilation.

57. Bibliothèque Nationale, ms. fr. 16630, fols. 523-24.

58. Daniel Roche, "La fortune et les revenues des princes de Condé à l'aube du 18e siècle," *Revue de l'histoire moderne* (1967); François-Charles Mougel, "La fortune des princes de Bourbon-Conti," *Revue de l'histoire modern* (1971).

59. Victor Champier and G.-Roger Sandoz, *Le Palais-Royal* (Paris: 1900), vol. 1, 152-54.

60. Minutier Central, xcii, 314.

61. With the exception of a few senior servants who, presumably, lived all the time at Saint-Cloud, the only other occupants of apartments who are actually named in the inventory were the noblewomen in direct attendance upon Madame, such as her *dame d'honneur* and her *dame d'atour*. Other members of the Orleans entourage were lodged, when they were at Saint-Cloud, most probably in a sequence of apartments indicated only by numbers in the inventory.

62. Minutier Central, xci, 554.

63. Maurice Lever, *Les bûchers de Sodome* (Paris: 1985), 181-82.

Police and Sodomy in Eighteenth-Century Paris: From Sin to Disorder

Michel Rey, PhD

Dark legend: in 1924, the second issue of *Inversions*, the first militant French homosexual periodical, appeared. A certain H. Gomero wrote an article titled "On Repression" in which he contended: "In 1580, two pederasts were burned on the Place de Greve. The Middle Ages were no longer indulgent. A few years before the Revolution, a Capuchin friar was burned."[1] The only punishment known: fire, on account of religious condemnation. Pascal, the friar burned in 1783, had killed a boy who defended himself against a rape attempt. Seven sodomites had been burned to death between 1715 and 1781, five of whom had also been accused of murder, blasphemy, and theft.

In his *Memoires*, the police lieutenant-general Lenoir estimated at 20,000 the number of Parisian sodomites in 1725, and Mouffle d'Angerville reported that in 1780 a police commissioner had shown his friends "a large book in which were listed all the names of pederasts known to the police."[2] He claimed that Paris had at that time "as many as it had prostitutes; that is 40,000." Even if these figures are exaggerated, they give an impression of a fear of being invaded. One wonders what kind of fate awaited all these men, obviously very numerous, who were not burned.

Dr. Michel Rey is associated with Ecole des Hautes Etudes en Sciences Sociales in Paris.

This paper is a summary of the first part of the author's master's thesis (*memoire de maitrise*) defended at the University of Paris, Section VIII, under the supervision of J. L. Flandrin. It was published in French in the *Revue d'histoire moderne et Contemporaine*, vol. 29 (1982); and has been revised.
Translated by Kent Gerard and Gert Hekma.

129

In 1671, La Reynie, the first lieutenant-general of the police, wrote to Louis XIV's minister Colbert:

No one can know how important it is for the service of the King, and for the contentment of the inhabitants of Paris, for calm to be maintained. . . . It is much easier to preserve it now than it would be to restore it once it is disturbed.

La Reynie thus attributed to the nascent police the role of the prevention of disorder. His successor, D'Argenson, accentuated this role by increasing the number of police spies and informers and by collecting detailed information on the private lives of many Parisians. D'Argenson undoubtedly created the police services whose archives we have retrieved. Their long-term descendant, the "group for the surveillance of homosexuals" of the Prefecture of Paris, has only recently been dissolved.

THE DOCUMENTS

The most important set of documents used for this article was found at the Archives de la Bastille preserved at the Bibliotheque de l'Arsenal. Seven cartons contain the police accounts of sodomites arrested in Paris. From these, one can distinguish two periods,[3] 1723 to 1747 and 1748 to 1749.

During the years 1723 to 1747, the reports come mainly from undercover agents, the *mouches* ("flies"), who would allow themselves to be accosted at known cruising sites, let their suspect talk, and then signal to have him arrested before he had done anything more. These agents were themselves former-accused who had been blackmailed, either in prison or undercover, by police officers. The conversations reported consisted of the same sorts of banalities used anywhere in this kind of rendezvous. The reports also contain notes on the identity of the suspect and the decision taken in each case, and often end with petitions filed at the request of the family and signed by respectable neighbors ("bourgeois," priests, employers).

In 1748 and 1749, the new lieutenant-general Berrier reformed the police system into a more efficient bureaucracy. Thereafter, the reports no longer provide a detailed account, but instead consist almost entirely of names: who denounced the suspect, who debauched him, whom did he denounce? Specific individuals become less visible, while the organization of a particular Parisian "milieu" becomes more readily discerned.

Since the completion of my thesis, I have consulted other documents kept at the Archives Nationales (series Y) that concern the second half of the century, in particular the reports of the *patrouilles* (patrols) *de pederastie*, these reports are included the papers of the police commissioners and those of the Swiss Guard of the Champs-Elysees between 1777 and 1781.[4]

POLICE PERSONNEL

By 1715, two officers were working full-time tracking Parisian sodomites. They paid the provocateurs, the mouches, whom they personally enlisted with the approval of the lieutenant-general, and made use of the available police personnel that they did not command (guards of the gardens, prisons, and night watch) to arrest suspects "in the act" ("sur le fait"). Their mandate appears to have been regularly renewed by their superiors. Many of the accused declared that this situation was peculiar to Paris: there were no mouches deployed elsewhere (at Rouen or in Brittany, for example).

Mr. Simonnet, a police inspector, directed the most important of these services between 1700 and 1740 with the assistance of two under-officers. His authority extended over the entire city of Paris, with the exception of royal domains such as the Tuileries. It did not extend to the suburbs. He was also occupied with other forms of profligacy, such as gambling. Simonnet gives the impression of an old fox, ineradicable, indispensable. He knew many sodomites, by sight and by name. Indefatigable, always on the lookout, he was a master of the terrain. He strove to be honest and scrupulous. The reports describe him resisting several attempts at corruption. In 1725, a nobleman from Bourgogne, de Sainte-Colombe, accused him of arresting innocents in order to get bonuses from de Pontchartrain, minister of the Royal House. Simonnet protested vigorously, produced testimonials from bailiffs and mouches, and wrote to the lieutenant-general:

If one does not oppose this [the attacks on his office], this work will be utmost disgraceful and dishonorable to those who have the honor to execute the King's orders, and the people will no longer have any respect for them.

When in 1727 a commissioner wrote in a report about a certain Fournier that "he has the look of a scoundrel," Simonnet made the following note: "It is not the physiognomy that reveals anything about the interior, but rather the evidence." Simonnet is mentioned for the last time in 1738; there are no extant documents for 1739 and 1740. Perhaps he had been removed in 1740, when de Marville became lieutenant-general. De Marville seems to have replaced many older officers from D'Argenson's tenure who did their work in the name of the king and religion and left their place to other administrators of public order.

Simonnet's successor, Framboisier, had assisted him since 1735. However, the scarcity of extant documents precludes exact knowledge of his activities until 1747. At the end of the major reorganization instituted by the new lieutenant-general Berrier, Framboisier was named *inspecteur* "charged with the execution of the King's order against sodomites." In a petition from December 1747, mention is made of the "Department of M. Framboisier." At the same time, other inspectors are in charge of the surveillance of Jews, priests, and so on. The work became more administrative: to verify, mainly by cross-checking, accusations provided by persons summoned by the police. This method had been used before, but not very often or with any regularity. It became the rule that informers were set free or given a mild sentence. It was a slow method, but one which allowed for the unraveling of circles of contacts, the nuclei of organized groups which were constituted at this time. It made each neighbor, each partner, a potential police auxiliary. But such evidence was indirect, and the confession of the accused remained necessary. Framboisier stayed at the police stations and lost the contact with the street that Simonnet apparently had had.

The other operation present in these archives is directed by Haimier, officer of the Provostship and general marshalsea of the Ile-de-France, and responsible for the Tuileries, the private domain of the King, where he was occupied equally with all forms of disorder. He worked there beginning in 1715; he disappears from the

sources at the same time as Simonnet. Much more so than his colleagues, he had the occasion to importune the well-to-do, or to render services to them. Thus, he had to be more sensitive to the social
situation of the people he interrogated: he quite readily set free
young men, men with families, and those involved in business. He
showed his respect for those societal units (family, parish, neighborhood) that could set back on the straight path those who had
strayed from it.

Both kinds of police operations depended directly on the lieutenant-general Chatelet. Flagrant misdemeanors of this type did not go
past Chatelet; the lieutenant-general, or rather his secretary, decided on the punishment. In this regard, the "first clerk" (*premier
commis*), Rossignol, also had a long career. Present in the sources
from 1723 on, he also disappears around 1740.

In the second half of the century, a police inspector was specially
charged with the surveillance of the known places where sodomites
congregated. His work was "presided over" by a special commissioner who interrogated the arrested persons and had the authority,
if he chose, to order them to prison.

Some people were arrested on the basis of denunciations, most
often made anonymously. But the abbot Theru, professor at the
College Mazarin, seems to have made spying his trade or his vocation. His zeal "for the glory of God and the good of the public"
was indefatigable. He spied especially on the ecclesiastical world
that he knew so well, working from 1723 until 1740. His style was
very preachy. He pressed hard on the lieutenant-general with stir-
ring appeals against "the ravishing wolves," "the corruptors,"
"public pests." He requested the harshest penalties: burning, deportation. In 1725, he wrote to Rossignol about the abbot Emery:

> It isn't necessary to release him as easily as has been done.
> Abbots must be examples, and one has to make them serve as
> examples. When they are the instruments and the angels of the
> devil, good laymen such as you have to act as apostles and
> angels of God.

Such language was already archaic by this period. Reference to God
is never made in the police reports. Examples are made instead in
the name of social order. Theru's illusion of a stable and sheltered

world was fading fast. Louis XIV was dead. The police listened to his lamentations only insofar as they were concerned about their control over the circulation of people in the new urban space of Paris.

PREVENTION OF SOCIAL DISORDER

The "Beau Vice"

In 1724, Theru was alarmed by the growing audacity of the sodomites:

> If one spares the corruptors too much . . . there will be great disorders . . . because all kinds of people will take off their masks, believing that everything is permitted for them, and they will organize leagues and societies, which will be disastrous, with respectable people in the lead. I have already heard of one, and when I am better informed about it, I will warn the magistracy.[5]

The greatest danger was the mingling of people of different social status; the aristocratic vice must not be allowed to spread from the Court to the city. In 1725 Haimier was concerned less with eradicating a vice than with preventing the spread of a form of disorder. He "had made a judgment about impeding the effect of the infamy . . . especially because he knew that the young man did not seem to be of the same status as the Count" (the Count d'Autry). In 1720 young noblemen were punished with exile for a party in the gardens of Versailles, and the Marshal de Richelieu believed it appropriate to write: "As this vice is unknown among the people, one [needed] a punishment that afforded no scandal."[6] In 1784, Mouffle d'Angerville considered the struggle lost:

> This vice, which used to be called the *beau vice* because it had only affected noblemen, men of wit and intelligence, or the Adonis, has become such a fashion that there is no order of society, from dukes on down to footmen, that is not infected.[7]

This entire discourse rested on the idea that sodomy was a vice of the aristocracy, an excess of libertines bored with permissible pleasures. But the police, in contact with the everyday reality of the Parisian streets, certainly had a more realistic perspective, as evidenced by the records they kept of sodomy arrests (see Table 1). The relative percentages in this social distribution show considerable stability over time, with the exception of 1737-1738, when the increase in the number of domestic servants stems from half of that number declaring themselves "unemployed servants." By this claim, they apparently hoped to avoid imprisonment in the *Hopital General* as beggars. The upper classes were far from being a majority, even in 1723. The main fear of the police was of collusion between different ranks, which in their minds would scramble the social and moral order.

THE TRIAL OF DESCHAUFFOURS: EXEMPLARY PUNISHMENT

In 1725, Benjamin Deschauffours was arrested for kidnapping, raping, and selling boys to French and foreign aristocrats. He had killed a boy who had importuned him and disguised the crime as an accident. In 1726 the lieutenant-general Herault, to whom all judicial authority in the case had been delegated, delivered a sentence of death. Deschauffours was burned at the stake on the Place de

Table 1: Social Distribution of Sodomy Arrestees

	1723	1737/38	1749
Nobles & Bourgeois	8	17	28
Small Merchants and Artisians	20	63	129
Domestic Servants	12	59	58
Unknown	4	7	29
Totals	44	146	244

Greve. Commentators were unanimous in asserting that only sodomy explained the sentence.

> M. Herault has decided and has shown that an example must
> be made, it not being possible to punish all those who were
> implicated, because that would cause too much trouble. And
> besides, it wasn't desirable to further illustrate this crime and
> to spread it, because most of the people do not even know
> what it is.[8]

The police themselves had posted placards in Paris printed with the
sentence, on which nothing but sodomy was mentioned[9] although
the original sentence had also mentioned "other enormous and detestable crimes." *Philosophes*, pamphleteers, and sodomites "of
the street" were outraged at the arbitrariness of the police, who
burned people without connections while allowing the powerful to
go free despite substantial charges against them. Voltaire drew a
juridical argument from this: "one must proportion the punishment
to the crime."[10] A manuscript play from 1739, *L'ombre de Deschauffours* (The Shadow of Deschauffours),[11] analyzed the trial as
an attack by the *conistes* (*con* = cunt) on the buggers.
    A few years earlier, in 1733, a pamphlet replete with anagrams,
Anecdotes pour servir à l'histoire sècrete des Ebugors (Bougres),
had martyrized (Deschauffours) a certain Fourchuda, portraying him
as having been sacrificed for an oppressed people:[12]

> Fourchuda, celebrated inhabitant of Spira, who in his zeal in
> defending a large army of Ebugors, was taken prisoner in the
> struggle, was condemned and thrown in the fire by the order
> and judgment of the principal partisans of the Cythereennes.

The fear that found expression in several memorials brought sodomites to a more radical expression of their desire: the idea of a
community founded on sexuality that would unite people of different social classes. In 1728, an adolescent tailor named Frementeau
declared "that he had not gone into the garden since a gentleman
had been burned for this kind of thing, that one would do best to
restrain these kinds of pleasures, that one could never get rid of."
Increasingly, sodomites came to explain their "pleasures" as a "in-

born" taste. The efforts of the police ran aground to the same degree that the people believed this explanation. In his *Memoires*, Lenoir, lieutenant-general from 1775 until 1785, repeated the time-worn story of the affair, but he also clearly described the position of the police regarding sodomy:

> I must remark here that at the time of the sentence, Paris numbered, as far as the police knew, more than twenty thousand individuals who offered examples of the vice for which Deschauffours mounted the scaffold. What was wanted was a public chastisement, and it befell, not the most criminal, but the least protected of the accused, and thus it is that the same people can boast of more virtue than the great. The executioner works to this end. In the long run, pederasty can only be a vice of gentlemen.[13]

All these often illusory discourses described an ideal society, parceled out, where everyone should stay in his place under the gentle surveillance of the police, the parish, the employer, the landlord, the family. The police would decide what was inconvenient in the streets and encourage everyone to stay at home. The birth of the concept of private space was inscribed at the same time with the protection of the individual and with the confinement of individuals for the sake of public order.

PROTECTION OF YOUTH AND FAMILY

In 1724, an anonymous denunciation of the abbot Dumay seemed to indicate, as an additional danger, that he lived "near a large college, several boarding schools and several tennis courts." Fear for the contagion of youth by adult sexuality rested on social reality. From quite an early age, boys went around Paris on their own, encountering prostitutes and dissolute couples on their way. Yet no one seemed to care about such a situation before the end of the seventeenth century. On the other hand, young boys were also subjected to teachers, employers, and colleagues at work who sometimes imposed on them relations that they would have preferred to refuse. Even so, the police did not interfere with these relations of dependency; such violence took place within established social relations.

The police feared far more the roving seducer because innocent boys could be corrupted without the boys' intelligent objections. This conception of youth (perhaps a new one) allowed the reading of dialogues in which boys spoke in a very realistic manner about their desires, while the authorities driveled about their pretended innocence. In 1726 and 1727, Simonnet arrested one fourteen-year-old boy three times. The third report related this interrogation:

Q: Who debauched him "at his age"?
A: Teenagers from his neighborhood, since his eleventh year [not adults, as the question suggests].
Q: Who was his "comrade" [*camarade*]?
A: The son of the grocer who lived in the same house with him. They performed their infamies in the commode, which consisted of mutual touchings.

The young Bergeron added that he went cruising on the wharves every Sunday, as well as every holiday.

Police preoccupation with moral corruption appeared to be inherited from the Church. In 1727, a certain Fournier was arrested at his home after being denounced. He was in bed with a young man from the provinces whom he presented as a paying guest, which the other confirmed: "Commissioner Divot remarked of Brassery [the provincial youth] that he seemed to him so naive that he did not dare to ask him questions from fear of teaching him things that he did not know." This was the typical problem of the confessor: how to uncover traces of sin without thereby teaching it to a perhaps still-pure soul. The notion of error with regard to divine law was slowly replaced by a notion of civic morality. In the course of the eighteenth century, treatises on proper behavior proscribed with increasing insistence those ambiguous situations of comradeship where, for example, two men shared the same bed.

Although in 1760 Dr. Tissot would become the instigator of the heroic battle against masturbation, as early as 1730 the police were noting the "losses of semen." In 1736, Simonnet arrested a fourteen-year-old workman, Saintard, who was masturbating in the street while watching a woman. On several occasions, young men spoke frankly about this practice to the police. In 1738, a certain Francois even admitted "that in his native region, there would be twenty boys bathing together and screwing each other." Such sexual games might keep the passion of bachelors—who were obliged to wait a long time after puberty before they could marry—at bay without danger; that is without fear of illegitimate births or future sexual "deviation."

Despite his surprise, Simonnet imprisoned children and had them scolded in the presence of their fathers, while Haimier, always respecting social hierarchies, would imprison young footmen yet release schoolboys, even if he had seen them cruising in the Tuileries all summer.

> Considering that they are two young boys, who were apt to indulge in some infamous talk without foreseeing the consequence, and who each gave their name and residence, the said Haimier has sent them away, choosing only to mention it to the magistrate.[14]

The police seemed to hold to an increasingly moralistic and paternalistic discourse with young men: they should stay in their families' homes, not run around in the streets, and not associate with people of different status who behaved differently. So, the number of youths arrested at cruising places grew. In 1723, of twenty-five persons arrested whose ages were recorded, one was under twenty years of age and eight between twenty and twenty-nine years, while in the period 1731 to 1738, of a total of forty-five, twelve were under twenty years old and fourteen between twenty and twenty-nine years. Can this variation be explained by a greater vigilance on the part of the police, or by a more significant real presence?

THE PROPER USE OF RELIGION

In the seventeenth century, the post-Tridentine Church mobilized all of its resources to reform the daily life of believers. In the eighteenth century, however, religion lost ground, especially in the large cities, where social control was more difficult. At the beginning of the century, the police took up the moral language of the Church, but they no longer functioned as its secular wing. Rather, it was they who now seemed to be using the Church to maintain urban social order. Since the 1740s, the police discourse acquired a certain autonomy.

Sodomy was a reserved case which could only be heard by the chief confessor of each diocese, who was designated by the bishop. "This passion was stronger than he was. He had been to the chief confessor, the other confessors no longer willing to hear him, which had also delayed him."[15] Thus, some people were unable to confess for several years: "He admits that it is his favorite sin, that he has also not had absolution for two years, and that that is just."[16] Sodomy was not seen by the priests as an irresistible "passion" (the starting point for a psychological justification). Instead, they saw it simply as a grave sin to which someone had surrendered, but which the will and the love of God would not allow to be committed any longer. They distinguished between the act and the person: "He has confessed it several times . . . often one has deferred absolution and allowed him a period of two or three months to see if he could not correct himself."[17] Masturbation was sanctioned in the same way.

Such postponement of the sacraments, this rejection from the fold of the Church, provoked extensive discomfort among pious people. In 1748, a wine merchant named Brugiere declared that "for two years he had had a mass said every Monday in order for God to do him the grace to correct himself." The police would then attempt to use an arrest as a means to reintegrate a culprit into this protective and normalizing framework. During Herault's tenure as lieutenant-general of police (1726-1739), his secretary systematically interrogated sodomites on their adherence to the confession. If they were worried about it, he sent them to the chief confessor. Guilt could prove a valuable emotion.

When the clergy did not play their role adequately, the police reacted. "He went to confess to a Nazarene monk, who gave him absolution. I had advised him to see the confessor at Notre-Dame."[18] It was often difficult to distinguish between the sincere responses and the merely tactical attitudes: everyone knew well that asking for a confessor could have a positive result. Religious indifference grew, and the cloisters, convent gardens, and so on were

seen—even without any thought of blasphemy—simply as convenient meeting places. Only older people mixed religion, morality,
and the police in their utterances, as did the sixty-year-old teacher
Thomas, in 1738: "He admitted the above facts, saying that he is a
miserable sinner, whom God would not want to ruin, that he had
permitted it [the arrest] to happen to him so that he would repent
and do penance."

At the beginning of the century, the police spoke in the same sort
of language, which also appeared in their denunciations: "The old
Duke de la Battue will die in sin, if someone in authority doesn't
have the charity to warn him to do penance and to renounce the
infamous love of boys." Simonnet responded in the same vein:

> To attempt to procure salvation for this man at the end of his
> days, it would be necessary to imprison him at Saint-Lazare or
> at Charenton, or else to banish him fifty leagues from Paris,
> for he is one of the most obstinate and infamous ones. I do not
> believe that the penalty of banishment could make him repent.

This preoccupation with religious confession dwindled over the
course of the 1730s. Herault had sodomites interrogated about their
religious beliefs for the purpose of social order. Under Berrier, this
type of questioning disappeared entirely.

THE EVOLUTION OF PUNISHMENTS

Although the death penalty for sodomy remained on the books
until the adoption of the *Code Penal* during the Revolution (1791),
by the eighteenth century the burning of sodomites at the stake
(symbolic of heavenly fire) was no longer viewed as appropriate for
the crime of sodomy. Deschauffours and Pascal, who was burned in
1783, had also committed other grave offenses. The case of two
other men sentenced to burning in 1750 seemed to be an anachronism.[19] They had been caught by surprise while in the act in the Rue
Montorgueil, as had many others. (In 1741, a similar unfortunate
experience had befallen a fairground stall-holder, but he had been
released on appeal.)[20] Their punishment should have been commuted to permanent detention at Bicetre "because of the indecency

of these sorts of examples which certainly teach the young that
which they should not know."[21] Nevertheless, "the execution [had]
taken place in order to make an example," but "the sentence [had]
not been publicly announced, apparently in order to avoid the name
and description of the crime. It had been publicly announced in
1726 in the case of Deschauffours's crime. . . ."

Various notions about punishment that reflect judicial discussions of the period concerning the role of public chastisement thus
seemed to clash, all based on the idea of prevention. Barbier stated
in passing the effect of the Berrier-Framboisier method: "As these
two workmen had no point of relation with people of distinction,
either from the court or from the city, and as they did not denounce
anyone else, this example could be made without any further consequences."

One can advance various hypotheses in attempting to explain the
exceptional rigor of the penalty. Judged directly by the judges of
Chatelet, and not by the lieutenant-general, the two men could have
been the victims of the smoldering conflict between the magistracy
and the police since the creation of the latter in 1667. On the other
hand, in the spring of 1750 a number of riots took place in Paris
because of a rumor that children were being abducted by the police.
Perhaps to appease the public, the police and the magistrates offered to execute or corporally punish several people, among whom
were these two men. The eventual result of this example can not be
traced, however, because this set of police dossiers end in 1749.

Besides burning at the stake, the harshest penalty for sodomy was
deportation to the colonies in the West Indies (Martinique, Guada-
loupe, Santo Domingo, and Mississippi), as was done with prostitutes. Theru often requested it in the case of indignant parents and
employers. However, no clear traces remain in the police archives
of such penalties, undoubtedly because such were usually imposed
only after the accused had already been imprisoned in Bicêtre.

The general rule for simple cases, those not involving prostitution, blasphemy, or violence, was to distinguish between people
who were merely thoughtless, those who had committed a mistake
for the first time but could be returned to their social milieu, thereby
preventing them from repeating it, and the hardened criminals, who
posed the risk of spreading evil and therefore must be neutralized
and kept away from Paris. Actual practice did not always follow

these principles. Until 1748, the sentences were often arbitrary, confused, indeed contradictory. Some people arrested six or seven times previously were released. Certain orders were never carried out. It was after 1748 that the administration of punishment became more precise. But the criterion for determining the severity of punishment changed: denunciations led to a systematic reduction in punishment.

In the minds of the accused, sodomy proper was much more serious than other erotic play between men. The police did not always make this distinction. Some people were arrested solely for their conversations in suspect places at "untimely" hours, particular attitudes and phrases; these were sufficient to indicate that one was "of the character" (six examples in 1723). The police were not persecuting individual acts, but were trying to control a particular social group and specific public behaviors.

All those who seemed susceptible to disseminating the vice (by debauching young men or by organizing prostitution) were sent to the Hospital General in Bicetre, south of Paris. Those who were wealthier paid for their own stay there. One could be released by displaying consistent signs of repentance. The police returned foreigners to their own countries, and sent provincials back to their regions of origin under the surveillance of bailiffs, provincial officials, or bishops. In times of war, one could be released by enlisting in the army. The soldier was then placed under the responsibility of his captain. For those imprisoned, it became essential to get out by any means possible because Bicetre had a very high mortality rate among its prisoners, particularly from scurvy. Families concerned about a less severe incarceration would request the favor of a transfer to Saint-Lazare, where they paid for the period of imprisonment.

Bicetre was above all a place for shutting people away, a dungeon, and the corruption that reigned there led to protests. Bicetre was also meant to control public morality, for it was the only place which was authorized to deal with venereal diseases; the general practitioners of medicine had no right to do so. This regulation promoted the propagation of disease because some people refused to seek cures for fear of being arrested. The quacks who attempted to make and sell remedies themselves were also imprisoned in Bicetre.

The majority of those arrested, except those of the upper classes or the very young, were compelled to serve their prison terms in secret. In principle, this was not a penalty, but a necessity in order to verify the prisoner's identity and whether the person had been condemned before for the same activities. Beginning with Berrier, imprisonment also served to make the accused speak: an initial interrogation would be conducted as soon as one was placed behind bars (*entre les quichets*). It is impossible to evaluate how violent these interrogations were. According to the police reports, they were mild, but people questioned for several days eventually gave further information and denounced more partners. In the period 1720 to 1730, those released had to sign a testimonial of repentance stating that they would no longer frequent public promenades. In 1723 the average period of imprisonment was eight days. It was increased to up to two months in 1737 and 1738 when the dismantling of gangs (*bandes*), networks of prostitution, was in progress. The same procedures as at Bicetre were utilized to accelerate this process, or to bring about a lenient verdict.

Noblemen, as well as lesser gentlemen, were never imprisoned *sur le fait*, but they knew that they risked a lot if their adventures became known. The king could amuse himself with the pastimes of his Court; at the same time, he had the obligation to maintain the honor and reputation of the State. Gentlemen risked not only a boring exile far from the pleasures of the Court, but also the loss of their offices and privileges, as well as lengthy imprisonment paid for by their wealthy families. La Riotterie, the son of the governor of Melun, and compromised by Deschauffours, was locked up for nearly twenty-seven years on the strict orders of his father.[22] Noblemen thus would appeal to officials to keep the news of their adventures from going beyond the cabinet of the lieutenant-general.

Many families of lower status also demanded the imprisonment of their sons in order to avoid dishonor, because sodomy was considered ignominious. The police reports often designated sodomites only as *infames*, those who "prostituted" their male bodies. In Parisian neighborhoods, everyone knew everyone else, and reputation played an important role. Thus, those arrested could be released more quickly if they were claimed by their families or neighbors. Anonymity was increasing in Paris, principally in the streets of the city center, but each quarter lived in part like a village, which also exposed sodomites to blackmailers.

The police also used the family and the neighborhood network as a means to monitor individual conduct more closely. It was undoubtedly the first time that a population was systematically supervised—through the reports in which earlier arrests were recorded and through the extensive lists of sodomites periodically updated.[23]

In the eighteenth century, sodomy was no longer considered a sin by the police, but an offense against the social order because of the furtive rendezvous, the social slippages that it seemed to allow, and also because of the long-term trend toward a revalorizing of the familial milieu and its enclosure within private space. It therefore became necessary to confine all deviant sexualities and to eliminate all situations which posed dangers in this regard. Mercier wrote in his *Tableau de Paris*:

> The police discover dangerous inclinations in certain souls, which may promptly lead them to misdeeds. Such a character already turns to crime; it is time to sequester him from society; and although it may be a very delicate judgment to prescribe, nevertheless it is impossible to leave punishment to the traditional forms of ordinary tribunals.

The philosophes were indignant at the excesses of a justice that rested on the fear created by spectacular punishments. Yet they approved of a well-run State, one where everyone could be happy if they stayed in their place. All of them protested against the stake, a penalty they believed disproportionate to the crime. Yet only Condorcet went so far as to write (in a footnote to the Kehl edition of the complete works of Voltaire): "Sodomy, when there is no violence involved, cannot be part of the criminal law. It does not violate the rights of anyone."[24] The "passion" of sodomites did not accord with the "mediocrity" of the happiness imagined by the philosophes.

Even the term sodomite disappeared. After 1738, the police use the term "pederast" more and more often. The new term was not of religious origin. It designated a type of person without making reference to a specific act. After having prompted their words, after having noted the minutest details of their sexuality, the police refused to listen to pederasts any longer. In subsequent years, the police were only interested in the geography of the urban body. The middle-class pederast could not, must not fascinate as did the liber-

tine and noble sodomite of earlier times. Instead, one started thinking in terms of "curing" the pederast.

At the beginning of the century in 1701, d'Argenson could still
doubt the madness of a certain young man imprisoned in Charenton. The young man's "habitual sodomitical obsession (*sodomitte
habituelle*) was his entire occupation, and even all his studies." He
spoke of himself, he claimed what he was: a madman. D'Argenson
wrote, "If he were dealt with as a man with all his reason, he would
deserve capital punishment, and he could not be placed among the
mad without injuring his mind, which is certainly intact."[25]

NOTES

1. Cited from G. Barbedette and M. Carassou, *Paris Gay 1925* (Paris:
Presses de la Renaissance, 1981), 196. The first date must be a mistake; nothing is
known about a double burning in 1580.

2. *Mémoires secrets*, vol. 23 (1784).

3. Cf. mss. 10,245, 10,225, and 10,256-10,260 concerning cases from
1715, 1723-30, 1733-34 and 1736-50 (especially many cases in 1749).

4. Archives Nationales 1589.

5. Desfontaines ms. 10,256.

6. De Richelieu, *Mémoires*, vol. 3, chap. 24.

7. *Mémoires secrets*, vol. 23 (1784).

8. Barbier, *Journal*, April 1726.

9. Ms. 10,918.

10. Voltaire, *Dictionnaire philosophique*, article "Amour socratique."

11. Bibliothèque Nationale, new French acquisitions no. 1562.

12. Ibid., Enfer no. 113.

13. Lenoir, *Mémoires*, vol. 1, 289.

14. Delacroix, 1724.

15. Descaves, 1737.

16. Clément, 1738.

17. Dubois, 1748.

18. Gaucher, 1735.

19. Archives Nationales, X2A 1114 and 764 and X2B 1006. These documents
were published by Claude Courouve in 1980.

20. Archives Nationales, X2A 1105 and X2B 989.

21. Barbier, *Journal*, June-July 1750.

22. Ms. 10,895.

23. Cf. Ms. 10,895, the great memory of 1726.

24. Note to *Prix de la justice et de l'humanite*, art. 19, "De la sodomie."

25. Bibliothèque Nationale, ms. Clairambault 985: J. F. de la Guillaumie.

The Personal, the Political, and the Aesthetic: Johann Joachim Winckelmann's German Enlightenment Life

Denis M. Sweet, PhD

There were two scandals in Winckelmann's life that appalled his contemporaries: his conversion from German Lutheranism to Roman Catholicism and his bloody end in Trieste at the hands of a murderer. Both of these events continued to pursue Winckelmann (1717-1768) in the written treatments of his life, throughout the nineteenth century and into the twentieth. A third and potentially more debilitating scandal, that of his homosexuality, was never admitted to by his contemporaries. Indeed, Winckelmann's homosexuality as a scandal is a product of twentieth-century fictional and biographical treatments. In a study by the West Berlin author Wolfgang von Wangenheim of the some thirty-four fictional treatments (novels and novellas, short stories, dramas and poems) in which Winckelmann has appeared as protagonist, a definite trend has been ascertained: homosexual desire as a subject for kitsch.[1] Here, the scandals can amalgamate, as in Frank Thiess's completion of the Winckelmann novel begun by Gerhart Hauptmann, where Winckelmann receives his just desserts in a violent murder because, as a homosexual, he can attain no other real satisfaction in life.[2]

By contrast, in the portrayals by Winckelmann's contemporaries, homosexuality as scandal was studiously avoided. The most telling

---

Dr. Denis M. Sweet teaches German in the Department of Foreign Languages and Literatures at Bates College, Lewiston, ME 04240 and is currently writing an intellectual biography of Winckelmann.

example is to be found in Goethe's *Skizzen zu einer Schilderung Winckelmanns* (Sketches Toward a Portrayal of Winckelmann). These "sketches," accompanying a selection of Winckelmann's letters that Goethe edited, are divided into sixteen mini-chapters usually of no more than a few pages each. The first five, with the headings "Entrance," "The Antique," "Pagan Aspects," "Friendship," and "Beauty," form a unit, a distinct logical progression in contrast to the mosaic nature of the remainder of the sketches, that has to do with the nature and function of eros in Winckelmann's life. Everything seems to be clearly named here. In the last of the five sketches, under the heading "Beauty," we read: "So finden wir Winckelmann oft in Verhältnis mit schönen Jünglingen, und niemals erscheint er belebter und liebenswürdiger als in solchen, oft nur flüchtigen Augenblicken."[3] [Thus we often find Winckelmann together with beautiful youths, and nowhere does he appear livelier or more gracious than in such, oftentimes but fleeting moments.] And yet the naming of names that seems to be taking place is misleading. It is only part of a profound stylization of Winckelmann in Goethe's hands—of Winckelmann as the "born pagan through and through." As such, friendships with other men are no more than part of the ancient aura that Goethe constructs about Winckelmann. Because Winckelmann, by this reckoning, is really an ancient somehow misplaced and born into the modern age, he seeks friendships along the ancient model. The issue at stake here is the construction of a normative, neoclassical aesthetics by Goethe and the Weimar Friends of Art bulwarked by a stylization of the famous archaeologist's life and character from the previous generation. The issue is not an uncovering of Winckelmann's homosexuality.

The stylization to which Goethe subjected Winckelmann extends throughout his life and into his death. In the last sketch, "Parting," Goethe writes: "Und in diesem Sinne dürfen wir ihn wohl glücklich preisen, dass er von dem Gipfel des menschlichen Daseins zu den Seligen emporgestiegen, dass ein Kurzen Schrecken, ein Schneller Schmerzihn van den Lebendigen hinweggenommen."[4] [And in this sense we can acclaim him fortunate that he ascended to the blessed from the height of human existence, that a brief fright, a quick pain, took him from the living.] Here, there are to be no scandals, not in

death, not in sexuality, not in religious conversion. The German
literary historian Hans Mayer was appalled. His book, *Outsiders*,
details Goethe's "forceful harmonization," an unwillingness to
confront the homosexual crux of Winckelmann's "double life."[5]

Another contemporary, this time one who had known Winckelmann personally, casts a different light on the matter. Walking
unannounced into Winckelmann's rooms in Rome one day, Giacomo
Casanova was witness to a scene — suppressed in earlier editions of
his memoirs — that he has described in detail. Casanova's account
must be taken seriously. Composing his memoirs after Winckelmann's death, Casanova had nothing to gain in misrepresenting
the facts, and the meticulous notes he kept with a view to later
memoir-writing suggest reliability. After Winckelmann had
straightened his trousers and the young man he had been surprised
with had beat a hasty retreat (Casanova remarks that this "Batyl-
los" — one of Anacreon's favorites — was indeed quite handsome),
Winckelmann approached Casanova with a smile and offered the
following justification:

> You know I am not only not a pederast, but for all of my life I
> have said it is inconceivable that such a taste can have so se-
> duced the human race. If I say this after what you have just
> witnessed, you will think me a hypocrite. But this is the way it
> is: During my long studies I have come to admire and then to
> adore the ancients who, as you know, were almost all bug-
> gerers without concealing it, and many of them immortalize
> the handsome objects of their tenderness in their poems, not to
> speak of superb monuments. They went so far as to bring up
> their taste as evidence of the purity of their morals, as for
> example Horace, who, in order to prove to Augustus and Mae-
> cenas that evil gossip could not injure him, defied his enemies
> to prove that he ever soiled himself by taking on an adulteress.
>
> With the clear realization of such truths, I cast a glance at
> myself and felt disdain, a kind of reproach for not at all resem-
> bling my heroes. I found myself, at least as far as my love life
> was concerned, as unworthy of esteem, and not being able to
> overcome this conceit by cold theory, I decided to illumine
> myself through practice, hoping that by analysing the matter

my mind would acquire the light necessary for distinguishing between true and false. Thus determined, it has been three or four years that I have been working at this business, choosing the cutest Smerdiases of Rome, but it has done no good. When I get down to it, *non arrivo*. I see in my confusion that a woman is preferable in any case, but outside of not caring about this I fear a bad reputation, for what would one say here in Rome, particularly where I am well known, if one could say that I had a mistress?[6]

Casanova's report could not be more nonchalant. The Italian phrase "non arrivo" in the middle of the original French text lends immediacy and seems to buoy up the authenticity of the account. Casanova kept detailed records of his encounters with an eye toward future memoir-writing; this is not an old man looking back over many years inventing details. The scandal of homosexuality is not in the memoir-writer's eyes who seeks to suppress or harmonize it, as Goethe had done, but has been introjected by Winckelmann himself. The fatuousness of the apology offered, experimenting with the model of the ancients without regard to his own true desires, makes it all too apparent.

Yet Winckelmann's life in Rome seems to stand in complete contradiction to Casanova's account. The one aspect that unites his letters from Rome is their encomium of Roman freedom and fulfillment. And they seem to suggest sexual fulfillment as well. Yet both Goethe and Casanova present a Winckelmann who is in some sense homoerotic, but whose relation to (homo)sexual practice is strangely refracted. Can it be that they do indeed reflect a problematic and contradictory life?

* * *

Johann Joachim Winckelmann had been born into utter poverty, a poverty that had overtaken the city of his birth. Stendal, one of the lights among the north German cities of the Middle Ages, had been pillaged and ransacked during the Thirty Years' War and had never recovered. Many of the houses had been abandoned or burnt down and never rebuilt. The Winckelmann family lived — typical for the place, the age, and their station — in a small one-room house that served as cobbler's workshop, living room, bedroom and kitchen.

Various institutions existed then to help defray the schooling of the destitute. These were the way stations of Winckelmann's youth: singing in a Latin boys' choir at all seasons on public occasions (Stendal), receiving free meals by supping together with worthy citizens who thus showed their charity for the poor (Berlin), and attending a university that was known to forego fees for the impoverished (Jena).

Prussian subjects who entertained hopes of receiving a position in the Protestant state church were obliged by royal decree to a two-year study of theology at the University of Halle. Three career avenues were open to the sons of the poor who had aspirations for an intellectual life in the Germany of that day (to say nothing of the prospects for their daughters): preacher, tutor, or librarian. Winckelmann's university education, study of theology at Halle, was with a view toward the first. It proved an utter rout. The anecdotes—that Winckelmann read Homer during sermon and lectures—merely stylize the seriousness of the rupture. His disinclination toward theology was evident from the start; it simply grew more and more unwieldly. The theological diploma made out to him and attesting to his studies is one embarrassment. "He attended classes," it says, "but we know nothing of what is in his heart. It is our hope that he has taken some benefit from his lessons."[7]

This diploma did not mark the beginning of a career, but an end. The young ex-theology student then moved on to the next course open to him: private tutoring, living with aristocratic families and tutoring their teenage sons. He was caught in the same lockstep as so many other young intellectuals in eighteenth-century Germany who entered the ranks of the *Hofmeister* after attending university, some of whom emerged years later as the progressive and critical writers of that century's rising bourgeoisie: Lenz, Hölderlin, Schiller. But it is also the place where Winckelmann's real and deepest inclinations come to the fore—where he discovered his loves.

The chief magistrate of Hadmersleben near Magdeburg engaged Winckelmann, who had just completed an additional year's study of mathematical medicine at the University of Jena, to tutor his son, Peter Friedrich Wilhelm Lamprecht. One biographer put it like this: "Bereits nach kurzer Zeit schlug in der Verbindung von Erzieher und Zögling die Flamme der Freundschaft durch: Unterricht und Erziehung wurden zu einer lebendigen Gemeinschaft. . ."[8] [After only a short while the flame of friendship shot up in the bond between educator and pupil. The boy's upbringing and formal instruction merged together into one living community. . . .] When Winckelmann left the Lamprecht family house in the spring of 1743 to take up a position as assistant headmaster in a school in Seehausen, the young Lamprecht followed, taking up residence in Winckelmann's room and continuing with his lessons. A visitor captured the scene: "After instruction from Winckelmann, the boy went to bed at ten and Winckelmann studied for himself till midnight when he put out the lamp and slept in his chair till four. At four he awoke, lit the lamp and studied alone till six when Lamprecht's lessons commenced anew, until time for school."[9]

The first draft of a letter to Lamprecht that is preserved dates from this period. It is in Latin and begins "ad delicias suas" — to his sweet delight. It is a love letter to the extent that it speaks of love and the heart, but it is also a letter from a teacher to his charge concerned with the latter's learning and exhorting him to greater efforts in Latin letters. "Write to me something not in French but in Latin, and not just one page either, but several," Winckelmann wrote, "so that I might see how your style is progressing." He would make corrections in the margins for the boy.[10] This friendship with the young Lamprecht was a composition in paedagogy and passion. Winckelmann continued to write after a break, yet all that remains are the drafts of his letters. One from the summer of 1746 concluded:

> Mein einziger Trost in meiner Verlassenheit, ist, dass sich etwas in mir befinden muss, das mich so fest mit Dir verbindet. Dieses muss das einzige sein, was sich grosses bei mir befindet. Ich werde Dich lieben, so lange ich lebe. . . .[11] [My sole consolation in my solitude is that there must be something in me that binds me so fast to you. This must be the sole thing in me that is great. I will love you as long as I live. . . .]

The unmistakable stylization in Winckelmann's letters to Lamprecht makes itself felt. One written in French the next year marks the highwater point:

Peu s'en faut que je pousse des plaintes amères contre le destin
qui va dissiper le doux espoir, dont se nourrit [notre rare] une
amitié peu connu dans un siècle entier ne pouvant secousser
leur fondement. Mille soupirs sont des temoins que je me
meure pour desir de celui, que j'aime eperdument.[12]

This is a document that speaks of the heart, and we must assume,
from the heart. But in these early letters to Lamprecht there has
already crystallized that which will be so characteristic of Winckelmann throughout his life and work: an ideal of love, society, and
art taken from ancient Greece; desire that blends eros, pedagogy,
and aesthetics; and, ultimately, an oscillation between same-sex
eros and politics.

After many trials, prolonged hesitation, and then finally conversion to Roman Catholicism, Winckelmann, now the author of a
short work on the imitation of ancient Greek art that had given him
a reputation in art circles, finally set out for Rome in 1755. He was
thirty-eight and had thirteen more years to live. From Rome he
appeared to his contemporaries as at the zenith of success: librarian
to a cardinal and great collector, papal prefect of antiquities, the
author of a history of ancient art, a guide to the Roman art collections sought out by princes on their grand tours. Strange, that it was
not so much the rise from penury and constriction in Germany to
fame in Rome that occupied Winckelmann's own accounts of his
life, though it played a role certainly. Rather, it was what he called
his great freedom in Rome that was the constant topic of his letters.
Italy, in the ensuing nineteenth century in particular, was the "underground tip" (Hans Mayer) to homosexuals throughout Europe.
Here was one place where their erotic desires might be lived out.
Peter Tchaikovsky and Hans Christian Andersen, who both led hidden, "proper" lives at home, were well-acquainted with Italian liberties. Yet the freedom Winckelmann meant seems to have been
another.

There was to be only one more Lamprecht in his life—twenty
years after the first. In 1762 when they met, Winckelmann was
forty-four; Friedrich Reinhold von Berg was twenty-five. It is curious that Winckelmann's whole circle of acquaintances, including
his correspondents in Germany and Switzerland, were immediately

informed. He was smitten with love, he wrote his friends: "I was in love, and how!, with a young Livonian . . . and would perhaps even have dedicated the *History of Ancient Art* to him had I been able to change it."[13] And yet, paradoxically, he also wrote that he only once put his arms around him during the young baron's five-week sojourn in Rome. What occurred here, and in the earlier friendship with Lamprecht, was a stylization of male friendship *sans pareil*. "Winckelmann war ja stets geneigt, die Freundschaft pythago-räisch als unbeschränkte Gemeinschaft im geistigen und leiblichen Sinn zu fassen," wrote his biographer Carl Justi.[14] [Winckelmann was ever inclined to conceive friendship in a pythagorean fashion, as an unrestrained community of both spirit and body.] But here exactly is the stylization: A full sharing of body and mind seems scarcely practicable with someone passing through town, except as an ideal. Winckelmann's friendship with Reinhold von Berg not only delineates a specific instance of homoerotic practice, and artic-ulates the boundaries of time, place, and circumstance, but also demarcates Winckelmann's place as a German Enlightenment thinker.

He dedicated his *Treatise on the Ability to Perceive the Beautiful in Art and Instruction in the Same* to "the nobly born baron." Its pedagogic intent is evident from the first page. "Your form let me deduce that which I wished, and I found in a beautiful body a soul fashioned for virtue, a soul which is endowed with the perception of the beautiful."[15] Addressed to Reinhold von Berg, it could just as well be addressed to any such promising young man. And it was addressed to them—to all the others Berg represented.

Berthold Vallentin, who more than any other biographer has sub-jected Winckelmann's friendships to close scrutiny (indeed, this is his chief aim), has concluded that Winckelmann may have had many kinds of friendly relations, but that there was only one friend-ship underneath them all.

So mochte man vielleicht sagen: Winckelmann hat vielerlei Arten freundschaftlicher Beziehungen gehabt, aber nur *eine* Freundschaft in allen. Er ist vielleicht weniger eines bestim-mten Freundes Freund gewesen als er selbst glaubte, aber dauernder Freund, der Freund an sich—einmal, im vorletzten

Jahre seines Lebens sagt er selbst: "Ich bin der Freund der Freunde" — das Person und Leben gewordene Bedurfnis nach Freundschaft, das sich in alle Verbindungen hineintrug, die ihn uberhaupt nur menschlich naher beruhrten.[16] [One could put it like this: Winckelmann entertained many kinds of friendly relations, but there was only *one* friendship at the bottom of them all. He is perhaps less the friend of a particular friend than he himself believed, but he was a lasting friend, the friend personified — once, in the penultimate year of his life, he himself said: "I am the friend of friends" — here was the need for friendship to become the life and blood that he brought to all relationships that touched him at all closely.]

The stylization of friendship at work here — Vallentin tends to see it more existentially — offers a key not only to Winckelmann's personality, but to his paedagogic program, which contained an aesthetic and, ultimately, a political impetus.

The friendships from antiquity that he celebrated again and again, starting with his first writings, were replete with homoerotic overtones, but the one pair of friends whom he raised up over all others for emulation, Harmodius and Aristogiton, stand out for one reason only: they were tyrannicides. Similarly, the ties to his friends in Switzerland were nourished by his admiration of that country's republican form of government, which he never ceased to praise. His own friendships with the young princes from Germany whom he had met and instructed in Rome were marked by the same elan and pedagogic purpose as his friendships with Lamprecht and Berg.

The most memorable of these was with Leopold III Friedrich Franz, the ruling prince of Anhalt-Dessau who was twenty-five when he sought out Winckelmann in Rome. This ruler, one of the most receptive to Enlightenment ideas, built up in his mini-state south of Berlin (700 sq. km., comprising some thirty-thousand inhabitants) a model of enlightened practices. Praised by the revolutionary Enlightenment thinker Andreas Riem as the "idol of Germany" (1796),[17] Leopold Friedrich Franz represented the kind of fulcrum Winckelmann was searching for to put his ideas into practice: a "programmatic friendship," if you will, with democratic and homoerotic undercurrents. Erhard Hirsch, the author of a recent study of early Enlightenment culture in Dessau (envisaged as "Irenopolis," the city of peace, by its eighteenth-century adherents), laments that this chapter of German cultural history, which offers a counterweight to Prussian militarism and expansionism, has been thoroughly forgotten. The letters by the commoner Winckelmann to Prince Leopold were burnt by the Prince's heirs as containing "nothing substantial" for art history. No, their intentions went well beyond that field.

The thread that runs through Winckelmann's *History of Ancient Art*, the first history to trace the rise and fall of the arts in antiquity, is that of freedom. Indeed, the topic of political freedom becomes so dominant for significant stretches at a time that the discussion of art and art works is overwhelmed by it. That had not always been the case in Winckelmann's writing. When Herder wrote in his 1777 encomium of Winckelmann (his submission to the prize question put by the Academy of Antiquities in Kassel, "At what point did Winckelmann find the science of antiquity and at what point did he leave it?") that Winckelmann's first writing, "Thoughts on the Imitation of Greek Works in Painting and Sculpture" (1755), contained the germ of all of Winckelmann's later writings, he erred on one point.[18] Freedom as a decisive factor in determining great art had not yet been articulated. Winckelmann's "Thoughts" delineated the superiority of Greek art works from a moral and aesthetic viewpoint, but the interwovenness of the rest of society, and political freedom in particular, with the arts, had not yet come so unequivocally to the fore. By the time the *History of Ancient Art* was published eight years later (1763), Winckelmann might be said to have become the writer of freedom. In this work, the visions characteristic of him intersect: those of beauty and those of political freedom.

The *History of Ancient Art* had a dual purpose and construction. The first part, Winckelmann explained, offers not history in the narrower sense, but rather a propaedeutic construct (Lehrgebaude); an introduction to aesthetics — not a theory of aesthetics in the abstract — through one's own direct viewing of the art works that Winckelmann selects. Strange that it should be so concrete. It is really nothing more than a selective tour of the Roman art collections of Winckelmann's day, the very task he carried out in person with visitors to Rome. Winckelmann offers no system. Instead, he seeks to school one's own sight. His treatise on the ability to perceive the beautiful in art written a few years later makes the point most succinctly: "Go there and open your eyes," it concludes. It was to be an education to beauty in art, and from art to the question of how it could arise, and from there to the ideal of a democratic state.

The descriptions of art works that contributed in no small part to Winckelmann's fame can be taken as examples *in nuce* of the many elements that come together in Winckelmann's characteristic discourse. Here, more than anywhere else, the personal sight that Winckelmann had meant to inculcate demonstrated itself—and captivated his contemporaries. What follows is a highly abridged selection of his description in the *History of Ancient Art* of the statue of Apollo in the Vatican Belvedere:

> The statue of Apollo is the highest Ideal of art amongst all works of Antiquity which have survived destruction. . . . His body is raised up over those men, and his stance gives witness to the greatness filling him. . . . Go with your spirit into the realm of incorporeal beauties, and try to become the creator of a Heavenly Nature, in order to fill the spirit with beauties which raise themselves up over nature. . . . No veins nor sinews ripple this body. . . . He has pursued the Python, against which he first used his bow, and in his mighty stride has reached and slain it. From the heights of his sufficiency there proceeds his lofty look, far past this victory, as if into endlessness: disdain sits upon his lips, and displeasure, which he draws inside, distends his nostrils of his nose, and journeys up in his proud brow. . . . and a mouth which forms that which inspired in beloved Branchus his delights.[19]

The efficacy of this description stems from the seemingly disparate elements that crisscross and reinforce each other: details from history and mythology; a precise, even tactile description that is nonetheless bathed in an ideal light; and the erotic overtones, both in the sensuous emphasis and in the homoerotic reference to Branchos.

Clearly, this is not an "objective" or nonpartisan description. The viewer's or reader's understanding of the statue increases step by step in a most convincing and self-reinforcing fashion, but what really made this and the other descriptions Winckelmann wrote so effective was their idiosyncratic vision. The man who wrote it was not an antiquarian in the usual eighteenth-century sense of a master of arcana, but someone who communicated to his European contemporaries an immediacy of art and a vision of antiquity, Greek antiquity in particular, that was so successful precisely because it was an amalgam of enthusiasm and disciplined order, sensuousness and precision, scholarship and ideology. There was no one else writing like this in Europe at the time.

The *History of Ancient Art* is not simply a history, or a work that is part history, part aesthetics. It is all of these, of course. Nor is it a document of personal, homosexual desire, though that is oftentimes a popular image that Winckelmann's work takes on in modern fictional treatments. Sensuousness is there, to be sure, and references again and again to homoerotic aspects of Greek mythology, but the image of ancient Greece generated there is driven by altogether different considerations. Winckelmann explains it very clearly in the second, historical, part of the *History of Ancient Art*: "In Absicht der Verfassung und Regierung von Griechenland ist die Freiheit die vornehmste Ursache des Vorzugs der Kunst."[20] [Considering the constitution and the government of Greece, freedom is the most principal cause of the superiority of art.]

The notion of freedom becomes so strong in Winckelmann's history of ancient art that it oftentimes monopolizes the text and brings the historical discussion of art to a standstill. "Durch die Freiheit erhob sich, wie en edler Zweig aus einem gesunden Stamme, das Denken des ganzen Volkes."[21] [Because of freedom the thinking of the whole people raised itself up like a noble bough from a sound trunk.] This is no longer an historical account, but wish fulfillment. What is more, it precisely situates a specific strand of German bourgeois ideology in the mid-eighteenth century that launched its attack upon absolutist privilege and rigid, hierarchical society by means of its own particular reception of antiquity — antiquity in the arsenal of the bourgeoisie.[22]

A long line of German writers followed in Winckelmann's footsteps who propagated a version/vision of antiquity that maximizes personal liberty and political freedom. Antiquity under their hand became politicized for the use of the present. In fact, the particular reception of antiquity, Greek antiquity in particular, among German writers and artists in the century that followed might be taken as a gauge of those writers' politicization and republican politics. In Friedrich Hölderlin's novel *Hyperion* (1797), for example, the subject matter is political liberty. Here, modern Greeks wage a war of liberation against Turkish domination. The motor and incentive that drives Hyperion is a vision of ancient Greece as a homeland, and this is Winckelmann's concept too, of high art and political liberty that has to be regained. The novel ends with an excoriation of the Germans, as if to make certain there is no misinterpretation: this is a work addressed to them and to their situation, despite the geographical displacement — a displacement that figures in so many other similar works of German literature for obvious reasons. Wilhelm Heinse's novel, *Ardinghello, or the Blissful Islands* (1787), is set both away from Germany and in the past — in Renaissance Italy. Its vision of antiquity blends personal and political liberty with eros in a manner far more radical than anything attempted by Hölderlin or Winckelmann. At its end, a republic based on free love and equality is founded on the blissful islands — a German vision of utopia as refracted by antiquity, Italy, and the Renaissance.

The German reception of Greek antiquity in the eighteenth and nineteenth centuries, however, did not always lead to politicization and delineate a progressive desire for liberty. Even a figure like Winckelmann himself was used by others for purposes of political consolidation and, later, nationalism and reaction. Goethe's own *Sketches Toward a Portrayal of Winckelmann* (1805) marks a first step in this direction. The Goethe of the sketches, now in his mid-fifties, is far removed from the young *Sturm und Drang* author who produced *The Sorrows of Young Werther*. The French Revolution and the disappointment, not to say horror, and rejection of it by wide circles of the German intelligentsia have intervened. Here, the progressive political impetus contained in Winckelmann's Enlightenment reception of Greek antiquity has been drained away. The discourse is no longer of political liberty and an art which reflects it, and of the necessity of somehow regaining or fashioning it anew, but rather of inward moral character. It is all too typical. This one writing of Goethe's on Winckelmann can be taken as an example par excellence of the turn inward, toward morality and an interior life, taken by the German bourgeoisie in a period of retrenchment. The ideals of an earlier generation were no longer sought after, and the situation worsened in the further course of the nineteenth century. By the 1840s, a text like the following was typical:

> Er hat das Hochgefühl deutscher Kraft und Volkstumlichkeit mit dem Musterbild seines eigenen Lebens ausgestattet. In dieser letzten Bedeutung als Musterbild einer unaufhaltsam strebenden deutschen Nation ist Winckelmann vielleicht nicht minder erfolgreich gewesen als durch die Leistungen seiner Forschung.[23] [He furnished the high feeling of German strength and national culture with the exemplary image of his own life. In this ultimate significance as the image that exemplifies an unstoppably striving German nation, Winckelmann has been perhaps no less successful than in the accomplishments of his studies.]

This Winckelmann was a cultural hero still, to be sure, but one pressed into the service of a militant German nationalism that saw in him simply the successful German, the first writer in the German language to attain a European reputation, who simply becomes a puppet in the use of hurrah patriotism — ignoring, of course, Winckelmann's repeated attacks on Prussian militarism and tyranny and his reference to Frederick the Great as a bloodsucker of humanity. A formula of inverse proportions might be set up: The more a turn toward reaction came to dominate the German political and cultural climate of the nineteenth century, the less the progressive political Enlightenment impetus to Winckelmann's thought was discerned. The changes made in Carl Justi's life of Winckelmann between the first edition, written under a liberal constellation in the 1860s, and the second, written after the founding of the German Empire in 1871, document this *in parvo* — Winckelmann, the stylized ancient scholar pressed into national service.

Already thus hollowed out, it is understandable that by the twentieth century Winckelmann was a figure ripe for caricature — and, in his case, caricature as a homosexual. What the earlier writers had stylized, avoided, or suppressed now became the scandal, above all in fictional treatments. Winckelmann's only English-language biographer treats the matter in the same way:

> In real life, Winckelmann may have been as unlikely to debauch young Adonises as his contemporaries among the German poets were to deflower the Chloes and Amaryllises at whose adorable little feet they, portly, middle-aged *Bürger* for the most part, lay all the ardent if stylized lover's plaints that are now gathering dust in anthologies of rococo verse.[24]

The homosexual Winckelmann, the progressive Enlightenment thinker who practiced a pedagogic eros, who ultimately meant utopian politics when he spoke of ancient art, has been effaced. In the nineteenth century, he was effaced by an effulgent German nationalism; in the twentieth century, by the strange scandal of homosexuality.

NOTES

1. Wolfgang von Wangenheim, "Winckelmann als Held" (Paper delivered at Winckelmann-Gesellschaft Colloquium, Magdeburg, East Germany, 26 October 1986).
2. Gerhart Hauptmann, *Winckelmann: Das Verhängnis*, vollendet und herausgegeben von Frank Thiess (Gütersloh: Bertelsmann, 1954).
3. Johann Wolfgang Goethe, "Skizzen zu einer Schilderung Winckelmanns," in *Winckelmann und sein Jahrhundert* (Leipzig: Seemann, 1969), 214.
4. Ibid., 231.
5. Hans Mayer, *Outsiders: A Study in Life and Letters*, trans. Denis M. Sweet (Cambridge, MA: MIT Press, 1982). Cf., the chapter "Winckelmann's Death and the Discovery of His Double Life."
6. Jacques Casanova de Seingalt, *Histoire de ma vie*, vol. 7 (Wiesbaden: Brockhaus, 1961), 197-98.
7. This document ("III. Theologisches Abgangszeugnis") is reproduced in the appendix by Carl Justi, *Winckelmann und seine Zeitgenossen*, vol. 1 (Leipzig: Vogel, 1923), 502.
8. Berthold Vallentin, *Winckelmann* (Berlin: Bondi, 1931), 97.
9. Johann Joachim Winckelmann, *Briefe*, vol. 4 (Berlin: de Gruyter, 1957), "Erinnerungen an Winckelmann und Gespräche," text by Konrad Friedrich Uden, 169.
10. Winckelmann, *Briefe*, vol. 1, letter of 16 February 1744, 56.

11. *Briefe*, vol. 1, 62.
12. *Briefe*, vol. 1, 69.
13. *Briefe*, vol. 2, 333.
14. Carl Justi, *Winckelmann und seine Zeitgenossen*, vol. 1 (Leipzig: Vogel, 1923), 369.
15. English translation in Denis M. Sweet, "An Introduction to Classicist Aesthetics in Eighteenth-Century Germany: Winckelmann's Writings on Art," PhD diss., Stanford University, 1978, 96 sqq.
16. Berthold Vallentin, *Winckelmann*, 124.
17. Erhard Hirsch, *Dessau-Wörlitz: Aufklärung und Frühklassik* (Leipzig: Koehler and Amelang, 1985), 7.
18. Johann Gottfried Herder, "Denkmal Johann Winckelmann's," in *Die Kasseler Lobschriften auf Winckelmann* (Berlin: Akademie, 1963), 31-62. [Winckelmann-Gesellschaft Stendal, Jahresgabe 1963.]
19. English translation, "Description of the Apollo in the Belvedere from the *History of Ancient Art*," in Denis M. Sweet, "Introduction to Classicist Aesthetics," 89-90.
20. Johann Joachim Winckelmann, *Geschichte der Kunst des Altertums* (Darmstadt: Wissenschaftliche Buchgesellschaft, 1972), 130.
21. Ibid., 133.
22. Johannes Irmscher, "Antikebild und Antikeverständnis in Goethes Winckelmann-Schrift," *Goethe-Jahrbuch* 95 (1979), 99: "Man hat von einer neuen Renaissance gesprochen, und dies insofern berechtigt, als dem erstarkenden Bürgertum erneut die Antike und insonderheit das Griechentum zum ideologischen Arsenal im Kampf um seine ökonomische, politische und geistige Emanzipation wurde."
23. Eduard Gerhard, "Festgedanken an Winckelmann," (Berlin, 1841), 4.
24. Wolfgang Leppmann, *Winckelmann* (New York: Knopf, 1971), 51.

Sodomy in Enlightenment Prussia: From Execution to Suicide

James D. Steakley, PhD

Beneath the known history of Europe runs a subterranean one. It consists of the fate of human instincts and passions suppressed and distorted by civilization.

Max Horkheimer
Theodor W. Adorno
Dialectic of the Enlightenment (1944)[1]

The history of sexuality in early modern Germany is largely as uncharted today as it was a generation ago, when Adorno and Horkheimer regarded their homeland from American exile and characterized the bureaucratic efficiency of Nazi extermination camps as the final outcome of the Enlightenment's dark side. Under the impact of that national and international trauma, what little German historiography of sexuality that has appeared in recent years has tended to focus on the quite recent past, indeed often on the Nazi period itself, while the pre-Napoleonic era has languished in obscurity.[2] In most respects, the state of our knowledge of eighteenth-century sexual practices and ideologies has advanced no further than the fragmented findings of historians at work in the pre-Hitler era.

What we can do, however, is seek to rearrange and reexamine certain long-established historical data in light of a new scholarly perspective that has been evolving over the past decade. Partly the result of the gay liberation movement, partly an area of specialization among academic historians, this new historiography of West-

Dr. James D. Steakley is Associate Professor, Department of German, University of Wisconsin-Madison, Madison, WI.

163

ern European and American sexual minorities has opened three key areas of investigation: (a) changing definitions of sexual crimes and state sanctions; (b) the establishment of urban homosexual subcultures; and (c) the emergence of a distinctly modern homosexual role or gay identity.[3]

The only study of Prussian sodomy prosecutions actually based on archival research that has appeared to date was authored by an interested physician, Dr. Hans Haustein, and published in 1930.[4] Examining both court records and royal edicts for the years 1700 to 1730, Haustein found that forty-three males and one female were charged with witnessing, being accessories to, or directly participating in sodomitical deeds, which comprised acts of bestiality as well as homosexuality. A number of these individuals managed to escape the long arm of the law; others got off lightly because of their young age or lack of evidence. It is noteworthy that in several instances when the judges called for lenience, King Frederick William I ("the Soldier King"), who personally reviewed all sodomy sentences, demanded that the guilty be punished to the full extent of the law (the Constitutio Criminalis Carolina of 1532 as affirmed by the Prussian State Law of 1620). The standard sentence was execution by sword, to be followed by burning the corpse. The animals involved in bestiality generally received the same treatment as well. During the thirty-year period examined by Haustein, nine individuals were executed for bestiality and three for homosexuality.

On 15 June 1704, Ludwig Le Gros and Martin Schultze were executed after confessing to homosexual "vice" (*Unzucht*) with each other.[5] On 31 January 1729, a thirty-year-old baker named Ephraim Ostermann was sentenced to death after confessing to have twice fellated a nineteen-year-old apprentice, Martin Köhler, who had subsequently died and whose death was attributed to exhaustion caused by the unnatural loss of semen. Ostermann also confessed to having fellated some twenty other men while they were asleep, "for this was his delight, and whenever he swallowed the seed of another, his own discharged at the same time."[6]

These executions stand in glaring contrast to the justice meted out to a nobleman, Baron Ludwig Christian Günther von Appel, who was twice acquitted of sodomizing farmhands on his estate. The first charge was brought by Jürgen Schlobach, a twenty-three-year-old, who claimed that the baron had seduced him two years earlier. In self-defense, the baron argued that sodomy was out of the question because his bed was too small for two people and, moreover, it was immediately adjacent to a door behind which his servants slept. After an eight-month investigation, Schlobach "admitted" that he had raised charges only because he hated the baron. Appel was acquitted, while Schlobach was sentenced to a flogging and payment of court costs. Two years later, the baron again successfully defended himself against charges brought by Jürgen Ludewig Lange, who testified that Appel had "twice stuck his member in his rear and once in his mouth; he'd gotten gooey (*labbrig*) and had to rinse out his mouth at the fountain."[7] For making a false accusation, Lange was sentenced to a flogging and eternal banishment from his homeland. When the court executioner began the flogging, Lange's father and brother attacked him with pitchforks, which brought them prison sentences of four and two months, respectively. Lange's mother was also sentenced to prison for claiming that Baron von Appel's wife had attempted to bribe her to keep silent by giving her a dress. That such patent injustice was not exclusively confined to cases involving commoners charging aristocrats is suggested by a final case from 1730, when a church secretary named Achenbach was acquitted of committing indecent acts with a fifteen-year-old and a thirteen-year-old. Because he had served the church directory "honorably" for seventeen years and had "always led a respectable life," the accusations of the two boys were dismissed as slander. However, the court also declared its intention to keep the records concerning Achenbach on file.[8]

Beyond demonstrating that all men were by no means created equal in the absolutist state, the early eighteenth-century court records also reveal that torture was regularly used to extract confessions from recalcitrant sodomites. These practices underwent considerable change upon Frederick II's accession to the throne in 1740. Among his first acts was the abolition of torture in Prussia. Such enlightened measures initially seemed to confirm Voltaire's characterization of him as the "Solomon of the North" and "the hope of mankind." In his memoir of his sojourn in Berlin as a guest of the young philosopher-king, Voltaire recounted an anecdote concerning a sodomy trial:[9]

Once some judges out in the provinces wanted to burn some poor farmer who had been accused by a priest of having a gallant adventure with his donkey; nobody was sentenced to death without the king confirming the judge's verdict, a very humane law now coming into practice in England and other countries; Frederick wrote under the verdict that in his states he granted freedom of conscience and of cock (*vit*).

Had Frederick actually granted the freedoms he so provocatively proclaimed, he would have made Prussia into Europe's first truly modern state by anticipating the French Revolution's creation of a private sexual sphere, a hallmark of the bourgeois state. But Prussia remained absolutist: torture was reintroduced after a short time, and the law against sodomy was neither repealed nor even revised during Frederick's forty-six-year reign. The lack of archival research leaves us in the dark as to how often the statute against sodomy was enforced, but there is every reason to suppose that the old double standard of aristocratic privilege versus bourgeois privation still prevailed.

In July of 1779, Frederick undertook one of his periodic journeys to survey the progress of "inner colonization," a program of creating new farmland and founding new villages by draining swamps and clearing forests. A telling exchange with two bureaucrats suggests how he regarded his subjects as chattels and bluntly, even tactlessly denied them any private sexual sphere:[10]

Fromme:	Your Majesty, this is Councillor Klausius from the Office Neustadt, under whose direction the colonies stand.
The King:	Well, well! Glad to hear it! Send him over! What is your name?
The Councillor:	Klausius!
The King:	Klau-si-us. Well, do you have a lot of cattle here in the colonies?
The Councillor:	1,887 head, Your Majesty! It would be far over 3,000 if there hadn't been the cattle epidemic.
The King:	Are the people increasing well, too?
The Councillor:	Oh, yes, Your Majesty, there are now 1,576 souls in the colonies.

The King:	Are you married, too?
The Councillor:	Yes, Your Majesty.
The King:	Do you have children, too?
The Councillor:	Stepchildren, Your Majesty.
The King:	Why not your own?
The Councillor:	I don't know, Your Majesty; that's how things turn out.

It would, of course, have been entirely unthinkable for the subject to ask the king why he failed to produce an heir to the throne.

Nationalistic biographers and historians have spent the last two centuries trying to defend Frederick against rumors that he was a sodomite. In the summer of 1986, both East and West German museums mounted major exhibitions honoring the many achievements of this great king on the two-hundredth anniversary of his death. The two opposing systems were united in the pained silence with which they passed over the topic of Frederick's erotic proclivities. Tour groups at Frederick's palace in Potsdam are informed by the official East German guides that Frederick never lived with his wife simply because he preferred the company of his faithful whippets to that of people, and there matters are allowed to rest. The conventional position seems to parallel the principle of Anglo-Saxon law that one is innocent until proven guilty; here, innocence is linked with heterosexuality, guilt with homosexuality. Yet it would be absurd to suspend any consideration of Frederick's sexuality simply because we lack the sort of forthright confessions extracted — under torture — from those sodomites who were sentenced to death. Indeed, the most detailed testimony was obtained in cases involving aristocrats who were later acquitted.

If Frederick's manifest homosexuality be granted as a working hypothesis, new interpretive possibilities open up in such diverse areas as the absence of a political network or entourage in his court, his growing misanthropy with advancing age, and his role as a patron and producer of the arts. Even within aristocratic circles, Frederick was locked into the role of outsider, a role which he developed into a style of living and governing. Soon after coming to the throne, he sought to escape from the constant intrigue of court life in Berlin by retreating to the rural isolation of Potsdam, where he could create his own pastoral Arcadia and redefine the natural and the unnatural. Upon dedicating Sanssouci, the Potsdam residence of his own design, he offered the following poem to his intimate friend, Count Kaiserlingk:[11]

> Dans ce nouveau palais de noble architecture
> Nous jouirons tous deux de la liberté pure,
> Dans l'ivresse de l'amitié!
> L'ambition, l'inimitié
> Seront les seuls péchés taxés contre nature.

Elsewhere in his poetic oeuvre, Frederick gave voice to his anticlericalism by describing a gang rape in a monastery, employing terms that are both ribald and erudite. Before the first monk forces himself upon the unwilling novice, he describes in glowing terms the distinguished company of sodomites he will soon join, citing the examples of Socrates and Alcibiades, Euryalus and Nisus, Julius Caesar, and—most shocking of all—calling St. John the Ganymede of Jesus.[12]

Frederick was never far from representations of Ganymede at Potsdam. A bronze statue of Ganymede from the late Hellenistic era was carefully positioned before his library window at Sanssouci so as to afford an unhindered view. He acquired this statue from the estate of Prince Eugene of Savoy, the homosexual commander of the victorious Hapsburg armies with whom he briefly studied the art of warfare as a crown prince, thus creating an aesthetic link with a role model of the previous generation.[13] A second Ganymede was the central figure in the ceiling fresco of the New Palace Frederick built in Potsdam after his victory in the Seven Years' War. Near this palace he erected a Friendship Temple decorated with portraits of Euryalus and Nisus, Orestes and Pylades, Heracles and Philoctetis, and Peirithoüs and Theseus.

In regal isolation at Potsdam, Frederick was able to indulge his aesthetic—and doubtless also his erotic—interests in a refined manner. The first account of a homosexual network that enabled Prussian commoners to pursue their Ganymedes dates from 1782, toward the end of Frederick's long reign. Entitled *Letters on the Gallantries of Berlin*, it was written "by an Austrian officer" who sought to remain anonymous but who has been reliably identified as

Johann Friedel, an author and Jacobin social critic of some note. Friedel's twenty-nine letters deal with the forms of demimonde entertainment and sexual promiscuity that await the visitor to Berlin, and three of the letters are entirely devoted to homosexual practices. Friedel's Berlin host takes him to a gathering one evening attended by a mixed company of men and women:[14]

> I noticed from time to time that the fellows embraced with the warmest tenderness, kissed each other, squeezed hands, and said such sweet things to each other as a fop might say to a lady. I took all these displays for merely a friendly tone, for true male sympathy or spirits. And regarded from that angle I admired the small band of intimate friends. But how astonished I was when I understood these friendship mysteries.

Friedel's host explains the peculiar behavior:[15]

> "Oh, you mustn't be surprised. These seven gentlemen are warm brothers." — Warm brothers? What's that? — "You don't know anything about that, and already four months in Berlin, that surprises me! I'll have to give you a small description of it. You must have read something about Socratic love?"

Friedel's host goes on to give a brief survey of the existence of homosexuality in classical antiquity, but firmly rejects any transfer of the morals of another time and place to Germany, attributing homosexual practices in late-eighteenth-century Berlin to excessive sexual lust and the desire to be stylish:[16]

> "And, friend — this swinish behavior is passed off as gallantry about which people joke in good company like they would about loving a girl; it is practiced completely without shame, and people don't even blush about it! Almost no good-looking boy is safe from these gentlemen. As soon as they spot one, they chase after him like a stag in rut . . . Even more! You will find here houses that exist under the honorable title of a boy establishment (*Knabentabagie*), in which lads of fourteen, fifteen, and older gather for this preoccupation . . . You will find

pimps and female procurers who wander the streets looking
for children and grown boys to tempt them into these houses
and make their profit."

This description makes Friedel curious, and his host consents to
take him to one of the boy bordellos on a following evening. Here
he sees:[17]

> . . . a gathering of ten to twelve boys of various ages, men of
> various character at their sides; on each face womanly lust;
> and so on. With astonishment I watched the embraces with
> which the older rams met the younger ones. Neither sweets
> nor expense was spared to win the lad. There a foursquare
> Bacchant toasted his Ganymede with full wine glass, there a
> second one cuddled against his boy with the warmest feeling
> of delight; here on the other hand a loose lad played with the
> belt of his Zeus, and there the victor disappeared with his
> Thracian booty. In short, my friend, it surpassed any expecta-
> tion you might have of this gathering's wild lust. For appear-
> ance's sake, a few worn-out dames appeared from time to
> time. If by chance it happens that a guest who is not drawn to
> boys should appear, they are the Graces who seek to hold him
> in Jupiter's entryway while this gray-bearded thunder god
> seeks his pleasure according to his taste behind the curtain.

Under the stern gaze of the Jacobin moralist, the mannerisms and
language of this establishment's habitues have a regrettable tendency to dissolve in a welter of metaphors derived either from the
animal kingdom or from classical antiquity, rendering difficult any
comparison of the Berlin boy bordello with the well-documented
homosexual subculture of such cities as London or Amsterdam. It is
also uncertain whether this bordello was known to and tolerated by
the police, how long it existed, and whether there were others like
it. During the nineteenth century, further accounts of homosexual
prostitution as well as of outdoor and indoor meeting places in
Berlin were published sporadically, tending to suggest that a fairly
continuous homosexual subculture was in place by the late eighteenth century.

The emergence of a visible homosexual minority in Berlin is

linked, of course, to urban growth: under the reign of Frederick II, the city's population doubled to more than one-hundred thousand. Like the policy of inner colonization, this expansion was directed from the throne because of Frederick's insight that more people meant more money, an insight quite contrary to the premodern view that sought to guarantee political stability through a stable population. Prussian pronatalism may well have combined with the Enlightenment critique of Christian orthodoxy to produce a general sense of greater (hetero-)sexual freedom; the gradual emergence of a public sphere of uncensored political discourse went hand in hand with the creation of a private sphere of bourgeois domestic intimacy.

All of these changes help account for the elimination of the death penalty for sodomy in 1794. Prussia thus joined Josephine Austria (1787) and revolutionary France (1791) in repealing this remnant of medieval Christianity. Under Paragraph 1,064 of the General Prussian State Law, "sodomy and such like unnatural sins" on the part of men or women were henceforth punishable by imprisonment for not less than one year, flogging upon entering and leaving prison, and banishment following the prison term. Although this statute was not published until eight years after the death of Frederick II (and thus redounds to the glory of his otherwise undistinguished nephew, Frederick William II), it was prepared by extensive legal discussions under his reign and may actually reflect de facto judicial practice for some years prior to its formal promulgation.

The flowering of the Enlightenment in Berlin was manifested not just in the changing situation of homosexuals, but also in the growing tolerance toward Prussia's Jewish minority. Because of his brilliant contributions to Kantian philosophy, the autodidact Salomon Maimon (1753-1800) was excommunicated by the Berlin rabbinate just as he was welcomed into the intellectual community that spurned both Christian and Jewish orthodoxy. With the distinguished author Karl Philipp Moritz (1757-1793), Maimon coedited what is generally regarded as the first German journal of psychology, the *Magazin zur Erfahrungsseelenkunde* (1783-1793). In its pages, writers from all over Germany published reports of their own dreams, fantasies, and states of mind, as well as observations concerning deaf-mutes, depressives, and individuals with psychic peculiarities of all kinds. And it was here that lovers of the same sex were first brought to the sympathetic attention of the German reading public.

In 1791, a nameless writer described the "unhappy passion"[18] of a fellow student whose temperament had been characterized by a tendency to "cold ridicule" and the firmness with which he "refused to allow his head to be influenced by his heart"[19] until the fateful day when a attractive newcomer enrolled at the same university. It was "as if he had been struck by an electric shock."[20] He did not initially venture to approach the newcomer, and his studies suffered while he observed him from afar. After the two finally became acquainted, he paid even less attention to his studies, but instead devoted himself to Shakespeare's sonnets, memorizing them in a short time and assuring the writer that "no one had ever understood the sonnets as well as he did."[21] He eventually became so incapable of work that he dropped out of the university, moved to a different town, and became "quiet and extremely melancholy."[22] The writer closed his report with two questions: "Does anyone have further examples of such a peculiar aberration of human nature? And how is my friend to be helped?"[23]

This remarkable appeal elicited a quick response from another nameless university student whose firsthand account had a far happier ending. He, too, felt an "attraction" to a newcomer, but could not find the resolve to make his acquaintance, so his affection festered and "finally degenerated into the most extreme passion."[24] He "felt the pain of the most extreme longing"[25] and even "occasionally fell into a kind of rapture (*Schwärmerei*)."[26] He emphasized that he "had no further, forbidden intention":

> I desired only the most precise union with him; indeed, in my rapturous seizures I wanted to draw myself into him completely, so that the two of us would make one person. Reason and religion, however, had too much influence on me for me to allow such forbidden wishes to emerge.

The writer noted that his "deadly restlessness" evaporated as soon as the two actually became acquainted: "I am glad and happy!"[27]

Yet he conceded that his emotional life was still aberrant and even offered an etiology:[28]

> If I look back through my life story, the causes of this, my aberration, lie clearly before my eyes. From my youth on, people had told me that I had an appealing appearance. As a child of five to six I was always embraced by adult persons, and as a boy of ten and twelve years by my schoolmates. This, and the totally lacking contact with persons of the other sex, caused the natural inclination toward the female sex to turn entirely away from it in me and toward the male; and I remember having tenderly loved some men already as a boy, for even now I am still rather indifferent toward women.

This remarkable confession simultaneously marks the highpoint of the German Enlightenment and the onset of what might be termed the Counter-Enlightenment. With its pronounced emphasis on subjective states, Moritz and Maimon's *Magazin zur Erfahrungsseelenkunde* turned the gaze from the outer to the inner world, from natural law to the lawless maelstrom of emotions. The emergence of Romanticism in late eighteenth-century Germany brought to an end the dominance of reason and the growth of tolerance, attitudes which came to be yoked with the Reign of Terror in revolutionary Paris, and later also with Napoleon's humiliating destruction of the Holy Roman Empire. German Romanticism signaled a backlash against rationality and the resurgence of Christian anti-Semitism, as well as the crystallization of modern sex roles in the bourgeois family.

In 1810, the Napoleonic Code was imposed on Prussia, completely eliminating any penalty for homosexual acts between consenting adults in private. One year later, a Prussian officer named Heinrich von Kleist, a member of the anti-Semitic Christian-German Table Society, killed himself in Berlin. The motivation for this suicide was many-layered. As a soldier, he was humiliated by the French occupation of his homeland; intellectually, he was brought to the verge of despair by Kantian philosophy; emotionally, he was troubled by the same feelings reported in Moritz and Maimon's magazine. The source of his feelings of inadequacy vis-à-vis increasingly rigid sex roles was poignantly documented in a letter he wrote to a fellow officer, Ernst von Pfuel, in 1805:[29]

> You recreated the era of the Greeks in my heart, you dear boy; thus my entire soul embraced you! I often regarded your beautiful body with truly *girlish* feelings when ever you climbed into the lake at Thun before my eyes. . . . Accept my proposal; if you don't do this, then I'll feel that no one in the world loves me.

To the extent that it was motivated by his homosexual desires, Kleist's suicide graphically demonstrated the internalization of moral codes that was accomplished by the domination of bourgeois norms.

At the very moment when the state completely removed itself from controlling homosexual practices by threat of death or imprisonment, the German citizenry took matters into its own hands. We search the early records of sodomitical behavior and subcultures in vain for any signs of shame or self-reproach. Such negative emotional responses appear, instead, to be characteristic only of modern society.

NOTES

1. M. Horkheimer and T. W. Adorno, *Dialektik der Aufklärung*, vol. 3 of *Gesammelte Schriften*, ed. R. Tiedemann (Frankfurt: Suhrkamp, 1981), 265.

2. The most ambitious undertaking of recent historiography is *Eldorado: Homosexuelle Frauen und Männer in Berlin 1850-1950* (West Berlin: Frölich and Kaufmann, 1984), a catalog prepared for an exhibition under the same title at the Berlin Museum from May to July of 1984. The group that mounted this exhibition has since constituted itself as "Verein der Freunde eines schwulen Museums" and recently published the first issue of a journal devoted to gay history, *Capri*. Its mailing address is Friedrichstrasse 12, 1 Berlin 61. See also George L. Mosse, *Nationalism and Sexuality* (New York: Howard Fertig, 1985), which contains a chapter on friendship in pre-Napoleonic Germany.

3. Cf. Randolph Trumbach, "Sodomitical Subcultures, Sodomitical Roles, and the Gender Revolution of the Eighteenth Century: The Recent Historiography," in *Unauthorized Sexual Behavior During the Enlightment*, ed. P. Maccubbin; special issue of *Eighteenth-Century Life*, n.s. 9 (May 1985): 109-21.

4. H. Haustein, "Strafrecht und Sodomie vor 2 Jahrhunderten," *Zeitschrift fur Sexualwissenschaft* 17 (1930): 98-105.

5. Ibid., 99.

6. Ibid., 104.

7. Ibid., 100.

8. Ibid., 105.

9. Voltaire, *Mémoires pour servir a la vie de M. de Voltaire, écrits par lui-même* (1759), vol. 1 of *Oeuvres complètes de Voltaire* (Paris: Garnier Frères, 1883), 28.

10. *Gespräche Friedrichs des Großen*, ed. F. von Oppeln-Bronikowski and G. B. Volz (Berlin: Reimar Hobbing, 1919), 188.

11. Frederick II, "Sanssouci," reprinted in *Friedrich der Große dem Strafgesetz verfallen?* (Berlin: Adolf Brand, 1921), 4.

12. Frederick II, *Palladion*, ed. Jurgen Ziechmann, 2 vols. (Bremen: Edition Ziechmann, 1986). See especially vol. 1, pp. 105-9.

13. On this statue of Ganymede, see the exhibition catalog *Friedrich II. und die Kunst: Ausstellung zum 200. Todestag*, ed. Generaldirektion der Staatlichen Schlösser und Gärter Potsdam-Sanssouci (Berlin: Tourist, 1986), 1:67.

14. *Briefe über die Galanterien von Berlin, auf einer Reise gesammelt von einem österreichischen Offizier* (Gotha: n.p., 1782), 147.

15. Ibid., 148.

16. Ibid., 152-54.

17. Ibid., 171-72.

18. "Zur Seelenkrankheitskunde," *Magazin zur Erfahrungsseelenkunde* 8 (1791): 9.

19. Ibid., 6.

20. Ibid., 7.

21. Ibid., 8.

22. Ibid., 9.

23. Ibid., 10.

24. Ibid., 101.

25. Ibid., 102.

26. Ibid., 103.

27. Ibid., 106.

28. Ibid., 105.

29. Heinrich von Kleist, *Sämtliche Werke und Briefe*, ed. H. Sembdner (Munich: Hanser, 1961), 2:749.

Sodomy in Early Modern Denmark: A Crime Without Victims

Wilhelm von Rosen, cand. mag.

What strikingly characterizes Denmark's gay history in the early modern period is the almost total lack of victims. Sodomy, of course, was a crime punishable by death by burning, but no Dane, as opposed to foreigner, was ever executed for having committed this crime with another man. Extremely few were tried and one or two, depending on how you look at it, received light sentences.

It is possible, but by no means certain, that sodomy was what led two Scottish mercenaries to the stake in Copenhagen in 1628. In 1744, one man was sentenced to two years of prison for "the sin of softness" (masturbation), while his much younger partner was considered sufficiently punished by having stood trial. Eleven men involved in a group of unnatural libertines, exposed in Copenhagen in 1814, got away with very discreet warnings, although most of them could have been sentenced to death. It was not until 1835 that, from a European point of view, a more ordinary looking series of trials for sodomy and attempted sodomy began.

Why was sodomy between men in practice a nonexistent crime in Denmark for more than two hundred years?

In Denmark the theoretical framework of sodomy did not differ from the rest of Europe. Law and jurisprudence were much the same. Canon law applied until the Reformation in 1526, but the canonical prohibition did not, as in Southern Europe, penetrate into medieval secular law, nor did the Inquisition have jurisdiction in the ecclesiastical province of Denmark.

As a consequence of Reformation, Canon law and the ecclesiasti-

---

Wilhelm von Rosen is associated with the National Archives, Copenhagen, Denmark.

cal courts disappeared, thereby leaving a vacuum that was filled by the secular courts and by a number of statutes promulgated during the next hundred years. None of these statutes, however, concerned sodomy. It was only with "Danske Lov" (The Danish Lawbook) of 1683 that Denmark got its first secular and statutory prohibition of sodomy: "Intercourse which is against nature shall be punished with death by burning" (art. 6-13-15).[1] A number of executions for sodomy with animals during the first half of the seventeenth century demonstrated that the absence of an explicit law against sodomy by no means meant that sodomy was tolerated.

"Danske Lov" is a comprehensive compilation of the provincial statutes of the Middle Ages and the national statues of the sixteenth and seventeenth centuries. Notes to the preliminary drafts of the lawbook give the references to previous statutes for the vast majority of the articles. But there is no information on what precisely inspired the lawmakers to include the article on sodomy. Legal historians have suggested Mosaic law, Canon law, or German law as the direct source. Certainly, these legal systems have to various extents influenced Danish law. The German criminal code of 1533, Constitutio Criminalis Carolina, is also considered a possible source for a few of the articles of "Danske Lov."[2] But it would probably be more to the point to say that the article prohibiting sodomy was an inevitable confirmation of what by 1683 was established legal practice.[3] Whereas a number of sodomy cases, in the sense of *bestiality*, are extant from the seventeenth century (mostly from accounts of local jurisdictions), the evidence of an actual legal practice concerning sodomy *between men* is very scant.[4]

The accounts of the Lord Lieutenant of Copenhagen tell of expenditures for the executions by burning in the square in front of the Castle of Copenhagen of a Scottish lieutenant-colonel and a Scottish "lad" (possibly meaning a servant), during a one-month interval in 1628. There is no indication of the crime for which the two Scotsmen, who were probably soldiers in one of the Scottish regiments hired for the war against Sweden, were executed. Similar but more detailed accounts from the Magistrate of Copenhagen for the burning of men in 1624 and 1641 explicitly stated the crime as sodomy with cows — the burning of which was an additional cost, of course. This, however, is not the case with the two Scotsmen.[5] In theory, they may have been burned for sorcery. (Incidentally, it should be mentioned at this point that charges in Denmark in sorcery cases contained virtually no allegations of orgies and sexual intercourse with the Devil, and therefore no nexus between sorcery and sodomy in the sense of committing sodomy by having sexual intercourse with the Devil and demons.)[6]

Regardless of the lack of evidence of actual proceedings in cases of sodomy with men[7] — besides the uncertain cases of the two Scotsmen in 1628 — it is quite safe to assume that the practice of burning for sodomy with animals also would have covered cases of sodomy with men, if there were any. The general European tradition of what sodomy was, with its various subdivisions, the definitions and comments of contemporary German jurists to the German penal code, and the later commentaries of Danish jurists of the eighteenth century, is sufficient evidence.

Seventeenth-century practice of executing man and animal rested not solely on tradition. A sentence for sodomy with a mare in 1767 stated that the man was sentenced to death "according to the Law of God" (i.e., the Bible), "as there is no explicit letter in our law about this."[8] Also, after the promulgation in 1683 of the "Danske Lov," sentences by the Supreme Court cited the "Law of God" as prescribing the death penalty by burning (1707).[9] In Denmark, as elsewhere in Europe, the Bible, notably the book of Leviticus, was regarded as a positive law, especially, but not solely, in carnal matters. The Reformation in Northern Europe meant, in this as in other theological matters, a return to the basis of Canon law; namely, to the letter of the Bible. Christian leniency of the Middle Ages gave way to a probably much more severe and brutal conception of how a Christian society should deal with sodomites.[10] The reason for considering this more a "tradition" than an influence of Mosiac law is that the latter did not prescribe death by burning, but seemed to prescribe death by stoning.[11]

An exposition of the laws that must prevail in a truly Christian state — namely, *all* the laws that can be found in the Bible — was published with royal approval in 1605 by a priest, Anders Mikkelsen. The explanation given here was the same as the one found in contemporary German commentaries on the penal code: God will punish a society that does not itself punish the few who are guilty.

There is, however, no specification of God's eventual punishment, corresponding to what German jurists like Damhouder (1601) and Carpzow (1636) meted out (e.g., famine, flood, earthquake),[12] and the author employed a comparatively mild and sober-minded language.

Among the prescribed and cited biblical laws, the ones concerning sex between men were certainly not omitted, but they did tend to drown among the hundreds and hundreds of, even for the seventeenth century, absurd Mosiac rules.[13] It therefore seems fair to say that in Denmark the practice of burning sodomites was a tradition that veiled itself in a selective and ideological use of Mosiac law. What is more interesting is that the practice of, and from a 1683 secular law the prescription of, death by burning for sodomy, was never put to actual use in cases of sodomy between men, even though that was in force until 1866. The two Scotsmen must be considered exceptions to a general rule, possibly explained by their being foreigners.

From 1660 Denmark was by written constitution and the grace of God an absolute monarchy. Implicitly, interpretation of the "Danske Lov" was considered a royal prerogative until the middle of the eighteenth century.[14] It was understood that no one had the right to suggest that the law needed clarification and comment, except of course the king and his closest servants. Questions from judges on how to interpret the rules in specific cases were usually answered by the Royal Chancery (Danske Kancelli) with an unhelpful order to follow the law.

During the eighteenth century the influence of natural law began to be felt in Denmark, mainly through the German school of Samuel van Pufendorf and Christian Wolff, which united absolutist rule and any law and regulation of an absolute monarchy with the Law of Nature. In his book, *The Duties of Man and Citizens According to the Law of Nature* (1675), Pufendorf explained the reason why sodomy was unlawful. Marriage was the first type of social contract, concluded in order to ensure and protect the reproduction of mankind. God had given human beings a strong inclination to unite with each other, but not for the purpose of bringing pleasure, as such would lead only to great disorder and be an abominable spectacle. The intention was to make marriage sweeter and more pleasurable, to teach the business of nature on which propagation depended, and to surmount the inconveniences of pregnancy and the trouble of rearing children. Any other use of the organs of reproduction was contrary to the Law of Nature, which condemned not only all those kinds of lust that had as objects the dumb beasts or persons of one's own sex, but any kind of carnal intercourse and shameful defilement outside of marriage.[15]

The most prominent person of the Danish Age of Reason, Ludvig Holberg (1684-1754) — a historian, man of letters, and writer of comedies whose work to this day is considered among the highlights of Danish literature — began his career as an author by rewriting Pufendorf in a very unoriginal way. His book, "The Knowledge of Nature in International Law according to the Principles of the most Excellent Jurists," first published in 1716, saw innumerable reprints and became the most widely read juridical work for a whole generation. His only addition to Pufendorf's exposition on the Law of Nature in its relation to sodomy was the observation that this "severe obscenity" used to be so rife among the ancient Greeks "that by law it could not be eradicated."[16]

The idea that there exists a natural system of law, an eternal justice implanted in man as a creature of nature, or by God, meant that, by contemplating "Reason," man could arrive at a conclusion of what law ought to be, or, rather, of how marvelous in accordance with "Reason" positive law happened to be. Empirical observation of history, geography, international differences in positive law, or psychology had no place in this system that culminated with the German philosophers Kant and Fichte. It was these deductive systems of natural law that, along with Roman law, dominated teaching at the Faculty of Law of the University of Copenhagen throughout the eighteenth century. Holberg's remark on ancient Greek customs showed that by the eighteenth century observation of actual fact, the lesson and experience of history, did not necessarily have to refer solely to the history of the Old Testament. Holberg himself wrote a follow-up on sodomy in ancient Greece in his collection of essays, the "Epistles," where in 1748 he raised the question: "Was Socrates a pederast?" It is not surprising that Holberg arrived at the conclusion that Socrates was not, considering that to him Socrates was the embodiment of a moral hero. The important aspect of the essay, the first original discussion of sex between men in Danish literature, is that the question was raised, that there was a discussion of pederasty without any reference to the Bible. Thus, the problem was secularized, although the historical framework had been removed to a safe place in ancient history, but thereby also removed from the concepts of sin and Christianity and into the somewhat more sophisticated sphere of the elite, where reason ought to reign. Although in this "letter" Holberg characterized Greek pederasty as "the vice with which a number of Greeks at his (Socrates') time were infested," the essay was probably pushing the limit of what was then acceptable. It demonstrated that emancipation from a purely biblical or juridical understanding of sexual behavior was by that time possible. The more than implied moral condemnation of pederasty was certainly inevitable in 1748.[17]

How extraordinary Holberg's literary treatment of Socrates' possible inclination to pederasty was can be seen from the way in which the authorities, a few years before the essay's publication, handled the probably one and only case of sodomy between men that was brought to court during the eighteenth century.[18]

Shortly after sundown on Whit Monday 1744, eighteen-year-old Laurids Frandsen and seventy-two-year-old Rasmus Væver[19] were discovered in a field near the village Boring in Northern Jutland by Laurids' father. They were lying on top of each other with their pants down. As later came to light, they had practiced interfemoral sex regularly for about ten years. The father complained to the local squire and accused Væver of being a hermaphrodite. A semiofficial survey of Væver's sexual organs was conducted a few days later by four men from the village. It was established that Væver was indeed a real man. Rumor of what had happened by then had run all over the parish, and soon thereafter the vicar made a visit to Frandsen's family and eventually got a confession that was repeated, written down, and signed by two witnesses. The squire then summoned Frandsen and Væver before the local court (herredsting) on the charge of having "sinned against nature." The case was heard behind closed doors and lasted for four months. Both of the defendants were imprisoned during the trial. However, Frandsen seems to have been treated lightly because at one point Væver complained that he (Væver) was in chains day and night and had to watch

Frandsen running around outside the prison, playing. Over the years of their relationship, Væver had supplied Frandsen with gifts such as a pipe and tobacco, a knife, mittens, a scarf and a shirt, and on Whit Sunday the pair of bluegray stockings that he later wore in court. Rasmus had promised Laurids that he would inherit his money and had shown Laurids' father a purse and told him that he would hide it in a secret place inside a chest that Laurids' father should buy from his estate. In this way, Væver's wife would not get the money, which was enough to buy a couple of heifers for Laurids.

The focus of the interrogation of the defendants was their sexual practice. They denied having ever done anything but Rasmus placing his member between Laurids' thighs from behind. Væver claimed that he had been impotent for ten years, and Laurids declared that he did not know whether "anything wet" had ever come from it. They were examined by two physicians, who declared that it was not possible to determine whether a member had been used for illicit and unnatural purposes. Both defendants denied that Væver had "placed his member in that place from where by nature uncleanliness is thrown out." It took a number of court sessions and the persuasion of a severe prison stay before Væver confessed. Both of the defendants claimed that they had not realized that what they had done was a sin and a crime.

So much for the facts, as they were established in court. A much tougher problem was the legal interpretation of those facts. Even the prosecutor and the judge were uncertain whether the acts were covered by the formula of the "Danske Lov," art. 6-13-15: "Intercourse which is against nature shall be punished with death by burning." In his written deposition, the prosecutor declared that "this sin" did not seem to be mentioned in the "Danske Lov," except that it might be considered "intercourse against nature." If so, it would have to be punished accordingly. He continued by citing Leviticus, "If a man also lie with mankind . . . they shall surely be put to death," and concluded from a literal understanding of "lie" that because the king had not given a law covering this, "which is probably sodomy," Væver would have to be condemned to death according to the law of God.

Considering the fact that during the interrogation the prosecutor

had been very keen to establish whether anal intercourse had occurred, he also must have realized that that was the decisive legal
factor. But as anal intercourse had not occurred, he was reduced to
trying to extend the areas of punishable acts to include what had
happened according to the confessions. He did not, however, claim
that sodomy had been attempted or intended, probably because attempt or intention did not enter the penal thinking of the "Danske
Lov," which was casuistic in its formulation of what constituted a
crime.

Both of the counsels for the defense dismissed the idea that this
was the case of sodomy or intercourse against nature. They maintained that it was necessary to distinguish between sodomy on the
one hand, and "mollitia" on the other. (They both used a Danish
term, literally "to be soft.")[20] The Counsel for Rasmus Væver
wrote in his deposition that he would be greatly to blame if he
explained more accurately what was meant by sins against nature,
but that it was necessary to do so. If this "gross sin" was what had
supposedly occurred, it was absolutely necessary to establish "res
in re," that is, that the thing had been inside the thing. He continued with a probably realistic description of sexual behavior and its
hypothetical legal consequences:

> If the sinful intercourse of the defendants is considered sins
> against nature, what would then prevent considering sinning
> against nature, thousands of other people whose sinful and by
> Satan inspired imaginations and unchaste movements of hands
> and other limbs, like pagans in their sinful freedom, all serve
> the same purpose as these defendants, the throwing out of their
> semen?

If this became known, the Counsel argued, "one would have reason
to fear that there would be too many executions by burning."

The judge then took the unusual precaution of sending a copy of
the minutes of the proceedings to the Royal Chancery in Copenhagen. There the case was handled by the Procurator General.[21] The
Procurator General responded to the judge by writing that, although
instruction of judges was outside of his powers, he could not with a

clear conscience omit to communicate his opinion and suggest a sentence due to the special circumstances of the case.[22]

The Procurator General agreed with the Counsels for the Defense on all the main points of the case. Nobody, he wrote, who had even the slightest knowledge of what was meant by the "Danske Lov," art. 6-13-15, had ever claimed that intercourse against nature covered everything outside of natural and usual intercourse between married people. The "Danske Lov," just like Leviticus, aimed solely at "coitus or intercourse . . . in the way a man lies with a woman." This was to be distinguished from the "peccatum onaniticum" or the "sin of softness." The onanistic sin he divided in three groups: (1) Masturbation with oneself or with some other male; (2) onanistic sins committed by married people; and (3) "if the member is inserted between thighs and the semen has been excited." Those who committed these, and similar "delicta contra pudicitiam," were what the Bible termed "malakoi" or "molles." The Procurator General concluded:

> If all those who through an incautious investigation, as in the present case, are found to have committed this last mentioned sin, should be sentenced by death by burning, a large part of humankind would have to be annihilated, something that no theologist or jurist has ever been ungodly enough to maintain.

Not only did the third group of the Procurator General's definitions of the onanistic sins fit the actual case very neatly, he also accepted Rasmus Væver's claim of having been impotent for many years and declared this a mitigating circumstance when onanistic sins had to be punished; that is, when they caused public offense.

The heart of the matter, as seen from the central, judicial administration in Copenhagen, was the scandal and the offense to the public. And there was no doubt about who the real culprit was: the vicar. This theme had been touched upon by one of the Counsels of the Defense who said that the vicar had to carry the burden of the responsibility "for all the many souls who because of this case have found occasion to let themselves be thoroughly eaten by the leaven of evil." The vicar and the squire should have known better than to initiate an investigation in the presence of witnesses and to bring such things to court. The vicar may have realized this because he never turned up in the court, despite being summoned as a witness several times.

The Procurator General began his instruction to the judge by deploring the blind and careless zeal that had made the matter known among the peasants — not to speak of having it investigated before a court "whereby more offence has been caused by these good men, especially the vicar, than any good that an investigation might bring, because the greatest offence in such cases, according to mine and the opinion of all upright people, is that it is made known." This was what made it necessary to sentence. The Procurator General suggested that the judge sentence Rasmus Væver to two years of prison, and that Laurids Frandsen be considered having "atoned" for his sins, by having endured arrest for five months. Laurids' release was motivated by the fact of his youth, his lack of knowledge that he had committed a sin, and the hope that by that time he had become disgusted with his previous acts. After the termination of his term of prison, Rasmus Væver was to be banished from the Province of Jutland. The judge pronounced this verdict immediately (23 October 1744).

According to the "Danske Lov," any verdict by a local court could be appealed by the Provincial Court.[23] The Procurator General, however, instructed the judge, immediately after pronouncing the verdict, to send it to the Royal Chancery in order to have the sentence confirmed by the king and thereby to prevent appeal. Legally this was possible because the king constitutionally was above the law. This very unusual procedure was accepted by the College of Chancery and by the Council of State,[24] and on 11 December 1744 the verdict was confirmed by King Christian VI.[25] The motivating factor behind this rather drastic administrative measure was the Procurator's wish to prevent gossip and public offense from arising due to the procedure at the Provincial Court.

The Procurator General, Jens Severin Wartberg, was a close friend of Ludvig Holberg and had a reputation for somewhat loose living. When he died in 1749, he not only left an exquisite library, but also (and more shocking in pietist Copenhagen) the largest and most elegant wardrobe ever seen. He was a co-manager of The Royal Theater, a keen party-goer, and a bachelor. His fear that "these things" were spread among the common people throws Holberg's Epistle of 1748 on ancient Greek pederasty in relief. But although Holberg has sometimes been called "the Danish Voltaire," his moralistic treatment is a far cry from Voltaire's frivolous poem "L'Anti-Gone" (published 1720)[26] or his tongue-in-cheek essay on the so-called Socratic Love, in Dictionnaire Philosophique.[27] Even so, Holberg's Epistle was probably slightly risque; there can hardly be any doubt that the authorities were scared that immoral conduct spread among the subjects.

The Procurator General was not a narrow-minded rural cleric, but a man of the world. His fear that this kind of knowledge would spread must be taken seriously and not considered just the banal fear of the ruling class that the governed would begin to behave uncontrollably. The fear of immorality, loose living, and unchastity can only have been a *real* fear, deeply felt by any Christian and loyal civil servant. Any sin, but especially the carnal sins, was a violation of God's and Nature's order (in this case a violation of marriage as an institution) and it was the duty of the state to prevent it from happening.

During the latter half of the eighteenth century, the idea of the social contract that the real and original source of political power lay with the people gained followers in high places and was, with all due circumspection and respect for the absolute monarch, included in works on the theory of government. For such early theorists of political science, to whom the idea of the sovereignty of the people was not a strange thought, it was, however, a matter of course that what in the end held society together and prevented its dissolution and corruption was *religion*. There was, at the same time, a veiled discussion, partly inspired by Montesquieu, of the pros and cons of absolute monarchy, but in the end it was agreed that a state consisted of people, and that whatever the type of government, the state would be as good or as bad as the sum of its individual parts. Laws and coercion, virtue and honor, tradition, education — none of these — sufficed. The real and final social bond was religion, "because we can have no more perfect rule than the command of the Highest Being who cannot will anything that is not in itself Good, and in accord with the Nature of Things.[28]

Prevention of and punishment for carnal vices between the sexes was a routine matter in the eighteenth century. There were rules and regulations to deal with that. Not so when it came to the "onanistic sins" that, as in the case from 1744, might develop uncontrollably. What was uncontrollable is not the fact of interest to us living in the twentieth century, but rather the fact that it involved two persons of the same sex. Yet the "homosexual" aspect of the case is really not mentioned in the records. The uncontrollable and feared factor in the case was the scandal, the offense to the public, the sinful thoughts, and the inspiration of a counter-religious nature that would follow from the publicity. The case developed the way it did not because two males were involved together in something of a carnal nature, but because some village residents believed that a hermaphrodite was in their midst. There was no law against that, but it was evidently a grave matter that the biological sex of a person was not certain.

There was no legal or administrative practice for the authorities to refer to when it became necessary to deal with "onanistic sins." But the Procurator General did, in his instruction to the judge, describe how the sin mollitia should be silenced: All sensible and enlightened theologists were of the opinion that Christianity and wise politics (*prudentia politica*) demanded that, when a rumor of such things occurs, a priest never should let it be publicly investigated, and certainly never referred to the courts. Instead, with the greatest of caution he should trace the rumor to its origin, expostulate with, punish, teach, admonish to conversion, and give absolution, to the sinner, and then smother the rumor. In other words, sex between men that did not qualify as consummated sodomy was, by tacit understanding, referred to the discipline of the church. Here lies part of the explanation as to why no cases were brought to court in Denmark for attempted or intended sodomy between men until well into the nineteenth century. And this administrative practice probably also explains why no case of sodomy between men has been uncovered during the Early Modern period.

The main reason, however, for the lack of cases of sodomy between men probably lay in the social structure of Denmark during that period. Denmark was an agricultural society consisting primarily of small towns. At the end of the eighteenth century, three-fourths of the population lived in rural areas.[29] As has been shown convincingly by E. William Monter, the crime of sodomy between men was, in the Early Modern period, a crime that was dealt with in cities, whereas in rural areas the concern with serious deviation in carnal matters was directed toward bestiality.[30] This seems to have been the case of Denmark. Throughout the seventeenth and eighteenth centuries, a fair number of cases of bestiality were brought before the courts. Until 1866 when the law was changed, those found guilty were sentenced to the stake. The last execution seems to have occurred in 1751; after that, death sentences for bestiality were commuted to prison for life, and then, from about 1800, commuted to two to ten years of prison.[31]

The most widely circulated devotional handbook of the pietist period, "Fear of God through Truth" (1737), was written upon royal command by the court-preacher and later bishop, Erik Pontoppidan. It was characteristic for such an agricultural society that under the heading "What Kind of Evil is Forbidden for Us by the Sixth Commandment?," there was no mention of intercourse against nature. Instead, more relevant and specific evils were mentioned: "bestial unchastity," "pollution of the body," "dancing," and luxurious clothes.[32]

Ludvig Holberg's book, *The Knowledge of Nature and International Law* (1716), was a general exposé of the theory of natural law, not a commentary on the "Danske Lov."[33] The first such comment on Danish penal law was published in 1760, by a judge from a rural area, C. D. Hedegaard, who had studied in Halle as a pupil of German jurist Bohmer. His remarks on the "Danske Lov," art. 6-13-15, were based on German and Roman law, not on the actual sodomitical crimes committed and brought to court in Denmark. His definition of sodomy followed closely the German penal code of 1533, but also included, with a reference to Damhouder and Carpzow, "the onanitical crime" as a subgroup that, with the other types of sodomy, was always punished with burning. But was such punishment by then obsolete?[34] In light of German tradition, it is not surprising that Hedegaard—without any argument of his own—distanced himself from Montesquieu's remark in "L'Esprit des Lois" (1748) that "Nature will probably correct and vindicate itself" in these cases. That Montesquieu rejected the death penalty for crimes against nature was not mentioned, nor that death sentences for bestiality were by that time regularly commuted to prison. It is ironic that cases of sex between men were actually handled by the authorities in exactly the way recommended by Montesquieu:

> La privation des advantages que la société a attachés à la pureté des moeurs, les amendes, la honte, la contrainte de se cacher, l'infamie publique, l'expulsion hors de la ville et de la société, enfin toutes les peines qui sont de la jurisdiction correctionnelle. . . .[35]

One observation by Hedegaard seems curious: "It has been noticed that the persons most devoted to this, as to other kinds of filthyness, are misers."[36] The rational explanation seems to have been that men who would not pay the costs of marriage might end up with a cow or another man. Is there evoked here an image of the bachelor living alone and in seclusion? In a case of bestiality before the Supreme Court in 1794, the defendant pleaded mitigation because of poverty. He could not afford a wife, so the court accepted this and added "poverty" as a mitigating circumstance.[37]

The end of the eighteenth century saw a number of comments on the Danish penal code. These comments were strongly influenced by the German school of natural law, and those concerning intercourse against nature were theoretical and learned, and lacked any foundation in the juridical reality of the court and the Chancery.[38] One of these comments, by Supreme Court judge and professor of law Christian Brorson, gave a more than usually detailed explanation of why intercourse against nature was a crime. In 1791 he wrote that the authors of the "Danske Lov" had been concerned with "the wrath of a Deity." Brorson argued that such intercourse was contrary to the innate duties of mankind and detrimental to the state:

> It [intercourse against nature] makes the guilty incapable of business of mind and body, inculcates abhorrence of marriage, the foundation of the state, causes either barrenness or produces an offspring that cannot be called anything but wretched. When perpetrated in secret it is very difficult to discover and here habit, more than in any other crime, defeats

Reason. These are the miserable consequences for civic community.[39]

The offended party now was not God or religion, but society and mankind. Central to the various reasons Brorson gave for prohibiting and punishing sodomy was the idea that it was an offense against the institution of marriage and prevented the intention of marriage, the production of offspring. Brorson's reasoning is interesting because he also considered sodomitical acts harmful to the person committing them. Such reasoning may have been the early foundation for the much later concept of "homosexuality" as a pathological condition.

Brorson also mentioned that it was an absolute precondition for the sentencing for sodomy that "res in re and effusio seminis" be proven. This was also argued in the case of 1744 by both the Counsel for Defense and the Procurator General. To the modern mind, imbued with the concept of "homosexuality," this legally very important demarcation of what constituted sodomy seems rather arbitrary, and one wonders whether ordinary people would have been aware of it. Yet they probably were. One should not forget that sodomy, especially in an agricultural society, included bestiality and that sodomy between men was seen as something much closer to bestiality than to sex and love between men — or, to be more historically correct, than to onanistical sins. For a man to love, kiss, and sleep with another man was probably no more sodomitical than to love, kiss, and sleep with a beloved animal. It must have been evident that the crime, the unacceptable act, was to put the thing into the thing.

From reading Brorson and other late eighteenth-century commentators of the penal code, one cannot see that the works of foreign criminologists of the more openly political and revolutionary French school of natural law, such as Montesquieu, Beccaria, Hommel, and Voltaire, were known in Denmark. Yet they were known, at least to some extent.[40] The ideas of the French Revolution were discussed in Denmark, even while "official" jurisprudence remained firmly planted in the wording of the "Danske Lov" and in a school of natural law that, from a metaphysical concept of liberty and equality, deduced and supported any and every existing political and legal situation—in this case absolute monarchy and Christian morality. Only in one instance, was a more radical opinion on sodomy publicly vented, that coming before September 1799 when freedom of the press was severely curtailed.

In February 1799 a former judge, Peter Collett, whose dismissal in 1797 had caused a scandal (he had advocated "virtuous atheism" and the principle of the right of resistance), published an article on the principles of penal law that was strongly influenced by the French philosophers and the revolutionary school of natural law. Collett's arguments were basically the same as those found in Anselm von Feuerbach's "Revision der Grundsätze und Grundbegriffe des positiven peinlichen Rechts," also from 1799. But Collett was not, as Feuerbach eventually turned out to be, steeped in his own moralist condemnation of sodomy. Collett argued that what made an act punishable was the violation of the security of the state, not the morality of an act. Also, if morality was the measure used for meting out punishment, the punishment would be much more severe than what was required to maintain the security of the state. As an example of this, Collett used intercourse against nature (and abortion) and found no reason to sacrifice such a supposedly criminal person on the stake. "The only duty neglected by this offender is an ethical duty, nothing more than a neglect of what is demanded by modesty and decency." It constituted no interference with the rights of others. To put the death sentence actually to use would be "without and against justice." This, he added, was accepted by "all civilized states," including Denmark, where the death penalty was never actually effected but always commuted to a term of prison. He concluded that it would be wise and just to abolish a law which was not observed. Collett continued by writing that if what was punished was not the immorality of an act, but the immorality of a person, a very severe punishment would be difficult, however, because in a case involving intercourse against nature one could not surmise "from a man's bizarre desires . . . his moral character in general."[41] Compared to the general and axiomatic disgust always voiced in connection with sodomy, Collett showed himself to be a representative of the best of the tradition of the Enlightenment: the ability to see, independently of prevailing morality, what is and is not to be considered a crime when the basic freedom of man is at issue.

A few months later, in October 1800, a commission was established to revise the penal code, the sixth book of the "Danske Lov." It was explicitly stated that this was to be done on the basis of natural law and the social contract. The commission's members were those civil servants who made up the judicial center of power in the State of Denmark: the Presidents of the Supreme Court and the Royal Chancery, the Procurator General, and two professors of law. The members agreed that certain very severe types of punishment had to be brought into more reasonable proportion with the seriousness of the crimes.

As punishment for intercourse against nature, the majority of the commission proposed flogging, followed by banishment or prison. The reasons given for suggesting banishment are interesting because they demonstrated the general difficulty in this period of how to reconcile the traditionally felt disgust and public offense with the realization that this crime violated neither the rights of the state or the citizens:

> The character of this crime is such that the person who has committed it causes offence by living in a place where his infamous deed is, or can be considered as known, notwithstanding that the criminal properly speaking cannot be considered as being dangerous to the public security, so that it is not for this reason necessary that he is punished with the loss of freedom.[42]

A minority of the commission considered banishment to be contrary to international law because the "depraved mind" of the condemned would make him just as bad a citizen outside of Denmark as he had been in his own country. Instead, the minority suggested solitary prison for life—first without labor, later with forced labor.

One member of the minority, Frederik Moltke, President of the Royal Chancery, who had taken the initiative to appoint the commission and who under the influence of Beccaria upheld a principal opposition to the death penalty, offered an argument for the detention of sodomites that foreshadowed the future: Intercourse against nature was not a crime and therefore could not be treated in criminal law. However, those "depraved" persons who because of ignorance or corrupted imaginations had become deaf to the voice of nature, but had not had any intention to offend, "ought in my opinion to be treated as lunatics or sick persons, and together with their acts hidden away in secluded places."[43] However foresighted this might seem, though, it was not yet possible to use sickness as a way out of the conflict between, on the one hand, the demand of natural law that only acts which violated the rights of citizens or the security of the state were crimes and, on the other hand, society's general feelings of disgust and offense toward intercourse against nature. Medical science had not yet devised a syndrome that fit this problem.

The work of the Commission of Penal Law of 1800 was not followed up and the results were soon forgotten. As far as intercourse against nature between men was concerned, all of the Commission's discussions were of a hypothetical nature anyway, as only cases of bestiality were brought before the courts.

Of much greater historical importance than either the Commission on Penal Law or the revolutionary writing of Collett was the appearance in Danish jurisprudence of a young man of immense juridical talent and energy, Anders Sandøe Ørsted (1778-1860). With the history of law the only exception, his voluminous writing covered every aspect of law, including penal law. As a judge of the Supreme Court, and later as a member of the College of Chancery of Procurator General, he gained insight into the actual working of the law. He is considered the founder of Danish jurisprudence. One of his earliest published articles was a review of Collett's above-mentioned article.

Ørsted agreed with Collett about the basic principles of penal law: the right of the sovereign to punish was not based on a right to establish a moral order, but instead based on a right and a duty, as head of state, forcibly to maintain equal freedom for all (i.e., uphold the security of the state and of the citizens). Nothing that exceeded this purpose could be forbidden or prescribed.[44] In accordance with this distinction between moral law and natural law, he wrote elsewhere (at the same time) that intercourse outside of marriage could not be considered illegal "since nobody's freedom suffer[s] thereby."[45] But he was not able to accept such extreme consequences of his basic tenets when it came to intercourse against nature and seriously contemplating what, if any violation of the security of the state and its citizens was involved.

> Besides the immediate disgust caused by such unnatural sins, it must be evident to anybody who applauds clean principles of morality that it is a real and a very gross crime to use the impulse which nature and reason have intended for the preservation of the species . . . as only a means for the satisfaction of beastial sensuality.[46]

In clear contradiction to the basic principles of penal law as elaborated in the very same article, Ørsted here deduced from "clean principles of morality" that intercourse against nature was a real crime. The idea that intercourse against nature was—as provocatively stated by Collett—only "a neglect of what is demanded by modesty and decency," was so far removed from Ørsted's concept of reality that he added that this could not possibly be Collett's opinion.[47]

Ørsted realized the contradiction, and his solution was radical: From then on he dropped natural law as the basic principle of jurisprudence. Since then, natural law has been considered something of a naughty phrase in Danish jurisprudence. The not very practical notion that liberty and equality were the basic principles of penal law disappeared. That the school of natural law which Ørsted wiped out was a scholastic and speculative system, hopelessly lost in the metaphysical fogs spread by Kant and Fichte made this inevitable in any case. In a note to the same review of Collett, Ørsted wrote that the right of the state to punish was not founded on any natural right that either the offender or the offended had possessed but subsequently agreed to hand over to the state via the social contract. The right of a state to punish was instead a direct consequence of the nature of a state: A state must by definition have laws, and for laws to have effect, punishment must be laid down.[48]

According to Ørsted, the purpose of the state, and consequently the purpose of penal law, was identical to the purpose of mankind: Achievement of the highest moral good.[49] It was therefore not enough that the penal law maintained the security of society; law had to be rooted in "moral law." This did not mean, though, that all human activity had to be regulated by law, or that the state could demand or forbid everything demanded or forbidden by moral law:

> Only that which directly or indirectly disturbs the basic pre-condition for all moral activity, namely the free and secure existence, can be forbidden by the laws of a state. . . . Such disturbances will not be punished because they are sins accord-ing to conscience, but because and in proportion to the degree in which they violate the peace and order of society.[50]

In relation to intercourse against nature, the question then be-came the meaning of the distinction between "direct" and "indi-rect" disturbance or violation of the security of society. In general, Ørsted did not doubt that direct violation of a good that society is committed to preserve (e.g., life and property) was more punish-able than those acts that were only an indirect violation—that is, contrary to an order established by law or a regulation serving the further protection of such a good.[51] That one's house does not burn was such a good, and to put fire to someone's house was a direct violation of this good and therefore punishable. But it was only an indirect violation of the same good if a neighbor neglected to have his chimney swept regularly according to regulation, and therefore punishable only to a lesser degree.

Ørsted did not, however, believe that all indirect violations of the security of society were under all circumstances less punishable than direct violations; this is where he disagreed with Feuerbach.[52] Other considerations, for example, the importance or the magnitude of the good that is put in danger by an indirect violation, might make such a violation as punishable or more punishable than a di-rect violation. As examples of this, Ørsted mentioned blasphemy, incest, unnatural sensuality,[53] and serious breaches of quarantine regulations as indirect disturbances "that probably should be pun-ished more severely than the less serious degrees of libel, bodily harm, and invasion of property, although no direct harm or viola-tion of any right is involved."[54] As a consequence, Ørsted did not think that it was possible in practice to distinguish, as Feuerbach did, between punishment for the direct violation of a right or a good (to be treated in a penal code), and an indirect violation (not to be mentioned in a penal code, but in police regulations only). The difference between law and regulation was a practical one of procedure and investigation, and of whether a breach was summarily and quickly dealt with by the police, or more thoroughly by a proper court. According to Ørsted, the reasons for prescribing the use of one or the other of these procedures should not have been based on whether a direct or an indirect violation of a right was involved, but rather on the difficulty of the investigation, the importance of the good that had been violated, and the degree of punishment involved.

For these reasons, Ørsted dissociated himself from Feuerbach who "maintain[ed] that sodomy is a smaller offence than even the slightest violation of a private right."[54] Ørsted was of the opinion that intercourse against nature violated the purpose of the state and the highest moral good. Therefore, it ought to be dealt with in a penal code. He considered the treatment of sodomy and blasphemy in the German penal law of the time as being too light. He agreed with the German jurist C. J. A. Mittermaier, that to refer such "despicable acts" to police regulations only "had a detrimental moral effect on the nation."[56]

In 1822 a draft of a new Bavarian penal code was published. Like the Bavarian penal code of 1813 written by Feuerbach, the draft of 1822 in principle decriminalized sodomy; sodomy was referred to in the second part where police regulations were dealt with, and was to be punished with imprisonment for one week to three months.[57] In a review of the draft, published in German, Ørsted wrote:

the theoretical system has had "the depraving consequence that acts causing a high degree of public offence, and which greatly contribute to the loosening of those bonds on which the order of society depends, are treated as trifles when they do not involve a violation of any right. It is outrageous that blasphemy and unnatural sensuality is punished with only a few days of simple prison." . . . It is "incomprehensible how such a crime can be treated in this reckless manner. An actual law that followed the draft in this, deserved to be counted among those books that are most offensive to morality and religion."[58]

This rhetorical outburst was *not* in character with Ørsted's usual phlegmatic and well-argued style; he must have been in the throes of his own disgust.

Feuerbach himself heartily agreed with Ørsted. Although Feuerbach was responsible for the theoretical considerations that decriminalized sodomy in Bavaria 1813, he by now had admitted the relevance of his own personal feelings of disgust and declared the decriminalization of sodomy in 1813 to be his own fault.[59] A harsh polemic ensued between Ørsted and the author of the draft, N. T. V. Gönner, and his supporters.[60] It is probable that this contributed to the fate of the draft. So the ironic effect of Ørsted's criticism was that the Bavarian penal code of 1813 — with no mention of sodomy at all — remained in force.

Ørsted's opinion was challenged and he was exposed to those impulses that might have made him reconsider tradition. But he didn't, mainly for two reasons. First, Ørsted was a devoutly religious man, and second, he was a practical man — in his words "a man of business." As a judge, and later as a member of the College of the Royal Chancery and as Procurator General, he did not see it as his task to overthrow tradition. Disgust, offense, religious and moral norms were part of the reality that he dealt with — in addition to the more or less revolutionary ideas of foreign authors. When in 1814-15 a "gay" subculture was discovered in Copenhagen and brought to the attention of the Chancery, Ørsted took part in the deliberations.

The revolutionary wars in Europe brought considerable commercial benefits to neutral Denmark, along with fugitives from the troubled parts of Europe. One of these was Franciscus Dumont from Paris, who settled in Copenhagen and became a successful milliner. He had a shop and a flat on the main street and could afford a pleasure farm outside Copenhagen. He also became the center of a group of "gays." By then, the City of Copenhagen had grown to over one-hundred thousand inhabitants, supposedly the size required to sustain a gay subculture.[61] According to police information, eleven persons were involved, all of them of respectable social standing (an actor, a civil servant who was also of noble family, a private secretary to a Minister of State, a physician, a wine merchant, a medical student, a cadet, a vinegar manufacturer, Dumont's assistant milliner). Three were foreigners. It is possible that a greater number than those mentioned in the Chancery file was involved, but it seems unlikely that this group constituted a gay subculture that recruited new and young members on a scale that would ensure its continued existence. (There is no mention in the records of fun houses or special cafés, only of parks, mainstreets, and private parties.)

The affair was investigated by a commission of two, the President of Police in Copenhagen and an especially appointed judge. Anal intercourse had occurred regularly within the gay group, and it was clear from the beginning that some of those involved would be sentenced to death if the case was brought before a court. But it was equally clear that the sentences would be commuted to prison sentences by the Chancery. The commission recommended to the Chancery that the affair not be brought to court, but that by royal resolution one of the foreigners be banished, that the cadet be removed from the army and from the city (he had "slept around" all over), and that the rest be warned. The reason offered for not taking formal action according to the "Danske Lov," art. 6-13-15, was that "the case would lead to publicity which is not suitable in a case of such offensive character."

The investigation took place in the private rooms of the President of Police. Dumont was not interrogated, however, because "we believe that, considering his profession, the mere investigation might lead to serious unpleasantness for him." In the Chancery, the case file was handled by members of the College only, and the file was stored along with a small group of particularly secret and potentially embarrassing files on such things as divorce in the royal family, a group of revolutionaries, and the possible exclusion from the order of succession of the heir presumptive to the throne.

For a number of reasons, Ørsted disagreed with the solution suggested by the commission; namely, to deal with the people involved through the instrument of a royal resolution that could be kept secret. Ørsted argued that it would be unjust to condemn and punish someone unless it was done according to law and in a court. In addition, rumors were circulating in the city of a "club" of highly placed pederasts that supposedly included civil servants who seduced young cadets. As Ørsted knew, the rumors pointed to the wrong people, one of them the President of the Chancery, who received an anonymous letter to that effect. Formal proceedings in court, Ørsted wrote in his opinion, would bring the truly guilty persons out into the open and absolve the innocent.

Nonetheless, the President of Chancery had made up his mind, and against the majority of the College of Chancery, he made Ørsted write the formal motion to the king. On 6 July 1816 His Majesty decided accordingly that the cadet was to be sent away (his father had by then shipped him off to the West Indies), the vinegar merchant was to be banished, and the rest were to be called before the President of Police, who would issue severe warnings and inform them that they would be held under observation. Subsequently, one by one they all signed a document to this effect.[62]

As late as the early 1800s, the authorities in Denmark maintained the attitude that Christianity, and certainly "wise politics," demanded that certain offenses should not be investigated in public — onanistic sins, nor consummated sodomy between men. Not until 1835 were cases of sodomy between men brought before the courts in formal accordance with the "Danske Lov."[63]

NOTES

1. *Kong Christian den Femtis Danske Lov*, 2d ed., ed. V. A. Secher (Coppenhagen: 1911), 942.

2. Ibid., xxxi and 1062.

3. 1663, if one counts the first draft of the "Danske Lov" that mentions "sodomy"; cf. Secher and Stochel, *Forarbejderne til Kong Christian V.s Danske Lov* 1 (Copenhagen: 1891-92), 143.

4. Poul Johs. Jorgensen, *Dansk retschistorie*, 2d ed. (Copenhagen: 1947), 144. V. A. Secher: "Bidrag til Københavns Rets- og Kulturhistorie," in *Historiske Meddelelser om København* 1 (Copenhagen: 1908), 592sqv.

5. V. A. Secher, *Forarbejderne*. Only the accounts are extant; the records of the Copenhagen Magistrates Court burned in 1728.

6. Merete Birkelund, *Troldkvinden og hendes anklagere – danske hekseprocesser* i, det og 17., Århundrede (Copenhagen: 1983).

7. The following editions of sentences from the fifteenth to the seventeenth century have nothing on sodomy with men: J. L. A. Kolderup-Rosenvinge (ed.), *Udvalg af gamle Danske Domme afsagt paa Kongens Retterting og paa Landsting* 1-4 (1477-1596), (1842-48). Troels Dahlerup (ed.), *Det kgl. Rettertings Domme og Rigens Forfølgninger fra Christian IIIs Tid*. 1-2 (1537-44) (Copenhagen: 1959-69). V. A. Secher (ed.), *Jucidia Placiti Regis Daniae Justitiarii. Samling af*

Kongens Rettertings Domme 1595-1614, 1-2 (Copenhagen: 1881-86). E. Reitzel-Nielsen (ed.), *Danske Domme 1375-(1608)*, 1-4 (Copenhagen: 1978-83).

8. Sjællandsfar landstings justitsprotokol 5 November 1676, Provincial Archives of Copenhagen.

9. Tage Holmboe, Højesteret og strafferetten, in *Hojesteret 1661-1961* 2 (Copenhagen: 1952) 142-43.

10. Evidence of the application of Canon law in pre-Reformation Denmark regarding sodomy is scant. Cf. Honorius III to the archbishop of Lund 4 February 1227, in E. Krarup (ed.), *Bullarium Danicum. Aktstykker vedrørende Danmark 1198-1316* (Copenhagen: 1932), 178; "Decreta Qvædam Arhusiensia, Qvae Ulricus Stykke Episcopus, cum consensu Capituli anno 1443 constituit . . . art. 55 Casus reservati," in G. J. Thorkelin (ed.), *Samling af Danske Kirke-Love* (Copenhagen, 1781), 13; Interrogationes in Confessione faciende (1514), in G. J. Thorkelin (ed.), *Statuta Provincialia . . .* (Copenhagen, 1778).

11. The European tradition of the burning of sodomites has been traced by Gisela Bleibtreu-Ehrenburg, *Tabu Homosexualität: Die Geschichte eines Vorurteils* (Frankfurt am Main: S. Fischer, 1978).

12. Ibid., 300sqv.

13. Andreas Michaelius, *Verdzlig Low oc Skikke efter hvilcke Gud selff haffde befallit Israels Folck oc Menighed at styres oc Regeris* (Copenhagen, 1605), 70.

14. Frantz Dahl, *Anders Sandøe Ørsted som Retslaerd* (Copenhagen: 1927), 22.

15. Pufendorf's "Duties . . . " (1675) was published in a Danish translation in 1742, cf. S. v. Pufendorf, *Et Menneskes og en borgers Pligter efter Naturens Lov* (Kiel, 1742), 360sqv.

16. Ludvig Holberg, *Naturens og Folke-Rettens Kundskab bygget paa de fornemste Juristers Principiis*, 5th ed. (Copenhagen, 1763), 286.

17. Ludvig Holberg, *Epistler*, Vol. 1, ed. F. J. Billeskov Jansen, 234-36 (epistle no. 54); cf. August Peterson, Den sokratiske Holberg, in *Tilskueren 1935* 2 (Copenhagen:), 125-38.

18. Voer-Nim herreds justitsprotokol 1744, fol. 121b-178b, Provincial archives of Viborg. It has, of course, not been possible to examine the rather massive amount of records from local jurisdictions of the eighteenth century. Nowhere, however, in a large section of literature on Danish legal history, local history, the few historical works on sexual mores (standard work: Georg Hansen, Sædelighedsforhold blandt landbefolkningen i Danmark idet 18. århundrede (Copenhagen: 1957), checked over the last five years, has any mention of a case of sodomy been found. The case in 1744 is first very briefly mentioned in J. R. Hübertz, *Aktstykker vedkommende Staden og Stiftet Aarhus* (Copenhagen: 1846), 325.

19. "Væver" means weaver, which was probably his profession.

20. Danish: "Blødagtighed."

21. The Procurator General was the judicial expert and adviser of the Royal Chancery and as such a member of the College of the Royal Chancery (Danske

Kancelli) which was the central administrative authority in judicial, ecclesiastical, educational, and other matters of the interior.

22. Danske Kancelli, Records of the Procurator General, *Erklæringsbog 1744-48*, National Archives, Copenhagen.

23. Danske Lov 1-6-9, cf. n. 1.

24. Danske Kancelli, Supplikprotokol 1744, 2.halvdel, nr.900; ibid., *Kancelliprotokol 1744*, fol. 415-16, National Archives, Copenhagen.

25. Danske Kancelli, *Jyske Tegnelser* 1744, fol. 324-25, nr. 104, National Archives, Copenhagen.

26. Oeuvres complètès de Voltaire 14, ed. Beuchot (Paris: 1833), 5-9.

27. Voltaire, *Dictionnaire philosophique 1*, ed. Julien Benda and Raymond Naves (Paris: 1937), 22.

28. Jens Schjelderup Sneedorff, Om den Borgerlige Regiering (Copenhagen, 1757), 105, cf. 120. Cf. Andreas Schytte, *Staternes Indvortes Regiering, Forste Deel* (Copenhagen, 1773), 257sqv; Jens Arup Seip, Teorien om det opinion sstyrte enevelde, in (Norwegian) *Historisk Tidsskrift 38* (1957-58): 410.

29. *Statistisk årbog* 6 (1965). By 1769 (the first census in Denmark) Copenhagen had about 80,000 inhabitants, provincial towns 78,911, and the rest of the country 638,673.

30. E. William Monter, Sodomy and Heresy in Early Modern Switzerland, in *Journal of Homosexuality* 6 (Winter 1980-81).

31. Tage Holmboe, *Hojesteret*, 194 n. 170; Georg Hansen, *Saedelighedsforhold*, 158-59.

32. Erik Pontoppidan: Sandhed til Gudfrygtighed, Cph. 1741, p. 37-41.

33. Cf. n. 16, *supp.*, 4.

34. The prominent German judge, Karl Ferdinand von Hommel, related that his colleagues in the 1750s had trouble deciding "if one should not burn these so-called onanites." K. F. von Hommel, Des Herren Marquis von Beccaria Unsterbliches Werk von Verbrechen und Strafen (Breslau, 1778): note, p. 166.

35. Montesquieu, L'Esprit des Lois suivi de la defense de l'Esprit des Lois, 12:4; cf. 12:6, "Que l'on prépare point ce crime; qu'on le proscrive par une police exacte, comme toutes les violations des moeurs."

36. C. D. Hedegaard, Forsøg til en Tractat Angaaende den Danske Criminal-Ret, Indeholdende den Siette Bog af Kong Christian den Femtes Danske Lov med Summarier, Paralleller og Amnerkninger, 2d ed. (Copenhagen, 1760); Chap. 1773, 708-12.

37. Records of the Supreme Court, Voteringsprotokol 1794B, no. 324, National Archives, Copenhagen.

38. Engelbrecht Hesselberg, *Juridiske Collegium Igjennemset og med Anmærkninger foroget af Jens Bing Dons*, 2d ed. (Copenhagen, 1773), 341; Lauritz Norregaard, *Natur- og Folkerettens første Grunde* (Copenhagen, 1776), 100; Jens Bing Dons, *Academiske Forrelæsninger over den Danske og Norske Lov*, 3, Deel (Copenhagen, 1780), 180; Lorentz Evensen, *Samlinger af juridiske og historiske Materier*, vol. 2 (Trondheim, 1785), 88; J. F. W. Schlegel, *Naturrettens eller den almindelige Retslæres Grundsaetninger* 2d ed. (Copenhagen, 1805), vol. 1, 146.

39. Chr. Brorson, *Forsøg til den Siette Bogs Fortolkning i Christian den femtes Danske og Norske Lov, samt Straffene efter de ældre Love* (Copenhagen, 1791), 341.

40. Cf. Stig Iuul, "Den danske strafferets udvikling i tiden efter ca. 1800," in *Kampen mod forbrydelsen*, vol. 2 (Copenhagen: 1952), 14. Beccaria, *Trattato dei delitti e delle pene* was translated into Danish in 1796, but was known earlier.

41. Peter Collett, "Betragtninger over Straffe i Almindelighed og Æresstraffe i Særdeleshed," in *Minerva* (1799).

42. Forestilling (motion to the king) 27 October 1803, see. n. 43.

43. Danske Kancelli G.123b, Dokumenter til kommissionens forhandlingsprotokol, National Archives, Copenhagen. Cf. Troels G. Jørgensen, "Kriminallovskommissionen af 1800," in *Nordisk Tidsskrift for Strafferet* (Copenhagen: 1946), 207-25.

44. A. S. Ørsted, "Anmeldelse af Betragtninger over Straffe i Almindelighed og over Aeresstraffe i Særdelesned af P. Kollett," in *Philosophisk Repertorium for den nyere Literatur* (Copenhagen, 1799), 262-63.

45. C. Goos, *A. S. Ørsteds Betydning for Moral- og Retsfilosofien samt Strafferetsvidenskaben* 1 (Copenhagen: 1904), 256. Fornication (lejermål) was illegal until 1812, adultery (hor) until 1933.

46. Ørsted, *Anmeldelse af Betragtninger*, 260.

47. Ibid.

48. *Anmeldelse af Betragtninger* note, p. 258.

49. Ørsted used the Danish, by now archaic, expression "det højeste sædelige gode." This implies something that is virtuous in a general moral sense, but also a high standard of purity in carnal matters, and of bourgeois respectability.

50. A. S. Ørsted, "Over de første Grundregler for Staffelovgivningen," in *Eunomia* 2d pt. (Copenhagen, 1817), 5-7, 137.

51. Ørsted, "Over de forste Grundregler," 182.

52. Cf. A. von Feuerbach, "Revision der Grundsätze und Grundbegriffe des positiven peinlichen Rechts," *Erfurt/Chenitz* (Erfurt, 1799-1800), 1:13-17; 2:226-27.

53. "Unnatural sensuality" (unaturlig vellyst) is the expression Ørsted mostly used. There is no reason to believe that he considered anything but "unnatural" *acts* to be punishable, but there are reasons to believe that he realized that habitude or habituation was involved.

54. Ørsted, "Over de forste Grundregler," 183-84.

55. Ørsted, "Over de forste Grundregler," 183-85, cf. 93-95. Cf. Feuerbach, "Revision der Grundsatze," 1: 312-13; 2: 227.

56. A. S. Orsted, "(Review of) Über die Grundfehler der Behandlung des Criminalrechts in Lehr- und Strafgesetzbüchern," von Dr. C. J. A. Mittermaier (Bonn, 1819) in *Nyt juridisk Arkiv*, vol. 30, chap. 1820, 34, 39.

57. The Bavarian penal code of 1813 had no second part. Feuerbach wrote a penal code, not police regulations.

58. A. S. Ørsted, "Ausführliche Prüfung des neuen Entwurfs zu einem

Strafgesetzbuche für das Königreich Bayern, erschienen in München 1822, Kopenhagen 1823,'' 63-64. Cf. Bleibtreu-Ehrenberg, *Tabu Homosexualitat*, 321.

59. A. von Feuerbach, ''Uber die Polizeistraf-Gesetzgebung überhaupt und den Zweiten Theil eines ''Entwurfs des Strafgsetzbuchs, München 1822,'' in Ludwig Feuerbach, ed., *Anselm von Feuerbach's Leben und Wirken aus seinen ungedruckten Briefen und Tagebüchern, Vortragen und Denkschriften* 2 (Leipzig, 1852): 353.

60. von Spies, *Kritik der Schrift des dänischen Staats-Raths Dr. Oerstedt über den Entwurf zu einem Strafgesetzbuche für das Königreich Baiern* (Landshut, 1825), 40. The several other books and articles, including Ørsted's rebuttal in 1826, did not mention the point of interest here.

61. Monter, ''Sodomy and Heresy,'' 51, n. 6. According to the census of 1801, Copenhagen had 100,975 inhabitants; cf. *Statistisk årbog* (1965), 6.

62. Danske Kancelli I. 58-59, Den deputeredes protokol med bilag, no. 16; Private Archives of Cosmus Bræstrup (no. 5232), C.1.a., National Archives, Copenhagen.

63. Records of the Supreme Court: Højesteretsordener 1797sqv; Voteringsprotokol 1835 litra A, No. 107; Voteringsprotokol 1835 litra c, No. 316, National Archives.

III. THE NETHERLANDS

Sodomy in the
Dutch Republic, 1600-1725

Dirk Jaap Noordam, PhD

The more than three hundred and twenty trials held in the early 1730s in Holland and other provinces of the Dutch Republic against perpetrators of sodomy and homosexual acts have received considerable attention since the eighteenth century,[1] including in recent literature.[2] The events of 1730 were totally unanticipated by people living there at the time. The trials were seen as an example of divine wrath. According to authors in the eighteenth century, sodomites were sometimes secretly executed in the seventeenth and early eighteenth centuries.[3] But traces of those horrible crimes were often erased when judicial records concerning sodomy were destroyed.

Although investigation into the different crimes recorded in the archives has not begun in earnest, it is clear that before 1730 not many sentences against sodomites were registered. At the court of the major textile city, Leiden, only five sentences out of more than five thousand were registered during the two centuries before the mass trials in the eighteenth century.[4] In the same period, the Court of Holland, which had jurisdiction over the central part of the cosmopolitan city, The Hague, sentenced only two sodomites to death, one of whom was tried for sacrilege and forgery as well.[5] In Breda, a small provincial town in the South of the Republic, only one sentence against a perpetrator of unnatural fornication was registered during the period 1626 to 1730.[6] Some of the sentences in these cities and in other cities as well, were executed in secret.[7] Entries in

---

Dr. Dirk Jaap Noordam is Lecturer in Social History with the Rijksuniversiteit, Leiden, The Netherlands.
The research for this article was done before December 1984.

207

the register sometimes mentioned that fact as well; thus, the record of that crime had to be erased.[8]

These absolute figures are not, however, valid indicators of social trends. The sentences also yield information about cases of sodomy that were not brought to trial. Apart from the criminal archives, some depositions before notaries contain material about those unnatural crimes. The starting point of my study is 1600 because of the fact that only from the seventeenth century, the "Golden Age" of the Dutch Republic, forward are systematic investigations of criminal records possible. This article deals with why such a small number of sentences against sodomites was entered in the registers, the way the perpetrators of this offense were regarded, and the foundation of this view. Was there a gradual development in the cases and the trials against sodomites, or does the period 1600 to 1725 have to be subdivided because some important changes in the treatment or the behavior of the sodomites occurred?

THE AUTHORITIES
AND THE CRIME OF SODOMY

That the judicial archives of the period from 1600 to 1725 contain so little about sodomy is partly due to the fact that the criminal system in the Republic was basically an accusatory one; the official authorities had no independent role in tracing and prosecuting criminal acts. They acted mostly under pressure from the civilian population. This was the case in 1653 when a mother brought charges before the Court of Holland against Jacobus Frederik Litius à Wieland, the teacher of her fourteen-year-old son whom she suspected of having anal contacts with the boy. The man was not sentenced and his case was dismissed for reasons not specified by the authorities.

Sometimes they were forced to investigate criminal cases. That happened in Rotterdam in 1717 when, in a "secreet" (a public lavatory), an unfortunate sodomite touched the private parts of the man next to him, who by sheer chance happened to be the second highest judicial officer in the city. He accused other men of sodomy during his trial. Two of them were banished for life, the others for a period of twenty or twenty-five years.

From these and other cases, it is clear that the courts undertook legal proceedings in which they collected information concerning sodomitic acts, without always sentencing the sodomites. Some of those files have been preserved. When sodomy sentences were registered, they were included in the ordinary sentence books along with other crimes. These files and registers were not burned, as the witnesses of the events of 1730 thought. Moreover, the crime itself was studied and commented upon in the seventeenth and the beginning of the eighteenth century. After the publication of the penal codes of Emperor Charles V and his son Philip, who were both lords over the Netherlands, many books treating criminal law were written.[9] Among the best known were the works of Joost De Damhouder and Benedict Carpzovius, but other treatises were written as well concerning penalties for and forms of sodomy. In judicial practice sodomy meant, first of all, anal penetration between men or boys.[10] The concept could, however, be given a far broader interpretation, for sometimes "carnal knowledge" between women was also labeled as such.[11] Anal penetration of a woman by a man was also considered a sodomitic act.[12] In addition, bestiality was seen as sodomy and punished as such.[13]

The legal foundation for the prosecution of sodomites was mostly found in very general wording such as "by virtue of divine and civil laws." A more detailed wording was in many cases not possible because in many jurisdictions no penal measures against sodomy existed.[14] Only during the prosecutions of 1730 and after the execution of the first sodomites did the provinces of Holland and Groningen enact criminal laws against anal contact between men. The local courts, such as the court of Amsterdam, the largest city of the Republic, had no laws condemning sodomy or sodomitic acts.[15] This official attitude was the rule until the 1730s and, in a sense, even after the trials during those years. They prosecuted based on charges brought by civilians, but after investigating those charges they did not always bring the accused to court. Moreover, the authorities pronounced judgment on acts which were commonly considered criminal but for which there were no punitive laws. This attitude was due to a certain lack of interest on the part of the officials in such crimes, which then were called "sins," and which are now called "offenses against morality." Generally speaking, the secular authorities in the seventeenth and the beginning of the eighteenth centuries were not much interested in such matters. Adultery and prostitution were criminal offenses, but the officials hardly felt inclined to prosecute, and therefore the number of sentences in such cases was relatively small. After the church assemblies had put pressure on the civilian authorities for more than twenty years, the States of Holland, which had the authority over that important province, in 1694 finally renewed the measures against "horrible and dirty crimes."[16] But the projected result, more numerous and severe sentences, did not come about.

Some changes in the attitude and actions of the secular authorities can be detected, however, during the period from 1600 until the middle of the 1720s. The renewal of the measures against sins is not the only example of change. It will also become apparent in the way sodomites were looked upon and how their cases were treated. A break in time around 1690 is the most logical division of the period.

1600-1690:
SODOMY AS A SECONDARY CRIME

The criminal proceedings against sodomites in the Republic during the period 1600 to 1690 differed markedly from such proceedings in subsequent years. In the seventeenth century, information concerning sodomy was only gathered and trials were only held in cases of suspected or attempted anal penetration. From a legal standpoint, one man's feeling the body of another man or masturbating, kissing or inviting the other to have sexual contact did not constitute triable offenses. Even the strong suspicion of repeated anal penetration with a minor did not often bring a man in court, as can be seen in the case of a boy in Amsterdam in 1633 who was kept by his master and was not given the work he was entitled to, as his working contract stipulated.[17] The only s/m-case known is that of a young man who was deported to the Dutch East Indies because, after being beaten by a sodomite, he had stood guard while the man penetrated his friend. In this case, which came to trial in Utrecht in 1676, the active part was played by the patrician Dirk De Goijer, a former burgomaster of the city. De Goijer fled before the sentence was pronounced and was banished for life. The young penetree was sentenced to death and secretly executed. This case is a good example of the kind of sodomitic relationships which were investigated and brought to court in the seventeenth century. It was based on the unequal relationship between a more than sixty-year-old member of the ruling class of the Netherlands and two young workers. Such young men usually received money for their willingness to be used sexually.

Other sodomitic relations as well were based upon or the consequence of inequality. In the 1680s, Captain Sigismund Pape made a habit of forcing young soldiers under his command in several parts of the Republic to submit to his advances.[18] Only occasionally was a subordinate grateful for those attentions, because they proved that his master loved him. In spite of a number of sworn statements against him, Pape was not convicted.

Yet the social, physical, or financial superiority of one man was not always enough to force another to consent to sexual contact. In 1645 in Leiden, a textile worker raped a boy with whom he shared his bed but who had resisted him stubbornly. Forty years later, the vice-bailiff of the same city was tried in absence for having used a boy by forcing him with a knife at the throat to surrender to his will. The man did not succeed and, in spite of his position, had no success with two others either. Both men in Leiden were banished for life. In all of those cases, the passive party was several years younger than the man who sought sexual contact. The men upon whom the attentions were forced were usually quite young, often small boys.

The authorities, however, did not always defend the weaker party in those assaults. Sexual abuse did not always lead to the conviction of the abuser. Several depositions against the teacher Litius à Wieland proved beyond doubt that he had penetrated his pupils anally. Nevertheless, his case was dismissed before coming to trial because he denied the charge and withstood torture, thus providing no evidence against himself. His dismissal is all the more surprising because he did not even produce any witnesses to testify as to his good conduct. In the years after his dismissal, Litius continued to display sodomitic behavior. Twenty years after he was taken into custody in The Hague, his widow took legal action to obtain the inheritance of a young man who had been sheltered in their home for years.[19] The young man, Ferdinand Viskofsky, had made no secret of his intention to leave the teacher after having spent the rest of Litius' money. The young Ferdinand had posed as a member of the Wieland family in order to make his behavior acceptable to the outside world, and it was on this fictitious relationship that the widow based her claims.

If men confessed to anal penetration, they were sentenced to death. The death sentence was not executed by fire, as was the custom during the Middle Ages,[20] but by strangling. In Breda in 1636, the painter Carel De Lasco received that sentence, along with the younger worker who had been penetrated anally. But the textile worker in Leiden who raped a boy in 1645 did not confess his crime. His punishment was less severe than that of a man who was tried for raping and assaulting a girl later on in the seventeenth century. The girl's attacker was severely flogged, then banished for life.[21] Most judgments were based on clear and sometimes extensive motivations. In the case of the patrician De Goijer, the court of the city of Utrecht even consulted outside criminal lawyers. Their advice concerning culpability and argumentation was published in a treatise later on[22] and served as a part of the jurisprudence during the trials of the 1730s.[23]

The picture of sodomy in the period would be distorted if the attention was focused only on male sodomites. In the seventeenth century, some females were also tried for sodomitic activities. In the Dutch Republic some eight hundred trials against sodomites are known before 1811, of which some thirteen were against females in Amsterdam between 1792 and 1798.[24] The only other cases in which female sodomites stood trial were held in the seventeenth century—in Leiden in 1606 (one), in Amsterdam in 1641 (two), and in Leiden in 1688 (two).[25] These trials differed greatly from those in the eighteenth century.

Between 1600 and 1690, only those women were brought to court who lived in a relationship resembling marriage, in which one woman played the part of the man and even wore men's clothes. In two instances couples tried to be married by the authorities; one of them was successful, and those women continued their relationship for years. A third couple, who lived in Amsterdam, also intended to get married if the authorities allowed it, which they did not. One of these women was Hendrikje Verschuur, who earlier in her role as a man had served as a soldier in the army of the Netherlands until she was discovered.[26] The record of two of the five women was tainted not only because they had gone around as men, but also because they had deserted their husbands. Nevertheless, the combination of sodomy, desertion of a husband, travesty, and a false marriage was punished in all cases by banishment only. It was a relatively light sentence, also in view of the confessions by the women that they had lain with a woman and done what men did. In 1688 the punishment of the women in Leiden amounted to twelve years of banishment for a combination of the four crimes mentioned above, which is hardly more severe than the sentences of six and ten years banishment, respectively, that a male bigamist received in 1697 and a female bigamist received in 1682. In every case against the female sodomites, the sodomitic activities seem to have barely influenced the judgment. Sodomy itself was not punished, but instead other activities, of which pretending to live in a normal relationship and faking a marriage seem to have been the most important.

Only in a few cases of male or female sodomites in the seventeenth century is it known what people other than the authorities and the informers thought about sodomitic acts and about the men and women who committed them. The vice-bailiff of Leiden had been practicing sodomy for years, and Captain Pape and the teacher Litius also had long-standing records of such activities. Those facts were known but only came out during trial and in depositions. Until then, the attentions younger men and boys received from them had not led to lawsuits. The same was the case with the patrician De Goijer, of whose sodomitic career little is known except that once, two years before his imprisonment and his subsequent escape, he had engaged in sodomitic activities.

Public reaction regarding sodomitic behavior was far less severe early in the eighteenth century than during the mass trials of the 1730s. Nor were the official authorities inclined to deal with sodomites in a harsh way. Gathering incriminating evidence did not always result in the trial of a sodomite, even if the evidence was heavily stacked against him. This explains why sodomy, which was one of the most serious offenses according to seventeenth century jurisprudence, only rarely led to a trial. Furthermore, it seems probable that when they did prosecute, the authorities did so not because of the sodomitic behavior of the accused, but because of the other offenses he or she had committed, such as rape, travesty, or bigamy.

1690-1725:
THE RISE OF SUBCULTURES

In the period 1690 to 1725, changes took place both in the way the courts conceived of the phenomenon of sodomy and the way they dealt with it. At the same time, patterns of sodomitic behavior evolved that can best be described as subcultural, meaning that the activities of perpetrators of sodomitic acts were, during that period, concentrated in certain areas, and the men involved developed a code to recognize people of the same kind and organized special meetings for having sexual contact.

The first traces of the rise of these subcultures are discernable in the trials held in Amsterdam in 1689 against four men accused of blackmail and extortion.[27] This gang of men in their early twenties would accost men in the neighborhood of the Exchange or of the town hall situated nearby, usually grabbing the victims' pants. Rarely did the gang actually handle their victims' private parts directly or indulge in any further sexual contacts with their victims. These corporal contacts only took place after changing and responding to the code; namely, stepping on one another's foot. Whatever else happened, the gang always extorted money from the men. Usually they were not content with the sum the victim gave, and after robbing him they followed him to his home or another place where he could get more money for them. The gang consisted of a fluctuating number of youngsters because sometimes members left Amsterdam under the flag of the East Indies Company. The head of the gang was hanged, and the other three youngsters were sentenced to detention in the house of correction.

The town hall of the biggest city in the Republic remained a cruising center for sodomites, as is shown by what happened some years later to Jan Van Lennep, a member of an important merchant family. He was accosted there by another man with whom he then committed sodomy in the building itself.[28] Another area for extortioners in Amsterdam was the public lavatories. There a gang of young men engaged in criminal activities in the middle of the 1720s.[29] Their victims were usually innocent but wealthy men, whom they treated even more insolently than their colleagues did forty years earlier (if that was possible). They succeeded in keeping their actions from the law for at least ten years. In 1735 they were finally brought to trial, and received the same sentences as the gang in 1689: the leader was hanged, his accomplices confined. In the 1720s, there were also other places in Amsterdam frequented by sodomites; for instance, the inn "The Serpent" at the fishmarket,[30] near the town hall.

During the interrogations held in 1702 before the Court of Holland, information came out that young men in The Hague also made a habit of extorting money from real or supposed sodomites. For these activities, not for his sodomitic acts, Gabriel Du Bergé was sentenced to death. The tactics he and his friends employed were the same as in Amsterdam, but with some differences in the geographical setting. The area in which the activities of this group of about five youngsters took place was the rectangle formed by the broad and shady lanes of the Voorhout and Vijverberg. This cruising area was situated in the vicinity of the city forest, the Haagse Bos, a place well suited for sexual contact. The lanes were frequented by sodomites, either in men's clothes or in travesty, and also by prostitutes of both sexes.

In 1702 the sodomites in The Hague had a code of recognition that differed somewhat from that used in Amsterdam: they pulled at the arm of another man, urinated, or waved their handkerchief. The phenomenon of criminal extortion of sodomites was then also internationally known, as is shown by a conversation held by Gabriel Du Bergé, the young extortioner who left the protection of his commander in the army in which he was serving. Gabriel invited a friend to go with him to England, where the possibilities of robbing sodomitic lords were even greater than in The Hague. The subculture and cruising area around the Vijverberg and Voorhout remained in existence throughout the eighteenth century and were mentioned not only during the trials of the 1730s, but also later on.[31]

Another trace left by the subculture dates from the beginning of that century. In 1702 in The Hague, a house was mentioned of which the inhabitants were sodomites who entertained friends. Somewhat later, in 1717, an inn existed in the city where it was possible to spend the night with a bedfellow of the same sex, which was allowed by the innkeeper, who was "of that sort of people" ("mede van dat volk") himself.[32]

In the same year, signs of a subculture in a third Dutch city, Rotterdam, became visible. According to two witnesses, the sexual activities in Rotterdam differed from those that were common in The Hague in that sodomy itself was seldom practiced in this harbor city.[33] Homosexual activities were concentrated in public lavatories, of which during the trials at least five were mentioned. Before the men engaged in mutual masturbation, it had to be decided if the other man was a sodomite, too. The signals of recognition could take different forms. For instance, they played with their own organ, thereafter with the other man's, or they moved close to the other and took his private parts directly. Although in 1717 no less than eight men were caught in Rotterdam, they were only a few of the many who visited the lavatories with the purpose of having sexual contact. Thirteen years later, two men confessed that they had indulged in masturbation with some of the men caught in 1717. However, they were not prosecuted.[34]

By the middle of the 1710s and the beginning of the 1720s, a similar subculture had developed around the lavatories of two smaller cities in Holland, Schiedam and Gouda.[35] In Leiden there was a cruising area alongside the Rapenburg, the principal canal.[36] Courting took place in that textile city at central places in the open air. Such was also the case in Amsterdam and Rotterdam. In Utrecht that purpose was served by, among other areas, the St. Janskerhof, a church tower in the vicinity of the Dom.[37]

The number of inns in which sodomites gathered rose gradually in Amsterdam and The Hague during those years,[38] and new inns of that kind could also be found in Utrecht.[39] Other places with a similar but more private character came into being so as to deter detection. In 1725 the most important such place in The Hague was that of Willem Van Schalen, who was employed by the States of Holland. The house of Van Schalen was a haunt of some fifty sodomites in the middle of the 1720s.[40] Van Schalen gave up his governmental duties at the age of forty and left the city.

From the beginning of the eighteenth century onwards, other similar forms of meetings existed. Circles of friends regularly met in most of the major cities, as is attested to by the interrogations of the 1730s. At that time, even the smaller provincial centers Leeuwarden and Zwolle had such circles of friends who met in one of their member's houses with the purpose of having sexual contact.[41] In the major cities, several of those groups flourished,[42] and had by then for decades.

Immediately after his settlement in Utrecht in 1700, a city of about twenty-five thousand inhabitants, the wine merchant Barend Blomsaet came into contact with a circle of friends who belonged, like he did, to the middle class.[43] Some years later, he joined another group consisting of men of the same social status. At the time of peace negotiations held at Utrecht in 1713, another circle existed around Jan Van Lennep, who had gone bankrupt in Amsterdam and who lived in his new city as a canon. Most of its members did not visit the house of Blomsaet or his friends.[44] A fourth circle of Utrecht prior to 1730 was formed by Dirk Vonk.[45]

In Haarlem, as well, a group of sodomitic friends had developed before 1724, but its members were recruited from among men with very different backgrounds.[46] A common weaver was a member of that circle, but also Willem Six, a member of the town council. A certain social hierarchy existed in this group, as is attested to by the election held by these sodomites. In a remote part of the city forest, the Haarlemmerhout, where the men gathered, a king was chosen. Not surprisingly, the election was won by Six, which gave him the right to be the first to withdraw with his favorite.

More permanent relationships sometimes developed between men in these circles who knew each other well. Some men lived together and were bedfellows for years, as was the case with Dirk Vonk and Rijk jerkroost in Utrecht.[47] More exclusive was the "marriage contract" that two young sodomites made in The Hague, which stipulated that they would have sexual contact with any third man only after the other partner was informed of such intentions.[48] In Leeuwarden these kinds of relations were based on strict monogamy; the sign that two men belonged to each other was the word "nicht" (female cousin), with which they addressed one another.[49] Such expressions were used in other places as well for indicating a fellow sodomite, and occasionally such terms bore a very local character. The term "vlaggeman" (flagman) was employed only by inhabitants of Rotterdam, whereas in The Hague "nichtje" (diminutive of female cousin) was the expression.[50] But the other world was wholly ignorant of the existence and the meaning of those terms.[51] The verb "kaleboeren" meant to masturbate[52] and was probably a corruption of a French word. More general, also among the common people, was the word "boegeren,"[53] the term for anal contact that has the same etymology and meaning as the English verb to bugger. In Dutch the anal penetrator or penetree was called a "bouger."[54]

The fact that someone took part in the meetings of a circle of friends, involving all sorts of exclusive habits and conversation, did not mean necessarily that he restricted his sexual contacts to members of that group. Barend Blomsaet, the wine merchant in Utrecht, often recruited men and boys in the streets. He usually gave some money for their service, but the amount differed, even for similar activities or for the same bedfellow. Sometimes he offered a drink in return instead of money, a meal, or shelter. This type of payment closely resembled heterosexual prostitution in Leiden in the eighteenth century, where no fixed prices for the services existed either and the reward was often something other than money.[55] The unequal relations so prominent among perpetrators of sodomitic activities prior to 1690 did not entirely disappear in the period afterwards. One man often depended on the other in that, for instance, he had a position in his house as footman or journeyman.[56] Those relationships could only exist when the dependent party was of a certain age. In Utrecht a man complained that it was very easy for him to earn a lot of money when he was sixteen years old, but that it was quite impossible to do so now, seventeen years later.[57] Other examples in the interrogations of the 1730s prove that boys were in great demand as long as they were young and handsome. After the boys' charms had dwindled, the sodomites among them could not earn their bread in that fashion any longer and had to satisfy their sexual needs by other means.

Yet it was possible to make contacts of an anonymous character in the streets;[58] for instance, in dark public lavatories. Other places could also yield contacts with men who were total strangers before the meeting. In the inns, at fairs, and in the neighborhood of the-aters where comedies were performed, it was rather easy to find a man willing to engage in some quick sex. Sometimes the actual sexual contact took place in the area where a man had been re-cruited. The town hall of Amsterdam, the Haagse Bos, and the Haarlemmerhout have already been cited as examples, but there were other spots along the cruising area, too.[59] These places were mostly used only for feeling and mutual masturbation, as there was always the risk of being discovered in those public areas. In order to have anal contact a room in an inn or at home was usually preferred.

In the period 1690 to 1725 more places than those named in the interrogations must have existed. Nowadays, though, it was almost impossible to determine where they were located. For a sodomite in the eighteenth century, however, it is possible to find such places after a short time, and even a stranger could join a circle of friends quite easily, as the example of Barend Blomsaet proves. Those groups had to be relatively open because they lost members, too, due to the fact that the population of the Republic was highly mo-bile, especially in the numerous cities spread all over the territory. Young men in their late teens and early twenties sometimes spent time away from their parents' home while learning a job. Some occupations demanded great geographical mobility, as was the case with footmen and soldiers. Two of the best known sodomites in 1730, Zacharias Wilsma and Casper Bersé, were members of those professions.[60]

Some older men also led transient lives, selling goods at market-places and fairs or working as comedians. Most of these sodomites were over thirty years old, were usually married and had children. In these respects they were not different from the men who engaged in sodomitic activities later on in the eighteenth century.[61] Some traits in their behavior were different from those detected before 1690. Examples of these differences have been cited: for instance, the concentration of sexual activities in certain places, the participa-tion in circles of friends, the signs and the code of recognition, the masquerade of men. An aspect which has not yet been mentioned was a form of womanly behavior or a way of speaking called "John girlish" ("op zijn janmeisjes").[62]

With our present knowledge, it would be too farfetched to retrace the modern homosexual back to what has been found in the archives of the period 1690 to 1730. Several examples of such men have, however, been found in the second half of the eighteenth century: men who declared that the sexual contacts they wished to have were with males or who stated that they were born that way.[63] Still, there were some sodomites in the period 1690 to 1725 whose lives differed even from those of common sodomites—whose lives, in turn were deviant from the lives of sodomites prior to 1690.

The best example of this was a certain Cornelis Boersema, who lived his whole life in De Hoorn, a small village near Warfhuizen in the Northern part of the province of Groningen, where he was born around 1645.[64] During the interrogations held in 1730, he stated several times that never in his long life had he slept with a woman or felt a female's private parts because he loathed such corporal contacts. His pleasure lay in touching men, in seeing and feeling their private parts. He continued these activities even after having been punished by the local priest, who had warned him that he could get the death penalty for such behavior. In spite of the fact that part of the punishment was sheer humiliation, sitting on the back benches in the church, he could not restrain himself from looking at young men and complimenting them on their good looks. Boersema got a rather light sentence because he had to pay a fine of 500 guilders.

Canon Jan Ven Lennep, born in Amsterdam but who lived most of his adult life in Utrecht, was not keen on women either. True, at the age of twenty-eight he married a lady belonging, like himself, to the upper classes of the Republic. But the marriage was childless and broke up after a short time. Thereafter, he spent his time with men only, walked around in drag from time to time, and entertained a circle of friends at his home. He had anal contact with some of them, but during the trial he wished to name only those who had already been executed.[65] He, too, was later executed.

Rijk Verkroost, born in Utrecht in 1690, is a third example of a man with new and different characteristics. He was said to have led a very active sexual life, during which, before he reached the age of forty, he had seduced more than one hundred men and initiated them into the pleasures of sodomy.[66] In addition, Rijk had a more or less exclusive relationship with Dirk Vonk. Dirk was the same age as Rijk and the two lived together for a couple of years. Rijk remained a bachelor after the first trials in 1730. It then became necessary to clear his name of the repeated allegations that he was an energetic sodomite. Although the marriage Rijk then contracted remained childless, he was not prosecuted for sodomy.

It can be concluded from these examples that sodomites could be detected by anyone who was observant. The characteristics of sodomitic behavior were so obvious that some of those men could even be recognized as deviating somewhat from the normal pattern. The fact that men were blackmailed for being sodomites makes it apparent that such behavior was stigmatized during the period 1690 to 1725. The men who were blackmailed usually were wealthy and probably feared losing their good name. However, they probably did not fear being considered a sodomite as much as they feared being discovered involved with people outside their social class. The allegation of breaking the barriers of the hierarchical society that the Dutch Republic had become at the end of the seventeenth century was a heavier menace than being looked upon as a perpetrator of sodomitic acts.

Neither stigmatization nor prosecution of sodomites was characteristic of the attitude of the official authorities in the Republic before 1725. Among the common people, apparent sodomitic behavior was not a reason for ostracizing someone. Nevertheless, some men got into trouble. Frequent visits of sodomites to a room or house could force a landlord to give notice to his apparently deviant teneant. Sometimes, sodomites were pointed at or, when denounced as "buggers," thrown out of an inn.[67] Reactions against apparent sodomites were usually limited to such actions; acts of physical violence were rarely mentioned. Even when a man did not respond to the sexual advances of a sodomite acquaintance, the two usually still maintained social contact.

Most of the passes and advances did not lead to judicial actions. However, when a sodomite was brought to court, it was often possible to draw up a long list of his offenses. In the course of such proceedings it became clear that sodomitic acts were more numerous than at first believed. This was frequently the case in the major cities, from which most of the facts date and where the climate for sodomitic behavior was probably more tolerant than elsewhere.

Nevertheless, the same tolerance was also found in smaller communities. Cornelis Boersema reached the age of 85 without legal steps taken against him for his sexual behavior. Similarly, inhabitants of the village of Hilversum or the small town of Woerden, who displayed the same pattern of activities, were left alone for years.[68]

It is difficult to compare the attitudes of the common people toward sodomy during the years 1690 to 1725 with the attitudes held prior to the 1690s because of a lack of sufficient data on the subject for the latter period. The perception and treatment of sodomites by the official authorities, on the other hand, are well known in both periods. Before 1690, the purpose of the judges (as stated earlier in this study) was not so much to punish sodomites, as to punish those guilty of rape, bigamy, and travesty — offenses linked in those cases with sodomitic acts. These three crimes were punished as heavily when they occurred in other relations. Sodomy, as such, was an action rarely dealt with by the courts. When a man confessed to having had active or passive anal contact, he was sentenced to death; women confessing the same were banished. Some of these sentences were executed in secret, but registered normally along with records of other crimes. Many such records have survived, even some that did not lead to a sentence.

In some respects, the attitudes toward sodomites and the administration of cases against them remained the same. In Amsterdam in 1710, the authorities did not press charges against a man who kissed another man in public and invited him to go upstairs with him.[69] In Rotterdam a year later, a man confessed to having committed sodomy, but he appeared mentally unstable, and perhaps for that reason was dismissed.[70] However, it was new that in most cases sodomy was no longer treated as a secondary crime, but as an independent offense. Proceedings were instigated where they had not been before, as was seen in Rotterdam in 1717 in which some men were accused of mutual masturbation. In more closed social circles, sodomy was handled harshly: in the same city of Rotterdam, a young man living in the municipal orphanage was sentenced to death in 1702 along with the younger boy with whom he had had anal contact. On ships, sodomites were sentenced to death. Five sailors who had sodomized one another were drowned in the canals of Den Helder in 1707.[71] Strangling, however, remained the principal form of executions of sodomites on land, just as in the seventeenth century.

The judicial criteria for sentencing sodomy were, as earlier, very vague and general. A new standard developed when the motivation of those accused became a factor in persecuting sodomitic acts. In Utrecht in 1676 a young man was beaten up, which was seen as a form of sodomitic action. It had to be considered as such because it was linked to two men who had committed sodomy on the same spot in the presence of the unfortunate youngster. In Rotterdam in 1717, a link between masturbation and sodomy was made although there was no clear reason for making masturbation punishable on that ground. Some lawyers did not consider masturbation a crime,[72] but it could be seen as such when connected with sodomy. In that sense the court of Rotterdam made masturbation a punishable offense and sentenced the masturbators to various terms of banishment. The theory of gradation developed here, defining masturbation as a preparation for or first step to anal penetration, was also used to sentence the less guilty Cornelis Boersema who had felt the private parts of men but not played with them. In his case, the sentence was given only upon the advice of several lawyers. Nevertheless, that opinion and the theory of gradation were subject to discussion later in the eighteenth century.[73]

Sodomy and other homosexual acts were certainly not seen and treated as the horrible crimes the witnesses of the trials of the 1730s and their successors thought them to be. Although systematic investigations into the criminal archives have as yet been limited, it is clear from all the examples cited that more trials for sodomy and sodomitic activities were held in the beginning of the eighteenth century than before. This greater interest manifested itself quantitatively and qualitatively: the records were more extensive and more detailed. This was due partly to the fact that all proceedings were based on firmer evidence and were better prepared, but this is not the complete explanation. The increasing attention to sodomy was also connected to the rise of certain other trials. All "offenses against morality" came to trial more frequently at the beginning of the eighteenth century. In Leiden, where it is possible to analyze the cases in detail, adultery was sentenced more frequently during that period.[74] In the 1720s, strong action was taken by the authorities in that textile city against prostitutes and some brothels. This wave proves that concern about sexual contacts outside marriage was increasing. In the seventeenth century, there was less reason to proceed harshly against sodomy, prostitution, and adultery because marriage then seemed to be an inviolable institution in Leiden. When, as elsewhere in the Calvinist Republic, the magistrate began allowing the dissolution of marriages and a general loosening of the bond of marriage — namely, legal separation — more and more married couples began living apart from the end of the seventeenth century onward.[75] Such separations were much more common among the lower classes than among the higher social classes. The ruling aristocracy of Leiden considered these developments not only as a violation of, but also as a potential threat to the whole social order of the country.

In the beginning of May 1730, a letter from the government of the city of Utrecht arrived in Leiden with the message that certain inhabitants of Leiden had been named as sodomites in the interrogations of Zacharias Wilsma. Small wonder, then, that the authorities in Leiden gladly accepted this information as an opening for them to proceed against this form of extramarital relations. (It goes almost without saying that the members of the ruling class, a burgomaster and a son of a former burgomaster, who were mentioned several times as sodomites, were spared in these actions.) It should be investigated whether this explanation, which strongly underlines the continuity of the developments in the seventeenth century and the beginning of the eighteenth century, and which is also proven by most of the legal actions and by the patterns of behavior of sodomites themselves, holds true for other cities and villages in the Republic as well. However, it is certain that the mass trials of 1730 to 1732 did not come out of the blue, but had solid roots in the past.

NOTES

1. See the survey in: L. S. A. M. Von Römer, "Der Uranismus in den Niederlanden bis zum 19. Jahrhundert, mit besonderer Berücksichtigung der grossen Uranierverfolgung im Jahre 1730. Eine historische und bibliographische Skizze," *Jahrbuch für sexuelle Zwischenstufen* 8 (1906): 424-91.

2. See L. J. Boon, "De grote sodomietenvervolging in het gewest Holland,

1730-1732," *Holland* 8 (1976): 140-52, and the articles in *Groniek* 12 nr. 66 (1980) and *Spiegel Historiael* 17 (1982): 545-603.

3. Contemporaries spoke of sodomites as "sometimes" having been executed in secret, see the advice of W. Van Erpecum and J. Stael of 17 June 1730: Algemeen Rijksarchief, Raad van State, nr. 796, 1 (date 4 July 1730). D. Van Hogendorp, who edited the translation in Dutch of B. Carpzovius, *Verhandeling der lyfstraffelyke misdaden en haare berechtinge* (Rotterdam, 1752), expressed the same opinion (p. 642). It was widely read J. Wagenaar, *Vaderlandsche historie* 19 (Amsterdam, 1748): 37, who replaced "sometimes" by "often." Boon, in *Sodomietenvervolging*, 140, followed Wagenaar, but added in "Het jaar waarin elke jongen een meisje nam; de sodomietenvervolgingen in Holland in 1730," *Groniek* 12 nr. 66 (1980), 16: that the judicial records concerning sodomy were destroyed and quoted as his source the advice of Van Erpecum and Stael. His opinion has been repeated in most studies since then.

4. D. J. Noordam, "Homosexualiteit en sodomie in Leiden, 1533-1811," *Leids Jaarboekje* 75 (1983): 77.

5. Both in the sixteenth century, in 1538 and in 1548.

6. J. van Haastert, "Beschouwingen bij de criminele vonnissen van de schepenbank van de stad Breda uit de jaren 1626 tot 1795," *Jaarboek van de geschied–en oudheidkundige kring van stad en land van Breda "De Oranjeboom"* 29 (1976): 56-106.

7. In Leiden in 1606, in Utrecht in 1676 and 1721, in Rotterdam in 1702 and 1717.

8. Gemeentearchief Rotterdam, Schepenarchief, nr. 207, fol. 128.

9. See A. H. Huussen, "Gerechtelijke vervolging van 'sodomie' gedurende de 18e eeuw in de Republiek, in het bijzonder in Friesland," *Groniek* 12 nr. 66 (1980): 18-33.

10. So in Rotterdam in 1702.

11. As in Leiden in 1606, and in Amsterdam in 1641.

12. Pieter Spierenburg, *The Spectacle of Suffering. Executions and the Evolution of Repression: From a Preindustrial Metropolis to the European Experience* (Cambridge: Cambridge University Press, 1984), 76.

13. In Texel in 1711.

14. Von Rëmer, *Uranismus*, 376-88.

15. Spierenburg, *Spectacle*, 125.

16. *Groot Placcaatboek*, vol. 4 (Den Haag, 1705), 340-41.

17. Gemeentearchief Amsterdam, Notariële archieven, nr. 447, fols. 30-30v, 33.

18. Algemeen Rijksarchief, Hof van Holland, nr. 5337-1.

19. Gemeentearchief Den Haag, Notariële archieven, nr. 448, 99; 472, 111-111v; 599, 139-139v; 621, 179; 791, 184, 200, 218-20, 246-48.

20. Dick Berents, *Misdaad in de Middeleeuwen. Een onderzoek naar de criminaliteit in het laat-Middeleeuwse Utrecht* (Bloemendaal: Amiciha, 1976), 108-9 and "Homoseksualiteit en criminaliteit in de Middeleeuwen," *Groniek* 12

nr. 66 (1980): 10-13, R. I. A. Nip, "Bengaert Say, een 15de eeuws ambtenaar," *Holland* 15 (1983): 67, 72.

21. Noordam, *Homosexualiteit*, 80.

22. I. Van den Berg (ed.), *Neder-lands Advys-boek inhoudende verscheide consultatien en advysen van voornaamste regtsgeleerden in Nederland*, vol. 2 (Amsterdam, 1722): 427-30.

23. *Requeste en deductie mitsgaders advisen en bylagen in de zake van Joan Lucas Bouwens inedaagde in persoon* . . . (Amsterdam, 1732?).

24. Theo van der Meer, *De wesentlijke sonde van sodomie en andere vuyligheeden. Sodomietenvervolgingen in Amsterdam 1730-1811* (Amsterdam: Tabula, 1984): 137-47.

25. The cases in Leiden were studied by Noordam, *Homosexualiteit*, 77-81; those in Amsterdam by Rudolf Dekker and Lotte van de Pol, *Daar was laatst een meisje loos. Nederlandse vrouwen als matrozen en soldaten, een historisch onderzoek* (Baarn: Ambo, 1981); and by Van der Meer, *Sonde*, 138-39. Gemeentearchief Amsterdam, Rechterlijk archief, nr. 304, fol. 236 and following also contains data on this trial.

26. See the studies mentioned in note 25 concerning Amsterdam.

27. See also for these trials the study by P. C. Spierenburg, "De dood op bevel van de rechter. Een verkennende historisch-sociologische beschouwing," in G. A. Banck (ed.), *Gestalten van de dood. Studies over abortus, euthanasie, rouw, zelfmoord en doodslag* (Baarn: Ambo, 1980), 131-32.

28. Gemeentearchief Utrecht, Secretariearchief II, nr. 2244, year 1730 I, deposition of 21 September 1730.

29. Gemeentearchief Amsterdam, Rechterlijk archief, nr. 393, fols. 12v, 15.

30. Boon, *Sodomietenvervolging*, 142.

31. D. J. Noordam, "Homoseksuele relaties in Holland in 1776," *Holland* 16 (1984): 11, 16-18.

32. Gemeentearchief Rotterdam, Schepenarchief, nr. 121, fol. 218.

33. Ibid., nr. 103, fol. 57; nr. 121, fols. 216v-217.

34. Ibid., nr. 123, fols. 151, 155.

35. Ibid., nr. 121, fol. 212. Algemeen Rijksarchief, Rechterlijk archief Woerden, nr. 16, deposition of 26 January 1731.

36. Noordam, *Homosexualiteit*, 95.

37. Gemeentearchief Utrecht, Secretariearchief 2, nr. 2236, period 1713-1727, 931; nr. 2244, year 1730 I, deposition of 1 September 1730 by Van Lennep.

38. Boon, *Jaar*, 16; Van der Meer, *Sonde*, 170.

39. L. J. Boon, "'Utrechtenaren': de sodomieprocessen in Utrecht, 1730-1732," *Spiegel Historiael* 17 (1982): 554.

40. Gemeentearchief Rotterdam, Schepenarchief, nr. 123, fols. 168-70. Gemeentearchief Haarlem, Rechterlijk archief, nr. 64 I, fol. 1v.

41. Rijksarchief Friesland, Hof van Friesland, GG 85, depositions of 19 September 1730 by Wilsma, of 6 October 1730 by Hansen, and of 13 October 1730 by Floris. Gemeentearchief Zwolle, Rechterlijk archief, nr. 601, 325-27, 417.

42. Gemeentearchief Zwolle, Rechterlijk archief, nr. 601, 342.

43. Gemeentearchief Utrecht, Secretariearchief II, nr. 2244, year 1730 I, deposition of 17 March 1730 and of 24 March 1730.

44. Ibid., deposition of 29 August 1730 by Van den Bosch.

45. Ibid., deposition of 28 June 1732.

46. Algemeen Rijksarchief, Hof van Holland, nr. 5420-23, deposition of 10 June 1730 by Van Stein, quoting the weaver Sonneveld, who died in 1724, according to Gemeentearchief Haarlem, Rechterlijk archief, nr. 64 I, fols. 32-32v.

47. Gemeentearchief Utrecht, Secretariearchief II, nr. 2244, year 1730 II, deposition of 1 September 1730 by Vonk and of 4 June 1732 by Pinckenie.

48. Noordam, *Homosexualiteit*, 82.

49. Rijksarchief Friesland, Hof van Friesland, GG 85, deposition of 17 October 1730 by Hansen.

50. Gemeentearchief Rotterdam, Schepenarchief, nr. 103, fols. 55v, 216; 121, fol. 189v.

51. Huussen, *Vervolging*, 22.

52. Gemeentearchief Rotterdam, Schepenarchief, nr. 121, fol. 189v.

53. Ibid., nr. 262, deposition of 18 April 1711.

54. Gemeentearchief Utrecht, Secretariearchief II, nr. 2244, year 1730 I, deposition of 19 January 1730 by Van Baden.

55. D. J. Noordam, "Prostitutie in Leiden in de 18de eeuw," in D. E. H. De Boer (ed.), *Leidse facetten. Tien studies over Leidse geschiedenis* (Zutphen: Waanders, 1982) 76-79.

56. Boon, *Sodomietenvervolging*, 144-45.

57. Gemeentearchief Utrecht, Secretariearchief II, nr. 2244, year 1730 II, deposition of 2 September 1730 by Van Renes.

58. Gemeentearchief Utrecht, Secretariearchief II, nr. 2244, year 1730 I, deposition of 24 February 1730 by Van Wijck and of 13 March 1730 by Blomsaet. Gemeentearchief Amsterdam, Rechterlijk archief, nr. 536, fols. 32v, 37.

59. Boon, *Sodomietenvervolging*, 142.

60. Boon, *Utrechtenaren*, 556; Huussen, *Vervolging*, 20.

61. Noordam, *Homosexualiteit*, 93-94, and *Relaties*, 21.

62. Boon, *Sodomietenvervolging*, 144.

63. Noordam, *Relaties*, 23, and *Homosexualiteit*, 72-76, 92-93; Huussen, *Vervolging*, 29.

64. Rijksarchief Groningen, Rechterlijke archieven, XL e*, depositions of 6 September and 23 October 1730.

65. Gemeentearchief Utrecht, Secretariearchief II, nr. 2244, year 1730 I, deposition of 18 September 1730.

66. Ibid., deposition of 21 March 1730 by Van Baden.

67. Boon, *Sodomietenvervolging*, 147. Gemeentearchief Utrecht, Secretariearchief II, nr. 2244, year 1730 I, deposition of 19 January 1730 by Van Baden.

68. Rijksarchief Noord-Holland, Rechterlijk archief Naarden, nr. 3044, depositions of 15 November 1730. Algemeen Rijksarchief, Rechterlijk archief Woerden, nr. 6, depositions of 26 January 1731.

69. Gemeentearchief Amsterdam, Notariële archieven, nr. 4393, 927-31.
70. Gemeentearchief Rotterdam, Schepenarchief, nr. 262.
71. Huussen, *Vervolging*, 20.
72. Algemeen Rijksarchief, Hof van Holland, nr. 5661, fols. 112-15.
73. Noordam, *Relaties*, 28.
74. Noordam, *Homosexualiteit*, 79-81, 90-92, 95-98.
75. Donald Haks, *Huwelijk en gezin in Holland in de 17de en 18de eeuw. Processtukken en moralisten over aspecten van het laat 17de- en 18de-eeuwse gezinsleven* (Assen: van Gorcum, 1982), 184-90.

Sodomy at Sea
and at the Cape of Good Hope
During the Eighteenth Century

Jan Oosterhoff, PhD

During the eighteenth century in the Netherlands, sodomy was heavily punished, generally with the death sentence if the act could be proven. Yet the number of sodomy cases was relatively low comparing the total number of criminal cases in the Netherlands. In Leiden during the seventeenth century, only five criminal cases against sodomy were recorded. Between 1731 and 1811 (the year the *code Napoleon* was introduced in the Netherlands) twenty-one cases in Leiden were recorded.[1] During the same period in Amsterdam, 119 persons were prosecuted for sodomy.[2] Between 1533 and 1811, only 47 out of 6,500 criminal records in Leiden concerned sodomy.[3] The Netherlands, however, formed an equal balanced sex-ratio society.

One can ask if punishment against same sex acts was more severe or more frequent in an almost male or male-dominated society because of the required discipline. Moreover, one can ask if the perception of homosexual practices like sodomy was different in such a community. For that reason, I have focused on the Dutch in the eighteenth century on ships of the Dutch East India Company (VOC). These ships were sailing between the Netherlands and Asia. Traveling both directions, they landed in the Cape Colony to take on supplies. At the same time, the ships left there the prisoners who could not be judged on board because of the severity of their crimes.

The Colony had been founded in 1652 as a supplies station. The intention of the Dutch East India Company was to trade with the indigenous people, the Khoisan. This plan never succeeded. The

Khoisan were slowly displaced by European, mostly Dutch farmers and reduced to the status of slaves. By the beginning of the eighteenth century, the Cape Colony had developed a characteristic economic pattern. The center was the port of Cape Town, built around the VOC castle. Between sixty and eighty-five ships sailed into the port every year during the first half of the eighteenth century. In the middle of the eighteenth century, about 6,000 adult males (including more than 3,400 slaves) and 1,700 adult women (including almost 900 slaves) lived in Cape Town.[4] According to a 1749 census, there were 344 men to every 100 women. The imbalance of the sex ratio was not so exceptional, however, because of the existence of Company slaves, about 650 in addition to the private slaves. There was also an unknown number of Khoisan. On the other hand, the number of inhabitants excluded the crews of the about seventy ships that spent an average of a month at a time in the Cape Colony. These figures led to the conclusion that many men, in any case those on the ships, could not have been able to find wives. The majority of these men were slaves and low-level Company sailors and soldiers.

I have used for my research the archives of the Dutch East India Company, the criminal records of the trials held before the Court of Justice in Cape Town. These documents form a continuous series from 1705 to 1792.[5] Each year about one to five sodomy trials were held out of a total number of about fifty to sixty trials. During that period about 150 sodomy trials were conducted against more than 200 men. Women were never prosecuted for sodomy in the Cape Colony. The percentage of sodomy trials here seems considerably higher than during the same period in Leiden in the Netherlands, about five percent compared with less than one percent in the last case.[6] The criminal records of the Court Justice in Cape Town ranged from desertion, mutiny, conspiracy, and violence to robbery, adultery, murder, and sodomy. The sodomy cases were never recorded in a secret file. The men who committed such crimes on ships were after arrival held in prison in Cape Town before they were led before the Court of Justice. There are no examples of prosecution for prostitution. According to contemporary reports, a large number of slave women of Cape Town were prostitutes, and a certain proportion of the slave men acted as pimps. The Company's slave lodge acted as the main brothel, mainly serving the soldiers of the visiting ships.[7] There is no evidence of male prostitution among the slave men.

The sodomy trials can be divided into those on bestiality and those on sodomy. More nonwhites (slaves) than whites were prosecuted for bestiality. There also were differences in sentences between whites and nonwhites. If the case could not be proven, slaves were flogged and sent home, whites were imprisoned at Robben Island near Cape Town. If the case could be proven, the convicted person was strangled and thrown into the sea, frequently tied to the animal in question (mostly dogs, but also cows, donkeys, or on ships, usually pigs). For example, in 1764 Jan Hansz van Elsevelde committed bestiality on boars while on a ship. After examination under torture (often inflicted by holding burning fuses between the person's fingers), he confessed. The sentence stands that the man was bound at a pile and whipped, and afterwards sent to the Robben Island to work in chains the rest of his life. But when he committed the same act with a sheep the following year, he was brought to a ship in the Table Bay, tied to the dead sheep, and thrown into the water with enough heavy weights attached to him to make certain that he would sink.[8]

One can divide the sodomy cases in the Cape Colony into several models. The most severe one was anal penetration in which the *effectio seminis* had been proven by the confession of the accused. A second group of sentences were those in which sodomy could not be proven, but where there was an attempt to commit the act. A third group were sentences concerning mutual masturbation.

An example of the first model is the 1753 trial against three criminals, a Dutchman and two slaves, who were held in detention in chains on Robben Island. The Dutchman, Nicolaas Modde from Amsterdam, and a slave from the Chormandel Coast in India had committed mutual masturbation at the chicken-house at Robben Island. But "not satisfied with their devilish frisky stimulation," they had also sodomized each other as well. The same also happened between Nicolaas Modde and another slave. Although there were no eyewitnesses, the commander of the guard heard it from one of the slaves. All three men subsequently confessed before the Court of Justice. So according to the sentence, all three men were bound together with weights and thrown overboard into the Table Bay.[9] This was the usual sentence against proven sodomy. This case is significant not only as an example of voluntary sodomy, but also as an example of an interracial sexual relationship.

A 1764 trial gives us an example of the second group, a case in which sodomy could not be proven completely. In December 1763, Reijnier van den Bergh and Christiaan Pruijsman, both ordinary seamen on the VOC ship *Imagonda*, had spoken about the female sex on a certain night. Their tempers became so heated that they committed mutual masturbation, and thereafter "without any shame" Reijnier had tried to sodomize Christiaan. Because in this case the act had not been committed fully, the Court of Justice had to deliberate on a milder sentence. Their first argument was a biblical one: "because the human seed serves to the procreation of the human race and by the fusion with the same sex this seed destroys the possible birth, therefore this man, like Onan, has killed himself, too. As the divine law requires here the death sentence, so does the law of this country." But according to the well-known law studies of Diderik van Hogendorp and J. de Damhouder,[10] on which the Court of Justice leaned, the crime of sodomy was so awful that even the attempted act had to be punished as heavily as if it had been committed fully. Only when one of the partners had made an effort to stop the other person—when sodomy had not been committed *in summa gradu*—could a less severe punishment be pronounced. In the case of Reijnier van den Bergh and Christiaan Pruijsman, because of their youth (their ages nineteen and fourteen respectively) and because the crime had not been carried out fully, both were whipped and banished to the Netherlands.[11]

The same sentence was executed in 1758 to two sailors, Willem Hendriksz from Bergen op Zoom and Adriaan Spoor from Hoorn, both at the VOC ship *De Gerechtigheid* (Justice). Here too the *crimen sodomiticum* had not been fully committed. When Adriaan Spoor had tried to "play" with a young sailer, Hendrik de Vogel, the latter refused to engage himself in mutual masturbation and said to Adriaan: "God save us! You are a bourgeois child like me, are you?" This young sailor had heard of the sodomy act between Willem Hedriksz and Adriaan Spoor. The Court could only prove the sodomy attempt and the *effectio seminis*.[12]

Another case in which the *crimen sodomiticum* had not been fully proven occurred in 1759 when Francois van Holte from Amersfoort and Carel Kosterman from Brussels, both soldiers, met in the lavatory of a hospital where both were confined at the time. First, they "played" together (mutual masturbation). Had it gone no further, there probably would not have been any problems. But they were not satisfied, and tried to sodomize each other. Because they were discovered during their act by another sailor looking through a hole in the lavatory's wall, the act was not fully committed. So they both received the same punishment: whipping and banishment to the Netherlands.[13]

An example of the third group, in which only mutual masturbation played a role, is the case of a sailor and two soldiers from the VOC ship *Leijden*. The sailor Gerrit Wijntjes had committed mutual masturbation with the two soldiers, Jan Hendrik Snijder and Jan Casper Boscenius. All three men confessed, but declared their innocence on the ground they did not know what sodomy was. They were bound to a stake and flogged, and afterwards sentenced to labor on the VOC ropery at Cape Town for one year.[14]

On board the ship *Vreeburg* in the year 1765, a fourteen-year-old boy Francois David La Pron, a young sail-maker, had tried to perform his "dirty passions" on the young ship's carpenter, Jan Tacke. Although Francois had only touched Tacke's feet and his trousers near his knees, the ship's carpenter, watching Francois, said: "Villian, what are you doing there? If you are trying to do here the same things as at Delft, then we are obliged to send you away from this ship." Francois asked for pardon, promising not to act toward another the same way again. The captain sent him ashore at Cape Town.

At home in Delft, Francois stayed with another sail-maker at the alderman's house of Cornelis Reijnevel. There, on one particular occasion after a conversation about prostitutes, he asked his companion, Frederik La Vigne, to lay on top of him as if La Vigne was the boy and Francois the girl. But Frederik refused to do that or to reverse the roles. Francois then tried to persuade Frederik to participate in mutual masturbation, saying "in doing so there is no harm," but his efforts were in vain. Finally, Francois followed Frederik to his bed and kissed him. At that moment, a servant entered and asked what he was doing. Francois was subsequently rebuked for kissing his male companion. In Cape Town, the Court of

Justice judged that because of his age, his innocence, and the fact
he perhaps had not intended to sodomize La Vigne, this was only a
case of "riggishness" and therefore not punishable. On the other
hand, the Court decided that Francois would have gone further if he
had not been discovered by the servant. Therefore, the Court sentenced him to a whipping and then banished him to the Netherlands.[15]

Some conclusions can be drawn from these trials. First, bestiality
appears to have been prosecuted more frequently in the Cape Town
Colony than in the Netherlands during the eighteenth century,
among both whites and nonwhites. There were also relatively more
sodomy cases (about five times higher) there as compared with the
Netherlands. Sodomy was seen within the biblical conception of
procreation and the man-woman relationship. As in the Netherlands, following the law studies of the seventeenth and eighteenth
centuries, punishment for "incomplete sodomy" was milder, generally taking the form of banishment. There are no indications for
the development of sodomite personality as is suggested for the late
eighteenth century in the Netherlands.[16] Mutual masturbation itself
seemed not to be punishable, but the possibility that it could lead to
sodomy recast it as a preliminary phase of sodomy — and therefore
criminal. Moreover, actions like kissing, embracing, or caressing
were considered feminine and could be used against the accused in
sodomy trials. Most condemned persons were of low social status —
common sailors, soldiers, and slaves. But there were also persons
of higher status, like the captain of the ship Termeijen, Hans Christiaan de Rotte from Flensburg (Germany). In 1754 he was condemned *in absentia*.[17] Finally, it seems likely that sodomy was noticed and punished sooner in a male-dominated society and on ships
than in a society where the sex ratio was balanced.

NOTES

1. D. J. Noordam, "Homosexualiteit en sodomie in Leiden, 1533-1811,"
Leids Jaarboekje 75 (1983): 72-105, esp. 85.
2. Theo van der Meer, *De wesentlijke sonde van sodomie en andere vuyligheeden. Sodomieten vervolgingen in Amsterdam, 1730-1811* (Amsterdam: Tabula, 1984), 201-9.
3. Noordam, "Homosexualiteit," 76.

4. R. Ross, "Oppression, sexuality and slavery at the Cape of Good Hope," *Historical Reflections/Reflections Historiques* 6 (1979): 421-33, esp. 421.

5. *Civiele en Criminele Regtsrolle benevens de Processtucken van de Raad van Justitie des Casteels de Goede Hoop,* archival nos. VOC 10907 to VOC 10992 (1705 to 1792), kept in the General States Archives in The Hague.

6. Noordam, "Homosexualiteit," 76.

7. O. F. Mentzel, *A Geographical and Topographical Description of the Cape of Good Hope,* vol. 2, ed. H. J. Mandelbrote (Cape Town: Van Riebeeck Society, 1925), 125; and vol. 2 (Cape Town: Van Riebeeck Society, 1944), 99. Abbe N. L. de la Caille, *Journal historique du voyage fait au Cap de Bonne Esperance* (Paris, 1776), 309-312. Cf. Ross, "Oppression," 430.

8. VOC 10964, f 24, f 26, and VOC 10965, f 34 ff.

9. VOC 10954, f 71 ff.

10. J. de Damhouder, *Practijcke in Criminele Saken* (Rotterdam, 1660); and Benedictus Carpzovius, *Verhandeling der lijfstraffelijke misdaden en haare berechtinge,* trans. Diderik van Hogendorp, 2 vols. (Rotterdam, 1752). The original text of Carpzovius dated from the seventeenth century.

11. VOC 10964, f 25-28, f. 36.

12. VOC 10957, f 50 ff.

13. VOC 10958, f 9 ff.

14. VOC 10949, f 55, f 61 ff.

15. VOC 10956, f 48 ff.

16. Noordam, "Homosexualiteit," 92, 98.

17. VOC 10953, f 26 ff.

Those Damned Sodomites:
Public Images of Sodomy
in the Eighteenth Century Netherlands

L. J. Boon

Former centuries did not discriminate between sexual acts between males and the mental condition of those who committed
those acts.[1] During the eighteenth century and before, a "sodomite" was not a person comparable to our present-day homosexual
(whatever this ambiguous term may connote) but someone who
willingly debased himself by temporarily obviating God's com-
mandments. Sodomy was foremost a sinful act. All sinners were
considered trespassers into the forbidden, but sodomites were more
than mere sinners: they committed *crimen laesae maiestatis tam
naturae quam divinae*, an offense to God and man alike, the most
heinous sin that could be imagined and one considered on a par with
heresy and witchcraft. As an offense against God, human nature,
and dignity, it was prosecuted by the courts—that is, when by
chance or in times of moral crusades it came to their attention. In
fact, sin and crime were one and the same thing. But, whereas all
sinners could be converted by doing penance, mere contrition was
not enough for a sodomite. The moral order, desecrated by ultimate
sin, demanded to be restored by cutting out the rotten member from
the community of believers. Yet, the unfortunate was not viewed as
someone predisposed to such horrible acts. Indeed, he was corrupt,

L. J. Boon died in 1986 without completing his PhD on the prosecution of
sodomy in 18th century Netherlands. His supervisor, Professor I. Schöftin, will
finish his important study.

This article was written for the conference *Among men, among women* (Amsterdam, 1983).

but only because someone else had corrupted him by initiating him into the techniques to which he had willfully consented.[2] In his turn, he could pass those techniques on to others, like a germ, and so the contagion could spread. This was pre-nineteenth century science regarding sodomy.

In the nineteenth century, a homosexual was not someone who *did* something, but either a sick person or a representative of the intermediate sex or someone who still suffered from disorders in infantile development. In either case, he was a person with a predilection for his own sex. Sin was out and so was crime, but predisposition came in. From then on, male homosexuality would characterize persons, body and mind.

Are these distinct ideal types mental constructs only, or serious ways to exemplify observable phenomena? Because all models or ideal types are instruments to order reality so as to reduce a bewildering multitude of phenomena to manageable proportions, this is the wrong question to ask. A better question would be: Were they good or bad constructs in the eighteenth and nineteenth centuries, respectively? Did people actually behave the way the constructs seemed to imply? In large measure they did; the types did not just express the discourse of the learned. Sodomy, in the sense of being an act perpetrated by an otherwise "normal" person, was not a mere chapter in theological treatises or the evidence in court, but the actual expression of homosexuality before the nineteenth century. In the same way, homosexuality as a disease was not just a chapter in nineteenth century medical or psychiatric textbooks, but an actual role that had developed historically before it came to the attention of physicians and psychiatrists. Examples from Dutch eighteenth century judicial archives illustrate this premise.

Large scale persecution of sodomites in most provinces of the Dutch republic, particularly in the provinces of Holland and Groningen, took place during the years 1730 to 1732. (To my knowledge there is no other example of a persecution against homosexuals of that magnitude.) The subject had been largely neglected until recently, perhaps because of scholarly taboo. With the exception of a pioneering article in 1906, a doctoral thesis on an aspect of the persecution, and some minor publications, there is nothing in

Dutch historiography on this subject. This is all the more surprising in view of the fact that the persecution claimed more than three hundred victims (some one hundred death sentences and at least two hundred judgments by default), no mean thing in a country reputed at the time for its tolerance in other areas.[3]

Highlights of the persecution were a series of arrest in the major cities of the country—Amsterdam, The Hague, Haarlem, Delft, and Utrecht—and a razzia-like drive in a rural village called Faan, in the northern province of Groningen. Knowledge of this persecution comes from the files of the proceedings and the transcripts of the interrogations in court that have been preserved, unlike the records of many other such cases which were destroyed. These files enable us to reconstruct in detail not only the proceedings themselves, but also the lives of the defendants before their arrests and the reaction of the population toward the sodomites' conduct. Moreover, the files reveal the existence of sodomite subcultures in the cities and of casual sodomitical acts in a peasant village, information from which a comparison of the two simultaneous phenomena can be made.

In pursuing their investigations, the prosecuting officers in the city courts discovered, to their utter dismay, a number of brothels of male prostitutes run by pimps and disguised as meeting places for gentlemen of esteem looking for valets and footmen. The Hague, the diplomatic center of the country and, to a lesser extent, Amsterdam, were the prime centers of these brothels.[4] These establishments were linked to one another by a network of traveling "valets" employed by the bosses of the *fun houses*, as these brothels were nicknamed in the homosexual slang of the time. The fact that the trade operated as an interlinked network of prostitutes and clients enabled the judges to reconstruct it as soon as they had arrested one of these prostitutes and gained his confession. The arrest of some former soldiers in Utrecht in January 1730, among whom was Zacharias Wilsma, a twenty-two-year-old Catholic, started the whole episode. The proceedings subsequently progressed from defendant to defendant, the former denouncing the latter. From the very beginning, the courts kept each other abreast regarding what their prisoners had confessed about their accomplices in other cities. The magistracy was astounded by the veritable cesspool that

opened up and, as the interrogations brought to light an ever accu-
mulating mass of incriminating evidence, the pit of immorality appeared to grow even deeper.

Some nonconclusive evidence suggests that the courts were not
as ignorant as it might appear about sodomitical activity and the
existence of fully developed urban sodomite subcultures. Of
course, the subcultures had been relatively closed circuits and participants in them could retain their anonymity only by virtue of the
general disapproval of their doings by neighbors and others, who
were very well aware of what went on. But the confessions also
reveal a considerable amount of indifference on the part of the general population. Similarly, the attitude of the authorities appears to
have been one of relative neglect, provided the persons involved in
sodomitical activity did not pass certain boundaries of decency and
provided no complaints were lodged against them.

It is interesting to note that the substance of the subcultures in no
way differs from what we know of similar phenomena in, for example, London and Paris at that time.[5] Meeting places, cruising areas,
bynames, relative promiscuity, and, above all, the delivery of boys
and young men to clients upon demand and a jargon fully understood only by insiders—all of these testify to the fully developed
nature of subcultural activities as can be gleaned from court archives that date back as far as 1710. A superficial search of the pre-
1730 archives would, however, lead to the opposite conclusion because there is no record of any indictment of a sodomitical offense
before 1730.

The persecution reached its peak with the promulgation in July
1730 of an edict of the States of Holland (the provincial assembly)
that once again affirmed[6] the penalization of sodomy as a felony,
offered premiums to denouncers, and made punishable by law those
who withheld information considered of vital importance to the administration of justice. This edict, together with the prior executions of the condemned in public, caused considerable commotion
among the population and triggered a torrent of popular broadsheets, pamphlets, gossip, cheap poetry, moralistic discourse, and
some theological treatises. It is from this publicity (a large amount
of gossip from hearsay was published abroad, primarily in England)[7] that we can gain a startling insight into the public image of

the sodomite as guilty of all the unexplained and bewildering adversities that had befallen the nation: commercial decline, rising unemployment, the demise of strict church practice, the rising influence of papism and, concomitant with papism, the overwhelming influence of French and Italian culture and *mores*. Exaggerated as this may seem from hindsight, the contemporary perception of these events is nonetheless historical fact.

Indeed, Dutch society appeared very much in distress at the beginning of the eighteenth century. To the Dutch, the peace treaty of Utrecht of 1713 heralded the beginning of the end of the Golden Age of superiority in many fields, including commerce, shipping, art, and science. A common explanation offered for the decline of Dutch hegemony during the 1720s and 1730s was ready at hand: foreign (French) cultural influence, which emasculated the nation; soft manners, which had corrupted the simple morals of the fathers; luxuriousness, laxity, and debauchery—a consequence of riches acquired during years of prosperity; and an easygoing lifestyle in the absence of common pursuits.

To a disturbed witness, the consequences were everywhere to be seen. The days of thanksgiving, prayer, and fasting were observed so leniently that taverns and public inns were overcrowded after sunset. The people appeared no longer to believe in penance in times of war, pestilence, flood, and unemployment, though these were seen as undeniable portents of what God had in store for the country if immediate action was not taken to eradicate evil. People had become effete and hunted for luxuries. The country had become indolent, profligate, and prone to debauchery; through an abundance of temporal blessings people reveled in the most shameful kinds of lechery and pagan abominations. Effeminacy expressed itself through clothing and the Dutch, once renowned for their simplicity and austere mode of life, now dressed in grand style and extravagant attire. Through unmanly French fashions, sodomites could display their perverse attitudes openly and unrestrained. Sodomy contaminated the entire society. Again, it was seen as an omen foreshadowing the final stage of the life of the people as a nation under God. The signs seemed to be unmistakable there. The Amsterdam stock exchange was in full decline, trade and commerce withered away, God's chastising hand had sent fevers, thunderstorms, and plagues, and worms were gnawing at the dykes which protected the country from floods. Ungodliness reigned supreme. Nothing highlighted the general mood and the moralistic conviction of the country better than the following poem, only one example of many that were divulged in the wake of the first executions:

> God stages wrath in the midst of this our country,
> submerged as it is in seas of wicked sins,
> Befoul'd by bands of dogs and dirty swine
> Whose poison spreads through its entrails like pestilence.
> Thus, by wordly fire, a hellish fire it put out,
> Nature's law's redressed, profaned by loathsome vices,
> Strains have been put upon a sinful, frantic rage.
> You may flee the land, but cannot escape God's hand.[8]

(Translation mine)

This image of the sodomite as a scapegoat, responsible for every disaster and misfortune, does not square at all with the picture of a man who had "only" committed the most disgraceful crime that could be possibly imagined, but who was not perverse in body and mind. It does not for various reasons, the most important being that the public image sketched above does not picture a single sodomite — that would not have given rise to a public outcry, but to occasional scandal at most — but a whole band of debauchees ready to destroy the vital basis of the nation, its morals and austere way of life. All of this is implied in the traditional story of Sodom, and the moral entrepreneurs and Protestant clergymen, who voiced public opinion, did not shun making the comparison between the biblical Pentapolis and the Netherlands.

The persecutions of the 1730s marked the dividing line between the image of the sodomite as an actor, a criminal, or a sinful "heterosexual," and the view that sodomites (the plural) constituted an interrelated network, a "fifth column" of profligates, the devil's henchmen, a vital threat to sanity, reasonableness, and purity — "that godless bunch of people," as one of the broadsheets put it. Contrast this image with the relative tolerance of sodomy as witnessed by the absence of trials in the decades before 1730 and the basic discontinuity in discourse about sodomy becomes abundantly clear. From that time forward, sodomites would be persons of a different type.

The summer of 1730 did not witness the end of the persecution. It merely put an end to the public executions of the convicted in most provinces of the Dutch republic. Around that time most people must have become aware of the seriousness of the situation and must have observed how deeply rooted the evil was — so deeply that even magistrates and noblemen had been affected. Most of the well-to-do had fled the country and gone south, thereby confirming the prevailing prejudice that sodomy was a vice imported from southern Roman Catholic countries.

That the persecution took most of its victims from the cities did not come unexpectedly, either, because sodomy was supposed to follow luxury. One did not encounter that in the countryside, but in the centers of depravity, the cities, channels of foreign influence. In fact, the structure of the persecution itself had been responsible for the idea of the urban basis of sodomy. The evidence, largely gleaned from court interrogations, came from customers of the brothels in the cities who, each in their turn, had denounced other *habitués*. So established, the network was to a large extent an urban network spreading over the entire country, but excluding the countryside.

The countryside was also infected, but this would not become clear until 1731. Who could have imagined that God-fearing peasants could be so corrupted and who could have believed that the contagion would be so pervasive as to infect part of the rural population of the undistinguished village of Faan in the Groningen province? Yet such was the discovery of the local *grietman* (country judge) Rudolphe de Mepsche in April 1731. His discovery took place after the persecution of sodomites in other parts of the country had already eased.

The affair started in April 1731 with a blind thirteen-year-old boy charging his nephew of the same age with attempted sodomy. The two boys were arrested that same night by De Mepsche. During the subsequent months, the stables of the De Mepsche's house filled with an increasing number of suspects (up to thirty-six) who by often unbearable torture (so it seems) were brought to confession. The structure of the *razzia*, a persecution on a smaller (geographical) scale in itself, was more or less the same as elsewhere. Suspects were pressed to indict their former accomplices, who in turn were brought to incriminate others. The affair, which can be compared to the Salem witch trials in 1692 in that an entire community was involved, continued until the horrible death (burning at the stake with prior strangulation) in September 1731 of twenty-four of those found guilty.[9]

The proceedings were extremely complicated. A full account of all the intricacies would far exceed the scope and space of this article and would require, among other things, the disentanglement of a web of local feuds. Suffice it to say that the suspects changed their confessions more than once during their trials, that not only were peasants involved, but also some well-to-do landowners, and that De Mepsche, as supreme judge in capital crimes, finally was let down by his colleagues in other jurisdictions. Because no court of appeal existed in the province, the verdicts were final.

The most striking thing in this context is not the mass process itself, but the content of the confessions in the court and the voice of the population. Given that the confessions were wrung from the unhappy suspects by intolerable means, they are nonetheless revealing as to their *circumstantial evidence.* In Faan, there were no brothels, no prostitutes, no customers (of course), no commercial exploitation of sodomy; instead, only honest fathers, hardworking farmhands, and the inevitable village eccentric, whom no one took very seriously. No one would formally have believed that the prisoners were capable of the crime of sodomy—with all the connotations that concept had acquired in the meantime. No member of any family could have conceived that his or her son, father, uncle, or cousin, would be involved in an underground conspiracy to undermine the health of the nation. Yet that is what popular ideology and the local minister, Henricus van Byler, with his treatise *Helsche Boosheit* (Infernal Lewdness) would have had them believe.[10]

The interrogations in fact disclosed exactly those furtive and casual "same sex acts" described at the beginning of this article. Sodomy was practiced in a ditch, near the barn of one's neighbor, or in similar settings after leaving the local tavern. "Shall we play the whore?" one boy had proposed to his friend after having finished the day's work. According to the transcripts of the interrogations by De Mepsche, the defendants came forward with incredibly long lists of acts of sodomy they had committed and specified the place, hour of the day, and date the acts had taken place. It would seem that a good number of the confessions were probably white lies, intended at least to evade the threat of physical harm from the court, aids if the defendants did not confess what the judges wanted them to. Close reading reveals that what they in fact confessed to were occasional acts of sodomy or mutual masturbation which no one seemed to have taken seriously as long as these had not been practiced too openly.

Thus, the trials both in Holland and in Faan, witnessed the tragic clash between the two perceptions of sodomy mentioned above. The "theories" did not fit the facts in both cases. Until the 1730s sodomy was a temporary lapse into sin; the interrogations in Faan seem to prove this theory. But to the detriment of the defendants in Faan, a thorough labeling process in the wake of the persecutions elsewhere in the country had accused sodomites of being perverted in body *and mind*, liable to commit any foul deed the imagination would dream up. Such was the view of the population (based on broadsheets and popular poetry) and the judges in Faan. Without the example set by Holland, De Mepsche would probably never have persecuted local sodomites on that scale. An incidental culprit would have been caught or an occasional death sentence pronounced. No expiatory communal purge such as that staged on 24 September 1731 would have taken place.

Significantly, the population in Faan reacted in a way radically different from what the broadsheets would have us believe. In Faan it was the judge, De Mepsche, his aides, and Van Byler who incurred the wrath of the population. In the years to follow, De Mepsche became known in popular legend as a brute and a scourge and as an executioner of innocent people. The families of the condemned voiced their indignation about what the judges implied about their relatives; namely, that they had not been obedient fathers and sons who occasionally "sinned," but instead a band of "dogs and dirty swine."

The two images of sodomy, one as an inherent quality of people depraved in body and mind, and the other as a casual (be it forbidden) act of single persons, are therefore closely linked with the various ways in which man-to-man relationships were expressed before 1730. Before the persecution, people did not bother to make the distinction let alone think about sodomites as a bunch of mean conspirators. True, there was the Sodom story and the idea that sodomy was a contagious disease, but there was no evidence that sodomites as a group could inflict damage upon a community or a nation. In everyday life a sodomite was a man of whose conduct you knew or did not know. In any case, people did not care – this evidenced by the confessions in Faan. This was the prevailing appearance of sodomy: half-hidden, half-known, known but not familiar, odd, and, in the view of the church and the court, sinful, criminal, and punishable.

Then came the persecution and consequent confessions that revealed highly developed sodomite subcultures not that different from those existing today. These subcultures constituted a covert network encompassing the major cities of the country. The educated and the magistrates reacted to the existence of these networks with increasing alarm. To my knowledge, this was the first time in history that the general public had become acquainted, not with the actual life of sodomites, but with the concept that sodomites were neither isolated individuals, nor lapsed "heterosexuals," but people with their own subversive ways.

During this time the public image of the sodomite changed quite suddenly. In 1734, two years after the persecution, the Dutch publicist Justus van Effen spoke about "hermaphrodites in their minds" and "effeminate weaklings," which are quite different kinds of persons from the single actors of the pre-1730 period.[11] As such, the altered perception of the sodomite both foreshadowed nineteenth century preoccupations with homosexuality ("a feminine mind in a man's body" is the actual wording in one of the pamphlets) and the fear of those others whom could never be trusted and who should be avoided whenever possible. An example of the far-reaching impact of such an attitude was the razzia De Mepsche held in his tiny resort of Faan. He was mistaken: he chased sodomites as a group where in fact only casual sodomy had more or less openly been practised following the pre-1730 model. That is to say, he chased a phantom.

The beginning of the eighteenth century was crucial in the formation of the subcultural groups among sodomites – as examples from

London, Paris, and the Netherlands have made abundantly clear. Dutch records show that subcultural groups as such existed only in the cities. In Faan, sodomites were not sodomites per se, but merely men who participated in varying sexual activities. Nonetheless, the peasants of Faan who participated in such activity suffered as a consequence of the appearance of a visible sodomite subculture in the Netherlands around 1730.

NOTES

1. Cf. Alan Bray, *Homosexuality in Renaissance England* (London: Gay Men's Press, 1982), 104 sqq. For "homosexual" in this essay read "male homosexual."

2. This point of view was most clearly expressed in the collection of broadsheets in rhyme that went off the press during the 1730 persecution in two bound volumes under the title *Schouw-toneel soo der Geexecuteerde als Ingedaagde over de verfoeilyke Misdaad van Sodomie*, s.l., s.a. The volumes also contain most of the court citations, the subpoenas of the defendants, and the verdicts.

3. The first single monographic article devoted to the subject was published in 1906 in German by the Dutch psychiatrist L. S. A. M. von Römer, "Der Uranismus in den Niederlanden bis zum 19. Jahrhundert, mit besonderer Berücksichtigung der grossen Uranierverfolgung im Jahre 1730, eine historische und bibliographische Skizze," *Jahrbuch für sexuelle Zwischenstufen* 8 (1906): 365-511. The article was followed by a dissertation in 1921 by G. M. Cohen Tervaert. The dissertation was published under the title *De Grietman Rudolph de Mepsche, Historisch-juridische Beschouwingen over een Reeks Crimineele Processen, Gevoerd in 1731, in den rechtstoel Oosterdeel-Langewold*, The Hague, 1921. This book considers the notorious proceedings by the local judge Rudolf de Mepsche against thirty-six defendants from a judicial point of view only.

4. As Margaret Jacob has made abundantly clear, The Hague in the beginning of the eighteenth century was a hotbed of European libertines and free thinkers of all shades. It would, in my view, go too far to assume a direct connection between those fashionable subversive ideas and the persecution as a kind of repressive backlash against libertinism as Jacob and, earlier, Gibbs have suggested. See Margaret C. Jacob, *The Radical Enlightenment, Pantheists, Freemasons and Republicans* (London: Allen and Unwin, 1981), and G. C. Gibbs, "Some Intellectual and Political Influences of The Huguenot Emigres in the United Provinces, *Bijdragen en Mededelingen betreffende de Geschiedenis der Nederlanden* 90 (1975): 255-87. There is no doubt, however, that there was a strong undercurrent of xenophobia during the persecution, *vide* the cheap poetry published in the *Schouw-toneel*.

5. For sodomite subcultures in this period, see Alan Bray, *Homosexuality in Renaissance England*, D. A. Coward, "Attitudes to Homosexuality in Eighteenth

Century France," *Journal of European Studies* (1980): 231-55; Michel Rey, "Police et Sodomie a Paris au XVIIIe Siecle, du Peché au Desordre," *Revue d'Histoire Moderne et Contemporaine* (1982): 113-14; Maurice Lever, *Les buchers de Sodome* (Paris: Fayard, 1985). For the best overview on this subject, and the article that coined this term, see Stephen Murray and Kent Gerard, "Renaissance Sodomite Subcultures?" in *Among Men, Among Women* (Amsterdam: University of Amsterdam, 1983), 183-96.

6. The edict of July 1730 in fact did no more than strongly confirm the condemnation of sodomy in Roman and Mosiac law statutes, which were rule of law in the Dutch Republic during the *ancien regime*.

7. The leading English newspapers published editorials and comments on the subject, e.g., *The London Gazette, The Daily Post Boy*, and the *St. James Evening Post*.

8. The poem was not published, but survives in written form in a broadsheet called *Groninger Pasquin* 73 (Groningen State Archive).

9. See Paul Boyer, Stephen Nissenbaum, *Salem Possessed, the Social Origins of Witchcraft* (Cambridge, MA: Harvard University Press, 1974).

10. H. C. van Byler, *Helsche Boosheit of Grouwelyke Zonde van Sodomie, om haar Affschouwelykheid en Welverdiende Straffe in Goddelyke en Menselyke Schriften tot een Spiegel voor Het tegenwoordige en Toekomende Geslagte Openlyk ten toon Gested* (Gropningen, 1731).

11. Justus van Effen, *De Hollandsche Spectator*, 10 March 1732, 71. *De Hollandsche Spectator* was the Dutch counterpart to Steele's "Spectator." In the same vein, Michel Foucault, some two-hundred forty years later, dubbed homosexuality "a kind of inner androgyny, a hermaphroditism of the soul"; see Michel Foucault, *Histoire de la Sexualité, I, La Volonté de Savoir* (Paris: Gallimard, 1976).

Prosecution of Sodomy
in Eighteenth Century
Frisia, Netherlands

Arend H. Huussen, Jr., PhD

Research on homosexuality in the nineteenth and twentieth centuries has tended to leave a gap between the period of the medical construction of homosexuality and the homosexual emancipation movement and the period in which homosexuality as plain "sodomy" led a marginal existence in the shadows. Some historians, however, feel we must not hasten to conclusions regarding the existence or nonexistence of a homosexual identity or of homosexual subcultures in the ages preceding the middle of the last century before we have examined closely the sources which may yield information on these topics. Several historians (e.g., Gilbert, Harvey, Oaks, Rey, Trumbach)[1] have already brought to light interesting material and have put forward stimulating hypotheses.

The purpose of this article is to present the results of my investigations into one specific source: court records. Relying on trial records in investigating the "crime" of sodomy implies, as Oaks rightly stressed, some evident dangers of distorting reality. Yet if used critically, the material also provides some striking advantages. First, the records must be researched serially over a long timespan. And second, other information—from church records and the contemporary literature of jurists, moralists, "spectators," and so forth—must be drawn within the scope of research.

Much research has recently been done in the Netherlands on a local or regional level into the existence of sodomy before the nine-

Dr. Arend H. Huussen, Jr. is Professor of Modern History, University of Groningen.

249

teenth century. One factor behind this phenomenon has been the study of crime and criminal justice in general. The sovereign court of the province of Frisia tried 7,886 criminal cases during the eighteenth century, until its extinction in February 1811 as a consequence of the annexation of the Kingdom of Holland by the French Empire. The jurisdiction of the Frisian Court was rather wide, including even cases of petty thefts committed in the country. Its jurisdiction was somewhat limited, however, by certain other specialized courts that dealt with "tax" crimes (fraud, smuggling) and with offenses involving the military, or students and professors at the University of Franeker.

THE COUNTRY

The sovereign province of Frisia was a member of the Union of seven Dutch provinces that constituted an independent confederation since 1581. Its territory was bordered on the north and west by the estuaries of the North Sea: the Wadden Zee and Zuider Zee. As has been shown by J. A. Faber in his masterly study on the economic and social developments in Frisia during the period 1500 to 1800, a secular trend can be established:

> The sixteenth and the first half of the seventeenth centur[ies] are characterized by population growth, rising prices, land reclamation on a large scale, more intensive farming, expansion in the peat-cutting industry and in shipping, trade and industry in general, an increase in the size of the towns, and the rise of a well-to-do middle class.
>
> After 1650 there are signs everywhere of stagnation and decline . . . a fall in the number of inhabitants, pressure on price levels, greatly diminished activity in connection with land reclamation, a tendency toward more extensive farming, stagnation in the peat-cutting industry and in shipping bound to the Sound and Norway, foreign trade, and various branches of industry. At the same time a certain rigidity becomes apparent in the social structure, with power and wealth increasingly concentrated among the members of a progressively smaller

and deliberately exclusive ruling class—the regenten, to give them their Dutch name.[2]

The second half of the eighteenth century was characterized by an upward trend in population growth, rising prices, an agricultural revival, and expansion in most branches of economic life. In the long run, concluded Faber, Frisian society was fairly stable: economic differentiation did not cause the province to lose its predominantly agrarian character.

Frisia consisted of eleven towns, the capital being Leeuwarden, and thirty landed districts of "grietenijen" (see Map 1). The demographic development is traced in Table 1. In the year 1749, the population was divided occupationally as indicated in Table 2. Before approximately 1800, Frisia was characterized by a remarkable religious homogeneity. See Table 3. The mean size of households in 1744, as computed by Faber, was between 3.11 and 4.43 persons. In the towns, the households tended to be smaller than in the country (3.11 to 3.62, and 3.57 to 4.43, respectively). In 1796, domestic servants constituted 11 percent of the population in the country and 6 percent in the towns (the census of 1744 did not specify their numbers).[3] No accurate information is available on the number of children or members of the family who were coresident. In general, however, most households were nuclear family units.

THE LAW

In 1701, the first year of our research period in the field of Frisian crime and criminal justice, there existed no special statute against the crime of sodomy. The law codified in the *Statuten* of 1602 (revised edition 1723) did not speak of the *crimen contra naturam*. The learned commentators of these statutes, Hamerster and Binckes, judges in the Court of Frisia, were silent on the subject.[4] Yet the crime was not unknown to jurists. Apart from biblical knowledge, of course this was due to the fact that, in the Republic, Roman law formed the basis of the academic study of law and supplemented the Frisian law practiced in the courts. In addition, the famous scholars of criminal law and the writers of commentaries on the Justinian *Digest* would often mention sodomy.[5]

Map 1: FRIESLAND (FRISIA)

Boundaries of towns (steden) and landed
districts (grietenijen) shown

Source: J. A. Faber, Drie eeuwen Friesland 2
(Wageningen: A. A. G. Bijdragen, 1972),
609.

Some pre-Republican laws regarding sodomy, such as the famous *Peinlich Gerichtsordnung (Constitutio Criminalis Carolina*,
1532) of the German Emperor Charles V,[6] or the *Criminele Ordonnantien* (1570) of the Spanish King Philip II, were widely quoted in
theory and in practice. The former decreed in Article 116: "Who
commits lewdness with a beast, or a man with a man, or a woman

Table 1

	1689	1714	1744	1796	1815	1848	1881
County	85,777	85,599	94,327	112,672	127,606	182,131	251,763
Towns	42,957	43,644	40,806	44,824	46,095	60,510	76,381

Table 2

	Agric.	Fishery	Trades & Industry	Peat-Cutting	Commerce	Public Services	Laborers
Country %	37	1	18	1	14	5	24
Towns %	4	1	45	-	27	17	6

Table 3

	Reformed		Mennonites		Roman Catholic		Other		Unknown/None	
	1796	1947	1796	1947	1796	1947	1796	1947	1796	1947
Country %	84.0	43.8	8.7	2.7	7.0	4.4	0.2	1.4	0.1	20.1
Towns %	73.7	29.9	6.6	3.1	16.6	13.7	3.0	4.2	0.1	34.1

(N.B., "New Reformed Church" in 1947: 27.6 and 17.7%, respectively)

Source of Tables 1, 2, and 3: J. A. Faber, *Drie eeuwen Friesland*, 1972.

with a woman, forfeats his life; according the customs those people ought to be burnt from life to death.'"[7]

Given this situation, it is not surprising to find sodomy mentioned in the description of Frisian jurisprudence by the famous seventeenth-century jurist Ulrik Huber (1636-1694). In his commentary (first edition, 1686) he stated:

> Secret lascivousness, committed with oneself, commonly called "the sin of Onan," is also not punished, on account, no doubt, of the multitude of offenders, though otherwise it is no less sin than ordinary fornication. But shameful intercourse between man and man, or woman and woman, is still punished at the present day with death, and the same applies to intercourse with animals.[8]

Huber's brevity on this topic was remarkable, given that he was a professor of law at the University of Franeker and during the years 1679 to 1682 himself a judge in the Frisian Court. Generally speaking, sodomy does not seem to have been a problem for the seventeenth century Frisian judiciary.

MASS PERSECUTIONS

The year 1730 marked a turning point. Although it is clear from theological and juridical sources that the sin and crime of sodomy was not an unknown phenomenon, the judiciary did not take much interest in it during the first two decades of the eighteenth century. This changed in 1730 when persecutions escalated dramatically beginning in Utrecht and Holland. The occasion seemed trivial enough: the custodian of the Dom church, irritated by the scandalous and noisy behavior of many people in and around the church, brought a charge against two men because of sodomy. He told the towncourt of Utrecht in January 1730 that he had identified one of the men who had perpetrated the act. The incident prompted investigations from which was learned that many men participated in a sinister interprovincial network of homosexual relations. The Utrecht court was shocked by the confessions of the accused. Correspondence with other courts was initiated. More accusations followed. It is noteworthy that the first delinquents were sentenced and put to death within a few months. Other provinces followed: the provincial Court of Holland and the town courts of Leyden and Amsterdam executed several sodomites from June 1730 onward.[9]

Persecutions began in Frisia also as the result of an isolated incident.[10] During this time there was a general sense of unrest among the people of the Republic. Several hundreds of sodomites fled their country. Many other people were alarmed by the extent of the "new" immorality in their midst. One such person, Marike Artens from Dronrijp, traveled to the nearby capital of the province, Leeuwarden, at the end of May or the beginning of June 1730, intending to confront Caspar Abrahams Bersé, a relative of hers, with rumors about his being a sodomite. She could not find him, so some time after she brought a charge against him. It was not until 12 July that Casper Abrahams was arrested by a policeman in the countryside – in spite of opposition from the local population. Caspar had traveled several times from Friesland to Amsterdam during the preceding few months, alarmed by the arrests of sodomites in Utrecht and Holland. He was so frightened that he even implored the policeman to kill him.

The confessions of Caspar Abrahams Bersé present the story of a typical sodomite during this period. Born about 1714, Berse became a servant boy with the distinguished Frisian families of the Van Burmania and the Grovestins at the age of ten. At thirteen, he became a drummer in a regiment, but after two years he quit to become a servant (*hereknecht*). He had sodomitic relations with several of his gentlemen. From his lovers, he received presents such as dresses and jewelry. He knew many patrician gentlemen intimately all over the Republic. One of his lovers was the famous hereknecht Zacharias Wilsma, who seems to have been at the center of several sodomitic networks during the 1720s. In 1730, Wilsma began cooperating with the judicial authorities. He was "lent" to the Frisian Court, and his confrontation with Casper Abrahams on 21 September 1730 formed the culmination of the preliminary examinations, during which the names of more sodomites were obtained. On 30 September Bersé was executed. Something of the feelings of horror the Court felt was indicated in the unusual motivation for the penalty:

> [T]he prisoner has led during many years an immoral and impious life, committing many wicked and abominable deeds with a named Zacharias Wilsma and other persons; the prisoner has even committed with the same Zacharias Wilsma during the years 1723 and 1724 on three different occasions really the most horrible, yes unnatural sin of sodomy; all this in such circumstances, the mere thought of which makes one shudder and frightened.

Another "incident" denunciation, was costly, though not lethal, for a Sijbe Meinerts of the village of Ferwert. He denied having committed the crime of sodomy – the counsel for the defendant going so far as to state his client didn't even know what "sodomy" meant – but on 14 July 1730 he confessed to having slept several times with men on one bed. Though this was not an unusual event, Sijbe's behavior apparently was: he, a man servant of his, and a day laborer had indulged in sexual games, "but without further intercourse or 'mixing' of seed." Sijbe Meinerts, who did not belong to any of the interprovincial networks of sodomites, was kept in custody during the following months. On 18 October, three weeks after the execution of Caspar Abrahams Bersé, he was punished with banishment from Frisia for one year because of "excesses."

At the same time, the Frisian Court was investigating the offenses of three men named by Zacharias Wilsma in his deposition of 19 September (in the case of Caspar Abrahams). Jan Obbis, Pijtter Floris, and Jurrian Hansen, all from Leeuwarden, confessed to having committed mutual masturbation with each other. But even under torture, they denied having perpetrated the crime of sodomy — anal penetration and ejaculation. The Court consequently acquitted them of accusation of committing the "real sin of sodomy," but punished them on 25 October for "filthy acts" with sentences of three to five years of prison labor.[11]

Meanwhile, two other cases of sodomy were investigated, both also the consequence of the Wilsma depositions of September 1730. He had accused Christiaen Feugen, a part-time military captain by then married and living in Leeuwarden, of very grotesque sexual acts with his man servant. Christiaen was a strong-willed man with excellent connections in the upper circles of Frisian society. He did not confess anything, even when confronted by Zacharias Wilsma and Caspar Abrahams Bersé. Yet there were some unequivocal depositions by witnesses; for example, a trustworthy usher of the Frisian Court who testified to his having been the object of repeated indecent proposals by the accused. The Court punished Christiaen Feugen with banishment for two years for not further specified "excesses."

The other accused, and the last one in the year 1730, was Jurrien Christiaens, nicknamed the hunchback. This forty-year-old man was not only named by the unenvitable Zacharias Wilsma, but he was also denounced by several ladies from Leeuwarden, one of whom testified having heard his name in connection with persons who had fled the country. Under torture, Jurrien Christiaens denied everything. However, he collapsed during the confrontation with Wilsma. At first he denied the "real sin of sodomy," but later on (perhaps under torture) he confessed to having played a passive role in his intercourse with a fugitive suspect named Jan van Wijngaerden. That confession put his case on the same level as Casper Abrahams'. Because Christiaens had, in addition, seduced many other men to sodomitic lewdness by exploiting a meeting house, the Frisian Court ruled that he should be executed.

This ended the persecution of sodomites in Frisia: of eight convicted, two were put to death. The judiciary had paid its tribute. No special law against sodomites, similar to those in neighboring Groningen or in Holland was enacted. If a panic had existed in Frisia, it was among sodomites, or people who were afraid of being classified as such. Many fled, then returned; some were arrested. Denunciation from the public, correspondence between the criminal courts of the Republic, and of course the central character of Zacharias Wilsma (who was kept alive for years) — all of these brought the sin of sodomy suddenly to the attention of the judiciary. By the early 1730s, sodomy seemed overall to be a criminal problem, one to be eliminated with speed and vigor. Given this, it is not surprising that no one spoke to oppose the notorious "sodomy" persecutions organized by Rudolf de Mepsche in the neighboring "Westerkwartier" of the province of Groningen (April-September 1731).[12]

The persecution of sodomites in Frisia was most widespread during the early 1730s. The judiciary in Utrecht panicked, as did hundreds of sodomites in the Republic and many theologians who wrote treatises on the subject in prose or verse. The unusual harshness of the punishment given those convicted during this period was, again, probably due to the public's fear that the evil of sodomy was contagious, its fear that God would seek revenge on them due to the presence of such evil, and its determination to extirpate this "new" crime, a move supported by the public press. Yet there must have been other reasons as well, because the prosecution of sodomites continued in the years following.

PROSECUTIONS SINCE 1730

Apart from two mentions of bestiality in the Frisian criminal court records (1731, 1746), ten instances of sodomy can be found in the period 1731-1811. Sixteen men were involved, one of whom was an old offender. On 20 November 1734 the court condemned Jan Obbis van Leeuwarden, who served a prison term of three years because of sodomy. He had been accused in the fall of 1733 by several fellow prisoners of seducing one of them, Idse Sakes, to indecent acts. Even under torture, Jan Obbis denied having committed "real sodomy." After protracted preliminary investigations, both men were condemned to public flogging, branding, and ten years of prison to be served in isolation apart from the other prisoners. After serving their prison terms they were banished for life. The other cases may be summed up in Table 4.

From this survey, it seems fairly obvious that the crime of sodomy was not the main priority in the maintaining of law and order in eighteenth-century Frisia. It is evident that sodomites were usually left alone. It is clear from the Frisian criminal records that the judiciary became involved in these cases only due to complaints from those men who were molested against their will. Yet in none of the cases could real sodomy be proven. In studying these records, one can discern a striking feature of this Frisian society: most men felt little need for privacy or physical distance. Men often slept together in one bed without any moral problem. In fact, one gets the impression that hospitality demanded this custom. The invitation to sleep in the (only) bed together seems to have been accepted without hesitation or afterthought.

CONCLUSION

The causes for the mass persecutions of sodomites in 1730 remain intriguing. Its specific origins in some locales may be indicated, as Noordam has shown for Leyden. (See his article in this issue.) He stressed the fact that from 1720 onward the city authorities and the town court of Leyden began to pay more attention to sexual offenses.[13] Yet in other regions, as in Frisia, this phenomenon may not be found. Moreover, one has to bear in mind that sodomy had been officially condemned even prior to 1700 as well. Therefore, by 1730 "real sodomy" was no longer a "new" sin or crime.

Among the consequences of the events of 1730 was undoubtedly a sharpened sensitivity to the crime of sodomy as such. But a

TABLE 4

Date of Sentence	Name of Suspect	Occupation of Suspect	Age of Suspect	Criminal Charge	Sentence
26/4/1757	Paulus Hichten van Amsterdam	comedian`	28	seduction to sodomy	acquitted
13/3/1759	Claes Wijbes van Dokkum	potter	29	attempting seduction to sodomy	acquitted
13/6/1766	Evert Jans van Leeuwarden	fisherman	?	attempting seduction to sodomy	7 years of prison labor
24/9/1766	Claas Clasen van Leeuwarden (married)	?	?	attempting seduction to sodomy	acquitted
23/10/1766	Christoffel Bosch van Leeuwarden	porter	70	seduction to sodomy	3 years of prison labor
8/12/1768	"	"	72	"	acquitted
12/10/1774	Adolph Jans van Oldeberkoop	customs officer	50	seduction to sodomy	banishment of 2 years
20/2/1775	IJpe Jacobs van Deinum	manservant (of Pals Palses)	18	toleration of sodomy	banishment of 3 years
20/2/1775	Sjouke Cornelis van Deinum	manservant (of Pals Palses)	16	toleration of sodomy	banishment of 3 years

259

TABLE 4 (continued)

Date of Sentence	Name of Suspect	Occupation of Suspect	Age of Suspect	Criminal Charge	Sentence
18/3/1775	Pals Palses van Deinum	farmer	41	seduction to sodomy	flogging, branding, 7 years of prison labor
21/10/1797	Reinder Pieters van Workum	?	56	seduction to sodomy	flogging, 10 years of prison labor (isolation), banishment for life
26/10/1798	Foppe Jans van Heereveen (married)	merchant	50	seduction to sodomy	10 years of prison labor (isolation)
23/2/1803	Lambertus G. G. de Wolf van Lochem	student (Univ. of Franeker)	?	forcing to lewd acts	1 month of prison, banishment of 1 year
23/2/1808	Johannes L. Tuinhout van Harlingen	student (Univ. of Franeker)	?	forcing to lewd acts	1 month of prison, banishment of 2 years
6/7/1809	Pieter Pot (at Leeuwarden)	?	46	seduction to sodomy, theft, violation of banishment	7 years of prison (isolation), banishment for life from the Kingdom of Holland

heightened awareness of the dangers of physical intimacy between men (sleeping together) cannot be demonstrated. On the contrary, one cannot but wonder about the low level of "painfulness" — in the terms of Norbert Elias[14] — in Frisia during the period under study. In essence, sodomy constituted a *quantité quasi négligeable* in eighteenth-century Frisian registered criminality.

NOTES

1. A. N. Gilbert, "Buggery and the British Navy, 1700-1861," *Journal of Social History* 10 (1976): 72-98; A. D. Harvey, "Prosecution for Sodomy in England at the Beginning of the Nineteenth Century," *The Historical Journal* 21 (1978): 939-48; Robert F. Oaks, "'Things fearful to name': Sodomy and Buggery in Seventeenth-Century New England," *Journal of Social History* 12 (1978): 268-81; Michel Rey, "Police et sodomie à Paris au XVIIIe siècle, du péché au désordre," *Revue d'Histoire Moderne et Contemporaine* 29 (1982): 113-24; R. Trumbach, "London's Sodomites: Homosexual Behavior and Western Culture in the Eighteenth Century," *Journal of Social History* 11 (1977): 1-33.

2. J. A. Faber, *Drie eeuwen Friesland. Economische en sociale ontwikkelingen van 1500 tot 1800* (Frisia during three centuries. Economic and social developments, 1500-1800), in 2 parts (Wageningen: 1972 AAG Bijdragen, 1972 vol. 17): pt. 1, 399.

3. Ibid., 1:34-38, 71-73; 2:425 and Table 2:26.

4. D. Hamerster, *Naukeurige en duidelijke verklaring over de Statuten, ordonantien, reglementen, en costumen van rechte in Friesland* (Accurate and clear explanation of the Statutes . . . of law in Frisia), 3 vols. (Leeuwarden: 1760-83); S. Binckes, *Verklaaringe van de Statuten, ordonnantien, reglementen en costumen van rechte in Friesland, anders genaamd 's Lands Ordonnantie . . .* , 4 vols. (Leeuwarden: 1785-86).

5. For example, Antonius Matthaeus II of Utrecht (1601-1654), in his *De criminibus ad Lib. XLVII et XLVIII Digestorum commentarius* (Utrecht: 1644), 460-61; and Dionysius Godefridus van der Keessel of Leyden (1738-1816) in his *Lectures on Books 47 and 48 of the Digest setting out the criminal law as applied in the courts of Holland (based on Cornelis van Eck) and on the new Criminal Code, 1809.* Latin text ed. and trans. into English by B. Beinart and P. van Warmelo, 6 vols. (Cape Town: 1969-81), (1:337; 2:569, 823, 857-65; 3:997 note; 6:2159 note, 2165).

6. John H. Langbein, *Prosecuting crime in the Renaissance. England, Germany, France* (Cambridge, MA: Harvard University Press, 1974), 165 ff.

7. Gisela Bleibtreu-Ehrenberg, *Tabu Homosexualität. Die Geschichte eines Vorurteils* (Frankfurt am Main: S. Fischer, 1978), 297-99.

8. Ulrik Huber, *The jurisprudence of my time (Heedendaegse Rechtsge-*

leertheyt), 5th ed. trans. Percival, 2 vols. (Durban: 1939), vol. 2, 424; Book 6, chap. 13, pars. 10-11.

9. L. J. Boon, "De grote sodomieten vervolging in het gewest Holland, 1730-1731" (The great persecution of sodomites in the province of Holland, 1730-1731), *Holland, regionaal-historisch tijdschrift* 8 (1976): 140-52; idem, "Utrechtenaren: de sodomieprocessen in Utrecht, 1730-1732" (Utrechters: Sodomy trials at Utrecht, 1730-1732), *Spiegel Historiael, maandblad voor geschiedenis en archeologie* 17 (1982): 553-58; idem, "Those Damned Sodomites: Public Images of Sodomy in the Eighteenth Century Netherlands," *Among Men, Among Women. Sociological and historical recognition of homosocial arrangements*. Papers delivered at the Gay Studies and Women's Studies University of Amsterdam Conference, Amsterdam, 22-26 June 1983 (Supp. 1, 19-22). D. J. Noordam, "Homosexualiteit en sodomie in Leiden, 1533-1518" (Homosexuality and sodomy in Leyden, 1533-1811) *Leids Jaarboekje* 75 (1983): 72-105; idem., "Homoseksuele relaties in Holland in 1776" (Homosexual relations in Holland in 1776), *Holland, regionaal-historisch tijdschrift* 16 (1984): 3-34. Theo van der Meer, *De wesentlijke sonde van sodomie en andere vuyligheeden. Sodomietenvervolgingen in Amsterdam 1730-1811* (The real sin of sodomy and other lewdness. Persecutions of sodomites at Amsterdam, 1730-1811) (Amsterdam: Tabula, 1984).

10. Based on the trial records in the Provincial Archives of Frisia at Leeuwarden, see my "Gerechtelijke vervolging van 'sodomie' gedurende de 18e eeuw in de Republiek, in het bijzonder in Friesland" (Prosecution of Sodomy During the Eighteenth Century in the Republic, especially in Frisia), *Groniedk, Gronings historisch tijdschrift* 66 (January 1980): 18-33.

11. A man named Tjerk Ottis was acquitted on the same day.

12. C. G. van der Kooij, "Rudolf de Mepsche en de Faanse processen" (Rudolf de Mepsche and the trials at Faan), *Spiegel Historiael, maanblad voor geschiedenis en archeologie* 14 (1979): 358-64.

13. D. J. Noordam, "Homosocial relations in Leiden (1533-1811)," *Among Men, Among Women* (see note 9): 218-23.

14. Norbert Elias, *The civilising process*, vol. 1, The history of manners (Oxford: Oxford University Press, 1977).

The Persecutions of Sodomites in Eighteenth-Century Amsterdam: Changing Perceptions of Sodomy

Theo van der Meer, Drs.

In 1730, for the first time in its history, the Republic of the United Provinces saw the heavy persecutions of sodomites. These persecutions started in January of that year with the complaint of the Custodian of the (former) Cathedral of Utrecht about unnatural practices taking place in the building. The judicial authorities in this city went into action: two soldiers were arrested and executed in secret. The confessions they had made led to the arrest of the former soldier and footman, Zacharias Wilsma, who had traveled throughout the Dutch Republic. He revealed to the authorities the existence of a network of sodomites, with branches in all major cities of the Republic. Wilsma's confessions produced a snowball effect: in different cities numerous suspects were arrested and put on trial. The persecutions reached a climax in the summer of 1730, but investigations went on as late as 1737.[1] However, the most notorious of these persecutions took place in 1731, in a small village in the north part of the country. On 24 September 1731, twenty-two boys and men from this and nearby other villages were executed by the country squire Rudolf de Mepsche.[2]

When the persecutions started, an Edict against sodomy was pro-

Theo van der Meer is affiliated with the Free University, Amsterdam.

This contribution is mainly an extensive summary of the author's study *De Wesentlijke Sonde van Sodomie en Andere Vuyligheenden. Sodomietenvervolgingen in Amsterdam, 1730-1811* (Amsterdam, 1984). Parts are, however, from the paper, "Legislation Against Sodomy in the Eighteenth Century Dutch Republic: The Acknowledgement of An Identity," presented at the *Sex and the State Conference*, 3-6 July 1985, Toronto, Canada.

mulgated in the Province of Holland. Modified in 1764, it was kept in force until 1811, after the annexation of the recently founded Kingdom of Holland by France.[3] Under this bill, sodomites were prosecuted, sometimes incidentally, sometimes in sequences of trials, especially in Amsterdam, by far the largest and most powerful city in the Republic. Between 1730 and 1811, at least two hundred and twenty-eight men and women, suspected of sodomy, sodomitical acts or of compliancy, stood on trial in two-hundred thirty-six cases. Of those two-hundred twenty-eight, one-hundred fifteen men were sentenced by default to lifelong exile.[4]

Most of the records of these trials are to be found in the last five out of eight so-called *Secret Confession Books* in the Municipal Archive in Amsterdam.[5] These books used to be concealed in a secret cabinet in the Alderman's room in the City Hall, the present Royal Palace in Dam Square, together with the minutes of the Alderman as well as letters and other manuscripts taken from arrested sodomites.[6] The letters and manuscripts have for the greater part been lost, but quotes from the letters can be found in the *Secret Confessions Books*.

Some of the records of trials against sodomites can be found in the standard *Confession Books* of the law court in Amsterdam, of which the Municipal Archive has preserved a collection, covering a period from 1534 to 1811. No serial works of these hundreds of *Confessions Books* are available, so it is possible that more cases against sodomites will come to light in the future. Therefore, the numbers of people persecuted for sodomy should be considered provisional.

Hundreds of references to the prosecuted sodomites or those who escaped, some of them containing only one small detail, others offering extensive additional information, are to be found in other sources in the Municipal Archive; for example, correspondence between the Bailiff and the Aldermen, the correspondence between the city's deputees in the States of Holland and the Burgomasters, the minutes of the Alderman, the *Warders Bills*, the *Sentence Books*, the *Bailiffs Roll* (mentions the sentences by default), and the Prison Archive, as well as the Archives of Orphanages and Notorial Acts. Copies of records of trials, probably intended for the Burgomasters, often contain annotations about legal grounds on which a sentence was based, or the vote of the Aldermen about the verdict. While the diary of the citizen Jacob Bicker Raije, who had for forty years (1732-1772) kept records of the gossip in the city, sometimes offers information about things or persons not mentioned in the judicial sources, the diary of Maarten Weveringh, Alderman between 1765 and 1777, supplies information about the courts. Together these sources give a detailed account of the lives and works of sodomites in the eighteenth-century Amsterdam, down to their very sexual acts, their subcultures, and their self-conceptions.

In this article, I will give an account of the persecutions, the lawsuits, the punitive measures, and the way of sentencing, as well as the public's reaction to and details about the subculture. I will also try to explain the persecutions. Quotations from original sources are translated as literally as possible. As a consequence, some expressions are as unusual in English as they are in modern Dutch: for example, "the shaking out" for masturbation.

THE LAWSUIT

Before going into any detail about the procedures against sodomites, the interpretation of the term used by the eighteenth-century court should be explained. (The question of whether or not an eighteenth-century sodomite was a homosexual in the modern sense of the word is considered elsewhere in this article.) Up until and throughout the seventeenth century, "sodomy" in common language and legal comments stood for any sexual technique that was not directed to procreation: oral and anal intercourse with male or female, masturbation, bestiality, and even sexual intercourse with Jews and Saracens.[7] In the eighteenth century, the courts used a more limited interpretation of the term. It considered sodomy exclusively as anal intercourse (or bestiality), and only then when the act had been committed to full: namely penetration and ejaculation in the body of a partner. When a suspect confessed to anal intercourse he was asked whether the act had been complete. Pieter Wagenaar, on trial in 1798, confessed that he had committed a coitus interruptus with a boy, but claimed he had never committed sodomy.[8] Nevertheless, the Judges as well as the suspects often got confused. Sodomites themselves called all their acts sodomy, perhaps due to the common use of the word.[9] For example, in 1764 Johannes Oudendijk told that he had committed sodomy. Later he specified that he and his accomplice had thrust their naked bodies against one another and "both of them had shaken out their own seed." Confronted with the legal definition of sodomy, he had said that he "had considered the filthy matters mentioned before as the sin of sodomy."[10] A year later, Hendrik Eelders said that he had believed, "that the shaking out belonged to the real sin of sodomy."[11] To avoid such confusion, the Judges sometimes drew a distinction between "the real sin of sodomy and other filthy matters." The difference was important because there was a correlation between the kind of act that a suspect confessed to and the punitive measure imposed. Only the "real sin of sodomy" was punishable by death.

In Amsterdam the court consisted of nine Aldermen and the Bailiff. They were chosen from the leading families of the city. The Bailiff was in charge of maintaining public order and tracking down criminals, and also acted as public prosecutor. A suspect did not receive legal assistance and once sentenced had no right to appeal.[12]

One of the main legal problems the court confronted in these cases was the fact that sodomy left no traces. There was no corpus delicti. To condemn a suspect, his confession was vital. To achieve this, the Bailiff confronted the suspects with witnesses or accomplices or used their statements. Those statements were part of the evidence, but to send a suspect to the scaffold, his confession was necessary.[13] The absence of one of the components, the confession or otherwise, did not automatically mean the dismissal of the suspect, but did exempt him from execution. In 1765 Hendrik Tulken denounced himself to the court and confessed to anal intercourse, but none of the accomplices he mentioned were found and he was only given a prison sentence.[14]

To obtain the confession of the suspect, the court had torture at its disposal. Allegations have been made that people suspected of sodomy were tortured to the extreme and confessed to things they had never done.[15] That seems, however, not to have been the actual case. The kind of torture used in Amsterdam was limited to shinscrews and whipping. From 1765 onward, whipping was the only kind of torture applied to sodomites in Amsterdam. Torture was also subjected to certain rules. It was only allowed when the

Bailiff had gathered so-called "full half proof." Though the meaning of this was not always clear, in cases against sodomites torture was until 1795 only applied when eyewitnesses or accomplices had testified of anal intercourse. Furthermore, the Bailiff had to ask the permission of the Aldermen before a person could be ordered tortured.[16] Once a suspect had admitted his crimes under torture, he had to resubmit his confession "free from pains and ties." Indeed, such was the question put forward to the confessor immediately after he had been released from the instruments of torture and again at the beginning of the next examination. So a kind of safety valve was built in — for what it was worth. Those who revoked a confession could be tortured again.

In 1764, Hermanus van Werkhoven confessed to anal intercourse. A week later, he revoked part of his confession and only admitted to mutual masturbation. Threatened with shinscrews again, he repeated his former confession. Explaining his revocation, he said that "he had remembered the sadness that would befall his poor wife if he was punished publicly by death, as he understood that this had to follow the crime of sodomy: on the contrary, he thought that if he confessed nothing but the shaking out, he was only to be confined for the rest of his life, where he could see neither sun nor moon."[17]

Torture applied to sodomites in fact seldom resulted in confessions. The Aldermen in Amsterdam gave their approval twenty times to torture people suspected of sodomy. Four men confessed before it had been applied. Only four others confessed under torture.[18] Lawsuits in the eighteenth century were quite intimidating, however, and torture was often not a necessity to "convince" suspects of their crimes. Besides, while society at large considered sodomy to be a most abominable crime, it is no wonder that those involved shared this concept, especially when brought in court and even more after a confession. Once a prisoner had confessed to sodomy, he often became very cooperative and up to the very moment of execution impeached accomplices or mentioned the names of people whose reputation he knew. He was encouraged to do so by the Bailiff and the clergymen that accompanied him during his last hours.

Some sodomites took this negative self-conception to its ultimate point by denouncing themselves to the court, like Hendrik Tulken mentioned before — though his action may have been a complicated attempt to commit suicide. It sometimes happened that people accused themselves of capital crimes they had not committed in order to be executed.[19] A more obvious case of self-denouncement was that of the twenty-two-year-old Pieter Didding and the twenty-three-year-old Willem Knieland. They stood on trial in 1743, some time after they had committed sodomy in the toilets of the orphanage where they lived. Pieter told his judges that he "committed it this one time and never again and also had not given any thought of doing it again, but that after the committed act, he had become very sad and that his conscience could not rest about it and such was the cause that he out of remorse had made it known to the fathers of the house and that the thing mentioned above had happened some five weeks ago and that he had since prayed day and night to the Lord to prevent him from such sins and that he had only been seduced to this atrocious fact by the before mentioned Willem Knieland."[20]

THE VERDICT AND THE PUNITIVE MEASURES

In the eighteenth century most legal sources — Roman law, Mosiac law, Jurisprudence, Legal Comments — conferred the death sentence on sodomy and stated that sodomites should be burned. The Edict promulgated by the State of Holland 21 July 1730, bore out the capital punishment, but left the method of execution to the discretion of the Judges.[21] As mentioned above, only anal intercourse was punishable by death and no difference was made between the active and the passive role.[22] Of all the people on trial for sodomy in Amsterdam between 1730 and 1811, sixteen men died at the scaffold, the last one in 1765.[23]

In the eighteenth century an "execution day" was held in Amsterdam two or three times a year, always on a Saturday. All the people sentenced to public punishment — capital or otherwise — were brought forward on that day. Capital executions were preceded by several ceremonies, which started the Thursday before. In the presence of the Aldermen, one of the Burgomasters, and the prisoner, who was escorted by constables and clergyman, the Bailiff put forward his capital requirements.[24] Everybody then left the room except for the Aldermen, who voted on the Bailiff's demand. Next, the Burgomaster brought the "learned advice" of the Burgomasters.[25] After that the Bailiff was informed whether or not his demand was granted him.

The following day the prisoner was informed by the Bailiff and one of the Aldermen in a new ceremony that the Bailiff would "summon him next morning at the high tribunal to hear his verdict." "The Bailiff admonished the patients in a Christian way, very sensitive, to think of their imminent end and to spend the rest of the short time left to them with true repentance; may God have mercy on these poor sinners," noted Weveringh in his diary, when in 1765 he assisted the Bailiff in notifying the sodomites Hendrik Eelders and Jan Kemmer of their execution.[25]

On Saturday morning in the Vierschaar, the marble courtroom on the ground floor at the front of the City Hall, the condemned were declared "children of death." All those involved – the condemned, the Judges, the Burgomasters, and Clergymen – met in the Room of Justice to say a final prayer. Then the condemned were executed on a removable scaffold, built against the front wall of the City Hall.[26]

In the eighteenth century, execution of a criminal was usually performed in accordance with the act he or she had committed; for example, somebody who had killed a person with a knife was hanged with a knife above his head. Concerning this habit, the act of sodomy of course presented a difficulty. That is probably why sodomites were almost always executed by garroting, in eighteenth-century Amsterdam a typical punishment for women.[27] The faces of two sodomites garroted in 1730 were scorched after their executions. Two others were drowned in a barrel on the scaffold, which according to a compiler of a list of persons executed in Amsterdam, was "a surprisingly harder death" than garroting.[28] While in the scorching a remnant of symbolic purification may be found, the drowning was meant to wash away the sins.[29]

Usually in the Republic, the bodies of the executed criminals were not buried but, like elsewhere in Europe, sent to a gallowfield – in Amsterdam the Volewijk – (Birdsdistrict), "given up to the influence of air and the birds of heaven." The exposure of the corpses was meant to set an example to potential criminals.[30] Besides, the existence of standing gallows, mostly outside the city walls, showed outsiders that this was a law-abiding city. In a society in which the constitutional state is as personal as an oligarchy like that of the Republic, standing gallows are also a part of the majesty of the authorities.[31] The same goes for the exposed corpse: it remained the property of the authorities.[32] The corpse of a sodomite obviously was not considered to be an ornament to the majesty of the authorities. The Edict of 1730 stipulated explicitly that the executed sodomites were to be either burned or thrown into the sea.[33] In Amsterdam the executed sodomites were thrown into the deepest part of the River IJ. After all, sodomy was also a *crimen nefandum*, a mute sin, of which it was better not to be reminded.[34]

The penalties for sodomites varied, depending on the kind of evidence and the precise acts they were accused of. Those that confessed only to mutual masturbation or against whom there was no complete evidence of the "real sin" were usually confined for decades.[35] Others, only charged with but denying mutual masturbation, were exiled or provisionally released.

In the men's prison in Amsterdam, prisoners manufactured powder, used in the paint industry, from a red Brazilian wood. The sodomites were not, however, allowed to take part in labor. They were kept in solitary confinement in the cellar of the building. It seems as if for these prisoners the same considerations were in force as for those sodomites that were executed. They were hidden.[36] Meanwhile, in 1806 the drafter of a concept report about the prison system complained about the fact that the imprisoned sodomites were "delivered up to lazyness and unemployment, the sources of all kinds of crimes and particularly those for which they were confined."[37]

The Prison Archive has only been partially preserved. What remains tells us that of twenty-eight sodomites confined in prison in Amsterdam between 1791 and 1811, twelve died in their cells. But some, like Jan Jansz, were to spend a long life down in that cellar. In 1741 at the age of seventeen he was confined for the rest of his life. He died fifty-seven years later, in 1798. Jan Schuyl, confined for fifty years in 1761 died in 1806.[38] Jan Hikke, imprisoned in 1764, was released in 1804.

Attempts to break out of prison were not unusual. Indeed, the sodomite Jan Mandel escaped from prison in 1745 after failing at a first attempt in 1740.[39] In 1792 two sodomites escaped, but one of them returned a week later and asked to be confined again.[40] Sodomites that were still imprisoned in 1811 when the French Penal Code came into force were not automatically released, though some of them received reduced sentences.[41]

When at the beginning of June, 1730, deliberations commenced in the States of Holland upon the Edict against sodomy, it appeared that a lot of suspects had taken refuge across the border. Lots of others, who were not even suspected, had also taken refuge. The Edict stipulated in Clause Five that refugees against whom there was evidence of sodomitical crimes had to be summoned three times, and when they did not appear in court should be sentenced by default to lifelong exile. According to Clause Six people that had disappeared without apparent reason within three months of 15 May 1730, were to be summoned and sentenced likewise.[42] It was precisely this last clause that necessitated a modified Edict in 1764, when once again heavy persecutions were taking place in Amsterdam. At the request of Amsterdam, from that time on Clause Six could be applied to those disappearing at times when sodomites were arrested.[43]

THE PERSECUTION OF SODOMY

The figures mentioned above about sodomites prosecuted in the eighteenth century in Amsterdam show that there never has been a systematic persecution of them. When in 1730, 1764, and 1776 sequences of trials took place, they were the result of a snowball effect. It always started with the more or less accidental arrest of a sodomite and his subsequent confessions. People could not be arrested on the merest suspicion.[44] As previously stated, the figures should be considered provisional, and hardly anything is known about preliminary examinations followed by discharge. That such things happened becomes apparent in the case of two "mindless" men from the Almony's Orphanage. They were accused of sodomy, but after consultation of the Bailiff, the Alderman, and the servants of the house, because of their mindlessness they were only confined for half a year in a courtyard of the Orphanage itself. The record of their case is not found in judicial sources, but in the minutes of the masters of the Orphanage.⁴⁵

On the other hand, repression is not measured by figures only. In January 1761, Jacob Bicker Raije noted in his diary:

> A boatman from Leiden has been fished out of the water near the Papenbridge, who had been missed for six weeks, as he was to marry a young lady who worked in a shop at the New Market and with whom he at that time was at the City hall to enter their names in the registry, when two brothers of the young lady seized the prospective bride, saying we will not allow you to marry a sodomite. At which the young lady struggled a little, but went with her brothers. And he, not to fall in the hands of the mob, as he was suspected there about by many people and perhaps felt guilty in his conscience, without speaking silently slinked away and has been missed from that time on and has thus been found perished.⁴⁶

In 1763-1764, a practice began to evolve of deliberately entrapping sodomites. This was first carried out by four night watchmen who started their activities in public toilets. Those toilets were built under the numerous bridges in Amsterdam and divided into men's and women's cubicles. Visitors took their places next to one another on a bench, furnished with holes, that emptied directly into the water below. Two women "forced by their poverty to keep residence at night in the common toilet . . . in the so-called women's cubicle"⁴⁷ had informed a lieutenant of the nightwatch of things happening next to them in the men's cubicle. On the night of 8 May four night watchmen concealed themselves with the women in their cubicle. When two men, Barend Jansen and Jan Heemskerk, entered the men's cubicle and started their usual activities, the night watchmen stormed the men's cubicle and arrested both men.

During trial, the witnesses declared that they had heard Jansen and Heemskerk, "their lips smacking whilst they kissed."⁴⁸ Jansen explained to the Bailiff that he produced the sound while he tried to remove with his tongue a piece of sausage lodged between his teeth. The gasping the witnesses had heard, he explained, was straining due to a laxative he had taken that day. The Bailiff was not impressed. Besides, Jansen could not deny what the night watchmen had seen when they stormed the cubicle. Both men stood with naked bellies, Heemskerk's hand on Jansen's penis. While only assault was proven, Jansen and Heemskerk were imprisoned for six and eight years, respectively. Heemskerk was considered the seducer. A year later when more evidence was gathered, Heemskerk was sentenced to death and Jansen, due to the fact that he had already been tortured twice, was imprisoned for another twenty years.[49]

From that time on, the night watchmen took the initiative themselves. One of them, Jan van der Marck, took to wearing a carpenter's apron at night because he thought he had noticed "how among those persons suspected by him, various have been with an apron before their body."[50] Dressed like that, he patrolled at night around the City Hall and tried to provoke sodomites near the urinals, placed at the back of building. His success was limited. In 1763 he arrested a cobbler, but before this man had made a full confession, he committed suicide in his cell.[51] In the year that followed, Van der Marck and his fellow night watchmen made several more arrests, but only one man arrested under these circumstances confessed to his crimes.[52]

The Persecutions of 1730

The persecutions started in January 1730 in Utrecht, and by 5 May the Utrecht magistry had informed other courts about suspects under their jurisdiction. On 18 May, the first suspect in Amsterdam, the merchant Dirk Cuyleman, was arrested but then provisionally discharged. By the time he was summoned again four days later, he had disappeared.[53] The day before, four other men had been arrested and immediately confronted with the main witness and accomplice, Zacharias Wilsma, brought to Amsterdam for that purpose. He charged all four of them with "the real sin of sodomy." In the weeks that followed, one after the other confessed. One of them, Pieter Martijn, turned out to have been in a key position in the sodomite network. He mentioned no less than forty names of accomplices.[54] On 22 June, all four of them were sentenced to death and executed two days later.[55] English newspapers informed their public of the execution, also making allegations that some days before, thirty men had been thrown into the river in sewn-up sacks.[56]

At the beginning of August, a new suspect, Lourens Hosponjon, was arrested. He was the protégé of Burgomaster Pieter Gijs of Leiden, probably his lover.[57] He was executed on 16 September. Hosponjon was the last of the sodomites to be executed in Amsterdam in the 1730s. One man and one woman were exiled because of compliancy to the act, while five others were discharged provisionally.[58] Between 1730 and 1732, thirty-five men were sentenced by default,[59] among them the brother of the Bailiff.[60] One of them returned to the city and committed suicide after being arrested.[61] Another one, the prominent merchant Jan Bouwens, was strongly defended by his family, friends, and a lawyer. They appealed without success to the Court of Holland, and so like the others, Bouwens was sentenced by default to a lifelong exile.[62]

The Persecutions of 1764

Though the persecutions in 1764 were, so to say, "in the air," as may be seen from the activities of the night watchmen in 1763, they started with the accidental arrest of a soldier in March 1764. This soldier, Jacobus Hebelaar, was the token unlucky person. In January 1764 he was courtmartialed in the garrison of Den Briel for theft. He was whipped and exiled from all the garrisons throughout the country. Two months later, he was court-martialed again because of taking up service in the army at the garrison of Zutphen. He was consequently branded and exiled a second time. He left for Amsterdam.[63]

On 23 March Jacobus Hebelaar had his ultimate run of bad luck. He had been drinking all day. Around half past eight that night he walked through the Warmoesstreet. At the corner of a passage he saw two men acting as if they were urinating. He positioned himself next to the smartest, urinated, pinched the man on his back, looked him in the eyes and said: "My Lord, why do you pretend to be simple? You're not as simple as you pretend." About the man's companion he said to the former: "Fy! Aren't you ashamed of yourself to take up with so low a fellow. He is a scalliwag."[64] Jacobus was told to clear off. He then went to the public toilet under the Papenbridge, and addressed himself to the first man that entered the men's cubicle, saying: "Rascal, scamp, sodomite. Art Thou there. I've waited so long for you."[65] He struck down the man and robbed him of his cloak, silver clasps, snuff box, corkscrew, handkerchief, and money and left the toilet. He was arrested shortly afterwards.

On trial, Jacobus maintained that "he had partly been robbed of his mind by the liquor and that Satan had taken what was left of it."[66] Then it turned out that the man he had made a pass at in the Warmoesstreet was no one less than the Substitute Bailiff. The man he had called a scalliwag was the night watchman Jan van der Marck who used to dress himself in a carpenter's apron. Both men were on their way to make an arrest that night and, to avoid being recognized, had acted as if they "were making water." After several interrogations, Jacobus Hebelaar confessed to the robbery. Concerning the occurrences with the Substitute Bailiff, he pretended ignorance. On 9 June 1764, Jacobus Hebelaar was hanged. His sentence records the robbery and the odd things that happened in the Warmoesstreet.[67]

Jacob Bicker Raije noted that very day in his diary that Jacobus "would have been executed a fortnight earlier, yet because of important discoveries he revealed to my Lords, that have been concealed from the common, justice had been postponed a fortnight."[68] Bicker Raije may not have known the ins and outs of the case, but the *Secret Confession Book* tells the facts. On 22 May Jacobus Hebelaar himself had asked to be examined by the court. "To unburden his conscience," he confessed that for seven years he had committed actively as well as passively "the gruesome sin of sodomy." He mentioned a number of accomplices, amongst whom was Barend Jansen, one of the men arrested a year before in a public toilet by the night watchmen.

It is obvious that the court, by its decision to hang Hebelaar instead of garroting him and by only mentioning the robbery, wanted to prevent Hebelaar's accomplices from taking refuge. Indeed, only a few days before Hebelaar's execution, the Bailiff started to round up other sodomites. Between the day of his execution and the summer of 1765, seven other sodomites were executed by garroting. Five were imprisoned, three were exiled, one was provisionally discharged, and sixty-four sentenced by default.[69] Bicker Raije wrote in his diary that more than one hundred men had fled from the city and that others had withdrawn themselves from the authorities by committing suicide.[70] One of those sentenced by default was rehabilitated in 1767 after his return to the city — as he pleaded that he had only left because of "the bad temper of his wife," whom he had just married.[71]

The Persecutions of 1776

In 1776, a new sequence of trials against sodomites started.[72] Once again, they resulted from accidental circumstances. In April of that year, Floris Husson and Hendrik Nederveen were arrested in Amsterdam, charged with selling forged bonds. Husson had stolen these bonds from the office of the General Receiver in The Hague, where he was employed.[73] His mother petitioned the City Holder William V to prevent the humiliation of a public punishment for her genteel family. In his advice to the Prince, the Bailiff stated that such atrocious crimes should not be left unpunished and that "at present we do live in the happy times, that the crimes are personal and the infamy following there from, is applied by right minded people only to the criminal himself and not to his innocent family."[74]

With this advice, the overture in the case was passed. At the end of May 1776, the Bailiff discovered eight letters in the luggage of Husson containing obvious references to sodomy. Among other things, all men mentioned in these letters were referred to by female names. Cryptic expressions turned out to be of a scurrilous nature, referring to the size of a penis or to special sexual qualities of certain men. One of the correspondents wrote that he had been called a "confounded child," "shitstamper," "assfucker." One expression is very cryptic indeed: "she is a nice person; when one touches her little hole she laughs very hard."[75] Asked for the meaning of this, Husson explained that the man in question was created by a man as well as a woman — to which the Bailiff responded that that was ridiculous.

Both Husson and Nederveen confessed to mutual masturbation. Nederveen admitted that twice he had tried to penetrate an accomplice, but that he had failed because he was "created too large." Husson and Nederveen were whipped and branded on the scaffold, before being imprisoned for twenty-five and thirty years, respectively.[76] The Alderman Weverinh noted in his diary that Husson took the punishment with "much impudence."[77] Fifteen years later, both men escaped from prison, but Husson returned, was confined again, and died in his cell in 1799.[78] During the trials of Husson and Nederveen, the Amsterdam court kept in close touch with other courts, especially the Court of Holland. Arrests were made in other cities as well, but especially in The Hague. Prosecutions lasted until 1779.[79] In Amsterdam, only two others were arrested. This time, sixteen were sentenced by default.

The Persecutions After 1795

Between 1795 and 1811, more sodomy trials were held in Amsterdam than in the preceding sixty-five years.[80] Most notorious were the years 1795 to 1798. During this period, for the first time women were put on trial for sodomy (or tribady, as it was also called). But another radical change can be seen in the persecution of sodomy after 1795. Before 1795, those that were accused of soliciting were usually discharged provisionally—if put on trial at all. As a lawyer in 1730 stated: The mere will to commit sodomy was not punishable.[81] After 1795, such people were put on trial, sometimes tortured,[82] and in several cases condemned even while they denied the crime.

On an evening in October 1795, a twenty-year-old footman and a fifty-year-old keyboard master met at a square in Amsterdam. They did not know each other, but the master addressed himself to the footman: "Good evening citizen. Where are you going to?" At the request of Visch, the master, they sat down. Visch took off the footman's hat, put it on himself, stroked the young man's hair, and said, "What hast thou beautiful hair, was it arranged while thou werest in thine service?"[83] Moments afterward, they were arrested by several night watchmen, who alleged that Visch's pants were loose and that his shirt was hanging out of them. Nothing had happened so far that justified either an arrest or a trial. But prosecutions started the day after the arrests. Visch denied that he had wanted to

seduce the footman. Then the unthinkable happened. The Prosecuter (as the Bailiff was called after 1795)[84] got permission to torture
Visch. Visch was whipped and asked whether or not he had wanted
to commit sodomy with the footman, to which he answered, "not
with him." With this answer, he gave himself away and, after several evasive remarks, he confessed to sodomy with other men and
was confined for fifty years. The footman was discharged provisionally.

A year later, Thomas Gouwes stood on trial. The matter in question must have taken place a year before. He was charged with
having said to a man in a pub that he "would like to fuck him."
And to the pubman he was supposed to have said, "Forgive me.
When I spoke to the fellow, I lost my nature."[85] Gouwes was
whipped, but denied the charges. The Prosecuter recommended a
provisional release, but the court sentenced Gouwes to two years of
solitary confinement.[86] The same happened in 1797 to Hendrik
Coerten, charged with caressing a number of men.[87]

These examples do not stand alone. Though some men were still
charged with and found guilty of homosexual acts after 1795, many
others were arrested for what was called a "tentamen sodomiti-
cam" or "an attempt to commit sodomitical acts." These expressions did not refer to an attempt to commit anal intercourse or other
undeniable sexual acts, but referred mainly to soliciting.

After 1795, people were no longer sentenced to death in Amsterdam for sodomy, and the average confinement went down from
more than thirty years in the period before, to twelve years (for
men) after 1795. But this decrease was mainly due to the "short"
confinements for "tentamina." When a sexual act was proven, a
confinement of twenty years or more was still the norm.[88]

Sodomitical acts were committed among all classes, but those
prosecuted usually came from the lower strata of society—even
though the judicial authorities tried to give the impression that they
treated their peers like anyone else. Indeed, among those sentenced
by default in 1730, there were a number of aristocrats and members
of the governing class: Baron Meeuwen van Huynsburg, Cornelis
de la Faille, Alderman of Delft, Jacob van Wouw, Bailiff in that
city, Cornelis Backer, Bailiff of Buuren and brother of the Amsterdam Bailiff, and Willem Six, City Father of Haarlem.[89] But it seems

unlikely that members of the governing class were prepared to meet their peers in a scandalous trial. Somebody like Pieter Gijs, Burgomaster of Leiden, continued his career in spite of charges brought against him.[90] Frederik van Reede van Renswoude, a prominent diplomat and President of the Knighthood in the States of Utrecht, returned undisturbed to his country seat.[91]

With the flight of a number of highplaced gentlemen, the governing classes were saved from too much embarrassment concerning the unequal treatment of the suspects. In fact, here they could demonstrate that they wanted to do justice impartially. The fugitives, coming from all strata, were exiled. But it does not seem to have been accidental that the same time in 1730 when the States of Holland promulgated an Edict against sodomy, the usual practice of confiscating the belongings of those that had fled the country was also abolished.[92] The possessions of the better situated sodomites remained unassailable. The aforementioned Cornelis Backer, brother of the Amsterdam Bailiff, left upon his death in England in 1748 a fortune of 160,000 guilders to his heirs in Holland.[93]

In dealing with upper-class people who did not belong to the governing class, the court made extraordinary rulings. No records are known to exist of the interrogation of the merchant Dirk Cuyleman, the first to be arrested in 1730 in Amsterdam. All that is left are two notes about his provisional discharge and his sudden departure from the city.[94] The question of why he was discharged provisionally remains unanswered. In 1732, another merchant, Anthony van Waart, stood on trial in Amsterdam and was confronted with a supposed accomplice, who accused him of anal intercourse. Although the Bailiff also had at his disposal a statement from an already executed sodomite against him, Van Waart denied everything. But why did the Bailiff not ask for permission to torture Van Waart? And why the discrepancy between the requirements and the actual verdict? The Bailiff wanted Van Waart to be imprisoned for the rest of his life, but the Alderman discharged him provisionally.[95]

In 1776 the Alderman Weveringh made detailed notes in his diary about a sodomy trial against another prominent citizen, Hermanus Kloek, one of the foremen of the highly esteemed soapboilers guild. He was one of the authors of the letters which when discovered caused the persecutions of 1776. Kloek was not arrested

at first, but when it was discovered that he was one of Floris Husson's correspondents, he was asked to pay a visit to the City Hall.
On his arrival, Kloek was interrogated and almost immediately confessed to mutual masturbation. However, the interrogation had to
be interrupted because of a legal problem. A person who appeared
in court voluntarily could not be placed under arrest. The Bailiff,
the Aldermen, and the Burgomasters decided to discharge Kloek,
but to put him under arrest as soon as he left the City Hall. But the
interrogation was halted once again when Kloek confessed that he
had once been assaulted by a gentleman. The Bailiff asked the Aldermen whether he should ask Kloek for the name of the gentleman. The Aldermen were in a dilemma, "while we feared that it
could be a man related to one of us."[96] Finally, they decided to have
the examination continued by the two Aldermen with the fewest
family ties in Amsterdam. The result was not at all reassuring. The
man turned out to be the former Alderman and present secretary of
the Amsterdam insurance department, George Clifford. The Bailiff
did not inquire any further into the matter and Kloek was exiled—
whereas people found guilty of mutual masturbation were usually
imprisoned for decades. When a couple of weeks later an accomplice of Kloek was arrested and confessed to masturbation with
Kloek, Weveringh noted the public opinion that Kloek had been let
off too lightly. For that reason, the Bailiff recommended forty years
of confinement for Kloek's accomplice, but in the end the Aldermen voted for having him exiled instead.[97]

Those sodomites who were punished with confinement or death
were from the lower middleclass or the working class, or were pau-
pers. They were shopkeepers, craftsmen, footmen, or peddlers,
professions that obviously alternated with begging.[98]

Children and Women

Anal intercourse used to be punished with death. However, age
could be an extenuating circumstance, and no man under twenty
was condemned to death because of sodomy.[99] In the period studied
eight boys charged with sodomy varying in age from eleven to eighteen stood on trial in Amsterdam. One of them was discharged.[100] In
1746 a seventeen-year-old boy was whipped on the scaffold and

forced to watch the hanging of his mature accomplice.[101] He and others suffered an average confinement of almost forty years. Even the eleven-year-old was confined for twenty years.[102] No doubt, these punishments were extremely severe, even in the eighteenth century. Children up to sixteen were seldom confined or put to the scaffold in this period. Even when their crimes were considered serious, they were almost always released after being whipped indoors on the so-called wooden horse, or else put in the hands of their parents to be castigated.[103]

It is obvious that the court did not consider sodomitical acts by children to be different from those by adults. Likewise, sodomitical acts between adults and children were not categorized separately. In 1761 Jan Schuyl confessed to assaulting two six-year-old boys and was confined for fifty years.[104] In 1806 the schoolmaster John Cocouault stood trial, accused of telling the children committed to his charge about married life and the seduction of a nine-year-old boy. Though he denied the charges, he was imprisoned for thirty years.[105]

Until 1792 only males were arrested on the suspicion that they had committed sodomy. However, a woman was exiled in 1730 after being convicted for being compliant to sodomitical acts in her pub.[106]

Quite a number of cases are known from the seventeenth and eighteenth centuries in which women, dressed as males, served in the army or the navy. In some cases, they even married other women and had sexual intercourse with them. Weveringh found in the old confession books the story of Hendrikje Verschuur. In the first half of the seventeenth century, she had served in the army of Prince Frederik Hendrik of Nassau and taken part in the siege of Breda.[107] Later, she was examined by Doctor Nicolaas Tulp, who discovered that "she had a clitoris the size of a child's penis and thickness of half a little finger and with that had carnal conversation with several women and amongst others Trijntje Barends, widow of Theunis Michielse (with whom she had begotten six children) and had been so besotted with one another that they would have liked to have been married if it had been possible."[108]

In 1792, for the first time a woman, Bets Wiebes, was sentenced because she had laid upon another woman "in the way a man is used to do when he has carnal intercourse with his wife." The court seemed not to know how to react to this situation. Bets Wiebes was not arrested for her "conversation," but on the suspicion of having murdered one of her girlfriends. Later it turned out that another girlfriend with whom Bets lived was the murderer. That woman, Bartha Schuurman, confessed "the envy she had entertained against [the murdered] was situated in a strong jealousy, born from the dirty lusts that had taken place between Bets Wiebes and the murdered and between Bets Wiebes and herself."[109] The court did not go to much trouble to find out exactly what had happened between the women. Bartha Schuurman was sentenced to death for murder and Bets Wiebes was exiled for six years because of her "dirty lusts."[110]

Sex between women was punished after 1795 — the same time after which soliciting between males became criminalized. Between 1795 to 1797, eleven women stood trial in Amsterdam because of "dirty acts" with one another. Eight of them were confined in women's prison. But their average confinement was much shorter than that of men: six versus twelve years during that period.[111] Besides, all of these women received a reduction of their sentences, whereas only some of the male sodomites still in prison after 1811 received similar reduction.[112]

The *Secret Confession Books* are as explicit about the sexual acts between the women as they are about sexual acts between males. For example, in 1796 Gesina Dekkers told that she "was lying on the floor with Engeltje Blauwpaard next to her, and when they were caressing one another, Engeltje Blauwpaard put her finger in the womanliness of she, [and] moved that finger up and down, which lasted about a quarter of an hour."[113]

All of these women — except for a certain Anna Grabout — were as poor as most of the prosecuted sodomites. Like them, the women peddled fruit and papers, gathered drywood, or turned in and out of prostitution. Anna Grabout, however, was married and fairly well-to-do. She supposedly promised another woman jewelry and other finery. The witnesses' testimony also suggested that Anna was a passionate woman. She was accused of having said to one of her girlfriends:

"I love you so much you should always be without your bonnet, then I love you so much. I shall take care that my old fellow leaves town and then you have to come to me, and we should be alone together, because I want to see you naked and if you do what I like, I shall support you. I shall give you anything your heart desires, because if I have drunk a glass of wine I'm as hot as fire."[114]

A sister of this girlfriend charged Anna with assaults and testified that Anna had said to her on such an occasion: "Pretty flower. You're not as pretty above your skirt as below. I don't feel any hair. It is like it's covered with cotton."[115] A third witness told in court that when on one occasion she and Anna were looking at a boy swimming naked in a canal, Anna said to her: "You do have something in your being which attracts both male and female. If I just see you, I come already and if you have me whipped tomorrow and branded the day after, I shall yet love you for it."[116] Though she denied the charges, Anna was confined for two years.

A rather exceptional case was that of Christina Kip in 1797. She was charged with raping a fourteen-year-old girl with an artificial penis. At the trial, women of her neighborhood testified that Christina had long been considered to be out of her mind. One of the women gave an example of Christina's supposed madness. She told that once she had asked Christina, "Chris, it amazes me that you don't marry." Christina's answer: "Just to fuck? If that's all I'm missing I can do it myself."[117]

The word "sodomy" was never used in the cases against these women. Most of the time, the Prosecuter spoke of "caresses and filthy acts." At least in one source the women were called "tribades."[118]

PUBLIC REACTION

The persecutions in 1730 were soon followed by massive publicity. In pamphlets and poems sodomites were made the scapegoats for all disasters that were supposed to wreck the country, the de-

cline of trade and the Bourse, and the decline of morals.[119] Clergymen tried to enlighten the public in books about sodomy, but their
version veiled the facts rather than informed the readers. These
books were about the destruction of Sodom and Gomorra and explained why the men of Sodom committed their wicked sins: pride,
the result of abundance, took away their fear of punishment. Copious food made the people lazy, incapable of doing their duty, and
seduced them to all kinds of sins. The lack of enemies of the state
caused idleness, the parent of vice. From Sodom, sodomy spread
across the world. In the West, this vice was limited at the outset to
Catholics and Italy, but now that the people of the Netherlands had
lost the austerity of their ancestors and lived in luxury, they had
fallen prey to this terrible crime. Everybody who had already succumbed to "the screaming sins" — card-playing, gambling, swearing and whoring — was likely to commit sodomy or to be seduced
into it and thus spread it further among the people.[120]

In 1730, it turned out that people had known of the activities of
certain sodomites long before. But when the persecutions began,
they became aware of the penalty for sodomy and in some cases
reported sodomites to the authorities.[121] This was not a common
practice, however. In Groningen, for example, the Burgomasters
promulgated an Edict summoning the citizens to denounce suspects
and even promised a reward and guaranteed anonymity. But the
Edict hardly worked out this way.[122] Even in later years, when the
awareness of the penalty for sodomy must have grown, people were
seldom very cooperative. Most of the time sodomites were only
reported when they made an indecent assault upon an unconsenting
person.

In 1749, Christiaan Kip was caught in the act outside the city
walls. He was severely abused by those who caught him, and a
bystander was noted to have said: "Oh, it is that rascal; he has had
that name for so long."[123] But Kip was not denounced until half a
year later when several young men who had hired a place to sleep in
his house accused him of assaulting them.[124]

In 1810, two men stood trial, charged with sodomy. A couple
living opposite them testified that a year before they had witnessed
from their window how one of the men had used the other "as his
wife."[125] But the couple was not responsible for their arrests. Their

arrest resulted from inquiries the prosecutor had made after the arrests of several others.[126]

However, in some cases people tracked down sodomites themselves, perhaps to gain a reward. The case of the two men in 1810, mentioned above, started with the arrest of six men in 1809. They had been tracked down by a man who acted almost as a professional detective. Once he had realized that sodomites were meeting in a certain house, he visited the house himself, then took other witnesses with him on subsequent visits. When testifying in court, he gave a vivid description of what he had seen and of the effeminate atmosphere he had encountered in this company.[127]

The fact that people did not often denounce sodomites did not mean that they approved of their behavior. When sodomites like the before-mentioned Christiaan Kip fell into the hands of the mob, they were often severely abused. Kip sustained a broken arm and leg on that occasion. On the other hand, this should not be explained as a kind of "queerbashing" *avant la lettre*. "To fall into the hands of the mob" (*in de maling geraken*) could happen to any suspected criminal caught in the act. The cry "hold the thief" could raise a mob in no time, and if such a mob laid hands upon the supposed perpetrator, the unfortunate was beaten up and often thrown into a canal (as indeed happened to the sodomite Gerrit ter Horstn 1799).[128] Numerous criminal case records noted suspects being assaulted by mobs or else being saved from mobs by constables. According to the Dutch legal historian Spierenburg, the mob justice was a relic of an older form of justice, the feud, which in the middle ages was an accepted form of settling scores between individuals without interference from the legal apparatus. Spierenburg argued that the practice reflected the fact that the authority of the ruling class had not yet been completely established.[129] This also might explain why people were not very cooperative with attempts by the authorities to track down sodomites.

Forms of violence against sodomites that came close to "queerbashing" did exist, however. Especially after 1795, people suspected of sodomy often testified in court that they had been victim to this kind of violence.[130]

Another less direct kind of violence was blackmail. As early as 1689, three young men were sentenced in Amsterdam because they had blackmailed men whom they had pretended to seduce in the City Hall and the Bourse.[131] In 1735 three other men confessed to having blackmailed people they had met in public toilets and accused of soliciting. Their practices went back as far as 1725.[132] In both cases, the perpetrators had been able to continue their practices for quite a length of time without being reported. In a case of blackmail in 1715, the victim obviously was less afraid to denounce his blackmailer, though the arrest of the perpetrator might also have been due to the fact that he caused a disturbance when he carried out his threat and informed the neighbors of his victim that the man was a sodomite.[133] In 1800 a shopkeeper hurried to leave the city when his blackmailers were caught.[134]

THE SUBCULTURE

Where homosexuality or sodomy is concerned, the use of the word "subculture" is often unspecified. Does it refer to places where those involved meet, to common practices, to habits? Can we even speak of "a subculture?" In this article I define "subculture" as a specific form of organization of sexuality which differs from what is dominant in a culture, as a means of passing on habits, norms, and values, and as a means to identify with one another. Here, I deal with the subculture that came to light in the Dutch Republic in 1730. This does not mean, however, that other kinds of subcultures in which sodomy was practiced did not exist. In fact they did; namely, among soldiers, sailors, and courtiers.[135]

What Zacharias Wilsma, mentioned earlier in this paper, revealed to the authorities in 1730 was the existence of a "nationwide" network of sodomites with a rather loose structure. Many of those sodomites knew one another, at least by reputation. They were involved in local networks, met one another in small groups, individually, or both, or had contacts in other cities. Some of them had tight relations, others, perhaps belonging to the periphery of the network, had only loose contacts. Members of the aristocracy often hired special footmen through people officially mediating between those looking for work and those that could employ them. People like Wilsma connected the different parts of the network.

Sodomites showed a remarkable mobility.[136] Some, like Pietar

Martijn (who was executed in 1730 in Amsterdam), had had contacts in different cities, like Hoorn or The Hague. Among his acquaintances he could count members of the aristocracy. Though by no means a prostitute per se, he sometimes rendered sexual services for money.[137]

The number of people that according to judicial sources belonged to the network may only have represented a fraction of those actually included. Throughout the century, people were put on trial who had only been involved in casual sexual contacts with members of their own sex—without belonging to any network.[138] If the number of people prosecuted was representative of the extent of the network, the one that came to light in Amsterdam in 1730 seems to have been considerably smaller than the one, for instance, in The Hague. The same goes for the "infrastructure" that supported the network. In The Hague, pubs, brothels, mediators, and public meeting places like parks and toilets were known to many sodomites. In Amsterdam, only two pubs and no public meeting places were mentioned in 1730.[139] This may be looked upon with some doubt. In the blackmail cases I described, toilets and cruising areas like the City Hall were referred to as early as 1689 and 1715.

Though the existing sodomite network was completely disbanded in 1730, new ones arose in the decades to follow. But if the judicial sources reflect reality, the new networks seemed to have been smaller, at least geographically, than the one existing in 1730. In the persecutions of 1764, which were limited to Amsterdam, only a local but coherent network was involved; in those of the 1790s coexisting networks were also involved.[140]

If the "infrastructure" in Amsterdam in 1730 seems to have been rather small, the one referred to in the trials of 1764 was by comparison much larger. Once again, the City Hall was often mentioned as a cruising area. According to *The Queen's Vernacular* the English "cruising" comes from the Dutch "kruisen," which sodomites as well as prostitutes used to describe their pick-ups.[141] The sodomites committed their acts in numerous public toilets. Some toilets had special names, like The Old Lady or The Long Lady.[142] In 1730, special pubs existed. In one of them, sodomites went to "dance and jump," as one sodomite confessed. When they found a partner, he told the Judges, they usually went to a public toilet—which they called "going to the office."[143] A decade later, the Balcony of the Comedy was mentioned, where, in the crowds sodomites pressed up against one another and caressed.[144]

During certain incidental trials in the early 1760s and the sequence of trials in 1764, the Bailiff and Aldermen showed a deep interest in how sodomites recognized one another, signaled each other, and then chose their partners. They obviously did not know that in 1689, in the first known blackmail case in Amsterdam, one of the blackmailers had told that "that kind of people" got in touch with one another near the toilets in the City Hall by kicking one another's feet.[145] That sign had been used in the Middle Ages for heterosexual contacts.[146] In 1702 in The Hague, in what was obviously also a blackmail case, another sign was described: patting one hand with the other. A witness told he had thought it meant an invitation for going to the whores.[147] (Today, that sign is still in use in the Netherlands as a mocking gesture to indicate that someone is a homosexual.) In 1764 Jacobus Hebelaar gave an extensive account of this kind of behavior in Amsterdam:

> The people had their particular signs for the places, they used to meet one another and that the signals proper for the arches of the City Hall were such, that a person who met another man, whom he thought to be a sodomite, looked the other stark in the eye and put his hands on his hips, which was answered by the other in the same way, after which they gave each other a nudge with the elbow. And the signals used at the back of City Hall were such, that if somebody doubted, he went to make water. The other did the same and having known one another in that way, the one went to a public toilet, where the other followed him immediately.[148]

No matter how much the authorities wanted to detect general patterns in the cruising behavior of sodomites or their choice of partners, one may doubt whether such patterns could be established. The evidence of the 1730 trials suggests that some sodomites who were good-looking but not very well-to-do sought the protection of rich, sometimes elderly men.[149] On the other hand, when prosecuted sodomites were confronted with such questions, their answers were, if not evasive, confusing because of their diversity. Whereas one sodomite claimed that he had chosen his permanent, much younger partner because he was so well educated in the gospel, another one, arrested at a toilet, stated that he would have done "it" with any man, indiscriminately.[150]

Promiscuity was one part of the subcultural behavior. On the other hand, little is known about protracted or even monogamous relationships. No one suspected of sodomy was ever asked whether he had been in love with another man. Only in cases in which the obvious affection between men could be used to "convince" a suspect is it mentioned in the records. For example, Lourens Hosponjon, executed in Amsterdam in 1730, and Hermanus Moljon, executed in The Hague in the same year, were said to have had an agreement (that they called a contract of marriage) in which they promised not to have sex with others without one another's knowledge and consent.[151] In 1802 Jan van Weert was confronted in court with quotations from what must have been a love letter from a friend. "Dear Jan, write me if your heart is still worthy of mine" and "Thou art faithful to me until death; who will separate us, nobody but the will of The Heavenly Father and we are tied in love forever."[152] In one of the last sodomy trials in Amsterdam against two men, testimony suggested that both men had been involved in a lasting relationship. One of them took considerable trouble to visit his partner or lover in the houses of his master in summer and climbed walls and strolled through gardens to visit him at night.[153]

Whether or not the subculture was a vehicle by which sodomites passed on their self-conceptions is difficult to ascertain. When the Judges became interested in the private motives of sodomites, the same problem arose as when they asked them to explain their signals to one another and their choice of partners. Some sodomites claimed to have been seduced, sometimes in their youth.[154] Others said they were possessed by the devil.[155] Some answers must indeed have bewildered the Judges. In a famous case in The Hague in the 1750s a man produced a prenatal cause for his behavior: when his mother was pregnant with him, in the absence of his father, his mother took to a great liking for men.[156] In 1798 an eighteen-year-old boy in Amsterdam, who had committed sodomy since he was thirteen (sometimes for money), said that he had done so because "the monsters" (women) did not want him because he had only one testicle.[157] A much older accomplice of this boy claimed to suffer from hypochondria and "weakness of the brains" due to his hopeless love for a married woman.[158] He was treated by doctors for his hypochondria and his neighbors testified in court on his behalf regarding his mental state.[159]

If such answers did not fit well with the prevailing discourses about "screaming sins" (onany, celibacy, seduction) as causes of sodomy, answers that seem logical may be looked upon with doubt. For example, the court considered sodomites to be "hooked on" the practice and asked a confessor for how long such had been the case. But did a positive answer come from a confessor's own convictions that he shared with others, or just as a reaction to the judicial discourse? Surely, sodomites talked among themselves about sodomy. Floris Husson told in 1776 that he and his friends had talked about "the badness" of "the real sin" and that he himself had always held himself back from it.[160] And Hendrik Eelders told in 1765 that he and his doctor, with whom he had committed sodomitical acts several times, had talked about the risks they were running. The doctor had told him not to worry because too many of "the great" were involved and that they seduced "the small."[161]

There is at least one subject for which the judicial sources do not fail to give us the answer: the sexual habits of sodomites — the ones prosecuted that is. The *Secret Confession Books* are very rich in detail about the sexual activities of sodomites, not only because of the correlation between different kinds of acts and the corresponding punishments, but also presumably because of the prurient curiosity of the Judges. In 1765 the Aldermen agreed no longer to take home secret material to copy it for their own use.[162]

Among the sexual habits of sodomites, mutual masturbation — "the shaking out," "the milking out," "throwing the seed with the hand" — seems to have been the favorite act. Next came anal intercourse — "the dirty work" — descriptions of which are often picturesque. In 1747 Jurriaan Stromberg told that his accomplice "had stuck his manliness into his foundation and had shot his seed into his body and that he was then very wet from behind."[163]

Though it is obvious that sexual acts could not be very innovative, it is surprising that few cases of fellatio are found in the confessions of the sodomites. Only some confessed to this kind of activity.[164] One of them, Hendrik Eelders, had learned this technique from his doctor when he had consulted him regarding some illness. The doctor had said afterwards: "Oh boy, I swallowed it."[165]

The ample description of other sexual acts justifies the conclusion that fellatio was not very popular among sodomites. The case of Hendrik Eelders was so extraordinary that the Judges had to decide whether or not "the real sin of sodomy" had been committed because one partner had ejaculated in the other's body.[166] Fellatio's lack of popularity was perhaps due to the lack of hygiene at that time. Sodomites seemed not to have thought of it and, unlike anal intercourse, were never asked about it by the Judges. In his highly doubtful book about sodomy among pirates,[167] D. R. Burg makes at least one notable point when he suggests that fellatio was considered to be an aristocratic vice.[168] Evidence from judicial sources suggests that members of the aristocracy committed this kind of act with their protégés. The case of Hendrik Eelders makes it obvious how such a habit was passed on through the subculture: once he had learned it from his doctor, he applied the technique to his partner Jan Kemmer, who in his turn applied it to him.[169]

One thing that certainly was passed on through the subculture was venereal disease. In 1764 a prisoner told that Barend Jansen was nicknamed Barend Coffeehouse, and that it was known among sodomites "that he had the clap and that his tap was leaking."[170] In 1796 Jan Weismuller confessed that he had suffered from gonorrhea and explained that "at a certain night he was committing filthy sodomitical acts in a cubicle under a bridge, with a person who's name he didn't know and that at the time he was to shoot his seed, he was interrupted, which caused him his gonorrhea."[171] The prosecutor did not believe him, instead thinking it to be the result of anal intercourse. Whether sodomites used pig's bladders as prophylactics to prevent venereal diseases (as was not uncommon in heterosexual intercourse) is not certain. Pieter Wagenaar, charged with sodomy in 1798, confessed that he had used a pig's bladder when he went to female prostitutes.[172]

In his study *Homosexuality in Renaissance England*, Alan Bray gives an ample description of effeminate behavior in the Molly houses in London at the beginning of the eighteenth century. Drag

seems to have been especially popular among the London sodomites.[173] Transvestism certainly existed in Holland, but none of the
sodomites arrested in Amsterdam confessed to it. Nevertheless, effeminacy among sodomites was noticed by witnesses, especially
because of the way the sodomites spoke to one another and the
nicknames they gave one another. Nicknames often were the feminine equivalent of the sodomites' male names, though they could
refer to certain qualities as well. A certain Jan was called "Janne
Nightglass in the Ass," and a man called Piet was nicknamed
"Pieternel Roundabout Beautiful."[174]

Sodomites often referred to the passive role in anal intercourse as
a female role. When this happened in court, one may ask whether
they came up to some unofficial legal discourse. But in at least one
case passivity was explicitly referred to as a female role. In 1796
Hendrik Coerten was accused by another man of asking "whether
he was male or female and that he [Caerten] was both male and
female."[175]

Something should be said here concerning the subculture of "tribades" (women homosexuals). The lack of trials against women
suggests that such a subculture did not exist in the eighteenth century. The women prosecuted in the 1790s in Amsterdam were either
arrested individually or in small groups. In only one case was such a
group said to meet at the house of one of the women involved. No
pubs or other meeting places were mentioned, and the records lack
a description of anything except the sexual acts the women were
accused of, which amounted to palpating, mutual masturbation, and
once to oral intercourse.

DISCUSSION

The faulty historiography of homosexuality in the Netherlands
illustrates how one myth produces another. It fit well with the nineteenth century romantic tradition to describe the seventeenth century as The Golden Age, whereas the eighteenth century was called
a century of weakness and decline, commonly denoted as "The
Wigs Era." The step from the eighteenth-century persecutions to
economic and political decline was easily made. Prosecutions of
sodomites were rare in the seventeenth century, which indicates it

must have been a time of, it not acceptance, meekness concerning homosexuality.[177] Such an attitude would explain why sodomy trials before 1730 were rare, would provide a motive for the persecutions of 1730, and would assimilate the eighteenth-century explanation, which held that the decline was God's revenge against a society that tolerated sodomy and the reason why sodomites had to be exterminated.

Historiography has made it clear, however, that economic decline certainly did exist in the contemporary perception, but not in reality, at least until far into the eighteenth century.[178] In cases of moral indignation, such a perception of reality might be more important than reality itself. But if this indeed was the cause of the persecutions, one would expect to witness a period of instigation and insinuation prior to the persecutions. Such instigation, and to a lesser extent insinuation, occurred, however, only when the persecutions began.

Certainly, the economy was stagnant in certain fields, but that had already begun in the second half of the seventeenth century.[179] It had also become obvious in 1713 at the Peace Treaty of Utrecht (to end the Spanish War of Succession) that the Republic had lost its once powerful position. But if one wants to look for political decline, the internal constitutional problems of the Republic had already been going on for one and one-half centuries.[180] No doubt, the sodomites were made the scapegoats for all disasters the Republic met with—the supposed decline, floods, the cattle plague, and so on. Yet sodomites were not specially selected as scapegoats, but rather were welcomed as such when they were publicly discovered. The sodomites may have for some time diverted attention away from the oligarchy's inability to work on constitutional rearrangements, and in Amsterdam sodomites probably served as a lightning conductor for some rousing financial scandals among the authorities.[181]

Persecutions in later years also cannot be explained by economic decline. As a result of what was called "the internal contraction of economy," Amsterdam became in the eighteenth century more important than ever in the Republic.[182] As a creditor to the antagonists, England and France, during the Seven Years' War (1756-1763), Amsterdam sailed before the wind. This resulted in a financial crisis in 1763. It was in that year that the legal authorities in Amsterdam started looking for sodomites. But in letters to the States of Holland they never referred to this crisis. Instead, they convinced themselves and the States that sodomy "had recently returned to the city."[183] By the time the actual persecutions of 1764 started, however, the city had already recovered from the crisis of the year before.[184]

Absolute decline started at the beginning of the last quarter of the century, but once again this cannot explain the increase in numbers of sodomites prosecuted in the 1790s. Economic problems were growing even more severe during the Napoleonic wars, while the numbers of prosecuted sodomites decreased after 1798.[185]

Therefore, if we have to look for a direct motive (which is something different from an explanation) for the persecutions, it seems logical that it simply was the discovery of a nationwide subculture in 1730 and something similar in 1764 or 1776 that caused the persecutions.

This raises the question why such persecutions had not happened before. For one thing, the existence of a sodomite subculture is not a self-evident fact. From the persecutions of 1730, it becomes obvious that the existence of the newly discovered network went back to the beginning of the eighteenth century. And in the blackmail cases previously described, public meeting places for sodomites were mentioned beginning from the last decades of the seventeenth century. Far from being just a part of an uninterrupted history, the very existence of such a network might mark a turning point in the history of homosexuality in the Netherlands, similar to the one Alan Bray ascertained for England.[186]

Foucault, Weeks, and others have stressed the fact that sodomy, as opposed to homosexuality, was considered to be a casual act, fleeting and undefined, a temporary aberration from the norm. However, when the medical sciences in the second half of the nineteenth century started to categorize sexual deviances, their very descriptions came to constitute the identities they sought to describe.[187]

I would like to argue, for reasons that will partly be considered later in this article, that such a sharp break in the perception of homosexuality in the nineteenth century from data provided by research in the Netherlands is not very likely. The description of the perception of sodomy by Weeks and others fits well enough with the outcome of research into the period before the persecutions of 1730. Sodomy had been incidentally prosecuted in the sixteenth and seventeenth centuries when rape or dislocation of marriages were involved.[188] In the blackmail cases before 1730, the authorities seemed not to bother with tracking down sodomites.

In the case in 1715, the blackmailer was accused of having said to the neighbors of his victim that he knew lots of places where sodomites met in Amsterdam, as well as in The Hague and Rotterdam. He was asked only whether he had said those kinds of things and the authorities were satisfied with his tentative answer. As far as his victim was concerned, they accepted without further inquiry his denial that he was a sodomite.[189] That could have resulted from the fact that for a long time, sodomy was hardly recognized as such because of the stigmas attached to it: it was associated with witchcraft, heresy, werewolves, and so on.[190] Who would consider himself, his neighbor, his son, or his spouse, to be such a monster?

According to Jeffrey Weeks, a subculture is likely to develop in response to the emergence of hostile norms and, in the case of homosexuality, of sharpening social control. Such a subculture has a two-fold function: It provides access to the outlawed sexual activity, provided that a collective need for such access is felt, and, by containing the outlawed behavior, it keeps the bulk of society pure.[191] Mary McIntosh reasons in much the same manner about the development of a recognizable homosexual role.[192]

The description Alan Bray gave about the activities of the *Societies for the Reformation of Manners* at the end of the seventeenth century fits with the reasons why Weeks thinks a subculture is likely to emerge, though he himself puts much more stress upon developments in the nineteenth century. These societies dealt with the tracking down of deviant (including sexual) behavior and brought pressure to bear upon the authorities to interfere, as indeed they did. For some people this put a clear threshold between licit and illicit behavior. For others it became a necessity to organize their sexuality in a relatively safe subculture.[193] Organizations like these societies did not exist in the Netherlands at that time, and neither church nor secular authorities worried about homosexuality before the persecutions started. In fact, the period lacks any sign of a clear antihomosexuality.

Maybe more stress should be put upon the role of secular authorities and the fact that they were called upon to deal with matters of morality. Kent Gerard and Stephen Murray did so in their article about the emergence of sodomite subcultures in Southern Europe from the fifteenth century onward. They called attention to the shifts in alliances between church and state.[194] Whether such a shift took place in the Netherlands is difficult to ascertain. One thing is sure, however: The ruling patriciat in the Netherlands rose to the peak of its power in the seventeenth century. And as Spierenburg argued, by this time the judicial system was firmly established in the hands of the rulers, which he ascribed to state formation processes.[195] This may have coincided with the gradual expansion of the control secular authorities had over the minds and bodies of their people. So the emergence of a sodomite subculture may not be ascribed to growing hostile norms, but to a growing secular power. As such, this emergence may be understood as the result of, or at least part of, state formation processes as well. Of course, this is all hypothetical, and even when confirmed by research other questions remain to be answered; for example, the relationship of developments between sodomy and gender, or between sodomy and family life.

If indeed the absence of a sodomite subculture and the general perception of sodomy as a casual act explains the "lack" of prosecutions before 1730, the trials held in that year bring us to a crossroad regarding the perception of homosexuality. Partly, old traditions and discourses were continued, as may be seen from the way in which the authorities wanted to dispose of corpses of executed sodomites or the secrecy surrounding the records of their trials. On the other hand, the concept of sodomy as a casual act was incompatible with the discovery of the network. The degree of organization of homosexuality revealed that sodomy was committed wantonly and intentionally and that the authorities dealt with people who had committed sodomy over and over again. Sodomites obviously stuck to their practices once they had committed sodomy, and after their confessions they often said for how long.[196] Sodomy had changed from a casual act into a mode of behavior. Yet it was not considered to be a state of mind. In a society that was deeply religious and explained behavior in religious terms, sodomy — a crime and a sin — now represented a permanent *state of sin*. As this was completely compatible with ideas about the surpassing steps of the screaming sins and seduction, sodomy was also considered to be a contagious sin which had and would continue to spread among the population. From then on, sodomy had to be prosecuted whenever it was discovered, never mind the age or mental state of those involved.[197]

This new perception may also have caused the massacre in the small northern village of Faan referred to earlier, an event which shocked judicial authorities. The country squire De Mepsche was accused of attempting to get rid of his political opponents—or at least their innocent adherents. The acts they were accused of and partly confessed to were exactly of the casual nature that used to be so common for so many forms of homosexual behavior. They did not even know that their acts were called sodomy—if they gave them a name at all. They certainly had nothing to do with the network that was discovered elsewhere in the Republic, but De Mepsche acted as if a well-developed urban subculture existed in his small village.[198]

Nevertheless, like Alan Bray, I would like to argue that the eighteenth-century subculture in the Republic was a relatively safe place. Allegations have been made that the eighteenth century Dutch Republic had witnessed a "gay genocide."[199] This is not only anachronistic,[200] but also is not true if a "genocide" is described as a ruthlessly carried out program of extermination. The total number of people prosecuted through the eighteenth century and throughout the Republic because of homosexual acts did not surpass six hundred.[201]

The stipulation in the Edict of 1730 that the vice and its perpetrators had to be exterminated was highly rhetorical, as may be seen from the fact that the authorities did not wish to condemn their peers to humiliating public punishments. It seems to be a misunderstanding of the judicial system at the time to suppose that the authorities could launch a continuous and rigorous pursuit of sodomites—even if they ever wanted to. First of all, they lacked the institutional apparatus to monitor even a major part of homosexual behavior. Secondly, because of the delicate balance between an oligarchy and the masses it was to rule, public executions not only served as a means to punish and deter crime, but to confirm the power of the oligarchy over the masses. This meant somehow that the masses had to be convinced of the guilt of those who were punished publicly (capital or otherwise), even if at some times (e.g., when the masses were rioting) the authorities had to display their power firmly by engaging soldiers to carry out the executions.[202] If the authorities had organized an uninterrupted pursuit of sodomites involving the frequent inevitable spectacle of executions of vast numbers of the accused, citizens witnessing the large-scale executions of their husbands, sons, friends, and neighbors would not have given credence to the acts the authorities accused those men of. Furthermore, it would have destabilized the country in an unacceptable manner. This indeed happened in Faan, the small village in the north. People did not believe the accusations, and De Mepsche could carry out executions only with the help of vast numbers of soldiers. (Or at least he thought so, as he feared an outright revolt.) And indeed, the persecutions did destabilize the province of Groningen to which Faan belonged. All of the legislative machinery in Groningen came to a standstill for nearly two decades.[203]

What the authorities achieved by their periodic persecutions was a strong awareness of permissible and impermissible behavior. With the irregular, though always sensational, executions of small numbers of sodomites, the ruling elites were confirmed in their rights to exercise power over the people's minds and bodies. One can speculate then that the consequences of the eighteenth-century persecutions of sodomites went far beyond the fate of that group alone. Like the emergence of a subculture, the persecutions were also a part of state formation processes.

NOTES

Key to Abbreviations: GAA = Gemeente Archief Amsterdam (Municipal Archive Amsterdam); RA = Rechterlijk Archief (Judicial Archive); PA = Particulier Archief (Private Archive); ARA = Alegemeen Rijks Archief (State Archive).

1. L. J. Boon, "De Grote Sodomietenvervolging in het Gewest Holland," *Holland* 8 (1976): 140-52; idem, " 'Utrechtenaren': De sodomieten-processen in Utrecht, 1730-1732," *Spiegel Historiael* 17 (1982): 553-58.

2. G. M. Cohen Tervaert, *De Grietman Rudolf de Mepsche* (The Hague: Mouton, 1921).

3. Th. van der Meer, *De Wesentlijke Sonde van Sodomie en Andere Vuyligheeden* (Amsterdam: Tabula, 1984), 36-43.

4. van der Meer, *De Wesenlijke*, apps. 1 and 2.

5. GAA RA 5061-533-540. The first three volumes of the *Secret Confession Books* contain all kinds of cases, of which it is not always obvious why they were kept secret.

6. This becomes obvious from annotations in the minutes of the Aldermen, GAA RA 5061-645, fo 151^v-152^r and RA 5061-538, fo 68.

7. E.g., J. de Damhouder, *Practycke in Crimineele Saken* (Rotterdam, 1660), 154. (Older copies of this legal comment are known.)

8. GAA RA 5061-539 fo 70.

9. In the *Secret Confession Books* and other sources, there is a recurrent mention of persons scolded as sodomites, without referring to anal intercourse. E.g, the case against Pieter Hageman, GAA RA 5061-536, fo 50^r or in the Notorial Act, NA 14262, no. 83.

10. GAA RA 5061-537, fo 245.

11. GAA RA 5061-538, fo 438.

12. In 1798 this procedure was changed. From then on the court could "receive" a suspect in "ordinary process" if it did not feel convinced by the prosecutor. The suspect got legal assistance in such a case. In fact, most people on trial for sodomy got such a process, but nevertheless, most of them were convicted.

13. S. Faber, *Strafrechtspleging en Criminaliteit in Amsterdam, 1680-1811* (Arnhem: Gouda Quint B. V., 1983), 30.

14. GAA RA 5061-538, fo 1-56. Also, M. Weveringh, *Aantekeningen betreffende het Verhandelde in de Schepenbank gedurende de jaren 1765-1777*, GAA Collection Handwritings no. 55, 21-23, 40-41.

15. R. A. P. Tielman, *Homoseksualiteit in Nederland* (Boom, 1982), 54. The only place where torture may have been applied to people suspected of sodomy without observing the rules seems to have been Faan. In this and other nearby villages the country squire Rudolf de Mepsche arrested more than forty men in 1731 and 1732. One, perhaps two, men died under torture. G. J. Cohen Tevaert, *De Grietman de Mepsche*, 80, 89-91.

16. Permission could be refused by the Aldermen, as in fact they did in those cases where the prosecutor required torture against women accused of same-sex intercourse.

17. GAA RA 5061-537, fo 371-372.

18. Th. van der Meer, *De Wesentlijke*, app. 1.

19. For this indirect form of suicide, see P. Spierenburg, *The Spectacle of Suffering* (Cambridge: Cambridge University Press, 1984), 95-96. Such an attempt was obviously also made by Johannes Hesterman in 1806 — he was brought to the hospital. van der Meer, *De Wesenlijke*, 55.

20. GAA RA 5-62-536, fo 43^{1r}. Apart from what Didding said, this case is obscured by the fact that not he, but his accomplice, denounced himself to the Masters of the Orphanages, as becomes obvious from their minutes. GAA RA 343, no. 7, fo 171.

21. *Groot Placcaatboek* 6 (Den Haag, 1746): 604-5.

22. This seems to be different from other countries. According to G. Rug-

giero, *The Boundaries of Eros* (New York: Oxford University Press, 1985), 121, the active role in anal intercourse was considered to be worse than passive role. I found annotations which indicated something like that on a copy of the records of the trial against Pieter Didding, but while he had committed sodomy actively as well as passively on the same occasion, he was condemned to death like his accomplice. GAA RA 5061-641M1.

23. Compare van der Meer, *De Wesentlijke*, app. 1. In 1798 the death penalty was yet required against two men, Hendrik Herderschee and Pieter Wagenaar. Instead, both were confined after an exhibition on the scaffold. Herderschee was also branded and whipped. See also, GAA RA 5061-620, nos. 102-3.

24. Obviously, the constables and clergymen were not obliged to secrecy concerning the things they heard during the ceremony. (The complete confession was read out.) In the case of Hendrik Eelders, the Bailiff asked to leave the constables and clergymen out because in Eelders' confession the names of prominent citizens were mentioned. For that very reason, the Aldermen let them in so that it would be known in the city that they had ruled impartially. Weveringh, *Aantekeningen*, 28.

25. The Burgomasters' advice could differ from the verdict of the Alderman, as can be learned in the case against Jan Kemmer (1765). They advised lifelong imprisonment, but he was executed. Weveringh, *Aantekeningen*, 32.

26. This description is not quite representative. The ceremony changed several times during the eighteenth century. P. Spierenburg, *Spectacle of Suffering*.

27. P. Spierenburg, *Judicial Violence in the Dutch Republic* (Amsterdam: 1978), 77.

28. *Naamlyst van alle personen, Die binnen Amsterdam seederd het Jaar 1693 tot 1764 Door Scherprechters Handen zyn ter Dood gebragt* (Amserfoort, 1766), 37.

29. P. Spierenburg, *Judicial Violence*, 77.

30. P. Spierenburg, *Spectacle of Suffering*, 57-58.

31. Ibid.

32. Ibid., 203. Spierenburg mentions a case in 1689 in which the body of an executed criminal was stolen from the gallows, probably by friends who wanted to bury him. Incidently, it was the body of a man who was involved in the first known sodomy-blackmail case in Amsterdam. GAA RA 5061-334 fo 77-275.

33. This clause prevented the authorities from showing any long suffering. It was not unusual to "grant" the body of an executed a burial. The request by the sodomite Hendrik Eelders to be buried was rejected without discussion. See Weveringh, *Aantekeningen*, 30.

34. According to some sources, the term "crimen nefandum" denoted the habit of burning the records of the trials with the perpetrator. L. J. Boon, "Het jaar waarin elke jongen een meisje nam," *Groniek* 12:6 (1980): 16. The disposal of the corpse might be remnant of this habit.

35. Compare van der Meer, *De Wesentlijke*, app. 1. In some countries only anal intercourse was punishable. For example, the Inquisition in Portugal considered mutual masturbation a sin, not a crime, and did not prosecute this kind of act.

L. Mott, "Report from Brazil," *The Cabirion and Gay Books Bulletin* 5:11 (1984): 14.

36. In 1777 "the hiding" of sodomites became a matter of discussion in two anonymous published pamphlets. One author suggested exhibiting the sodomites every now and then in order to remind the public of the awfulness of their deeds. See A. Perrenot, *Bedenkingen over het straffen van zekere schandelyke misdaad* and *Nadere bedenkingen over het straffen van zekere schandelyke misdaad* (Amsterdam, 1777).

37. "Conceptrapport over de Gevangen en Tuchtuizen te Amsterdam, 23 Augustus 1806," GAA PA 345, no. 3.

38. GAA PA 345, no. 1, fo 1.

39. "Annotatien van mijn schepenschap," Archief de Vrije Temminck, GAA RA 5061-641 F and G, mentions the first attempt. Bicker Raije noted the escape in 1745 in his diary, *Notitie van het Merkwaardigste Meijn bekent dat in de Jaren 1732-1772 is voorgevallen*, GAA Library, B 54, p. 79. He refers to Mandel as a servant of Jews imprisoned because of sodomy. Mandel was arrested in 1739 after blackmailing two Portuguese Jews for whom he had worked. By accusing them of having committed sodomy with him, he accused himself as well and was imprisoned. GAA RA 5061-399, fo 100^v-138^r and 5061-400, fo 8^r.

40. GAA PA 345, no. 1, fo 6.

41. van der Meer, *De Wesentlijke*, app. 1.

42. Clause 6 was especially considered to be arbitrary. After all if people answered the summons of courts, they could only be charged with their disappearance. van der Meer, *De Wesentlijke*, 40.

43. GAA RA 5061-647, fo 59^v-60^r and GAA 5021, Missiven van Gedeputeerden ter Dagvaart, 1763-1766.

44. R. A. P. Tielman (*Homoseksualiteit*, 54) says that people could be arrested at the merest suspicion. Only an Edict by the Burgomasters of Groningen (14 July 1730) gives reason to suppose something like that. It guaranteed anonymity to those who denounced others and even promised a reward. Yet it hardly worked out that way. The number of people prosecuted in the city of Groningen was limited. L. S. A. M. von Romer, "Der Uranismus in den Niederlanden bis zum 19. Jahrhundert," *Jahrbuch für Sexuelle Zwischenstufen* 8 (1906): 373-75, 404.

45. GAA PA 343, no. 7, fo 165.

46. J. Bicker Raije, *Notitie van het Merkwaardigste*, 256.

47. GAA RA 5061-536, fo 115^v.

48. Idem., fo 116^{2v}.

49. GAA RA 5061-537, fo 289, 377.

50. Idem., fo 18.

51. Arnoldus Menschen, idem., fo 34-35.

52. Hermanus Smit, idem., fo 100-289.

53. GAA RA 5061-535, fo 20^v-21^r.

54. GAA RA 5061-536, fo 31^v-34^v.

55. GAA RA 5061-611, nos. 163-66.

56. *The Old Dublin Intelligence*, 10 July 1730, and *York Courant*, 7 July 1730.

57. GAA RA 5061-536, fo 23ᵛ-27ᵛ. Also, D. J. Noordam, "Homosexualiteit en sodomie in Leiden, 1533-1811," *Leids Jaarboekje* 75 (1983): 82.

58. van der Meer, *De Wesentlijke*, app. 1.

59. Idem., app. 2.

60. The summoning of citizens of Amsterdam by the Court of Holland caused a sharp dispute between Amsterdam and the before-mentioned Court. This kind of dispute was part of a traditional antagonism between the cities and the Court of Holland, but the fact that the brother of the Amsterdam Bailiff was among those summoned may have contributed to the dispute. GAA 5029, Missiven van en aan Gedeputeerden ter dagvaart, 1730. The dispute was settled when the Court of Holland agreed that Amsterdam was to summon its own citizens. Cornelis Backer, brother of the Bailiff, was officially summoned by the Substitute Bailiff, Dirk van der Meer. GAA RA 5061-644, fo 102ʳ. Also, J. E. Elias, *De Vroedschap van Amsterdam, 1578-1795*, Repr. Amsterdam, 1963, vol. 2, 509.

61. Klaas Vermeulen, GAA RA 5061-388, fo 66ᵛ-67ʳ.

62. *Requeste en Deductie mitsgaders Advisen en Bylagen inde zake van Joan Lucas Bouwens, Ingedaagde in Persoon.*

63. GAA RA 5061-422, fo 453-512 and 5061-423, fo 1-105.

64. GAA RA 5061-537, fo 38-40.

65. GAA RA 5061-422, fo 481.

66. Idem., fo 479.

67. GAA RA 5061-615, no. 155.

68. J. Bicker Raije, *Notitie van het Merkwaardigste*, 293.

69. van der Meer, *De Wesentlijke*, apps. 1 and 2.

70. J. Bicker Raije, *Notitie van het Merkwaardigste*, 292. I have found no evidence of the suicides. They were usually reported to the secretary of the Court, in 1764 the notary Beels.

71. Pieter Weeber, GAA RA 5061-647, fo 70ᵛ.

72. These persecutions have been extensively described by D. J. Noordam, "Homosexuele relaties in Holland in 1776," *Holland* 16 (1984): 3-34.

73. GAA RA 5061-442, fo 145-380.

74. GAA RA 5061-647, fo 175ᵛ.

75. GAA RA 5061-538, fo 104.

76. GAA RA 5061-617, nos. 14, 40.

77. M. Weveringh, *Aantekeningen*, 307.

78. GAA PA 345, no. 1, fo 6.

79. See note 72.

80. Compare van der Meer, *De Wesentlijke*, app. 1.

81. *Requeste en Deductie (. . .).*

82. Compare van der Meer, *De Wesentlijke*, app. 1. Torture, as explained, was only allowed in cases of capital crime when a substantial part of the evidence was already gathered. Soliciting, even if proved, certainly did not constitute a capital crime.

83. GAA RA 5061-538, fo 271.
84. In 1795 the office of the Bailiff was divided between a Prosecutor and a "Maire," head of police. At the same time, the Aldermen court was changed into a "Committee of Justice."
85. GAA RA 5061-538, fo 374-75.
86. It was the first time in a sodomy case that the verdict of the Court went further than the requirements of the Prosecutor.
87. GAA RA 5061-539, fo 1-7.
88. E.g., compare van der Meer, *De Wensentlijke*, app. 1.
89. L. J. Boon, *De Grote Sodomietenvervolging*, 141.
90. D. J. Noordam, *Homosexualiteit en Sodomie*, 82.
91. L. J. Boon, *Utrechtenaren*, 553.
92. J. Wagenaar, *Vaderlandsche Historie*, Amsterdam, 1790-1796, vol. 19, 41.
93. J. Elias, *De Vroedschap*, vol. 1, 509.
94. GAA RA 5061-535, fo 20^v-21^r.
95. GAA RA 5061-536, fo 37^r-43^r.
96. M. Weveringh, *Aantekeningen*, 286.
97. Idem., 309.
98. Compare van der Meer, *De Wesentlijke*, apps. 1 and 2.
99. At least in Amsterdam. Of those executed by the country squire De Mepsche in Faan in 1731, eight varied in age from 15-20. The only exception was made for two fourteen-year-old boys. They were imprisoned. G. M. Cohen Tervaert, *De Grietmen*, 78-80.
100. Compare van der Meer, *De Wesentlijke*, app. 1. See for the discharge the case against Abram Leemans in 1798, GAA RA 5061-539, fo 61-67.
101. Gurriaan Stromberg (1746) GAA RA 5061-536, fo 435^r-43W^v.
102. Hendrik de Groot (1741) GAA RA 5061-536, fo 43B^r-43G^v.
103. P. Spierenburg, *Spectacle of Suffering*, 160-62.
104. GAA RA 5061-536, fo 80^v-88^v.
105. Jan Cacouault had already stood trial in 1804 for the same kind of charges, but was discharged provisionally. GAA RA 5061-539, fo 275-313.
106. Bartha Wagener, GAA RA 5061-536, fo 10^r-21^v.
107. R. Dekker and L. van de Pol, *Daar was Laatst een Meisje Loos*. (Baarn: Ambo, 1981), 82. By the same authors, "Maria van Antwerpen (1719-1781), een transseksuele vrouw uit de achttiende eeuw," *Documentatieblad Werkgroep Achttiende Eeuw* 17 (1985): 103-17.
108. M. Weveringh, *Aantekeningen*, 297. The case was considered of medical importance as it was quoted in Tulp's work, *De drie boeken der medicijnsche aenmerkingen* (Amsterdam, 1650), 244. But it also constituted a case of jurisprudence even in cases in male sodomy, as can be learned from Weveringh's quotation as well as from annotations of a copy of the records of a trial involving heterosexual sodomy. (Willem de Boer 1702) GAA 5061-640i II.
109. GAA RA 5061-459, fo 240.
110. GAA RA 5061-538, fo 251-256.

111. Th. van der Meer, *De Wesentlijke*, app. 1.

112. Ibid., and GAA RA 5061-636. (Op en afslagboek van tuchtelingen.)

113. GAA RA 5061-538, fo 341.

114. GAA RA 5061-539, fo 30.

115. Idem., fo 33.

116. Idem., fo 34.

117. Idem, fo 21.

118. GAA RA 5061-640A (Het boekje van De Melander).

119. *Alle de Copyen van Indagingen als mede alle de Gedigten op de Tegen-woordige tijd Toepasselyk*, 2 vols. (Amsterdam, 1730). *Schouw-toneel so der Geexecuteerde als Ingedaagde voor de Verfoeilijcke Misdaad van Sodomie*, 2 vols. (Amsterdam, 1730). For the persecutions of 1764: *Het Regtveerdige en Goodelyke Wraak-Toneel* (Amsterdam, 1764). See also: W. Knuttel, *Catalogus van de Pamflettenverzameling in de Koninklijke Bibliotheek*, 7 vols. (Gravenhage, 1889-1920).

120. Among other works L. Beels, *Sodoms Zonde en Straffe en Streng Wraak-recht over Vervloekte Boosheidt* (Amsterdam, 1730); A. Royaards, *Nodige en Tijdige Waarschouwing tegens de Gemeenschap van Sodoms Grouwelyke Zonde en Vreeselyke Straffe* (Arnhem, 1731).

121. L. J. Boon, *De Grote Sodomietenvervolging*, 148.

122. See note 44.

123. GAA RA 5061-536, fo 67^r.

124. Idem., fo 64^r.

125. GAA RA 5061-540, fo 13.

126. In 1809 six men were arrested, all of them at the same time. One of them was accused of having sexual contacts with one of those two arrested in 1810. GAA 5061-539, fo 328-368, and 5061-540, fo 1-42.

127. GAA RA 5061-539, fo 369-374.

128. Idem., fo 184-95.

129. P. Spierenburg, *Spectacle of Suffering*, 11.

130. E.g., Coenraad Visch (1795), GAA RA 5061-538, fo 272-90, Jan Weis-muller (1796) idem., fo 317-58; Gerrit van der Sluis (1799), GAA RA 539 fo 167-83.

131. Jacob Brouwer, Jacobus van Santen, Jan Wouters. GAA RA 5061-334, fo 77^v-275^v.

132. Abraham de Leeuw, GAA RA 5061-392 fo 94^r and 5061-393, fo 11^v-29^v.

133. GAA RA 5061-372, fo 116r-119r and 5061-608, no 291.

134. See for the blackmailers: Joseph Langeveld and Anthonij van Kerkhoven GAA RA 5061-490, 5061-491, fo 2-179.

135. For sodomy among sailors see the contribution of Jan Oosterhof else-where in this issue. Works that deal with sodomy among courtiers are of a rather doubtful quality. A. L. Rowse, *Homosexuals in History* (New York: Macmillian, 1977); R. de Ruig, *In de Schaduw van de Grand Seigneur* (Utrecht: E. J. van Himbergen, 1984).

136. For this network see the following: (1) L. J. Boon (1976), (1980), (1982); (2) D. J. Noordam (1983), (1984); (3) A. H. Huussen, "Gerechtelijke vervolging van 'sodomie' gedurende de 18e eeuw in de Republiek, in het bijzonder in Friesland," *Groniek* 12 (1980): 1833, and "Strafrechtelijke vervolging van 'sodomie' in de Republiek," *Spiegel Historiael* 17 (1982): 547-52; (4) van der Meer, *De Wesentlijke*, 91-103, 163-75.

137. GAA RA 4061-536, fo 6^v-34^v.

138. E.g., Mathijs Mulder and Hendrik Voogt (1730), GAA RA 5061-536, fo 12^v-21^v for the trials between 1741-1762.

139. L. J. Boon, *De Grote Sodomietenvervolging*, 142. van der Meer, *De Wesentlijke*, 170.

140. Trials in 1764 and 1765 were all connected with one another. See for the coexisting networks van der Meer, *De Wesentlijke*, 123-28 and app. 1.

141. B. Rodgers, *The Queen's Vernacular* (San Francisco: Straight Arrow Books, 1972), 56.

142. GAA RA 5061-537, 537, fo 36.

143. GAA RA 5061-537, fo 252.

144. GAA RA 5061-538, fo 150.

145. GAA RA 5061-334, fo 94^r.

146. W. L. Braekman, *Int Paradijs van Venus*, Sint Niklaas, 1981, 22e van de Jongelinghs vragen.

147. ARA Hof van Holland 5374.

148. GAA 5061-537, fo 87-88.

149. L. J. Boon, "Dien Godlosen hoop van menschen," *Onder Mannen, Onder Vrouwen* (Amsterdam: SUA 1984), 59.

150. GAA RA 5061-537, fo 17.

151. Idem., fo 25^r.

152. GAA RA 5061-539, fo 265.

153. Gerrit Voogt, GAA 5061-540, fo 7-75.

154. E.g., Johan Hesterman, RA 5061-537, fo 287-373.

155. Hermanus Smit, GAA RA 5061-537, fo 123.

156. A. H. Huussen, *Strafrechtelijke*, 551.

157. Hendrik Herkerschee, GAA RA 5061-539, fo 82.

158. Pieter Wagenaar, Idem., fo 125.

159. NA 14273, no. 18; NA 17513 no. 554; NA 17882 no. 398.

160. GAA 5061-538, fo 181.

161. Idem., fo 22.

162. GAA RA 5061-645, fo 151^v-152^r.

163. GAA RA 5061-536, fo 43T^v.

164. Most notably it was mentioned in the "pedofile" cases against Jan Schuyl (1761), GAA RA 5061-536, fo 80^v-88^v, and Jan Cacouault (1806), 5061-539 fo 302-303.

165. GAA RA 5061-537, fo 426.

166. Annotations in the copy of records of the trial against Jan Kemmer, RA

5061-640 M2. The same question arose in Portugal with the inquisition. L. Mott, *Report from Brazil*, 14.

167. D. R. Burg, *Sodomy and the Pirate Tradition* (New York: New York University Press, 1984), deals in such a speculative manner with his subject that he cannot be taken seriously.

168. Idem., 135.

169. GAA RA 5061-537, fo 384-451, 5061-538, fo 9-55.

170. GAA RA 5061-537, fo 97.

171. GAA RA 5061-538, fo 349.

172. GAA RA 5061-539, fo 102.

173. A. Bray, *Homosexuality in Renaissance England* (London: Gay Men's Press, 1982), 86-87.

174. GAA RA 5061-536, fo 47^v.

175. GAA RA 5061-538, fo 349.

176. van der Meer, *De Wesentlijke*, 137-147 and app. 1.

178. J. de Vries, *De Economische Achteruitgang der Republiek in de 18e Eeuw*, 2d pr. (Leiden: 1968), Introduction.

179. Idem., 19.

180. I. L. Leeb, *The Ideological Origins of the Batavian Revolution* (The Hague: 1973), 24.

181. S. Dudoc van Heel, "Vervolging was Mogelijk Politieke Manoeuvre," *SEK* 13:9 (1984): 11.

182. de Vries, *De Economische*, 40.

183. GAA RA 5061-647, fo 58^r.

184. de Vries, *De Economische*, 75-76.

185. van der Meer, *De Wesentlijke*, app. 1.

186. A. Bray, *Homosexuality in Renaissance England*, 114.

187. M. Foucault, *De Geschiedenis van de Seksualiteit*, vol. 1. (Nijmegen: SUN, 1984), 40. J. Weeks, *Coming Out*, (1982; Repr., London: Quartet Books, 1983), 12.

188. D. J. Noordam, *Homosexualiteit en Sodomie*, 35. In 1648 the Italian Jeronimo Colonna was expelled from Amsterdam for fifteen years because he had committed sodomy with boys and girls. GAA RA 5061-534 and 5061-580, fo 106^v.

189. GAA RA 5061-372, fo 116^r-119^r.

190. A. Bray, *Homosexuality in Renaissance England*, 76-80.

191. J. Weeks, *Coming Out*, 36.

192. Mm. McIntosh, "The Homosexual Role," *Social Problems* 16 (1968): 183-84.

193. A. Bray, *Homosexuality in Renaissance England*, 100-2.

194. Stephen Murray and Kent Gerard, "Renaissance Sodomite Subcultures," *Among Men, Among Women* (Amsterdam: University of Amsterdam, 1983), 193.

195. P. Spierenburg, *Spectacle of Suffering*, 200-7.

196. P.g., Maurits Schuring, GAA RA 5061-536, fo 9^r.

197. Though, as said, age and mental disorder were considered to be extenuating circumstances when it came to punishing those involved.

198. Tervaert, *De Grietman*; Boon, *Dien Godlosen*, 65.

199. L. Crompton, "Gay Genocide from Leviticus to Hitler," in *The Gay Academic*, ed. L. Crew (Palm Springs, CA: ETC Publications, 1978), 67-91.

200. This kind of anachronistic use of terms is to be found in most works dealing with the history of homosexuality. Implicitly, they usually represent an essentialist point of view.

201. Compare figures, von Römer (1906); Boon (1976); Huussen (1980, 1982); Noordam (1983, 1984); van der Meer (1984).

202. Spierenburg, *Spectacle of Suffering*, 100-9.

203. Tervaert, *De Grietman*, 107.

IV. ENGLAND

"In the House of Madam Vander Tasse, on the Long Bridge": A Homosocial University Club in Early Modern Europe

G. S. Rousseau, PhD

". . . my acquaintance here, it lies chiefly almost wholly among the gentlemen that lodge with Mr. Vanderlas"[1]
(Mark Akenside to Jeremiah Dyson, April 17, 1744)

The annals of early modern European social history are not so detailed that the existence of a homosocial university club fraternized by young men who in their maturity would become public figures in their respective countries can be overlooked. Individual homosexual males have long been identified in the European Enlightenment[2] — the epoch of greatest interest to me in this essay — and, upon occasion, have even identified themselves: as when William Beckford, then presumably England's wealthiest man, called attention to his eccentric style of life and strange physical surroundings at his ruined abbey in Fonthill. And, more recently, scholars have been calling attention to the fact that the countries involved — Britain, France, Holland — were experiencing an unusual degree of anxiety over the question of sodomy in the eighteenth century. But the activities of homosocial cliques and clubs in this period, which may have encouraged members to engage in overt homosexual behavior, are less well charted and barely understood.

One club developed at two universities — Leiden and Utrecht — during the mid-eighteenth century. Fortunately for modern students many of the manuscripts (letters, diaries, papers) of the individual

Dr. G. S. Rousseau is Professor of 18th-Century Studies, Department of English, University of California, Los Angeles, 405 Hilgard Avenue, Los Angeles, CA 90024.

members are extant in the Department of Manuscripts of the British Library; these, in addition to Alexander Carlyle's abundant memoirs, permit the members to speak, as it were, for themselves.[3] Although the group has been mentioned briefly by Professor Margaret Jacob,[4] its members and their complex entanglements have never been described and interpreted. Such analysis is my purpose here.

While reconstructing the "club" and lives of its members I continued to wonder to what degree these youths were libertines and I constantly asked myself: if libertines precisely what type of libertines? Libertines in the seventeenth-century sense of Rochester et al., men who were drawn to women as well as boys, with anal penetration their final act of defiance? Libertines or rakes of a newer type, so vividly described in the anonymous *Satan's Harvest Home* (1749)—men who sodomitically relished male whores but who could not abide being kissed by other men? Or libertines in name only but in reality men who were merely homosexual in the Platonic sense—that is, homoplatonic—men who romantically idealized same-gender friendships? If the last, then the group may be among the early representatives of a complex form of homosocial behavior that flourished in the nineteenth century, especially among women, but which was less developed in the eighteenth. My conclusion after reconstruction is that the group, considered collectively, had clear tendencies in the direction of the first and last of these varieties but not in the second. At least I have found no trace of the second—no evidence that male whores were involved but abundant proof that "kisses and hugs" among themselves were. More than this I cannot say about their specific version of libertinism because the evidence does not warrant it. The present reconstruction has been a case where the extant evidence is neither consistent nor complete. Unfortunately it does not permit the grand generalizations most of us like to make and, to a greater degree, like to read.

I. PASSIONATE FRIENDSHIPS

"I think as much upon you as you can do upon me," the older Scottish philosopher and itinerant tutor Andrew Baxter wrote to a young male medical student at the University of Leiden on June 23, 1745.[5] The letter is emotionally charged—permeated with abrupt fits and starts, as if they captured the author's turbulent state of mind. Baxter's letter may have been less noteworthy if it had been addressed to an obscure student, the type of "Youth to Fortune and to Fame unknown" whom the poet Thomas Gray had invoked in his "Elegy in a Country Churchyard," composed at approximately this very time. But the student addressed is none other than John Wilkes, the great radical political statesman of mid-Georgian England, who was a household name to his contemporaries. How can this chapter in the prominent Wilkes's career have been overlooked by all his biographers? It is a disturbing question, charged with overtones of intentional neglect if not outright homophobia: those biographers who knew but would not address the issue.[6]

Actually, Baxter wrote more rhapsodically in this letter than I have owned. Insisting that he had ruminated about Wilkes more than about any other man alive, Baxter continued: ". . . it is my most serious Business to think of you."[7] The reason provided by the philosopher-tutor is surcharged with libidinal thrusts and direct references to the gender involved: "In short never man was thought so much upon by another, I dare say: tho' a woman perhaps may. This is all a Riddle—No 'tis Literal." A riddle it may have seemed to Baxter, but Baxter could not conceal his passionate friendship any longer. In the fits and starts from "I think" to "'tis Literal," he discloses his purpose: revelation of his passionate interest in his correspondent and the response it will elicit from the young Wilkes.

Baxter's letter also reveals his awareness of the ancient tradition of Platonic admiration for virtuous males.[8] This acknowledgement, indeed, is what he intends by the afterthought of "tho' a woman perhaps may." Yet what can he mean by the "Riddle," followed by his sudden reversal, "No 'tis Literal?" True, riddles are rarely literal, and Baxter means to contrast ambiguous riddle from literal truth here. To paraphrase him, his love puzzles him, because it is so overwhelming. But Baxter also intended something else: the notion that a man can esteem another man in this erotic way and to such a profound degree is the basis of the riddle. And the riddle is "literal" because however puzzling this erotic passion is, it is nonetheless true. It is a "Literal Riddle" because of the degree of its truth.

This discovery appears to galvanize Baxter, at least for the moment. Even the ambiguity embedded in the grammatical antecedent of "This" in "This is all a Riddle" understates his wonderment at the truth of his discovery: the knowledge that his "love" (Baxter's word) for Wilkes is as patent — and hence as "literal" — as any passionate love between the two sexes.

Any ambivalence later disappears in Baxter's love letter. "I think more upon you," he confesses, using the same seductive trope he has invoked before, "without leting [sic] you know it."[9] What is more conclusive for our purposes is his statement "till now you have wrested my Secret from me." The "Secret" is not the information that Baxter is ill in Utrecht and cannot accept Wilkes's invitation to visit him in Leiden — the letter makes this clear — but rather that Baxter's "love" for Wilkes is no different from the love of a man for a woman. The rest of Baxter's correspondence, never published but still extant in manuscript in the British Library, makes evident that as Baxter lay ill in Utrecht, his malady was not entirely physical. Somatically ill he may have been, but his concurrent illness was love-sickness for his new young friend: the soon-to-be notorious British politician, John Wilkes.

If the passionate love letters of male friends in previous epochs have not commanded interest, why, we may ask, should these between Baxter and Wilkes? The answer is bipartite: only recently — in our time — has the history of friendship come into its own;[10] moreover, the Baxter-Wilkes correspondence represents letters between illustrious personages of the past revealing at the least a homosocial, and possibly a homosexual, international network of students.

The network — a "club" in Baxter's words — consisted primarily of British students and their tutors in the two Dutch universities, although Baron d'Holbach, the German-born philosophe of the Enlightenment, who would later pronounce so vigorously against the church in favor of materialism, was also a member. D'Holbach's letters to Baxter also survive in the British Library. They make clear that d'Holbach prized nothing "so much as friendship,"[11] even more than the radical "philosophy" he hoped eventually to generate, or the "little Physic" [i.e., medicine] he believed would be useful for his medical education at Leiden. Mark Akenside, the pre-Romantic English poet and author of *Pleasures of Imagination*

(1744), was also a member of the "club," as was his close friend and eventual lover (in our modern sense) Jeremiah Dyson. That it was a society based, at least in part, on "tears" and "Kisses," on hugs and caresses, there can be no doubt unless this group has deluded itself by leaving documents that report untruths: the numerous letters of erotic devotion from an older married man to a young magnetic man; the outpourings of the students to one another, as in d'Holbach's extant correspondence; the copious diaries of Carlyle, who was then a student himself; and the fact that two members of the group, Akenside and Dyson, were lovers in later life.

A long and expressive letter from d'Holbach to Wilkes, dated August 1746, provides a clue to the range of emotions these youths enjoyed.[12] Here d'Holbach divulges a dream he has had. While passing his summer holidays in solitude on the family estate in Heze, near Spa in current-day Belgium but then in the German Palatinate, d'Holbach engages in daytime reverie. It is impossible to tell whether he has imagined this dream or actually dreamed it. He remembers "those delightful evening Walks at Leyden" with Wilkes. "It is a dream, I own it," d'Holbach confesses, imagining himself at Aylesbury, in Buckinghamshire, where Wilkes has gone to be with the woman his family has prearranged for him to marry. D'Holbach is wracked with jealousy; he fears that future separations from Wilkes will resemble his own first "parting" from Wilkes and "the club" at Christmas in 1744.

At this removal of time we wonder what the intimacy between these two young men can have entailed to elicit this intensity of language. "What a Hurry of Passions! Joy! fear of a second parting! What charming tears! What sincere Kisses . . . but time flows and the end of the Lay [sic] is now as unwelcome to me, as [it] would be to another to be awaken'd in the middle of a Dream wherein he is going to enjoy a beloved Mistress."[13] D'Holbach's jealousy of the "beloved Mistress" (now Wilkes as "Mistress") far away in England is precisely what wracks him.[14] He continues romantically: "the enchantment ceases, the delightfull [sic] images vanish, and nothing is left to me but friendship, which is of all my possessions the fairest." But Platonic friendship remains a bogus substitute for the exiled lover (d'Holbach in Germany, Wilkes in England) pining for his beloved, and d'Holbach's rhetoric barely conceals his yearning to fuse with Wilkes no less than did the Keatsian poet with his nightingale.

D'Holbach's letter is unequivocal. However, his youthful ebullience notwithstanding (he was then 21), he may or may not have sexually expressed his passion for Wilkes while they were in Leiden. Like Baxter, d'Holbach invokes the term "club" to describe the society's existence. In those days students banding together from different nationalities referred to their clubs as "nationes."[15] Even Boswell's journals record how the Hungarians and Poles banded together at Utrecht.[16] The British may or may not have been one of these "nationes"; more significant than the label are its activities and beliefs. Andrew Baxter and the young Baron d'Holbach have left enough clues in their letters to reconstruct both. During Christmas 1747, while again passing his holidays on his wealthy family's estate, d'Holbach wrote to Wilkes: "Mr. Dowdeswell being left alone of our Club at Leyden, I Desir'd him to come to Spa."[17] Are these invitations all suggestive of an active sexuality? It is impossible to know inasmuch as the club's daily activities, like the sexual practices of its various members, remain in doubt. I certainly do not suggest that the members were exclusively homosexual: extant evidence does not prove they were. But they were unusually homosocial, even considering the conventions of the day.

The identities of the club members are not difficult to reconstruct. These include Andrew Baxter, John Wilkes, Baron d'Holbach, Mark Akenside, Jeremiah Dyson, as well as William Dowdeswell, Andrew Leeson, Charles Townshend, Anthony Askew, Alexander Carlyle, James Johnstone, John Freeman, all of whom were together in Holland during the years 1743-47.[18] Not all were in residence simultaneously, nor did they all know each other well; but they were sufficiently bound, in different combinations, to validate using the term "club" for their group. It is crucial to fix this membership with precision as many grew up to become important personages. Three or four—especially Wilkes, d'Holbach and Akenside—were household names in their time, known to every educated person, although one doubts if the extensiveness of their homosocial component was ever divulged. These three illustrious figures have been the subjects of many biographies, whereas less is known about the students in the list from Dowdeswell to Freeman. Given the nature of the extant material, the best way to understand the group and its significance for the history of homosocial behavior, is briefly to reconstruct the lives of its members.

II. THE TUTOR: ANDREW BAXTER (1686-1750)

Baxter was a mainstay of the group, not only because he had brought his two students to Holland, but also because of his role as mentor and father figure. A master seemingly destined to attract young disciples, he provided authority and validated the society's sentimental excesses. Nearly sixty in 1745, he was obviously the most experienced member of the group, as well as the one most affected by the passionate attachments of discipleship.

Baxter is known as a Scottish moralist to students of Enlightenment civilisation.[19] His contemporaries thought of him as one of the philosophers who attempted to refute the basic premises of Locke and Berkeley. His own contribution to the history of ideas remains a wild, if mystical, theory that dreams are caused by the actions of spiritual demons capable of causing motion in matter. But Baxter was also a professional tutor who had an immense influence on a large number of Scottish students, including John Hay of Drummelgier Scotland, in whose family vault Baxter was eventually buried.

Baxter's life before migrating to Holland with his students in 1741 was uneventful. Well-educated, he had supported himself in Scotland by tutoring the sons of wealthy noblemen. This vocation was much sought after at the time, as it offered a guarantee of a secure living and could even become a perpetual sinecure for the fortunate; it was especially attractive to homosexual tutors who naturally found work with young men ideally suited to their temperaments. As his son's brief account remarks,[21] Baxter was extremely studious, but he refused to take orders in the Church of England. No offers of immediate preferment could tempt him. He enjoyed the company of young men who found him to be an excellent companion and among whom he was immensely popular. In 1741 he decided to leave his wife and children to travel to Utrecht with John Hay and Lord Blantyre, both youths under 20. The choice of Utrecht is not mysterious: this ancient university, like its neighbor at Leiden, had attracted British scholars and students from all over Europe; its canals and coffee houses, libraries and bookstalls, provided romance and a perfect setting for foreign students and their travelling tutors.

Utrecht was attractive also because of its geographical location: Holland. The province, as well as its surrounding lowlands, was by the 1740's a place that some Britons — certainly those in this circle — equated with toleration and libertinism, and for decades known as a haven for all types of political and sexual freedom.[22] The execution there of some two-hundred sodomites during 1730-32 had, it is true, cast a chilling fear among homosexuals throughout Europe, especially among those committed to sodomitical practices but by the late 1730's Holland gradually reverted to her pre-1730 tolerationist reputation. By 1741, when Baxter and his students arrived, the events of 1730 were nearly forgotten: it had been an inquisition that could recur, of course, but it was generally viewed as an unfortunate sequence of events whose chance of recurrence was small.

After 1741, other Scottish students joined Baxter, Hay and Blantyre. The group lived in close quarters in Utrecht, sharing bedrooms and — perhaps — even beds, their tutor residing no further away than a fellow student.[23] The group studied and travelled together, frequently making excursions into the nearby Dutch countryside in Gelderland and the Achterhoek (i.e., "outside hook") near the German-Belgian border. On one of these outings to Spa in the summer of 1744, Baxter fortuitously met John Wilkes, then a youth of 19. Baxter's attraction to Wilkes was instantaneous: from the moment he encountered Wilkes, Baxter continued to profess that he had never met such a precocious youth. Their friendship was to last until Baxter's death, although it seems not to have been reciprocated by Wilkes with the intensity Baxter would have wished for.

Wilkes was a student at Leiden, approximately thirty miles from Utrecht. In an age when trekschuits (passenger barges drawn over canals by horses walking on an adjoining path) were the cheapest and most effective means of travel in the Netherlands, one could spend the better part of a day travelling from Utrecht to Leiden.[24]

Baxter must have been aware of the insurmountable difficulties involved in cultivating a steady friendship with Wilkes; he was nevertheless determined to win the youth's affections at whatever cost.

Win them he did, although there was a natural limit to Wilkes's affection for a man nearly old enough to be his grandfather. Deep affection set in; each man was able to display it to the other. Moreover, Baxter met Wilkes's circle of friends — including d'Holbach — at Leiden; similarly, Wilkes and company met Baxter's group of students at Utrecht. Deeply moved and inspired by his new friend, and intent upon memorializing the passionate friendship, Baxter began to compose his final philosophical treatise casting Wilkes as one of his main antagonists.[25] Five years later, as Baxter lay dying in his native Scotland, it was Wilkes, rather than any member of his family, who occupied his thoughts; a moving letter to Wilkes, dated April 10, 1749, makes this evident. "My first desire . . . my dearest Mr. Wilkes, is to serve virtue and religion; my second and ardent wish to testify my respect to Mr. Wilkes."[26] Furthermore, the very last letter Baxter wrote was addressed to Wilkes on January 29, 1750. Three years after Baxter's death, the faithful Wilkes printed this letter and distributed it to Baxter's friends.[27]

As I suggest above, it may be going *too* far to link the onset of Baxter's ill health with Wilkes's departure from Holland and his subsequent marriage in 1747 to Mary Mead, the daughter of Wilkes's wealthy patron at Aylesbury. But there are reasons to connect these two events, even if direct cause and effect cannot be proved. As one of Wilkes's recent biographers has written, "face or no face, he [Wilkes] could charm a bird off a tree."[28] Wilkes may have been among the homeliest of men, yet his charisma was irresistible. It proved to be irrepressible to the senescent Baxter, who could not erase the image of the youth from his thought. Baxter died on the estate of his tutee Hay, in Whittingham near Edinburgh, holding a copy of a book he had written in his last illness, dedicated to Wilkes and ostensibly the record of their first conversation in the Capuchine's Garden in Spa. The new book — his last — may not have been a Gidean *Corydon* or Wildean *de Profundis*, but it was Baxter's best way of immortalizing his love for Wilkes.

III. THE RADICAL YOUNG LIBERTINE:
JOHN WILKES (1725-97)

Wilkes arrived at Leiden University during the first week of September, 1744, to matriculate as a medical student. He was accompanied by his contemporary Hungerford Bland, the son of a Yorkshire baronet, and the Reverend Matthew Leeson, Wilkes's tutor who was by this time rather aged and intellectually feeble. Unlike Baxter, who was Church of England, Leeson was a dissenting minister, but little in his dissension, or free-thinking, inspired the young Wilkes. Wilkes's father had arranged for Leeson to take the boys to Holland. The three settled into rooms in the center of the ancient university town and decided to make a tour of the Rhineland via Spa before the term began early in October.

While dining at an inn outside Liege, they linked up with Baxter and his two students. The four students were approximately the same age: 19 to 22; Leeson was a decade older than the sexagenarian Baxter. The symmetry of tutors and tutees, old and young, must have seemed nearly perfect to both groups, who shared so many common interests, not least their national British origin. However, Baxter was repulsed by Leeson, and never could develop an interest in the man; but he was magnetically drawn to the charismatic Wilkes. The two groups decided to carry on together to Spa, which was well-known for its secluded garden called "the Capuchine's." The young homoerotic Baron Poellnitz himself had previously wandered through this garden and rhapsodized about it as "the prettiest Walk at Spa."[29] From that moment on Baxter seemed never to be able to erase Wilkes — nor did he wish to! — from his memory and imagination. The figure of Wilkes became an obsession with him, an *arrière pensée* lingering at the back of his mind.

After leaving Spa, the group carried on to Aix-la-Chapelle (now Aachen in West Germany), also a favorite spot for its architecture and springs, and then on to Cologne, where they boarded a boat and sailed up the Rhine back to Holland. The itinerary was convenient: Utrecht and Leiden are both situated on this long river; neither group would have to make a detour.

Tutors and tutees returned to Holland at the end of September, the six having become friends, but Baxter's attraction to Wilkes

surpassed mere friendship. During that fortnight Baxter was personally regenerated and intellectually inspired; he returned to Utrecht
deciding to compose a metaphysical dialogue called "Histor" with
Wilkes in the role of chief interlocutor.[30] "My greatest endeavour,"
he communicated to Wilkes just a few weeks later from Utrecht,
"is to make you speak and think [in the dialogue] with as much wit
and sprightliness, with as much solidity and good sense as you deserve."[31] It is clear that Wilkes also wrote letters to Baxter but they
apparently do not survive; it is therefore difficult to gauge how the
younger man responded to the older. In attempting to appraise his
response, we must cautiously bear in mind Wilkes's physical characteristics (his homely face, poor features, the famous squint), as
well as his subsequent maturation into one of England's most notorious rakes and libertines. Yet in actuality these characteristics
probably did not compound an already bisexual nature; they may
have permitted Wilkes to indulge a homosexual drive whose tug he
would have felt anyway. Wilkes's recent biographer has prudently
written: "how much the squint, like the crippled foot of Lord
Byron, accounted psychologically for the drive behind his vora-
cious appetite for women, we cannot truly tell."[32] Nor can we tell
for men two centuries later because the biographical evidence isn't
sufficient and probably has little to do with sexual disposition or
appetite. Wilkes's homoerotic affair with Baxter may have been a
passing phase, or—more likely—bisexual behavior encouraged by
the little club at Leiden to whose collective homosocial exuberance
Wilkes succumbed. All then that can be said with confidence is that
although he became primarily heterosexual in his maturity, Wilkes
seems to have been bisexual or homosexual at this time. During his
stay at Leiden he clearly allowed himself to become attached to
Baxter: whether the liaison represents a passing phase of gerontophilia (love for an older man), an ingrained bisexual disposition,
or some deeper need to replace his distant father and feeble tutor
Leeson, is a matter on which those with psychoanalytic training can
better decide.[33]

In any event, by October, 1744, sworn friendships had developed. In Leiden Wilkes's party (Wilkes, Bland, Leeson) did not
reside at Madam van de Tasse's but around the corner.[34] Yet Wilkes
and Bland remained on good terms during that academic year

(1744-45) with the five Britons who resided there, especially with William Dowdeswell, who later was invited to Spa by d'Holbach in 1747, and a "Mr. Freeman, a man of fortune, Sedate and Sensible,"[35] who also matriculated that autumn. While Baxter's group attended lectures in Utrecht, these meetings did not intercept frequent travel to Leiden. As time passed, the young Wilkes was increasingly attracted to Baxter's theory of the immortality of the soul and his belief that physical spirits cause dreams, while growing increasingly intolerant of Leeson's incompetence. The problem was not merely that Baxter shone, whereas the intellectually defective Leeson repelled many of those who came near him by his combination of advanced age, decrepit manner, and intellectual incompetence. It was also that Baxter's encouragement of homosocial, and possibly even homosexual, behavior appealed to Wilkes's libertinism. Baxter, it seems, had captured Wilkes at just the right moment in his own homosocial development. Leeson was no rival for Baxter in this capacity. Wilkes was also touched: he had never experienced the type of passionate devotion now shown him by an older man.

While Leeson faded into the background, Baxter stole the limelight. As Wilkes grew to be acquainted with Baxter's two tutees, they in turn fraternized with Bland and the five Britons on the "Long Bridge in Leiden." During holidays the group travelled together, often staying with d'Holbach in Heze. They exchanged presents as well as intellectual ideas and emotions. On October 3, 1745, Wilkes presented Baxter with an English set of the works of Spinoza, the radical Dutch Jewish philosopher, for which Baxter immediately thanked him. "Your kind Present of Spinosa's [sic] whole works, and more kind letter of September 29th," Baxter wrote, "romantically charmed me."[36] Baxter's letters to Wilkes also contain asides, indicating that the friends have developed a cryptic language of their own — a secret code boys and adolescents sometimes use to disguise, in Wilde's phrase, "the love that hath no name." In the same letter, on October 3, 1745, Baxter told Wilkes that he (Baxter) and Leeson would "pluck a Graw together when we meet. He will not understand this Language: but he'll know very well what it means."[37] The meaning of "plucking a Graw" is not clear from the letter's context, and one can only guess how Baxter is using the term "Graw." But Baxter, enduring Leeson's company if it could bring him closer to Wilkes, made a point to derogate Leeson's intellect: "He will not understand." Baxter's letters indicate he won Wilkes's mind in part by intellectual glitter; he thought he could secure it by assuring Wilkes that he (Baxter) was the most suitable proxy anywhere for Leeson.

By Christmas 1745, Baxter and Wilkes were on intimate terms. They would have spent the holidays together if Baxter had not grown ill; yet Baxter was not too sick to write to Wilkes about "the force of Bodies moving in free spaces." Baxter's language in these letters rarely misses an opportunity to couch his metaphysics in erotic terms. In the same Christmas letter he writes of the physics of motion that "if ye be against this Whim (which a passionate Love for you has brought me to bed of) I shall drop it. But if you will allow of it, I will do it more sincere Friendship than ever anything like it was done."[38] The sentence is grammatically tortured but makes its point through explicit references to passionate friendship and images of "bedly" love.

During the winter of 1746, Baxter and Wilkes continued to exchange gifts, usually books. By this time Alexander Carlyle had arrived in Leiden (he matriculated in November 1745) and had moved in with the van de Tasses, as had Charles Townshend, who appeared in October; the former eventually to become the leader of the Broad Church Party in Scotland, the latter the Chancellor of the Exchequer in England and the key figure in Pitt's second ministry. During a heightened state of consciousness brought on by illness on February 6, 1746, Dowdeswell wrote a strangely confessional letter to Wilkes indicating that their "club" had become blissfully intimate;[39] he suggested that their intimacy was based on similar sociopolitical principles, including radical Whig politics and libertine ethics. On May 10, Baxter thanked Wilkes for another present, a copy of John Balguy's *Tracts*, a compendium of sermons and essays defending the then dissenting positions of Samuel Clarke.

By June, 1747, Wilkes prepared to return to England with Leeson and Bland, a departure that gave Baxter much pause. Once Wilkes left Holland, Baxter would have only d'Holbach among his tutees with whom to discuss philosophy and to become enraptured. Baxter was not sufficient reason to keep Wilkes in Holland; when he left, Baxter lost his own desire to travel and began to dream of returning home himself; he also became cynical and sharp. On August 21, 1747, descanting to Wilkes about Parliament, now that Wilkes was back in London, Baxter said, "It were worth our Legislator's while, to take care that the British Youth should have all their Education in their own Country, for which they come abroad. They return full of foreign airs, disgusted with the manners of their own Country, and important foreign vices; which is called *Seeing the World*."[40] This is a very different tune from the strain Baxter had sung six years ago, when he abandoned his wife and children to travel on the Continent in the name of breathing the free and tolerant Dutch air, and to wander through the lowlands with youths less than half his age. "Seeing the World" had been precisely what he wanted. Wilkes's departure from Holland left a void for Baxter that nothing could fill, not even further travel.

From this time onward—1746-47—Wilkes's biography is well documented: his rapid marriage, its precipitous failure, his heterosexual promiscuity and his leading role in the satanic activities of the Monks of Medmenham, causing at least one biographer to refer to him as "that Devil Wilkes."[41] In this regard, it is impossible to accept the conclusion of his most recent biographer when she writes of these satanic monks that "whatever the rituals and whatever the form of the lecheries, there is no real indication either of 'group sex' or of perversions such as homosexuality, although these have been claimed by some purely sensational writers. Eighteenth-century vice tended to be heartily heterosexual . . ."[42] The matter of homosexuality as a deviation or perversion aside, what is the evidence for these sweeping assertions? Given Wilkes's earlier career in Leiden, there is no reason to outlaw homosexual activity as a possibility for him. Indeed, the transition from Leiden to West Wycombe Park (where the monks assembled in Sir Francis Dashwood's ruined Gothic abbey) would not have been abrupt for Wilkes. His little homosocial club in Holland had prepared the way, even if his biographers have not known, or said anything, about it.

IV. THE BARON D'HOLBACH (1723-1789)

Paul-Henri Dietrich Thiry, the famous Baron d'Holbach and eventually one of the most influential of the eighteenth-century

French philosophes in view of his materialism and anti-clericalism, arrived in Leiden at the age of 21 during the winter of 1744. His biographers suggest that he selected this place for university studies as a consequence of its international reputation for excellence, as well as its attraction for large numbers of foreign students.[43] Wealthy, patrician, well-educated, radical in his politics and libertine in his ethics; eventually a fervid and unparalleled Anglophiliac; the young d'Holbach concluded in old age that he had chosen wisely when deciding to matriculate at this particular Dutch university.

The central, inner city of Leiden in the 1740s was still a small place, the university buildings clustering around a few modern-day blocks in the vicinity of the Rapenburg Canal or as students then and now call it, "de Rapenburg." Students quickly identified similar types of radicalized libertines in the bars and clubs that dot the alleys permeating the small quarter between the Rapenburg and Old Rhine. Wilkes and d'Holbach could have met in any of these places; or their radical politics could have brought them together in the clubs of students where political orientation was a consideration. Once friends, it was inevitable that d'Holbach and Baxter would eventually become acquainted: any friend of Wilkes was sooner or later destined to become a friend of Baxter's. Baxter soon became extremely fond of d'Holbach, but even after encountering d'Holbach's brilliant, analytic mind, he was never to be as taken with the young patrician baron as he was with the charismatic Wilkes. D'Holbach's philosophical materialism differed from his own, it is true; but then Baxter's Aristotelian theory of motion and matter brought d'Holbach's own Newtonianism into greater relief, as it were, and made it more tenable for the young German. It is also certain, in view of d'Holbach's extensive correspondence with Wilkes and Baxter (still extant in the British Library), that d'Holbach was a regular member of the homocentric "club" described so well in retrospect by Carlyle: "We pass'd our time in General very agreeably, and very profitably too, for ten or 12 of us held Meetings at our Lodgings, thrice a Week in the Evenings, when the conversations of Young Men of Good Knowledge, intended for Different professions, could not Fail to be Instructive."[44]

D'Holbach's participation in the club, and especially his interest in Wilkes, was also homosocial. While in Leiden he constantly sought out Wilkes; even when Wilkes returned to Clerkenwell, in London, for holidays, d'Holbach bombarded him with frequent letters. "Direct your first letter to me," he summoned Wilkes on December 3, 1746, after Wilkes had returned to England for Christmas, "under the covert of Mr. Dowdeswell at Miss Alliaume's in Leyden."[45] Under "the covert" because it was wartime — the War of the Spanish Succession — and all students, not merely the British, ran the risk of being identified as spies. A few months later, "No more at Mr. Van Sprang's," d'Holbach wrote to Wilkes,[46] "like you used to do," that is, because d'Holbach had moved, but still imploring Wilkes to stay in close touch. Leiden without Wilkes became a lonely place for d'Holbach, as it was also for Baxter; d'Holbach often fled Holland, as in February 1747, fast on the heels of Wilkes. A troika of Baxter-Wilkes-d'Holbach: on more occasions than one it must have been evident to Wilkes that Baxter and d'Holbach were competing for his intimate friendship. Wilkes somehow satisfied both men and remained on close terms with his fellow student for two decades. *Quant à* d'Holbach, and viewed from his perspective, the affair with Wilkes was something he was never to forget. Wilkes and Leiden were inextricably entwined for him, a high moment whose excitement never left him, not even when as a famous old man he contemplated his youth.

In the most detailed study of d'Holbach's coterie in Paris written to date, Alan Kors has commented that "it is perhaps to the Baron's remembrances of his student milieu [in Leiden] and the pleasures, and not to a Parisian tradition of salon life, that the coterie holbachique owed its inspiration."[47] This is a daring hypothesis, but Kors has placed his finger on an important matter. The point takes on special significance when the homosocial basis of this particular "student milieu" is brought into sharp relief: this aspect enhanced not only its intellectual ferment and radical politics but also the emotional interactions between individual members. There can be no doubt that d'Holbach was familiar with the group who lived at Madam van de Tasse's house and their British satellites elsewhere, for d'Holbach vividly recalled the character of one of their group, and took pains to inquire of Wilkes about this Briton — Jeremiah Dyson — after Dyson had left Leiden.

D'Holbach's relations with other members of the group are best narrated below, especially his ties to Akenside, Dyson, and Dowdeswell. Suffice it to say here that he won the confidence of all its chief supporters, in whose service he placed his family estate. Although he may have cultivated other British students with whom he enjoyed a less intense friendship,[48] d'Holbach's intense Anglophilia probably began during these years in Leiden as a direct consequence of the experience with the club. But Wilkes and Baxter, as well as Akenside and Dyson, occupied a special place in his psyche. He was never to forget them.

V. MARK AKENSIDE (1722-1770) AND JEREMIAH DYSON (1722-1776)

If the extant evidence does not indicate precisely when Akenside and Dyson met Wilkes and d'Holbach, there is no question that each group not only knew the other, but that they developed a great familiarity with each other. In January-February 1747, d'Holbach wrote to Wilkes (who was now back in London) inquiring about Jeremiah Dyson. "I wish to know," he asked, "if Mr. Dyson since his return to his native country [i.e., England], continues in his peevish cross temper."[49] In context the passage makes clear that the question arises from firsthand knowledge of the subject of the peevish temper; and if d'Holbach was on such familiar terms with Dyson, it is inconceivable that he had not also become acquainted with Dyson's closest friend Mark Akenside; the two were practically inseparable while in Leiden from 1743-47.[50] At the very least, Wilkes and d'Holbach knew a good deal about Akenside, the precocious young poet who was also the most brilliant medical student in the group and eventually one of the most intuitive medical thinkers of his epoch.

The latter possibility—that they knew *about* Akenside rather than actually knew him firsthand—is insupportable in view of the club's established (i.e., through the extant correspondence) intimacy. Other evidence further diminishes its probability. For example, Akenside refers to his intimacy with Wilkes in a letter to Wilkes, dated May 21, 1745. It has now disappeared, but one of Akenside's earliest biographers printed it and long ago demonstrated that it assumed a close friendship in Leiden.[51] Moreover, Akenside and Charles Townshend (see section VI below) were on close terms in Leiden: as a result of this friendship, Townshend became Akenside's patient in London, and Akenside dedicated two odes to him. Akenside also knew the physically handsome John Freeman from Jamaica, who has been vividly described by Carlyle in his memoir of the group: "There was another West Indian there [at Leiden], a Mr. Freeman, a Man of Fortune, Sedate and Sensible. He was very Handsome and well made. Having been 3 Years [i.e., 1742-45] in Leyden, he was the best Scater there."[52] On April 21, 1744, Akenside wrote to his patron-lover Dyson, then back in London and thirsty for news of the club: "Mr. Gronovius tells me, what perhaps you do not know, that Mr. Freeman is to return to Leyden: by which I judge he has intirely dedicated himself to Greek . . ."[53] Why would Dyson care to know about the Creole Freeman if, first of all, the three had not been friends, and, more importantly, if Freeman's physical beauty had not elicited much attention among club members? I fail to see how Dyson would have otherwise understood the unannotated reference to Freeman. But Freeman was most certainly a regular member of the club, and Akenside's inclusion of this piece of information suggests how homoerotic the group was.

More crucially, Akenside and Dyson, like Baxter, were actually homosexual, eventually becoming (in our terminology) lovers and living together.[54] The reasons for Akenside's sexual orientation must be discussed elsewhere: whatever their psychological basis, perhaps they were affected by the club foot he shared in common with Byron, his eccentric but not effeminate dress, the incommensurability of his own precocity, from his parents' lack of education and social standing. Whatever the reasons, Akenside leaned on other men; turned to them so pronouncedly that one wonders if he, unlike his contemporary poet Thomas Gray, was more misogynist than homosexual. In view of all the evidence, then, it is clear that Wilkes and d'Holbach knew Akenside and Dyson rather well, were members of the club centered in the house of the van de Tasses, and that through this association d'Holbach was first exposed to Akenside's great poem, *Pleasures of Imagination* (1744), which d'Holbach translated into French and published in 1759.[55] Who then were Akenside's friends in Leiden? As he continued to assure Dy-

son, when Dyson went back to England: "my acquaintance here
. . . [are] the gentlemen that lodge with Mr. Vandertas,"[56] and they
remained those gentlemen.

Akenside's life as one of England's best known poets is so well
known that there is no need to restate it here. His stature as perhaps
the most gifted poet writing between Pope and the Romantics, as
well as his brilliant dual career in literature and medicine, has been
the subject of frequent commentary. But the philosophical contents
and political implications of his poetry, as well as the biographical
details of his life with Jeremiah Dyson are less well understood.
Here documentation exists in so circumspect and erratic a manner
that more questions are posed than can be answered. The likelihood
is that Akenside and Dyson, like Baxter, were homosexuals, rather
than merely homosocial men. For example, Smollett, the comic
novelist, vigorously reinforced this notion of Akenside's homosexuality. In *Peregrine Pickle*, his second novel published in 1751,
Akenside figures as a physician in love with the Greeks and all
things Grecian, as with republican political principles, blatant references to Akenside's two best-known idiosyncrasies. While travelling in France on the Grand Tour, Peregrine and his companions
link up with a "physician" — Dr. Akenside — who invites them to
"An Entertainment in the Manner of the Ancients," where epicu-
rean delights preside, especially homosexual debauchery. Smollett
may have preferred to name Akenside himself in this illicit act, but
he dared not — the reference would be unequivocal, subject to the
law of libel and slander. Instead, Smollett conveniently invented an
Italian marquis and German baron who are prominent among Akenside's party and who are caught in the very act. Readers in 1751 did
not overlook Smollett's insinuation about Akenside's sexual company: chapter 49 speaks all too clearly about the sodomitical Euro-
peans with whom Akenside associates. In addition to Akenside,
who was enraged at the allegation (true as it probably was), Smollett's publisher objected, as did several of the reviewers; and Smollett prudently removed, or was compelled to remove, this scene
when the novel was reprinted in 1758. Yet his purpose was accomplished: by 1751 Akenside's link to homosexuality was established
at home, in England, in a best-selling novel. From the vantage of

social history, homosocial behavior was indeed normative among educated youths during this epoch, but Akenside and Dyson went beyond this norm.

Dyson, older and wealthier than Akenside, courted him with patronage and eventually won whatever romantic affection Akenside was capable of. After financing Akenside's medical education in Holland and personally subsidizing his medical practice in England, Dyson purchased a house for him where the two could live as companions — while Mrs. Dyson remained in another house — and he remained emotionally loyal until he buried the 48-year-old Akenside in 1770. Oddly, only one recent commentator has been willing to describe this relationship for what it was: a practicing American physician, Dr. Ober, who unfortunately published his study in an obscure medical journal.

It needs to be emphasized that Akenside and Dyson already were on intimate terms in England before arriving in Holland. Indeed, they may have decided to matriculate in Leiden, as I have suggested elsewhere,[58] to kill two birds with one stone: to complete their studies in an academically excellent and internationally fashionable university, while enjoying the tolerant libertine atmosphere there without restraints they would have felt at home. This is not to imply that they escaped to Holland out of a feeling of desperation. Not at all: on the contrary, the Leiden medical and law faculties (Dyson matriculated in law) were as excellent as could be found anywhere. But Leiden offered academic excellence *in addition to* toleration and freedom. No British university, not even Edinburgh, where both Dyson and Akenside had already studied and which was unquestionably the most distinguished British university of the day, could rival Leiden for offering both types of experience.

They certainly could not rival Leiden as a place for sexual experimentation and university libertinism. For Oxbridge at mid-century was not only in serious academic decline — as Gibbon, who was there roughly at that time (1752-53), noted: Oxford was a place "steeped in port and prejudice." The Oxford fellows, still reeling from the recent attempted rape of William French, a commoner at Wadham, by Robert Thistlethwayte, a doctor of divinity and the Warden of the college, were now more cautious with their students than they had previously been. If no similarly notorious case had arisen at Cambridge, the masters of the Cambridge colleges nevertheless continued to warn their fellows of the harsh consequences that would now follow if they lusted after their students. A desire for homosexual libertinism probably existed at Oxbridge as well as anywhere else, and possibly in more intense versions given the nature of the expensive, segregated, all-male schools from which most of the students were drawn. But the possibility of attaining it with impunity was slight. All sorts of student clubs thrived at the two English universities but always under the palm, as it were, of inquisitive masters and moral tutors. Furthermore, the colleges in Cambridge and Oxford were constantly under local and governmental surveillance, especially in the aftermath of the 1745 and the accusation then that groups of students had seditiously functioned as Jacobite spies. In the Dutch universities there was neither actual surveillance or the perception of it; and the relatively recent Oxbridge regulation that students sleep one to a bed had never crossed the North Sea. The Dutch authorities, then as now, were largely tolerant of all expressions of social behaviour, all arrangements for sleeping, provided that they did not interfere with Dutch commercial interests or fly in the face of ancient Calvinist-Catholic hostilities. The homoerotic libertinism of a small number of British students in Leiden or Utrecht was of no interest whatever, so long as the foreign youths continued to convert their English shillings into Dutch guilders and not interfere with local Dutch law. Tolerance even abounded in the legal realm since all matriculated university students in Leiden, whether Dutch nationals or foreigners, were not subject to many of the local city ordinances. The freedom, then, offered to British tutors and their students who travelled and studied abroad, and who especially possessed an alibi for libertinism while travelling on the Grand Tour, was greater than anything that could be hoped for in England.

The duration of Akenside's residence in Leiden is crucial to this argument. It was not "less" than six months, as the literary critic Samuel Johnson thought,[59] or "about" six months, as some recent scholars have concluded,[60] but a sporadic residence for at least three years, as the matriculation records of the University make clear.[61] Akenside certainly returned to England during these three years; he also frequently went back to Holland. Although the precise chronology of his movements, as well as his reasons for making them, cannot be considered entirely apart from his involvement with the group, other incentives could have attracted him to come back. Among these, Dyson remains the key figure.

Dyson matriculated in civil law at Leiden in October 1742, having crossed over to Holland without Akenside. William Courtauld, an early biographer of Dyson, surveys the chronology as briefly and carefully as anyone: ". . . eighteen months later [April 1744] Mark Akenside, still engaged in learning medicine, joined him [Dyson] there, thus renewing an acquaintance which had been originally established at Edinburgh. They lived together while in Holland, and returned together to London [in 1745], when Dyson was called to the bar . . ."[62]

The chronology is accurate and revealing: at the least it requires a gloss. First and foremost, "living together" did not preclude frequent visits of each party across the North Sea. Moreover, Dyson was Akenside's patron, paying for Akenside's expenses. Akenside had good reason, first to follow Dyson to Holland in 1744, and then to continue to pursue Dyson in England. Finally, both men were deeply interested in the Greeks and Romans, and Holland remained the best source anywhere for the purchase of Classics books, Leiden being at the time at least as good a place for book purchase as Amsterdam. The availability of these books was a genuine inducement for Akenside. It is therefore inaccurate, or at least inchoate, to suggest that *either* man made his residence in one and only one of these countries during the years in question, 1742-47. The evidence suggests that both men readily came and went, sea passages being easy to obtain despite wartime, with Dyson's money being placed in Akenside's service. This financial arrangement was crucial for Akenside's survival.

A coincidence of political views probably contributed to Akenside's love for his patron. Even if their views had differed, Akenside may have initiated the relationship because he was in such desperate need of patronage. But they seem to have agreed, as their extant letters reveal, that the best patriot was the one who had acknowledged the benefits of the republican revolution of the previous century, the one who would ensure England's liberty in the future by defending revolutionary principles now. Akenside's politics were mysteriously transformed later on, during the 1760s, when he suddenly denounced the Whigs and declared himself a Tory, but this alteration need not concern us here. During the 1740s, his political philosophy reflected a radical Whig belief that republicanism, of the type he had seen in Holland, practiced within a commercial setting, was best for England. Unfortunately, the Holland Akenside saw then had fallen into decay, and Akenside's monolithic negativity in his letters from Leiden towards everything Dutch reflects his awareness of this decline. But he was clever enough to distinguish between the political form of government and the exigency of the day. If Holland had not lived up to her seventeenth-century promise as the paragon — indeed the miracle — of nations, this was owing to alliances and competition from other countries, not to her basic republican commitment.

Dyson and Akenside held these views in common with others in the club: with Wilkes, d'Holbach, Townshend and Dowdeswell, but not with Baxter.[63] The subject must have been a constant one while the War of the Spanish Succession raged; and the youths must have thrashed out opposing positions in the coffee and ale houses where they met, as well as in the rooms of the van de Tasses. The precise route by which this radical republican politics combined with the libertine ethics of free homoerotic involvement and bisexual activity must be surmised as the documents provide no clue. Even so, it would be a mistake to keep national and sexual politics apart, especially insofar as these British students in Leiden were then more homoerotic than the Dutch.

By 1747, Akenside and Dyson had left Holland permanently. At least neither is known ever to have returned, and it is interesting to notice how their passionate, personal friendship subsequently evolved. Dyson bought a fashionable townhouse in Bloomsbury for Akenside, and provided him with an annual allowance of £300, an amount whose purchasing power today translates into about $50,000. Akenside's medical career progressed well, owing to the favors of his patron-lover as well as to his own brilliance in the theory and practice of medicine (although he was remarkably cruel to indigent patients).[64]

A remaining question regards Akenside and Baxter. Why is there no extant evidence that they knew each other? Surely Akenside knew who Baxter was, even if he never met him; Wilkes and d'Holbach, Akenside's good friends, would have seen to that. But it may be that Akenside wished to give Dyson no offense by offering the possibility of a competing patron. Given Baxter's attraction to men of this age group, as well as to personal charisma and intellectual dazzle, he may have found Akenside – despite his club foot and formal dress – appealing. If Baxter were favorably impressed by Akenside, Dyson could grow jealous. Perhaps d'Holbach sensed this potential rivalry between Baxter and Dyson: can this intuition possibly be the source of d'Holbach's strange interrogation of Wilkes about Dyson's "peevish cross temper," discussed in the beginning of this section (see page 327)? Baxter had none of Dyson's financial resources (Dyson's father had left him a fortune), and Akenside would have known that itinerant tutors, like Baxter, travelled at the discretion of their sponsors. Still, Akenside may have been playing things cautiously without taking any risks: by 1745 Dyson had already been financially generous to him and given every indication that he (Dyson) would remain a loyal patron. These are two of many possibilities, and they do not definitively answer the question about the relation of Baxter and Akenside. Their connection, alas, remains a puzzle.

VI. CONCLUSIONS

Further questions about the club are of a general nature, and relate to dealing with its time and place in the history of homosocial behavior. In approaching these questions, it is crucial to recall that by 1744-47 the University of Leiden – however tolerant it may have been – was established in 1579, and was by then an old institution. It was particularly attractive to British students because of its international student body, then virtually unique among European universities, and it appealed to medical students from far-flung corners because of the legendary fame of Hermann Boerhaave, the Newton of medicine, who was then the leading medical educator anywhere. At Leiden, students could fraternize with students from other countries while receiving a first-class education. For students with a pronounced Whig bent, Leiden held a further attraction: for at least two decades it had been a republican/liberal breeding ground for the children of prominent Whigs. It had developed a reputation for offering the best education in an environment especially sympathetic to those with a Whig bias. All this contrasted to the universities in Oxford and Cambridge, also ancient but then declining in prestige and hardly aligned with republican causes. More significantly, Leiden accepted students of all religions and personal beliefs, and accorded them the same rights and privileges as other students. For homosexual or bisexual students and their masters, this was an obvious boon.

Also, the club of Baxter, Wilkes, d'Holbach et al. thrived during wartime, and its shared beliefs about war may have loomed larger than I have so far suggested. The area of active combat lay to the southeast of current-day Holland, along the border of France and Belgium; this was the Spanish Netherlands, so-called because, by 1745, the Spaniards and Austrians had fought for these lands for almost a century. Students in the club received news of the war almost daily; their allegiances were to Britain, their native country, and the political positions they held must be viewed within a national framework. In 1744-45 all Europe was at war, but Holland's position remained ambiguous. Though a member of the Anglo-Austrian alliance, Holland remained curiously neutral, a posture that elicited comment among the club members. The question was not merely whether Holland ought to have adopted this position, but whether republican politics naturally led to such political stances. Wilkes and d'Holbach were eager to debate the connection between neutrality and republicanism.

Carlyle's diary, used so preeminently in reconstructing the club, is indeed a war diary in that it contains abundant references to these debates among the members; and the letters of Baxter and d'Holbach reveal their authors' awareness that every time they travelled between Leiden and Spa, they inevitably came closer to soldiers and guns. The relationship between political and personal beliefs entails the pressures wartime places on social, and especially sexual, behavior.[71] War in civilian zones, among other things heightens romantic emotions and strengthens human bonds. No observer could contend that the club depended on war for its existence; but it is reasonable to suggest that the fact of war nearby — only a couple of hundred miles to the southeast against a French

enemy who was advancing north into the Lowlands — intensified
these interpersonal relationships and elicited homosocial arrangements that otherwise may have lain dormant. Of course, it should
be noted that none of the club members was French or particularly
pro-French. Akenside had been resident in Leiden for only a few
weeks when he wrote to Dyson, in April 1744, that he greatly "fa-
voured the war against France." His reason was that the "cause of
justice would be served" because he had not "the least doubt of the
superiority of our national [English] spirit, and consequently of our
success in general."[72]

In this political context, 1745 also marked the year of the last
attempt at a Jacobite revolt: the attempt to return the English crown
to the House of Stuart. Bonnie Prince Charles, the son of James II,
and his cohorts in Culloden, Scotland, threatened to take England
by storm. The Jacobite plot had widespread European repercus-
sions, especially rekindling old questions about the degree to which
the manifestoes of the English Revolution had been executed.
Those — like Wilkes and other club members — who practiced radical politics and who preached new revolution, found Leiden an ideally tolerant environment in which to thrash out their differences.
For over a century the Netherlands, a miracle in the development of
modern republicanism, had symbolized toleration of alternative
views; in Holland the radical discussants could air their views without fear of apprehension or retaliation. Their status as temporary
emigrés (exiles does not accurately reflect their position) was
equally crucial, in that emigrés are almost always reinvigorated by
the novelty of foreign soil. The alien views of the Dutch — alien at
least to most Britons — and the felt presence of a European continent
whose past had been so different from Britain's, combined to regen-
erate the revolutionary principles of these young men.[73] This was
indeed reinvigoration of a profound type, and it may have cemented
friendships that otherwise would have been less intense and romantic. Even the sentimentally homoerotic Baxter, whose politics were
much more conservative than Wilkes's or Akenside's, must have
succumbed on more than one occasion to the temptation of revolution at home: to the bandwagon of Bonnie Prince Charles and his
army.

So far these matters explore the public dimensions of the club.

The execution of some 200 Dutch homosexual sodomites in the decade before the club thrived need not be discussed here because overt sodomy was probably not among the club's primary programs. The club was indeed homosocial and bisexual: Baxter was in love with Wilkes; Akenside and Dyson were possibly engaged in a physical relation; d'Holbach's pinings — "those sincere Kisses" — would seem to represent more than fleshless Platonic memories. Still, it cannot be proved beyond a shadow of doubt that the members were fundamentally homosexual, with the exception of Akenside and Dyson. Yet it would be a mistake not to observe how passionate friendship and politics combined in the personal ethos of individual club members.

In summary then, in this group emotion was endorsed rather than discouraged. Indeed, Wilkes felt himself as comfortable giving presents to, as receiving presents from, Baxter; d'Holbach felt similarly at ease when describing the rhapsodic thrill he felt upon imagining himself reunited with Wilkes. The interpretations I offer above may suffer from caution rather than its opposite; some may see in the d'Holbachean dream analyzed above a wish that d'Holbach could become Wilkes's surrogate bride. This element of exchange — of genders as well as sexual roles — may or may not be unconsciously present in d'Holbach's outpourings. But even among those club members who were less homoerotic than Baxter and d'Holbach, and less homosexual than Akenside and Dyson, positive encouragement was offered to those who displayed sexual longings. By contrast, one searches in vain among young upper-class Britons in this period for other clubs whose ethos was as homocentric and whose politics were as republican.[74] My hypothesis here is that the club's radical politics was its starting point after the obvious fact of common British nationality. From a similitude of political beliefs, individual members justified their own intense friendships. In a few cases members (d'Holbach) whose homosocial components were small permitted themselves to indulge homosexual emotions they may otherwise never have allowed to surface.

That most of the members later married and had children is irrelevant, as is the information that some members engaged in heterosexual relations at the very time they were sworn devotees of their club. As Erik Erikson has commented: "to a considerable extent adolescent love is an attempt to arrive at a definition of one's identity by projecting one's diffused ego image on another and by seeing it thus reflected and gradually clarified. This is why so much of young love is conversation,'"[75] including, Erikson might have added if he were commenting on the club, conversation in the form of outpourings in letters. Here Wilkes served as the center of attention in the number of letters he received. Given his libertine views, the others could project on to him their own diffused egos. In Leiden, these men could have passionate friendships with other young men without agonizing about their future state, especially their future professional niches. In this sense, their Leiden life was an existence apart: detached from the past and future and existing without any of the anxiety and guilt they would have felt had they tried to flourish as a subterranean club at one of the British universities.[76] Wilkes and d'Holbach both married; both fathered children. But this did not preclude their subsequent friendship; the two men retained their Leiden ties, and Wilkes visited the Baron in Paris many times, remaining with him for long periods of time.

It would be an error, though, not to notice the significance of the tutor-student relation. Parents of British students permitted their children to matriculate in a foreign university because their tutors accompanied them. In the case of Dyson and Akenside, the arrangement was different: the two fellow students existed in the relation of patron and patronee. Historians have noted how little of a sociological nature is understood about the institution of patronage in early modern Europe,[77] and elsewhere I have noticed that almost nothing has been written about the relations of the tutors and their charges, especially their homosocial arrangements in an epoch when young men and women could not travel together.[78]

These ties point to discipleship, especially to its natural history. Since Socratic times, when the erotic element was inherent in teacher (master) student (slave) relations, discipleship has remained a vexed issue. When Plato's Phaedrus comments that Eros lies at the center of discipleship, he identifies a problem that has lingered for thousands of years. Yet the Christianization of discipleship is a subject no modern scholar seems brave enough to tackle, perhaps because it disturbs the center of so many of our contemporary institutions: education, apprenticeship, the professions. Discipleship is a complex enough matter even when viewed apart from its religious contexts. Judeo-Christian discipleship is more troubled than pagan Greek varieties because the built-in erotic element produces such terrific, if unconscious, anxiety and guilt. That is, in pagan versions initiation and eros seem to coexist with a minimum of anxiety, as even Plato's dialogues demonstrate. But when discipleship becomes Christianized, as it were, a whole new order of guilt is introduced. The rituals of Christian initiation show that the erotic element must be eradicated if the apprentice-student is to be properly introduced. Indeed, initiation is often tantamount to destruction of the erotic element itself. But in certain instances in Judeo-Christian society it cannot be, and in the cases of homoerotic and homosexual youths eradication proves detrimental to the learning process, as we are gradually beginning to discover in the late twentieth century.

Yet the effect of Christianization impinges on the story of those who gathered in Leiden and Utrecht where masters and students engaged in the romantic explorations of discipleship. Had Wilkes's Leeson been more Socratic—in the academic as well as erotic sense—Wilkes would not have been so readily disposed to replace him with Baxter. Likewise, if Baxter's tutees had possessed a grain of Wilkes's radical verve and personal charisma, Baxter may not have felt the compulsion to abandon his charges in Utrecht and devote his energy to a Leiden student. But Baxter's homoeroticism was entirely directed to younger men, especially his students, and the most difficult aspect in reconstructing his situation lies in imagining the moral verdict we would attach today—in the 1980s—to someone in his situation.

If my own moral cowardice has manifested itself anywhere in this essay, surely it lies in refusing to put Baxter on trial here. Viewed by the standards of the 1980s, he would be found guilty of unprofessional conduct: we are taught that teachers, even tutors, should not allow themselves to fall in love with their students and then act out that love. Judged by the laws and norms of the mid-eighteenth century, Baxter would have been found even guiltier: he may not have been an outright sodomite; he may not even have committed any overt sexual act with his students let alone sodomized them; he may only have romanticized the teacher-student relation in his vocation of discipleship. Still, his passionate attachments to young men would have been viewed as disgraceful by most of those asked to judge him. Only in earlier times—the Renaissance, Greek Antiquity—would he perhaps have been exonerated. So it is just as well that I have not put him on trial here.

My point has been that the vitality of the club needs to be seen in the light of these complex developing institutions of discipleship and patronage, as well as in their more obviously local contexts: as a group of young men willing to express their homoerotic attachments in enduring passionate friendships. The club thrived because it integrated a complex web of needs. The libertinism of these men cannot be viewed, ultimately, in an absolute sense: that is, as the result of purely internal libidinal needs. Youthful drive was obviously present; it flourished because the environment was so conducive. But if any aspect of the cultural climate had altered (i.e., different time, country, university, student body, economic and social class), the other conditions may have changed so much in turn that the club would not have existed. For this reason, rather than simply listing names and describing activities, it has been crucial to present the club and its members within a broader context.

NOTES

1. Quoted in C. T. Houpt, *Mark Akenside: A Biographical and Critical Study* (Philadelphia: Pennsylvania, 1944), p. 62. Akenside wrote "Vanderlas," meaning "van de Tasse," but his first biographer, Alexander Dyce, misread the handwriting and the error has been propagated ever since; see Alexander Dyce, *The Aldine Edition of Akenside's Poems* (London: Aldine, 1835), p. xx. British students almost never learned Dutch in the eighteenth century; thus the variety of spellings given to the van de Tasses. The phrase about "the House of Madam Vander Tasse" in my title is found in Carlyle (see below), p. 85. Madame van de Tasse ran a boarding house for British students on the site of the present Lange Brug (Long Bridge) in Leiden's old quarter between the Rapenburg and the New Rhine. Alexander Carlyle has provided a full description of her premises: "Vandertasse's was an accustom'd Lodging House, her Father and Mother having carried on that Business, so that we [the British students] liv'd very well there at a moderate Rate—That is 16 Stivers [a stiver was then worth an English penny] for Dinner, 2 for Coffee, 6 for Supper and for Breakfast. She was a Lively little French Woman about 36, had been tolerably Well Looking, and was plump and in Good Condition. As she had only one Maid Servant, and five [British] Gentlemen to Provide for, she Led an Active and Laborious Life; Insomuch that she had but little time for her Toilet, except in the article of the Coiff, which no French

Woman omits. But on Sundays when she had Leisure to Dress herself for the French Church [in Leiden], either in the Morning or Evening, Then, Who but Mademoiselle Vandertasse! She spoke English perfectly well, as the Guests of the House had been mostly British: But it had cost her Something to Learn the Language. As I had come Last, I had the worst Bedchamber. Besides Board, we [the British students] paid pretty High for our Rooms, and Dearest of all for Fewel, which was chiefly Peat. We had very Good Small Claret, at a Shilling a Bottle; Giving her the Benefit of our Exemption from Town Duty [students were then exempt from all sorts of ordinry taxes], for Sixty Stoups of Wine, for every Student. Our House was in high Repute for the best Coffee so that our Friends were pleas'd when they were Invited to partake with us in that Delicious Beverage. We had no Company to Dinner, but in the Evenings about a Dozen of us met at one anothers Rooms in Turn 3 Times a Week and Drank Coffee and Smoak'd tobacco, and Chatted about politicks, and Drank Claret and supped on Bukkam (Dutch Red Herrings) and Eggs and Sallad, and never Sate later than 12 a clock.'' See Alexander Carlyle's *Anecdotes and Characters of the Times*, first published in 1860 under the title *Autobiography* and edited by J. H. Burton. I have used the modern scholarly edition, edited with an introduction by James Kinsley and published by the Oxford University Press in 1973, pp. 85-86; for "Club Suppers" see p. 88. The middle-aged Miss van de Tasse was sexually promiscuous and may not have objected to the libertinism of her boarders; see Carlyle, p. 91. Subsequent references are to this edition and appear as Carlyle, *Anecdotes*.

I consistently spell Leiden with an i despite its common British form as Leyden, but in quotations cited I retain the spellings found there. Before March 25, 1752 dates could be listed in old or new style; all dates here are new style; therefore, an old style version as February 1, 1744-45, is here listed new style as February 1, 1745. In this essay I define terms as follows:

sodomy	anal penetration of either sex (i.e., homosexual or heterosexual sodomy) not necessarily with personal homosexual involvement
homosexuality	an umbrella term to designate all forms of homosexual behavior including homosexual sodomy
homoerotic	referring to male-oriented friendship not necessarily oral or genital
homosocial	referring to relations which are less than homoerotic friendship, thus a weaker form of homoerotic behavior
homocentric	male oriented, male centered, male dominated

Of these working definitions the term "homosexual(ity)" is problematic and anachronistic. Homosexuality is a late nineteenth-century concept denoting a psychological frame of mind that exists independent of action, and a general orientation that may or may not correlate to specific patterns of behavior. A homosexual, in this sense, primarily describes a mental set rather than a prescribed course of action or predisposing bio-anatomical conditions. But the eighteenth century had no such concept of homosexuality, and nowhere in this essay do I claim it did.

Avoidance of all forms of the words homosexual would therefore have been historically more precise, especially since much of my discussion is clearly not about persons who were then labelled sodomites—i.e., males in the eighteenth century who had anal relations with other males—but about males who were in remarkably varying degrees homoerotic and homosocial, whether passively (the mid-century's constant reference to pathics) or actively. Yet I have permitted the anachronism to remain for a number of reasons, ideologically explosive though the concept homosexuality is today; not least of which reasons is my aim to convey to readers that I attempt to survey a broad spectrum here: not merely those who actually engaged in sexual acts with another person of the same sex, but also those who were homoerotic and who cultivated the homosocial dimensions of friendship. Also, I have tried to reach a broad readership that does not consist exclusively, I presume, of historians of sexuality, and which may be as interested in this wide repertoire of same-sex relations as in the more extreme sodomitical ones. An alternative usage was consistent resort to the umbrella phrase homosocial arrangements: a cumbersome literalism presenting its own hurdles, if not of anachronism then of misleading implications for a late twentieth-century readership—among which is the remote sound of the phrase and the unfortunate suggestion that those involved were "arrangers"—i.e., consciously arranging something. On balance, the roadblocks created by such a literalism are as formidable as the use of the anachronistic noun homosexual; and ultimately less confusion arises for contemporary readers by use of the familiar noun and adjective homosexual, so long as readers are warned well in advance that the noun, especially, is an anachronism. Still, the reader who wishes to avoid this interpretative crux can eradicate all traces of the anachronism by substituting "homosocial arrangements" for every use of homosexual, and can also substitute the noun sodomite; provided it is clear that the concept sodomy in the eighteenth century was itself very much in flux, as I show—so much so that by the end of the century it had altogether different connotations from the beginning. These changes by 1800 are so pronounced, and by now (i.e., 1800) so riddled with class distinctions and vocational resonances, that one wonders if the preference of sodomite over homosexual for someone living between 1700 and 1800, is a safe choice after all.

2. See A.L. Rowse, *Homosexuals in History* (New York: Macmillan, 1977); H. Mayer, *Outsiders*, trans. D.M. Sweet (London, MIT Press, 1983); the various articles of Randolph Trumbach, Philippe Aries, Michel Rey, Leo Boon, Gert Hekma, Louis Crompton, and now G.S. Rousseau, "The Pursuit of Homosexuality in the Eighteenth Century: 'Utterly Confused Category' or Rich Repository?" *Eighteenth Century Life*, X (1985-1986), pp. 132-168, reprinted now in R. Maccubbin (ed.), *'Tis But Nature* (Cambridge; Cambridge University Press, 1987).

3. The two major sources are: BM Add MSS 30,867 and Carlyle's *Anecdotes*.

4. Margaret C. Jacob, *The Radical Enlightenment: Pantheists, Freemasons and Republicans* (London: Allen & Unwin, 1981), p. 263. I realize from the outset that comparisons between this group and the one centered around Byron in the early nineteenth century could usefully be made. Space does not permit this

but fortunately there now exists a fine study of the later group; see Louis Crompton, *Byron and Greek Love* (Berkeley and Los Angeles: Universities of California Press, 1985).

5. BM Add MSS 30,867, f. 8.

6. See, for example, Percy Fitzgerald, *The Life and Times of John Wilkes,* *M. P.*, 2 vols. (London: Ward and Downey, 1888); L. Kronenberger, *The Extraordinary Mr. Wilkes* (New York: Doubleday, 1974); A. Williamson, *Wilkes* (London: George Allen & Unwin, 1974); John Brewer, *Party Ideology and Popular Politics* (Cambridge: Cambridge University Press, 1976).

7. BM Add MSS 30,867, f. 8.

8. For the tradition see Thomas Gould, *Platonic Love* (London: Routledge & Kegan Paul, 1963).

9. BM Add MSS 30,867, f. 8.

10. See Stuart Miller, *Men and Friendship* (Boston: Houghton Mifflin, 1983); John Lehmann, *Three Literary Friendships: Byron and Shelley, Rimbaud and Verlaine, Robert Frost and Edward Thomas* (New York: Holt, Rinehart and Winston, 1984); Leo Rangell, "On Friendship," *Journal of the American Psychological Association*, 11 (1963): 3-54.

11. BM Add MSS 30,867, f. 14.

12. *Ibid.*, letter dated merely "August 1746."

13. *Ibid.*; all quotations in this paragraph are found on folio 14.

14. Wilkes left Leiden in the spring of 1747 to marry Mary Mead in Aylesbury in Buckinghamshire.

15. For a description of the "nátiones" see the anonymous *Description of Holland* (London; Knapton, 1744), p. 337.

16. See F. A. Pottle (ed.), *Boswell in Holland 1763-1764* (New York: McGraw Hill, 1952), p. 161.

17. BM Add MSS 30,867, f. 21.

18. Carlyle provides most of these names in his *Anecdotes*, p. 86.

19. There is no biography of Baxter but see the brief sketch by Leslie Stephen in *The Dictionary of National Biography*, ed. by L. Stephen and S. Lee, 22 vols (Oxford: Oxford University Press, 1917), I: 1345.

20. Andrew Baxter, *An Enquiry into the Nature of the Human Soul: wherein the immateriality of the soul is evinced from the principles of reason and philosophy* (London: Millar, 1733), which went through three editions by 1745. William Warburton, the influential critic and collaborator of Pope the poet, wrote to his constant correspondent, Bishop Hurd, from Grosvenor Square in London on March 3, 1759, that Baxter's preposterous theory of dreams had been the cause of his own neglect. "This [dreaming]," Warburton noted, "has been the very fate of Baxter. His noble demonstration [i.e., about the immateriality of the soul] has been neglected, because he wrote of 'dreaming.'" See Richard Hurd, *Letters from a Late Eminent Prelate to one of his Friends* (Kidderminster, 1808), p. 283.

21. *Biographia Britannica*, 6 vols. (London: W. Innys, 1747-1766), I: 239.

22. See Margaret C. Jacob, *The Radical Enlightenment*, note 4 above, and the recent excellent anthology edited by Gert Hekma, *Among Men, Among Women*

344   *G. S. Rousseau*

(Amsterdam: University of Amsterdam, 1983), which contains essays dealing
with these matters. The image of Holland among the British during the 1740s is a
complicated matter. The British press had covered the Dutch persecutions in considerable detail during 1730-32 as part of an ongoing anti-Dutch political campaign, but the English were accustomed to these onslaughts and did not necessarily change their minds about the traditionally tolerant Dutch. Furthermore, these
students were too young in 1730-32 to appreciate the significance of the persecutions; they, unlike their parents, would not remember them. Baxter was much
older and would of course have remembered. In any case, at stake is not the
genuine historical atmosphere then prevailing in Holland, but *British perceptions*
of that atmosphere. The two phenomena are very different indeed.

23. A search in the Municipal and University Archives of Utrecht has not
produced more information about their living quarters than what is described here
and below.

24. Travel in the 1740s by trekschuits from Leiden to Utrecht is described in *A
Description of Holland* (London: Knapton, 1744), pp. 323-331.

25. A dialogue called *Enquiry into the nature of the human soul, wherein the
principles laid down there are cleared from some objections* (London: Millar,
1750), which he completed in the next two or three years.

26. BM Add MSS 30,867, f. 44.

27. [John Wilkes], *A Letter from Mr. Baxter, author of an Enquiry into the
Nature of the Human soul . . . to John Wilkes, Esq.* (London: Strahan, 1753).

28. See A. Williamson, *Wilkes* (London: Allen & Unwin, 1974), p. 13. For
valuable information of a psycho-biographical nature, see Lewis B. Namier and
John Brooke, *Charles Townshend* (London: Macmillan, 1964).

29. See Karl Ludwig Poellnitz, *Les amusements de spa: or, the gallantries of
the Spaw [sic] in Germany* (London: S. Birt, 1745), p. 42.

30. Baxter published this late in 1745 as *Matho . . . A dialogue, in which the
first principles of Philosophy and Astronomy are accommodated to the capacity of
young persons, or such as have yet no tincture of these sciences*, 2 vols. (London:
Millar, 1745). In the dialogue, Matho and Histor are the main characters. Two
years later, on August 21, 1747, Baxter explained his larger purpose to Wilkes: "I
designed to attack the Dutch *Philosophers* . . .who had endeavoured to undermine
the *English philosophy* by unfair arguments," that is, Dutch scientists who
claimed precedence over Newton in physics and mathematics. Baxter was actually
anti-Newtonian; see BM Add MSS 30,867, f. 23.

31. BM Add MSS 30,867.

32. A. Williamson, *Wilkes*, p. 13.

33. But see the interesting discussion of gerontophilia in B. Lapouge and J. L.
Pinard-Legry, *L'enfant et le pederaste* (Paris: Seuil, 1980), many of whose conditions Wilkes's early life satisfy.

34. In the Klok Steeg; see *Leiden University Senate Archives*, v. 115, under
"Johannes." By 1746 Carlyle was on familiar terms with Wilkes and Leeson and
was carrying some of Leeson's belongings, as a favor to Wilkes, over the North
Sea; see Carlyle, *Anecdotes*, p. 95.

35. To whom Carlyle was most physically attracted; see Carlyle, *Anecdotes*, p. 90. His return to England in the spring of 1746 was surcharged with sexual adventures of all types. On board, he met "3 Forreigners of Different Ages, who had under their care a Young Person of about 16 very Handsome." Carlyle took him "for a Hanoverian Baron," and was delighted when a gale at sea caused the group "to Take to our Beds in the Cabbin." Carlyle discovered that "The Young Person was the only one of the Strangers, who had a Berth there." He was further delighted when discovering that "My Bed was Directly opposite to that of the Stranger." "But," Carlyle's account continues, "we were so Sick that there was no Conversation among us, till the Young Forreigner became very frightened in Spite of the Sickness, and call'd out to me in French, if we were not in Danger." But the "beautiful person," the presumed lovely male, turned out to be a female disguised as a youth, and was none other than "Violletti the Dancer, who was engaged to the Opera in the Hay-Market." Still, Carlyle remained loyal to the foreigners and helped them clear customs in Harwich and Colchester. The whole account is found in Carlyle's *Anecdotes*, p. 95.

36. BM Add MSS 30,867, f. 9.

37. *Ibid.*, f. 9.

38. *Ibid.*, f. 10.

39. *Ibid.*, f. 11.

40. *Ibid.*, f. 23.

41. Raymond Postgate, *That Devil Wilkes* (London: Constable, 1930; rev. ed. Dobson, 1956). There was a huge, if not grotesque, phallus in the garden of Medmenham Abbey which caused Wilkes to comment that "the favorite doctrine of the Abbey is certainly not penitence." Wilkes was obsessed with that grotesque phallus — seems to have been unable to dislodge it from his mind. I have often thought he would have been an ideal reader of Payne Knight's *Discourse on the Worship of Priapus* (1786) and he certainly lived long enough to read it, but I have searched in vain among the vast collection of extant Wilkeana without discovering any trace that Wilkes in old age had read the phallic masterpiece.

42. A. Williamson, *Wilkes*, p. 38.

43. See Pierre Naville, *Paul Thiry d'Holbach et la philosophie scientifique au xviiie siecle* (Paris: Gallimard, 1943), p. 18; Virgil Topazio, *D'Holbach's Moral Philosophy* (Geneva: Institut et Musee Voltaire, 1956), p. 15, and many others too numerous to cite here.

44. Carlyle, *Anecdotes*, p. 89, a crucial passage for understanding of the club's structure.

45. BM Add MSS 30,867, f. 18.

46. *Ibid.*, f. 19.

47. See Alan C. Kors, *D'Holbach's Coterie: An Enlightenment in Paris* (Princeton: Princeton University Press, 1976), pp. 11-12.

48. D'Holbach's Anglophilia is discussed by Kors, pp. 12-13. It is germane to note that La Mettrie, the radical materialist philosopher, was also in Leiden during these years; he is omitted in this discussion because no evidence suggests that he interacted with any of the British students in the club.

49. BM Add MSS 30,867, f. 21-22.

50. Dyson officially completed his studies at Leiden before Akenside began his, but they continued to visit each other, either on the English or Dutch side of the North Sea. The notion, therefore, that Dyson had already returned to England by the time Akenside arrived is inaccurate.

51. Alexander Dyce, *Akenside's Poems* (London: Aldine, 1835), pp. xxvi-xxvii. Dyce's life prefixed to this edition and based on oral as well as printed sources remains an authoritative source for Akenside's biography.

52. Carlyle, *Anecdotes*, pp. 90-91. See section VI for further discussion of Freeman's physique and homosexual appeal.

53. Dyce, *Akenside's Poems*, p. xvii. Abraham Gronovius (1695-1775) was then the University Librarian in Leiden and a distinguished classicist, and should not be confused with his brother Johan, a botanist.

54. Dyson bought a house for Akenside in Bloomsbury, London and (in our jargon) kept him for several years.

55. *Les plaisirs de l'imagination. Poeme en trois chants. Traduit de l'anglois* (Amsterdam: Arkstee & Merkus; Paris: Pissot, 1757). D'Holbach may have been an impassioned Anglophile but he did not translate all English works randomly as his list of translations shows; he had his reasons for turning to Akenside's long poem.

56. See n. 1.

57. See William Ober, M. D., "Mark Akenside M. D. Physician and Philosophic Poet," *New York State Journal of Medicine*, 68 (1968): 3167-3175.

58. G. S. Rousseau, "The Pursuit of Homosexuality in the Eighteenth Century," *Eighteenth-Century Life*, X (1985-86): 132-168.

59. G. B. Hill (ed.), *Lives of the English Poets by Samuel Johnson*, 3 vols. (Oxford: Clarendon Press, 1905; rev. ed. 1935), III. 412. Johnson got Akenside's dates in Leiden altogether wrong.

60. C. C. Barfoot, "A Patriot's Boast: Akenside and Goldsmith in Leiden," in Jan van Dorsten (ed.), *Ten Studies in Anglo-Dutch Relations* (Leiden: Sir Thomas Browne Institute, 1974), pp. 197-98.

61. *Leiden University Senate Archives*, vols. 116 (1745), 117 (1746), 118 (1747), under "Marcus," n. p. Akenside is also listed in the *Album Studiosorum Academiae Lugduno Bataviae* (n. d.).

62. W. Courtauld, "Jeremiah Dyson," in Leslie Stephen et al. (eds.), *The Dictionary of National Biography*, 22 vols. (Oxford: Oxford University Press, 1922), 6:299. Dyson and Akenside lived in the house of Jan Silvius in the Pieterskerksteeg, a few hundred yards from the van de Tasse house; see *Leiden University Senate Archives*, vol. 114 (1744), under "Jeremias," n. p.

63. Dyson and Akenside were both dissenters whose sense of patriotism and liberty were shaped by their radical, republican Whig views; as Samuel Johnson wrote: "[Akenside] certainly retained an unnecessary and outrageous zeal for what he called and thought liberty;" see G. B. Hill (ed.), *Lives of the English Poets*, III. 411. Baxter's views, on the other hand, derived from his anti-Newtonian physics and anti-Lockean psychology, and drove him into a position of con-

servative Whiggism that especially derogated atheism and pantheism. Baxter's views therefore considerably differed from the clubs'. He probably coped with this disparity by not permitting it to interfere with his homoeroticism.

64. Dyce, p. xxxii, suggests that there was a great deal of contemporary gossip about this financial arrangement, as there must have been about Akenside's rough treatment of female medical patients.

65. Carlyle, *Anecdotes*, p. 86. For Townshend, see note 28.

66. Dyce, pp. xvi-xvii.

67. Carlyle, *Anecdotes*, p. 91.

68. BM Add MSS 30,867, f. 21.

69. Carlyle, *Anecdotes*, p. 88.

70. Ibid., pp. 90-91. Carlyle's attraction to Freeman, like that to the foreign youth on board ship, is so intensely described in the *Anecdotes* that one wonders to what degree he himself was homosexual.

71. Magnus Hirschfeld, *The Sexual History of the World War* (New York: Panurge, 1934), p. 167.

72. Dyce, p. xxii.

73. As it must have also regenerated them for certain Dutchmen; on this matter see Simon Schama, *Patriots and Liberators: Revolution in the Netherlands, 1780-1813* (New York: Knopf, 1977), ch. i.

74. There were, of course, plenty of student clubs in the British universities during this period, but I am not aware of any whose printed or manuscript materials contain so many homosocial and homosexual references. There were also clubs in Leiden at this time, as has been mentioned, but whether they were as homocentric as this one I do not know.

75. See Erik Erikson, *Childhood and Society* (New York: Norton, 1963, 2nd rev. ed.). p. 262.

76. There must have been, one would think, homosocial, and possibly even homosexual clubs in the British universities during the eighteenth century but these have not yet been studied in any detail by scholars.

77. See S. N. Eisenstadt and L. Roniger, "Patron-Client Relations as a Model of Structuring Social Exchange," *Comparative Studies in Society and History*, 22 (1980): 42-77; G. F. Lytle et al., *Patronage in the Renaissance* (Princeton: Princeton University Press, 1981); M. Foss, *The Age of Patronage* (London: Hamish Hamilton, 1971).

78. See G. S. Rousseau, "The Pursuit of Homosexuality in the Eighteenth Century," *Eighteenth-Century Life*, X (1985-86): 132-168.

Sexuality and Augustan England: Sodomy, Politics, Elite Circles and Society

Dennis Rubini, PhD

Recent studies dealing with sodomy in pre-industrial England have usually focused upon the development of a sodomitical subculture within the lower and lower-middle classes. Mary McIntosh, Alan Bray, and Randolph Trumbach, while disagreeing over the timing, concur that by 1700 there had developed in London a reasonably well-developed sodomitical subculture replete with special walkways, parks, and molly houses (inns in which the almost exclusively male subculture was tolerated in part or all of the premises). Some molly-house patrons employed a special vernacular and displayed deviate mannerisms, usually of an effeminate nature.[1] London, with a population of a half-million, was unique among English cities in being able to provide the anonymity seemingly required to create a subculture.[2]

What the attitude toward sodomy was elsewhere has been a subject of some debate. Mock heterosexual roles and sodomitical acts may or may not have been common: below stairs, among the sexually mature but unmarried servants, between youths in the boarding schools and universities, between preachers and choirboys. They existed, as Bray puts forward, but the limited data base leaves the question of degree uncertain. Trumbach asserts that sublimation, drinking, rioting, harassment of prostitutes, and charivaris may have been the norm.[3] For those who were caught, it appears that perhaps being forced to move was thought of as punishment enough. It appears that in moving, one Gloucestershire sodomite

Dr. Dennis Rubini is affiliated with Temple University.

349

had tried (and temporarily succeeded) in leaving his old sodomitical reputation behind.⁴ Although the degree of sodomy occurring throughout the land was problematic in the Augustan era, there were probably no more than several thousand men who thought of themselves as mollies and only a few hundred who had permanently adopted that lifestyle.

London, moreover, was unique in being a focus for Northern European sodomy. It was much the same size as Paris or Amsterdam and hence provided a similar degree of urban anonymity. In considering the other point of traditional sodomitical development, the privilege of the court, the English court was overshadowed by Versailles, which had a large and flourishing sodomitical subcourt ruled by the king's brother, Phillipe.⁵ But neither the French nor the Dutch courts were located in their nation's principle city, whereas England's was. In London alone, then, could the anonymity that allowed for the development of the city's subculture reinforce the privilege of the court.

Under the closer observation of the populace, the English court under certain Stuart rulers had become associated with promiscuity (Charles II), and earlier even sodomy (James I). Furthermore, in London the sins of heterosexual or bisexual lust had given certain areas of the metropolis the title of "Little Sodom."⁶

Subtle changes were taking place, however. In the Elizabethan period there was a toleration for bisexuality among the urban elite which was to diminish considerably by 1700. More importantly, however, the attitude toward those who were promiscuous, but exclusive, heterosexuals had improved. Trumbach notes, for example, that by 1700, being a profligate womanizer did not detract from one's reputation, but rather enhanced it. Similarly, he has come to concur with Kent Gerard and Steven Murray in finding that while there had been a continuous European adult male sodomitical subculture since the Renaissance, the overt effeminacy of the sodomitical subculture in the Augustan age was something new.⁷ Heterosexual lust received greater toleration, while hostility towards sodomitical practices increased, particularly outside the limited confines of the subculture, a trend which began to divide heterosexuals and homosexuals. The reasons for the change are debatable. The quasi-militarized society created during the first two global wars (1689-1697 and 1702-1715) may well have created a setting that moved the effete fop off stage, leaving the scene to the proper sexual beings: the hearty married man and the rake.[8]

The declining power of women was also clearly a factor. As Hilda Smith and Ginnie Smith point out, it was a time when the pamphlets of sectarian writers on women's incapacities such as Thomas Tryon dominated social thought. Women were clearly the weaker vessels, their minds deemed unsuited even for the complexities of midwifery.[9] The conceptualizing of the sodomite was possibly affected by this change, in that the old alliance of witches, midwives, and sylvan sodomites was greatly diminished in power. The aggressive woman of the Augustan age, as Susan Gubar argues, was seen as an aberration—a monster—and was to be dealt with accordingly.[10]

The development of London's molly houses caused concern because such appeared to be an aspect of the frightening and quite possibly God-forsaken phenomenon of effeminacy, monster women, and urbanization.[11] On the other hand, being commercially based, the molly houses provided the petty bourgeois mantle of protection required at the birth of capitalism; molly-house patrons were consumers, and the tavern owners, businessmen. But for many, the existence of even such a limited subculture was unacceptable.

That the capital city should share some of the avowedly sodomitical aspects of Sodom and Gomorrah was bad enough. While, as Bray infers, the molly houses may have existed since the 1650s,[12] they had not found an echo in the capital's centerpiece, the court. Under the austere Protectorate, as well as under the heterosexual and promiscuous court of Charles II and the staid quasi-Jansenist court of his brother, James, the court's image was certainly far from sodomitical—although it surely contained some sodomites. This image perhaps kept attention from focusing upon the subculture in general, and on the molly houses in particular. But William's court appeared in quite a different light: as foreign, expensive, and rather sodomitical. William's two principle favorites gained over a quarter-million acres of land, allegedly in part for sodomitical sexual services rendered to the monarch.[13] Attempts were made to bring the matter to the attention of what has generally been termed the political nation; that is, the three to five percent of the populace who were engaged in the electoral process.[14] Anti-court satirists were quick to point out, for example, that parallels existed between the alleged sodomy of the court and the mollies. One peer, satirized as a court supporter, was said to "skulk about the alleys/And is content with Betty's, Nan's and Molly's."[15]

Subsequently under Queen Anne, lesbian coteries allegedly developed and engaged at one point in a pamphlet battle.[16] If in Anne's reign there was no considerable disquiet owing to alienation of land to foreign favorites or a greatly enlarged subculture, nor was there a reversal of the sodomitical image London and the court shared.

THE COURT AND SUBCULTURE
AND THEIR OPPONENTS

The Societies for the Reformation of Manners:
The Country Party

The organized forces opposed to the development of a sodomitical subculture focused their attention upon both London and, albeit more indirectly, the Court. In the city, puritanical forces appeared which declared that the sodomites were a blot upon the Divine Providence that was creating the new English supremacy. Providence worked through the normal succession or through conquest, and it was to Providence that England owed the successes of the Glorious Revolution.[17] The Societies for the Reformation of Manners, a reformist group founded in the Tower hamlets at about the time of the Glorious Revolution, were directed by such leaders as the Reverend Thomas Bray and developed support from such allies on the Bench as Sir Henry Dutton Colt. But even after twenty years of effort, the Societies, while commending themselves as being helpful in restraining prostitution, swearing, and cursing, found the sodomitical subculture to be an obdurate challenge. Indeed, Bray characterized it as "an evil force invading our land."[18]

Bray and his supporters ostensibly took no notice of palace affairs because the Societies felt that royal support was an essential part of their being. They were, after all, on the side of Providence and saw William as part of Providence's work in shaping a better and more Godly England. Others, however, particularly Jacobite/ Country party satirists and other polemicists, took William to task for his alleged sodomy.

Why palatial sodomy had the potential for creating such resentment among the country gentry is, at first, not easy to fathom. The reason basically rested upon several interrelated factors that, it was hoped, would create anti-Williamite sentiment, if not at once, then when opinion toward the court soured (as it was to do from 1697 to 1701, during the years between the wars). Principle to the satirist's argument was that sodomy brought in Catholicism and monasteries,[19] much as Catholicism and monasteries were associated in the English mind with absolutism. In part, this association was designed to foment fears among the electorate, fears which were both rational and irrational. The association of sodomy with the Catholic Mediterranean had some foundation, if not in the manner usually thought.[20] Both Charles I and James II had found Catholicism to be to their advantage owing in no small part to the fact that it provided them with a pretext to take back the vast monastic landholdings alienated under Henry VIII. Through *quo warranto* proceedings, that is, by challenging the title to virtually all landholdings where the leases did not predate the 1540s, the central government might resume the lands through reestablishing the monasteries and, by inference, move toward the absolutist alliance of church and state on the Continental model. To aid in establishing this fear, pamphleteers pointed to William's past absolutist tendencies, his alleged sodomitical practices, his foreign favorites, and the willingness of the Dutch to compromise their religion to get what they wanted. William, who was to be termed the savior of Protestant Europe, was seen as being less anti-Catholic than anti-French. Pamphleteers pointed out that Dutch merchants had changed their religion to gain a foothold in Japan; thus, might they not become papists in England if it was to their material advantage?[21] Further, William's cardinal victory over James II at the Battle of the Boyne was simply a Protestant victory. Indeed, it caused the Spanish envoys to send the good news on to the Pope (who, with the Spanish, was fearful of the Sun King's ambition).²² In pointing to William's past behavior in the Dutch Republic, the pamphleteers noted that he threatened certain provincial rights.

More importantly, a torrent of tracts in the late 1690s claimed that maintaining a standing army in peacetime posed a very real threat to English liberties. Just as the satirists' job was to link sodomy to the monasteries, and these in turn to *quo warranto* proceedings, so, too, they attempted to reaffirm the link to Continental absolutism by showing William's court as sodomitical, viz.: "Why were your arms not turned towards Italy?/ . . . There had each sodomite his brother's best" and found it little change to have "old popery/turn'd out and replaced by almighty sodomy."²³ Various events, including almost simultaneous attacks on the molly houses and those connected with the court, were used to reinforce this connection.

The seeming aim was to appeal to the sentiments of the gentry and aristocracy, who had made the vicarage and marriage the centerpiece of society to keep their Sceptered Isle free not only of sodomy—thought so common in papist and barbarous nations—but also to keep from losing their lands. With proper timing, court opponents might be made to propagate connections between *quo warranto* proceedings, the re-establishment of the monasteries, their alleged endemic sodomy, and the growing sodomitical subculture of the molly houses in the contiguous environs of the allegedly sodomitical palace government.²⁴

The Treaty of Ryswick (1697), moreover, left much to be desired from an English perspective, and was concluded in secret. William wisely opposed the creation of triumphal Roman columns, arches, and obelisks at the time of signing, which would have made the city resemble what the satirists had been trying to create in the mind of the political nation: associations with second-century Rome and certain emperors. Nevertheless, prints of William were circulated in which he appeared in Roman armor wearing a full-bottomed wig.²⁵ His young favorite, Van Keppel, made matters a bit more public, wearing both perfume and a grand wig on his travels, which made him appear to take on some sartorial aspects of the effeminate patrons of molly houses.²⁶

The Standing Army Issue, Captain Rigby's Sodomy Case, and Further Anti-Sodomitical Attacks Upon Court and Subculture

Even during wartime, Parliament attempted to reduce the size of the army. The navy received larger appropriations, being less of a threat to English liberties (although it was morally suspect).²⁷ The only truly revered military institutions were the county militias led by squires, who were above suspicion of Catholic absolutist tendencies and the squires who ideally took their turn in sitting in the commons for their counties (which they often called their countries) as knights of the shire. These provincial potentates were obstensibly the leaders of the country party who could, if they decided to, overwhelm any faction allied with the court.

With the coming of peace in 1697, the standing army became the most important issue of the opposition's agenda and remained a bone of contention until the resumption of a war footing in 1701. William was reluctant to disband the army and rely upon a militia. Further, he attempted to maintain some forty thousand troops composed completely of mistrusted foreigners, disbanding only the English forces. Pamphleteers of the old country-whig school (not at all associated with Jacobitism), such as Sir John Trenchard, attacked the standing army with a rare ferocity during the 1698 session. A year later, the king found himself with but seven thousand troops, all of whom were English. For William, the 1698 session was an ugly one followed by a yet uglier one. At the same time, sodomy and the military was becoming a public issue.

At first, it might seem inconsistent to worry about sodomy (now associated with effeminacy) sapping the vitality of the military when the chief concern was the overwhelming strength of a standing army. But the political nation always wanted a strong militia composed of hardy yeomen and tenant farmers defending their own land or that of their "betters." A standing army, particularly one composed of foreigners, was something leading to absolutism, and a decadent force. Sodomy in such an institution would point to a growing need for a strong militia. In 1698, Captain Rigby, a military officer accused of attempted sodomy, was to be put in the public pillory. It would have been even worse for the court, of course, if he had been a Dutch army officer rather than an English naval officer. The event did not occur aboard ship, however, but on land in central London. There were associations to be made if the king wished, or even if he did not. During William's military campaigns in Flanders, for example, satirists made overt and covert references to William's satisfaction in being in the all-male company of the military.[28]

After a court-martial, Rigby was acquitted, which was probably where the king wanted the matter to end. The issue had come up in the midst of the disbandment crisis, and further attention would play into the opposition's hands. Oblivious to such considerations, or in league with the opposition (the event was noted in the correspondence of the leader of the country party),[29] the Society for the Reformation of Manners had moved ahead on its own.[30] Bray acted in concert with one of his parishioners, the master of a servant approached by Rigby some months after his acquittal on the first offense, and concerted plans with a sympathetic justice. They worked out a plan with the constabulary that all but entrapped Rigby in the act. When ensnared, Rigby blasphemed at the arresting officers, leading to a second charge when his case came up at the Old Bailey.[31]

Nor did the case fail to receive a strong reaction from the London government; shortly afterwards, the Lord Mayor, addressing his aldermen, spoke against the moral depravity being seen in the city. Moreover, the speech was circulated in a tract, providing added grist for the Societies' mills.[32] Convicted, Rigby was sentenced by Justice Colt to three sessions in the pillory, a year in jail, and a one-thousand-pound fine. In addition, he was forced to pay sureties to insure good behavior for seven years, a severe sentence made despite the gentility of Rigby's showy appearance in the pillory. Defoe, no true friend of the Societies (and who was to run afoul of them early in Anne's reign) mentions that Rigby even had a defense tract circulated, which A. G. Craig has conjectured may have aided Rigby in avoiding the worst effects of the pillory.[33] Rigby's trial also led to a poem being published that had a motif similar to other poems to be discussed, namely the complaint of a woman as an aggrieved sex object forsaken owing to the sodomitical interests of the time. The ladies demand that Rigby recant and that the soldiers henceforth do "their duty,"[34] both as soldiers and as creators of future soldiers (or more properly, militiamen-to-be) through the impregnation of females.

The theme of sodomites being women haters and a corrupting force upon the military was taken up anew after raids upon the molly houses in 1699 and 1707; both raids occurred under distinctly similar circumstances.[35] As promised, the Societies for the Reformation of Manners entrapped individuals such as Rigby and hired informants to infiltrate the highly porous borders of the subculture and to note the times and places of meeting, thus facilitating raids by the constabulary.[36] Reaction to both raids was similar. The Societies sought to capitalize on the Rigby case by publishing "The Sodomites Shame and Doom . . . ," a tract telling the sinners to reform by "avoiding plays, bad books and frivolous company." More importantly, the tract stated that it knew who many of the sodomites were and would publish their "places of abode" if they did not reform. Further, the Societies stated that they knew the location of the "scandalous haunts," which would be visited, they hoped, by the forces of justice, who would punish them for their crimes.[37]

Following the 1707 raid, a political tract appeared entitled "The Women Hater's Lamentation or a New Copy of Versus on the Fatal End of Mr. Grant, Woolen Draper and Two Others that Cut Their Throats or Hanged Themselves in the Counter [a prison] with the discovery of near hundred more that are accused for unnatural despising the faire sex and intriguing with one another to the tune of Ye Pretty Sailors All."[38] The tract is quoted in Appendix 1.

Whether women really wanted the attention of men was beside the point in the Augustan age. Women wanted sex because men controlled society and said that women wanted it. To say that sodomites were women haters was, again, another instance of patriarchal assumptions distorting the facts. True, many did not desire women as sex objects, but then it was a question of whether a woman — or any person — really enjoys reification. From a sexist perspective, the real charge may have been that sodomites were unwilling to aid the forces of sexism through marriage and the impregnation of females.

The Societies aided patriarchy through their antisodomitical raids and entrapments, which came to have a life of their own, as did the antisodomitical judiciary which they encouraged. In 1702, for example, Lord Chief Justice Colt, Rigby's old nemesis, ordered the execution of four sodomites at Maidstone, Kent assizes.[39] Some of these measures were supported by the country party and landed interests to counter the seemingly sordid developments of a commercial and urban society with which the Williamite court was closely associated. The molly houses provided large numbers of reliable scapegoats; high personages on even greater challenge. Indeed, the antisodomitical sentiments may even have had an effect in driving away the principal secretary of state, and aided in an attempt upon the heads of the king's "second self," the earl of Portland, and that of his closest English minister (and lifelong bachelor), Lord Chancellor Somers.

CHATEAU DE DERRIERE?

The Politics

Liselotte, wife of Louis' brother, was asked if the English court had not become a "chateau de derriere."[40] After Mary's death in 1694, William's court even came to look embarrassingly monastic, being almost totally devoid of females. In addition, while monks and priests were pledged to at least *de jure* celibacy, William's favorites were not, and their offspring could inherit. The fact that much of the land was in Ireland and that no Englishman lost the lands he currently held was a redeeming feature. But even such court supporters as Bishop Burnet found that William's grants could not withstand scrutiny. After the Peace of Ryswick, there was an attempt to resume the Welsh and Irish grants. When the honors of Denbigh, Bromfield, and Yale were resumed, the king stated that he would show his favor in some other way, which he was to do with the Irish grants, totaling as they did over two-hundred forty thousand acres.[41] The success of the Commons in resuming the Welsh grants was highlighted when one outspoken member stated bluntly that the grants were suited only for a "Prince of Wales"; Parliament's stand again resuming the Irish grants, clearly drained the king's energies.[42]

The attack upon the court gained momentum when it included one of the innermost English members, Charles Talbot, earl and (in 1694) duke of Shrewsbury, one of the "immortal seven" who had signed the invitation for William to invade. Shrewsbury never married (d.s.p., 1718). He is painted by Dorthy Somerville as the ultimate in eligible bachelors.[43] In "The Reflection" (1689), satirists portray him first as having an adulterous relationship with the queen (neglected by her sodomitical husband): "Whilst William van Nassau, with Benting Berdasha,/Are at the old game of Gomorrah,/Wise Tulla his wife, more pious of life [i.e., a supporter of procreative sex],/With Shrewsbury drives away sorrow."[44] But by the end of the year, he is depicted in "A Litany for the Reducing of Ireland" in a more ambiguous role: "In a Court full of vice may Shrewsbury lay molly on/Whilst Nanny enjoys her Episcopal stallion/and Billy Benting does play the Italian. . . ."[45] The alleged unification of the court behavior with that of the city's surrounding sodomitical subculture is particularly worthy of note. In "Jenny Cromwell's Complaint Against Sodomy" (1692), Shrewsbury appears even more clearly as a sodomite.[46]

While compiling and editing hundreds of letters in Shrewsbury's political papers, I found no overt reference to anything discrediting Shrewsbury's heterosexuality. But then, there was little affirming it, either. The principal correspondent, James Vernon, his undersecretary and then replacement, provides some clues as to why Shrewsbury was to resign the seals. While besmirched in the Commons with allegations of treasonable correspondence with the exiled court, Shrewsbury may have found too much to bear in several letters discussing Rigby's case; although the letters simply reported the events, Shrewsbury resigned the seals in the very midst of the case.[47] One cannot but suspect that the sodomy question was a factor that played a role in Shrewsbury's decision to distance himself further from the antisodomitical winds prevailing against William's allegedly sodomitical palace and the contiguous subculture of London's mollies.

Rigby's session in the pillory and Shrewsbury's resignation, followed by one successful and one thwarted attempt upon Portland's and Keppel's landholdings, were succeeded by an attempt on the lives of Portland and Somers. Against the wishes of the rival minis-

terial factions, and to placate the country party, Portland's name
was included, albeit temporarily, in the list of ministers to be impeached in 1700. As Portland was the king's "second self," this all
but amounted to a direct attack upon the king. The proceedings had
echoes of Wentworth's attainder in the 1640s. As Charles had followed Wentworth, would William follow Portland? Seemingly to
aid in this development, pamphleteers provided an echo of the trial
and execution of the earl of Castlehaven for sodomy in 1637.[48]

   Although Portland's proposed impeachment had more to do with
Wentworth's trial than Castlehaven's, there were enough connections for a special edition of "The Tryal and Condemnation of . . .
Castlehaven." The tract had a warning in the preface stating that
the sins "which rage amongst our English debauchees" would
bring England to be consumed like the "cities of the plains" unless
there was complete reformation of manners. The Sodom and Gomorrah warning included a discussion of Rigby's sodomy case, and
it was republished in 1699.[49]

   While in the end Portland was able to extricate himself, it was a
close call, close enough for the king to think of giving up the English throne and returning to the Netherlands.[50] In the end he stayed,
but this was largely owing to the return of a war footing, with
Louis' recognition of the Pretender and the need for William's military skills.

   Although William remained as king, Lord Somers was not recalled to office. If purely political factors played a critical role, the
gentle bachelor statesman may have been confronting problems associated with the new emphasis upon maintaining the appearances
of an uncompromising heterosexual lifestyle. His renowned interests in literature and the arts were out of keeping with the less refined tastes of the other ministers — much less the rustic country
gentry. Exceptionally soft mannerisms had played no small role in
his success as the only English minister to become truly close to the
king.[51] He was suited for much the same reason to take on the role
of administrator/consensus-taker for the egocentric, rapacious junto
statesmen. His close association with Shrewsbury may likewise
have had a varied effect.[52] He probably was removed from office
and included in the impeachment proceedings primarily as a junto
leader, as well as due to his ungentlemanly emphasis upon the law

and legalisms.[53] As interest in war waxed, however, and fortune returned to the junto interests, questions of his unmanly lifestyle and interests may have been reinforced by the effect of the antisodomitical attitudes affecting the city and palace. For many of the same reasons Somers had gained the royal favor, he may have been unable to return to office.

The Evidence

The question raised for Liselotte is not easy to resolve because firm evidence is difficult to find. For example, in their Williamite biographies (1968), Steven Baxter and Nesca Robb deny all but the most undeniable. Kenyon (*The Stuarts*, 1957) has less trouble in accepting that William had a David and Jonathan relationship with Van Keppel. Henri and Barbara van der Zee (*William and Mary*, 1973), while their work was termed "journalism" by Baxter,[54] concur with Kenyon, noting that their view was more in keeping with the outlook of William's contemporaries in the 1690s than with that of his 1960s biographers (Baxter and Robb). To take just two of Baxter's examples which seem overly defensive, he sees no problem in first Portland, and then Keppel, employing specially designed adjoining bedrooms, alleging that this arrangement simply facilitated late-night conferences and had no secret sexual purpose such as facilitating unnoticed trysts. Similarly, the fact that Lord Villiers tried to arrange a marriage between Rochester's daughter and Albemarle is given as further evidence. Baxter alleges that Villiers would never have aided in such a match if he had believed the accusations. For tens of thousands of acres, however, one might overlook a good deal of bad reputation (which was certainly the case in the sodomitical French subcourt of Le Monsieur and Le Chevalier). In one satiric poem, moreover, Villiers is said with others to be "mimicks to the crown,/They to each other put their breeches down" hoping to have their "bums" blessed by a more powerful sodomitical courtier.[55]

The rivalry between Portland and Keppel once heated up to the point where swords were said to have been drawn and the king was obliged to separate them. But William is absolved by Baxter owing to the fact that he drew in the Vaudemonts to reconcile the differences. Baxter finds this to be "the strongest single argument for his innocence."[56] In part, Baxter rests his case on William's fear of exposure if the charges were true, but the moral rectitude of the mediators is seen as a critical factor; the Vaudemonts would not have allowed themselves to be drawn into the disputes if they did not believe William was innocent. Mediators are usually drawn into messy situations, however, and what would constitute the truth in a sodomy charge in one case might not in another.[57] Indeed, if it had not been for political considerations, the best person to have handled such a squabble would have been Louis XIV, the Sun King himself, whose brother (a family man) was alleged to be the best-placed sodomite on the Continent. Louis was frequently involved in settlements involving his brother's male favorites, most notably the Vaudemont's relative, Phillipe, who was also a Prince of Lorraine.[58]

It may have been Phillipe's relationship that provided William with an idea of just how far one could go in having publicly recognized male favorites in the first place. Of course, there were also differences, some of which William might not have recognized; for instance, William was a king, Phillipe but a prince. Obviously, too, elements within the Third Estate which did take notice could not take political advantage of the situation owing to the discontinuance of the Estates General since 1614 (a parallel situation being provided in the instance of Buckingham, James I, and the prolonged prorogations of Parliament). But the aforementioned geographic factor brought the behavior of the English court to the attention of the puritanical bourgeoisie, for better and, in 1699 (and under somewhat similar circumstances under Anne in 1707), clearly for worse, both for court and subculture.

William's unwillingness to let Englishmen into his confidence raised suspicion, which may have grown after Keppel was reported to have told an English courtier that the king spoke more freely at night in the company of his bottle and his Dutch friends.[59] His Dutch courtiers were not of the Amsterdam burgher class, but of aristocratic Brabant families of old Burgundian lineage, and were accustomed to the privilege and prerogatives of the court. If we accept the premise that William's loosened tongue might have given away too much about his own sexuality — in addition to state secrets, then conversing intimately only with those whom, owing to their nationality, were utterly dependent upon him, makes even more sense in a reign when rival ministerial factions tried to proscribe, and occasionally execute, each other. English politicians such as Mathew Prior might have been fine drinking companions, yet utterly deadly when they became court opponents, as Prior was to become in 1700.

Chroniclers present problems, too. In 1683 Sir Constantyn Huygen's chroniclers reported a suspicious relationship between William and a young Dutch army officer, Captain Dorp. (Huygens was told that nothing was going on, but that he should not mention it to anybody.)[60] Bishop Burnet, an ardent court supporter, wrote that William "had no vice, but of one sort, in which he was very cautious and secret."[61] Jonathan Swift, commenting on Burnet's remark, noted acidly that "the vices were of two sorts—male and female—in the former he was neither cautious nor secret."[62] In discussing the matter some years ago with the noted ecclesiastical historian, G. V. Bennett, Dr. Bennett argued that the vice to which Burnet referred was alcohol. It could be put forward, however, that alcohol was simply a third vice that jeopardized the secrecy of the other two. Certainly, if we can trust Liselotte's observation that William kissed Keppel's hand before all the court, then Swift would be even closer to the mark than Burnet. Even if there had been greater discretion, rumors would probably have circulated, though in not so virulent a manner. George I, for example, was rumored at the time of his accession not simply to have "given the queen the pox" but to keep "two Turks for abominable uses."[63]

Baxter is elliptical, and Robb seems unimpressed over William's virtual admission of Kenyon's analysis noted earlier that he and Keppel had a David and Jonathan relationship. William dealt with the question with characteristic regal candor: "It seems to me a most extraordinary thing that one may not feel regard and affection for a young man without it being criminal."[64]

Mary had felt equally strong passions for a woman, Frances Apsley. Seven years older than Mary, Frances was also worshipped for a time by Mary's sister, Anne. However, Mary's relationship was more lengthy and was marked by correspondence containing such phrases as "Your loving obediant wife" and "loved blest husband.''[65] Allusions to lesbian interests among some of Mary's maidens in early poems of the reign also lend support to a belief in Mary's female interests.[66] Mary seemingly became more discreet, and the theme of these poems was discontinued. The harsh judgment of Anne's companion, Sarah Churchill, over Mary's character, namely that she "lacked bowels," might have become more injurious had Mary maintained her open enthusiasm for her own sex (as will be seen with Sarah's expressed views toward Anne's behavior with Abigail Masham in 1707). One wonders, then, if the confidential papers which Mary kept tied to her person and periodically burned, might not have included lesbian material.[67]

Perhaps hesitant at first over the physical aspects of her marriage to William, Mary *may* have sensed his alleged sexual orientation on their wedding night,[68] and by and large welcomed it. A lack of compulsory heterosexual relations (except for anticipated role fulfillment) and attempts at procreation that Mary might initiate[69] may well have suited her needs. Moreover, Mary also found William's scant interest in women helpful for her sense of self-esteem. William's selection of his one unofficial "mistress," Elizabeth Villiers,[70] may have reflected interests less physical than psychological and political. Further, rumors of relations with a token mistress may have dampened more serious sodomitical allegations.

Same-sex social worlds, however, clearly encompassed most of Mary's and Anne's time. The two clearly enjoyed the female world of love and ritual of a court that in many ways paralleled the sexually segregated society of nineteenth-century America discussed by Carroll Smith-Rosenberg.[71]

Further Satirical Insights

The satirical poems provide insights less into what was truly occurring, than what the satirists thought would seem credible and influence the political nation. In some respects, for example, William's masculinity was impugned because of his marriage to Mary. In marrying above his station, he was thought to owe much of his strength to a woman, and Mary was highly demanding emotionally. Their relationship may have seemed too close (mother/son?) to contemporaries. Too close a proximity to women, it was thought, could debilitate a man and cause effeminacy. Because it was ostensibly a joint monarchy, the temptation to poke jibes at the gender identity of the monarchs was irresistible.

"A Description of Hampton Court Life" (1689) depicts the monarchy as heresy to the sexual dimorphism of the age: "Man and Wife are all one/In flesh and in bone, . . . /The Queen drinks chocolate to make the king fat/the king hunts to make the Queen lean." The deprecatory inference that William was but Mary in drag and vice versa was supplemented by the usher of the Black rod (the official who led the king into Parliament) now leading William into his "box" (closet?). There he is "uplocked" until supper by "Benting," presumably to cross-dress. The use of the term "Benting" is seemingly a *double entendre* on Bentinck and may be an early use of the English term "bent" as an indicator of unnatural sexual proclivities; that is, not straight or heterosexual. The author may be implying, then, that Bentinck was "bending" the king into an unnatural, transvestite role (as some thought the Chevalier was forcing Phillipe into effeminacy).

The term "bent" was not, however, clearly associated with effeminacy, as were the terms "molly" and "queen." If this interpretation of "bent" is correct, then McIntosh's assessment of "bent" being similar to "molly" and "queen," indicating an effeminate twentieth-century male, may need revision.[72] On the one hand, in "Jenny Cromwell's Complaint" (discussion follows), "bent" is used almost interchangeably with "bardash" (an English variant of several terms coming from the Arabic and then subsequently applied to the transvestite Indians in the American colonies). On the other hand, while the berdache Indians were effeminate, Bentinck clearly was not. Baxter's and Robb's biographies use the term to indicate that suggestions of Bentinck being an effeminate (?) homosexual were utterly ludicrous. While the *Oxford English Dictionary* dates the entrance of the term "berdache" into the English language as 1726 (the year of the largest of the early raids on the molly houses), it is clearly evident in the lampoons of thirty to forty years earlier and may be added to Wayne Dynes's and Warren Johansson's findings on the subject.[73]

William's masculinity was also impugned in a variant of another poem entitled "The Night Bellman off Picadilly." Some copies of satires have versions with slightly different wordings, which give a poem a totally different, and in this case burlesque, meaning. One version of the poem is a eulogy to the tories' favorites, Anne and Prince George, while a slight modification allows it to become a satiric, antisodomitical attack through the deft transition of the gender of the principle: "Welcome Great Prince [not Princess as in *POES*] to this lonely place? Where injured loyalty must hide its face/. . . God Bless your Queen! And I may moreover,/ Own you our Queen in Berkeley Street and Dover./ May your Great Prince, and you, live numerous years!/ This is the subject of all our loyal prayers."[74] Whether William had nocturnal wanderings that, like the Caesars, brought him to the periphery of the sodomitical subculture is problematic.[75]

Even if William had been completely heterosexual in orientation, he may have suffered the satirists' barbs, albeit less painful ones. The charge of satyriasis was, as J. H. O'Neill points out, employed against Charles II as a sign of overwhelming ambition; that is, his ambitious politics, like his penis, were overwhelming all other considerations as he sought more and more power.[76] But then again, the politics of nostalgia may have allowed a Restoration vice to become an anti-Williamite virtue and perhaps aided in making heterosexual promiscuity quasi-acceptable in the Augustan era.

Similarly, "The Anniversary, or Pious Memory" effected an anti-Williamite attack, with prostitutes undertaking a retreat to the tomb of Charles II. Their clients having abandoned them owing to the court-inspired support for sodomitical practices, they evoke "burning dildoes" hoping for a return to Restoration sexuality.[77] The theme of women considering themselves aggrieved as foresaken sex objects is also taken up in "Jenny Cromwell's Complaint Against Sodomy." If Burnet was cautious in his remarks regarding William's sexuality, overstatement was the hallmark in this parody of Dryden's "Absalom and Achitopel." Although available in several repositories, the editor of *POES* found it complex and included it in the list of poems not published.[78] Seven folio pages in length, it deteriorates rapidly after the first folio page, becoming insipid as it moves from satiric sexual attacks to those more political in nature. It is a blast at many who might be included in the 1692 honors list. Nevertheless, there is good material, and the whole poem is useful for synopsis. Appendix 2 deals largely with William and Portland, and makes a cryptic reference to Sarah [Churchill?] and the way in which the court is said to intermesh with the popular sodomitical subculture. The remainder of the poem analyzes the subculture by summarily listing six discernible types of discredited elite circles. Several of the categories were echoed in other poems of the period, highlighting the emphasis satirists placed upon sexual deviance, decadence, and the impending decline of England unless it rejected the mores of second-century Rome.

The listing in "Jenny Cromwell's Complaint" provides a data base of thirty-five leaders and supporters of the court that can be divided into six elite circles, as follows:

Elite Circle A (N = 11): Sodomites, pretenders to sodomy, condoners of sodomy and possible lesbians.
Bardash [Bentinck]
The King
Brithwaite (?): namely, Blathwayte, an aggressive sodomite
Shrewsbury (see earlier discussion)
Wentworth: Raised from being a page and now haughty, possibly an aggressive sodomite
Scarsdale: Charged with impotency and sodomy through default owing to impotency; said to be afraid of being cuckolded owing to lack of virility, and found "to skulk about the alleys/ And is content with Betty's, Nan's and Molly's
Rosse [Ross], Roberts, Villiers, and Cornwallis: Said to be pretenders to sodomy to fit into the elite circles of the king of Wentworth; namely, "Thinking they must be mimicks to the crown,/ They to each other put their breeches down/ If Wentworth one of these with bum will bless,/ He's not a little proud of his success"
Sarah [Churchill?]: Condoner of sodomy, and by association seeming to support sodomites in that she collaborates with the others in rejecting Jenny's complaint

Elite Circle B (N = 6) Only marginally heterosexual; stated or inferred impotency and not fulfilling the masculine role; effete or a fop.
Feilding ("Debigh's brother"): Insipid and therefore possibly

stupid enough to be caught by a sodomite (?) such as Braith-
waite [Blathwayte]
Devonshire: Of him it is said that even if "the Nymph be so fair
or willing/ His limber weapon is too weak for killing"
Heningham: Said to be "not fit for fucking"
Berkeley (see also under cupping)
Denbigh: Effete
Bellen: Fop

Elite Circle C (N = 8): Cowardice and being reduced to having sex
only with professionals, only bragging about heterosexual con-
quests, being involved in a heterosexual scandal (indicating inca-
pacity of clearly besting male rivals in the sexual subjugation of
females), spurious birth.

Manchester and Kingston: Cowardice and whoremongering; both
said to find "fighting for a mistress out of fashion" so they
meet at Pyes "and trust their fate to her arbitration"
Reresby: Heterosexual whoremongering and being undone by
same
Clent and Savil [Savile]: Being involved in a heterosexual scandal
Ployden [probably Francis Plowden]: Pretender to masculinity
and promiscuity
Richmond: Liar, braggart, and heterosexual only owing to having a girl (see below, under Marsh)
Marsh [March]: A bastard; "Tis well you've [the Earl of Rich-
mond] got a girl, for it'd be harsh/ If Shrewsbury had got an
Earle of Marshe"

The link between groups A, B, and C indicates primarily a lack
of aggressiveness with females at best, and sodomy at worst, with
the active sodomite being held in much less contempt than his passive partner or prey. The separation between these elite groups and
elite groups D, E, and F (discussed below) is important in showing
that various forms of sexual aberration were thought more important than serious forms of nonsexual deviance; namely possible
treason, bribery, plagiarism, or remarkable stupidity.

Elite Circle D (N = 8 [10]): Indicating flawed character which
might also lead to sexual impropriety.

Warwick: Cowardice
Guy: Bribery
Kildare: A villainous leech
Culpepper, Essex, Sandwich, Yelverton (?): Witless, stupid, or
   "fit only to hold a chamberpot"
Berkeley: Counted in elite group B, cupping (probably drinking
   excessive amounts of liquor or aiding in the surgical proce-
   dure); also said to be "not fit for fucking" (see above)
Leveson: So worthless as to gain a peerage by being a cattle thief;
   also a traitor
Bellen (counted as a fop in elite group B) and Mulgrave: Snobs

Elite Circle E (N = 2 [4]): Defective in literary aspects; also in being
supporters of some or all of the elite circles.
   Scarsdale: Authors of stolen or poor wit, some of whom are also
      scandal-mongers
   Berkeley (counted in elite group B)
   Ployden (counted in elite group C)
   Unnamed others: "and the rest" including Robin, poetic aide to
      scandal-mongers

Elite Group F (N = ?): Unnamed others are referred to as "game-
sters, sharpers, bullys." Owing to its undetermined size, this last
group has not been included in the data base. Further, there are
others who evidently are not thought worthy of mention, seemingly
because they are such a common species of politician. Whether this
could include Carmarthen, the coalition leader of the time, is problematic.

   Impotency was, as discussed, a rather grievous charge. One
notes that one member is said to have a penis too "weak for killing." This failing brings to mind the still common military practice
of teaching male soldiers the difference between rifle and gun by
having them stand on the parade ground holding rifle in one hand
and penis in the other, chanting: "This is my rifle, this is my gun:
this is for killing, this is for fun." (One might also consider a
French phrase for sex, "la petite muerte.") The charge of being
unwilling to fight for women is also seen in a negative light, seemingly because those who do not fight for their property in flesh

might be unwilling to fight for their country — a serious sin as England was embarking upon a war footing.

The reference to the days of Master Horner in the earlier stanzas of the poem is clearly an appeal to the rakish hero of Wycherley's "The Country Wife." The use of the allusion might indicate that the development of the Societies for the Reformation of Manners did not find their labors countered by pronounced court interest in heterosexual involvement. Rather, it was that alleged homosexual interests were seldom portrayed except in defiance of the court during either William's reign or, to a lesser degree, during Anne's reign after 1708, when lesbianism came to the attention of the political nation (see below).[79] Sir John Vanburg's play, "The Relapse or Virtue in Danger" (1696), was thought irreverent owing to the homosexual allusions reflecting upon the Williamite court.

ANNE'S COURT AND THE ATTACK
UPON THE SUBCULTURE IN 1707,
WITH COMMENTS ON THE CLOSE
OF THE AUGUSTAN ERA

Heterosexuality was compulsory for women in the Augustan age, even more so than in our own time. Anne was obliged not only to marry, but to bear seemingly innumerable children, none of whom reached maturity. Some historians infer that Anne was the only lesbian monarch who spent virtually her entire childbearing years in an almost perpetual state of pregnancy.[80] If she had been an Augustan Joan of Arc and granted lavish grants to foreign favorites, there might have been a refrain from the antisodomitical years of William's reign. She ably fulfilled, however, a role that society had prescribed for women, the role of brood mare.

While providing an heir, preferably a male heir, to strengthen her position was Anne's paramount motivation, it may have been reinforced by other considerations. Despite their obvious discomforts, near-constant pregnancies would have provided those disinclined to heterosexual intercourse the advantage of prolonged respites from conjugal duties. Both during the later period of pregnancy and the lengthy lactation period which follows, sexual relations become difficult. In the later case, unless the mother wore a nursing halter, many a male partner still considers physical intimacy a rather messy and unpleasant experience. Having a large number of children, particularly when they continually fail to reach maturity, could indicate a desire to *avoid* recreational or romantic heterosexual intercourse. Simultaneously, Anne may have enjoyed the social and personal benefits of being a mother—one with virtually unlimited household help available to care for and rear them.

As Anne's reign progressed, her companion of long-standing, Sarah Churchill, now duchess of Marlborough, became increasingly overbearing. Anne turned to her excellent hairdresser and nurse, Abigail Masham, for emotional and physical support. (Sarah had made the mistake of introducing Abigail to the court some years earlier.) A conflict ensued as Sarah noted Anne's developing closeness with Abigail's politically artful second cousin, Robert Harley. Harley, the noted opposition leader in William's reign, developed new alliances under "the squire queen,"[81] becoming the court manager of the Commons. Some conjectures have been made about Harley's sodomitical tendencies, and while there is no mention of such an aberration in Angus McInnes's biography (which portrays him as the ultimate puritan),[82] there is the question of how Harley, an opposition leader, had been able to have conferences, occasionally at night, with William on an almost annual basis if they did not have special mutual interests.[83] While I have not found anything clearly sodomitical when reading over virtually all of Harley's correspondence in William's reign, what does catch my attention is his cold calculation over his heterosexual relations and his seeming lack of romantic interest in the opposite sex. I also note the very feminine art of making deft alliances, including one as important as that which he had with his second cousin, Abigail, whom he noted could "break" any politician.[84]

Perhaps it was the possible homosexual bond between Anne and Abigail that Sarah found so threatening and that most historians glossed over. In any case the Masham/Harley alliance was a valuable one for Harley, who in 1711 was to become earl of Oxford and Mortimer and Lord Treasurer.[85] Sarah certainly realized the threat and tried to remove Abigail from the queen's affections with much the same fervor as Bentinck had tried to remove Keppel from William's affection a decade earlier, though with the belief that the pen

was mightier than the sword. Satirical poems were written as the
two sides battled vindictively in 1707. When the final break occurred a year later, there was hardly any question regarding lesbianism as far as Sarah and her circle were concerned. In one poem,
attributed to Sarah's propagandist, Arthur Maynwaring, little is left
unsaid. Designed to provide alternate lyrics to a popular ballad of
the time, the ending has a provocative stanza: "Her secretary she
was not/ Because she could not write/ But had the Conduct and
Care/ Of some dark deeds at Night."[86] Not only did Sarah show
such lampoons to the queen, but she also followed them up with a
long letter that left little unsaid: ". . . nor can I think the having noe
inclination for any but one's own sex is enough to maintain such a
character as I wish may still be yours."[87] Unlike Portland, who
phrased his letters—if not his behavior—more tactfully, Sarah
acted belligerently toward Anne, which eventually caused a permanent break between the two. The matter came to the attention of the
political nation, the tracts finding their way into the coffee houses.

In 1707, there were three other matters which might also have
had antisodomitical moral ramifications. While 1706 was a year of
military victories, 1707 was a year of reversals, and the commercially oriented junto whigs took advantage of the situation to force
themselves back into office. Specifically the commercial interests
were challenging the more purely landed interests, such not having
occurred since 1694-97.[88] In addition, 1707 was the year of the
Union with Scotland, and London was the center of the festivities
that culminated in the early autumn. It may have been a good time,
in short, to make certain that the capital was "cleaned up." One
suspects, then, that the stress of the military reversals, the pressure
from ministers of the purely landed interests in defending their positions, and the need to make the capital of Great Britain look as
though it was truly blessed by Providence may have created a climate of antisodomitical moral fervor, and the Societies for the Reformation of Manners did what they could to help, producing the
second major raid on the molly houses with the estimated "near a
hundred men being found" and the publication of the previously
discussed "Women Hater's Lamentation."

Anne reigned, and took quite an active role in the day-to-day
proceedings of government, but William was probably the last En-

glish monarch truly to rule. William was victimized by the very changes the new commercially oriented society was creating, one change in making it obligatory to ostensibly avoid bisexuality as a lifestyle. William's survival as king had depended, to no small degree, on his abilities as a general; Baxter considers him one of the best of the age (although this judgment has been considered over-enthusiastic by some). By winning his battles, William defied the new stereotype of the effeminate sodomite. Later, as power shifted in the Augustan period to the ministries, only the focus changed. The alliance between Walpole and Lord Hervey was attacked owing to Hervey's overt effeminacy.[89] The English losses at Preston Pans in 1745 were thought to be due to Cope's indecisiveness, which Smollett argued to be a sign of effeminacy, charging that Cope had gained his position at court owing to his "prolific bum."[90] Similarly, there was a raid on the molly houses in 1776, and then sodomitical questions were raised about Sackville regarding his role in the losses of the American colonies.[91]

Always having to win places one on a precarious perch. Such a must-win mentality must have caused severe anxiety among suspected sodomites, lesbians, and nonvirile males in governmental positions, as well as among scapegoated members of the sodomitical subculture at the same time, and in strikingly similar ways.

NOTES

1. M. McIntosh, "The Homosexual Role," *Social Problems* 16 (1968); also readily available in *The Making of the Modern Homosexual*, Kenneth Plummer, ed. (Totowa, NJ: Barnes and Noble, 1981), 30-49. (See esp. 37, where it is said that there was a move from speculation about individuals to descriptions of homosexual life, in which apparently no distinction was made between homosexuality and transvestism. Citations are to Plummer's edition.) Alan Bray, *Homosexuality in Renaissance England* (London: Gay Men's Press, 1982), esp. Chap. 4. Trumbach, "London's Sodomites: Homosexual Behavior and Western Culture in the Eighteenth Century," *Journal of Social History* 11 (1977): 9-31. (See esp. 11, where Trumbach argues that the transition was not as dramatic as McIntosh asserts; that is, effeminacy was apparent earlier in the century.) Wayne Dynes and Warren Johansson have found a mixed subculture, employing Richard of Davizes' descriptions of Medieval life in the twelfth century: "London's Medieval Sodomites," *The Cabirion and Gay Books Bulletin* 10 (1984), esp. 5-7.

2. The next four largest cities taken together had a population of but one fifth

that of London. In the provincial towns, Trumbach argues that "sodomitical network" is a more applicable term. We look forward to Kent Gerard's findings regarding the provincial metropolises.

3. "Sodomitical Subcultures, Sodomitical Roles and the Gender Revolution of the Eighteenth Century: The Recent Historiography," 18. (This paper, which I had the privilege to read over, incorporates portions of a paper presented at the American Historical Association meeting in 1984.)

4. An examining magistrate found that in his previous residence he "had been notorious for the practices formerly." David Rollison, "Property, Ideology, and Popular Culture in a Gloucestershire Village, 1660-1740," *Past and Present* 93 (1981): 72.

5. Louis's brother Philippe, while twice married and having several children, apparently revelled in the role of resident sodomite and transvestite with his acknowledged male consort, the Chevalier de Lorraine (see following notes).

6. Bray, *Homosexuality in Renaissance England*, 14. This fame in notoriety was limited to only certain parts of London; indeed, London had one of the lowest bastardy rates in the country (although all of London may have been thought to be sexually progressive to those living in the more rustic areas).

7. "Sodomitical Subcultures" esp. 18. Kent Gerard and Stephen Murray, "Renaissance Sodomite Subcultures," in *Among Men, Among Women* (Amsterdam: University of Amsterdam, 1983). Gerard and Murray document the continuity of the European subculture through such hard evidence as court records, and so on. See esp. 183-96.

8. See Susan Staves, "A Few Kind Words for the Fop," *Studies in English Literature* 22 (1982): 413-28.

9. Hilda Smith, "Gynecology and Ideology in Seventeenth Century England," in *Liberating Women's History*, ed. Berenice A. Carroll (Evanston, IL: University of Illinois Press, 1975), 97-115. Ginnie Smith, "Thomas Tryon's Regimen for Women: Sectarian Health in the Seventeenth Century," in the London Feminist History Group's *Sexual Dynamics of History* (London: Pluto Press, 1983), 47-65.

10. "The Female Monster in Augustan Satire," *Signs* 3 (1977): 380-94.

11. True, many Londoners had rural roots, but an increasing number did not.

12. Bray, *Homosexuality in Renaissance England*, 80.

13. See my discussion in *Court and Country*, esp. chap. 7 relating to the size and nature of the grants, as well as the development and debate that occurred over the Irish Forfeitures.

14. The political nation as a concept indicates simply the small proportion of the population which held political power in the Augustan era. Under Charles I and James II it was clearly smaller, while during certain periods of the Civil Wars, especially at the time of the Putney debates, it might have been far larger. H. J. Habbakuk and J. H. Plumb have indicated the reduction of political instability during the Augustan period while David Rollison ("Property, Ideology, and Popular Culture . . .") has indicated the fragility of the stability, particularly beyond

the Home Counties. See too, Rubini, "Party and the Augustan Constitution, 1694-1716: Politics and the Power of the Executive," *Albion* 10 (1979): 194-206.

15. See "Jenny Cromwell's Complaint Against Sodomy," Appendix B.

16. See note below, under "Anne's Court in 1707."

17. It was not until late in the eighteenth century that Locke's concept of natural law gained supremacy, at least among Anglican polemicists. Natural law was used in the Augustan era by dissenting clergymen.

18. G. Straka, "The Final Phase of Divine Right Theory in England, 1688-1702," *English Historical Review* 77 (1962): 638-58. See Thomas Bray, "For God or For Satan; Being a Sermon Preached at St. Mary's Le Bow before the Society for the Reformation of Manners, 27 December 1708" (1709), 30.

19. See the comment about sodomy and monasteries in "Jenny Cromwell's Complaint Against Sodomy," Appendix B.

20. Several studies have indicated that it took a much smaller population in the Mediterranean countries to create a sodomitical subculture than in Northern Europe. See especially Guido Ruggiero, who concerns himself with the timing of the developments of the sodomitical subculture in *The Boundries of Eros* (Oxford: Oxford University Press, 1985). See also, P.H. LaBalme, "Sodomy and Venetian Justice in the Renaissance," *Legal History Review* 52 (1984): 21-54.

21. Note particularly, W. J. Cameron, *Poems on Affairs of State*, vol. 5 (1971), 224.

22. See the letter of the Marquis of Cogolludo to Ronquillo, 2 August 1690, discussed in Macaulay's *History of England*, vol. 4 (1893), 1892.

23. See the discussion of the whole poem below under the "Further Satirical Insights."

24. The poetic connection between mollies and the court is discussed in "Jenny Cromwell's Complaint," Appendix B.

25. *POES*, 6:6. See discussion of the Treaty of Ryswick.

26. C. Huygens, *Journalen van 1688-1690*, vol. 2 (1876-77), 626-27.

27. Arthur Gilbert has published a series of articles in the areas of naval morality, the most important of which is "Buggery and the British Navy, 1700-1861," *Journal of Social History* 10 (1976): 72-98.

28. See, for example, the satiric barbs in B. L. Osborne, Mss. W. 46 ff. 23-7 and 262.

29. See B. L. Portland Loan 29/163 for the "Account of Robert Harley's Conduct with Reference to the Revolution and Succession" (folder 3). While written in a clerk's hand, there are corrections by Harley, and while composed in the third person, there are occasional lapses into the first.

30. See A. G. Craig, "The Movement for the Reformation of Manners, 1688-1715" (PhD diss., Edinburgh University, 1980), 168-70.

31. Ibid., 169-71.

32. Guildhall Broadside, March 1699.

33. Idem, 169-71.

34. "The Women's Complaint to Venus" (1698).

35. See the following discussion of Anne's court in 1707.

36. "Account of the Progress of the Reformation of Manners in England, Scotland, and Ireland" (1703). See esp. 26-28.

37. "The Sodomites Shame and Doom Laid Before with Great Grief and Compassion by a Minister . . ." (n.d.). We might add a fourth purge in the lent judicial term in 1704, although that set of cases occurred in the Maidstone, Kent assizes.

38. Guildhall Broadside collection.

39. "Account of the Progress of the Reformation of Manners in England, Scotland and Ireland" (1703), see esp. 26-28.

40. It was said that while William was thought to have been a member of that brotherhood, he was less interested in it than previously. Duchess D'Orleans, *Letters from Liselotte*, ed. and trans. M. Kroll (1970), 70. If this was true, his interest was soon to revive, particularly as his intimacy with Albemarle became more overt.

41. See "Irish Forfeitures," in Rubini, *Court and Country*, Chap. 7.

42. Ibid.

43. *The King of Hearts* (1962).

44. *POES*, 5:60.

45. Ibid., 70. The other possible interpretation is that Shrewsbury was fornicating with Mary (Molly), but that seems less likely, particularly owing to the subsequent satirical jibes discussed below.

46. See below, "Chateau de Derriere?," subsection "Further Satirical Insights."

47. The case is discussed in letters of 8 and 13 December, leaving Vernon as sole secretary for both departments. See *Letters from James Vernon to the Duke of Shrewsbury, 1696-1708*, ed. Dennis Rubini (1981), 55.

48. Castlehaven's sodomy case had many unique complications, most notably him being a sometime-Catholic, of having his wife raped by a member of the lower orders for voyeuristic purposes, and his wife's possible ambition to get his lands. These have been discussed by Caroline Bingham in "Seventeenth Century Attitudes toward Deviant Sex," *Journal of Interdisciplinary History* 1 (1971): 445-72.

49. "Tryal and Condemnation of Mervin Lord Audley, Earl of Castlehaven . . ." (London, 1699), preface.

50. The country party leadership took note of the earl of Sunderland's remark: "O Silly, Silly, had they left alone Lord Portland and the civil list, they might have hanged the other three in a garret." B. L. Portland loan 29/163.

51. Burnet, iv, 388. *The Freeholder* 39. In the biography by William Sachse, *Lord Somers: A Political Portrait* (Madison, WI: University of Wisconsin Press, 1975), it is noted that Somers was, by legend, raised by a doting aunt rather than his father, who lived in the same village (an arrangement deemed "extraordinary"). He remained reasonably close to his mother until her death in 1710, when he inherited the family estates. Sachse does not speculate as to why he remained a bachelor, but finds it unusual, particularly for his later years. While looking through the Somers papers in Reigate and elsewhere, I found nothing impugning

his heterosexuality—but then nothing affirmed it, either (cf. Somers Papers, Reigate Corporation, Sussex).

52. Sachse, *Lord Somers*, 155.

53. Members learned in the law are still subject to some derision from the gentlemen of the Commons, who occasionally refer sarcastically to barrister MPs as "learned members."

54. In his "Later Stuarts" entry in *Recent Writings on British History*, ed. Richard Schlatter (1984), 165.

55. See "Further Satirical Insights," below.

56. *William III*, 352.

57. Without penetration, the statute (5 Elizabeth c. 6), while not requiring *emissio semenis*, would allow for interfermoral sex, although this provision could be swept away with a deft *ubi lex non distinguit, ibi non distinuendum*, as the earl of Castlehaven and his servant learned, to their demise. The judiciary was not fully independent at this time, as has been pointed out in Rubini, "The Precarious Independence of the Judiciary," *Law Quarterly Review*: 344-45.

58. Their special relationship was publicly acknowledged in such records as the *Dictionnaire de Noblesse. L. De Rouvroy, duc de St. Simon*, vol. 26, ed. A. De Boislisle (1879-1930). Of the many entries dealing with Phillipe, note particularly that of 1695 (vol. 2, 258-59). The chevalier was said to have controlled Phillipe from the public acknowledgment of their relationship until the chevalier's death in 1701.

59. Carte papers, *cit*. Strickland, *Lives of the Queens of England*, vol. 7, 218-20. See discussion in Van der Zee.

60. *Journalen*, vol. 3, 78-81.

61. Burnet, *Own Times* (1838), 429, and *Supplement* (1922), 191.

62. Swift, *Works* (1883), vol. 12, 205-6.

63. From J. Percival to n.n., 26 January 1714/15. B. L. Add. Mss. 47028f. 7v.

64. N. Japikse, *Correspondentie van Willem III en Hans Villem Bentinck (1927-37)* 199-201 (noted in Van der Zee, 419, with a provocative discussion).

65. Robb, *William of Orange*, see esp. 91-93. Cf. also B. Bathurst, *Letters of Two Queens* (1924), 91 and 122.

66. *POES*, 5 (app. of unpublished poems).

67. See Robb, *William of Orange*, App. A (Mary's Papers). Why did she not burn such highly provocative, but purely political manuscripts?

68. That at least is the inference one might draw from the discussion in Robb, *William of Orange*, 99-100 and 125-27, noting Verney's comments on Mary's behavior. Robb's discussion, although quite thorough, reflects a reluctance to deal with continuity of sexual orientation. William's poor health, and the likelihood (until stricken by smallpox) of Mary's own succession, may also have reinforced the need to gain acceptance. The fecundity of her sister Anne was certainly impressive (notwithstanding the brief life spans of the infants).

69. See Robb, *William of Orange*, esp. 133 and 148; and H. M. C. Dartmouth, 39. Mary tended to overeat (see "Further Satiric Insights" below), and overweight may have aided in the credibility of false pregnancies.

70. Elizabeth was brilliant, and an obvious mine of information about the politics of the maidens and the wives of the ministers at court. But with Mary's death, William seemingly felt free to tailor the court to his own tastes. Villier's dismissal may have been as much a reflection of that change as one of respect for his lost companion who had so aided his fortunes.

71. Carroll Smith-Rosenberg, "The Female World of Love and Ritual: Relations between Women in Nineteenth-Century America," *Signs* 1 (1975): 1-29.

72. Japikse, *Correspondentie*, passim.

73. "The Word 'Berdache'," *Gay Books Bulletin* 8 (1982): 18.

74. University of Chicago, Misc. Eng. Manuscripts, "A Collection of All the Secret Poems and Lampoons wrote during the Reigne of the Late King William," f. 57.

75. The *POES* version was clearly the principle version. An accompanying map shows the locale in which Anne and George inhabited (*POES*, 5:333). The two poems may well have been circulated together, making an even greater impact on the reader.

76. *POES,* 5:16-17.

77. *POES,* 5:17. There is also the sexist assumption, to be sure, that women enjoy being penetrated by penises and revel in the roles of sex object and prostitute. In a period when women were prevented from entering the more lucrative crafts and guilds, such assumptions may not have been out of line with reality.

78. A complete manuscript is available in the Portland Collection at Nottingham University Library, and an incomplete version in the University of Chicago Library, Miscellaneous English Manuscripts.

79. See Katherine Kendall, "Queen Anne's Reign: The Golden Age for Women Playwrights" *Theatre Southwest* (October 1985), 5-10. The death of one woman playwright and the cessation of another's writing at about the time of Anne's break with Sarah are also considered important factors.

80. Ibid., and taped discussion with Katherine Kendall on 13 January 1986 over her thesis in progress relating to "An Analysis of the Social Conditions Contributing to the Success of Women Playwrights in Queen Anne's Reign," University of Texas (Austin).

81. See Rubini, "The Squire Queen," in the revision of Churchill's *History of the English Speaking People* (1977).

82. Robert Harley, *Puritan Politician* (1982), passim.

83. "Account of Robert Harley's Conduct," B. L. Portland Loan 29/163, folder 3.

84. McInnes, 237.

85. E. Gregg, *Queen Anne*, 237.

86. Ibid., 275.

87. Ibid., 275-76.

88. It would be hard to underestimate the abilities of the Junto Whigs in forwarding their own monetary enterprises at the expense of country party proposals and the anger these efforts had created in the country opposition. See Rubini, "Politics and the Battle for the Banks," *English History Review* 85: 693-714.

89. Pulteney, writing under a pseudonym, in "A Proper Reply to a Late Scurrilous Libel Entitled Sedition and Defamation Displayed" (1731), 6 and 27-28.

90. "Advice," *The Works of Thomas Smollett*, ed. John Moore (1799), see vol. 1, passim.

91. Humphrey Nettle (pseud.), *William Jackson, Sodom and Onan.*

APPENDIX A

The Women-Hater's Lamentation . . .
(London, 1707)

[To the Tune of, *Ye pretty Sailors all*]

I.   Ye injur'd *Females* see
           Justice without the Laws,
        Seeing the Injury,
           Has thus reveng'd your Cause.

II.   For those that are so blind,
           Your Beauties to despise,
      And slight your Charms, will find
           Such Fate will always rise.

III.   Of all the Crimes that Men
           Through wicked Minds do act,
     There is not one of them
           Equals this Brutal Fact.

IV.   Nature they lay aside,
           To gratifie their Lust;
     Women they hate beside,
           Therefore their Fate was just.

V.   Ye *Women-haters* say,
           What do's your Breasts inspire,
     That in a Brutal way,
           You your own Sex admire?

VI.   *Woman* you disapprove,
           (The chief of Earthly Joys)
    You that are deaf to Love,
           And all the Sex despise.

VII.   But see the fatal end
                 That do's such Crimes pursue,
            Unnat'ral Deaths attend,
                 Unnat'ral Lusts in you.

VIII.   A Crime by Men abhor'd,
                 Nor Heaven can abide
            Of which, when *Sodom* shar'd,
                 She justly was destroy'd.

IX.   But now, the sum to tell,
                 (Tho' they plead Innocence)
            These by their own Hands fell,
                 Accus'd for this Offence.

X.   A Hundred more we hear,
                 Did to this Club belong,
            But now they scatter'd are,
                 For this has broke the Gang.

XI.   Shop-keepers some there were,
                 And Men of good repute,
            Each vow'd a Batchelor,
                 Unnat'ral Lust pursu'd.

XII.   Ye *Women-Haters* then,
                 Take Warning by their Shame.
            Your Brutal Lusts restrain,
                 And own a Nobler Flame.

XIII.   *Woman* the chiefest Bliss
                 That Heaven e'er bestow'd:
            Oh be asham'd of this,
                 You're by base Lust subdu'd.

XIV.   This piece of Justice then
                 Has well reveng'd their Cause,
            And shews unnat'ral Lust
                 Is curss'd without the Laws.

APPENDIX B

Jenny Cromwell's Complaint Against Sodomy

In pious times, e're bug-ry did begin
When women only rul'd at in and in
When Britains did encounter face to face,
And thought a back stroke trecherous and base.
Then Punch reign'd uncontrol'd, but now she plys
In hackney coach at Chaives's and LaFayes
Calls Sarah out, and sends in her petition,
Hoping that someone will pity her condition
Which since she finds rejected, home she goes
Swearing to publish all the truth she knows,
Cries, damms and curses Bardash 'k and all
That ere were instrumental in her fall
And since all lovers have a leave to rail
She thus begins her lamentable tale.
With the respect that's due to Majesty,
Why were your armies not turned towards Italy?
And since your business was a father's *throne*,
Why not your father's Antichrist at *Rome*
There you had your peaceful goverm't,
And placed your throne on downy fundam't,
There had each sodomite his brother Best,
And with lascivious lust his joy exprest
For ere great change to find old Popery
Turn'd out and replaced by Allmighty Sodomy
But here content with our own homely joys,
We had no relish of the fair fac'd Boys.
Till you came in and with your Reformation,
Turn'd all things Arsy Versy in the nation.
And now the greatest grievance I have told,
With underlings I hope I may be bold.

Sodomy and Male Honor:
The Case of Somerset,
1740-1850

Polly Morris, PhD

There is a lengthy literary tradition that takes the relation between male honor and permissible behavior as its subject, but the rich descriptions of this literature are absent from the legal records upon which historians rely. In one regard, however, the literary and legal sources of the eighteenth century are in agreement: an unblemished sexual reputation was not of the same importance to men as it was to women. Smollett's creation, Matthew Bramble, could denounce a man as "a brutal husband, an unnatural parent, a harsh master, an oppressive landlord, a litigious neighbour and a partial magistrate."[1] This catalogue of dishonor, devoid as it was of sexual vice, would not have been out of place in a contemporary libel suit. The lack of concern with illicit heterosexual activities is nearly universal—and encompasses men of all classes—in eighteenth-century novels. Among fictional men, only the uncomfortably religious and the Scottish (when in Scotland) value their sexual propriety.

In practice, this disinterest emerged more slowly, especially outside the upper classes. It is in the second half of the eighteenth century that one can see the boundaries of sexual honor being redrawn in accordance with more polar definitions of masculinity and femininity. While the simple epithet "whore" became sufficient to damage a woman's character, men instead took umbrage at and sought legal redress for a variety of accusations related to their hon-

---

Dr. Polly Morris was awarded her PhD in History at the University of Norwich, England.

383

esty, bravery and ability to govern, rather than to their sexual activities.[2]

Even among the plebeian clientele of the Somerset church courts, the incursion of the double standard is visible. These small tradespeople and artisans were slower than the novelists suggest to abandon a sexual culture in which the same misbehavior could lead to loss of reputation in men and women. Yet between the 1730s and the 1850s, the vast majority of plaintiffs in local defamation suits (which were entirely concerned with sexual insult) were women, and by 1781 men had ceased to use these courts to defend their reputations.[3] By the late eighteenth century, alleged heterosexual transgressions could enhance any man's reputation, and it was only when fornication or adultery were exacerbated by other crimes that they excited notice.

As interest in male heterosexuality waned, two aspects of male sexuality remained important to the definition of male honor: the whore, if she had a counterpart, found him in the cuckold and the sodomite. As the adoption of the double standard released men from the direct defense of their sexual reputations, it simultaneously shifted attention to the reputations of married women and probably increased male sensitivity to the charge of cuckoldry. In Somerset, the proportion of wives among women bringing defamation suits begins to rise unevenly in the 1770s and reaches a peak of 72% in the decade 1840-1849.[4] And if men could ignore the consequences of their heterosexual acts, their participation in unnatural acts continued to lead to dishonor and even death. What remained of the sexual component of male reputation centered on charges of abandoning the male role. Men could do this in two principal ways. The passive cuckold or the effeminate sodomite blurred the increasingly firm line between masculinity and femininity and the buggerer — regardless of the sex or species of his partner — violated the distinction between men and beasts.

In this essay I will use prosecutions for committing unnatural acts — sodomy and bestiality — and for the blackmail of sodomites to explore an important and changing aspect of male honor. The county of Somerset contained a rural hinterland as well as the notorious city of Bath, and the legal records enable us to approach themes related to buggery and male honor from these distinct vantage points. In the pages that follow I will examine alterations in popular attitudes toward and definitions of sodomy and I will discuss the implications that new definitions of gender roles, and consequently of male honor and sexual reputation, had for sodomite activity and the prosecution of sodomites in the years between 1740 and 1850.

I.

Abhorrence for unnatural crimes was widespread enough to seriously endanger the reputations and even the lives of men who were accused of committing sodomy or bestiality. Smollett describes the reaction of a crowd to "a certain effeminate beau" who was taken for a woman when his chair overturned; when the rescuers discovered their mistake, "their compassion was changed into mirth, and they began to pass a great many unsavoury jokes upon his misfortune, which they now discovered no inclination to alleviate; and he found himself very uncomfortably beset."[5] When Henry Hunt, the radical, was incarcerated in Ilchester he launched an inquiry into intolerable conditions at the Somerset prison. Anxious to expose the moral environment in the jail, Hunt was able to play upon the prisoners' notorious antipathy to buggerers (as well as their disregard for the legal distinction between attempt and commission of the crime) when he called them as witnesses.[6] Jeremy Bentham, who considered buggery in the context of his penal reform scheme and also as part of his project of submitting morality to utilitarian analysis, recognized that the severity of the punishment and the general moral antipathy to sodomy made it a useful weapon to the extortionist, particularly because circumstantial evidence was not required to prove any offense short of a rape. (Bentham also supposed that men only chose beasts as their sexual partners in desperate circumstances and that decriminalization, which he also advocated for sodomy, would disarm blackmailers without encouraging the spread of the vice.) Innocence was no protection to the accused sodomite, and proof of commission of the crime was not critical to popular judgment. "Whether a man be thought to have actually been guilty of this practise or only to be disposed to it," wrote Benthan, "his reputation suffers equal ruin."[7] Indeed, the accusation, according to

Randolph Trumbach, rendered all the standard evidence of good character dubious and made legal defense that much more difficult.[8]

Yet moral antipathy to sodomy and bestiality, while general, was qualified in ways Benthan does not suggest. (The unfortunate beau described above, for instance, was saved by the intervention of the eponymous hero, Peregrine Pickle.) Deviant sexual practices were tolerated within certain communities or among particular class, occupational and age groups — women were treated ambigously under the sodomy statutes and no women were prosecuted in our period — and this had important implications for the maintenance of a good reputation.[9] Temporary homosexuality, such as the adolescent homosexuality countenanced across Europe, did not challenge definitions of masculinity and lead automatically to dishonor. Jeffrey Weeks, in his exploration of male prostitution, identified other worlds symbiotic with homosexuality. The Guards, "notorious from the eighteenth century and throughout Europe for their easy prostitution," and members of certain working-class groups were considered "indifferent to homosexual behaviour." The prostitute recruited from their ranks discovered that he could make money with "little effort and with no risk of stigma by his fellows." The crucial factor here was the ability to participate in homosexual acts without forfeiting one's self-definition as a man.[10]

The navy, too, represented an area in which sodomy was severely punished and yet practically tolerated to some degree. Arthur N. Gilbert, in his investigation of the *Africaine* courts-martial, turns up considerable evidence that sodomy was widely practiced aboard the ship and that some crewmen, far from expressing antipathy to buggery, considered it acceptable sexual behaviour. Interestingly enough, the officers who were court-martialled claimed in their defense that their loathing for the crime would have prevented them from committing it. This fissure between officers and men reminds us that attitudes could be determined by circumstances and that the disgust for buggery could be suspended under the proper conditions.[11]

Where enclaves exist in which sexual norms differ, definitions of reputation are adjusted to accommodate them. Consequently, reputation only suffers when their insulation from the outside world is breached. The London sodomite subculture that Trumbach has documented, with its own meeting places, customs and argot, was vulnerable to the waves of religious fervor that produced the moral crusades of the eighteenth and nineteenth centuries. It was also vulnerable to the poor choice of a partner by a member, or to the pressure upon members, once accused of sodomy or some other offense, to ransom their necks at the expense of turning informer on their sodomite companions. It is unlikely that even the city of Bath supported a sodomite subculture of these dimensions, and neither the first nor the last of the circumstances mentioned by Trumbach is immediately obvious in the Somerset sodomy prosecutions, but the misjudged advance undid many local men.

The Somerset material is too thin to enable use to do more than identify the limits of sexual tolerance which in turn defined the risk to a man's reputation of pursuing variant sexual practices. Any speculation as to the meaning of the bestiality prosecutions must be based on the very rudimentary data offered in indictments and the stray comments of upper-class observers such as Hunt and Bentham. The sodomy prosecutions, on the other hand, leave a body of case material that includes informations and examinations. This evidence suggests that popular definitions of buggery differed sufficiently from the official, legal ones to permit considerable latitude in sexual practice—enough, certainly, to save many men from being identified as sodomites and felons.

Though legal records do not indicate that prosecutions for bestiality were malicious, it is likely that a blurring between what was tolerated and what was not resulted in the arrival of twenty-five Somerset men in court, charged with attempting or committing bestiality a total of twenty-seven times. Of the twenty-five, eighteen were identified as laborers, one as a mason and a laborer, and one as a carpenter.[12] In the three cases where ages are given, the defendants are uniformly young: 23, 22 and 14. Their crimes were committed almost entirely in the summer months, and their partners were common farm animals.[13] It is possible that these young male laborers, many from small rural parishes, were representative of those who practiced bestiality without getting caught, and that their prosecution was related to the aggravation of their crimes, the coupling of this offense with other antisocial behavior, or detection by those who did not share in the prevailing tolerance.[14] The latter point would be more easily determined if we knew something about the witnesses in these cases; as it is we have no more to go on than gender and a single occupational reference. Names of thirty-two witnesses survive, of whom eight were women and one was a clergyman. Women, of whatever class or occupation, may have been automatically excluded from this male sexual subculture.[15] Clergymen would have opposed it on scriptural as well as legal grounds.[16] The conviction rate, which need not have been high to interest blackmailers in such a potent weapon, was higher than for sodomy (see Table I). Eight men were found guilty (six of attempting bestiality and two of committing it) and an equal number were acquitted, though one of these last was required to find "two sureties for the space of five years to be approved by two of His Majesty's Justices of the Peace for this county to be bound himself in the sum of £100 and each surety in the sum of £50" — a directive that may have amounted to a jail sentence for a poor man.[17] One indictment was quashed, five indictments resulted in no bill (three for bestiality, and one on both charges) and four indictments were returned true without information being given on the ultimate outcome of the cases.[18]

The human participants in bestial acts differed in many ways from the sodomites named in indictments and informations. The forty-two sodomites included a gentleman, six clergymen, six yeomen, an apothecary, four tradesmen (a victualler, a brewer, a corndealer and a clothier), a tailor and twelve laborers.[19] The preponderance of clergymen may be attributed to many factors: anti-clericalisms, the ancient association between buggery and the priesthood, the concentration of clergymen in Bath (where opportunities for illicit sexual activity of all kinds were greater), and a visibility that made it difficult to merge into whatever protective grouping existed. Bath and its environs supplied twelve defendants who committed sixteen offenses and another eight men (eleven offenses) came from market towns. With occupational diversity probably came a greater variation in age; the four given in jail books range from 21 to 68. Witnesses listed in thirty-seven cases included sixty-two men and fifteen women and the most common witness was the man or boy who had brought the complaint. Of these cases, it is those that bear most directly on the problem of reputation, that

Table I: Convictions*

	Sodomy				Bestiality			
	Pro-secutions	No. of Defend-ants	Convic-tions	True Bills	Pro-secutions	No. of Defend-ants	Convic-tions	True Bills
1740-9	2	2		1	2	2		
1750-9	3	3		1	1	1		
1760-9	7	5		3	0	0		
1770-9	4	3			2	2		
1780-9	3	3	3		1	1		
1790-9	8	4	1	2	1	1		2
1800-9	6	6		1	1	1		1
1810-19	12	9	5	5	8	8	4	
1820-29	8	6	1+1	2	6	4	4	
1830-39	2	1			2	2		1
1840-49	0	0			3	3		3
	55	42			27	25		

*This includes felonies and misdemeanors; some of the sodomy convictions were for common assault or aggravated assault. True bills are included as possible convictions. Assize causes are included until 1828.

define the limits of tolerance and confront the issue of blackmail, that will be considered below.

II

Among the threats that blackmailers could choose from, perhaps none was more dangerous to a victim than the offer to expose him as a sodomite. Smollett observed that the city of Bath was furnished "with those who lay wanton wives and old rich widows under contribution, and extort money, by prostituting themselves to the embraces of their own sex, and then threatening their admirers with prosecution."[20] Men were susceptible to blackmail for sexual practice that were, according to statute law, unnatural and therefore capital offenses, and buggery, whether with man, woman or beast, was proscribed under a law that originated in the reign of Henry VIII.[21] While the evidence for a link between sodomy and blackmail in Somerset exists, it does not for bestiality. Suspected bestiality may have been equally damaging to male reputation, but, in addition to the evidentiary problems, the age and class of many offenders would have made them inappropriate targets for extortionists.

There are two patterns that emerge from the information given in sodomy indictments that suggest that blackmail was neither difficult to accomplish nor infrequently attempted.[22] The first involves the witnesses: in seventeen of the cases under study the complainant was the sole informant or witness, and in only two of the cases for which names of witnesses survive does the victim fail to give evidence.[23] Nor were the additional witnesses likely to have been present at the event, but instead were masters, fellow servants, friends, relatives or law officers who had been approached by the victims sometime afterward. There is no doubt that the evidentiary requirements for acts of attempted sodomy were minimal (sodomy itself was difficult to prove, and only six men were charged with the offense in Somerset) and though the conviction rate was low, there is no correlation between the number of witnesses and the success of the prosecution.[24] The second factor is belated prosecution, or even reporting, of the crime. While the observed pattern of self-witnessing may be in part justified by the circumstances under which attempted sodomy might be expected to occur, the reasons for keeping an actual sexual advance secret were more complex and cannot be divorced from a concern with reputation on the complainant's part. If the prosecution of a sodomite almost invariably required the victim to expose himself, one must consider the ways in which this inhibited men from acknowledging their participation in homosexual acts.

Informations and examinations make it clear that complainants were reluctant to reveal that they had been accosted or assaulted, and some admitted that they had participated in a number of encounters before informing anyone of their problem. This unwillingness to go to law (probably the inevitable outcome of a disclosure) may have had a mercenary foundation; some may have been at least temporarily satisfied with the common offers of money or employment, and others may have glimpsed ever-widening opportunities for extortion. But one must also consider the position of complainants vis-à-vis their seducers, their sexual attitudes and their fears for their own reputations. Some complainants, in a variation upon the archetypal heterosexual seduction scenario, were approached by masters upon whom they were dependent. Young complainants could claim ignorance of the significance of their acts, and older ones occasionally exhibited indifference. Sexual acts short of anal penetration were not necessarily recognized as buggery by the population at large, and this may explain the coexistence of a widespread and well-documented horror of the crime and a tolerance for certain homosexual acts in practice. Several statements made by complainants suggest that even though they knew they had participated in irregular sexual activity, they did not see themselves committing buggery.[25] At the same time, people do not seem to have distinguished between commission of the crime and attempted commission. Once caught, a man was as likely to be stoned to death in the pillory for attempted sodomy as for committing the crime, regardless of the law.

When William Bence, a mason doing a job of a few months duration for the Rev. W. Conybear, was accosted in the hayloft by Joseph Beckett, one of Conybear's servants, he told him, " 'to go to Bath and get a Whore.' " Yet neither Bence nor Joseph Butler, a carpenter similarly employed, felt they could say anything in the village about Beckett's repeated solicitations and assaults for fear of being discharged from their work.[26] James Philip, a servant to Mrs. Peck of Walcot, had been approached by the Rev. John Graves three times and had taken 2s. in drinking money from him, despite his reported efforts to discourage his advances, when a man knocked at his mistress's door and declared: "it is reported all over Town that Mr. John Graves has used a person ill in the buggering way" and that the young man inhabited that very house. Philip's immediate response was to warn the man that "people ought to be very cautious how they talk of such things" and to deny any knowledge of the incident. Philip also claimed that he did not discover his persecutor's name until later that day. He made his information before the mayor three days later.[27]

James Bane, who turned a man who claimed he was the Rev. G. Morgan over to the Walcot watchman after a midnight walk across the city during which Morgan made his intentions more than clear, was quick to assert that "he had been with a female" prior to encountering the clergyman.[28] The fear of compromising one's reputation, whatever one's private feelings about a little fondling or kissing, was a strong deterrent to men who participated, willingly or not, in homosexual acts and who considered prosecuting their partners. While fear of exposure must have set limits to the activities of sodomites, the risks inherent in reporting the crime must have protected many who might have otherwise gone to jail or to the gallows.

Most sodomites were well aware of the dangers they ran in approaching other men — of loss of reputation, death in the pillory, or hanging — and few informations are without a reference to the defendant's injunctions of silence, often reinforced by offers of money or employment.[29] Some, like the Rev. G. Morgan, went even further. He offered £1 to the Walcot watchman who apprehended him to enable him to escape, and when he was recaptured he was willing to exchange £5 for his freedom. If practicing sodomites were willing to ensure the discretion of prospective partners and to bribe law officers in this way, it is not surprising that extortionists could make exorbitant demands on them.

When writing on pederasty, Bentham could not avoid the topic of blackmail. He described the man of resolution who, where "incidental circumstances are favourable, . . . may stand the brunt and meet his accuser in the face of justice," but observed that "the danger to his reputation will . . . be considerable."[30] William Tyler may have been one such man. He certainly met his accusers, but he also may have suffered imprisonment and loss of reputation for a crime he may not have committed.[31] William Teyler otherwise Tyley, identified as a yeoman of Bedminster, was charged with assaulting and attempting to bugger William Mason, aged 21, on 21 April 1795. His indictment came up at the same Sessions as a bill accusing Mason and Samuel Davis, both described as Bristol laborers, with intending to deprive Tyler of his "good Name Fame and Credit" and with attempting to extort money from him by conspiring to falsely charge him with "unnatural and immoral practises."[32] James White, a victualler and a constable of Bedminster, gave an information the day after the supposed buggery occurred in which he described two men coming to his house at nine o'clock in the morning. When he confirmed that he knew Mr. Tyler, one man said:

> "he ought to be hung" and addressing himself to the other Man desired he would shew this Informant whereupon the said other Man shewed his private parts which appeared a little swelled which he said was caused by . . . Mr. Tyler having the evening before taken him into a private place in . . . Bedminster and used him in a violent and indecent manner.

White suggested they confronted Tyler with this accusation; Tyler "appeared much surprized" and offered to vindicate himself before a magistrate. White then asked Mason and Davis in private what they wanted of Tyler and Mason replied "£100" and Davis "immediately said they would have £50 which he would be damned if Mr. Tyler should not pay before they quitted the room." When White communicated these demands to Tyler, he replied that he would not give them fifty farthings, "but would go to Justice." White and Tyler went, as appointed, but Mason and Davis failed to appear before the magistrate.

Tyler admitted to drinking with Mason the night before in two pubs across the county line in Bristol, but claimed that they had parted at the Coach and Four in Redcliff Street about ten o'clock.

He had never been anywhere else with Mason. Davis was unknown to him when he came the next day with White to make "a charge against him of an indecent and unnatural kind." Davis and Mason were charged with extortion on the oaths of Tyler and White, and rapidly committed, though they were bailed prior to Bridgewater Sessions, where a true bill was found against them.[33] Mason and Davis nevertheless brought their charge against Tyler, telling a magistrate that Tyler had put his hands into Mason's breeches and fondled his private parts. Again, the jury found a true bill. The final decision as to the guilt of Tyler's accusers is not recorded.

The single member of the titled classes to be implicated in a sodomy cause, Sir Thomas Swymmer Champneys, was also a victim of blackmail. In 1821, Champneys, then identified simply as "Esquire," charged George Messiter, a gentleman of Frome, with trying to aggrieve and financially burden him by persuading four men to falsely testify at Assizes that Champneys had attempted to commit buggery.[34] (Neither Messiter nor Champneys were new to the law. The previous year a man of the same name, parish and occupation as Messiter had charged Samuel Wheeler with libel for posting rewards for his capture, and in 1815 Thomas Swymmer Champneys, Esq., of Orchardleigh, had been charged with assault.)[35] All four, and Charles Harrison, were listed as witnesses in the extortion trial, which was removed from Quarter Sessions by a writ of certoriari.

Whatever the outcome of the proceeding (and there is no record of the earlier charge against him, which indicates that Messiter only threatened to take him to court), Champneys, now identified as a baronet, late of Ilchester, was arraigned before the Lent Assizes in 1826.[36] There he was described as having a

> lewd wicked depraved and abandoned mind and disposition and wholly lost to all sense of shame and decency and devising and intending to vitiate the mind and corrupt the morals of one Henry Bragg and to excite in his . . . mind filthy lewd unchaste and abominable desires and inclinations.

Champneys tried, according to the indictment, to solicit Henry Bragg to commit buggery with him on two recent occasions. The tenor and wording of the charge suggest that Bragg was a minor, though he is listed as the sole witness. No bill was found, but whether we should attribute this to Champney's innocence or influence is uncertain, for the sexual molestation of children, of either sex, was universally deplored. The baronet's legal entanglements, unique to his class in the county, may have stemmed from a number of sources.[37] First, Champneys may have been a sodomite, if an unconvicted one. Second, he may have been alone among his peers in resisting blackmail. (William Beckford, more typically, fled the country.) Finally, the original extortion trial may have marked him as a suspected sodomite, and left him open to subsequent accusations.

Victims could go to great lengths to entrap sodomites, but we only know of those cases in which the entrapment was intended, probably from the outset, to result in arrest or at least a cessation of advances, rather than in blackmail. John Shipton, a shopman to a Bath linen draper, met James Williams in the Gravel Walk as he went to and from an errand on the evening of 15 or 16 September 1813.[38] Shipton sat and walked with Williams, protested mildly when Williams caressed him, and arranged to meet him again the following Sunday. Shipton then went home and informed his master of all that had passed. Two days after the appointed meeting, Shipton again encountered Williams, followed him into a field behind Marlboro Buildings and submitted to more kissing and caressing. Once again, Noah Coward, Shipton's master, was informed. On the evening of 24 September, Shipton met Williams, as previously arranged, at the Crescent. This time, their activities in the fields were interrupted when Williams heard a noise. As he tried to escape, Shipton "gave a signal to some Officers who were in waiting" and Williams was taken into custody.

John Shipton and James Reader, the informant in the following case, may have been quite young. Reader was a servant to Mr. Richard Nossiter Burnard, a surgeon of Crewkerne, and he was made aware of the Rev. George Donnisthorpe's sexual interest after he applied to him for a job in 1802.[39] In addition to being offered liquor and money, Reader was told that "if he (Donnisthorpe) were

a Lady and had ten thousand a year he would bestow it all on him.''
During this meeting Donnisthorpe took Reader's "private Member
in his hand, knelt down on one knee and put it into his Mouth,'' an
act which Reader did not equate with buggery. Reader only began
to resist when Donnisthorpe tried to lay him down on a sofa.
Though he did not depart immediately, Reader was uneasy. Later,
when Susanna Lye, a fellow servant, asked him if he was going to
Donnisthorpe's to live he said, "no he would not if Mr. Donnisthorpe would give him a hundred a year, that he had a particular
reason for it,'' and then he told her of his experience. The following
Sunday, 29 August, he revealed his secret to Mr. Nicholas Baker,
Mr. Burnard's assistant. Baker promised to write a letter to the
offender if Reader would carry it. Reader saw Donnisthorpe at least
four more times before Baker wrote, and during the final visit, on 3
September, he engaged in drinking and sexual play before presenting Donnisthorpe with the letter.

Despite Baker's reported distaste for Donnisthorpe's acts – when
Reader first told Baker of them he said "he would lend him a knife
to amputate the offending Member, if he would use it and at the
same time expressed his Abhorrence of the crime'' – he was willing
to warn Donnisthorpe off with a strong letter. (That it was not a
blackmailing letter is suggested by Baker's having shown it to a
local attorney before reading it to Reader and giving it to him to
deliver.) It was not until the clergyman denied the charges that
Reader and Baker went before a magistrate. As a result, Donnisthorpe was indicted for attempting buggery with James Reader on
three occasions.

The choice between silence, confession and blackmail was surely
influenced by the relation between a seducer and his victim. In the
case of clergymen, deference might be reinforced by respect for the
cloth or even the knowledge that parsons frequently avoided punishment in these cases. Had Baker's initial impulse to castrate the
offender been tempered by this final consideration, he would not
have been far wrong. The case, like so many in which clergymen
were defendants, was removed from Quarter Sessions – and beyond
the control of a servant and a surgeon's assistant – by a writ of

certoriari.[40] We hear no more of the Rev. George Donnisthorpe in the local legal records.

III.

Though most historians of sexuality agree that attitudes towards buggery underwent a change between the seventeenth and twentieth centuries, few are agreed on the nature or even the direction of that change. In many ways, this is as much a problem of evidence as of interpretation. Historians who have relied upon statutes, commentaries, manuals and other examples of official opinion have been struck either by the tone of vehement abhorrence for a crime condemned in the Bible or by the terseness of the treatment of the subject.[41] Historians who have studied prosecutions in the aggregate have been better able to describe the waxing and waning interest taken in buggery, though they are unable to determine the relationship between prosecution and practice. A. D. Harvey, who has consulted national data on sodomy prosecutions and convictions from 1804 and the London and Middlesex material from the mid-eighteenth century, has located the multiplication of both trials and executions of sodomites in the first third of the nineteenth century. Where executions in the metropolis had averaged less than one per decade between 1749 and 1804, they became yearly occurrences until they ceased altogether in the mid-1830s.[42]

The number of individuals indicted for committing or attempting to commit sodomy or bestiality was also increasing in Somerset in the early decades of the nineteenth century. The Somerset material, however, does not explain whether the horror evoked by anal intercourse and by sodomites was predicted upon the biblical coupling of sodomy and catastrophe; the medieval association of sexual deviance with heresy; concern for the maintenance of marriage, family and reproduction (procreation was of particular significance during wartime); or upon the belief that bestiality "threatened the firm dividing-line between men and animals" and resulted in monstrous conceptions.[43]

Nor does it point unambiguously toward any of the previously offered explanations for an increase in either the practice or the prosecution of sodomy. E. William Monter demonstrates that in Geneva, from the mid-sixteenth century to the late seventeenth century, a period when sodomy trials were at their height, men outnumbered women in the city; while in the rural canton of Fribourg, where cows outnumbered humans, there were thirty-two trials for bestiality between 1599 and 1648.[44] The delayed age of marriage and a paucity of pre-marital sexual opportunities may have had some bearing on the practice of bestiality in the Somerset countryside, where young agricultural laborers may have reconciled themselves to the inevitable wait with animal partners, but in the city of Bath, where women consistently outnumbered men, the impulse to commit sodomy must have had some other origin.

Economic disaster, the outbreak of war and religious revival have been suggested as factors influencing the number of prosecutions and convictions for buggery and the harshness of the punishment meted out. Gilbert has attempted to link persecution of sodomites with "perceived or imagined social disaster," and for the early nineteenth century points to

> an intensification of fear of deviance that parallels involvement in the long and threatening Napoleonic Wars. Pressure on homosexual men was particularly intense in 1810, when war weariness and fear of anti-religious and revoluntionary French ways were combined with economic strife.[45]

The year 1810, however, was not as significant in Somerset as it was in London: only one information against a sodomite is recorded. The rise of Calvinism, the Catholic counter-reformation and the crusades of the Societies for the Reformation of Manners have been credited with the proliferation of prosecutions in Geneva, Fribourg and London in earlier periods.[46] In Somerset, the growth of Methodism and Evangelicalism may have had a similar effect: Bath in particular was noted for its religious revivalism and experimentation. Trumbach has also suggested that the development of an organized police force had an impact on the apprehension of sodomites in the nineteenth century, but Bath, unlike London, had been unusually well-policed in the eighteenth century.[47] Finally, Harvey offers a range of explanations for the increase in prosecution and persecution he has described. These include intolerance arising from the hardening of gender roles, but he eventually fastens upon the "sexual neurosis" of the period as the source of the observed increase in hostility towards sexual deviance.[48]

If we descend from the legal treatises and statistics of prosecution to the realm of popular conceptions, it appears that the horror inspired by buggery, though nearly universal, was susceptible to modification. The eighteenth century marked a period in which the variety of sexual cultures that thrived in the wake of Puritanism were gradually resolving into the new sexual consensus of Victorianism. This merger of popular and polite sexual culture had many facets, and can be seen in the abondonment of a rudimentary plebeian sexual egalitarianism in favor of the double standard and more rigidly defined gender roles. Perceptions of buggery, too, changed. The exclusive link between buggery and anal intercourse was well-established in the popular mind in the seventeenth century and continued to flourish, according to the Somerset evidence, during much of the period under study. Likewise, the rare and largely urban creature, the sodomite, conformed, in the popular imagination, to the effeminate or transvestite stereotype evoked by Smollett. A new definition of homosexuality, however, as a pathological alternative to masculinity and a vice pertaining to persons rather than to acts, was gradually evolving. It owed its wide dissemination to greater literacy, exposure to urban life and improved communications. As a definition, it effectively eliminated temporary or circumstantial homosexuality and weakened the connection between buggery and anal intercourse, thus drastically narrowing the scope for popular tolerance. Weeks and other historians of homosexuality contend that the modern homosexual (who could be pitied as a deviant rather than abhorred and punished as a criminal) did not fully emerge until the late nineteenth century. But the transition from sodomite to homosexual was a long one and its early echoes in popular consciousness may be detected in the multiplication of prosecutions, in Somerset and elsewhere, in the first third of the nineteenth century.[49]

In Somerset, there had been sufficient horror of buggery in the eighteenth century to guarantee a small stream of prosecutions. The consequences of the accusation were great enough to encourage blackmail and false prosecution and to discourage reporting the crime. The anxiety to avoid the charge on the part of victims and defendants is more clearly illustrated than a readiness to shun certain acts; homosexual advances are often seen as symptoms of a lustiness that could find its outlet in a partner of either sex. In such a climate, male reputation was vulnerable to attack and many men were no doubt willing to pay off their accusers rather than to resist and risk revealing themselves. Yet the charge was one among several. A man could also be condemned — though with less danger — as a whoremonger or a father of bastards.

Tolerance, if prosecutions are any indication, was on the decline in the nineteenth century. There was an upward trend in both sodomy and bestiality prosecutions in the county most pronounced in the period 1810 to 1830. As long as sodomy and bestiality remained capital offenses, as they did until 1861, and as long as the attempt to commit these acts was severely punished, the opportunities for blackmail and extortion did not cease. Popular tolerance for some unnatural acts was never sufficient to erase the threat of prosecution for all men, and it is likely that the tolerance predicated on popular definitions of buggery waned as the boundaries between popular and forensic definitions dissolved and buggery became a well-defined offense associated with a specific kind of individual, the homosexual. Though individuals undoubtedly benefitted from local and limited tolerance, sodomy and bestiality remained the most serious threats to male sexual reputation in this period.

NOTES

1. Tobias Smollett, *The Expedition of Humphry Clinker* (Harmondsworth: Penguin Books, 1967), p. 205. I would like to thank Randy Trumbach and the members of the seminar on European Social History at Columbia University for their comments on earlier drafts of this paper.

2. For a fuller discussion of the divergence of male and female sexual reputation, particularly among the plebs, see Polly Morris, "Defamation and Sexual Reputation in Somerset, 1733-1850" (Ph.D. dissertation, University of Warwick, 1985).

3. *Ibid.*, Chapter 5.

4. *Ibid*, p. 281.

5. Tobias Smollett, *The Adventures of Peregrine Pickle*, 4 vols., The Dalquhurn Edition of the Works of Tobias Smollett (New York: George D. Sproul, 1908), 4:122-23. For the effeminacy of eighteenth-century sodomites and sodom-

ite stereotypes, see Randolph Trumbach, "London's Sodomites: Homosexual Behavior and Western Culture in the 18th Century," *Journal of Social History* 11 (1977-8):11;13; and A. D. Harvey, "Prosecutions for Sodomy in England at the Beginning of the Nineteenth Century," *The Historical Journal* 21 (1978):943. Thus, the passivity of the sodomite was related to his supposed effeminacy rather than to his role in the sexual act.

6. For Henry Hunt's homophobia, see his *Memoirs*, 3 vols. (London: T. Dolby, 1820-22), espec, vol. 3, pp. 582-83; *A Peep Into a Prison: Or, the Inside of Ilchester Bastile. 1821*, Ilchester and District Occasional Papers, no. 11 (Guernsey: The Toucan Press, 1979), p. 19; *Investigation at Ilchester Gaol in the County of Somerset into the Conduct of William Bridle, the Gaoler, Before the Commissioners Appointed by the Crown* (London: Thomas Dolby, 1821), passim; and the letters he published from prison, "To the Radical Reformers, Male and Female, of England, Ireland, and Scotland" between 1820 and 1822.

7. Louis Crompton, ed., "Jeremy Bentham's Essay on 'Paederasty' Part 2," *Journal of Homosexuality* (hereafter *J. Homosex.*):4 (1978):99; 102; 100.

8. Trumbach, "London's Sodomites," p. 21.

9. Though in Europe lesbians were punished along with male homosexuals, the English statute was interpreted to exclude women. Women were not, however, exempt from the bestiality clauses. Charges of bestiality, directed at women, do occasionally appear in defamation libels in the records of the ecclesiastical courts of the diocese of Bath and Wells, lodged in the Somerset Record Office (hereafter S.R.O.) though insults involving bestiality or sodomy were not, in theory, actionable in the church courts because they involved capital crimes. For a very complicated local cause involving anal intercourse between a husband and wife, based upon the subsequently withdrawn complain of the wife, see DD/TB box 18 F.T.7 (Carew papers, S.R.O.). And Mary Hamilton, who became notorious for passing as a man, came before the local authorities for marrying another woman: S.R.O. Q/SI 366 (Taunton, 1746).

10. Jeffrey Weeks, "Inverts, Perverts, and Mary-Annes: Male Prostitution and the Regulation of Homosexuality in England in the Nineteenth and Early Twentieth Centuries," *J. Homosex.* 6 (1980-1):122; 125.

11. Arthur N. Gilbert, "The *Africaine* Courts-Martial: A Study of Buggery and the Royal Navy," *J. Homosex.* 1 (1974):111-22.

12. Five occupations not given; one man charged three separate times.

13. Of the nineteen cases for which a month is given, fifteen occur between April and August, and two each in December and March. Named partners include four mares, five she-asses, three sows, two cows, one ewe, one heifer and one duck. Of course, most of these animals could be found as easily in parts of Bath as in a rural parish. The two prosecutions from Bath (Lyncombe and Widcombe parish, which still contained farms) named a cow and a she-ass, while mares, sows and a duck were among the animals named for others towns. Robert F. Oaks, " 'Things Fearful to Name': Sodomy and Buggery in Seventeenth-century New England," *Journal of Social History* 12 (1978):275, also notes the preponderance of young men and boys in bestiality indictments.

14. Parish of residence not given in five cases. Two cases originated in Lyn-combe and Widcombe, and four more in market towns. Eight of the parishes had fewer than 600 inhabitants; three had less than 1000; ten had more than 1000.

15. There is one piece of evidence that suggests that men may have become identified with a deviant sexual subculture as a result of the stigma attached to assuming, willingly or not, the passive role in the sexual act. John Pickford, a yeoman of Pilton, was charged with attempting to bugger George Pike in 1809. The witnesses to the indictment were Pike and James and John Dunkerton; no bill was found: ASSI 25/9/20 (Public Record Office, hereafter, P.R.O.). Three years later, Pike himself was found guilty of attempting to bugger a mare at Pilton. Pike, aged 14, was sentenced to twelve months in jail and two public whippings. The witnesses were James and John Dunkerton: P.R.O. ASSI 23/9 (Summer, 1812); 25/9/10; 25/9/20; 24/44 (Summer, 1812).

One of the two seventeenth-century Somerset sodomy prosecutions discovered by G. R. Quaife involves an innkeeper who not only had a long history of attempt-ing buggery and achieving sexual satisfaction with men, but who puportedly inter-spersed his assaults on the local blacksmith with attempts on the horses he was shoeing and invitations to watch him bugger his sow: *Wanton Wenches and Way-ward Wives; Peasants and Illicit Sex in Early Seventeenth Century England* (Lon-don: Croom Helm, 1979), pp. 175-77. The man's lengthy and public career as a sexual deviant in a small village raises interesting questions about tolerance and its cessation. B. R. Burg, in "Ho Hum, Another Work of the Devil: Buggery and Sodomy in Early Stuart England," *J. Homosex.* 6 (1980-1):71-4, uses the trial of this man to show that it was an "aggregate of social behavior," including crossing class boundaries in the search for sexual partners, that led to harsh punishment. According to Burg, the defendant was accepted by witnesses as a long-time bug-gerer, but his attempt at bestiality was too much for them.

16. In the case where a clergyman was to give evidence, the cause originated in a parish of barely fifty inhabitants, none of whom joined the parson as wit-nesses: P.R.O. ASSI 23/10 (Summer, 1813); 25/10/13; 24/44 (Summer, 1813); 25/10/4.

17. Of the guilty, one was to hang. He was simultaneously charged with three offenses committed over a period of six years, though no bill was found for the two earlier offenses: P.R.O. ASSI 25/17/21; 23/10 (Summer, 1822). Another man was reprieved, and the remaining six received jail sentences of one or two years and were ordered to be whipped, sometimes publicly, usually twice a year. The sureties case is in P.R.O. ASSI 23/6 (August, 1747).

18. The quashed indictment involved the duck and was quashed for insuffi-ciency. This may have been a malicious prosecution, or it may demonstrate a tendency to tolerate sexual deviance among the insane: P.R.O. ASSI 25/11/21. There is one remaining indictment for which no information as to outcome exists. As to the charges, thirteen were charged with committing bestiality (including four misdemeanors at Quarter Sessions which, like attempted bestiality, were lesser charges); eight were charged with the attempt; and six with both. Of these

six, two were acquitted, three found guilty of the attempt and one of the commission.

19. The sodomite community, particularly in Bath, must have been far larger than this figure suggests. Some cases may have come up at Bath Quarter Sessions (John Haddon, *Bath* (London: B. T. Batsford Ltd., 1973), p. 101, refers to an alderman charged in a " 'Sodomiticall Attempt' " in 1740) and many sodomites avoided brushes with the law. Occupation was not given in eleven indictments. Occupational designations are not very accurate, and while this does not alter the general pattern, it does disguise significant occupational diversity: see the Tyler case, below. The total number of offenses was fifty-five; one man was charged by four plaintiffs, three men by three each, and four men by two each.

20. Smollett, *Peregrine Pickle*, 2:292.

21. For some of the more notorious cases of homosexual blackmail in the late eighteenth and early nineteenth centuries, see H. Montgomery Hyde, *The Love The Dared Not Speak Its Name. A Candid History of Homosexuality in Britain* (Boston: Little Brown and Company, 1970), pp. 69-70; 77-8. Because reputation is our major concern in the pages that follow, I will not always distinguish between attempted sodomy or bestiality (a lesser crime) and commission; both charges were extremely damaging to a man's reputation.

22. Trumbach has uncovered far more attempted blackmail in London than I have in Somerset. He also notes that the London subculture, while it screened men from prosecution, made them more susceptible to blackmail: "London's Sodomites," p. 21. In 1810, a year in which prosecutions and convictions reached a high level in London, extortion trials showed a similar increase: Arthur N. Gilbert, "Sexual Deviance and Disaster during the Napoleonic Wars," *Albion* 9 (1977): 104. Subculture is probably a strong word to use for any local sodomite activity, even in Bath. Yet Bath offered an extraordinary degree of anonymity and mobility because of its medical-leisure orientation. Informations suggest that the city had its own topography of sodomy: safe fields, pick-up streets, etc. See especially the case of John Shipton, below.

23. No names survive in sixteen cases; the two non-testifiers may have been minors, though some minors did testify.

24. Two men were charged with both attempt and commission, two men with committing sodomy together, and two with sodomy alone. Of these, only one was convicted, in 1825, and his punishment was not recorded. The remaining men were charged with a variety of misdemeanors, most frequently attempted buggery. Punishments were harsher than those meted out in eighteenth-century London and generally involved jail terms of one or two years in addition to periods in the pillory (in a very aggravated case of 1811), solitary confinement (1814-5) and occasionally astronomical sureties and recognizances. Cf. with Trumbach, "London's Sodomites," p. 21: he records a higher conviction rate (3/5) and lesser punishments for attempted sodomy as well as a higher conviction rate (1/2) for sodomy. Punishments in London in the early nineteenth century were more in line with Somerset punishments; evidence of the latter is too spotty to show a worsening trend: cf. Gilbert, "Sexual Deviance and Disaster," p. 109. On a national

scale, for the years 1810 to 1818 inclusive, 102 men were committed for trial on the charge of sodomy, thirty were convicted, twenty-eight were acquitted and no bill was found for forty-four: Harvey, "Prosecutions for Sodomy," p. 948.

25. Arthur N. Gilbert, "Conceptions of Homosexuality and Sodomy in Western History," *J. Homosex.* 6 (1980-1): 63; 65, suggests that in the eighteenth and nineteenth centuries sodomy came to be identified with an act, anal intercourse, rather than with homosexual relations. The anal sex taboo stems, he argues, not from its non-procreativity, but from the association of the anus with excrement, beasts, death and evil. Others date this development earlier. Robert Oakes, "Perceptions of Homosexuality by Justices of the Peace in Colonial Virginia," *J. Homosex.* 5 (1979-80):37, feels that Coke made it clear that buggery was anal intercourse between men. Caroline Bingham, "Seventeenth-Century Attitudes Towards Deviant Sex," *Journal of Interdisciplinary History* 1 (1971):459, cites the chief justice's attempts to persuade the reluctant jury in the trial of the Earl of Castlehaven (1631) that emission, rather than penetration, was sufficient proof of buggery. Gilbert and Oakes are discussing legal and moral conceptions. But as Bingham's evidence shows, popular conceptions, even those of the upper-class jurors in the Castlehaven case, linked buggery with anal intercourse, probably exclusively, as early as Coke did. For a clear description of the metamorphosis of the sodomite into the homosexual — in moral, legal and medical terms and in the popular mind — see Jeffrey Weeks, *Sex, Politics and Society; The regulation of sexuality since 1800* (London and New York: Longman, 1981), pp. 99-102. Both Trumbach, in "London's Sodomites" and Weeks, in "Inverts, Perverts, and Mary-Annes," argue that though there was considerable pressure on sodomites to adopt a permanent role, the distinctions were far more fluid.

26. S.R.O. Q/SR 396 (Easter, 1815).

27. S.R.O. Q/SR 366 (Wells II, 1798).

28. S.R.O. Q/SR 390 (Michaelmas, 1813). Walcot was one of the parishes that made up the city of Bath.

29. Stoning in the pillory, sometimes to the point of death, was an obvious indication of public abhorrence for the crime. Convicted sodomites desperately offered to turn informer to be excused from their hour in the pillory; its use in the cases was discontinued in 1816. John Latimer, in *The Annals of Bristol in the Eighteenth Century* (Printed for the Author, 1893), pp. 148; 185, cites the case of a local Poor Law guardian sentenced for "a filthy offence" in 1732 who hired 100 colliers to protect him, wore an iron skull cap and covered his body with heavy brown paper for his hour in the pillory; he was nonetheless released early because of the riot that erupted. For hangings, see Louis Crompton, "The Myth of Lesbian Impunity: Capital Laws from 1270-1791," *J. Homosex.* 6 (1980-1), p. 17. The only conviction for sodomy in Somerset that may have resulted in an execution involved a Bath laborer who was found guilty of buggering George Maggs the younger. Maggs was not among the six witnesses, two of whom were women, facts which suggest that Maggs was a child: P.R.O. ASSI 25/19/4 (Lent, 1825).

30. Crompton, "Bentham's Essay, Part 2," p. 100.

31. Outcome unknown, but a William Tayler otherwise Tayley was convicted

of an unspecified misdemeanor at the next Sessions and sentenced to solitary confinement for two years and until he had paid a £50 fine. This is close to the standard sentence for attempted sodomy: S.R.O. Q/SR 363 (Taunton, 1795).

32. S.R.O. Q/SR 363 (Bridgewater, 1795): Informations of James White and William Tyler, dealer in corn. James White's information reveals that Mason was a servant to Mr. Harris, a malster of Bristol, and that Davis was a servant to Mr. Jacobs, a glasscutter of the same city.

33. S.R.O. Q/SI 415 (Bridgewater, 1795).

34. S.R.O. Q/SI 441 (Easter, 1821).

35. S.R.O. Q/SI 436 (Epiphany, 1816). A true bill was found.

36. P.R.O. ASSI 25/19/6 (Lent, 1826).

37. Trumbach, "London's Sodomites," pp. 19-20, suggests that aristocrats maintained their own homosexual network which benefitted from their greater geographical mobility. Nonetheless, aristocrats were linked to the sodomite sub-culture, and some of its less savory zones, through blackmail and prostitution, and Sir Thomas's legal problems may represent such a link. Champneys was not the only sodomite of note in the county. William Beckford, the heir to an enormous sugar fortune and M.P. for Wells, fled the country in 1785 after the scandal caused by his suspected liaison with the seventeen-year-old William Courtenay made life in England unbearable. Though the evidence was insufficient for a prosecution, it was enough, when taken up by the Press, to permanently ruin Beckford's reputation. An outcast, estranged from his family, Beckford spent the final twenty years of his life in Bath: Boyd Alexander, *England's Wealthiest Son. A Study of William Beckford* (London: Centaur Press, Ltd., 1962), pp. 107-18. This and other sodomite scandals were not easily erased from popular memory: Hyde, *Love That Dared Not Speak Its Name*, p. 88.

38. S.R.O. Q/SR 390 (Michaelmas, 1813).

39. S.R.O. Q/SR 370 (Taunton, 1802).

40. S.R.O. Q/SI 422 (Taunton, 1802). Hyde claims that clerical sodomites were invariably granted bail by magistrates, so that many of them fled abroad: *Love That Dared Not Speak Its Name*, p. 82.

41. A comparison between the lenient punishments handed down in incest cases with the stiff penalties imposed on buggerers in Elizabethan times leads Lawrence Stone to say that "there is reason to think that sodomy and bestiality were more repugnant to popular standards of morality than breaking the laws of incest": *The Family, Sex and Marriage in England 1500-1800* (New York: Harper & Row, Publishers, 1977), p. 491. This is not always the most productive approach to popular morality because among other things, it obscures the popular definitions of these crimes that formed the basis for complaints and prosecutions. Bingham, "Seventeenth-Century Attitudes Towards Deviant Sex," assumes that Englishmen of that period would unquestioningly take the biblical view and abominate sodomy, largely because the prosecutor in the trial of the Earl of Castlehaven did so. Unfortunately, she overlooks the jury's verdict: only fifteen of the twenty-seven peers voted to convict on the sodomy charge. These and other weaknesses in Bingham's article are pointed out by Bruce Mazlish in his comment,

Journal of Interdisciplinary History 1 (1971) and by Burg in "Ho Hum." Burg, however, defends the other extreme. He asserts that there was "little hostility or opprobrium" attached to acts other than bestiality or homosexual child molestation, unaware, perhaps, that taboos on buggery may have accounted for legal authors' seeming lack of interest in the matter.

42. Harvey, "Prosecutions for Sodomy," p. 939.

43. On the separation of animal and human spheres, see Keith Thomas, *Man and the Natural World; Changing Attitudes in England 1500-1800* (London: Allen Lane, 1983), pp. 39, 134-35.

44. E. William Monter, "Sodomy and Heresy in Early Modern Switzerland," *J. Homosex.* 6 (1980-1): 43-4; 47.

45. Gilbert, "Conceptions of Homosexuality," p. 61, and "Sexual Deviance and Disaster."

46. Monter, "Sodomy and Heresy," pp. 45-50; Trumbach, "London's Sodomites," pp. 10-11. Trumbach, in opposition to Monter, argues that sodomy, far from being desacralized in the eighteenth century, continued to excite religious horror.

47. Trumbach, "London's Sodomites," p. 23.

48. Harvey, "Prosecutions for Sodomy," pp. 946-47.

49. Weeks, *Sex, Politics and Society*, p. 103: "The latter part of the nineteenth century, however, saw the clear emergence of homosexuality although the elements of the new definitions and practices can be traced to earlier periods."

Sodomitical Assaults, Gender Role, and Sexual Development in Eighteenth-Century London

Randolph Trumbach, PhD

Twenty years ago, Mary McIntosh distinguished between societies where homosexual behavior entailed the assumption of a special role and those where it did not. She also proposed that the role of the queen—or the effeminate, exclusively homosexual adult male—had appeared in Western societies only with the organization of urban, homosexual subcultures in the early eighteenth century.[1] Ten years later, I sought to modify this schema in two directions. First, in societies that were not Christian, all adult males were allowed to engage in homosexual acts, provided they took what was perceived as the penetrator's role, and provided they continued to have sexual relations with women. But their passive partners were obliged to be either boys in the temporary condition of adolescence, or adult males who were permanently transvestite, with one or other of these patterns of passivity prevailing in a society. The effeminate male of Western society—the male who performed acts that were forbidden, no matter what his role in the sexual acts—was, on the other hand, a phenomenon that could be found as early as the twelfth century, when a distinctly western European culture first emerged. In the light of this presumption, I analyzed the sodomitical subculture of eighteenth-century London.[2]

In the years since my essay, a considerable literature has appeared, which I recently summarized and criticized.[3] It shows that by 1700 in the great cities of Europe with populations of 500,000

Dr. Randolph Trumbach is Professor of History, Baruch College, City University of New York, 17 Lexington Avenue, New York, NY 10010.

407

there had emerged sodomitical subcultures that differed significantly in scale and in behavior from the sodomitical networks and subcultures that had existed between 1100 and 1700 in the somewhat smaller European cities of that earlier cultural epoch. By 1700, sodomites were meeting each other in the parks and the latrines, the public arcades and taverns of London, Amsterdam, and Paris. They used verbal and gestural signals to indicate their interest in each other. Sexual acts were increasingly between two adult males rather than between an adult and an adolescent male, as had been the pattern, for instance, in Renaissance Florence.⁴ The sexually passive adult was often effeminate and sometimes transvestite. Many males, whatever their role in the sexual act, took on effeminate gestures, speech, and nicknames and were likely to compare themselves to whores. Some men were exclusively interested in men, whereas other men were married and had children. But in the public estimate, all sodomites were effeminate and exclusively interested in men. This was a belief that on both scores significantly differed from the presumptions about effeminacy and sodomy that had prevailed between 1100 and 1700.

Effeminacy had been (in the earlier culture) characteristic of both the man who sexually cared too much for women, as well as of the male who took the passive role in sexual intercourse. Sodomy had been an act of which all men were capable, given the beastliness of human nature; consequently, the sodomite was often pictured, and could be found, with his whore on one arm and his boy on the other. By 1700, however, the new image had largely replaced this old one in men's minds, if not in actual behavior.

The new image was sufficiently well accepted, and sufficiently dangerous to those who might be tainted by it, that a flourishing trade in blackmail against the known sodomite, or the apparently passive male, emerged in all the great cities. Those who policed the great cities were convinced that they faced an unparalleled problem. In England and Holland, more men were put to death for sodomy between 1700 and 1850 than in the previous six hundred years. (The policing in Paris was more diligent, but less violent.) More importantly, the men who lived in the great cities were increasingly certain that the truly masculine man could never feel sexually interested in another man. They accepted implicitly that this was a condition that was achieved, not given; they took for granted that adolescent males had to be taught this position and that adolescents were peculiarly subject to seduction by sodomites until their socialization was complete. Even the adult man whose desires were (what they would have called) natural was subject to sodomitical assault because sodomites, in their universal passivity, were likely to seek an active sexual object. Sodomitical seduction was, therefore, the act most regularly punished by the courts. Couples who were discovered engaging in mutual sodomy were also prosecuted. And sometimes (e.g., in London in 1698, 1707, 1762-27, 1763-65, 1776, 1798, and 1810), there were raids made on the taverns and other meeting places of the sodomitical subculture. By the end of the eighteenth century, however, sodomitical behavior came to be most effectively controlled by denying its existence and by severely limiting all public description or discussion of the behavior.

In this essay I wish to deal with only one of these principal points; namely, the seduction by sodomites of adolescent and adult males who either did not conceive of themselves as sodomites or who were not seen to be such by others. By doing this, I hope to show the relevance of the study of sodomy for the history of society at large. The study of these seductions reveals two things about the history of the general male population: first, a history of the stages of sexual development in males, starting at the age of ten; and secondly, a variety of male gender identities constructed around the acceptance or rejection of sodomitical acts and desires.[5]

* * *

The majority of boys who were seduced by sodomites had just reached the age of puberty. In the eighteenth century, this would have been around fifteen. One physician estimated that this was the age of menarche in girls, though he also said that many girls showed signs of it at thirteen or fourteen.[6] Aristocratic boys were often taken away from school at fifteen or sixteen because puberty had begun. One mother referred to her fifteen-year-old son as being at "his dangerous time of life." Schoolmasters agreed. William Gilpin, for instance, was inclined to refuse to educate boys after they had come to what he called "the age of right and wrong." Fifteen was the age when many boys started to run after whores,[7] and it was from such considerations perhaps that the lawyers declared the age of sexual consent for boys to be fourteen, after which a boy's sexual passivity in sodomy made him as equally guilty as his active partner.[8]

But then, a sixteen-year-old boy could still be remarkably innocent. When Richard Branson attempted to seduce James Fasset, he began, after the usual offer of a drink, by trying to excite the boy with sexually charged conversation. He "asked me," Fasset said, "if I never got any girls, or if I never f[ucke]d them." The boy replied no, that he "was not old enough and had no such thoughts." Branson then tried, without success, to put his hand into the boy's breeches. So he kissed him instead, putting his tongue into his mouth and sucking his lips. This the boy allowed, but kept a firm grip on the waistband of his breeches. Branson meanwhile turned from whores to masturbation, and asked Fasset if "I never frigged myself; to which I answered, No." But the boy did not really understand the question; when Branson asked about frigging a second time, he said "I did not know what it meant." Whereupon Branson offered "if I would go back, he would learn me." But Fasset would not. Apparently excited by this innocence, by the boy's sober, quiet ways (his headmaster said he was the most orderly boy in his college), and by what Branson told the boy were his soft, warm hands, Branson then "asked me if I had my maidenhead." Knowing the answer by now, he continued that "if I had, he should be very glad to take it from me, but supposed I saved it for a young woman." The thought of violating innocence was too much to leave alone, however, and so Branson asked again, "if he should ravish me? I answered no. He said he would not against my will."[9]

Branson was found guilty, though matters never went further. The Methodist preacher Charles Bradbury, on the other hand, was acquitted of the charge of sodomizing fourteen-year-old James Hearne, even though he had probably used the boy's innocence and his own authority, first to seduce the boy, and then to force from him in court a recantation of his evidence. Hearne was a Roman Catholic who had only recently come from France in 1755. He went with a fellow apprentice to hear the Methodist preacher in Glover's Hall in Beech Lane. After Bradbury had gotten rid of the rest of his congregation at about nine o'clock in the evening, he took the boy on his knee, kissed him, put his hand into the boy's torn breeches, got up, put out the candle, and then "unbuttoned his breeches and bid me play with his y[ar]d." The boy grew worried that his master would scold him for being late, but the preacher assured him that he would find him another place. Eventually, the boy told his master that he did not like the trade. The preacher first found him a lodging, where he spent the night with the boy, and "first tried with his finger to enter my body, then he tried with his y[ar]d, and did enter as far as he could, and his s[eed] came from him." This occurred four or five more times. Bradbury took to paying the boy's expenses and eventually moved him into the house where he lodged himself.

Then, Bradbury tempted fate and preached a sermon against Sodom and Gomorrah. After hearing the sermon, the boy began having qualms of conscience. The minister had already been observed, by a woman in the congregation, to kiss another boy, Billy Cook, a little too fondly. (Cook and the first boy, Hearne, had in fact been involved together with the preacher.) Hearne collapsed and told Mrs. Whittaker everything after she observed that the way Hearne kissed a baby in her house was "the way Mr. Bradbury kisses Billy Cook." The minister made various attempts to have the boy retract his statement: he accused him of theft, reminded him that his father had disowned him for changing his religion, got him to sign a recantation, and sent him for a month to France. Nonetheless, upon his return, Hearne pressed charges, but only to break down weeping at the trial, declaring that Bradbury was innocent and saying that "he wished he had never been born, and was sorry he had charged a person who had been his best friend." (Best friend was what sons called fathers.) Bradbury was acquitted.

It is evident that the court had some difficulty in crediting the boy's sexual innocence. He was asked whether he did everything that Bradbury bade him do. He answered yes. He was asked whether he did not know these things were wrong. He answered that as it came from a minister, he did not. So, he was asked his age and replied that the had just turned fifteen, and, further, that he would not have thought these matters a sin with anyone else. Then, the questioning turned to his religious background. His father was a papist, but Hearne had not received much instruction in the principles of religion. He had heard prayers read, had been at confession and at mass, yet he still had not known that sodomy was a crime. It was, in fact, only Bradbury's own sermon that had brought him to that belief, because he had never heard the papist priests talk of sodomy, nor had he read about it in any book.

The tack of the questioning then changed. Why had he gone to bed with Bradbury? "Because I was afraid of him, and I had no other friend but him in the world to stand by me." Did they talk about the acts? "He asked me whether I could bear it . . . I did." Bradbury also asked whether the boy had done the same with anyone else, and told him not to speak about it to anyone. That a fifteen-year-old boy in England should have been so innocent before Bradbury's sermon was evidently difficult to believe, but the boy had lived in England for only a year. True, he had been good friends with his fellow apprentice. But when he was asked, "Did you never talk about mollies?" he replied, "No."[10]

The seductions described in the two cases above were of boys who had just reached puberty, and were seductions founded on the attempt, at least, of forging a romantic relationship. In addition, there was another pattern in which a man intimidated a group of boys into having sexual encounters with him over some length of time. These boys were usually, by eighteenth-century standards, prepubescent. The first case involved Michael Levi, a young man esteemed by his fellow Jews as a virtuous and sober fellow, religious and observant of the sabbath.

Levi lived in Holborn and had a stall under an alehouse called the Baptist's Head. As he shut up his stall one night, he asked Benjamin Taylor, a twelve-year-old and the son of a tailor who lived forty yards away, to help him carry his boxes up to the room he had in the alehouse. Once they were in the room, Levi locked the door, unbuttoned the boy's breeches, threw him face down on the bed, and entered the boy. This went on for a quarter of an hour, the boy crying out in pain. The boy later told one of his playfellows what had happened; that boy told his father, who told another boy's father, who in turn told the injured boy's father. Taylor's father spoke to his son, telling him not to be ashamed or afraid to tell the truth. This all took a week.

Soon, the other boys started to come forward. A fourteen-year-old school fellow of Taylor's, Thomas Lambard, said that the same thing had happened to him two months before. He seems to have had no understanding of semen, though, because "when he got up he thought the prisoner had pissed on him." (Girls in rape cases in the Sessions Paper sometimes used the same expression to describe what had happened to them. Similarly, a thirteen-year-old boy testified to a naval court martial in 1706 that after James Bell had "put his cock in his arse, he wriggled about and pissed in his arse."[11]) A third, boy, Samuel Tidmarsh, thirteen, had, according to his father, been treated in the same way a year before. When questioned, Benjamin Taylor said that he had not spoken before because he was ashamed to, but that he thought at the time that what Levi was doing was wrong.[12]

In a second case, Isaac Broderick was accused of assaulting the boys who attended the school he taught for the Coopers' Company. Broderick had been educated at Trinity College and had a reputation for being pious and regular. But within a fortnight of being in the school, he sent eleven-year-old William Han upstairs, lowered the boy's breeches, and put his member between his thighs. William claimed that Broderick also did the same to four other boys. William's father usually questioned him about his day at school, and at first took William's dislike of the master to mean that he had been whipped. After the boy's mother examined him, the story came out. Edward Calley, who was ten, said that the master took down his breeches and "felt all about my body, gave me a gentle stroke or two, and bid me not cry out, he would not hurt me." Calley told his bedfellow but not his grandfather, fearing that if word of his disclosure got back to the schoolmaster, the schoolmaster would beat him. When his grandfather finally questioned him, Calley knew how to categorize his master's behavior: "the boy replied his master had served him as the two men had served one another that stood in the pillory."[13]

At this point, we might pause and ask whether it is appropriate to distinguish (as I have done) the first two cases from the last two. Was sixteen-year-old James Fassett, who did not know what frigging was, any different from fourteen-year-old Thomas Lambard, who did not know the difference between urine and semen? How could fifteen-year-old Thomas Hearne say that he saw nothing wrong with what he had done with the minister, but twelve-year-old Benjamin Taylor say that he knew that what Michael Levi had done to him was wrong? And how could Hearne say that he had never talked with other boys about mollies, but ten-year-old Edward Calley be able to say that his master had done to him what the two men who had stood in the pillory had done to each other? There are a number of possible answers to these questions.

A boy's sexual knowledge must have varied considerably according to how familiar he was with the sexual life of the London streets, and the degree to which he was a participant in a circle of peers. The latter point was especially relevant to masturbation. Men confessed to the author of the *Onania* that they had started the practice anywhere from eleven to seventeen. Some had learnt it on their own; some had started before they could ejaculate. But the majority claimed to have begun around fourteen or fifteen, and usually in a circle of friends.[14] Consequently, it is very likely that a sodomitical approach to a ten-year-old, and to a fifteen-year-old, raised very different questions in each boy's mind. It probably had a much greater effect on Thomas Hearne (even without the complication of his filial feelings toward the man) when he placed his actions with the Methodist preacher into the category of sodomy, than it did on Edward Calley when he made his casual, and probably not very thoughtful, comparison between his master and the sodomites in the pillory (however much the act may have reinforced his feelings of shame).

Moreover, the men who approached the boys in the first two cases were probably motivated by somewhat different feelings than the men in the second two cases. The two men who had used varying degrees of force against the boys in their circle probably did not individuate the boys to any great degree. Nor, perhaps, were they overly aware of the gender of the boys, just as individuals who are attracted to prepubescent children in the twentieth century (when the heterosexual-homosexual distinction has been fully developed) often do not distinguish between male and female in their sexual objects.[15] Presumably, however, a boy who is not sexually approached because he is a boy undergoes a different experience than a boy who is sought out because of his emerging masculinity. The eighteenth-century cases were complicated by the probable continued existence of the older pattern in which, in sexual terms, boys were thought of as equivalent to women.

This was what the men on board eighteenth-century naval vessels who seduced boys continued to do. These prepubescent boys, most of whom were twelve or thirteen according to Gilbert, were transformed into women. Charles Ferret testified that when he was awakened by the noise of the sexual exertions of Henry Newton on Thomas Finney's body, "[I] put my left hand up and got hold of both his stones fast, the other part was in the body of the boy, I asked him what he had got there, he said cunt, then I said you are worse then any beast walking in the fields."[16] The London public probably would have agreed wholeheartedly and made short shrift of these distinctions, seeing all four cases as sodomitic attacks — an evil which had to be stopped. But as Crown counsel said of Richard Branson, "had he prevailed with this lad, now sixteen years old, to commit this horrid and most destable crime, he would have infected all the others; and as in the course of years they grew big enough, they could leave the college to go into the world and spread this cursed poison."[17] What happened to a boy as he entered fully into sexual life at puberty was more important than what had occurred before. The danger lay in the fact that adolescent males of fourteen, fifteen, and sixteen, were still malleable as to their sexual direction.

By the age of seventeen (when a boy, if he was going to masturbate, had begun to do so) a boy's sexual orientation was probably set. He might still allow a man to treat him, flirt with him, and perhaps even have some sexual contact with him. But if the man attempted to continue the relationship, the boy would eventually turn on him. On the other hand, some boys were probably happy to be seduced because their desires lay basically in a sodomitical direction. Some evidence even suggests that effeminate adolescents were sometimes identified as future sodomites. They were sometimes used by men who did not identify themselves as sodomites and who were likely to brush aside a boy's objections. Such contacts were usually made either in the streets at night or in a shared bed.

First, let us go into the streets at night. Richard Spencer invited seventeen-year-old William Taylor to have a drink and talk over some of the affairs of his master. After the first drink, Spencer asked Taylor how big his cock was. He did not reply. Spencer held out his little finger and asked if it was as big as that, and then pulled out his own cock and asked the boy to lie on his side. When Taylor would not, "he said he would f[uc]k me that night." He then asked the boy what county he came from, and when he replied Hereford- shire, Spencer kissed him several times and said that he would take the boy there "in a coach, and make you drunk as an owl and all the way you go." (Traveling by coach, and indeed, having sex in a carriage, could be a highly charged sexual suggestion.) Later, when the second pint of drink was brought in, the boy went out and brought back a constable. The constable called Spencer a "black- guard old rascal for making such an attempt on a boy," and threw him out of the tavern. However, such a reprimand for Spencer was not enough for the deeply offended Taylor, who said "I did not think he had punishment enough, ran after him, and with assistance brought him back again, and gave the constable charge of him, and he was committed."[19]

In another instance, John Holloway met Henry Wolf while he was on an errand for his master and asked Wolf for directions. Wolf took him around the waist, tickled him, and offered him a drink. As they drank, Wolf put his hand under the table and into the boy's breeches, but stopped when the maid noticed. He then took the boy into a bye-alley, but there they were interrupted by a passer-by and ran away. He then offered the boy a pint of wine to keep silent and bought him a nosegay and a penny custard. As they passed Bedlam, he pulled the boy in to see the mad folks. Shortly after that, he took him into the necessary house (or toilet), pulled down both their breeches, and fellated the boy. He told the boy he hoped to see him often and came to his master's house several times. They arranged to meet on Sunday, at which time the boy brought three of his friends along. Wolf gave the boys the slip in the Posthouse Fields and looked unsuccessfully for a place where no one else would disturb them. But the three boys returned. Wolf suddenly became suspicious and dashed away, with the four boys in pursuit. A young man asked what was the matter, and they said "there was a sodom- ite." The young man caught Wolf, Holloway went for the constable and Wolf was taken to the justice.[20]

The third boy, John Meeson, was much more willing than the

boys in the other two instances. John Dicks met him as he stood in the churchyard watching them lay the first stone for St. Martin's Church and repeatedly invited him to have a drink. The boy reported that after he became fuddled at the first alehouse they went to, Dicks kissed him, put his hand into his breeches, and put the boy's hand into his own breeches. They then went to a cellar in the Strand. At that point, the boy told Dicks that he had to deliver some goods in Fleet Street but that he would return if Dicks waited for him.

When the boy returned, they went to two other alehouses looking for a more private location. Dicks settled for an apartment at the Golden Ball near Fetter Lane. Meeson later said that at this point he was drunk, vomited, and then lay down to sleep. Dicks unbuttoned his breeches, turned him on his face, and tried to enter his body, though (no doubt to save his honor) he declared that whether Dicks had entered him or not "I was not sensible enough to know." Three people on the other side of the thin partition — a man, a woman, and the alehouse boy — had no doubt themselves. They heard Dicks kiss the boy, call him his dear, his jewel, and his precious little rogue, and saw him "withdraw his yard from the boy's fundament" after making the usual humping movements. When Dicks was about to enter the boy a second time, the woman cried out that she could "look no longer — I am ready to swoon — He'll ruin the boy." They rushed in and seized Dicks as he lay on the boy's backside.[21]

The boy in our first example was offended by lewd talk and a few kisses. The second boy was willing to be shown a good time and to be fellated — once. This third boy, however, liked the initial flirtation enough to return for more, and once drunk enough, he was willing to be sodomized.

It would be interesting to know whether the third boy became an adult sodomite. In the four cases of bedfellow seduction, it is clear that one became a confirmed sodomite, that two others were probably effeminate boys who had begun at an early age to enact (probably without full realization) their sexual orientation, but that in the fourth case, the two young men seduced stoutly resisted.

William Curtis came to London in 1728 and went to live as a servant with a printer in the Old Bailey. Six months later, John Ashford, also a printer, came to live in the same house. He shared a bed with Curtis, who by then must have been about seventeen. According to Curtis, within a month Ashford began kissing him, calling him his dear Billy, fondling his privates, and giving him money to keep quiet about it all. Ashford promised to make Curtis his heir to a small estate and to cut off his own brother. After three months, "he over-persuaded me" (the same word that John Meeson, the boy who got drunk and then was sodomized, used to describe his reaction to John Dicks) "to let him bugger me," which he proceeded to do frequently. Curtis left the house when he became acquainted with other sodomites whom he eventually denounced to the magistrate. He said that he would also have denounced Ashford at that time, but was paid not to do so. Curtis had probably become (in the years of the fiercest attacks against the London sodomitical world) one of those sodomites mentioned by James Dalton who blackmailed their own friends.[22]

Thomas Pryor, who was apprenticed to a currier near Leicester Fields, buggered his master's servant, William Porter. Porter insisted that he had not consented, but his questioning was clearly aimed to show that he had not resisted as he might have. "I bid him not do it," Porter said, "I did not bid him do it, he did it of his own self. He did do it indeed. He did put it in." But still, he was asked, "Did you not strive to hinder him?" "No, Sir." "So you was as willing as he?" "No, I was not." "Why did you not endeavour to hinder him?" "He would do it." "Then you let him do what he would?" "I did not bid him do it." Surely, the aim of these questions was to establish Porter's receptive passivity in the face of his probable effeminacy — there was perhaps also a certain shrillness to his speech. His master and mistress had in fact heard the bed creaking in which the two men lay together. The wife had gone to investigate and she had stopped the noise, but she did not come to the trial. Only her husband came, and he had not seen anything. The master said that his accused apprentice had been a good worker until "he got acquainted with a gang of young wenches." And so with Pryor's liking for girls established, and Porter's effeminacy taunted, the jury acquitted Pryor of the sodomy he had very probably committed on the unwilling Porter.[23]

Joseph Churchill and Charles Horn (who was twenty) were both apprenticed to a watchmaker in East Smithfield and were accus-

apprenticed to a watchmaker in East Smithfield and were accustomed to sharing the same bed. They quarreled one night. Horn
would not let Churchill into their bed, and so he was forced to share
a bed with two Portuguese sailors. One of them, Emmanual Rose,
buggered Churchill in the night. The boy said he cried out to Horn
that Rose "will ruin me if you do not come to help me out." (The
woman witness in the alehouse scene had described what Dicks did
to Meeson with the same word—ruin.) But Horn ignored his cries.
The boy eventually told his mother, and by this means the matter
came to court. Here, as in the previous case, the court felt that the
boy had deserved his treatment because of his effeminacy. John
Basset, the master, described Churchill as a "very silly empty
boy," and said that the other apprentice, Horn, whom he called "a
good civil lad enough," had complained that he did not care to
sleep with Churchill because he was always hugging and kissing
him. (One man's kissing another, after all, had become a sign of
sodomitical inclinations.) Churchill had also once said to Horn,
"you are very rankey, it is a wonder you do not love me as old Bell
did," and then taken hold of the other's private parts. (Horn denied
this last gesture—it was perhaps too compromising to admit.) Churchill also hung over Horn in the kitchen and insisted on kissing him
until the other knocked his head away. After such testimony, the
jury acquitted the sailor. This was a world where men who would
themselves have started away at the touch of a sodomite were prepared to accept the sodomitical abuse of an effeminate young man
by men whose interest in women had been vouched for. Pryor, in
the previous example, had gone with wenches; Rose, in this one,
was said to have a venereal disease "because he cannot go to the
whores our way but what he must get it immediately."[24]

Unlike the previous three, in the last case of bedfellow seduction
it was the active partner who was the confirmed or suspected sodomite. George Duffus met both Nicholas Leader and Mr. Powell at
sermons on a Sunday evening and had religious discussions with
them afterwards and on several other occasions. In both cases, the
discussion having continued very late into the evening, Duffus
asked to share a bed for the night. Once they were in bed, he made
his advances. In Leader's case, Duffus first hugged and kissed him,
called him his dear, and when asked what he meant, answered,

"No harm, nothing but love." He tried several times to get on top of the other, and eventually seized him by the throat, turned him over, and entered him briefly. But the continued struggle caused Duffus to ejaculate in his own hand, which he then wiped on the tail of Leader's nightshirt, telling him "now you have it." Leader said he allowed Duffus to stay the rest of the night so as not to disturb his sleeping grandmother, and that the following morning Duffus told him "that I need not be concerned at what he had done to me, for he had done the same to several others, and named in particular, a cabin-boy."

Duffus's approach in bed with Powell was similar. He told him that his wife was out of town and asked to stay. In bed, he began to kiss Powell. He took hold of his privates and said, "How lean you be. Do but feel how fat I am," but Powell would not touch him. When Powell turned away, Duffus got on him, held him down, put his penis between his thighs, and ejaculated. He then offered the same sort of moral reassurances that he had made to Leader, that Powell "need not be troubled or wonder at what he had done, for it was very common, and he had often practiced it with others." But Powell, after refusing an offer of reciprocation, said that he "was a stranger to all such practices," and that if he "had known what sort of man he had been, I would never have lain in the same bed with him."[25]

Duffus was a pious, self-confident, aggressive, married man who was evidently accustomed to getting his way with the pious young men with whom he had established his moral authority and whose scruples he was certain he could calm. He might have had to use a little force initially, but eventually he expected to succeed. He had, presumably, succeeded in the past, but in these two instances he had, unfortunately for him, misjudged the moral pliability of his companions. For Duffus, sodomy was a thing to which any man might be brought. It was no sin, but an act of love. Yet it seems unlikely that Duffus was tied to the traditional libertine culture that had allowed Pryor and Rose to sodomize the boys with whom they shared a bed. Duffus's kissing and his offer of reciprocal sex probably made him a modern sodomite, even though he met his friends in a meeting house and not in a molly-house. In contrast, Powell must have felt that a man who would do such a thing at all was a different kind of man than himself.

If, however, Duffus was in fact a new sodomite rather than an old libertine writ large, he did not live up to expectations in two regards. He was not effeminate; Powell had not been able to tell in advance what kind of man he was. And he was not sexually exclusive; his wife was out of town. One thing, however, was certain about Duffus. He was very religious, like a number of other individuals in these examples, including John Dicks who, though he might bugger John Meeson on the alehouse bench, at his trial "often turned up the whites of his eyes in a very devout manner." Such a characteristic has often been noticed in the twentieth-century sexual deviant: the devout Catholic father who cruises the highway toilet, the religious husband who thinks sex with his daughter is preferable to adultery. This "breastplate of righteousness" protects an individual from his own negative judgment of himself, as well as from the judgment of others. Or else, an individual committed to a rigid moral system says to himself that once one rule is broken, none of the rules apply.[26] In which case, for instance, if Duffus found himself adulterous, why not be sodomitical as well. Yet there is a further possibility; namely, that Duffus, as a man accustomed to religious discussion, formed an independent conscience for himself and thus found sodomy "no harm, nothing but love."

All of this material on sexual behavior, role, and consciousness can be sorted into four different stages, according to age, and then into at least three major late-adolescent sexual orientations or roles and three or four major adult roles. First, one might distinguish three adolescent stages: prepubescent boys between ten and fourteen, early pubertal boys between fourteen and seventeen, and settled adolescent boys of seventeen to twenty. Adult males over twenty are put into a single category because the material for men does not come so highly discriminated according to age. (It is likely, however, that there were differences because in the twentieth-century the heterosexual-homosexual distinction seems to be more important to men in their twenties, for example, than to men in their fifties.)

In the prepubescent stage, boys might or might not have known of the sexual role of the sodomite or the molly. Even if they did, it could not have played much of a role in the lives of boys who did not understand what masturbation or semen were. Early pubertal boys were likely to have had active discussions among themselves of what mollies were and likely to have heard adults express their disapproval of the role in conversation and in sermons. Once masturbation had begun, however, the desire for sexual experience sometimes outweighed the fear of the molly's role. Settled adolescent boys seem to have sorted themselves out into three types: (1) boys who could not tolerate being touched by another man; (2) boys who could enjoy an occasional encounter with a man, but who would resist any continuation of the activity which might threaten their assignment to a deviant role; and (3) effeminate boys who, according to both sodomitical and nonsodomitical men (even though, sometimes not yet in the boys' minds) seemed to display signs of sodomitical desire.

It is also useful to think of adult men as having fallen into three, or perhaps four, groups. First were the men attracted to prepubescent boys who were probably indifferent to the gender of the boys. Rather, they were attracted to boys because men could easily control them. Second were the traditional libertines, interested in both women and boys, who were prepared to have sex with boys who were prepubescent or pubertal, provided that either their bodies (in the very young) or their effeminacy (in those who were older) made it possible to categorize them as feminine. Age for these men was not as important as gender transformation—and the question of who was available in one's bed. Third were the men attracted to early or late adolescent boys (and mainly the latter) whose desire for either a reciprocal relationship, expressed in kissing[27] or mutual sodomy, or for a passive role through fellatio or sodomy, branded them (despite their sometimes being married) as sodomites. These men excluded women from their desires and were seen as effeminate in their behavior. Finally, there were the men who were not conscious of desiring boys of any age or behavior, and who were profoundly upset by men who did, even one suspects, if such men were traditional libertines. The libertine was, in the eighteenth century, a dying breed. The other three were new, and increasingly divided the world among themselves.

The sodomite, however, desired not only the adolescent and his fellow sodomite, but also his fellow adult nonsodomitical male. Therefore, we must also consider the seduction of this category of males. In most of the complaints made to the magistrate concerning attempted sodomitical seduction (or assault, as it was called), it is not possible to tell which were made by late adolescents and which by adult males. (It is easier to spot those made on the behalf of younger boys.) These complaints make up the overwhelming bulk of the manuscript materials in the quarter-sessions' rolls. The printed material deals much more with adolescent seduction and raids on the molly houses, presumably because such cases were more likely to sell and were more likely to come to trial at the Old Bailey, rather than being made up, dismissed, or tried at petty sessions, as most attempted seductions of adults were. As described in the small percentage of cases where more information is given than who is charged by whom, such attempted seductions usually took the form of obvious lunges made at another man's privates while drinking in a public house, though they were also made in a public latrine or in the street. Sometimes more than a lunge was made and the encounters lasted for some time, implying a degree of initial interested consent, which later changed to anger or alarm. Even after charges had been made, they were sometimes withdrawn in instances involving drinking companions. In 1788, William Green charged that Thomas Impey had attempted an unnatural crime while they were drinking together. The next day, however, Green refused to maintain his charge, saying that he had been drunk and could not recall the matter. The magistrate had no choice but to discharge Impey. He fined Green five shillings for being drunk by his own confession. Similarly, Peter Campbell charged that Francis Philpott had touched him several times in Catherine Street and unbuttoned his breeches in Fleet Market. Because they had then agreed to go together to have a drink in a public house in Fleet Street, the magistrate dismissed the matter.[28]

The aggressive sexual acts of sodomites against other men took two forms across the century. Either the sodomite pushed his hand into the other man's breeches and took hold of his privates, or he took out his own penis and put it into the other man's hand. Either action might occur in the street or in a public house and be accompanied by kisses or enticing words. In 1704, Humphrey Bower said that William Gage met him in the street, touched him, and affectionately invited him to have a drink in a shop near Charing Cross. Gage, "being willing to see what his meaning was," went along.

When they were seated in an inner room, Gage put his hand into Bower's codpiece and "used all the enticing actions he could." After they left the house and were in the street again, "Gage drew his yard privately and put it into Mr. Bower's . . . hands." In the same year, John Hodges and Henry Turner met Thomas Turner in the street at one o'clock in the morning. Thomas Turner claimed that Henry Turner had assaulted him. The other two said that Thomas Turner had put his privates into the hands of John Hughes and tried to persuade Hughes to bugger him.[29] In 1726, Thomas Coleman put his privates into the hand of Richard Hudson. Another man did the same thing to Bartholomew Cornell in 1727, and nearly fifty years later, Godfrey Walley made the same complaint of John Batten.[30]

Three men complained together that Samuel Dassell put his hand into their breeches in 1707. In 1727, William Saise unbuttoned the breeches of Thomas Batterton, took hold of his privates, and asked him several times to lie with him. In the same year, Thomas Beach did exactly the same things to William Gibson.[31] In another part of town, also in 1727, John Harvey forced his hand into the breeches of Isaac Hughes, took hold of his privates, kissed him, and asked him to lie with him. Thomas Chamberlaine also kissed Edward Radvell, putting his tongue in his mouth, but in this case, Chamberlaine made the other take hold of his privates. William Davenport was more explicit in his acting out: when he took hold of John Marshall's privates, he also put his bare backside into Marshall's lap. Fifty years later, men were still thrusting their hands into other men's breeches, as John Weston did to Robert Amstrong.[32]

The enticing words that usually accompanied these aggressive actions, as well as the occasional kisses,[33] show the vulnerability of the initiators of these scenes. Other sodomites used a different kind of force to fulfill their desires. William Oliver forced William Siddall down on the ground, shoved his hand into his breeches, and pulled out his privates. John Blair went further. He met Samuel Beakley at two o'clock in the morning in Sudney's Alley and then violently beat him when he refused "to submit to his sodomitical practices."

In one contrasting instance, extreme force in a sodomitical assault was probably used not by a sodomite against a man who was not a sodomite, but by a group of whores and libertines against a sodomite. Here, Richard Renale, Robert Welch, and William Mott, with the help of Susannah Nutley and Susan Cooks, violently attempted to bugger Thomas Lile.[34] In other words, the aggressive sexual overture was not limited to sodomites, but was an ordinary part of the sexual life of the streets and alehouses. The rolls from which most of these examples have come include a far greater number of reports involving prostitutes who came up to men and thrust a hand into their breeches as a means of enticing their prospective customers, as well as the names of many men who thrust a hand down women's bosoms or up their skirts, or who even took out their private members and laid it in women's hands.

What is interesting in the approaches of sodomites to men who were not is that they occurred in places where access was not limited to sodomites. We must therefore presume either that all these assaults were made by men who were trying such a thing for the first time (which in some cases may have been so), or that these seductions were attempted because such initiatives had in the past succeeded with some adult men who were not thought to be sodomites either by themselves or by their male partners. The boundaries between the sodomitical world and its opposite (for which there is no convenient name) was, in other words, not yet so finely drawn as it came to be in the two subsequent centuries. It ought also to be noticed that the men who brought these charges of assault still felt free enough to bring them. They had not come to feel, as Polly Morris plausibly suggests they did, that they would be compromised even by admitting they had been found appealing by a sodomite. But finally, one must recall that in a given year, only four or five men at most[36] made these charges in a city with a population of from five-hundred thousand to a million.

The end result of these developments was that, by 1800, the male world was divided into three groups: the sodomite, the adolescent, and the adult male. The sodomite might try to seduce the adolescent still, as the traditional libertine had long done. But the new effeminate eighteenth-century adult sodomite was also interested in adult men, and was, therefore, that much more dangerous than the old libertine. In Europe, sodomy itself was as illegal as it had always been, but its enactment had changed from one of the world-wide patterns to the other: from the passive adolescent male, to the permanently effeminate passive adult male. This demonstrates the difficulty all human societies have of conceptualizing sexual behavior outside of male-female roles.[37] Sodomy also probably provided a new focus for irrational anxieties in a society that had more or less ceased to believe in witches. The sodomite, therefore, had to be kept at bay in order to protect adults and adolescents from his advances. Consequently, by around 1810, the London House of Correction was providing separate galleries for sodomites, apprentices, and soldiers, so that under the conditions of a modern total institution (where in the twentieth-century the homosexual-heterosexual distinction cannot be maintained) the sexual distinctions of the modern world might be kept secure. Unfortunately, isolating the imprisoned sodomite did not take away the need for human consolation, and it was found that one boy, Robert Jones became venereally infected because he had "almost constantly slept" with another young man named Joseph Bowyer.[38]

NOTES

1. Mary McIntosh, "The Homosexual Role," *Social Problems* 16 (1968): 182-92.

2. Randolph Trumbach, "London's Sodomites: Homosexual Behavior and Western Culture in the Eighteenth Century," *Journal of Social History* 11 (1977): 1-33.

3. "Sodomitical Subcultures, Sodomitical Roles, and the Gender Revolution of the Eighteenth Century: The Recent Historiography," *Eighteenth-Century Life* 9 (1985): 109-21; reprinted in *'Tis Nature's Fault. Unauthorized Sexuality During the Enlightenment*, ed. R. P. MacCubbin (Cambridge: Cambridge University Press, 1987).

4. Michael J. Roche, " 'They have lost all shame': San Bernadino on Sodomites in Fifteenth-Century Florence," *Journal of Homosexuality* 15(3/4).

5. I have previously tried to sketch something of this theme in my *The Rise of the Egalitarian Family* (New York, 1978), 281-84, and in "Kinship and Marriage in Early Modern France and England," *Annals of Scholarship* 2 (1981): 113-28. Antony Simpson, "Masculinity and Control in Eighteenth-Century London" (Ph.D. diss., New York University, 1984) is, in a sense, concerned with a similar question but in a different way. Certain abbreviations are used in the following notes: Greater London Record Office (GLRO); Corporation of London Record Office (CLRO); *Proceedings in the Old Bailey* (SP); Session, Roll (SR); *Select Trials* (*Select Trials at . . . the Old Bailey* [London, 1742], 4 vols.; in vol. 21, pts.

1 and 2, *Select Trials*, ed. R. Trumbach, Garland reprint (New York: Garland, 1985).

6. William Brodum, *A Guide to Old Age* (London, 1795), 2 vols., 2: 69-70.

7. Randolph Trumbach, *Egalitarian Family*, 259-62, 280. I was not fully aware that what was being described in this material was the onset of puberty.

8. E. H. East, *A Treatise of the Pleas of the Crown*, 2 vols. (London, 1803), 1:480, cited by Simpson, "Masculinity and Control," 429.

9. *The Trial of Richard Branson for an Attempt to Commit Sodomy on the Body of James Fasset* (London, 1760), 5-10; in vol. 24, *Sodomy Trials*, ed. R. Trumbach, Garland reprint (New York: Garland, 1986).

10. SP, no. 7, pt. 3 (1755), 317-23.

11. Arthur N. Gilbert, "Buggery and the British Navy," *Journal of Social History* 10 (1976): 76; and another example of the same response by a boy, 96, n. 83.

12. SP, no. 5, pt. 2 (1751), 186-88.

13. Ibid., no. 5 (1730), 10-13. In a third case, James Johnson enticed the neighborhood boys into his father's house, threw them down on the kitchen chairs or the bed, and "put his cock" in their "fundaments." One ten-year-old boy was assaulted twice. Another boy escaped twice by crying out. But a third boy, who as he was eighteen was hardly a boy in the same sense, was successfully assaulted on the kitchen chairs. (GLRO: MJ/SP/April 1707, no. 66.) Simpson says that in only four of the seventy-one prosecutions for sodomy at the Old Bailey between 1730 and 1830, were boys younger than fourteen involved—in 1742, 1757, 1772, and 1778 ("Masculinity and Control," 429, n. 8; 828-29). He does not, however, seem to have counted the 1751 case. Considering ages of some of the boys in the last two cases discussed, one finds it curious that in 1757 William Williams was acquitted because twelve-year-old Thomas Smith did not understand the nature of an oath, and so was unable to testify (SP, no. 6, pt. 2 (1757), 262).

14. *Onania* (London, 1723), 34, 37, 41, 47, 48, 60, 64, 149, 108, 159, 173; *A Supplement to the Onania*, 58, 83, 87, 90, 96, 100, 113, 123, 127, 139, 152; both in *Masturbation* vol. 12, ed. R. Trumbach, Garland reprint (New York: Garland, 1985).

15. Jean Renvoize, *Incest* (London: Routledge and Kegan Paul, 1982), 3, 30, *et passim*.

16. Gilbert, "Buggery and the British Navy," 74-75.

17. *Trial of Richard Branson*, 24-25.

18. Some additional cases of boys this age: (1) in 1726, Charles Kennet assaulted fifteen-year-old Isaac Kelson, kissing and hugging him and forcing him into several dark alleys (CLRO: SR (August, 1726), Recogs. 23, 29); (2) in 1729, John Wynn, the fourteen-year-old son of a laborer, was assaulted by Henry Hambleton, a perriwigmaker (GLRO: MJ/SR/2513: New Prison List, Bond of John Wynn; MJ/SR/2514, indictments 17, 82); (3) in 1737, Claudius De Magnay put his hand into the breeches of George Smart and Francis Batty, rubbed their breasts, arms, knees, and thighs, gave them plum cake and pudding, wrote out his address, invited them to come and lie with him, and asked them to let him into

their master's house between midnight and one o'clock when the rest of the family was in bed (GLRO: MJ/SR/2679, Recog. 28); (4) in 1765, James Trevor assaulted the young son of John Clark (GLRO: MJ/SR/3167, Recog. 3167); (5) in 1723, Charles Banner, a schoolmaster, was accused of trying to pick up fifteen-year-old Nicholas Burgess in the street at night, the boy and his father unsuccessfully attempted to entrap Banner, and the parents of his pupils came to his defense (*Select Trials*, 1:329-30); (6) Henry Lloyd was probably of the same age — he sang in St. James' Chapel — when James Williams tried to seduce him (SP [7-14 December 1726], 6).

19. SP, no. 6 (5-10 July 1749), 127-28.

20. SP, no. 5 (1735), 82.

21. *Select Trials*, 1:158-60, Captain Rigby's attempt to seduce the nineteen-year-old John Minton, is, of course, part of this history (*A Compleat Collection of Remarkable Tryals*, 2 vols. (London, 1718), 1:236-42).

22. SP, no. 7 pt. 2 (1732), 217: The jury acquitted Ashford; James Dalton, *A Genuine Narrative* (London, 1728), 31-43.

23. SP, no. 1 (1742), 17-18.

24. SP, no. 3, pt. 2 (1760), 121-23.

25. *Select Trials*, 1:105-108. Thomas Chamberlain was another young man approached by a sodomitical bedfellow (SP [30-31 August, 1 September 1727] 6).

26. Ibid., 1:160 Laud Humphreys, *Tearoom Trade* (Chicago: Aldine, 1970); Revoize, *Incest*.

27. Kissing and caressing were understood to transform and make sodomitical acts on board Dutch ships much worse; see Jan Oosterhoff, "Sodomy at Sea and at the Cape of Good Hope During the Eighteenth Century," *Journal of Homosexuality* 15(3/4). In England, kissing between men became an important sign of sodomitical affections and effeminacy. Englishmen in the late seventeenth and the early eighteenth century had kissed each other in greeting, but as the century wore on, Continental visitors had to be warned that mutual male kissing had a different meaning in England. Even kissing between two brothers, and between two women, came to be frowned on. (See: *Satan's Harvest Home* (London, 1749), 51-54; in vol. 20, ed. R. Trumbach, Garland reprint (New York; Garland, 1985); Louis Crompton, *Bryon and Greek Love* (Berkeley, CA: University of California Press, 1985), 295, 295-96, n. 26; Antony Simpson, "Masculinity and Control" (Ph.D. diss., New York University, 1984), 742-43).

28. CLRO: Guildhall Justice Room Book, Notebook 37 (9 August 1788), Notebook 29 (12 January 1785).

29. GLRO: MJ/SR/2032, Recog. 72; CLRO: SR (September 1704), Recogs. 30, 31.

30. CLRO: SR (August 1726) Poultry Compter List; SR (July 1727) Poultry Compter Kalendar; GLRO: MJ/SR, 3266, Recog. 256.

31. CLRO: SR (October 1707) Newgate Calendar; SR (May 1727), Recog. 12, and Poultry Compter List; SR (July 1727), Wood Street Compter Kalendar.

32. One of the objections to kissing was that when used as a form of greeting,

it allowed "vile catamites" to "make their preposterous address even in the very streets" (*Satan's Harvest Home*, 52).

33. GLRO: MJ/SR/2481, New Prison List, MJ/SR/2483, Recog. 137, Bond, 7; CLRO: SR (May 1727), Recog. 21; GLRO: MJ/SR/3363, Recog. 118.

34. GLRO: MJ/SR/2483, New Prison List; MJ/SR/2841, Gatehouse List, no. 7; MJ/SR/2223, Recog. 45.

35. Polly Morris, "Sodomy and Male Honor: The Case of Somerset, 1740-1850," *Journal of Homosexuality* 15(3/4).

36. I have consulted the sessions rolls for the City of London for 1704, 1707, 1720-1729, 1737, 1770, 1777; and those for Westminster and Middlesex for 1704, 1714, 1720-1729, 1734, 1737, 1745, 1755, 1765, 1770-1779, 1785. Much of this work was made possible by three faculty awards from the Research Foundation of the City University of New York, and a summer stipend from the National Endowment for the Humanities. My thanks to these institutions.

37. Salvatore Cucchiari, "The Gender Revolution and the Transition from Bisexual Horde to Patrilocal Band: The Origins of Gender Hierarchy," *Sexual Meanings*, ed. S. B. Ortner and H. Whitehead (Cambridge: Cambridge University Press, 1981), 32-79.

38. *The Third Report from the Committee on the State of Police of the Metropolis* (London, 1818), 13, 37, 50, 76, 85, 87, and 168.

V. OVERVIEWS

Sodomites, Platonic Lovers, Contrary Lovers: The Backgrounds of the Modern Homosexual

Gert Hekma, PhD

The pursuit of sodomy in early modern Europe brought to the fore some very important changes in the conceptualization and practice of homosexuality. The eighteenth century was a key age for the revision of ideas on sodomy and for the self-awareness of sodomites, especially in northwestern Europe. During the Enlightenment (and especially in France) a radical transition took place in thinking and practices regarding "Socratic love," as Voltaire called it. But in addition to the better-known philosophers of the Enlightenment, such as Montesquieu, Voltaire, Beccaria, Rousseau, and later on in England, Bentham, two other important currents in political philosophy also concerned themselves with Socratic love: first, the radical scoundrels of the Enlightenment, Sade and Lamettrie; and second, the German Counter-Enlightenment, a more or less Romantic and antirationalistic tradition from Hamann to Goethe and Platen.

The philosophes not only put forward ideas, they also proposed practical policies: for government, for social life, for criminal law, for sexuality. Their discussion of onanism is only one example.

Dr. Gert Hekma is affiliated with the University of Amsterdam. Address correspondence to: Gert Hekma, Gay Studies, Sociologisch Instituut, Oude Hougstraat 24, 1012 CE Amsterdam, The Netherlands.

A shorter version of this article was read at the "Sex and the State" conference in Toronto, 4 July 1985. The author wishes to thank especially Jim Steakley and Michael Dallas for their comments.

One Dutch author, A. Perrenot, wrote a small treatise in the best Enlightenment tradition on the crime against nature and proposed basic measures to combat the vice, which was no longer "unmentionable" but, as he put it, "infamous." At the same time, a distinctly new organization of sodomy, a half-hidden subculture of sodomites, had been developing since the end of the seventeenth century, and with it sodomitical self-awareness.

In this article I seek both to unravel the changes taking place in the eighteenth century with regard to Socratic love and to assess the importance and scope of this shift. I will discuss to what extent the development from Thomistic "sodomy" to the medically defined "homosexuality" and "the homosexual" was inevitable, and what alternatives existed. Moreover, I will point out that homosexuality and sodomy are not completely homogenous or unitary social phenomena; there has always been a certain range of variance in practices and philosophies surrounding them.

MORAL THEOLOGY: SODOMY

The concept of sodomy, its implementation, and its judicial invocation can be traced back to the Middle Ages. All of them are still in force in some parts of the Western world, though in modified form.[1] According to medieval moral theology, sodomy as a sexual act was the exact reversal of the lawful way of having sex. Men sought from behind what they ought to find in front: they were to propagate. In its strictest sense, sodomy referred to anal penetration, including the transmission of semen; in its broadest sense, it could apply to every emission of semen not intended for procreation. The range of meanings of sodomy, this most horrible sin, made and continues to make it difficult to grasp the actual practices which were considered sodomitical. (See other articles in this collection.)

Secular law as derived from biblical texts was in most countries clear in its policies concerning cases of sodomy. The guilty were to be punished by death — usually by burning, hanging, or strangling. The actual enforcement of these laws in early modern Europe seems to have been rather limited, however, (as the articles in this issue show). Venice and probably other Italian cities in the Renaissance, the Spanish cities after the colonization of America, Paris, London, and the urbanized parts of the Netherlands in the eighteenth century are the most important examples of places with a rather extensive history of persecuting sodomy. But even though many sodomites were put to death, the records brought to light up to now do not make it possible to speak of mass persecutions or mass murders — the "gay genocide" invoked by some historians.[2] No more than several hundred executions for sodomy have been uncovered, and there is little reason to believe that many more will turn up in the archives.

As awful of an episode in European history as it may have been, the persecution of sodomites does not approach the proportions of the slaughter of Jews, gypsies, witches, or heretics. Even the number of men murdered on account of their homosexuality by the Nazis in Germany may ultimately prove to be greater than all the sodomites put to death in Europe from the thirteenth through the nineteenth century.[3] On the other hand, a new topic for research on sodomy could be the European persecution and murder of American, African, Asian, and Australian "savages" because of their unnatural vices.[4] But that is a rather different topic due to the divergent political and cultural backgrounds involved; it concerns an intercultural as opposed to an intracultural clash.

Although an official policy of church and state concerning sodomy did exist, the interpretations and applications of it differed immensely, as did the social realities in which they had to take shape. Beyond the diverse social philosophies and policies regarding sodomy, different conceptualizations and social realities of homoeroticism also existed.

THE CLASSICAL HERITAGE: SOCRATIC LOVE

Throughout the early modern period, the most important philosophical tradition involving homoeroticism was the study of the history of classical antiquity, especially Neoplatonism (as Dall'Orto observes in this issue with regard to the Italian Renaissance). At a time when Latin was the spoken language at universities, intellectuals — libertines as well as puritans — were well aware of the classical philosophy and literature on eros, from Plato to Martial, Petronius, Galen, and Suetonius. The European intellectuals indeed used classical authors for their philosophies, for their self-awareness, and for medical theories.[5] Dall'Orto points this out for the fifteenth and sixteenth centuries in Italy, but in other countries and at other times, intellectuals also used the classical heritage to propose a certain variant of homoeroticism. Just like Ficino, most of these philosophers and classical historians condemned sexual intercourse between men and translated eros in terms of spiritual love or asceticism. Eros became synonymous with "platonic love," especially in heterosocial relations.[6]

During the early modern period, sodomy was not well-defined, nor was the concept of male eros derived from classical history. The first was a term of contempt, the other one of reverence. Between those two conceptualizations there existed a gray zone which seems to have been used by sodomites, an undefined free area that could cover (to give only some sexual examples) mutual masturbation and intercrural intercourse. Studies of Italy and Portugal reveal that sodomites abstained from anal penetration to avoid the danger of criminal prosecution.[7] Despite abundant historical material concerning sodomy in the Netherlands, these particular sexual tactics cannot be documented in that country, not even for a later period, perhaps because the persecution of Dutch sodomites came suddenly after a long period of almost no indictments for sodomy.[8]

In eighteenth-century Germany (as well as the Netherlands), there was a remarkable revival of philosophical and historical interest in male eros. Prior to this revival, a handful of English, French, and other authors began anew to speak about the vice which was ascribed to Socrates, but they denied that he had been a pederast.[9] Stimulated by the art historian J. J. Winckelmann, a new interpretation of Socrates' life began with that typically German mixture of Counter-Enlightenment and Romanticism of the late eighteenth century: Hamann, Jacobs, Herder, Meiners, Rajmdohr, Ehrenberg.[10] This current had a Dutch counterpart in Hemsterhuis, de Pauw, van Limburg, Brouwer, and Kneppelhout. This revival of Platonism further paved the way for the earliest works, both Swiss, which can retrospectively be called homosexual and emancipatory: Zschokke's *Eros oder über die Liebe* (1821, Eros, or on Love) and

Hossli's *Eros. Die Männerliebe der Griechen* (vol. 1, Glarus, 1836; vol. 2, St. Gallen, 1838; Eros. The Male Love of the Greeks).

J. G. Hamann, J. G. Herder, and F. H. Jacobs, the leading philosophers in the eighteenth-century German Counter-Enlightenment, all wrote on male love. They were contemporaries and acquaintances of each other and also of Kant, but were fiercely opposed to Kant's rationalism. Hamann focused his criticism on the duality of rationality and sensuality implied in Kant's work and proposed to bridge this gap by focusing on language, in which reason gains a sensual quality. With his first publication, *Sokratische Denkwürdigkeiten* (1750, Socratic Memorabilia, subtitled "For the tedium of the public, compiled by a lover of tedium"), he was a predecessor of the Counter-Enlightenment as well as of German Romanticism (Goethe, Schiller). His book contained a defense of male eros, indeed the most radical in this tradition.[11] He wrote, "through the art in which Socrates was educated (i.e., sculpture), his eyes were so accustomed to and trained in beauty and its touches that his lust for well-formed youths must not surprise us." Hamann argued that it would be foolish "to exonerate Socrates of a vice, rather our Christianity would do better to overlook it in him." Nevertheless, he continued, Socrates hated that vice, although he was well aware that he himself had a sinful heart (vice, in German *Laster*, was not gone into further). But most interestingly, according to Hamann: "One cannot experience a vital friendship without sensuality, and perhaps a metaphysical love sins more grossly (*grober*) against the fluids of the nerves (*Nervensaften*) than does a bestial love against flesh and blood. Thus, Socrates must have suffered and struggled over his desire for harmony between inner and outer beauty."[12] Hamann's defense of a sensual friendship is extremely noteworthy. Contrary to the tendency of later philosophers, Hamann clearly opposed an ascetic interpretation of the Platonic eros. Love and friendship must be sensual, and therefore homoerotic. However, Hamann was not clear about how far that sensuality could go.

Both his friends Herder and Jacobs published on the male eros of the Greeks, but their contributions pale in comparison with Hamann's. Writing thirty years later, Herder called it a disorder, arisen from the "crazy" Greek love for beauty. He remarked fur-

ther that his eros would have been more deleterious to Greek society
if it had been practiced "secretly" — this opinion perhaps a critique
of the customs of his time.[13] Jacobs' contribution dates from still
later and was published in 1829, a decade after his death. This was
even more negative about the male eros of the Greeks. He denied
that it had to do with the arethe, male virtue, and explained it not in
terms of a desire of beauty, but in terms of the vehemence of Mediterranean passions — which could be positive as well as negative —
and the organization of public life in Greece.[14]

When we consider these three philosophers of the German
Counter-Enlightenment, we see a slow retreat from a defense of
male eros and of sensuality in male friendships. Such apologies
seem to have become more problematic with time. An explanation
for this change can probably be found in the rise of Enlightened
rationalism that found philosophical expression in Kantian philosophy and political expression in the French Revolution of 1789 (see
next section).

After Hamann, the next important contribution on Greek love
was set forth by the Dutch philosopher Frans Hemsterhuis (who
also influenced eighteenth-century Romanticism) in his *Lettre sur
les desires* (1770, Letter on Desires). In it he made clear why the
classicists had such difficulties in defining male eros. "Love and
Friendship had among them (the Greeks) about the same meaning
as with us, but their tact or their extreme sensibility gave all their
virtues and their vices a splendor that dazzles us." As for their
vices, Hemsterhuis cited the standard series of forensic medicine:
"pederasty," bestiality, and the unbridled lust for statues. According to him, vices as well as virtues originated from the same source,
the "site of concupiscence." Therefore, it became very difficult to
trace a dividing line between, for example, a loving friendship and
pederasty. To put it simply, would mutual masturbation have been
for Hemsterhuis a vice or a virtue?[15]

Other authors simply denied that the Greeks sexually pursued
youth. Cristoph Meiners maintained in his essay "Betrachtungen
über die Männerliebe der Griechen" (1775, Considerations on the
male love of the Greeks) that their adoration — "schwärmerische
Liebe" — for the beauties of the male sex was a spiritual love which
only gradually degenerated, especially among the Romans, into "a

love that violated the holy laws of Nature."[16] The Dutch classical historian Cornelis De Pauw tried to explain "this grotesqueness of Nature, which was so lavish with its favors to one sex which did not need them, and so stingy toward the other which could not do without them." De Pauw noted that the explanation could not be the nudity of the youths in the gymnasia, for the myths of pederastic seductions were far older than the customs of sports and gymnasia. On this point he seemed to argue against other authors such as Voltaire who explained Greek eros through these customs of nudity. According to De Pauw, pederastic love was so widespread because of the ugliness of the Greek women and their fashions.[17]

Very complicated and verbose arguments were set forth by Friedrich Wilhelm Basic von Ramdohr in his *Venus Urania. Ueber die Natur der Liebe, über ihre Veredlung und Verschönerung* (1798, on the nature of love, on its ennoblement and enhancement). According to his theory of sexual attraction—heavily informed by Greek examples—love between males could be natural. But nature was not the basis of social life, and he opposed male eros because it was "contrary to reason and morals." At the same time, he defended the sensuality of friendship. The Romantic tradition was against dichotomization of body and mind, and so a certain ambiguity could exist concerning the sensuality of male eros, with "pederasty" (most probably understood as anal penetration) the only social phenomenon no one would endorse.[18]

After 1800, the debate on the Greek tradition of male love took several directions. First of all, there was the pure, narrative history of Greek love, as in the works of M. H. E. Meier and P. van Limburg Brouwer, both of whom acknowledged the widespread existence of male sexual passions in Greek history and tried to arrive at an understanding of the existence of these vices in an otherwise revered people.[19] Secondly, such pedagogues as von Humboldt in Prussia, and in the Netherlands the members of the Groningen-school, used the platonic philosophy of eros, mostly implicitly, for the development of an educational system, the German and Dutch "gymnasia" with their ideals of humanism and *Bildung* (self-cultivation).[20] Moreover, for homosexual artists such as the poets Platen and Byron, the sculptor Thorvaldsen, and as late as Gloeden, the tradition of Greek love meant a certain homoerotic self-awareness.

And lastly, the Socratic tradition was put to use in apologies for male love.

In the first of these apologies, *Eros oder über die Liebe* (1821), Heinrich Zschokke considered whether male love could be called "natural," and in a Symposium-like dialogue he came to the conclusion that this was not possible because acknowledging the naturalness of male love would be tantamount to legitimating homosexual passions. This discussion of eros was motivated by the execution in 1817 of Franz Desgouttes, who had murdered his beloved male secretary out of jealousy. Heinrich Hössli figured in this dialogue as "Holmar," the judge who disagreed with the other judges in the court on the sentence.[21] His ideas on Desgouttes were articulated by Zschokke in a very Romantic tone: "Alas, when as an infant he still slumbered in his cradle, he was already destined for the most infamous fate, because his true nature was a crime against the present-day world. His existence was his crime. . . . The law, instituted through the delusions of the world against natures which it did not know, is unjust."[22] In the end, Zschokke would only admit the naturalness of male love if Hössli could prove that this passion did not always become submerged in the sensual.[23]

Two ideas of love, mostly separate from each other, seem to have existed in the German-speaking world, the spiritual and the corporeal. In the early Romantic tradition (Hamann, Hemsterhuis), the rational and the sensual were not as separate as they later became. Nevertheless, no author endorsed sodomy as a sin of the flesh. At the end of the Romantic tradition, Zschokke as well as Hössli linked both theories again, but in their discussion the attention shifted from the dualism of sensuality and spirituality to the naturalness of male eros as a legitimation of a psychological identity. And while Zschokke opposed the idea of the naturalness of male eros because of the dangers of sensuality, Hössli defended it, not only as Holmar in Zschokke's *Eros oder über die Liebe*, but also in a publication of his own, *Eros. Die Männerliebe der Griechen*. Here, he mostly defended the naturalness of male love. What he did not specify was the extent to which this other love implied sensuality or sexuality. His apology for male love was formulated in classical terms and not, as would be the case with all later authors, in the vocabulary of the natural sciences.

ENLIGHTMENT: SOCRATIC LOVE

Peter Gay has stated: "In its treatment of the passions . . . the Enlightenment was not an age of reason but a revolt against rationalism."[24] His assertion seems to be affirmed by the negative way most philosophes spoke of the "crime of nature" (Montesquieu) or "Socratic love" (Voltaire). They opposed the Christian views on sodomy and the criminal consequences, but the best policy toward it was, according to these philosophes, prevention. Stockinger has already delineated the ambivalent position of the Enlightenment philosophes vis á vis homosexuality, but he sought to defend them despite their inelegant judgments by pointing to their difficult situation in light of the severe condemnation of sodomy by church and state alike.[25] Still, this explanation seems insufficient. It was not so much the Christian church or its confederates who tried to indict the philosophes by allegations of sodomy. It was the philosophes who used such accusations to incriminate their opponents: Voltaire in his *Anti-Giton* (1714), Diderot in *The Nun* (1760), Rousseau in his *Confessions* (1784).

The most important exception to the philosophes' ambivalent politics of the body was D. A. F. Marquis de Sade, who based his political philosophy precisely on sodomy. In the Enlightenment "the great chain of being," divine law, was being sundered, and reason and nature were becoming the cornerstones of social philosophy and social life. Sade radicalized this philosophy of rational and natural law by questioning whether prostitution, murder, theft, or sodomy were truly contrary to nature or reason. He argued that waste was within the normal course of things, so that wastage of semen was in accordance with nature. There was no purpose inherent in nature or social life, he argued, so there was no need to link sexuality to propagation. Sade used sodomy as a particularly good example of that which seemed to be unnatural, unreasonable, and purposeless, but which could in no way be proven to be against nature or reason.

Sade's *Philosophy in the Boudoir* (1795) was a clear apology for the decriminalization of pederasty and sodomy—far more radical than any apology in the nineteenth century would be.[26] Sade emphasized that there were no rational arguments against any form of sexual behavior, be it prostitution, lust murder, or sodomy, and he strongly opposed the suggestion that theft, prostitution, sodomy, or lust murder were against nature. He undermined the idea of "natural law" as put forward by the church as well as by enlightened philosophes (Beccaria). His critique was radically negative and was not balanced by a positive attitude toward the state, the law, homosexuality, or anything else. But in his literary works, he wrote extensively about sodomy as a supreme way of pleasure, for example in *The 120 Days of Sodom*. In this respect he was even more radical than any apologist either of platonic eros or of homosexual love in the tradition of Ulrichs and Hirschfeld, all of whom did not dare to defend the act of sodomy.

Sade was not only a libertine writer, he was also a libertine in his everyday life, indicted for sexual excesses with and torture of prostitutes, and moreover for sodomy. In 1772, Sade was sentenced to death for sodomizing his manservant and for poisoning prostitutes (with cantharides intended as an aphrodisiac). He and his servant were burned in effigy on 12 September of that year in Aix-en-Provence, while the Marquis himself was in Italy with his sister-in-law, whom he kept as a wife.[27] In 1778, when Sade was apprehended, the death sentence was commuted but his long imprisonment in Vincennes and in the Bastille began. Sade's mother-in-law had asked for and obtained a royal restraining order intended to prevent him from committing further sexual debauchery. Some months after the French Revolution, he was set free (1790), but under the Jacobin and Napoleonic regimes he was reimprisoned (1793-94 and 1801-14). He died in the Charenton lunatic asylum in 1814. Nothing is known about his homosexual proclivities except for the sodomy with his manservent and his writings. But his most scrupulous biographer, Gilbert Lely, has asserted that he was a homosexual with no remorse.[28]

Only in this century has Sade's contribution to sexual politics and philosophies come to be acknowledged by such French philosophers as George Bataille, Pierre Klossowski, Michel Foucault, and Roland Barthes.[29] But Sade has not to this day been claimed by the gay movement as one of its forerunners, and that is a loss. That he still cannot be acclaimed as a gay emancipator makes clear how extreme a philosophical position Sade took during his time.

HOMOSEXUAL POLICIES
OF THE ENLIGHTENMENT

I will use a relatively unknown, anonymously published text by the Dutch Enlightenment philosopher A. Perrenot, *Bedenkingen over het straffen van zekere schandelijke misdaad* (Considerations on the Punishment of a Certain Infamous Crime, Amsterdam, 1777), in order to illustrate enlightened sexual politics. To my knowledge, this pamphlet is the most elaborate of any text on the infamous love from an enlightened point of view. It also reiterates many points advanced by various philosophes.

Perrenot was vehement in his disapproval of the "unnatural crime," which he indeed considered contrary to nature. Like Montesquieu and Beccaria, he opposed the severe and public punishment of sodomy, which only attracted unwholesome curiosity.[30] According to Perrenot, these vices arose from habit and corrupt imagination. The causes were social: a shortage of women (through the institution of polygamy, as in some foreign cultures); the prohibition of contacts with women (as in monasteries and boarding schools); and the corruption of morals.[31] Then he came to the heart of his argument. The unnatural crime should not be severely punished, but should be prevented. The best method of prevention was a "closely watched civil household."[32] Prevention was necessary because this crime endangered society. Severe punishments — solitary and lifelong confinements — were needed only for those who seduced others. As preventive measures, he suggested a relaxed sociability between men and women, the facilitation of marriage, and a pious education.[33] Thus, heterosexuality was propagated against homoeroticism. By means of such practical measures, the vice could be checked and the natural order restored. Like Voltaire and Michaelis before him, Perrenot attributed greater danger to Mediterranean and southerly climates than to the northern zones, such as the Netherlands and England. This greatly influenced how society attempted to prevent or else punish sodomy.[34] He also offered a lengthy discussion of the death penalty, which he opposed, believing that Mosaic law applied only to Jews.[35]

Perrenot received an immediate reply from another anonymous author in the tract *Nadere bedenkingen over het straffen van zekere schandelijke misdaad* (Further Considerations on the Punishment of a Certain Infamous Crime, Amsterdam, 1777). This writer did not want to disagree with Perrenot on the severity of the penalties, but he did wish to stress the enormity of this sin against nature's wise division of humanity into two sexes made for each other.[36] The men who normally committed this vice were effeminate and useless to themselves and to society because they did not propagate.[37] Their vice was much worse than theft because, unlike the desires of a thief, their desires could never be stilled and could only be satisfied through the seduction of ever more and different men.[38] This anonymous author was also in favor of prevention through measures to be taken in boarding schools and religious congregations.[39] But whereas Perrenot had defended private punishment for the sodomites, this author favored humiliating public penalties aimed at deterring others, especially youths, from these vices. According to him, private sentences and punishments belonged to tyrannic regimes.[40]

These two obscure writers, who both worked in the enlightened tradition and approvingly cited the philosophes, outlined a politics of the body to deal with the infamous crime. First of all, the state was to prevent these vices by promoting a closely watched civil household; and secondly, when these crimes were committed, they were to be punished severely, especially in cases of seduction. The strict policies put forward by these Dutch thinkers were an elaboration on the ideas developed by the French philosophes. Their strategies did not constitute a break with enlightened traditions, as some authors would like to argue, but were instead a consequence of those traditions.

The eighteenth-century debate on onanism is a case in point. The horror stories about masturbation were, in my opinion, not a digression from or a marginal feature of enlightened thinking, but were central to it. Rousseau's interest in Tissot's writings, the article on onanism in the *Encyclopedie*, the belief in the inherent goodness of human nature, and the emphasis on social education all indicated a horror of masturbation as the lonely sin of children beyond the benevolent control of their educators.[41] The negative attitude of the enlightened philosophes toward certain forms of sexuality (sodomy, onanism) was central to their politics of the body, and it was the obverse of their regard for natural propagation and marriage. They were opposed not to sex, but only to certain forms of sexuality. Rousseau flatly stated at the beginning of the *Social Contract*: "The oldest form of society — and the only natural one — is the family."[42] For the leading thinkers of the French Enlightenment, sodomy remained unnatural. It was against their family politics and their limited rationalism, as well as against the church and its institutions, that Sade rebelled — albeit without much success — thus beginning a political struggle for the rights of pederasts.

THE TURN OF THE CENTURY

Thus, at the turn of the nineteenth century three important philosophies of homoeroticism existed: the moral theology of sodomy, the cultural history of male eros, and an enlightened vision of Socratic love. As we have seen, the platonic tradition in time became more prudent and emphasized sensuality less — probably due to the rise of enlightened philosophies of sexuality and their political application after the French Revolution. This same revolution put an end to the criminal laws condemning sodomy in large parts of the Western world, and moral theological views on sodomy lost their general validity. The Enlightened tradition achieved a strong position and influenced religious notions and practices.

Other traditions also existed or came into being in the eighteenth century concerning homoeroticism. First of all, there was since 1700 the sodomite subculture in the larger cities of Western Europe, which developed a certain style and self-awareness.[43] Especially in France, sodomites even produced some ambiguous tracts, such as *L'Ombre de Deschauffours* (The Shadow of Deschauffours, not published until 1978)[44] and, after the revolution, *Les Enfants de Sodome a l'Assemblee Nationale* (The Children of Sodom to the National Assembly, Paris, 1790) and *Les petits Bougres au Manege* (The Little Buggers in the Manege, Paris, 1791).[45] The latter two treatises discussed in a mocking fashion the rights of pederasts, sodomites, or buggers. The second stated that the lovers of the ass would return to the cunt if whores were to be regularly medically examined and their orifices reduced to the same width as boys' asses.

A second, international trend in discussing the nameless vice, dating back to the sixteenth century, was the book of travels, in which mention was sometimes made of strange, homoerotic customs of "primitive" peoples, mostly involving cross-dressing and male initiation. Although the philosophes used the travel story to criticize European morals, they did not extend their remarks of European or "savage" homoeroticism.[46] The only way in which information about "native" habits was put to use was as a justification for condemning and massacring other peoples, but the full scope of these writings and killings remains unknown and is clearly an important subject for further inquiry in gay studies. To my knowledge, the ethnographic tradition did not bring forth an apology for the nameless crime until the end of the nineteenth century (Sir Richard Burton's "Terminal Essay").[47]

A third, English innovation was the development of the Gothic novel, which Eve K. Sedgwick described as follows:

> The Gothic novel crystallized for English audiences the terms of a dialectic between male homosexuality and homophobia, in which homophobia appeared thematically in paranoid plots. Not until the late-Victorian Gothic did a . . . body of homosexual thematics emerge clearly, however. In earlier Gothic fiction (especially Beckford's *Vathek*, Walpole and Lewis) the associations with male homosexuality were grounded most visibly in the lives of a few authors, and only rather sketchily in their works.[48]

Like travel literature and the massacre of non-European peoples, the Gothic novel constitutes an important topic for further gay studies research. The same was true of the tradition of the dandy, which started around 1800 with Beau Brummell and ended with Oscar Wilde and Max Beerbohm.[49]

In her study, Sedgwick has delineated still other institutions of male homosocial desire, which hug the line between the homoerotic and the homophobic. In Western societies of the eighteenth century, the separate homosocial worlds of men and women must have yielded different forms of sensual desire among men: on board

ships, in armies, in boarding schools, in monasteries, in work-
shops. Burg has made some suggestions on the life of pirates, and
Jan Oosterhoff has found a considerable amount of material regarding the sailing vessels of the Dutch East Indies Company.[50] Many
prosecutions for sodomy involved homosocial institutions, for example officials of the Catholic church, orphanages, and the army.
Nevertheless, the abundant and precise materials we have on
present-day homosocial institutions are totally lacking for the early
modern period.

In the eighteenth-century campaign against onanism, mutual
masturbation was almost never mentioned, although the situation in
boarding schools was very conducive to it. Writers on onanism such
as those of the Philantropine School (Basedow, Campe) would have
had good reason to campaign against the sin when it involved two,
just as they did when it was committed in solitude.[51] Chandos reported that only after 1850 were moral sanctions strengthened and
corporal intimacies between boys acted against in English boarding
schools. Beds for two were replaced by single beds.[52] At the same
time, in most countries of Europe intimate contacts were made impossible in prisons through the introduction of the cellular system.
Two decades earlier, physical proximity between males and females and between youths and adults began being restricted in such
institutions.[53]

Why were the responsible authorities all over Europe (or so it
seems) so lax in their struggle against intimate relations among men
in homosocial situations, especially in total institutions? Although
they considered this vice one of the worst they could think of, and
although the philosophes of the Enlightenment had indicted homosexual desires in homosocial institutions of the Roman Catholic
church, the authorities did little against it. Yet it is clear from mid-
nineteenth-century sources that homosexual intimacies were common in homosocial environments. In any case, the interest in such
relations that did arise at that point coincided with the beginning of
medical debates on perverse sexuality (Michea 1849, Casper 1852,
Ulrichs 1864-1870). But even so, why did it take practically a century after the emergence of interest in Socratic love during the En-

lightenment for a general discussion of homosexuality to get under way?

THE NINETEENTH CENTURY

Only toward the end of the nineteenth century did a systematic interest in the sexual perversions develop within the medical profession. The publications of the 1880s marked this new intervention, which concentrated on "sexual inversion"—Moreau, 1880; Tarnowsky, 1885; Krafft-Ebing, 1886; Ball, 1888; Binet 1888.[54] This medical interest in *psychopathia sexualis* made use of some important principles of the Enlightenment, especially its emphasis on rational attitudes and on the natural sciences (as the biological determinism of Lamettrie had already indicated). But in order to explain why it took a century to elaborate those ideas into sexology, other factors must be examined.

One possible explanation for the mid-nineteenth century shift in ideas on sexual life was the transition in urban social policies, which had two important aspects with regard to the politics of the body. First of all, the state no longer existed for the welfare of its citizens, as Rousseau's *Social Contract* had more or less assumed. Instead, the welfare of the state depended on the behavior of its citizens. The balance of power shifted from the citizen to the state, notwithstanding developments in democratization in the same century. Thus, after criminal prosecution of homosexual acts in private had been abolished in Enlightened states (France, Bavaria, and the countries dependent on France under Napoleon) at the beginning of the nineteenth century—on grounds of the principle of noninterference in private affairs—a process of recriminalization of such homosexual acts slowly developed in the same century, this time on the grounds that they were detrimental to the welfare of the state. As Feuerbach, the reformer of Bavarian criminal law, himself suggested, such acts endangered the state because they hindered propagation and caused the "enervation" of the individuals in question. Although he himself was the initiator of the decriminalization of the sin against nature in Bavaria, he nevertheless emphasized the dangers homosexual desires posed for the state and the need to combat them.[55]

The Dutch specialist on public health, Anthonij Moll, wrote in an article entitled "What Is Political Medicine": "The State [is] the whole of individuals, the body in which each individual participates, although the participation of each individual is not of equal import for the general vitality of the state ('algemeene Staatsleven'); but his participation is necessary and indispensable to its complete and intact organization and its perfectly smooth functioning. . . ."[56] What individuals did, even in private, influenced the well-being of the state.

The second aspect of the new politics of the body was its medical implementation. The flourishing of medical specializations under the designation of "public health" indicated a revived interest of doctors in social policies. City politics had always involved health regulations, but what was new to the science of public health was its stress on prevention, and consequently on social measures. Halfway through the nineteenth century, the medical profession in continental Europe ascended, after a long struggle, to a new and higher position, one which was recognized by the general public and by state officials. The doctors attained their new position not because of successes in curing disease, but by virtue of their promises of a social policy of public health, and because they had become by then the foremost specialists on the human body and were acknowledged as such by lawyers, clergymen, and politicians.

After the revolution of 1848, the "social question" and socialism became central in political discourse. Through the social question the liberal distinction between private and public faded. The private life of the citizen—and thus also sexual life—became a matter of public interest. The rise of the social question with its medical counterpart in public health, appears to have been pivotal for the nascent "psychopathia sexualis."[57]

An important precondition for the growing influence of public health doctors evolved from the grand reconstructions of the European cities that began in the middle of the nineteenth century with the demolition of the city fortifications. In medical science itself, the rise of public health policy was stimulated by the development of theories concerning social life and the human body; for example, Morel's theory of degeneracy, which served as a model for the nascent sciences of criminal anthropology (C. Lombroso) and sexual psychopathology (R. von Krafft-Ebing).[58] The first manifestation of public health in sexual politics was the medical regulation of prostitution, which began to develop under the Napoleonic regime and underwent systematic implementation after the publication of Parent-Duchatelet's book on the topic.[59]

The combined influence of two other trends further stimulated the medical interest in sexual perversions: first, the rapid growth and professionalization of the urban police force, resulting in the apprehension of a much larger number of sexual criminals, and second, the involvement of forensic psychiatrists in the criminal justice system. Previously, doctors had functioned as medical experts and limited their juridical involvement to diagnosing anal penetration. But from the 1850s onwards, they concerned themselves as well with the mental constitution of criminals (sexual and otherwise) and began their battle with the criminal law experts on the responsibility of the accused.[60]

It was in this ferment that sexual psychopathology originated, arising out of biologist and rationalist traditions stemming from the Enlightenment (and dependent on the existence of subcultures of "wrong lovers"), but brought into existence by changes in urban and medical policies. The concept of what enlightened authors in the eighteenth century — fearing contamination by the infamous vice — shrewdly developed as a correct civil household was incorporated into the practice of politics of the body halfway through the nineteenth century. Thus, the practical philosophy of the French Enlightenment was finally put into social practice a century later within the framework of a new urban politics.

Psychopathia sexualis was also in keeping with the growing individualization, psychologization, and sexualization of Western culture. It stemmed directly from psychiatry and developed at the same time as Lombroso's criminal anthropology, the science that discovered the criminal behind the crime. It was the social opposite of the *fin de siecle* aesthetics, with its "art for art's sake," its individualism, its dandyism — and at the same time its passion for the seamy side of the urban life (Baudelaire, Lautreamont, Wilde). The medicalization of homosexuality was a result of both the urbanization of the group cultures of wrong lovers that was a long-term process dating back to the early eighteenth century, as well as of the social policies of municipal and medical authorities that originated in the 1850s.

The gradual shift from the enlightened philosophy of Socratic love to the psychopathia sexualis was not imperative and inevitable. There were other alternatives. German Romanticism of male bonding, for example, lived on into the twentieth century, but all those variations of homoeroticism remained on the outer fringes of social politics. Moreover, moral-theological definitions of unnatural vice and buggery survived in penal laws, but other factors accounted for this.

With the Enlightenment, a new social philosophy of Socratic love came into being that stressed criminal law reform and preventive measures. These policies became social practice in the nineteenth century in connection with the restructuring of the continental urban centers, and were implemented by means of architecture (housing, prisons, "boulevards"), which in turn influenced public and private behavior. Municipal life became more complicated, and its subjects had to accommodate themselves to it lest they be accommodated by it. As a result of municipal policies, the obligations of civic life became universal and the idea of the "correct civil household" a norm. Individuals who failed to make the needed psychic and social adjustments to accommodate themselves to the new standards became subjects of the human sciences. The contrary lovers who did not live up to the *social* norms entered the correctional system through criminal justice; inverts who did not succeed in mastering the *psychic* requisites of social behavior entered it through the private practices of psychiatrists. Psychopathia sexualis could thus take shape from two sources, the lower-class and the middle-class.

In the turmoil of urban politics, Socratic love became an outdated ideal. Male bonding was reduced to a fashion for the countryside, a sentimental journey beyond the new urban styles, and Sadenian philosophy persisted only as a romantic fashion.[61] Due to the overpowering influence of sexual psychopathology on nineteenth century social policies, other currents of homoerotic philosophy could survive only on the marginal fringes of modern society. It was on one of those fringes that the homosexual emancipation movement first began.

NOTES

1. Cf., D. S. Bailey, *Homosexuality and the Western Christian Tradition* (London: Longmans, Green, 1955); H. J. Kuster, *Over Homoseksualiteit in Middeleeuws West-Europa* (Utrecht: n.p., 1977); J. Boswell, *Christianity, Social Tolerance and Homosexuality* (Chicago: University of Chicago Press, 1980), 163-209.

2. L. Crompton, "Gay Genocide from Leviticus to Hitler," in *The Gay Academic*, ed. L. Crew (Palm Springs, CA: ETC publications, 1978), 67-91.

3. R. Lautmann, ed., *Seminar: Gesellschaft und Homosexualität* (Frankfurt: Suhrkamp, 1977), chap. 8.

4. Cf., J. N. Katz, ed., *Gay American History* (New York: Thomas W. Cromwell, 1976): pt 4; and J. N. Katz, ed., *Gay/Lesbian Almanac* (New York: Harper and Row, 1983), pt. 1.

5. Cf., the interesting re-edition and commentary on "De mollibus" of Caelius Aurelianus: P. H. Schrijvers, *Eine medizinische Erklärung der männlichen Homosexualität aus der Antike* (Amsterdam: 1985).

6. Nineteenth-century Dutch dictionaries gave this meaning to "Platonic."

7. If applied to present times, this material would suggest that sexual promiscuity can survive the AIDS panic by simply turning to sexual techniques other than the dangerous ones.

8. T. van der Meer, *De wesentlijke sonde van sodomie en andere vuyligheden* (Amsterdam: Tabula, 1984).

9. Cf., F. Charpentier, *La Vie de Socrate*, 3d ed. (Amsterdam, 1699); C. A. Heumann, *Acta philosophorum* 1 (1715): 121-22; G. Cooper, *Life of Socrates*, French trans. (1751), 69. All these books are cited in J. G. Hamann, *Sokratische Denkwurdigkeiten* (Gutersloh: Erklart von F. Blanke, 1959), 114. The original edition of Hamann's work was Amsterdam (i.e., Konigsberg) 1759. See also J. M. Gesner, *Socrates Sanctus Paederasta* (lecture in 1752), Utrecht, 1769, who denied Socrates had been a pederast.

10. On Winckelmann, see the article by Denis Sweet in this issue. Both Goethe and Schiller wrote on homosexual love, Schiller in his plays *Die Maltheser* (unfinished), in *Schillers dramatischer Nachlass*, G. Kettner, ed., (Weimar: 1895), and *Don Carlos*; and Goethe with his famous poem "Der Erlkönig," and in *Winckelmann und sein Jahrhundert* (Tübingen, 1805).

11. Cited after the edition of Blanke, see note 9.

12. Ibid., 112-18. In this edition the paragraph was titled "Sokrates und die Knabenliebe" (Socrates and Boy Love).

13. J. G. von Herder, *Ideen zu einer Geschichte der Menschheit*, vols. 1-4, 1784-91. About the Greek eros, book 13, chap. 4: "Sitten- und Staatsweisheit der Griechen" (The Wisdom of the Greeks concerning morals and the state), vol. 3, 209-27.

14. F. H. Jacobs, *Schriften* 3 (Leipzig, 1829): 212-54.

15. _____ Hemsterhuis, Paris (i.e., The Hague) 1770, 31-32; on Hem-

sterhuis: L. Brummel, *Frans Hemsterhuis. Een philosophenleven* (Haarlem, 1925).

16. In *Vermischte Schriften* 1 (Leipzig) 61-119.

17. C. de Pauw, *Recherches philosophiques sur les Grecs* (1787) (Berlin, 1788): 120-23. On de Pauw, cf. *Biographie universelle, ancienne et moderne* 33 (Paris, 1823): 227-30.

18. Ramdohr made a distinction between strength (*Stärke*) and tenderness (*Zartheit*). Attraction could exist between equals and opposites. (Leipzig, 1798, 3 vols.; quotation from vol. 1, 115-20). Strength and tenderness were associated with male and female, but it was not a necessary link, so that boys and old men could be inclined to tenderness. His ideas have some resemblance to Weininger's sex theory (ibid., 151). Ramdohr illustrated his theory with fits of lust of older men for boys "that morals condemn because they endanger the sense of shame and the population"; these men would feel "enervated" (*entnervt*) by their "debaucheries" (ibid., 152). In the third volume of his work, Ramdohr continued with the line of thinking of the Socratic school on love. "The ennobled love of the Athenians displayed itself in relations among men in a way that does not fit with our climate, our organization, our morals, and our form of government" (*Staatsverfassung*; ibid., vol. 3, 134). But the sexual instinct of males for each other was in agreement with Ramdohr's theories (for example, the love of strong men for tender boys), and he therefore could not condemn it as "degeneration of sensuality" or "an error of nature," but only because it is "contrary to reason and morals." So for him debaucheries were not crimes against nature, but against reason (ibid., 137). He differed in opinion from Plato, finding Plato's theory of the noble love egoistic: "The lover uses the beloved as a means to ennoble himself" (ibid., 230). In light of Ramdohr's opposition to the spiritualization of male love and his acknowledgment of passions between men, he seemed to defend in the best Romantic tradition the virtue of male bonding, including its sensual aspects. Unfortunately, I have never seen F. Ehrenberg's *Euphranor. Ueber die Liebe*, 2 vols. (Leipzig, 1805-6.) The Socratic tradition also had meaning in personal life, cf., the biographical notes of manlovers in Moritz' *Magazin für Erfahrungsseelenkunde*, vol. 8 (1790), 6-10 and 101-6, and H. Bender, ed., *Das Insel-Buch der Freundschaft* (Frankfurt: 1980) with diverse diary entries and letters which testify to the sensuality of German friendships.

19. M. H. E. Meier, "Paederastie," in *Allgemeine Encyclopaedie der Wissenschaften und Künste*, 3, sec. 9 (Leipzig: Theil, 1837): 147-89; P. van Limburg Brouwer, *Histoire de la Civilisation Morale et Religieuse des Grecs*, vol. 2, 2 (Groningue, 1838): 244-75.

20. Cf., on Bildung: O. Brunner, W. Conze, and R. Koselleck, eds., *Geschichtliche Grundbegriffe*, vol. 1 (Stuttgart: 1972); for the "Groningen-school," P. G. van Heusde, *De Socratische school of Wijsgeerte voor de Negentiende Eeuw*, 4 vols. (Utrecht: 1834-39).

21. F. Karsch, "Quellenmaterial zur Beurteilung angeblicher und wirklicher Uranier," in *Jahrbuch für sexuelle Zwischenstufen* 5, pt. 1 (1903). Pages 449-

556, Heinrich Hössli (1784-1864), and pp. 557-614, Franz Desgouttes (1785-1817).

22. H. Zschokke, "Eros oder über die Liebe," in *Ausgewählte Novellen und Dichtungen* (Aarau: 1841), 207.

23. Ibid., 236.

24. P. Gay, *The Science of Freedom*, vol. 2 of *The Enlightenment* (New York: Knopf, 1969), 189.

25. J. Stockinger, "Homosexualities and the French Enlightenment," in *Homosexualities and French Literature*, ed. G. Stambolian and E. Marks (Ithaca, NY: Cornell University Press, 1979), 161-85.

26. D. A. F. Marquis de Sade, *La Philosophie dans le boudoir* (Paris, 1795), especially 5th dialogue.

27. G. Lely, *Vie du marquis de Sade*, new edition (Paris: 1965), chap. 7.

28. Ibid., 350.

29. G. Bataille, *L'Erotisme* (Paris: Gallimard, 1957); P. Klossowski, *Sade, mon prochain* (Paris: 1947); Michel Foucault, passim, in *Les Mots et les choses* (Paris: Gallimard, 1966); R. Barthes, *Sade, Fourier, Loyola* (Paris: Gallimard, 1971); M. Blanchot, *Lautreamont et Sade* (Paris: 1963).

30. Perrenot, *Bedenkingen over het straffen*, 9.

31. Ibid., 14.

32. "Eene nauwkeurige burgerlijke huishouding," "huishouding" also meant economy, ibid., 12-14.

33. Ibid., 17.

34. Ibid., 28-29.

35. Ibid., 25.

36. Anonymous, *Nadere bedenkingen*, 5.

37. Ibid., 6-8.

38. Ibid., 9.

39. Ibid., 27.

40. Ibid., 28-32.

41. Cf., T. Tarczylo, *Sexe et liberté au siècle des Lumières* (Paris: Presses de la Renaissance, 1983); P. Lejeune, "Lecture d'un aveu de Rousseau," *Annales ESC* 29 (1974): 1009-22.

42. J. J. Rousseau, *The Social Contract*, trans. G. Hopkins (London: 1960), 241.

43. Cf., A. Bray, *Homosexuality in Renaissance England* (London: Gay Men's Press, 1982); and T. van der Meer, *De wesentlijke sonde von sodomie*, n. 8.

44. Edited by C. Courouve (Paris: n.p., 1978).

45. It listed as place and date of publication: *a Enculons* (Let's fuck), *l'an second du rêve de la liberté* (In the Second Year of the Dream of Liberty), i.e., 1791.

46. Cf. J. N. Katz, *Gay American History*, n. 6; M. Herzer, *Verzeichnis Homosexualität* (Berlin: Verlag Rosa Winkel, 1982).

47. Cf., S. W. Foster, "The Annotated Burton," in *The Gay Academic*, n. 2, 92-106, and further F. Karsch, *Das gleichgeschlechtliche Leben der Naturvölker*

(München: Seitz and Schauer, 1911), and E. Carpenter, *Intermediate Types Among Primitive Folks* (London: Allen and Unwin, 1911).

48. *Between Men. English Literature and Male Homosocial Desire* (New York: Columbia University Press, 1985), 92.

49. Ellen Moers, *The Dandy. Brummel to Beerbohm* (New York: University of Nebraska Press, 1960).

50. B. R. Burg, *Sodomy and the Perception of Evil. English Sea Rovers in the Seventeenth-Century Caribbean* (New York: New York University Press, 1983); see also J. Oosterhoff in this issue.

51. Cf., J. M. W. van Ussel, *Geschiedenis van het seksuele probleem* (Meppel: Boom, 1968), 207-57.

52. J. Chandos, *Boys together. English Public Schools 1800-1864* (New Haven, CT: Yale University Press, 1984).

53. M. A. Petersen, *Gevangenen onder dak* (Leiden: 1978).

54. G. Hekma, "De strijd om homoseksualiteit. De oprichting van een Janusbeeld," *Groniek* 77 (1982): 7-15.

55. P. J. A. von Feuerbach, *Lehrbuch des gemeinen in Deutschland gültigen Rechts* (Giessen, 1801), par. 467.

56. A. Moll, "Wat is staatsgeneeskunde?" *Tijdschrift voor Staatsgeneeskunde* 1 (1843): 4. The terms "staatsgeneeskunde" (medicine of the state) and "medische politie" (medical police) were popular in the 1840s and preceded "openbare hygiene" (public health), which became popular in the 1860s.

57. J. Donzelot, *La Police des Familles* (Paris: Gallimard, 1977), and J. Donzelot, *L'Invention du Social* (Paris: Gallimard, 1983).

58. B. A. Morel, *Traité des dégénérescences physiques, intellectuelles et morales de l'espèce humaine* (Paris: 1857); cf. J. E. Chamberlain and S. L. G. Gilman, eds., *Degeneration. The Dark Side of Progress* (New York: Columbia University Press, 1985). The 1850s saw the emergence of all kinds of evolutionary theory, e.g., Marxist socialism, Darwin's biological theory, and Gobineau's theory of the races.

59. A. Parent-Duchatelet, *De la Prostitution dans la ville de Paris*, 2 vols. (Paris: 1836).

60. Cf., J. L. Casper, *Handbuch der gerichtlichen Medizin*, vol. 2 (Berlin: 1858), and A. Tardieu, *Etude medico-legale sur les attentats aux moeurs* (Paris: 1857).

61. M. Praz, *The Romantic Agony* (London: Oxford University Press, 1933), chap. 4.

Homosexual Acts and Selves
in Early Modern Europe

Stephen O. Murray, PhD

In the introductory volume of *The History of Sexuality*, Foucault offhandedly included a "specification" of homosexual individuals in his examples of the elaboration of medical discourse about sexualities during the closing decades of the nineteenth century. Without providing even anecdotal evidence of the relationship between the "knowledge" about the "species homosexual" in the late-nineteenth century medical discourse and social control ("power") over those who were conceived within the new medical categories, Foucault suggested an important rupture occurred:

> As defined by the ancient civil or canonical codes, sodomy was a category of forbidden acts; their perpetrator was nothing more than the juridical subject of them. The nineteenth-century homosexual became a personage, a past, a case history, and a childhood in addition to being a type of life, a life form, and a morphology. . . . Homosexuality appeared as one of the forms of sexuality when it was transposed from the practice of sodomy onto a kind of interior androgyny, a hermaphroditism of the soul. The sodomite had been a temporary aberration; the homosexual was now a species.[1]

The paragraph from which this quotation is taken seems to have inseminated the minds of a goodly number of social historical theorists and researchers, who have produced a voluminous discourse in which both the late-nineteenth century rupture and the predomi-

---

Address correspondence to Instituto Obregón, 1360 De Haro, San Francisco, CA 94107-3239.

nance of discourse have been taken for granted. Foucault's exemplars and methodological pronouncements prior to *The History of Sexuality* (see especially *Discipline and Punish* and *Power/Knowledge*[2]) suggest that if he had followed up his paragraph on the medicalization of social control of homosexuality, these hypotheses would have been problematics rather than assumptions. Unfortunately, Foucault did not live to research the rupture he thought he glimpsed, and no one else seems to have examined earlier medical literature to sort out earlier conceptions of homosexuals in, for instance, Galenic medicine, to understand what was the discursive *status quo ante*.

At least in the United States, where the conflict between "fundamentalist" Christians and "scientific" medicine for control of what the one conceives as "immorality" and the other as "pathology" has been extensively discussed,[3] the medical conception of homosexuality seems to have spread from discourse to power only toward the end of the Second World War.[4] Interestingly, after the challenge to the legitimacy of that medicalization (viz., psychiatricalization) of homosexuality,[5] the remedicalization of the 1980s has returned to a focus on acts ("unsafe sex")[6] as the object for extirpation.

The studies collected in this issue concern the far side of the alleged medical rupture. Just as examination of recent history shows a continued focus on homosexual acts to be forbidden by medical authority and by Christian churches, examination of earlier history shows conception of homosexual persons, a homosexual species even.

Let us start the examination of evidence in this issue bearing on this question from the top—both of the map and of the social structure—with William and Mary and their courtiers. There is no record of homosexual acts involving either king or queen. Each was obviously homosocial and each bountifully rewarded same-sex favorites. William's standing army and his large land grants to court favorites threatened the power and status of the landed gentry. Indeed, the institution of an independent crown had been opposed by vassals whenever England was not at war, and sometimes even when it was.

The long-running conflict between the central power of the crown and large landowners was supplemented in William's time by an increasingly powerful bourgeoisie easily rallied against the aristocratic affectations of the royal court. William's enemies (who were united only by shared ethnicity, but had class interests antagonistic to each other) did not need any evidence of effeminacy, nor of sodomitical acts, in order to charge him (and his courtiers) with being sodomites. The successful general who wore the crown was transformed into a queen, "bent" (over) by Bentinck and Wentworth in satires discussed by Rubini.[7] The character of a sodomite was imputed to William (et al.). His sodomy, as conceived by his enemies, was not an act, nor a series of sexual acts from the great flux of human sexual potentiality.

The masculine company William kept, not any observable effeminacy, was threatening. That is, his army and the rewards of his male favorites were not symbolic affronts to the nation's masculine honor — which he successfully upheld with military victories. What was of concern to William's subjects was that the cost of his *masculine* success was his maintenance of countervailing powers (army and courtiers) to the power of the landowners and merchants, who were, thus, paying for loyalty to the king rather than to their own interests.

Rubini rightly places the discourse he analyzes in the political context of the era in which the discourse was produced, as I think Foucault would have, and as other authors in this collection also do in focusing on patronage.

Not only was the effeminacy of Philippe de France, duc d'Orleans, public knowledge, but his sexual "master," the chevalier de Lorraine, was publicly designated as his favorite. Oresko does not instance application of the label "sodomite" to Phillipe. He was a "pathic," not a "sodomite." The term "sodomite" was instead applied by his second wife, Elisabeth Charlotte, to the marquis d'Effiat. She was worried that her son might be believed to be d'Effiat's mistress (as her husband was the chevalier de Lorraine's). D'Effiat was a notorious debaucher of young men. Monsieur was unusual less in squandering everything to enrich the lewd boys (*bursch*) of increasingly lower status (who, according to his wife, ruled him) than in his notorious effeminacy.

Louis XIV tolerated his brother's appearance, behavior, and even extravagant gifts to his favorites. Whatever outrage there was for such favoritism did not tarnish the prestige of the Sun King. Indeed, invidious contrast with his brother may have enhanced Louis' prestige and perceived indispensability. Oresko suggests another political reason for Louis to go along with the gifts and grants of offices Monsieur and other princes made to their male favorites: enhancing ruling class cohesion. Whereas the patronage of the "foreign" king William was a threat to the "political nation" of England, Louis XIV worried less about intranational homosexual liaisons than about patronage opportunities within his own circle by those with "close family ties to dynasties on the other side of the Rhein and the other side of the Alps."

In seventeenth-century Portugal there was a named role for effeminate homosexual males, *fanchono*. Like the British mollies of the same time, *fanchonos* used female nicknames. The author of the letters Luiz Mott uncovered did not use a woman's name, and, indeed, began the very first letter by distinguishing himself from women. Whether Francisco Correa considered himself a *fanchone* or a sodomite or had no label for his sexual orientation, the vicar who denounced him to the Inquisition termed him a "fatuous whore of a sodomite." Like the other sodomites encountered in this issue, Francisco Correa lavished gifts on his fickle beloved. Unlike sodomites from other places and time, but like Monsieur, he was the *paciente* (in intercrural intercourse, in which the other "has his way").

Moving forward in time and back to merrie, but not gay England, Morris claims that gender roles hardened in England during the 1740-1850 period (during which the Somerset records she examined were produced), although her evidence hardly bears on this contention. There was a slight rise in prosecutions for attempted sodomy with intermittent convictions between 1780 and 1819. After 1829, there were hardly any more prosecutions and no more convictions at all. Between 1810 and 1829, there was a burst of nineteen bestiality prosecutions, most of which resulted in conviction. The correlation of peaks in bestiality and sodomy prosecutions suggests a heightened general anxiety about sexual crimes, but does nothing to establish either the contents of a code of male honor nor changes in it over time. No evidence is provided of effeminacy being attributed to those accused of either crime.

In the cases of attempted sodomy Morris discusses, the older man of higher status attempted to bugger a younger man of lower status.[8] The sodomites did not play the molly role. There is no question there was an effeminate stereotype by the mid-eighteenth century, at least in London, as Trumbach showed. However, in the popular view, mollies were buggered, not buggerers. If filling orifices other than those of human females reduced the honor of a Bath gentleman, circa 1800, no evidence is presented from literary records, legal records, or contemporary letters to justify considering Somerset's sexual honor code's distinctive from codes of male honor in other times and places in which sexual activity is masculine, whereas known sexual receptivity is not. There is also no evidence bearing on how the accused buggerers (of man or of beast) conceived of themselves, specifically, of their masculinity.

Morris' cases do undercut Trumbach's contention that gender-defined homosexuality had replaced age-graded homosexuality by 1700 and that "sodomites" were conceived of as effeminate. The "sodomite" was indeed "often pictured and could be found with his whore on one arm and his boy on the other" right through the first half of the eighteenth century, at least in Bath, despite the urban effeminates intermittently revealed by the Societies for the Reformation of Manners during the same era. However, such a libertine presumably was the "insertor" into both the boy and the whore. "Universal passivity" makes little sense in connection with "sodomitical assault" either, unless Trumbach is using only the narrow legal (non-)sense of "assault." Pubescent boys (in London, and all over Europe) were seduced by sodomites; the boys were not conceived of by anyone, least of all by themselves, as *being* the sodomites. James Fassett's "maidenhood" may seem ambiguous, but the Rev. Bradbury's yard in James Hearne is not. The Rev. Bradbury does not fit a characterization of "universal passivity." Nor can Michael Fly, who "unbuttoned the [twelve-year-old] boy's breeches, threw him face down on the bed and entered the boy." Other boys reported the same treatment: Dicks' yard was in Meeson's fundament, Spencer spoke of fucking Taylor, Ashford buggered the servant boy Curtis, and young apprentice Joseph Churchill was buggered by Portuguese sailors. Isaac Broderick's intercourse with schoolboys seems to have been intercrural rather than anal, but there is no question about who was on top, nor about who initiated the sexual encounter. George Duffus "was a pious, self-confident, aggressive, married man, who was, evidently accustomed to getting his way."

What modern sexologists call insertee behavior was exemplified by only one of the adult males (Holloway, who fellated a boy) whom Trumbach discusses. In none of these cases is any mention of effeminacy made in regards to the accused sodomite (e.g., Duffus). Similarly, there is no mention of evidence in the case records that those who kissed their adolescent prey "excluded women from their desires." It seems to me that along with the contention that it did not matter whether they were fucking boys or girls (which does not fit easily with the male exclusivity Trumbach also contends), the "universal passivity" of "sodomites" must derive from an a priori theory, not from the evidence presented.[9] Here, neither Morris nor Trumbach analyzes nonforensic sources in which sodomites and other species of libertines are, perhaps, described.

In the Dutch cases reported by Noordam, all cases of sodomy prior to 1730 involved older and wealthier men on top of boys: "In all cases the passive party was several years younger than the man who sought sexual conduct. Mostly, the men upon whom the attentions were forced were quite young, often even small boys." Also, a king rather than a queen of a sodomite club is elected. In Huusen's table, no one older than eighteen was accused of taking the passive role, and what little evidence of age is visible in Van Rosen's Danish data is also age-graded (a lieutenant colonel and his "lad"; a seventy-two-year-old and an eighteen-year-old). Oosterhoff's Dutch South African data focuses on mutual masturbation (which came to be glossed as "trying to sodomize each other" or as foreplay to sodomy), but where age data is included (Reijnier attempting to sodomize Christiaan), the elder is the insertor. Hendrik de Vogel appears to have been scandalized at the possibility of breaking from age-graded roles. Even as late as 1795 in the case of Visch discussed by Van der Meer, and in cases of "attempted sodomy" from still later, the elder is the putative "sodomite." There is no evidence of effeminate elders sexually servicing masculine youths in any of the Northern European cases discussed in this issue. Far into the eighteenth century, the sodomite was an insertor.

OTHER DISCOURSES

One fifteenth-century discourse in which sodomy was far more than a category of forbidden acts is the corpus of San Bernardino's sermons, in which there is a species "sodomite" who hates women and is enflamed (in Bernardino's simile, like a male dog on a bitch in heat) by attractive adolescent males. Michael Rocke shows with Florentine data from half a century later that the age-graded homosexuality bewailed by Bernardino existed. Those younger than fifteen *(fanciulli)* invariably took the passive role. With only one exception, those older than sixteen *(giovani)* took the active role. The latter were sodomites, the former were not, although according to Bernardino they were especially likely to be sodomites when they grew up (and took on the role of lover). Bernardino did not explain how the role transition occurred during the late teen years. That a change in sexual role was possible is implicit in his discussion, though he attributed the low Tuscan birthrate to habitual sodomy which could not be "cured" by marriage. Forty-five percent of the men aged between thirty and fifty involved in sodomy cases were married, and Bernardino recognized that marriage did not foreclose continuing to sodomize attractive boys.

He seems to have been less concerned with punishing sodomy than with reducing temptation, viz., provocative effeminate dress and the eagerness of parents to see their boys become objects of lust, avenues to patronage (civic offices), and recipients of gifts and money. Although he does not estimate the extent of the wealth of Florence which was redistributed to the families of sodomites' favorites, Rocke does estimate that one in twelve Florentine youths between ages twelve and twenty-five was denounced to the Officers of the Night between 1478 and 1483. There were concerted attempts to oppose what was indisputably a custom of age-graded Tuscan sodomy in the late fifteenth century.

Dall'Orto examines fifteenth- and sixteenth-century Italian neoplatonist discourse on *amor socraticus* (cf. Holberg's *Epistles* discussed by George Rousseau). Innate homosexuality, not merely isolated acts of sodomy, was conceived and defended by Ficino and his followers. Indeed, some men "naturally love men more than women and those nearly adults rather than children." One of the "natural" forces noted was birth during the conjunction of Venus and Saturn. The author of this explanation certainly conceived of—indeed embodied—the type of love he theorized, without the benefit of the revelations of late-nineteenth-century medical discourse. Fincino was himself enflamed by desire for an idealized youth, but sought to defend (his own) boy-loving nature by distinguishing spiritual from carnal love.

Dall'Orto shows that records of Socrates' and other ancients' behavior and philosophy legitimated same-sex love in which carnal union could not easily be kept distinct from its transcendence—"a very strange place and time are the bed and the night to admire boys' pure beauty," as one of Castiglione's characters remarked.

By the late sixteenth century, Socrates had been debased to exemplifying a sodomitical pedant, "an everlasting enemy of the female sex." Even so, his love for boys was called a natural inclination, and certainly was not conceived to have been random acts with no meaning from within undifferentiated sexual potentiality. Even though the platonic rhetoric was increasingly distrusted by the pious, it was used to legitimate homosexual behavior by Michelangelo Buonarrati and Benedetti Varchi. The homoeroticism expressed in Michelangelo's art was not unknown to the artist: the artist celebrated rather than unconsciously sublimated his homophile inclination.

It is not anachronistic to see that men (and presumably women, though they left fewer records) in the past sought to understand and justify homosexual desire, even if fifteenth- and sixteenth-century Italians may sound too "modern" to those catechized with the creation myths in a paragraph of Michel Foucault or an article of Mary MacIntosh.

In addition to the neoplatonist legitimation of same-sex love Dall'Orto found the records of a 1550 trial in Brescia in which the twenty-two-year-old defendant had sought the example of Jesus Christ in relation to his "catamite" or "bardache," John, "the beloved disciple," as precedent for adoring boys and taking "a lovely bum" as his altar, a view the defendant said came from *La cazzaria*. This libertine was on trial for exalting sodomy not for penetration or emission of seed into one of those "lovely bums."

That is, the sixteenth-century juridical focus was not on acts of sodomy, but on their rationalization.[10]

George Rousseau shows that by the late eighteenth century, alongside the traditional role of married tutor enamored by a student, "brought to the bed of" the student by "a passionate love," there were sexual relationships between some of the young men, one couple going on to live together in London. That the enduring relationship between Dyson and Akenside was not a total departure from earlier models is indicated by the continued presence of patronage. Dyson financed Akenside's medical education, subsidized his practice, gave him an annual stipend, and bought him a house where the two lived apart from Mrs. Dyson.

That Baxter's *Enquiry into the Nature of the Human Soul* does not provide an explicit rationalization for same-sex love should not be taken as evidence that Baxter's libido was "aim-inhibited." Rather, it should be viewed in the context of a social climate in which neither Bentham nor Byron could express their views on love between men.[11] Dyson was not an ideologist, and we do not know how he conceived of his relationship with Akenside. We know it was important to him from his investments in it: an enduring bond is not plausibly based on isolated acts of sodomy of no importance or meaning to those involved. As with the ongoing relationships mentioned by van der Meer, there is no indication of effeminate behavior in or out of bed by either partner.

BACK TO COURT

Pedro de León's compendium of Inquisition cases in Seville shows clerics and other sodomites taking poor youths home, giving them presents, dressing them up (sometimes effeminately) and sexually "using" them. A sheriff kept a gambling house with boys to sodomize. Departing from this pattern, one Negro (case 308) reported being paid to take the active role, and Perry suggests that a group of fifteen men burned together in 1600 (but not reported on by de León) and a *quadrilla* of eight men burned in 1585 were all a part of an effeminate subculture (like the mollies), rather than traditionally masculine sodomites. Whether a shift in cases represented a changing organization of homosexuality, or whether class and age-

graded sodomy continued apart from a growing effeminate subculture, cannot be determined, at least from the evidence Perry
reviewed here or in her earlier book. However, she points to a discourse (*picarós*) in which the question may be pursued.

Perry shows that while the religious rhetoric focused on the idleness and depravity of noblemen, the offices of the holy inquisition
endeavored to avoid trying nobles or priests. As in Venice (see
Ruggerio's book reviewed by Trumbach, and mentioned by Bray),
care was taken to prevent the defense of the faith from being turned
into an assault on social or religious orders, as was to occur in
England from Henry VIII's seizures of church lands to the decapita-
tion of Charles II.

A similar protection of the upper classes seems to have averted
prosecution in Denmark in 1816, and to have dampened prosecu-
tory zeal in the eighteenth-century Netherlands—permitting many
of those of the upper class who were accused to flee into exile;
usually, if not always, averting visibly special treatment of the governing classes; and not seizing the property of those who had fled to
avoid prosecution. The spectacle of exemplary punishment, as useful as it was for distracting popular unrest, had to be balanced (by
the ruling elites) against the potential disruption that might follow
from demonstrating moral laxity in the "superior" strata of society
and thereby nurturing resentments against the rich and powerful. As
in Seville, a fortuitous arrest would intermittently unroll a list of
other partners, and the networks thus revealed sometimes extended
to other cities (although the spectacular set of executions in Faan
were unrelated to the urban subcultures and conceptions). Those
with the bad luck to be remembered when a former sexual partner
was forced to name names had engaged in homosexuality "intentionally" and repeatedly. Eighteenth-century Dutch tribunals rou-
tinely asked about the entire sexual careers of those who confessed
to sodomy and were usually told about what van der Meer calls a
"mode of behavior," which the judges interpreted as demonstrating a permanent state of sin, not an isolated act.

Transvestism was not characteristic of those prosecuted in Amsterdam (or at the Cape of Good Hope). In Leiden and Frisia, only
class and age-graded relations are visible in the cases detailed by
Huusen and Noordam, and the aristocrat and his sexually complai-

sant footman form a pair repeated regularly in van der Meer's data. The mutual masturbation he reports from Amsterdam is not characteristic of either the sodomite patron role nor the molly role.[12] For that matter, without penetration there was no act of sodomy in medieval law. Nonetheless, van der Meer argues, without proof of the act, sodomites were vigorously prosecuted in the Netherlands—not for acts of sodomy, but "because they were supposed to be wells of contamination from which the vice would spread." (Huussen, Boon, and Oosterhoff make similar arguments, and Rey shows increasing arrests of "suspicious" people in "suspicious" locales within Paris, who had committed no sexual acts.)

Such beliefs remain salient for some people in the twentieth century who reject biological and psychological explanations of homosexual character and use their own versions of nominalism to demand that their children be safeguarded from homosexual recruitment (without which, in their view, homosexuality would vanish). Although "contagion" would seem to be a medical concept, its relationship with homosexuality long preceded late-nineteenth-century medicalization—as long ago as Justinian. In contrast, the eighteenth-century shift (without a specifiable "rupture") in forensic practice from prosecuting "complete sodomy" to "attempted sodomy," which Van der Meer, Boon and Oosterhoff note, has no discernible relation to "medicalization." The simultaneous shift from keeping track of sodomites to tracking "pederasts" in France, which Rey discusses, was similarly devoid of medical rationalization.

CONCLUSION

It seems to me that those gay intellectuals most attached to the "social constructionist" explaining away of homosexuality consider homosexual categories in isolation from other categories and in ignorance of the long philosophical conflicts between advocates of nominalism and realism, relexified as "social constructionism" and "essentialism." If anything, Dynes underestimated the extent of "social [de-]constructionists" ignorance of intellectual history when he noted:

In ignorance of the extensive eighteenth- and nineteenth-century German *Methodenstreit*, social constructionists have credited Foucault with inventing the wheel. Unable because of linguistic barriers or defects of training to monitor earlier discussions, SC advocates are forced to rely excessively on the Parisian polymath, although it was of course the Germans who as long ago as Herder in 1774, under the rubric of *Historismus*, insisted on the essential uniqueness of all historical situations.[13]

Those who would approach history as sites for infinitely variable social construction of homosexuality seem to lack familiarity not only with the historical debates, but also with the perennial debates about the reality of categories in philosophy and in incipiently professional social science (especially the discourse about differences between the sexes[14]); or with debates in contemporary biology, in which the punctuated equilibrium challenge to the neo-Darwinian synthesis questions whether there are species or merely inter-breeding populations on which evolution operates.[15] I have argued that it is intellectually dishonest to treat homosexual categories as uniquely social/historical/arbitrary.[16]

All categorical schema are to some extent arbitrary, infused with historical residues (if only from the very slowly changing organizing principles of human languages), learned and created by human beings with particular purposes in relation to others. Discovery of cultures that do not distinguish blue from green does not seem to have moved anyone to suggest abandoning the distinction in English. Whether labeled a raven, a crow, or "that black bird I see flying over the valley," there is a black bird visible out my window. *All* kinds of categories are "fuzzy sets"[17] and only the most trivial ones are exceptionless. Just as there are no exhaustive taxonomic slots for all plants or animals, or slots for every possible arcane geneological combination, there are fewer roles than behaviors in any culture. Regularities of cultural schema have been proposed (to take the meta-nominalist tack) or discovered (to be a meta-realist).[18]

Recent ethnology has gone beyond univariate descriptive statistics to identifying recurrent types of social organization of (mostly cognitive) domains. Not "Every society does A," but rather "There are organizations A, B, C, D attested in human societies; B and C develops from A; D develops from C; A never follows B, C, or D" is the form of argument. For homosexuality, gay organization has emerged where gender organization was, gender organization where age-graded organization was. The prominence of one, of course, does not entail the total disappearance of earlier organization.[19]

Roles

We do not even know how a young "catamite" graduated, let alone how one societal organization spawns another, but I think we know enough to see that claims for a universal effeminate homosexual role are unsupportable, whether the Freudian aetiology is offered, or a biological basis posited.[20] There not only have been, but *are* different conceptions of sexuality within European cultures and only a few different homosexual roles in all the world's cultures. Articles in this issue show that in early modern Europe the sodomite role did not entail exclusive homosexuality. The sodomite took his sexual pleasure from the catamite. The catamite — or his family — received gifts, including public offices, in exchange for this pleasure. As in the age-graded homosexuality described in Melanesia by Herdt[21] and in earlier epochs in Europe, with increasing age, the catamite role ceases to be available, and the older boy becomes an insertor, whether into younger boys or women. The molly (*mollitia* in Denmark) role resembles that of the *maricón* with expectations of feminine gender presentation and of insertee sexual behavior.[22]

Perhaps the dominant culture's equation of homosexuality and visible effeminacy served as a camouflage for homosexuality not accompanied by gender nonconformity, as Whitehead, and Callendar and Kochems argue was the case for homosexuality distinct from the *berdache* role in native American cultures.[23] As Trumbach noted, "Descriptions of the [molly-house] subculture which were intended for the general public always emphasized its effeminacy." With a stress on the "intended for the general public," such a conception may have permitted other homosexualities, including the traditional age-graded use of boys, to continue undisturbed. Even the majority of participants in the molly-house subculture "could not have been effeminate, let alone transvestite."[24] This is not to deny that there was a molly role in addition to the sodomite role; both of them were conceived and enacted considerably before any nineteenth-century medical discourse "constructed" homosexuality, or late-twentieth-century discourse denied knowledge about or enactment of any "homosexual role" until after the alleged medical revelation.

This late twentieth-century discourse is remarkable for hypostatizing the sociological concept of "role." Insofar as role is a technical term in social science, it contrasts with "essence" or "self" or "personnage." Indeed, the plurality of roles an individual plays was advanced by sociologists *against* psychologists' notions of fixed "personality."[25] In the discourse from which the term was borrowed, theater, an actor plays many roles over the course of a career, and sometimes over the course of a single evening. Not only do they enact different roles in different plays, but the actors are not always on stage, nor completely engulfed by a role even on stage. Analogously, a "homosexual role" may sometimes be enacted in appropriate settings by persons who play other roles at other times or in other places. Role distance is possible, as well as ignorance of role expectations.[26] Roles exist in a conceptual space between random behavior and psychic or social determinisms, except for social (de-)constructionists, who take anything less than full-time and total commitment to being "homosexual" as evidence for the lack of any "homosexual role."[27] As a defender of the heuristic value of the concept "role" argued against a realist, "The role formulation, emphasizing adult learning of sexual scripts and behaviors, allows for varied sexual experiences and consequent changes in self-identity in the course of an adult's lifetime."[28]

Historical data in this issue demonstrate normative (patterned) behavioral expectations about homosexual behavior, both on the part of "agents of social control" and of those trying to find sexual partners in early modern Europe. It should be obvious that sodomite is to sodomy as actor is to act. If there were only acts without any conception of their patterning, there would have been no need for the word "sodomite" (or "bugger" or "catamite"). There could not have been "suspicious" congregations of men at particular locales if a pattern of behavior was not conceivable, yet there is evidence that favored cruising locales were known to authorities in the seventeenth and eighteenth century in Northern Europe, and much earlier in Southern Europe. Possibly, those seeking homosexual liaisons noticed the same patterns of their behavior which were noticed by police and vigilantes, although social constructionists insist those involved were lost in the fogs of preconsciousness until medical discourse of the late nineteenth century revealed/constructed homosexuality.

There were roles (the complementary sodomite/catamite roles; the molly role). There were apologias for "Socratic love," and appeals of the sort "That's how God/nature made me. That's the way I am" which go beyond "secondary deviance" to what Kitsuse[29] calls "tertiary deviance"; that is, affirmation/legitimation of the "primary deviance" and challenge to the legitimacy of the stigma. Dall'Orto describes a Christian apologetic, as Boswell has others. Dall'Orto, Mott, Oresko, Rubini, Rousseau, and Rey point to sustained relationships. Rey, in particular, shows a consciousness of consciousness among those who "understand" (as in contemporary Spanish *entendido*, literally "in the know") and "think along those lines." Even the *mouches* noticed more than isolated acts of sodomy.

Forensic Records

Of course, behavior sometimes departs from norms (and the norms may be upheld even by those whose behavior departs from them). According to Durkheim, a certain amount of variance from norms is "natural" and necessary to show the boundaries of acceptable behavior. The spectacle of exemplary punishment is one demonstration of the power of society. A steady stream jades spectators and undercuts the plausibility that extreme punishment was deserved for extraordinary violation of man's, nature's, or God's laws. Perhaps more saliently, early modern European elites were loath to loose mobs, especially those whose destructive fever was stoked by punishment of members of the elite, including the ostensible moral elite of priests and monks. Authorities in various locales were also concerned that trials and executions might publicize forbidden sexualities rather than provide edifying (Durkheimian) moral lessons.

Most work done on the history of homosexuality has drawn data from forensic records. This may account for the popularity of neo-Durkheimian views about exemplary punishment, boundary maintenance[30] and acceptance of "normal deviance." The preponderance of forensic records as data sources perhaps also provides good reason for some skepticism about any generalizing about "real sexual patterns" from unsystematic (indeed, often seemingly accidental) prosecutions. Certainly, the fluctuations in rates of prosecutions *cannot* be taken as indicating changes in rates of homosexual behavior. Before the late seventeenth century, there does not seem to have been any European police force attempting systematically to monitor sodomy (and thereby providing social historians of later centuries some sort of random sample). As Rocke and Hekma note, Christian institutions were willing — indeed eager — to persecute sodomites, but they lacked the twentieth-century technological capacity for mass murder.

In the early modern period and before, arrests were not randomly distributed, nor were individual arrests even remotely orthogonal.[31] Indeed, until the rise of the Societies for the Reformation of Manners in England, fluctuations from one year to another mostly can be resolved into a chain of accusations within a network. The arrest of a key informant with many connections to other sodomites recurrently led to a spate of criminal cases, more spectacularly in the Dutch "pogrom" of 1730. In another year, elsewhere, someone without connections simply may have groped the wrong person, so his arrest led to no others. Trumbach suggested those unfamiliar with the subculture were more likely to make mistakes about where and to whom to make sexual approaches.[32] Such arrests did not trigger chain reactions and probably were more common than arrests of "acculturated" denizens of urban subcultures.

Case rates are not valid indicators of the criminalized behavior, and those arrested or convicted are unlikely to be representative of the population of those who commit the act, even those who commit it recurrently. Contemporary sociologists and criminologists do not generalize about "gay people" or "criminals" from examining clinical or incarcerated people: being caught or being treated indicates someone is not a typical member of these conceptual classes. I can think of no reason to suppose that the set of those who came to the attention of the criminal justice system in earlier, less rational- ized epochs is any less biased a sample from which to extrapolate. What the accused are reported to have said or done can show that a conception or behavior was present in the society, but cannot estab- lish how typical it was nor what was the range of variation within that society.

I have reviewed some indications of how people thought and be- haved in early modern Europe, but I would like to finish by warning that neither court records nor the writings of ideologists (for church, state, or for same-sex love) should be accepted as capturing the essence of how homosexuality was generally understood by those actually involved in recurrent homosexual behavior in any of the places discussed. Historians are creating "homosexualities" every bit as much as the often-mentioned medical discourse, and at times with as distorted a basis for generalization. It is possible to overesti- mate the flux of the past and the extent of attested intercultural variation.[33] It is possible to evaporate/deconstruct a term by so nar- rowing its definition that it is necessarily devoid of empirical con- tents, and then finding that it doesn't fit a particular case, as has been done to "homosexual role" in early modern Europe.

Reification is not the only danger a social historian faces.

NOTES

1. Michel Foucault, *The History of Sexuality* (New York: Pantheon, 1978), 42-43.

2. Idem., *Discipline and Punish* (New York: Pantheon, 1977); *Power/ Knowledge* (New York: Pantheon, 1980).

3. Richard Hofstader, *Anti-Intellectualism in American Life* (New York: Vintage, 1964); Paul M. Starr, 1983. *The Social Transformation of American Medicine* (New York: Basic Books); Irving K. Zola, "Medicine as an Institution of Social Control," *Sociological Review* 20 (1972): 487-504; Vern L. Bullough, "Homosexuality and the Medical Model," *Journal of Homosexuality* 1 (1974): 99-110; Peter Conrad, "The Discovery of Hyperkinesis," *Social Problems* 23 (1975): 12-18; Peter Conrad and Joseph W. Schneider, *Deviance and Medicaliza- tion* (Toronto: Mosby, 1980); Joseph W. Schneider, "Deviant Drinking as Dis- ease," *Social Problems* 25 (1978): 361-72.

4. Edwin H. Sutherland, "The Diffusion of Sexual Psychopath Laws,"

American Journal of Sociology 56 (1950): 142-48; George Chauncey, Jr., "From Sexual Inversion to Homosexuality," *Salmagundi* 58/59 (1982): 114-46. Chauncey shows the lack of medical categories in a homosexual scandal just after the first world war in "Christian Brotherhood or Sexual Perversion?" *Journal of Social History* 19 (1985): 189-211.

5. Ronald Bayer, *Homosexuality and American Psychiatry* (New York: Basic Books, 1981); Ronald Bayer and Robert Spitzer, "The Status of Homosexuality in DSM-III," *Journal of the History of the Behavioral Sciences* 18 (1982): 32-52.

6. Kenneth W. Payne and Stephen J. Risch, "The Politics of AIDS," *Science for the People* 16 (1984): 17-24; Philip M. Kayal, "'Morals,' Medicine and the AIDS Epidemic," *Journal of Religion and Health* 24 (1985): 218-38; Martin P. Levine, "The Medicalization of 'Sexual Compulsiveness,'" Society for the Study of Social Problems, Washington, DC, 1985; Stephen O. Murray and Kenneth W. Payne, "The Remedicalization of Homosexuality," Society for the Study of Social Problems meetings, Washington, 1985; Idem., "The Political Semantics of AIDS," *Medical Anthropology*, in press; Conrad and Schneider, *Deviance*.

7. Although Wentworth is unambiguously a "top" in *Jenny Cromwell's Complaint*, "Bardash" and "Beating Berdasha" are difficult to credit as locutions for "top" (see Claude Courouve, "The Word 'Berdache,'" *Gay Books Bulletin* 8 [1982]: 18-19). I read Scarsdale and Shrewbury not as being mollies, but as mounting them.

8. The Rev. Donnisthorpe committed fellatio, which no one seems to have equated with buggery. It was when Donnisthorpe tried to lay Reader down, that resistance, which eventually led to charges of attempted buggery, began.

9. This is at odds with Trumbach's earlier discussion of stigmatization in his justly famed "London's Sodomites," *Journal of Social History* 11 (1977): 1-33, and with the recurrent observation that "queens" cruised the "studs" in pregay North American homosexuality, just as *pasivos* take the initiative in finding and picking up *activo* partners in Latin America (see Stephen O. Murray, *Gai Saber Monograph* 5, 1987). In interpreting the reports of penises in hands, I would propose the commonsense interpretive principle that which penis is in whose hand signifies the intent of whoever put it there. Thus, if A took hold of B's privates, A intended B to be the insertor. If C put his own penis in D's hand, C intended to be the insertor. For reasons unclear to me, Trumbach interprets the initiator of either (A and C) to be passive. Only the second case seems to have been treated as part of "sodomitical assault," leaving what A, B, or D were regarded as (by themselves, by their peers, or by the courts) unrecorded.

10. There was a clear concern with acts of heresy, but also with determining what Francesco Calcagno believed; that is, whether he was a "heretic."

11. Louis Crompton, *Byron and Greek Love* (Berkeley: University of California Press, 1985).

12. Although van der Meer is notably cautious about generalizing from foren-

sic evidence to everyday life, he does not consider whether the preponderance of mutual masturbation was the favorite sexual act for confessing to or for engaging in. (He also takes the lack of evidence in forensic archives for evidence of a lack of any lesbian subculture.)

13. Wayne Dynes, "Reply," *SGC Newsletter* 46 (1986): 9-10; also see, idem., "Of Slide Shows, Local History and the Social Constructionist Theory," *SGC Newsletter* 45 (1985): 6-9.

14. Rosalind Rosenberg, *Beyond Separate Spheres* (New Haven, CT: Yale University Press, 1982).

15. Ernst Mayr, *The Growth of Biological Thought* (Cambridge, MA: Harvard University Press, 1981).

16. Stephen O. Murray, "Fuzzy Sets and Abominations," *Man* 18 (1982): 396-99; Idem., *Social Theory/Homosexual Realities* (New York: Gay Academic Union, 1984).

17. Paul Kay, "Tahitian Words for 'Race' and 'Class,'" *Publications de la Société dé Océanistes* 39 (1978): 81-91; Linda Coleman and Paul Kay, "Prototype Semantics," *Language* 57 (1981): 26-44; Lofti Zadeh, "Fuzzy Sets," *Information & Control* 8 (1965): 338-53.

18. On color see Brent Berlin and Paul Kay, *Basic Color Terms* (Berkeley: University of California Press, 1969). On ethnobiology see Brent Berlin, "Reflections on the Growth of Ethnobotanical Nomenclature," *Language in Society* 1 (1972): 51-86; Cecil H. Brown, "Folk Zoological Life Forms," *American Anthropologist* 81 (1979): 791-817. On kinship see Alfred L. Kroeber, "Classificatory Systems of Relationship," *Journal of the Royal Anthropological Institute* 39 (1909): 81-84. On social organization of homosexuality see Trumbach, "London's"; Stephen O. Murray, *Social Theory*; Barry D. Adam, "Age, Structure, and Sexuality," *Journal of Homosexuality* 11 (1986): 19-34.

19. The rise to prominence of one does not completely erase the existence of other relations. Not only were there simultaneously homosexual samurai and kabuki in Togukawa Japan, there is age-graded, queenly, and gay homosexuality in U.S. cities, circa 1986. It is not clear to me from the literature on France whether the change from sodomite to pederast in the forensic records represents a relexification of a role, or a different "species."

20. Frederick L. Whitam and Robin M. Mathy, *Male Homosexuality in Four Societies* (New York: Praeger, 1986); Joseph Harry, "Defeminization and Social Class," *Archives of Sexual Behavior* 14 (1985): 1-12.

The inadequate basis for generalization from these samples has been succinctly stated by Joseph M. Carrier, "Childhood Cross-gender and Adult Homosexuality," *Archives of Sexual Behavior* 25 (1986): 87-91.

21. Gilbert H. Herdt, *Guardians of the Flute* (New York: McGraw-Hill, 1980); idem., *Ritualized Homosexuality in Melanesia* (Berkeley: University of California Press, 1984); idem., *Sambia* (New York: Holt, 1987).

22. Joseph M. Carrier, *Urban Mexican Male Homosexual Encounters*. Ph.D. diss., University of California, Irvine (1975); Stephen O. Murray, *Male Homosexuality in Central and South America* (New York: Gay Academic Union, 1987);

Idem., "Lexical and Institutional Elaboration: The 'Species Homosexual' in Guatemala." *Anthropological Linguistics* 22 (1980): 177-85.

23. Trumbach, "London's," 17-18. Attempts to argue homosexuality out of the gender nonconformity of the berdache role include Harriet Whitehead, "The Bow and the Burdenstrap" in *Sexual Meaning*, Ed. S. Ortner and H. Whitehead (Cambridge University Press, 1981), 80-115; Charles Callendar and Lee Kochems, "The North American Berdache," *Current Anthropology* 24 (1983): 443-70; idem., "Men and not men," *Journal of Homosexuality* 11 (1986): 165-78.

24. Trumbach, "London's," 18.

25. Stephen O. Murray, "Edward Sapir and 'Chicago School' Studies of Personality and Language," *History of Sociology* 6 (1986): 75-108; idem., "The Reception of Anthropological Work in American Sociology," *Journal of the History of the Behavioral Sciences*, 1987.

26. Erving Goffman, *Encounters* (Indianapolis: Bobbs-Merrill, 1961), 85-152.

27. Attempts to elevate the requirements for use of the term "subculture" and "community" similar to those made to remove "role" from any historical/empirical exemplification have also been made. Evidence from systematic attempts to extirpate cruising grounds in various European cities in the fifteenth, sixteenth, and seventeenth centuries are reviewed Stephen O. Murray and Kent Gerard, "Renaissance Sodomite Subcultures?" *Among Men/Among Women* (Amsterdam: University of Amsterdam, 1983): 182-96.

Also see Michael Goodich, *The Unmentionable Vice* (Santa Barbara, CA: Ross-Erikson, 1977); Patricia H. LaBalme, "Sodomy and Venetian Justice in the Renaissance," *Legal History Review* 52 (1985): 217-54; and Guido Ruggerio, *The Boundaries of Eros* (New York: Oxford University Press, 1985).

For the eighteenth century, evidence of a subculture is overwhelming; see Trumbach, "Sodomitical Subcultures, Sodomitical Roles and the Gender revolution of the Eighteenth Century," *Eighteenth Century Life* 9 (1985): 109-21. On the applicability of the social science technical term "community" to contemporary urban life in North America see Stephen O. Murray, "The Institutional Elaboration of a Quasi-ethnic Community," *International Review of Modern Sociology* 9 (1979): 165-78.

28. Richard C. Omark, "A Comment on the Homosexual Role," *Journal of Sex Research* 14 (1978): 273-74. On the misuse of the ineractionist concept "role" by both constructionists and realists, see Stephen O. Murray, "The 'Homosexual Role,' Homosexual Roles, and 'Homosexual Occupational Roles,'" American Sociological Association, Chicago, 1987; idem., "Role," *Encyclopedia of Homosexuality*, ed. Wayne Dynes (New York: Garland Press, 1988).

29. John I. Kitsuse, "Coming Out All Over," *Social Problems* 28 (1980): 1-13.

30. There is something very odd about simultaneously claiming homosexuality was not differentiated as a concept before the late nineteenth century and that sodomy cases represent the sort of boundary maintenance posited by John I. Kitsuse, "Societal Reactions to Deviant Behavior," *Social Problems* 9 (1962): 247-

56; and Kai Erikson, *Wayward Puritans* (New York: John Wiley and Sons, 1966). The Essex School at once embraces Durkheim and denies the existence of "social facts."

31. John I. Kitsuse and Aaron V. Cicourel, "A Note on the Use of Official Statistics," *Social Problems* 11 (1963): 131-38, discussed the fallacy of taking such data as indicating rates of criminal behavior and stressed that "criminal statistics fail to reflect the decisions made and discretion used by law enforcement personnel" (p. 138). In regard to sodomy in early modern Europe, considerable discretion was exercised in deciding whom to prosecute; see Trumbach, "Sodomite Subcultures," van der Meer, and Perry in this issue. Sociologists have eschewed countable cases and drawn on literary records as more likely sources of historical conceptions; see the work of so formidable a quantitative criminologist as David Greenberg as well as that of McIntosh and her sociologist followers.

32. Trumbach, "London's," 10.

33. The same writers tend to underestimate intracultural variance in behavior and meaning, even now.

BOOK REVIEWS

HOMOSEXUALITY IN RENAISSANCE ENGLAND. Alan Bray.
(*London: Gay Men's Press, 1982, 149 pp.*)

In his book, Alan Bray charts the contours of male homosexuality from the Elizabethan through the Stuart eras, offering a convincing description of its place within English society. Bray argues that until the end of the seventeenth century, homosexuality lacked its own distinctive social forms and institutional networks. Rather, ordinary homosexual behavior was contained within broader, already existing social relations and cultural structures; that is, same-sex institutions such as schools and the military, dependent relations of work, education, church, patronage, household, and family.

At the same time, societal notions of sodomy and buggery were couched in general terms as forms of debauchery into which all were potentially subject to fall. This concept of debauchery formed an integral part of the elaborate symbolic system of Renaissance England, expressed in an apocalyptic demonology which associated homosexuality, and indeed all forms of "sexual excess," with the evil forces of disorder: witchcraft and sorcery, heresy and papism, treason and subversion. All of these posed a continual threat to the divinely ordained order of nature and nation. Yet it was the extreme and other-worldly character of these symbolic associations that allowed the participants and observers of everyday homosexual interactions to avoid making any cognitive connection between their behavior and perceptions and the devastations of plague, famine, and earthquake assumed in the Sodom myth.

As a result of this cognitive divorce of the commonplace from cultural symbol, existing forms of homosexual behavior (which I label "embedded" homosexuality) were left largely unmolested by the repressive forces of crown, church, and community. Only when they transgressed the social boundaries or power structures beyond the merely sexual sphere were homosexual individuals attacked, and no mass persecutions took place. Indeed, as Bray argues, very real benefits for social stability flowed from the allowance of embedded homosexual relations, though this allowance was in no sense a conscious tolerance.

By the late seventeenth century, however, a new situation had emerged with the formation of urban homosexual subcultures in London and elsewhere. London's homosexual clubs, known as "molly houses," the established networks of public cruising areas, a distinctive sexual semiotics of slang, dress, and gesture — all of these could be seen as forerunners of modern gay subculture. With the rise of molly culture, homosexual males now had an organized support structure, a social role, and an identifiable public presence. Such visibility and concentration allowed public exposure and persecution, but the periodic waves of repression that ensued also worked to encourage subcultural solidarity and consolidate subcultural forms.

Here Bray's account runs into problems. He cannot explain the transition from the embedded homosexuality of the Stuart era to the sodomite subcultures of the late seventeenth and early eighteenth centuries. He attempts an explanation in terms of larger changes in intellectual and religious culture, of a transformation of world view from unitary conceptions to particularistic individualism, by alluding to the scientific revolution and by citing John Locke at length.

Offered, however tentatively, by way of conclusion to an otherwise intriguing work, Bray's interpretive leaps come as a decided disappointment. He passes over the more important large-scale changes in economic and social relations and, more obviously, fails to relate the homosexual transition to the broader reorganization of sexual culture taking place within English society: the simultaneous rise of libertine subcultures as a sort of heterosexual complement to sodomite subcultures; the development of commercial markets in pornography, prophylactics, and sexual devices; the beginnings of the two-century-long "war against masturbation"; the emergence of moral purity movements. Bray's approach is substantially influenced by Foucault, but he seems too enamored of the earlier archaeological phase of Foucault's research, with its emphasis on terms and categories. Bray does not go far enough beyond this (albeit very necessary) type of investigation to be able to offer a compelling interpretation of changing social and institutional practices.

A few lesser sins of omission also afflict Bray's book. While he skillfully manages to incorporate an enormous variety and quantity of Elizabethan and Stuart sources, Bray unaccountably ignores certain bodies of important evidence. This particularly affects his account of English attitudes toward effeminacy and cross-dressing — which he shows to be important constitutive elements in the social life and public image of mollies. While he adequately demonstrates that these characteristics were not associated with homosexual behavior before the late seventeenth century, his analysis could have more easily, and more convincingly, been buttressed through an examination of the anti-transvestite tracts of the Stuart era (e.g., the series of pamphlets published in 1620 that included *Hic Mulier: or, the Man-Woman* and *Haec Vir: or the Womanish-Man*).

Bray also leaves unaddressed a subject that has received extensive historical investigation during the 1980s, the role of cross-dressing and gender reversal in rituals of popular protest — rituals, it turns out, that were taken over by the mollies and transformed for their own purposes. An approach similar to that of those social historians (such as N. Z. Davis) who have been utilizing concepts and methods derived from cultural anthropology would be particularly well-suited to the analysis of this sort of historical material.

Despite these flaws and missteps, Bray's book is a remarkable achievement, breaking new ground and offering fresh perspectives on an era in English homosexuality which has bedeviled many of the best researchers in gay history, including McIntosh, Trumbach, and Weeks. Bray's prose is a joy to read, clear and direct, unencumbered by jargon. The handful of illustrations provided are nicely reproduced and serve well to elucidate and reinforce the insights of the text. The extensive notes and bibliography will be welcomed by all scholars of the period. Only the lack of an index (a regrettable economy measure) mars this otherwise superb reference source. Produced outside the academy (Bray is a civil servant and gay activist in London, until recently unaffiliated with a university), the quality of this work not only rivals but surpasses that of all but a handful of professional historians.

Kent Gerard

SODOMY AND THE PERCEPTION OF EVIL: ENGLISH SEA ROVERS IN THE SEVENTEENTH-CENTURY CARIBBEAN. B. R. Burg. (*New York: New York University Press, 1983. 215 pp.*)

Burg's book has an intriguing title and opens up a new and exciting area of historical investigation: homosexual behavior in an autonomous male society of pirates, in which men for the most part lived by their own choice without women (things go better with men). The point of this history is simple: homosexual behavior in seventeenth-century England was hardly condemned or persecuted. The English pirates of the Caribbean at times lived extravagantly and had multifarious unproblematical homosexual contacts.

The persecution and condemnation of homosexuality is, according to Burg, a phenomenon of a later time period. This is a very interesting thesis, but one questions how much material exists to substantiate it. Actually, Burg offers only speculative proof to support his proposals. Such speculation is sometimes contradictory and often fails to rise about the level of twaddle. His primary evidence relates to the casually permissive stance of seventeenth-century English authorities with respect to sodomy between adult men, and with twentieth-century research about all-male associations, especially prisons. Despite the inadequacies of this evidence, it seems that the arguments against it are even more problematical.

A second objection to Burg's book must also be noted. Although at the outset he posits that homosexuality is a cultural geography, later in his book he repeatedly invokes the notion of a biologically determined homosexuality. After he has made it plausible that the death penalty for sodomy was handed down only in exceptional cases in seventeenth-century England — for example, those involving the seduction of minors — he then uses this argument to prove the relatively free homosexual behavior among pirates. It turns out, however, that most homosexual relations among pirates were indeed entirely pederastic, and thus punishable.

Burg's speculations in the final chapter about possible connections between homosexuality, piracy, sadism, and effeminacy are striking principally for their banality, and are frequently based on outdated research. Although Burg allows that homosexuals are no more sadistic or effeminate than heterosexuals, and that pirates were masculine, not sadistic, he does not shrink from recording several gruesome instances of their cruelty. As a criterion of cruelty, Burg uses the English criminal law of the era. This issue also is treated too hastily and casually.

Despite Burg's dubious arguments and casual use of concepts, this remains a pioneering work. First, of all, Burg does point out the relative tolerance toward homosexuality in seventeenth-century England. In *Homosexuality in Renaissance England* (London: Gay Men's Press, 1982), Alan Bray emphasizes precisely the homophobic character of the times. Yet at the same time he notes that extensive persecution of homosexual behavior is not evident until the eighteenth century. Although more research is needed, there seems to be a paradoxical simultaneity between the Enlightenment, a golden age of "reason," and the onset of extensive persecution and strict condemnation of homosexual behavior. There is a strong caesura in the history of homosexuality around 1700: after that point, alongside "enlightened" ideas about homosexual practices and the beginning of active opposition to certain homosexual acts, there is the origin of an explicitly homosexual subculture. All of this raises questions substantial enough for an entire cohort of gay studies scholars.

Burg's work is also interesting, even innovative, on another level. Up until now, homosexual relations in all-male associations have not yet been studied by historians, despite the considerable attention given to the navy, the military, and monastic societies, to mention just the best known "homosocial" ways of life. Burg's book demonstrates that investigating more than just the homosexual minority would be advantageous to gay studies and would advance the quality of its analysis. Closer study of homosexual arrangements throughout history could broaden the perspectives of this area of research.

Gert Hekma

SODOMY AND THE PERCEPTION OF EVIL: ENGLISH SEA ROVERS IN THE SEVENTEENTH-CENTURY CARIBBEAN. B. R. Burg. (*New York: New York University Press, 1983: repr. 1985 under the title* Sodomy and the Pirate Tradition.)

Burg's thesis is that, during the late seventeenth century, ". . . homosexual acts were not integrated with or subordinated to alternate styles of sexual contact. They were the only forms of sexual expression engaged in by members of the buccaneer community" (xvii).

Burg sees as the original impetus to such a society the lack of women sexually available to the following groups in Stuart England: (1) the lowest orders (vagrants, vagabonds, and apprentices); (2) sailors, in an age in which shore leave was virtually nonexistent; and (3) English settlers in the Caribbean. Those who would become buccaneers had already been exposed to homosexuality and had chosen either or both the single-sex environments of long-distance ocean voyaging or Caribbean settlement.

Having built a plausible (if unsubstantiated) argument for the selective recruitment of buccaneers from those with a homosexual preference, Burg has rather little to say about the kind of homosexual society that developed. Surprisingly, having emphasized how different sexual conceptions and social life in the late-seventeenth century were from ours, and having emphasized that the buccaneer community was unique in not having to build a homosexual enclave within a majority heterosexual society, Burg proceeds to extrapolate 1960s studies of prisons and sex offenders to explain this unique and vanished society.

Burg contends that what he is doing is "archaeology," yet it is as if his excavation consisted of bulldozing an abandoned junkyard that was built on an ancient burial mound, and then making no attempt to distinguish between the two very different sources of the material thrown up. Real archeologists may work from fragments (and Burg's actual data on pirate sexuality consist of a very few fragments), but they are preoccupied with distinguishing among strata (and with specifying what changes from stratum to stratum). Certainly, Foucault's archaeology does not garble epochs like this, either.

A list of preconditions for a social formation is no substitute for a description of its history and structure, but the former is all Burg supplies. I hope the next investigator of this topic will be more interested in historical facts, and less interested in speculations based on inapt analogies to modern prison populations. Even Burg's opaque prose cannot entirely disguise an intriguing historical phenomenon.

Stephen O. Murray

DE WESENTLIJKE SONDE VAN SODOMIE EN ANDERE VUYLIGHEDEN. SODOMIETEN-VERVOLGINGEN IN AMSTERDAM 1730-1811. *Theo van der Meer. (Amsterdam: Tabula, 1984. 128 pp.)*

Beginning in 1730, the Netherlands was witness to the routine persecution of sodomy. Several publications on this topic have already appeared.[1] Recently, Dirk Jaap Noordam described the persecutions of sodomites in Leiden during the period 1533-1811.[2] In the near future, Professor I. Schöffer will publish the late Leon Boon's dissertation on the sodomy trials throughout the Netherlands in the period 1730-31. With his book, *De wesentlijke sonde von sodomie en andere vuyligheden. Sodomieten-vervolgingen in Amsterdam 1730-1811* (The essential sin of sodomy and other filthy deeds. Sodomy persecutions in Amsterdam 1730-1811), Theo van der Meer offers a stimulating contribution to the historiography of sodomy.

The story of the persecutions is now fairly well known. For moral theologians and pastors, sodomy was the complete inversion of divine law and nature. For criminal justice, this sin was a capital offense. John Boswell has convincingly argued that the negative outlook on sodomy was not firmly established until the thirteenth century, thus challenging the simplistic notion that homophobia was first and foremost an unalterable result of Judeo-Christian tradition.[3]

But what was sodomy? According to van der Meer, this term was used prior to 1700 for any sexual act that did not have procreation as its goal, whereas after 1700 it came to mean, above all, anal penetration. He takes this notion of sodomy from Joost de Damhouder's *Practijcke in Criminele Saken* (Practice in Criminal Affairs), which saw numerous printings in many languages in the sixteenth and seventeenth centuries, and also derives it from his own research. Because he uses no other sources for the period 1300-1700, his descriptions fail to convince. In addition, his explanations of the sodomy persecutions dangle because of the lack of information about the period before 1700. Van der Meer writes more about the notions of sodomy in the eleventh century than in the seventeenth, leaving a regrettable gap.

The Dutch sodomy trials got underway in Utrecht in 1730 when two sodomites were apprehended *in flagrante* in the cathedral. Due to the confession of a certain Zacharias Wilsma, the persecution quickly took on a national character and spread to include Amsterdam. In 1730, three sodomites were strangled there and two were drowned, while many others were banned *in absentia* or were released due to lack of evidence. The Amsterdam persecutions continued at irregular intervals until 1811, the year in which the crime completely disappeared from the penal law. Between 1743 and 1765, the court handed down ten death penalties due to sodomy. The standard mode of execution was strangling, a typical punishment for women; the court apparently found it entirely appropriate for sodomites, who did not conform to the male role.

After 1765, the Amsterdam court no longer handed down any death sentences, but the number of prosecutions against persons who did not flee increased dramatically. Especially after 1795 (i.e., after the Batavian Revolution and the pseudoflowering of Enlightenment ideals), the number of sodomy convictions increased greatly. The punishments were less severe, yet on the other hand the acts of which suspects were accused took on a different character. Before 1795, the court condemned sodomites after they confessed to anal penetration; after 1795, attempted or intended homosexual seduction itself was punishable.

Here lies van der Meer's first noteworthy research finding. The widely hailed Enlightenment, in which God had to make space for so-called "reason" and "nature," had a more double-edged effect than the adepts of rationalism and humanism like to believe. In the first place, the theories of such enlightened philosophers as Montesquieu, Voltaire, Rousseau, and Perrenot certainly do not manifest "enlightenment" on homosexual relationships. Perhaps they quarreled with the death penalty. At the same time, they thought it would be possible to eliminate sodomy through preventive measures against homosexual acts. Van der Meer shows convincingly that even the practical consequences of enlightenment ideals by no means produced unambiguous progress with respect to moral-theological theory and practice. The regime of reason proved to be no less terrible for sodomites than the regime of the Bible. In the eighteenth and nineteenth centuries, humanism and rationalism brought about an important breakthrough that would later serve as the basis for the homosexual emancipation movement. At the same time, the Enlightenment brought about a rationalization, humanization, and expansion of social control, so that each individual could now either benefit or become a victim, depending on the situation.

EMERGING IDENTITY

In addition, the book contains an extensive anecdotal topography of the homosexual subculture in Amsterdam. One problem is van der Meer's definition of subculture, that which "arises in those situations in which homosexuality does not fit within any legitimate form of meeting and of organizing of sexuality." First of all, the question seems to be whether every form of meeting was excluded for eighteenth-century homosexuals. In addition, the description is too negative — as though a subculture exists only by virtue of a prohibition. The lifestyles of sodomites can be described as a way of organizing surplus within their group in a social situation of scarcity (and not of illegality per se).

Unfortunately, the topography of the subculture does not yield a sociography. The ages and marital status of homosexuals charged or convicted in court are not shown. The author also did not have courage to distinguish between the various group cultures and their resistance to social reprisals. It would have been interesting if he had tested Noordam's suppositions about marriage, homosexuality, and bisexuality.[2] The latter author suggested an increasing uncoupling of marriage and homosexuality in the eighteenth century.

The question of homosexuality and marriage is intriguing because it is related to a question that van der Meer does discuss extensively; namely, the creation and social acceptance of the homosexual. On this point, he polemicizes to some extent against those (such as Jeffrey Weeks and the present writer) who claim that modern homosexual identity is a nineteenth-century medical creation. He posits that as early as the eighteenth century, a shift can be seen with respect to the persecution of sodomites. To an increasing extent, judges begin to busy themselves with the question of who the sodomites are rather than what they have done. Doubtless—and this I must grant van der Meer—elements of homosexuality of a later date do exist as early as the eighteenth century. But the theoretical creation of the homosexual, with all its practical consequences, did not come about until the "psychopathia sexualis" of the late nineteenth century.

John Marshall, incidentally, has nuanced the idea of the creation of the homosexual from another angle. According to Marshall, the definition of the homosexual as someone with a sexual preference for persons of the same sex did not become established until the past few decades.[4] Paralleling Marshall, I, too, believe that the social acceptance of homosexuality as an exclusive proclivity of a minority of people is something typical of recent years. Only an upper stratum of doctors, homosexuals, and jurists were acquainted with the theory and practice of "psychopathia sexualis" around 1900.

The question of marriage and homosexuality plays an important role in the creation of the homosexual. Their gradual uncoupling since the eighteenth century would support van der Meer's theory that homosexuality began around that time to be seen as an exclusive motive for behavior. After all, the definition of homosexuality as a special sexual proclivity or orientation means that homosexuality and marriage are incompatible. By examining the marital status of sodomites, van der Meer could have tested his subtle description of what he terms the sociogenetic approach to homosexuality.

PERSECUTIONS

Another interesting part of his book deals with the interpretation of the sodomy persecutions. He brings two possible theories to the fore, one materialistic, one sociogenetic. He opens the discussion by positing that they do not have to be mutually exclusive, thus removing the scholarly tension in advance. Still, it emerges from his discussion that the type of materialistic interpretation he employs — the persecution of sodomites due to economic recession — does not apply to eighteenth-century Amsterdam. The most violent persecution in 1764-65 took place during a period of economic growth. Van der Meer shows that the idea of economic recession did indeed play a role in the instigation of the persecutions. However, the factual situation was less important. Historical fact points not to a materialistic, but rather to a sociogenetic or ideogenetic explanation of the processes.

Sodomy persecutions began in France and England, where there was anything but an economic recession, at the same time as in the Netherlands. Thus, it would almost be easier to show that government agencies turn to persecutions of deviant sexual behavior in times of economic growth. Elisabeth Pavan has shown that it was precisely in the fifteenth century, the flowering of the Italian Renaissance, that persecutions of sodomy began in Venice.[5] And in Spain, the trials of the Inquisition began shortly after 1500 and were more a result of economic growth than of decline. Further, large scale campaigns against (homo)sexual crimes were launched in France, Germany, and the Netherlands during the rise of industrialism at the end of the nineteenth century.

Such general analyses of homosexuality and economy remain, however, incomplete and simplistic. It seems more sensible to specify the individual elements of a theory about the relationship between homosexuality and society. True, government policy can be used to discourage, limit, affirm, encourage, to control society officially and unofficially. More specifically it can, for example, be used to restrict anal penetration or homosexual pornography. The effects of government policy are, however, almost always local and partial, not general and total — a point to keep in mind in analyses of discrimination and emancipation. It is nonsense to talk about *the* oppression of *the* homosexual in the eighteenth century. Noordam goes too far in the opposite direction when he posits that homosexual behavior was completely socially acceptable in Leiden in the period 1500-1730, as intriguing as his notion may be. Moreover, it is regrettable that van der Meer does not refer to radical forms of repression comparable to the sodomy persecutions in the same period, such as the extermination of the gypsies in 1720-30 or the round-up of the legendary outlaw band of Limburg.

In his explanations, van der Meer inclines toward a sociogenetic approach when he points out the importance of changes in "experience, perception, and the organization of homosexual behavior," which were fostered by certain social developments (the Enlightenment, nationalization). He emphasizes the individuation and increasing autonomy of homosexuality in the sodomite. Social labeling of the sodomite has two important results: the rise of a fairly exclusive group culture, and the persecution of the labeled behavior. However, because an adequate apparatus for persecution was lacking in the eighteenth century (it emerged only in the nineteenth century) the range of sodomy persecutions remained limited. At the same time, a clearer image of the sodomite developed within the legal apparatus, so that the court no longer concerned itself solely with the sodomite's admission of anal penetration. Instead, his further behavior and intentions were taken into account in sentencing. The shift of legal interest from anal penetration to same-sex behavior in general also had an important consequence for female homosexuality: in 1791, the court began prosecuting tribadic amusements.

PARADOX

Van der Meer's book is a substantive contribution to the historical writing on homosexuality. It contains an abundance of material to refine the long-range perception of homosexual emancipation. Although the reader may occasionally lose his way in its juridical byways, sodomitic labyrinths, and stiff prose, this study skillfully analyzes the nuances of Enlightenment rationality, humanitarian-. ism, and faith in progress in order to focus on the hypothesis of the making of the homosexual. In his book, van der Meer documents aspects of the everyday life of sodomites that had been all but forgotten. For instance, they married each other, never had oral sex, at times lived an extravagantly sexual life, and completely lacked "gay pride."

Finally, consider a paradox of gay liberation and gay studies. Up to the present day, the history of homosexuality seems to be defined by discrimination and victimization—life in the lion's den. Gays and gay scholars sometimes embrace misfortune and misery to such an extent that they remain parasitically attached to these tragic lives. Historical ideas and social practices in the area of sodomitic self-organization and "gay pride" have scarcely developed beyond this initial point. A masochistic preoccupation with discrimination is once again evidenced in the works of Pieter Koenders[6] and Theo van der Meer. Each ends his book with a sigh of relief; things weren't so awful after all.

Discrimination and persecution appear to be comprised in the term "homosexuality" itself. Would not people who are forced to call themselves "homosexual" because of some kind of social pressure be better able to find their well-being and happiness in other places and in other terminology? Why are gay scholars content to drag these cancerous twins of liberation and discrimination along behind them, never realizing that they have been paradoxical from the outset, that freedom per se has never existed, that finer analyses of homosexuality and society are possible and necessary? Instead, they too often allow the forked tongue of liberation and discrimination do all the speaking.

Gert Hekma

NOTES

1. L. S. A. M. von Römer, "Der Uranismus in den Niederlanden . . . ," *Jahrbuch für sexuelle Zwischenstufen* 6 (1906): 365-511; G. M. Cohen Tervaart, *De grietman Rudolf de Mepsche* ('s-Gravenhage: Mouton, 1921).

2. D. J. Noordam, "Homosexualiteit en sodomie in Leiden, 1533-1811," *Leids jaarboekje* 75 (1983): 72-105.

3. John Boswell, *Christianity, Social Tolerance, and Homosexuality* (Chicago: University Chicago Press, 1980).

4. John Marshall, "Pansies, Perverts, and Macho Men," in *The Making of the Modern Homosexual*, ed. K. Plummer (Totowa, NJ: Barnes and Noble, 1981), 133-54.

5. Elisabeth Pavan, "Police des moeurs, société et politique à Venise à la fin du Moyen Age," *Revue historique* 104 (1980): 241-88.

6. Pieter Koenders, *Homoseksualiteit in bezet Nederland* (Amsterdam: SUA, 1984).

SOCIAL THEORY, HOMOSEXUAL REALITIES. Stephen O. Murray. *(New York: Gay Academic Union, 1984, 83 pp., $6.95.)*

The aim of this short but ambitious book is to show the failure of "the grand tradition" of social theory to account for the emergence of ethnic and quasi-ethnic identities and communities: "The macro-historical processes projected by Marx and Durkheim from their consideration of [nineteenth-century] European history have not been enacted elsewhere as predicted, nor have subsequent events in Europe followed their scenarios" (p. 6).

Despite the extensive homogenization of "mass society," intergroup differences and loyalties have persisted, re-emerged, or (in the most interesting cases in the book under review) emerged for the first time. Identifications, "notably those based on gender and sexual preference — inconceivable to the fathers of sociology — have appeared, and have become more salient bases for mobilization than class" (p. 8). Murray suggests that the emergence of gay and lesbian communities is a particularly clear anomaly to the explanations of "world historical changes in systems of domination" (this is his statement of the central concern of macrosociology, p. 5), and thus deserves the sustained attention of social theorists, who have thus far been oblivious to it.[1]

Although he is critical of Foucault's superficial account of medical discourse forming homosexual self-perception, Murray's work is clearly Foucaultian in attempting to examine concrete historical changes in systems of power and domination.[2] This Foucaultian approach to the problematic "grand tradition" is not content with a singular explanation such as class, or with generalizing a singular revolutionary transformation ('*La Revolution*' in 1789). Murray more pointedly criticizes the functionalist notions of inevitable harmonization of interests within increasingly complex divisions of labor, and rejects the functionalist notion that there is a single moral universe in modern (or post-modern) states. Although he also criticizes the "deviance" conceptions common in symbolic interactionist theorizing, the work by Laud Humphreys and Kenneth Plummer on challenging and transforming social stigma derives from the symbolic interactionist tradition, rather than from the Neitzschean discourse on the transvaluation of values that influenced Foucault.[3]

Following Humphreys, Murray sees three necessary components of a cognitive revolution among those involved in homosexuality:

> (1) that there is a common condition, (2) that the present treatment [and status] of one's kind is intolerable, and (3) that change [in 1 and 2] is possible. These conceptions now seem so obvious that we are tempted to forget they were recently widely unrecognized, when the sinfulness or sickness that was homosexuality was perceived to be eternal, inevitable, and just. (p. 22)

Murray argues that the influence of professional discourses, including the Kinsey reports as well as psychiatric literature, has been overestimated by intellectuals who "like to believe that the Truth will make men (and possibly women as well) free and that books change the world" (p. 23). Given his stress on the necessity of a cognitive revolution before the status of homosexuals in North America could be raised, it is surprising that Murray dismisses the influence of the Kinsey report, which did much to establish that homosexual behavior was fairly common (condition 1 above). Instead of this directly cognitive source, Murray stresses the exposure of Americans to more tolerant European and Oceanic cultures, and to the concentration of a "critical mass" of "homosexuals" in major American port cities.[4]

Although World War II may have accelerated these processes, Murray argues that World War I may have provided a significant impetus away from rural American ethnocentrism. At this juncture, it is exceedingly difficult to document the movement of those with homosexual inclinations and experiences from rural areas to cities after they served in World War I. Examining published biographies of homophile leaders, Murray disputes claims about rural-urban migration occasioned by World War II service, while accepting that mass armies and the industrial mobilization of women fostered considerable wartime homosociality.

In regard to a second "gay liberation" revolution, Murray is still more Tocquevillean than when questioning World War II as a watershed for the emergence of North American gay and lesbian communities. He again stresses continuities across the supposed epistemic rupture of "the Stonewall rebellion." In particular, he shows that organized resistance preceded the much-publicized "Stonewall riot." He suggests that the latter has become a symbol mostly because it occurred in New York City, where American publishing is centered, and where tangible gay political gains have been few, leading to the defensive compensation of a foundation myth of a heroic Gay Liberation Front. He also stresses growth and diversification of gay institutions as more important than sectarian conflicts among unsuccessful New York gay politicos, whom he sees as perpetually out of touch with those they claim to represent.

The gradual shift from homophile to gay movements and self-identification is of central interest to Murray, as it is to historians of the movements.[5] Indeed, the de-assimilation of lesbians and gay men, whose primary socialization occurs within heterosexual families, is the phenomenon anomalous to sociologists' theorized universal assimilation, and the puzzle he challenges social theorists to take up. The homophile-gay transformation did not occur over the course of a single Manhattan summer night, however.

After describing (but without explaining) the masculinization of gay men during the 1970s, Murray turns to a concise review of the "social organizations of homosexuality" attested in anthropological and historical literature: age-graded, gender-defined, and egalitarian/gay (exemplified, respectively, by Melanesian, Polynesian, and contemporary urban North American homosexualities). These ideal types are clearly societal expectations of roles. The extent to which the roles are assumed by those engaged in homosexuality in various societies, and the extent of intracultural variability, remain empirical questions. For instance, all three organizations of homosexuality exist in contemporary North America. Anti-homosexual propaganda here focuses on the affronts to the fundamentalist Christian moral order of "corrupting" children into effeminacy, little as that has to do with the coupling of hypermasculine adult men.

Even though the three conceptual organizations of homosexuality coexist, Murray argues that the trichotomy is heuristic because "the typology seems to encompass the empirical variance that has been observed; i.e., there do not seem to be hundreds, or even dozens of differing organizing principles of homosexual relationships in human societies" (p. 46). This thrust obviously is intended to correct the view of sexual desire as undifferentiated flux that readers may encounter in the more hyperbolic writings of social constructionists (which through typesetting vagaries or ignorance of English geography has been transplanted from Essex to Sussex on pages 19 and 20 of the book). The parsimonious typology also permits one to raise questions about historical transformation in social emphasis from one type to another. Age-graded homosexuality has temporal priority in Europe — as Murray argues in his conclusory essay in this issue. He argues that the sodomite did not become the molly, but that the sodomite's pederasty receded from center stage as the gender-crossing (or - mixing, or -bridging) molly role attracted the spotlight — or the flashlight — of the Society for the Reformation of Morals). In recent years, a gender-crossing role has been rejected by those identifying themselves as gay or lesbian.

These transformations in societal conceptions and in lived experience are important problematics for social history, whatever the interest in medical texts may be for intellectual history. Murray suggests that the gender-gay transformation can now be observed in Latin America and in Polynesia, or can be recovered through oral history and collections of personal documents from lesbians and gay men living today. Although he is himself a historian of social science and a vocal critic of the conceptualization of AIDS in medical discourse, Murray's implicit program in his book is to gather data on the experiences and perceptions of the lesbian and gay rank and file, rather than to celebrate the Homitern leadership or sort through medical discourse. The book, then, provides legitimation (specifically, providing the materials needed to assess and improve social theory about the emergence of countertraditions) for the many oral history projects underway. Published medical literature is not going to disappear. Our prospective informants and their memorabilia do.

For earlier transformations, it is also the self-conceptions and lived experiences of those involved, not official discourse and explanations, that interest Murray. He accuses John Boswell[6] of obscuring the pederastic nature of the "gay people" for whom Boswell claims there was "tolerance" prior to some inexplicable popular change that the Church could not resist:

> [Boswell] lumps together any trace of homosexual desire or behavior—even in other species!—under a wholly ahistoric, invariant label "gay," and invents a counter-tradition that is a projection into history of the theological posture of Dignity, c. 1979. Boswell's True Faith—carefully and completely segregated from the practices of Christian institutions, prelates, and emperors in history—has nothing against gay people, not least because there was no notion in the periods Boswell describes that such an entity existed. (p. 51)

This critique might seem similar to social constructionists' critiques of "essentialism," but Murray criticizes what he deems social (de-)constructionists' bad faith in deconstructing solely homosexuality apart from a general analysis of social categorization almost as harshly as he attacks Boswell (see pp. 19-21, 45).[7] Bray is charged only with failing to see a transformation from one end of his book (and of the seventeenth century) to the other:

> but avoiding the Scylla of labeling everyone anywhere who engages in homosexual behavior as a "homosexual" or a "gay person" (as Boswell follows psychoanalysts in doing), exposes one to the opposite [social constructionist] danger, the Charybdis of arguing that there is no category at all. (p. 44)

As the quotations in this review show, Murray writes vividly, and gleefully flays the sacred cows not only of his own discipline (sociology), but also gay movement mythology (e.g., regarding the symbol of Stonewall), the dominant paradigm in gay studies (social constructionism), and anything else that seems to him to constitute an obstacle to understanding past or present homosexual realities. The primacy Murray accords to changes in North America over the course of the past half-century seems ethnocentric, however. Given his espoused interest in world-historical transformations, he devotes little attention to the world system and changes in production and distribution.

Murray's preference for idealist rather than materialist explanations, and for status rather than class as heuristic, evidences a nostalgia for Weberian analysis. While Murray explicitly rejects the Marxist and Durkheimian streams within "the grand tradition," he does not take on the ghost of Max Weber. Indeed, he suggests that "a feminist, vaguely neo-Weberian claim that social acceptance of homosexuality is a function of the status of women explains some of the variance among nonindustrialized societies in which 'passive' homosexuality is considered to be feminizing" (p. 57), although he also notes that such an account begs the question of why homosexuality is feminized in some cultures (e.g., North American Berdaches) and masculinized in others (e.g., Japanese samurai lovers, ancient Greek, or precontact Highland New Guinea warriors).

This short book contains astonishingly concise reviews of a vast amount of discourse on homosexuality. The cross-cultural contrast of conceptions of homosexuality is particularly remarkable — even if its location at the end rather than the beginning of the book is puzzling. In a mere nine pages, Murray describes the basic conceptions, proposes an order for their transformation, and lays out the outstanding questions requiring further research. This work is a model of conciseness. In some places, however, the price of conciseness may be readability; there are often too many ideas per sentence and per page. This severe compression may prove daunting to those not used to paying close attention to what they read. I suspect that, contrary to his expressed hopes, Murray's book will not succeed in explaining social science work on homosexuality to any of the gay "laity" who lack a college reading level.

Professional readers will be distressed by an inordinate number of typographical errors, even in section headings (e.g., Sussex for

Essex, a disconcerting "i" added to epigones). The value of the extensive bibliography is similarly compromised by inverted digits in references to D'Emilio and Lockwood, the crediting of a 1983 article by George Chauncey to Sherri Cavan, and the dropping of a millennium from Miller and Humphreys, 1980 — to list just a few of the errors. Despite some production problems and an overestimation of the rate at which readers can absorb ideas, this is an important book deserving careful attention from those engaged in anthropological, historical, linguistic, or sociological work dealing with homosexuality. The brevity of text, proliferation of suggestions for research projects, and completeness of bibliography recommend it as a text for courses on sex, gender, social theory, and social history.

Kent Gerard

NOTES

1. The importance of de-assimilation for social theory, along with explanations of the concepts "quasi-ethnic" and "institutional elaboration" are detailed in Stephen O. Murray, "Institutional Elaboration of a Quasi-ethnic Community," *International Review of Modern Sociology* 9 (1979): 165-78.

2. A challenge of the Weeksian appropriation of what were tentative hypotheses for Foucault is contained in Note 12 of the book under review. The basis in a conversation with Foucault a few months before his death is elaborated in Stephen O. Murray, "Remembering Michel Foucault," *Sociologists' Gay Caucus Newsletter* 43 (1985): 9-12.

3. See Laud Humphreys, *Out of the Closets* (Englewood Cliffs, NJ: Prentice-Hall, 1972); and Kenneth Plummer, *Sexual Stigma* (Boston: Routledge and Kegan Paul, 1975). Murray is particularly critical of any necessary connection between homosexual behavior ("primary deviance" in labeling theory), labeling, and gay identity ("secondary deviance"). Empirical data are adduced in Stephen O. Murray and Robert C. Poolman, Jr., "Folk Models of 'Gay Community,'" *Working Papers of the [University of California, Berkeley] Language Behavior Research Laboratory* 52 (1982).

4. Murray also stresses material factors such as the diffusion of automobiles and penicillin, and (perhaps overly optimistically) the valuation of a free press in American culture.

5. The most nearly definitive history of the homophile movement (John D'Emilio's *Sexual Politics, Sexual Communities*, Chicago: University of Chicago Press, 1983) was in press when Murray was writing his book. Murray reported

(personal communication, 1985) that he was using D'Emilio's *Body Politic* series
to guess what the contents of the book would be.

6. John Boswell, *Christianity, Social Tolerance and Homosexuality* (Chicago:
University of Chicago Press, 1980).

7. Also see Stephen O. Murray, "Fuzzy Sets and Abominations," *Man* 19
(1983): 396-99, a general challenge to neo-Durkheimian explanations of anti-
homosexual persecution and the partial perspectivism of "the Essex School of
homosexual deconstruction."

THE BOUNDARIES OF EROS: SEX CRIME AND SEXUALITY
IN RENAISSANCE VENICE. Guido Ruggiero. *(Oxford: Oxford
University Press, 1985.)*

On Christmas Day, 1497, Marin Sanuto, a citizen of Renaissance
Venice, went to church. The sermon he heard that day was delivered by a certain Timeoto da Lucca of the Order of the Observants
of Saint Francis. Its subject was the plague. The Doge does well,
Timeoto said, to close the churches for fear of the plague, but he
would do better to remove the horrible sins which have brought the
plague down on this city: blasphemy, usury, the corruption of justice, and the societies of sodomy. It was, Sanuto later noted in his
diary, a good sermon.[1]

This entry in Sanuto's diary left me, at the very least, thoughtful
and unsettled, but I shall come back to it. However, it is best to
begin by recounting the thesis that lies behind Guido Ruggiero's
book, for its origin is in those terrifying years in the 1340s when the
plague of which Timeoto was preaching first came to Venice. The
plague that swept over Venice haunted the imaginings of this city,
but Ruggiero draws our attention first to its tangible effects on Venice's social and material life. With the simplicity of a natural force,
the waves of immigrants who came in the wake of the plague replaced the artisans and laborers who had died and joined those who
were being drawn in by the growing vitality of the Venetian economy. It made for an unstable society. Yet alongside this, the fourteenth century saw in Venice's elite a growing desire to centralize
and tighten the city's government. The result was, on one side, the

breakdown of a traditional society and, on the other, a government concerned to exercise its authority over ever wider aspects of the city's life. Within these two boundaries, Ruggiero argues, the sexual life of Renaissance Venice was shaped. The effect was "the gradual definition of two distinct milieus of sexuality—a licit one that hinged on marriage and childbirth, and an illicit one" (p. 10). But the boundaries between the two worlds fitted poorly, and Ruggiero goes on to paint a picture of Renaissance Venice in which the illicit culture played a functional role, a way out of a regime that was sometimes impractical, due in part to the fact that the boundaries of Eros are hard to define, much less legislate.

The "societies of sodomy," Ruggiero believes, were part of this illicit culture, but the intense persecution homosexuality began to arouse at the beginning of the fifteenth century distinguished it from the other sexual crimes he describes, which were treated more leniently. It was "the one sexual crime where stern language and stern punishment coincided" (p. 144).[2] The reason for this, in Ruggiero's view, was an alarmed reaction on the part of the ruling elite to a homosexual subculture emerging in Venice in the fifteenth century. As long as homosexuality was regarded merely as a step on the way to adult heterosexuality, the authorities regarded it lightly. Yet "a growing awareness and fear of a homosexual subculture crystallized the perception that some continued to prefer homosexuality to heterosexuality as they grew older" (p. 160). The result was persecution, the ferocity of which corresponded, in the minds of those who instigated it, to the fierceness of the plague which the societies of sodomy had brought down on Venice.

Ruggiero argues his case well. His primary sources are the legal records of the Archivio Di Stato in Venice, which contain an immense collection of court documents, beguiling in their detail, depicting Venice in the fourteenth and fifteenth centuries. From among them Ruggiero has labored to produce an intelligent and scholarly work and his basic thesis is largely convincing.[3] But its unspoken assumptions are troubling and ultimately limit this book. His casual use of the term "homosexuals" in writing of this period accompanies his apparent assumption that if there is evidence of homosexual behavior, there will be a subculture of some kind in which "homosexuals" can meet each other. Ruggiero questions whether persecution reduced this subculture to marginality, which he believes occurred in the fourteenth century, or whether it was again becoming visible and accessible, which he believes began to occur in Venice around the beginning of the fifteenth century. Unfortunately, he does not account for the fact that the assumptions underlying his argument are quite modern ones, nor does he consider the cultural relativity of the social forms homosexuality can take.[4]

The result is to leave some important questions unasked. One of these is the question of what kind of homosexual subculture this was.[5] It is a pity Ruggiero does not question his assumptions in regard to Renaissance Venice, for the descriptions he provides strongly suggest that this was not a homosexual subculture per se but rather a culture marked by drinking, gambling, and other criminal activities, and that within the culture the unruly sin of sodomy found a place. When the authorities attempted to regulate the pastrymakers' shops, which were social gathering places and had a sodomitical reputation, they claimed that "in the shops of pastrymakers in this our city many youths and others of diverse age and condition come together day and night; there they hold games, drink and commit many dishonesties and sodomy" (p. 139). The authorities used similar terms when closing, or at least attempting to light more fully, various porticos of churches and shops that had a sodomitical reputation, where "it was dark and shadowy so that many in those shadows unknown commit illicit deeds" (p. 139). Indicative of this association of ideas was the arrest in 1477 of two teenagers for sodomy when they were discovered playing cards together in a private place (they were eventually released for lack of evidence) (pp. 195-96, n. 133.).

A second, and perhaps more important, question is prompted by that entry in Sanuto's diary because we get a different picture of this particular citizen in a report of the Mantuan ambassador (p. 189, n. 15). The ambassador appears to be telling us that Sanuto was himself a sodomite — or rather, that he was in the habit of having sexual relations with one of his male servants and that his inclination to this vice was public knowledge (apparently without his ever being charged for it). Was his diary entry, then, hypocrisy? It is difficult to see why it should be. If not, we are left with the conclusion that somehow Sanuto did not connect his behavior with that frightful image of the sodomite in the sermon that Christmas morning. This is perhaps a surprising conclusion, but it is just such a discontinuity which I frequently felt compelled to recognize in my own studies of homosexuality in the society of Renaissance England.[6]

The question Ruggiero has not asked is how the individuals involved understood for themselves what they were doing. The enticing but misleading evidence of court records, when taken alone, presents a problem because it is situated at precisely that point where the word and the thing named came together. They tell us about the regulation of sexuality, but whether they tell us more is a different matter.

If Sanuto did not understand his acts as sodomitical, how did he understand them? He does not say. But another individual who appears in Ruggiero's book does tell us directly what what he had done meant to him: a boy of thirteen named Antonio, who was charged with sodomy in 1368 together with a man called Benedicto, who was teaching him to be a herald (p. 116).[7] It was "friendship" said Antonio, because Benedicto was "teaching him like a master." In Renaissance Europe, "friendship" did not refer simply to an emotional attachment between two individuals (although it could involve that). The term characterized the relationship between master and servant, patron and client, even the king and his people. More broadly, friendship was also a relationship of two people who were linked by a common interest. To be someone's "loving friend" was to assure them of your influence and protection. Such friendship is present in Ruggiero's book not only in Antonio's remarks, but also as a social form present in several of the cases Ruggiero mentions: a boatman and his servant (pp. 115-16), a barber and his servant (p. 137), two servants sharing a bed (pp. 110-11), and a sailor and his young shipmate (p. 190, n. 31). It is also present in what we hear of Sanuto and his servant in the Mantuan ambassador's report.

Antonio's remarks echo the words of a young servant named Jean de Bayonne, who in the London of the early 1560s was sharing a bed with a visitor to the house in which his master lodged. As people do in such intimacy and darkness, they talked as they might not have done during the day.[8] Jean's master had been in the habit of having sexual relations with Jean, as Sanuto had had with his servant. But a few days before this night, Jean's master had been married, and Jean was curious about the sexual attractiveness of his new wife, whom the visitor knew. Jean asked his question. The question seems to have been a salacious one, and so was the reply. She would be well satisfied, remarked Jean, because her new husband "is very powerful and strong." [9] "From these words," the visitor later said, "I guessed the youth knew something." He pressed his questions and Jean revealed all.[10] But most interesting is what Jean's remarks tell about the way he appears to have understood his sexual relationship with his master. In the words he used, he linked not only an undifferentiated heterosexual and homosexual potency, but also the roles of his master as both master and husband. It was in these terms he appears to have comprehended his master's relationship with him. "Clients love masculine men," wrote a client in a formal letter to his patron, "as wives love their husbands."[11]

Did this provide an alternative frame of reference, very different from our own modern conceptions, in which homosexuality could be understood? There is a set of documents in the Guildhall Library in London which show this process at work.[12] They concern a certain Anthony Death, who was a schoolmaster at Oundle School in 1624-25, and was charged

> to take sundry of his scholars (being the most pretty and amorous boys) to take of them over and over one alone into the study at the end of the school and to send for some of them to his chamber at his lodgings and after a jerke or two [a blow with a rod or a whip] to meddle with their privities . . .

Anthony Death's reaction to this charge was not to deny that he had touched the boys; given the detailed evidence several of them provided, he was hardly in a position to do so. Yet he protested his innocence and stated his eagerness to go to court, where he said he was confident he would be acquitted. Does the explanation lie in that phrase "after a jerke or two"? In Anthony Death's mind, did these blows give the subsequent acts their meaning? Physical contact was part of a schoolmaster's relationship with his pupils: he was supposed to chastise them. Nonetheless, was what Anthony Death did sodomitical, or was it part of his pupils' chastisement? The argument was not about what happened, but about what it meant.

The court records involved have not survived. However, we do know from Anthony Death's subsequent career that nothing untoward happened in court, which is not surprising. Considerable evidence shows that homosexuality was widely institutionalized in the educational system of Jacobean England, and yet in that context ignored. When a charge was brought, it was usually not taken seriously.[13]

The terms Jean de Bayonne used were not those of sexuality but of power, and in fact corresponded closely to the social form in which his sexual relationship with his master was expressed. I am inclined to think they fit a good deal of the material Ruggiero has handled also. My main concern, though, is that questions of this kind should be asked. What *kind* of homosexual subculture was it? How did each individual understand what he was doing? Such questions fit poorly with our own sexual categories, and perhaps even with the notion of sexuality itself. But it is in asking questions like these that the history of homosexuality becomes more than the study of the past for its own sake because the answers such questions will bring are a measure of the relativity of the imaginative world in which we ourselves live.

Alan Bray

NOTES

1. Guido Ruggiero, *The Boundaries of Eros: Sex Crime and Sexuality in Renaissance Venice* (Oxford: Oxford University Press, 1985), 113. Unless otherwise stated, all subsequent page citations refer to this work.

2. My focus in this review is on Ruggiero's treatment of homosexuality. His book also deals at similar length with the shaping of other aspects of sexuality within his overall thesis of the two cultures, the licit and the illicit.

3. I think that Ruggiero misreads some of the evidence, however. Signs of homosexuality in the educational system (p. 138) are not evidence for a homosexual subculture, but rather for the reverse: that to this extent it was institutionalized within the existing social architecture of the culture. The group arrests which

began in the early fifteenth century, and the sodomitical reputations of certain public places, are more significant indications of the existence of a subculture.

4. The literature on this is now extensive, but the classic statement is still Mary McIntosh's "The Homosexual Role," *Social Problems* 16 (1968): 182-92; reprinted in *The Making of the Modern Homosexual*, ed. Kenneth Plummer (Totowa, NJ: Barnes and Noble, 1981), 30-44.

5. One modern author, for example, has described a working-class homosexual subculture in New England in as late a period as the 1910s that differed startlingly from any homosexual subculture in the United States today. See George Chauncey, Jr., "Christian Brotherhood or Sexual Perversion? Homosexual Identities and the Construction of Sexual Boundaries in the World War One Era," *Journal of Social History* 19 (1985): 189-211.

6. Alan Bray, *Homosexuality in Renaissance England* (London: Gay Men's Press, 1982), 67-80.

7. I have learned much about the history of friendship through conversations with Dr. Michel Rey of the University of Paris.

8. A. G. Kinder, *Casiodoro de Reina: Spanish Reformer of the Sixteenth Century* (London: Tamesis, 1975), 27-37 and 99-120. Kinder understandably questioned the extent to which the evidence against Casiodoro de Reina (Jean de Bayonne's master) may have been concocted. Yet the material I gathered together in Bray, *Homosexuality*, bearing on the social forms in which homosexuality was expressed, now inclines me to give the allegations more weight. They fit too well to have been merely an invention. The apparently orderly relationship of master and servant was not the image sodomy conjured up in the Elizabethan mind, but it was a social form in which homosexuality was widely expressed (Bray, *Homosexuality*, 13-32, 44-51).

9. Kinder, 108: "quippe qui magna vi et potentia sit praeditus."

10. Kinder, 109.

11. Antonio Perez, *Antonii Perezii ad Comitem Essexium . . . Epistolarum Centuria Vna* (Paris: n.d.), Epistola 61: "amant enim clientes, sicut vxores maritos viros viriles."

12. Guildhall Library, 11588/3/295-98. (I have modernized the text.) W. G. Walker transcribed part of these documents in *A History of Oundle Schools* (1956), 125-29, with a note on Anthony Death's subsequent career. I am grateful to Keith Thomas for this reference.

13. Bray, *Homosexuality*, 51-53.

THE BOUNDARIES OF EROS: SEX CRIME AND SEXUALITY IN RENAISSANCE VENICE. Guido Ruggiero. *(New York: Oxford University Press, 1985, 223 pp.)*

If one sets out systematically to study sexual behavior in the Renaissance or the Enlightenment, two kinds of source material can be used: the letters and diaries of individuals, and the legal materials generated by trials for illicit sexual acts. Both have their benefits and limitations. Diaries and letters have usually been produced by members of the elite, are limited to periods ranging from a year to a decade, and survive capriciously as far as period and place are concerned. Their great benefit is that they allow one to fit sexual behavior into a total pattern of life. By contrast, legal material can often trace patterns of behavior yearly over long stretches of time, and will often display the behavior of all classes of society. However, this material has two limitations: what does the behavior of those who broke the law and were caught tell us about the majority, and how are we to understand single acts by individuals about whom we usually know nothing either before or after their arrests?

Venice in the fourteen and fifteenth centuries did not produce diaries similar to those of seventeenth- and eighteenth-century England. Therefore, Ruggiero has to base his study of sexual behavior on arrests for illicit behavior. Five of his seven chapters study fornication, adultery, sex crimes against God (i.e., the seduction of nuns, sex between clerics and laypersons and between Jews and Christians, and sexual acts in sacred places), rape, and sodomy, with the greatest number of pages (35 of 128) devoted to the topic of sodomy.

In a concluding chapter, Ruggiero attempted to examine what normal, legal sexuality was like if illicit sexuality was as the preceding chapters described it. It is an entirely acceptable way of proceeding. That he did not discuss prostitution, on the technical ground that it was a legal (though sinful) activity, is the only disappointment because it makes it difficult to judge the cogency of one of the book's most interesting contentions.

Ruggiero says that the fourteenth and fifteenth centuries saw the emergence of two sexual worlds: the world of marriage and procreation, and the libertine world in which women were raped, prostitutes pursued, nuns seduced, and boys sodomized. Some men and most women would have passed all of their lives in the first world. An unspecified number of men and a minority of women, on the other hand, lived either wholly in the second world, or went back and forth between the two according to their stage of life. These two worlds coexisted in European society, Ruggiero maintains, until the second was more or less destroyed in the twentieth century by the changing position of women.

These two worlds did exist, but it is likely that there was a profound rearrangement of their relationship to each other well before the twentieth century. The change would have occurred, instead, around 1700 with the emergence of modern culture. At that point, the rise of egalitarian ideas and their impact on an older patriarchy began to change the nature of marriage, gender, and sexual relations, and opened the way for the development of romantic and companionate marriage, the concept of gender equality, and the division of the world into a heterosexual majority and a homosexual minority. Historians who write about periods subsequent to this great change are wise not to introduce anachronistically the presumptions of their own culture when they analyze, for instance, the world of Renaissance Italy. Ruggiero is most aware of this when he deals with marriage and sexual relations between women and men, and least aware of it when he deals with sexual relations between men and boys. Sexual relations between men and women have, after all, recently been far more demythologized than have relations between members of the same gender.

Ruggiero's chapters on fornication and rape are more satisfactory than the one on sodomy. He is aware that one cannot go looking for modern marriage in the Renaissance sources. He argues that the Venetian state prosecuted fornication either to force a couple to marry, or to clarify a couple's marital relationship. Such coercion was necessary in a society where there was no single unambiguous act that made a marriage official, and where couples often lived together who had not made use of this ambiguity to declare themselves married. But the state was not concerned with the immorality of the act, and therefore did not punish patrician men who seduced poor women.

Ruggiero explains that enduring sexual relationships and marriages often began with violent seductions that could be legally classified as rape. Consequently, the rape of young women of marriageable age received the lightest punishment of any sexual crime. On the other hand, violence against children, the elderly, or one's relatives was more harshly punished. The rape of a noblewoman by a plebeian, or the seduction (as it was presented) of a nobleman from his familial duties by a common woman—these were taken most seriously of all because the patricians who applied the law were interested not in upholding Christian morality, but in defending patrician honor and family continuity. This also probably explains why the seduction of nuns was more severely punished than any other sexual crime between men and women. Ruggiero is, however, unable to explain this other than by pointing to Venetian horror that the brides of God should be taken away from the most powerful males of all, that is, God himself.

But Ruggiero has previously shown that nuns were almost always patrician girls whose families placed them there in order to lessen their parents' familial responsibilities. Once in the convent, however, many young women had their circle of lovers (bettered only by the legal prostitutes) and their bastard children, often choosing their lovers from men of lower social standing. That their women should choose such men was unbearable to the patrician men who applied the law. In retaliation, the patricians severely punished men outside of their own class who raped noblewomen and seduced noble nuns.

This class concern for power and masculine domination could also largely explain why sodomy between men and boys was by far the most severely punished sexual crime, in that, as Ruggiero shows, most prosecutions were for an assault by a man on a boy, many made on a noble boy by a man of lower social status. Ruggiero cannot see this because he applies to his sodomy cases a model of homosexual behavior which became current in Western society only after 1700. This modern model presumes that there is a minority of men in society who alone feel sexual desire for men; who are sexually passive, feminine in behavior and transvestite in dress; who feel no desire for women; and who most often meet each other in the illicit subcultures of cities. Ruggiero is partially aware that the men in his cases do not much resemble this model. He mentions a number of times that in Venice it was the active adult partner, rather than the passive boy, who was most severely punished, and that this runs contrary to what he calls the usual pattern of punishing the passive partner more severely. That usual pattern exists only after 1700, when those passive partners, who are adult men not boys, are seen as seducing active males (whether adolescent or adult) who otherwise supposedly feel sexual desire only for women. Ruggiero misses this.

The author goes on to suggest that the homosexual subculture of the fifteenth century was more developed than the one in the fourteenth century because during the fifteenth century there were more group arrests of sodomites. To enforce this point, he presents his most revealing piece of misinterpretation, the case of Rolandina from the fourteenth century (p. 136). This individual had breasts and looked more like a woman than a man. As a man, he married a woman who left him because he could never have an erection. He then went to Venice and became a woman, where as Rolandina she was a successful female prostitute. Ruggiero comments that, "If there had been a homosexual culture to join, Rolandina might have had more chance to survive as a transvestite." It is a well-intentioned, but unwise comment. Rolandina was not a transvestite homosexual, a role produced by modern culture. Rolandina was an individual who changed from a man to a woman and was, by the standard of her culture, a hermaphrodite. She was guilty of sodomy because her culture held that individuals with the physical characteristics of both men and women were obliged to choose, and remain within, one gender or the other. If they did not, if they switched as Rolandina did, they were guilty of sodomy. (See Pierre Darmon, *Damning the Innocent: A History of the Persecution of the Impotent in Pre-Revolutionary France* [New York: Viking Press, 1986], chap. 2.)

Ruggiero's interpretation of his evidence, however, is even more hampered by his failure to ask whether his adult male sodomites were not also as interested in women as in boys. No doubt, this is partly because he rarely knows very much about the lives of his individuals apart from their sodomy cases. In the two instances where he does report such information (pp. 116, 120), the adult men involved with boys also had sexual relations with women. Art historians who study the full lives of individuals have a great advantage in this regard over a study like Ruggiero's. James Saslow can show that a great number of painters had sexual relations with both boys and women. (See his *Ganymede in the Renaissance* [New Haven: Yale University Press, 1986].) A biographer like Howard Hibbard can show the same thing in the person of Caravaggio (New York: Harper and Row, 1983), though Hibbard displays an unnecessary anxiety about whether this could mean that his subject was a "homosexual."

It is likely that the majority of Renaissance painters, like the actors and playwrights of Renaissance England, lived in Ruggiero's second sexual milieu. It is also likely that in that milieu, the same individuals sodomized boys and pursued prostitutes. It is a world as Saslow shows, that came to an end in the seventeenth century.

Randolph Trumbach

GANYMEDE IN THE RENAISSANCE: HOMOSEXUALITY IN ART AND SOCIETY. James M. Saslow. *(New Haven, CT: Yale University Press, 1986, 265 pp.)*

The Italian Renaissance ranks as a peak epoch in the history of Western art. It is also an era in which a number of major artists are known to have engaged in homosexual behavior or held homophile sentiments. The *garzone* system, whereby artists employed teenaged boys in their studies as assistants and models, offered many opportunities. Consequently, clarification of the psychosexual dimension of the lives of such artists as Donatello, Botticelli, and Michelangelo would seem to be of commanding importance—not only for the interpretation of their art, but for understanding the social context of homosexuality in this pivotal epoch. Yet obstacles arise, due above all to the need that the artists—together with their humanist confrères and patrons, many with similar proclivities—felt to hide their erotic preferences in the face of Christian intolerance.

The fourteenth century was marred by a wave of antisodomy enactments in the North Italian city states, rulings which laid groundwork for what was to become a pan-European trend toward the extension and secularization of such legislation. While the enforcement of these laws was, at first, often lax, their venom flowed at full strength in periodic surges of puritanical rigor, of which the Savonarola episode in late fifteenth-century Florence is only the most notorious. Ultimately, rigorism triumphed throughout Catholic Europe as a result of the implementation of the directives of the Council of Trent in the late sixteenth century (the Counter-Reformation). The encroachment of the law into the artists' lives benefited historians by providing documented instances of known or suspected homosexual behavior.

On another level, efforts by psychiatrists to probe the psyche of these artists have produced a meager yield, despite an early, problematic paper by Freud himself on Leonardo, first published in German in 1910. Moreover, for reasons that cannot be explored here, a kind of institutional timidity continues to inhibit art historians from examining sexual themes. Apart from the biographies of artists, the synchronic context remains clouded, for despite an abundance of evidence, there is still no general history, in any language, of homosexual behavior in Renaissance Italy.

Another avenue of investigation presents itself: the subject matter employed by the artists. Here, the writer of this review made a modest *sondage* ten years ago in a contribution on the myth of Orpheus read at an art historical symposium (published as "Orpheus without Euridice," *Gai Saber* 1 [1978]: 267-73). More recently, James Saslow of Columbia University has presented the case in full for one salient theme, Ganymede, the beautiful Phrygian youth who was kidnapped by Zeus to be his cupbearer and bedmate in Olympus. The story appealed to the Renaissance intelligentsia by force of its pederastic character, corresponding to the dominant form of male homosexual behavior. This point must be stressed because modern investigators of Renaissance same-sex behavior often unwittingly import their own androphile assumptions into the epoch.

One of the main elements of Renaissance civilization was the revival of classical antiquity, especially mythology. To be sure, this mythological heritage had persisted in the Middle Ages, though wrapped in hostile antiquity. Beginning with Boccaccio's *Genealogia deorum* of 1375, the Renaissance elaborated a new mythographic tradition. Though not bereft of Christian preoccupations that lingered sometimes for the sake of prudence, but also out of genuine syncretistic conviction, this trend aimed to recover the full richness of Greek and Roman mythology. The restored imagery harbored many homoerotic motifs, above all the amours of the gods, Apollo for Hyacinth, Dionysus for Ampelos, and Zeus for Ganymede — to name only three pairs of a numerous company.

Supplementing Renaissance mythography was the emblem book, an entirely new form combining text with pictures. The first was that of Andrea Alciati (1531; frequently enlarged and reissued), which contains an important Ganymede emblem. Readily portable, these books enjoyed great popularity with artists and poets alike from the sixteenth through the eighteenth centuries.

It is against this background that the achievements of the painters and sculptors must be seen. James Saslow views the profile of the Ganymede images in Italy as a bell curve, starting with the fifteenth-century revival of classical antiquity, reaching its apogee in 1530 to 1550, and then declining as the chill winds of the Counter-Reformation made themselves felt.

Boldly yet aptly, Saslow begins his account with the greatest artist of all, Michelangelo Buonarroti. He rightly insists on the homoerotic core of the master's drawing of *Ganymede Abducted by the Eagle*, which the artist presented to Tommaso de' Cavalieri, a young Roman nobleman for whom Michelangelo conceived, in his fifty-seventh year, an almost boundless though unconsummated passion. With this recognition, Saslow does not neglect the other associations which the drawing evoked, especially the idea — stemming from Xenophon in the fourth century B.C., — that the ascent of Ganymede is a metaphor of the yearning of the contemplative soul for union with the divine. In this chapter, one might dissent somewhat from Saslow's affirmation of Michelangelo's Neo-Platonism, which has been increasingly questioned by specialists in recent years. Then there is the writer's dalliance with psychoanalytic speculations, including the dubious claim, advanced by Robert

Liebert in his *Michelangelo: A Psychoanalytic Study of His Life and Images* (New Haven, CT: Yale University Press, 1983), that Michelangelo's homosexual feelings were generated by his lifelong search for a father substitute. Because Michelangelo's homoeroticism was, as far as is known, expressed exclusively toward young men, in keeping with the dominant pattern of the times, this notion seems to be a piece of gratuitous psychoanalytic projection.

Saslow's second chapter examines the great Correggio painting of *The Abduction*, as seen against a concern with androgyny and the libertine atmosphere of northeastern Italy during this period. Spurning any effort to recruit, posthumously as it were, any artist for homosexuality, Saslow holds that Correggio was entirely heterosexual because he had a wife and a family. But then, so did John Addington Symonds, the Victorian homosexual writer so often cited in the book. A private communication from a major contemporary scholar has suggested that Correggio may well have been bisexual, a theory that may warrant further research.

Chapter 3 extends the investigation to Parmigianino, Giulio Romano, and their circles, presenting some of the most overtly sexual images of the entire book. Among the topics discussed are the conflation of Ganymede and Apollo, the rivalry of Hebe and Ganymede, misogyny, the eroticism of male buttocks, and the fusion of Ganymede and Cupid.

The following chapter treats the sculpture of a master whose bisexuality is well documented, Benvenuto Cellini. Saslow holds that his Ganymede sculptures have as their subtext the then "current social pattern of close and often erotic relationships between masters and their servants or apprentices" (p. 10). By nature flamboyant and boastful, this Florentine lived on into an era in which rising pressures compelled outward conformity — an adjustment whose necessity was made brutally clear by Cellini's imprisonment.

The final chapter looks briefly at the later phases of the development, which saw the spread of the Ganymede image throughout western Europe, accompanied by its trivialization and desexualization. Nonetheless, in view of the story which he has so skillfully and eloquently recounted, James Saslow is justified in his final conclusion: "Amid the ignominious decay of former beauty and position, transfigured by the consolation of divine memory, Ganymede had known the highest honor and greatest love of any mortal man, and he rose in a last apotheosis to take his eternal place in the firmament of history" (p. 202).

In one of those synchronisms that often mark the progress of scholarship, the publication of Saslow's work—which had been substantially completed several years earlier—was preceded by the printed version of a Hamburg doctoral dissertation, Anette Kruszynski's *Der Ganymed-Mythos in Emblematik und mythographischer Literatur des 16. Jahrhunderts* (Worms: Werner, 1985). This volume, while generally offering a slighter and more selective treatment of the same material, does provide some complementary vistas. Emphasizing the sources in the emblematic tradition, Kruszynski shows how multilayered the textual presentation of Ganymede could be, owing in large measure to the "Aesopic" language that even those who were prepared to discuss the sexual facets felt compelled to adopt. In fact, they were so successful in obfuscating the homoerotic aspects that the theme of Ganymede could be repeatedly conscripted for political allegories glorifying reigning sovereigns. (Surely some embarrassment must have attached, however, to a French print of 1622 portraying the French King Louis XIII—the target of gossip because of his favorites—as Ganymede, the bringer of prosperity.) Thus, desexualization, which Saslow treats as a late feature, was present from the beginning. Basically, by *not* emphasizing the erotic element, Kruszynski implies that a completely balanced picture of the theme, a task to be accomplished only by some future historian, would show a more complex embedding of the erotic in a network of other concerns. Saslow goes only so far in this regard.

But enough caviling. Clearly organized and fluently written, Saslow's book raises appreciably the level of scholarship on homosexual themes in art. Indeed, it is hard to avoid the conclusion that his monograph stands as the only truly serious work in this late-emerging area. The quality of Saslow's accomplishment speaks for itself. However, the fact that it has no peers reveals major blind spots in both art historical and homosexual research. His successors, who must fill many gaps, will be immeasurably indebted to his sensitive and widely informed example. And despite Saslow's modest disclaimer that he has not written a general work on the Renaissance, social and intellectual historians will find much to ponder here.

Wayne Dynes

BETWEEN MEN: ENGLISH LITERATURE AND MALE HO-
MOSOCIAL DESIRE. Eve Kosofsky Sedgwick. *(New York: Columbia University Press, 1985, 244 pp.)*

   Eve Kosofsky Sedgwick, a professor of English at Amherst College in Massachusetts, is to be commended for being the first critic-
scholar, it would seem, to attempt a serious practical criticism
based on anthropological categories of homosocial desire and its
less-than-apparent modern antithesis, homophobia (against males).[1]
More specifically, she is the first critic to build on recent feminist
replies to, and harsh critiques of, Lévi-Strauss's controversial hypothesis that when two men pursue the same woman, they may
desire each other in some primitive way.
   The high priest of twentieth-century cultural anthropology had
generated a version of this notion (not the form we find here) under
specific archaeological conditions: the genesis of the family, primitive marriage, ancient and elementary institutions of kinship. But he
never used the word "desire" in any way remotely proximate to the
forms employed here, and he never intended to apply this triangle
universally, insofar as universal application would diminish its
most rudimentary thrust: elementary, patriarchal relations among
primitive societies. He would be surprised to discover how feminists have contorted his meaning from an *apercu* (male-centered
and patriarchal though it may have been) about primitive societies
and fatherhood in early family structures, into a polemic about ma-
triarchy and mothering. Equally relevant here, Lévi-Strauss never
interested himself, unlike Freud, in the homosexual dimensions or
implications of his discipline (cultural anthropology) and he never
invoked or referred to the word homosocial or any concepts derived

from it. Indeed, the notion of "homosocial" relations predicated on innate erotic desires, as well as post-Deleuzean versions of desire itself, is intrinsically foreign to his whole system of cultural anthropology.

But even if Lévi-Strauss had pronounced on these matters, and even if he had been able to incorporate them into some version remotely proximate to the forms found here, what would it mean to generalize diachronically, and in the face of radically altered social institutions among sophisticated societies, that whenever two men follow the same woman they want each other erotically? Circumspect (almost cloistered) in the range of his vision, Lévi-Strauss was ironically also too farsighted to postulate such sweeping historical laws. His notion about the structure of these triangles (he never elevated his observation to the status of the law) was rather intended as a symbolic synchronic force. More consequentially, he harbored no sense that one could rummage through the art and literature of advanced Christian societies like those of the European Renaissance and Enlightenment, let alone ours, and apply these triangles as a type of universal Einsteinian, or Freudian, law.

Yet in building on these feminist critiques of Lévi-Strauss (by Nancy Chodorow, Luce Irigaray, Dorothy Dinnerstein, and, most importantly, Gayle Rubin, whose phrase "the traffic in women" has fired up Sedgwick's imagination), Sedgwick applies them, almost wholesale, to a large chunk of British literature: from Shakespeare down to the twentieth century, from the historical Renaissance and English Restoration to Henry James's London and Whitman's Brooklyn, concluding that schematic though her book may be, her "resulting structure [i.e., in *Between Men*] represents a continuing negotiation between the book's historicizing and dehistoricizing motives." This "continuing negotiation" eludes me, but Sedgwick's approach nevertheless remains an original one that yields results, as when she notices (about the Gothic literature of the late eighteenth century) that "the Gothic novel crystallized for English audiences the terms of a dialectic between male homosexuality and homophobia, in which homophobia appeared thematically in paranoid plots." Even so, closer examination and more discriminating judgment shows that the method adopted is fundamentally flawed. However persuasive the approach may appear at first, and whatever the author's talents (which include a critical intelligence capable of drawing subtle distinctions), the approach itself needs to be dismantled and ultimately rejected. Sedgwick's feminists no doubt believed that they had latched on to something profound about the structural signification of love triangles, but the appearance in English literature of a phenomenon as complex as male homosocial desire needs to be captured and demonstrated in other ways if we hope to develop a meaningful definition of, and demarcation of, the boundaries of homosocial desire. Otherwise, the concept will remain, as it does in this book, an impossibly elusive domain.

If *Between Men* is a disappointing book, the reason is owing in no small part to the author's constant digression from her ostensible subject, male homosocial desire, into the most controversial realms of feminist methodology, and to her almost perverse refusal to gaze at homosocial desire through any other lenses than those of these radical feminists. (She does lean heavily upon René Girard's book *Deceit, Desire and the Novel*, published in 1972, for its method of application from the social sciences to literary criticism and for an antecedent discussion of erotic triangles. But it is the feminist critique of Levi-Strauss' elementary kinship that guides her rudimentary formulation.) In this connection, one wonders if Sedgwick would have reached the same conclusions by invoking the new feminist critique of Freud's (phallocratic) paradigm that predicates the understanding of adult sexual roles and sexual motives on double pairs composed of two males and two females. Would this more complex pursuit, two men and their women, have altered the nature of the men's desire for each other? Or is the essential fabric of homosocial interaction such that (according to the feminists invoked here) it can only be enacted, let alone unconsciously imagined, when two men pursue the *same* woman? It isn't at all clear why multiple women could not serve as well, and whether the age of males plays any significant role in the transaction (the ages of males in Sedgwick's texts is not given any weight).

A greater aberration than this comes from Sedgwick's eschewing of all social history and local custom, to say nothing of the mighty sway of diverse religion and politics, which naturally took their collective tolls over four centuries. These facets cannot be minimized or ruled out, despite all of Sedgwick's protests to the contrary. There is also the arbitrariness of the selected texts. Why these works, the inquiring reader asks without any straightforward assistance from the author, except to be assured, paradoxically, that there is no such thing as a separate male-homosocial literary canon. "In fact, it will be essential to my argument to claim," Sedgwick writes, "that the European canon as it exists is already such a canon, and most so when it is most heterosexual." Splendidly brave of her to strike out in this way, but if this allegedly heterosexual canon is necessarily homosocial, especially when in the extremes of heterosexuality, then what is new here? View it otherwise. If advanced societies are fundamentally homosocial, particularly when most heterosexual, then little light is shed except the introduction of a new word (homosocial) for an old concept (heterosexuality). But who, except the pious and fundamental, ever doubted that conventional heterosexuality included a touch of the homosocial?

The matter of texts is consequential: it is not merely that the texts (Shakespeare, Wycherley, Sterne) seem to have been selected without any contemplation or discussion of the alternatives, considering the vast corpus over many centuries from which Sedgwick could have selected, but rather that the whole question of choice has been abrogated. The author cannot, of course, have written about everyone. But why these particular writers? And even if the canon is *already* inherently homosocial (a crucial matter to which not every critic will assent), the question about the choice of texts still continues to arise. Nor does Sedgwick demonstrate awareness (at least none adumbrated in *Between Men*) of how the category homosexuality was itself constituted in the long diachronic period she covers.

I suspect that those contemporary readers with gay mind-sets (assuming that one can neutrally and meaningfully posit such mentalities) who assess the book will discover a Sedgwick less interested in the gay male's plight, to say nothing of the monumental contemporary homosexual dilemma, than in contemporary radical feminism, so committed is she to the preponderantly heterosexual triangles at whose center lies a solitary *female* waiting to be courted, abused, or seduced. An author who bothers to write about erotic triangles composed of two men and a woman will inevitably be sympathetic to gay causes in ordinary, mundane life; it is hard to imagine a Sedgwick who is otherwise. The problem here is that she has focused so exclusively on the *woman* between two essentially heterosexual men that she never proceeds to homosexual desire itself. For lesbian and gay readers, *Between Men* will appear to have been the work of a heterosexual feminist critic writing about heterosexual women for heterosexual women in a mold that is ultimately as politicized as it is arbitrary and open-ended.

Sedgwick's method is curious. Selecting her texts without explaining why she has selected them from literally dozens of other equally heterosexual (or in her terms homosocial) candidates, she proceeds on the currently fashionable assumption that literary criticism thrives best when guided by epistemological indirection and cognitive metonymy, as if the subject itself — males half in love with each other — must not be named. What this subject *is*, and how it came to be conceptualized in early Modern Europe, remains the issue here, and those readers who hope to come away from the book having learned something about "male homosocial desire" will find themselves disappointed. They will discover a great deal about the feminist critique of patriarchy and how an anthropological concept can be imported and then schematically applied in literary criticism (especially under radical feminist sponsorship), but they will learn little about actual "male homosocial desire" in the literature treated. Insofar as this issue concerns itself with homosexuality in early Modern Europe, I will limit my comments here to those aspects of the book dealing with the period before 1800, stretching the limits of early Modern European culture as far forward as the French Revolution and covering Sedgwick's first five chapters.

Sedgwick's four-part introduction develops her signposts: (1) homosocial desire, (2) sexual politics, (3) sex or history or both (her radical, Marxist-feminist discussion does not resolve the or), and (4) "What This Book Does." It is necessary to comprehend each category to clarify in what jeopardy her method lies. The goal to clear territories is salutory, but what follows is less definition or working assumption rather than a labyrinth of semantic puzzles couched in feminist jargon. The effort to distinguish among various *types* of sexual desire, as Roger Scruton (the philosopher of sex) would emphasize,[2] is laudable (and not a task most of us would gleefully will upon ourselves), yet no sooner does Sedgwick pronounce on something concrete than the enervated result becomes apparent:

> The example of the Greeks demonstrates, I think, that while heterosexuality is necessary for the maintenance of any patriarchy, homophobia, against males at any rate, is not. In fact, for the Greeks, the continuum between "men loving men" and "men promoting the interests of men" appears to have been quite seamless. It is as if, in our terms there were no perceived discontinuity between the male bonds at the Continental Baths and the male bonds at the Bohemian Grove [the all-male summer camp in California's Russian River for leading American business men] or in the board room or Senate cloakroom. (p. 4)

A "seamless" continuum among Greek lovers and Greek patriarchs? How can Sedgwick know? Greek homosexuality, as K. J. Dover, its most learned student in recent times, has shown,[3] exists in such a primitive state of knowledge that one must be at least cautious before rhapsodizing its conditions, let alone analogizing its relation to the Continental Baths. And to propose that its bonds were "seamless," or in any psychological or other state resembling the organic indivisibility suggested by "seamless," is to pretend that one knows much more than one actually does, and to place ideas dangerously in the service of words. Then, to leap forward by thousands of years to a contemporary bath house (which I assume Sedgwick has visited because she speaks about it with such authority), and to compare its secular "male bonds" to cloakrooms in the United States Senate, is to compare everything with everything else, to jumble Western Civilization into units that make grammatical but little substantive sense.

Sedgwick is more persuasive on homophobia (against men) and homosexual panic, especially as the former appears in her first endnote (p. 219). These are subjects whose recent history she comprehends well, but here, too, she relies excessively on etymology (e.g., "the word [homophobia] is etymologically nonsensical") and language to convey sign systems that are often metalinguistic or

cannot be fully understood by their being reduced to linguistic pa-
rameters. Sedgwick's attention to "sexual politics" (time alters so
rapidly in feminist discourse that Kate Millett's phrase and book
Sexual Politics aren't even mentioned here or in the bibliography)
comes in sequence as the second of Sedgwick's signposts, for her
argument is that homosocial desire cannot be understood without
also considering what is at stake in "sexual politics."

When Sedgwick proceeds to her third signpost, "sex or history?" she introduces a question she cannot answer, one that impossibly complicates the matter of the already *heterosexual* homosocial desire. "For the purposes of the present argument," she
writes, "I am going to be assimilating 'French' feminism — decon-
structive and/or Lacanian-oriented feminism — to the radical-feminist end of this spectrum." Perhaps the labels are necessary, but it
is hard enough to integrate homosocial desire and Lacanianism. To
compound such an already elusive desire with these hybrid versions
practically defeats the purpose of clarification (is elucidation of
male homosocial desire the purpose at all?). Then, as if French
feminism were not sufficiently recondite, we are offered several
other types, including Marxist and radical versions, as it becomes
evident that male homosocial desire construed in this heterosexual
way is merely a pretext for approaching the genuine subject of this
discourse: the varieties of contemporary feminist theory. "The
choice of sexuality," Sedgwick maintains, "as a thematic emphasis
of this study makes salient and problematic a division of thematic
emphasis between Marxist-feminist and radical-feminist theory as
they are now practised." If Sedgwick could write without an ostensible subject (i.e., male homosocial desire), she might do so. When
she pens dejargonized sentences in the introduction she is often perceptive, as in this admission: "Marxist feminism has been of little
help in unpacking the historical meanings of women's experience of
heterosexuality, or even, until it becomes legally and medically visible in this century, of lesbianism" (p. 12). It is true: historical
Marxism has been altogether unable to interest itself in gender differentiation, even less so to concern itself with the fate of sexual
minorities. But the last thing Sedgwick offers in this introduction is
an answer to her own question about "sex or history." The range of
possibilities hasn't even been raised.

Book Reviews

"What This Book Does," the last part of the introduction, is no afterthought and is grounded, happily, in the relatively concrete. "Necessarily because of my particular aptitudes and training, if for no better reason, the historical argument almost throughout is embodied in and guided by the readings of the literary texts." *Helas* for the texts, even if Sedgwick will not tell us how she chose them. She does not, however, plunge into their analysis without an inserted chapter (one), described as "Gender Asymmetry and Erotic Triangles," a "focus on male homosocial desire within the structural context of triangular, heterosexual desire." These are the already mentioned anthropological constructs, but no sooner do we dip into the chapter than we discover them to be composed of "boundaries between the genders" — anything *but* homosexual love triangles. And this practice proves true of the book at large: whenever we think the author is about to make a pronouncement — a forging ahead — about homosexuality, she diverges on another road paved with anything but the stones of homosexuality. "What This Book Does," then is mediate between feminism and the still impossibly nebulous homosocial desire; more specifically, meditate self-reflexively upon the signatures that evolve when a feminist possessed of ambivalent Marxist proclivities ponders male homosocial desire.

> My intention throughout has been to conduct an antihomophobic as well as feminist inquiry . . . In the absence of workable formulations about the male homosocial spectrum, this literature [about the boundaries that lie between women and male homosexuality] has, with only a few exceptions, subscribed to one of two assumptions: either that gay men and all women share a "natural," transhistorical alliance and an essential identity of interests (e.g., in breaking down gender stereotypes); or else that male homosexuality is an epitome, a personification, an effect, or perhaps a primary cause of woman-hating. I do not believe either of these assumptions to be true.

It is reassuring to recognize that the same Sedgwick who denounces homophobia as an intellectually indefensible construct also decries, for lack of a better word, heterophobia, but the reader must also learn, the sooner the better, that the forms of alliance between feminism and antihomophobia constitute the true subject of the book. Yet why then call the book *Between Men* when a more accurate title would have been *Between Men and Women*? And why pretend, as in the subtitle, that "Male Homosocial Desire" forms a weighty part of the discussion when feminism (of whatever version) commands the author's most urgent call? One can understand that Sedgwick wanted to satisfy her patrons on Broadway and 116th Street, the directors of the new series on gender and culture ("A Series of Columbia University Press"), under whose auspices this volume has been published. But it is procrustean to suggest that male homosocial desire is sustained by antihomophobic, heterosexual women, when the "English Literature" presented here does not support that particular contention.

The primary literature discussed, which was written before 1800, includes Shakespeare's *Sonnets*, a Restoration comedy (Wycherley's *The Country Wife*), Sterne's *Sentimental Journey*, and Gothic fiction at the end of the eighteenth century. Sedgwick is so much more effective when dealing with English literature than she is in the theoretical sections at the beginning of the book that one wishes she would have omitted those altogether and begun *in medias res*. Yet even here she lacks a persuasive method of procedure and soon lapses into feminist cant. Beginning with the old saw about Whitman's having been "a Victorian homosexual shibboleth" (when did he become a shibboleth if most literary critics still write without acknowledgment of his homosexuality?), Sedgwick discusses the sonnets in the context of the anti-Lévi-Straussian triangle.

My point is of course again, not that we are here in the presence of homosexuality (which would be anachronistic) but rather (risking anachronism) that we are in the presence of male heterosexual desire, in the form of a desire to consolidate partnership with authoritative males in and through the bodies of females. (p. 38)

It may be so, yet what does it amount to? Is there any virtue, practical or theoretical, in educating heterosexual males about this subterranean heterosexual desire? If the desire is indeed essentially het-

erosexual, then the transaction (among males) may entail many
other consolidations as well, not merely those of partnership. The
parentheses are as riddled, not merely in view of their several inherent contradictions, but rather because the crucial matter ("my
point") about the sonnets and "male heterosexual desire" is placed
in such jeopardy by Sedgwick's sudden interest in anachronism. If
diachronic anachronism, or any other historical exigency, had been
of concern then why project "male homosocial desire" all the way
back to the Greeks? Finally, does Sedgwick really believe that just
because there was no name for "the love that dare not speak its
name" in Shakespeare's time, or any other epoch, that homosexuality did not exist? Surely, capitalism, communism, and individualism (to name but three) thrived long before words for these conceptions entered the English language. The word homosexuality,
which Sedgwick knows as well as anyone, was introduced into English in the late nineteenth-century by Havelock Ellis, yet it was a
concept reasonably well comprehended (in other terms) by many
persons long before that.[4]

　　If Sedgwick fails to say much that is new about Shakespeare's
sonnets, or refrains from explaining why she chose the poems rather
than the plays, or other Elizabethan or Caroline literature, she pene-
trates to a new area for research in her chapter on Restoration
drama. His conclusion is worth citing:

> It is enough . . . to re-stress three things in The Country Wife:
> the compulsory and double-edged involvement of women in
> the all male homosocial bonds, the absence of direct genital
> contact between men, and the cognitively hierarchical, author-
> itarian, "transcendant" nature of the homosocial bond signal-
> ized by cuckoldry. The homosociality of this world seems em-
> bodied fully in its heterosexuality; and its shape is not that of
> brotherhood, but of extreme, compulsory, and intensely vola-
> tile mastery and subordination. (p. 66)

　　This perception could give rise to several doctoral dissertations
on the triangles found in plays from Etheridge to Congreve in that
era of libertinage, even if Sedgwick has not directed us to the obvious locus of Nathaniel Lee, whose Greek and Roman dramatic set-

tings barely disguise his homosocially charged scenes. Sedgwick has put her finger on a crucial aspect of the plots of these works (extending in time beyond *The Country Wife*) when she notices the prescribed nature of the homosocial bond. These socioeconomic attachments are so persuasive, if obviously not homosexual (in the sense of any genital activity), in *some* of the plays and novels of the period that the topic becomes unwieldy unless controlled by an externally imposed structure. The apparent controls originate in the social history of the time, when the genders were under terrific stress owing to a number of complex developments. But Sedgwick chooses another path. Limiting herself to one work of Restoration drama, she seems to believe that the triangles she has found owe more to Wycherley's invention than to the response of his wit to the socioeconomic pressures of the day. Sedgwick, consistent with her plan announced at the beginning, is forced away from the very concrete social history that she promised us in "Sex or History?" she would avoid.

This third chapter raises another question even more central to current research in Restoration drama. Among the varieties of exploration, a great deal of energy is now being expended on its gender ties and social milieu—precisely the nexus designated by Sedgwick when she refers to the involvement of women in all-male bonds. Yet practically all the scholars engaged in this type of analysis are female, as if to suggest that a type of gender distance is necessary if men are to see themselves (in whatever historical epoch) for what they really are. The fact is significant comment on patriarchal power itself today: the observation that male scholars do not wish to study male-centered texts (virtually the Restoration dramatists in the accepted canon) for reasons that they themselves never provide.

The fourth chapter selects its text even more arbitrarily than its predecessors. Omitting the wide body of English literature between 1700 and 1760, from the death of Dryden to that of Fielding and Richardson, Sedgwick latches on to Laurence Sterne, the sentimental, if eccentric parson from Yorkshire. Why, when Swift, Fielding, and Smollett are as likely, and when *Tristram Shandy* is the accepted masterpiece of the canon? The author of *Tristram Shandy* would appear on the surface to be a bizarre choice to represent

literature of the Age of Enlightenment, although when we recollect
(hard to do in a book calling itself a study of *Male Homosocial
Desire*) that *Between Men* deals with male-*female* alliances that are
essentially *heterosexual*, it is less difficult. *Tristram Shandy* is the
first-person memoir of a nearly mutilated but nonetheless sentimental hero who attempts to get born. Built into its gallery of charming
living-room characters is the triangle of an insubstantial Mrs.
Shandy, elided between a rigidly patriarchic (and presumably homophobic) Mr. Shandy and an exquisitely *anti*-homophobic Uncle
Toby (so kind that he would not harm a fly let alone a homosexual).
Although the novel sums up just about every trend of the Enlightenment, including its major sexual currents and even some of the un-
derbelly of sexuality then, there is virtually no trace of any sodomitical strain within it (to invoke the anachronism of homosexuality
Sedgwick has decried). It would have served Sedgwick's purposes
better, however, than Sterne's thinner volume, *A Sentimental Journey*, no epic-length novel but a short and sentimental travel book.
    There is little of a textual nature in Sterne on which Sedgwick can
hinge her heterosexual alliances and homosocial matrices, and this
may be why her writing goes out of control so often in this chapter,
wandering erratically and digressing into commentary about the English-language T-shirts that are popular in Japan today. The only
meaningful association she isolates is that between Parson Yorick
and his French man-Friday, LeFleur, but, as Sedgwick herself notices, this relation is so conventional, and for Sterne so weighted
down by quixotic resonance, as to render any point about homosocial desire (of whatever type) supererogatory unless the whole
(male) canon of English Literature is based on homosocial desire.
Further, the passages discussed about Yorick's sensation of blood
circulating in his veins, and the nervous pleasure he experiences
while in the monk's company, have so little to do with homosocial
desire (they have plenty to with the physiology of a more general
sexual desire) that one wonders if Sedgwick would not have done
better to look elsewhere in the vast ocean of eighteenth-century English literature. "What makes it worth plonking ahead with this
book," Sedgwick comments, "is, I think, that the techniques by
which it disarms analysis are themselves in the very closest relation
to its sexual-political meaning." Yet Sedgwick offers so little anal-

ysis of this "meaning," this "very closest relation" which she claims to have discovered, that one wonders if the whole chapter is not displaced. It is merely another case of her propensity to relate everything to everything else through the gymnastic pyrotechnique of linguistic jumble, as in "the lambency of Yorick's eros," which, she pathetically contends, "makes it especially difficult to isolate homosocial elements as distinct from heterosexual ones." Indeed it does. That has been the problem all along, and in more cases than one it seems as if all we have here is substitution of a "homosocial" vocabulary for a heterosexual one to tell us the things we knew long ago.

In the last chapter I will discuss, the one dealing with Gothic fiction, Sedgwick has put her finger on something crucial that I think will bear fruit for a long time: the introduction of the concept of homophobia in relation to the "terrorism and homosexual panic" that surfaces in the Gothic novel. At last we get homosexual, as distinct from merely homosocial, panic. And even the paranoia that surrounds the ambience of every demonstrable Gothic tale, it is not surprising that a variety of homosexual "panic" should permeate the world of these horror stories. Reminding us that for Freud, "paranoia is the psychosis that makes graphic the mechanisms of homophobia," Sedgwick suggests that at the heart of every Gothic fiction lies one or more males who are enslaved to, or persecuted by, other males.[5] The same cannot be said for any other prose genre, certainly not for novels written before Dickens. The result, for Sedgwick, is that such unequivocally Gothic novels must embody "strongly homophobic mechanisms." When she couples this with the probability that the three most influential early Gothic novelists (Walpole, Beckford, Monk Lewis) were probably homosexual themselves, she seems to be on the verge of something important: a point about gender demarcation in the Enlightenment. Students of the rise of the English novel will begin to understand why the early novel, from Defoe to Richardson, is a literature primarily written about women for women, with men — no matter whether lovers or not — hovering powerlessly in the background, while the later novel of the 1770s and 1780s, including the Gothic novel, remains a genre written about men for men. (Clara Reeve warned her female reader in 1785 to refrain from reading Gothic thrillers lest it might corrupt their female prudence.) This isolation of a crucial feature of Gothic fiction leads to the further identification of a form of paranoia that Sedgwick interprets as "homosexual panic." It is this panic, coupled with the paranoia, that jells into the most original idea Sedgwick has in this book.

Yet just when we are on the verge of a literary-critical breakthrough, the jumbling urge proves too irresistible and Sedgwick quickly jolts us back to the twentieth century, having lost (here as in dozens of other places in the book) any anachronistic reticence she may have once harbored:

> To put it in twentieth-century American terms, the fact that what goes on at football games, in fraternities, at the Bohemian Grove, and at climactic moments in war novels can look, with only a slight shift of optic, quite startlingly "homosexual," is not most importantly an expression of the psychic origin of these institutions in a repressed or sublimated homosexual genitality. Instead, it is the coming to visibility of the normally implicit terms of a coercive double bind . . . For a man to be a man's man is separated only by an invisible, carefully blurred, always-already-crossed line from being "interested in men" . . . The question of who is to be free to define, manipulate, and profit from the resultant double bind is no less a site of struggle today than in the eighteenth century, however. (p. 89-90)

It is not the struggle that most intrigues, but the manipulators in the double-bind. Yet the matter is how best to approach the net of involvement. After the magisterial interventions and widespread ideologies of Romanticism, Darwinism, Marxism, Freudianism, Structuralism, Feminism, and now a rampant Pluralism, is it still no less a struggle? What can history be if its arrangements "between men" are durable enough to withstand these monumental alterations? And has all sense of a retrievable past disappeared if one can conceptualize the "double bind" so facilely, so adroitly, without an iota of attention paid to the real manipulators and manipulated beings who are the stuff of real history? These are admittedly rhetorical questions. But why not, along these principles, conveniently contend that the whole of Judaeo-Christian history, from Exodus to the New Jerusalem, from ancient Phoenicia to modern San Francisco, has been one vast phallocratic coercion, with American or Parisian women now no better off than they were when they were slaves scrubbing down the Agora? Or is this contention, cast as a feminist polemic, precisely the point? If it is, Sedgwick's account seems to entail, at the least, a sorely defective historicism: one not only capable of collapsing decades of meticulous scholarship that argues to the contrary, but also leading to a whole body of tenuous literary criticism if it can hover in the atmosphere of such imperfectly documented notions.

Were it not that Sedgwick's pages regularly abound in fascinating, if by now predictably feminist, ideas, it would be easy to dismiss her preponderantly heterosexual "male homosocial desire" as another figment of the fecund feminist imagination. But her intelligence is too pronounced for that, her intuition too highly developed a barometer of gender relations. Clearly, she perceives something dire in the current discussion of genders in imaginative English literature, especially in the emergence of homosexual panic that first appears at the end of the eighteenth century. This filiation may be paradigmatic in the evolving history of sexuality, and Sedgwick has put her finger on a phenomenon, homosexual panic, all too feebly understood by the psychiatrists and too timidly represented by the social scientists (especially the Marxist theorists). Now, if she will just gaze more closely at more *nineteenth*-century literary texts — Tennyson, Hopkins, Dickens, Carlyle, both Jameses, Whitman, and particularly the Henry James about whom she has written such a perceptive essay, in the *English Institute Essays*[6] — where "homosexual panic" and "double bind" really do exist; and if she will perform a heroic service to contemporary criticism by disabusing those blindly patriarchal leaders (or tyrants, as the case may be) who lord over the Academy and who continue to lie to their students (by silence and stealth) about an essentially "heterosexual" James and a primarily "straight" Whitman — if she will do these, then she will have more than redeemed herself from the flaws evident in her work here.

G. S. *Rousseau*

NOTES

1. Eve Kosofsky Sedgwick, *Between Men: English Literature and Male Homosocial Desire* (New York: Columbia University Press, 1985), in the series entitled *Gender and Culture*.

2. Roger Scruton, *Sexual Desire* (London: Oxford University Press, 1985).

3. K. J. Dover, *Greek Homosexuality* (New York: Random House, 1980).

4. When Lady Mary Wortley Montagu, the eighteenth-century Bluestocking and woman of great independence, claimed that the races of mankind contained not two but three sexes, she had something clearly in mind even if she could not conceive of our concept of homosexuality.

5. The approach was anticipated by Pamela Kaufman in "Burke, Freud, and the Gothic," *Studies in Burke and his Time* 8 (1972): 2179-92.

6. Eve K. Sedgwick, "The Beast in the Closet: James and the Writings of Homosexual Panic," in *Sex, Politics, and Science*, ed. R. B. Yeazell (Baltimore: The Johns Hopkins University Press, 1986), 148-86.

Index